13th Annual Meeting of the Special Interest Group on Discourse and Dialogue 2012

(SIGDIAL 2012)

Seoul, South Korea
5-6 July 2012

ISBN: 978-1-62276-499-0

Printed from e-media with permission by:

Curran Associates, Inc.
57 Morehouse Lane
Red Hook, NY 12571

Some format issues inherent in the e-media version may also appear in this print version.

Printed by Curran Associates, Inc. (2012)

For permission requests, please contact the Association for Computational Linguistics at the address below.

Association for Computational Linguistics
209 N. Eighth Street
Stroudsburg, Pennsylvania 18360

Phone: 1-570-476-8006
Fax: 1-570-476-0860

acl@aclweb.org

Additional copies of this publication are available from:

Curran Associates, Inc.
57 Morehouse Lane
Red Hook, NY 12571 USA
Phone: 845-758-0400
Fax: 845-758-2634
Email: curran@proceedings.com
Web: www.proceedings.com

Introduction

It is our great pleasure to present the Proceedings of the SIGDIAL 2012 Conference, the 13th Annual Meeting of the Special Interest Group on Discourse and Dialogue. The conference is held in Seoul, South Korea, July 5-6, 2012, and is co-located with the 50th Annual Meeting of the Association for Computational Linguistics (ACL).

We received sixty-three submissions: forty long paper submissions, nineteen short paper submissions, and four demo submissions. The members of the Program Committee did a superb job reviewing the submitted papers. We thank them for their advice in selecting the accepted papers and for helping to maintain the high quality of the program. Special thanks go to Giuseppe Di Fabbrizio and Christophe Cerisara for helping out with last minute review requests.

In line with the SIGDIAL tradition, our aim has been to create a balanced program that could accommodate as many favorably rated papers as possible. Of the fifty-nine paper submissions, thirty-eight were accepted: eighteen of forty long paper submissions were accepted as long papers for oral presentation, seven were accepted as long papers for poster presentation, and two were accepted as short papers for poster presentation. In addition, eleven of the nineteen short paper submissions were accepted for poster presentation, for a total of twenty posters. Three of the four demo submissions were accepted.

SIGDIAL continues to serve as a publication venue for research that spans many aspects of discourse and dialogue. This year, the program contained oral presentation sessions and poster papers on discourse structure, paralinguistic features of dialogue, natural language generation and natural language understanding, evaluation, and statistical models of dialogue, as well as on the SIGDIAL 2012 special theme, "characterizing dialog coherence". We particularly thank the two keynote speakers for their contributions to research on coherence and dialogue: Professor Tatsuya Kawahara (Kyoto University) and Professor Diane Litman (University of Pittsburgh).

We thank Kallirroi Georgila, Mentoring Chair for SIGDIAL 2012. The goal of mentoring is to assist authors of papers that contain innovative ideas to improve their quality regarding English language usage or paper organization. This year, nine of the accepted papers were mentored. We thank the Program Committee members who volunteered to serve as mentors: Ron Artstein, Srinivas Bangalore, Michael Johnston, Kristiina Jokinen, Vincent Ng, Andrei Popescu-Belis, David Schlangen, Amanda Stent, and Michael Strube.

We thank Minhwa Chung, Local Arrangements Chair, and Hyung Soon Kim, Jungyun Seo and Sunhee Kim, the members of the Local Arrangements Committee, for taking care of the many details of the local arrangements. We also thank the student volunteers for on-site assistance. We are grateful to ACL PCO Nuricom for designing the conference bags.

We thank Jason Williams, Sponsorships Chair, for recruiting and liaising with our conference sponsors. Sponsorship makes possible valuable aspects of the SIGDIAL program, such as the invited speakers, conference reception and dinner, and best paper awards. We gratefully acknowledge the support of our sponsors, including AT&T, AVIOS, Honda Research Institute, IBM Research, KT Corporation, Microsoft Research, NHN Corporation, and Seoul National University.

We would like to thank last year's Program Co-Chairs, Joyce Chai and Rebecca Passonneau, last year's General Co-Chairs, Johanna Moore and David Traum, and last year's Local Chair, Peter Heeman, for their helpful advice and answers to questions.

We thank Priscilla Rasmussen at the ACL for handling the financial transactions for SIGDIAL 2012, including advance registration.

We gratefully acknowledge SoftConf for use of the START conference management system.

We also thank the SIGDIAL board, in particular Tim Paek, Amanda Stent, and Kristiina Jokinen, for their advice and support.

Finally, we thank all the authors of the papers in this volume, and all the conference participants for making this event such a great opportunity for new research in dialogue and discourse.

Gary Geunbae Lee and Jonathan Ginzburg
General Co-Chairs

Claire Gardent and Amanda Stent
Technical Program Co-Chairs

SIGDIAL 2012

General Co-Chairs:

Gary Geunbae Lee, POSTECH, South Korea
Jonathan Ginzburg, Université Paris-Diderot, France

Program Co-Chairs:

Claire Gardent, CNRS/LORIA Nancy, France
Amanda Stent, AT&T Labs - Research, USA

Local Chair:

Minhwa Chung, Seoul National University, South Korea

Local Arrangements Committee:

Hyung Soon Kim, Pusan National University, South Korea (KSSS liaison)
Jungyun Seo, Sogang University, South Korea (KIISE liaison)
Sunhee Kim, Seoul National University, South Korea (SNU liaison)

Mentoring Chair:

Kallirroi Georgila, University of Southern California Institute for Creative Technologies (ICT), USA

Sponsorships Chair:

Jason D. Williams, Microsoft Research, USA

SIGDIAL Officers:

President: Tim Paek, Microsoft Research, USA
Vice President: Amanda Stent, AT&T Labs - Research, USA
Secretary/Treasurer: Kristiina Jokinen, University of Helsinki, Finland

Program Committee:

Hua Ai, Georgia Institute of Technology, USA
Jan Alexandersson, German Research Institute for Artificial Intelligence (DFKI GmbH), Germany
Ron Artstein, University of Southern California Institute for Creative Technologies (ICT), USA
Srinivas Bangalore, AT&T Labs Research, USA
Luciana Benotti, Universidad Nacional de Cordoba, Argentina
Nate Blaylock, Florida Institute for Human Machine Cognition (IHMC), USA
Dan Bohus, Microsoft Research, USA
Johan Boye, KTH Royal Institute of Technology, Sweden
Kristy Boyer, North Carolina State University, USA

Harry Bunt, Tilburg University, The Netherlands
Sandra Carberry, University of Delaware, USA
Jennifer Chu-Carroll, IBM T. J. Watson Research Center, USA
Mark Core, University of Southern California Institute for Creative Technologies (ICT), USA
Heriberto Cuayáhuitl, German Research Institute for Artificial Intelligence (DFKI GmbH), Germany
David DeVault, University of Southern California Institute for Creative Technologies (ICT), USA
Barbara Di Eugenio, University of Illinois at Chicago, USA
Myroslava Dzikovksa, University of Edinburgh, UK
Maxine Eskenazi, Carnegie Mellon University, USA
Raquel Fernández Rovira, University of Amsterdam, The Netherlands
Katherine Forbes-Riley, University of Pittsburgh, USA
Matthew Frampton, Institute of Cancer Research, UK
Kallirroi Georgila, University of Southern California Institute for Creative Technologies (ICT), USA
Agustin Gravano, University of Buenos Aires, Argentina
Nancy Green, University of North Carolina at Greensboro
Alexander Gruenstein, Google, USA
Curry Guinn, University of North Carolina at Wilmington, USA
Joakim Gustafson, KTH Royal Institute of Technology, Sweden
Peter Heeman, Oregon Health and Sciences University, USA
Julia Hirschberg, Columbia University, USA
Michael Johnston, AT&T Labs - Research, USA
Kristiina Jokinen, University of Helsinki, Finland
Arne Jönsson, Linköping University, Sweden
Pamela Jordan, University of Pittsburgh, USA
Simon Keizer, Heriot-Watt University, UK
Alistair Knott, University of Otago, New Zealand
Kazunori Komatani, Nagoya University, Japan
Stefan Kopp, Bielefeld University, Germany
Ian Lane, Carnegie Mellon University, USA
Sungjin Lee, POSTECH, South Korea
Oliver Lemon, Heriot-Watt University, UK
James Lester, North Carolina State University, USA
Anton Leuski, University of Southern California Institute for Creative Technologies (ICT), USA
Diane Litman, University of Pittsburgh, USA
Ramón López-Cózar, University of Granada, Spain
Wolfgang Minker, University of Ulm, Germany
Sebastian Möller, Telekom Innovation Laboratories, TU Berlin, Germany
Mikio Nakano, Honda Research Institute, Japan
Ani Nenkova, University of Pennsylvania, USA
Vincent Ng, University of Texas at Dallas, USA
Tim Paek, Microsoft Research, USA
Olivier Pietquin, Supélec - Metz Campus, UMI 2958 (GeorgiaTech - CNRS), France
Paul Piwek, Open University, UK
Andrei Popescu-Belis, Idiap Research Institute, Switzerland

Matthew Purver, Queen Mary University of London, UK
Antoine Raux, Honda Research Institute, USA
Norbert Reithinger, German Research Institute for Artificial Intelligence (DFKI GmbH), Germany
Hannes Rieser, Bielefeld University, Germany
Carolyn Penstein Rosé, Carnegie Mellon University, USA
Alex Rudnicky, Carnegie Mellon University, USA
David Schlangen, Bielefeld University, Germany
Elizabeth Shriberg, Microsoft Research, USA
Candace Sidner, Worcester Polytechnic Institute, USA
Gabriel Skantze, KTH Royal Institute of Technology, Sweden
Manfred Stede, University of Potsdam, Germany
Svetlana Stoyanchev, Columbia University, USA
Michael Strube, Heidelberg Institute for Theoretical Studies, Germany
Marc Swerts, Tilburg University, The Netherlands
Takenobu Tokunaga, Tokyo Institute of Technology, Japan
Thora Tenbrink, University of Bremen, Germany
Joel Tetreault, Educational Testing Service, USA
Gokhan Tur, Microsoft Research, USA
Marilyn Walker, University of California at Santa Cruz, USA
Nigel Ward, University of Texas El Paso, USA
Jason D. Williams, Microsoft Research, USA
Ingrid Zukerman, Monash University, Australia

Additional Reviewers:

Timo Baumann, University of Hamburg, Germany
Christoph Broschinski, Bielefeld University, Germany
Hendrik Buschmeier, Bielefeld University, Germany
Christophe Cerisara, CNRS/LORIA Nancy, France
Nina Dethlefs, Heriot-Watt University, UK
Giuseppe Di Fabbrizio, AT&T Labs - Research, USA
Ulle Endriss, University of Amsterdam, The Netherlands
Rivka Levitan, Columbia University, USA
Alejandra Lorenzo, CNRS/LORIA Nancy, France

Invited Speakers:

Tatsuya Kawahara, Kyoto University, Japan
Diane Litman, University of Pittsburgh, USA

Table of Contents

Conference Program

Thursday July 5, 2012

9:00 AM Welcome and Opening Remarks

9:15 AM Keynote 1

Multi-modal Sensing and Analysis of Poster Conversations: Toward Smart Posterboard
Tatsuya Kawahara

10:15 AM Coffee Break

10:45 AM Oral Presentation Session 1: Evaluation

10:45 *An End-to-End Evaluation of Two Situated Dialog Systems*
Lina M. Rojas Barahona, Alejandra Lorenzo and Claire Gardent

11:10 *"Love ya, jerkface": Using Sparse Log-Linear Models to Build Positive and Impolite Relationships with Teens*
William Yang Wang, Samantha Finkelstein, Amy Ogan, Alan W. Black and Justine Cassell

11:35 *Enhancing Referential Success by Tracking Hearer Gaze*
Alexander Koller, Konstantina Garoufi, Maria Staudte and Matthew Crocker

12:00 PM Lunch

1:00 PM Oral Presentation Session 2 (Theme Session): Coherence

1:00 *Unsupervised Topic Modeling Approaches to Decision Summarization in Spoken Meetings*
Lu Wang and Claire Cardie

1:25 *An Unsupervised Approach to User Simulation: Toward Self-Improving Dialog Systems*
Sungjin Lee and Maxine Eskenazi

1:50 *Hierarchical Conversation Structure Prediction in Multi-Party Chat*
Elijah Mayfield, David Adamson and Carolyn Penstein Rosé

Thursday July 5, 2012 (continued)

2:15 PM Poster Session 1 "Madness"

2:30 PM Poster Session 1

Thursday July 5, 2012 (continued)

2:30 PM Demo Session

A Demonstration of Incremental Speech Understanding and Confidence Estimation in a Virtual Human Dialogue System
David DeVault and David Traum

Integrating Location, Visibility, and Question-Answering in a Spoken Dialogue System for Pedestrian City Exploration
Srinivasan Janarthanam, Oliver Lemon, Xingkun Liu, Phil Bartie, William Mackaness, Tiphaine Dalmas and Jana Goetze

A Mixed-Initiative Conversational Dialogue System for Healthcare
Fabrizio Morbini, Eric Forbell, David DeVault, Kenji Sagae, David Traum and Albert Rizzo

4:00 PM Sponsor Presentations 1

4:25 PM Oral Presentation Session 3: Discourse Structure

4:25 *Towards Mediating Shared Perceptual Basis in Situated Dialogue*
Changsong Liu, Rui Fang and Joyce Chai

4:50 *Global Features for Shallow Discourse Parsing*
Sucheta Ghosh, Giuseppe Riccardi and Richard Johansson

5:15 *A Reranking Model for Discourse Segmentation using Subtree Features*
Ngo Xuan Bach, Nguyen Le Minh and Akira Shimazu

Conference Reception and Dinner

Friday July 6, 2012

9:00 AM Announcements

9:15 AM Oral Presentation Session 4: Statistical Models of Dialog

9:15 *Landmark-Based Location Belief Tracking in a Spoken Dialog System*
Yi Ma, Antoine Raux, Deepak Ramachandran and Rakesh Gupta

9:40 *Probabilistic Dialogue Models with Prior Domain Knowledge*
Pierre Lison

10:05 *Exploiting Machine-Transcribed Dialog Corpus to Improve Multiple Dialog States Tracking Methods*
Sungjin Lee and Maxine Eskenazi

10:30 AM Coffee Break

11:00 AM Keynote 2

Cohesion, Entrainment and Task Success in Educational Dialog
Diane Litman

12:00 PM Lunch and Business Meeting

1:30 PM Oral Presentation Session 5: Paralinguistic Features

1:30 *A Bottom-Up Exploration of the Dimensions of Dialog State in Spoken Interaction*
Nigel G. Ward and Alejandro Vega

1:55 *Using Group History to Identify Character-Directed Utterances in Multi-Child Interactions*
Hannaneh Hajishirzi, Jill F. Lehman and Jessica K. Hodgins

2:20 *Adapting to Multiple Affective States in Spoken Dialogue*
Kate Forbes-Riley and Diane Litman

2:45 PM Poster 2 "Madness"

3:00 PM Poster Session 2

Dialog System Using Real-Time Crowdsourcing and Twitter Large-Scale Corpus
Fumihiro Bessho, Tatsuya Harada and Yasuo Kuniyoshi

Automatically Acquiring Fine-Grained Information Status Distinctions in German
Aoife Cahill and Arndt Riester

A Unified Probabilistic Approach to Referring Expressions
Kotaro Funakoshi, Mikio Nakano, Takenobu Tokunaga and Ryu Iida

Combining Verbal and Nonverbal Features to Overcome the "Information Gap" in Task-Oriented Dialogue
Eun Young Ha, Joseph F. Grafsgaard, Christopher Mitchell, Kristy Elizabeth Boyer and James C. Lester

Semantic Specificity in Spoken Dialogue Requests
Ben Hixon, Rebecca J. Passonneau and Susan L. Epstein

Contingency and Comparison Relation Labeling and Structure Prediction in Chinese Sentences
Hen-Hsen Huang and Hsin-Hsi Chen

A Study in How NLU Performance Can Affect the Choice of Dialogue System Architecture
Anton Leuski and David DeVault

Integrating Incremental Speech Recognition and POMDP-Based Dialogue Systems
Ethan O. Selfridge, Iker Arizmendi, Peter A. Heeman and Jason D. Williams

A Regression-based Approach to Modeling Addressee Backchannels
Allison Terrell and Bilge Mutlu

Improving Sentence Completion in Dialogues with Multi-Modal Features
Anruo Wang, Barbara Di Eugenio and Lin Chen

Friday July 6, 2012 (continued)

4:00 PM Sponsor Presentations 2

4:25 PM Oral Presentation Session 6: NLG and NLU

4:25 *Combining Incremental Language Generation and Incremental Speech Synthesis for Adaptive Information Presentation*
Hendrik Buschmeier, Timo Baumann, Benjamin Dosch, Stefan Kopp and David Schlangen

4:50 *Focused Meeting Summarization via Unsupervised Relation Extraction*
Lu Wang and Claire Cardie

5:15 *Markov Logic Networks for Situated Incremental Natural Language Understanding*
Casey Kennington and David Schlangen

5:40 PM Best Paper Awards and Concluding Remarks

Multi-modal Sensing and Analysis of Poster Conversations toward Smart Posterboard

Tatsuya Kawahara
Kyoto University, Academic Center for Computing and Media Studies
Sakyo-ku, Kyoto 606-8501, Japan
`http://www.ar.media.kyoto-u.ac.jp/crest/`

Abstract

Conversations in poster sessions in academic events, referred to as poster conversations, pose interesting and challenging topics on multi-modal analysis of multi-party dialogue. This article gives an overview of our project on multi-modal sensing, analysis and "understanding" of poster conversations. We focus on the audience's feedback behaviors such as non-lexical backchannels (reactive tokens) and noddings as well as joint eye-gaze events by the presenter and the audience. We investigate whether we can predict when and who will ask what kind of questions, and also interest level of the audience. Based on these analyses, we design a smart posterboard which can sense human behaviors and annotate interactions and interest level during poster sessions.

1 Introduction

As a variety of spoken dialogue systems have been developed and deployed in the real world, the frontier of spoken dialogue research, with engineering applications in scope, has been extended from the conventional human-machine speech interface. One direction is a multi-modal interface, which includes not only graphics but also humanoid robots. Another new direction is a multi-party dialogue system that can talk with multiple persons as an assistant agent (D.Bohus and E.Horvitz, 2009) or a companion robot (S.Fujie et al., 2009). While these are extensions of the human-machine speech interface, several projects have focused on human-human interactions such as meetings (S.Renals et al., 2007) and free conversations (K.Otsuka et al., 2008; C.Oertel et al., 2011), toward ambient systems supervising the human communications.

We have been conducting a project which focuses on conversations in poster sessions, hereafter referred to as poster conversations. Poster sessions have become a norm in many academic conventions and open laboratories because of the flexible and interactive characteristics. Poster conversations have a mixture characteristics of lectures and meetings; typically a presenter explains his/her work to a small audience using a poster, and the audience gives feedback in real time by nodding and verbal backchannels, and occasionally makes questions and comments. Conversations are interactive and also multimodal because people are standing and moving unlike in meetings. Another good point of poster conversations is that we can easily make a setting for data collection, which is controlled in terms of familiarity with topics or other participants and yet is "natural and real".

The goal of the project is signal-level sensing and high-level "understanding" of human interactions, including speaker diarization and annotation of comprehension and interest level of the audience. These will realize a new indexing scheme of speech archives. For example, after a long session of poster presentation, we often want to get a short review of the question-answers and what looked difficult for audience to follow. The research will also provide a model of intelligent conversational agents that can make autonomous presentation.

As opposed to the conventional content-based indexing approach which focuses on the presenter's

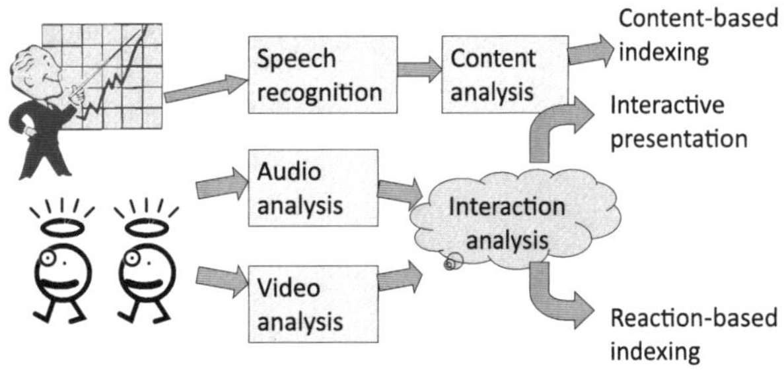

Figure 1: Overview of multi-modal interaction analysis

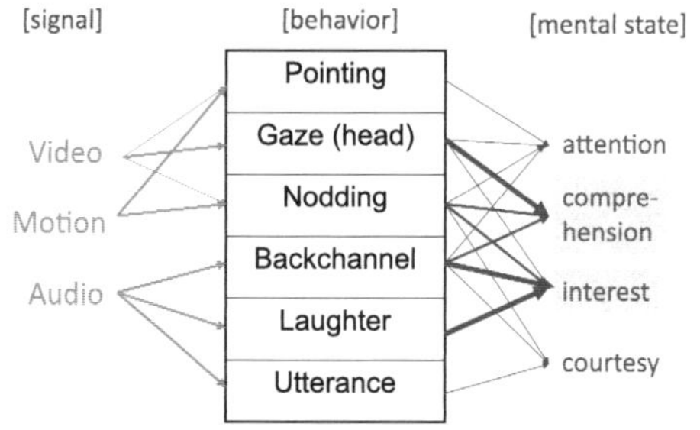

Figure 2: Flow of multi-modal sensing and analysis

speech by conducting speech recognition and natural language analysis, we adopt an interaction-oriented approach which looks into the audience's reaction. Specifically we focus on non-linguistic information such as backchannel, nodding and eye-gaze information, because we assume the audience better understands the key points of the presentation than the current machines. An overview of the proposed scheme is depicted in Figure 1.

Therefore, we set up an infrastructure for multi-modal sensing and analysis of multi-party interactions. Its process overview is shown in Figure 2. From the audio channel, we detect utterances as well as laughters and backchannels. We also detect eye-gaze, nodding, and pointing information. Special devices such as a motion-capturing system and eye-tracking recorders are used to make a "gold-standard" corpus, but only video cameras and distant microphones will be used in the practical system.

Our goal is then annotation of comprehension and interest level of the audience by combining these information sources. This annotation will be useful in speech archives because people would be interested in listening to the points other people were interested in. Since this is apparently difficult to be well-defined, however, we set up several milestones that can be formulated in objective manners and presumably related with the above-mentioned goal. They are introduced in this article after description of the sensing environment and the collected corpus in Section 2. In Section 3, annotation of interest level is addressed through detection of laughters and non-lexical kinds of backchannels, referred to as reactive tokens. In Section 4 and 5, eye-gaze and nodding information is incorporated to predict when and who in the audience will ask questions, and also what kind of questions. With these analyses, we expect that we can get clues to high-level "understanding" of the conversations, for example, whether the presentation is understood or liked by the audience.

2 Multi-modal Corpus of Poster Conversations

2.1 Recording Environment

We have designed a special environment ("IMADE Room") to record audio, video, human motion, and eye-gaze information in poster conversations (T.Kawahara et al., 2008). An array of microphones (8 to 19) has been designed to be mounted on top of the posterboard, while each participant used a wireless head-set microphone for recording voice for the "gold-standard" corpus annotation. A set of cameras (6 or 8) has also been designed to cover all participants and the poster, while a motion capturing system was used for the "gold-standard" annotation. Each participant was equipped with a dozen of motion-capturing markers as well as an eye-tracking recorder and an accelerometer, but all devices are attached with a cap or stored in a compact belt bag, so they can be naturally engaged in the conversation. An outlook of session recording is given in Figure 3.

2.2 Corpus Collection and Annotation

We have recorded a number of poster conversations (31 in total) using this environment, but for some of them, failed to collect all sensor data accurately. In the analyses of the following sections, we use four poster sessions, in which the presenters and audiences are different from each other. They are all in Japanese, although we recently recorded sessions in English as well. In each session, one presenter (labeled as "A") prepared a poster on his/her own

Figure 3: Outlook of poster session recording

academic research, and there was an audience of two persons (labeled as "B" and "C"), standing in front of the poster and listening to the presentation. They were not familiar with the presenter and had not heard the presentation before. The duration of each session was 20-30 minutes.

All speech data, collected via the head-set microphones, were segmented into IPUs (Inter-Pausal Unit) with time and speaker labels, and transcribed according to the guideline of the Corpus of Spontaneous Japanese (CSJ) (K.Maekawa, 2003). We also manually annotated fillers, verbal backchannels and laughters.

Eye-gaze information is derived from the eye-tracking recorder and the motion capturing system by matching the gaze vector against the position of the other participants and the poster. Noddings are automatically detected with the accelerometer attached with the cap.

3 Detection of Interesting Level with Reactive Tokens of Audience

We hypothesize that the audience signals their interest level with their feedback behaviors. Specifically, we focus on the audience's reactive tokens and laughters. By reactive tokens (*Aizuchi* in Japanese), we mean the listener's verbal short response, which expresses his/her state of the mind during the conversation. The prototypical lexical entries of backchannels include "*hai*" in Japanese and "yeah" or "okay" in English, but many of them are non-lexical and used only for reactive tokens, such as "*hu:n*", "*he:*" in Japanese and "wow", "uh-huh" in English. We focus on the latter kind of reactive tokens, which are not used for simple acknowledgment.

We also investigate detection of laughters and its relationship with interesting level. The detection method and performance were reported in (K.Sumi et al., 2009).

3.1 Relationship between Prosodic Patterns of Reactive Tokens and Interest Level

In this subsection, we hypothesize that the audience expresses their interest with specific syllabic and prosodic patterns. Generally, prosodic features play an important role in conveying para-linguistic and non-verbal information. In previous works (F.Yang et al., 2008; A.Gravano et al., 2007), it was reported that prosodic features are useful in identifying backchannels. Ward (N.Ward, 2004) made an analysis of pragmatic functions conveyed by the prosodic features in English non-lexical tokens.

In this study, we designed an experiment to identify the syllabic and prosodic patterns closely related with interest level. For this investigation, we select three syllabic patterns of "*hu:N*", "*he:*" and "*a:*", which are presumably related with interest level and also most frequently observed in the corpus, except lexical tokens.

We computed following prosodic features for each reactive token: duration, F0 (maximum and range) and power (maximum). The prosodic features are normalized for every person; for each feature, we compute the mean, and this mean is subtracted from the feature values.

For each syllabic kind of reactive token and for each prosodic feature, we picked up top-ten and bottom-ten samples, i.e. samples that have the largest/smallest values of the prosodic feature. For each of them, an audio segment was extracted to cover the reactive token and its preceding utterances. Then, we had five subjects to listen to the audio segments and evaluate the audience's state of the mind. We prepared twelve items to be evaluated in a scale of four ("strongly feel" to "do not feel"), among which two items are related to interest level and

Table 1: Significant combinations of syllabic and prosodic patterns of reactive tokens

		interest	surprise
hu:N	duration	*	*
	F0 max		
	F0 range		
	power		
he:	duration	*	*
	F0 max	*	*
	F0 range		*
	power	*	*
a:	duration		
	F0 max	*	
	F0 range		
	power	*	

other two items are related to surprise level [1]. Table 1 lists the results (marked by "*") that have a statistically significant ($p < 0.05$) difference between top-ten and bottom-ten samples. It is observed that prolonged "*hu:N*" means interest and surprise while "*a:*" with higher pitch or larger power means interest. On the other hand, "*he:*" can be emphasized in all prosodic features to express interest and surprise.

The tokens with larger power and/or a longer duration is apparently easier to detect than indistinct tokens, and they are more related with interest level. It is expected that this rather simple prosodic information is useful for indexing poster conversations.

3.2 Third-party Evaluation of Hot Spots

In this subsection, we define those segments which induced (or elicited) laughters or non-lexical reactive tokens as hot spots, [2] and investigate whether these hot spots are really funny or interesting to the third-party viewers of the poster session.

We had four subjects, who had not attended the presentation nor listened the recorded audio content. They were asked to listen to each of the segmented hot spots in the original time sequence, and to make evaluations on the questionnaire, as below.

Q1: Do you understand the reason why the reactive token/laughter occurred?

Q2: Do you find this segment interesting/funny?

Q3: Do you think this segment is necessary or useful for listening to the content?

The percentage of "yes" on Question 1 was 89% for laughters and 95% for reactive tokens, confirming that a large majority of the hot spots are appropriate.

The answers to Questions 2 and 3 are more subjective, but suggest the usefulness of the hot spots. It turned out that only a half of the spots associated with laughters are funny for the subjects (Q2), and they found 35% of the spots not funny. The result suggests that feeling funny largely depends on the person. And we should note that there are not many funny parts in poster sessions by nature.

On the other hand, more than 90% of the spots associated with reactive tokens are interesting (Q2), and useful or necessary (Q3) for the subjects. The result supports the effectiveness of the hot spots extracted based on the reaction of the audience.

4 Prediction of Turn-taking with Eye-gaze and Backchannel Information

Turn-taking is an elaborate process especially in multi-party conversations. Predicting whom the turn is yielded to or who will take the turn is significant for an intelligent conversational agent handling multiple partners (D.Bohus and E.Horvitz, 2009; S.Fujie et al., 2009) as well as an automated system to beamform microphones or zoom in cameras on the speakers. There are a number of previous studies on turn-taking behaviors in dialogue, but studies on computational modeling to predict turn-taking in multi-party interactions are very limited (K.Laskowski et al., 2011; K.Jokinen et al., 2011). Conversations in poster sessions are different from those in meetings and free conversations addressed in the previous works, in that presenters hold most of turns and thus the amount of utterances is very unbalanced. However, the segments of audiences' questions and comments are more informative and should not be missed. Therefore, we focus on prediction of turn-taking by the audience in poster conversations, and, if that happens, which person in the audience will take the turn to speak.

[1] We used different Japanese wording for interest and for surprise to enhance the reliability of the evaluation; we adopt the result if the two matches.

[2] Wrede et al.(B.Wrede and E.Shriberg, 2003; D.Gatica-Perez et al., 2005) defined "hot spots" as the regions where two or more participants are highly involved in a meeting. Our definition is different from it.

Table 2: Duration (sec.) of eye-gaze and its relationship with turn-taking

	turn held by presenter A	turn taken by B	C
A gazed at B	0.220	**0.589**	0.299
A gazed at C	0.387	0.391	**0.791**
B gazed at A	0.161	0.205	0.078
C gazed at A	0.308	0.215	0.355

We also presume that turn-taking by the audience is related with their interest level because they want to know more and better when they are more attracted to the presentation.

It is widely-known that eye-gaze information plays a significant role in turn-taking (A.Kendon, 1967; B.Xiao et al., 2011; K.Jokinen et al., 2011; D.Bohus and E.Horvitz, 2009). The existence of posters, however, requires different modeling in poster conversations as the eye-gaze of the participants are focused on the posters in most of the time. This is true to other kinds of interactions using some materials such as maps and computers. Moreover, we investigate the use of backchannel information by the audience during the presenter's utterances.

4.1 Relationship between Eye-gaze and Turn-taking

We identify the object of the eye-gaze of all participants at the end of the presenter's utterances. The target object can be either the poster or other participants. Then, we measure the duration of the eye-gaze within the segment of 2.5 seconds before the end of the presenter's utterances because the majority of the IPUs are less than 2.5 seconds. It is listed in Table 2 in relation with the turn-taking events. We can see the presenter gazed at the person right before yielding the turn to him/her significantly longer than other cases. However, there is no significant difference in the duration of the eye-gaze by the audience according to the turn-taking events.

4.2 Relationship between Joint Eye-gaze Events and Turn-taking

Next, we define joint eye-gaze events by the presenter and the audience as shown in Table 3. In this table, we use notation of "audience", but actually these events are defined for each person in the audience. Thus, "Ii" means the mutual gaze by the presenter and a particular person in the audience, and "Pp" means the joint attention to the poster object.

Table 3: Definition of joint eye-gaze events by presenter and audience

who		presenter	
	gazes at	audience **(I)**	poster **(P)**
audience	presenter **(i)**	**Ii**	**Pi**
	poster **(p)**	**Ip**	**Pp**

Table 4: Statistics of joint eye-gaze events by presenter and audience in relation with turn-taking

	#turn held by presenter	#turn taken by audience (self)	(other)	total
Ii	125	17	3	145
Ip	320	**71**	26	417
Pi	190	11	9	210
Pp	2974	147	145	3266

Statistics of these events at the end of the presenter's utterances are summarized in Table 4. Here, the counts of the events are summed over the two persons in the audience. They are classified according to the turn-taking events, and turn-taking by the audience is classified into two cases: the person involved in the eye-gaze event actually took the turn (self), and the other person took the turn (other). The mutual gaze ("Ii") is expected to be related with turn-taking, but its frequency is not so high. The frequency of "Pi" is not high, either. The most potentially useful event is "Ip", in which the presenter gazes at the person in the audience before giving the turn. This is consistent with the observation in the previous subsection.

4.3 Relationship between Backchannels and Turn-taking

As shown in Section 3, verbal backchannels suggest the listener's interest level. Nodding is regarded as a non-verbal backchannel, and it is more frequently observed in poster conversations than in simple spoken dialogues.

The occurrence frequencies of these events are counted within the segment of 2.5 seconds before the end of the presenter's utterances. They are shown in Figure 4 according to the joint eye-gaze

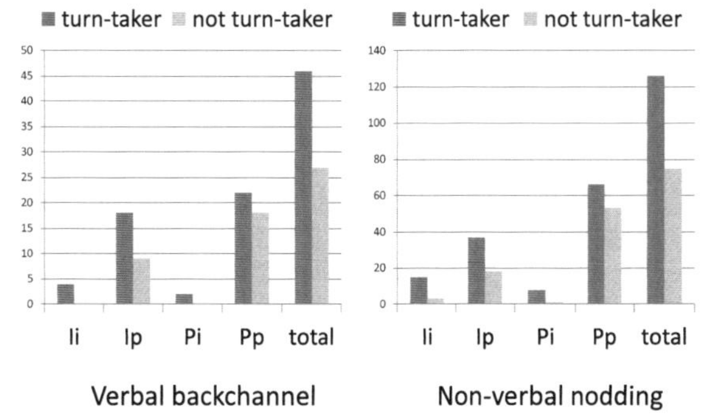

Figure 4: Statistics of backchannels and their relationship with turn-taking

events. It is observed that the person in the audience who takes the turn (=turn-taker) made more backchannels both in verbal and non-verbal manners, and the tendency is more apparent in the particular eye-gaze events of "Ii" and "Ip" which are closely related with the turn-taking events.

4.4 Prediction of Turn-taking by Audience

Based on the analyses in the previous subsections, we conduct an experiment to predict turn-taking by the audience. The prediction task is divided into two sub tasks: detection of speaker change and identification of the next speaker. In the first sub-task, we predict whether the turn is given from the presenter to someone in the audience, and if that happens, then we predict who in the audience takes the turn in the second sub-task. Note that these predictions are done at every end-point of the presenter's utterance (IPU) using the information prior to the speaker change or the utterance by the new speaker.

For the first sub-task of speaker change prediction, prosodic features are adopted as a baseline. Specifically, we compute F0 (mean, max, min, and range) and power (mean and max) of the presenter's utterance prior to the prediction point. Backchannel features are defined by taking occurrence counts prior to the prediction point for each type (verbal backchannel and non-verbal nodding). Eye-gaze features are defined in terms of eye-gaze objects and joint eye-gaze events, as described in previous subsections, and are parameterized with occurrence counts and duration. These parameterizations, however, show no significant difference nor synergetic effect in terms of prediction performance.

Table 5: Prediction result of speaker change

feature	recall	precision	F-measure
prosody	0.667	0.178	0.280
backchannel (BC)	0.459	0.113	0.179
eye-gaze (gaze)	0.461	0.216	0.290
prosody+BC	0.668	0.165	0.263
prosody+gaze	**0.706**	0.209	0.319
prosody+BC+gaze	0.678	0.189	0.294

SVM is adopted to predict whether speaker change happens or not by using these features. The result is summarized in Table 5. Here, we compute recall, precision and F-measure for speaker change, or turn-taking by the audience. This case accounts for only 11.9% and its prediction is very challenging, while we can easily get an accuracy of over 90% for prediction of turn-holding by the presenter. We are particularly concerned on the recall of speaker change, considering the nature of the task and application scenarios.

Among the individual features, the prosodic features obtain the best recall while the eye-gaze features achieve the best precision and F-measure. Combination of these two is effective in improving both recall and precision. On the other hand, the backchannel features get the lowest performance, and its combination with the other features is not effective, resulting in degradation of the performance.

Next, we conduct the second sub-task of speaker prediction. Predicting the next speaker in a multi-party conversation (before he/she actually speaks) is also challenging, and has not been addressed in the previous work (K.Jokinen et al., 2011). For this subtask, the prosodic features of the current speaker are not usable because it does not have information suggesting who the turn will be yielded to. Therefore, we adopt the backchannel features and eye-gaze features. Note that these features are computed for individual persons in the audience, instead of taking the maximum or selecting among them.

The result is summarized in Table 6. In this experiment, the backchannel features have some effect, and by combining them with the eye-gaze features, the accuracy reaches almost 70%.

Table 6: Prediction result of the next speaker

feature	accuracy
eye-gaze (gaze)	66.4%
backchannel (BC)	52.6%
gaze+BC	**69.7%**

5 Relationship between Feedback Behaviors and Question Type

Next, we investigate the relationship between feedback behaviors of the audience and the kind of questions they ask after they take a turn. In this work, questions are classified into confirming questions and substantive questions. The confirming questions are asked to make sure of the understanding of the current explanation, thus they can be answered simply by "Yes" or "No".[3] The substantive questions, on the other hand, are asking about what was not explained by the presenter, thus they cannot be answered by "Yes" or "No" only; an additional explanation is needed.

This annotation together with the preceding explanation segment is not so straightforward when the conversation got into the QA phase after the presenter went through an entire poster presentation. Thus, we exclude the QA phase and focus on the questions asked during the explanation phase. In this section, we analyze the behaviors during the explanation segment that precedes the question by merging all consecutive IPUs of the presenter. This is a reasonable assumption once turn-taking is predicted in the previous section. These are major differences from the analysis of the previous section.

5.1 Relationship between Backchannels and Question Type

The occurrence frequencies of verbal backchannels and non-verbal noddings, normalized by the duration of the explanation segment (seconds), are listed according to the question type in Tables 7 and 8. In these tables, statistics of the person who actually asked questions are compared with those of the person who did not. We can observe the turn-taker made significantly more verbal backchannels when asking substantive questions. On the other hand,

[3]This does not mean the presenter actually answered simply by "Yes" or "No".

Table 7: Frequencies (per sec.) of verbal backchannels and their relationship with question type

	confirming	substantive
turn-taker	0.034	**0.063**
non-turn-taker	0.041	0.038

Table 8: Frequencies (per sec.) of non-verbal noddings and their relationship with question type

	confirming	substantive
turn-taker	0.111	0.127
non-turn-taker	0.109	0.132

Table 9: Duration (ratio) of joint eye-gaze events and their relationship with question type

	confirming	substantive
Ii	0.053	0.015
Ip	**0.116**	0.081
Pi	0.060	0.035
Pp	0.657	**0.818**

there is no significant difference in the frequency of non-verbal noddings among the audience and among the question types.

5.2 Relationship between Eye-gaze Events and Question Type

We also investigate the relationship between eye-gaze events and the question type. Among several parameterizations introduced in the previous section, we observe a significant tendency in the duration of the joint eye-gaze events, which is normalized by the duration of the presenter's explanation segment. It is summarized in Table 9. We can see the increase of "Ip" (and decrease of "Pp" accordingly) in confirming questions. By combining with the analysis in the previous section, we can reason the majority of turn-taking signaled by the presenter's gazing is attributed to confirmation.

6 Smart Posterboard

We have designed and implemented a smart posterboard, which can record a poster session, sense human behaviors and annotate interactions. Since it is not practical to ask every participant to wear special devices such as a head-set microphone and an eye-tracking recorder and also to set up any devices attached to a room, all sensing devices are attached

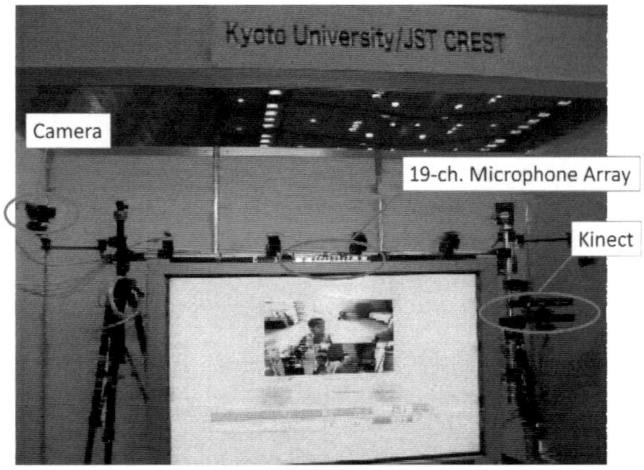

Figure 5: Outlook of smart posterboard

to the posterboard, which is actually a 65-inch LCD display. An outlook of the posterboard is given in Figure 5.

It is equipped with a 19-channel microphone array on the top, and attached with six cameras and two Kinect sensors. Speech separation and enhancement has been realized with Blind Spatial Subtraction Array (BSSA), which consists of the delay-and-sum (DS) beamformer and a noise estimator based on independent component analysis (ICA) (Y.Takahashi et al., 2009). In this step, the audio input is separated to the presenter and the audience, but discrimination among the audience is not done. Visual information should be combined to annotate persons in the audience. Voice activity detection (VAD) is conducted on each of the two channels to make speaker diarization. Localization of the persons in the audience and estimation of their head direction, which approximates their eye-gaze, are conducted using the video information captured by the six cameras.

Although high-level annotations addressed in the previous sections have not been yet implemented in the current system, the above-mentioned processing realizes a browser of poster sessions which visualizes the interaction.

The Kinect sensors are used for a portable and online version, in which speech enhancement, speaker localization and head direction estimation are performed in real time.

We made a demonstration of the system in IEEE-ICASSP 2012 as shown in Figure 5, and plan further improvements and trials in the future.

7 Conclusions

This article has given an overview of our multimodal data collection and analysis of poster conversations. Poster conversations provide us with a number of interesting topics in spoken dialogue research as they are essentially multi-modal and multi-party. By focusing on the audience's feedback behaviors and joint eye-gaze events, it is suggested that we can annotate interest level of the audience and hot spots in the session.

Nowadays, presentation using a poster is one of the common and important activities in academic and business communities. As large LCD displays become ubiquitous, its style will be more interactive. Accordingly, sensing and archiving functions introduced in the smart posterboard will be useful.

Acknowledgments

The work presented in this article was conducted jointly with Hisao Setoguchi, Zhi-Qiang Chang, Takanori Tsuchiya, Takuma Iwatate, and Katsuya Takanashi. The smart posterboard system has been developed by a number of researchers in Kyoto University and Nara Institute of Science and Technology (NAIST).

This work was supported by JST CREST and JSPS Grant-in-Aid for Scientific Research.

References

A.Gravano, S.Benus, J.Hirschberg, S.Mitchell, and I.Vovsha. 2007. Classification of discourse functions of affirmative words in spoken dialogue. In *Proc. INTERSPEECH*, pages 1613–1616.

A.Kendon. 1967. Some functions of gaze direction in social interaction. *Acta Psychologica*, 26:22–63.

B.Wrede and E.Shriberg. 2003. Spotting "hot spots" in meetings: Human judgments and prosodic cues. In *Proc. EUROSPEECH*, pages 2805–2808.

B.Xiao, V.Rozgic, A.Katsamanis, B.R.Baucom, P.G.Georgiou, and S.Narayanan. 2011. Acoustic and visual cues of turn-taking dynamics in dyadic interactions. In *Proc. INTERSPEECH*, pages 2441–2444.

C.Oertel, S.Scherer, and N.Campbell. 2011. On the use of multimodal cues for the prediction of degrees of involvement in spontaneous conversation. In *Proc. INTERSPEECH*, pages 1541–1545.

D.Bohus and E.Horvitz. 2009. Models for multiparty engagement in open-world dialog. In *Proc. SIGdial*.

D.Gatica-Perez, I.McCowan, D.Zhang, and S.Bengio. 2005. Detecting group interest-level in meetings. In *Proc. IEEE-ICASSP*, volume 1, pages 489–492.

F.Yang, G.Tur, and E.Shriberg. 2008. Exploiting dialog act tagging and prosodic information for action item identification. In *Proc. IEEE-ICASSP*, pages 4941–4944.

K.Jokinen, K.Harada, M.Nishida, and S.Yamamoto. 2011. Turn-alignment using eye-gaze and speech in conversational interaction. In *Proc. INTERSPEECH*, pages 2018–2021.

K.Laskowski, J.Edlund, and M.Heldner. 2011. A single-port non-parametric model of turn-taking in multi-party conversation. In *Proc. IEEE-ICASSP*, pages 5600–5603.

K.Maekawa. 2003. Corpus of Spontaneous Japanese: Its design and evaluation. In *Proc. ISCA & IEEE Workshop on Spontaneous Speech Processing and Recognition*, pages 7–12.

K.Otsuka, S.Araki, K.Ishizuka, M.Fujimoto, M.Heinrich, and J.Yamato. 2008. A realtime multimodal system for analyzing group meetings by combining face pose tracking and speaker diarization. In *Proc. ICMI*, pages 257–262.

K.Sumi, T.Kawahara, J.Ogata, and M.Goto. 2009. Acoustic event detection for spotting hot spots in podcasts. In *Proc. INTERSPEECH*, pages 1143–1146.

N.Ward. 2004. Pragmatic functions of prosodic features in non-lexical utterances. In *Speech Prosody*, pages 325–328.

S.Fujie, Y.Matsuyama, H.Taniyama, and T.Kobayashi. 2009. Conversation robot participating in and activating a group communication. In *Proc. INTERSPEECH*, pages 264–267.

S.Renals, T.Hain, and H.Bourlard. 2007. Recognition and understanding of meetings: The AMI and AMIDA projects. In *Proc. IEEE Workshop Automatic Speech Recognition & Understanding*.

T.Kawahara, H.Setoguchi, K.Takanashi, K.Ishizuka, and S.Araki. 2008. Multi-modal recording, analysis and indexing of poster sessions. In *Proc. INTERSPEECH*, pages 1622–1625.

Y.Takahashi, T.Takatani, K.Osako, H.Saruwatari, and K.Shikano. 2009. Blind spatial subtraction array for speech enhancement in noisy environment. *IEEE Trans. Audio, Speech & Language Process.*, 17(4):650–664.

An End-to-End Evaluation of Two Situated Dialog Systems

Lina M. Rojas-Barahona
Inria, LORIA, UMR 7503
Villers-lès-Nancy
F-54600, France
lina.rojas@loria.fr

Alejandra Lorenzo
Université de Lorraine
LORIA, UMR 7503
Vandoeuvre-lès-Nancy
F-54500, France
alejandra.lorenzo@loria.fr

Claire Gardent
CNRS, LORIA, UMR 7503
Vandoeuvre-lès-Nancy
F-54500, France
claire.gardent@loria.fr

Abstract

We present and evaluate two state-of-the art dialogue systems developed to support dialog with French speaking virtual characters in the context of a serious game: one hybrid statistical/symbolic and one purely statistical. We conducted a quantitative evaluation where we compare the accuracy of the interpreter and of the dialog manager used by each system; a user based evaluation based on 22 subjects using both the statistical and the hybrid system; and a corpus based evaluation where we examine such criteria as dialog coherence, dialog success, interpretation and generation errors in the corpus of Human-System interactions collected during the user-based evaluation. We show that although the statistical approach is slightly more robust, the hybrid strategy seems to be better at guiding the player through the game.

1 Introduction

In recent years, there has been much research on creating situated conversational characters i.e., virtual characters (VCs) that look and act like humans but inhabit a virtual environment (Gratch et al., 2002; Hofs et al., 2010; Traum et al., 2007; Johnson et al., 2005; Traum et al., 2008; DeVault et al., 2011).

In this paper, we focus on French speaking, situated conversational agents who interact with virtual characters in the context of a serious game designed to promote careers in the plastic industry (The Mission Plastechnologie game or MP). We present and compare two state-of-the art dialogue systems. The first system (H) is a hybrid approach that combines an information-state dialogue manager (Larsson and Traum, 2000) with a classifier for interpreting the players' phrases. The second system (QA) is a question/answering character model which predicts the system dialog move given a player's utterance (Leuski and Traum, 2008). Both systems use a generation-by-selection strategy (Leuski et al., 2006; Gandhe and Traum, 2007) where the system's utterances are selected from a corpus of possible outputs based on the dialog manager output. While previous work focuses on relatively short dialogs in a static setting, in our systems we consider long interactions in which dialogs occur in a setting that dynamically evolves as the game unfolds.

We evaluate the two dialog systems in the context of the 3D game they were developed for and seek to determine the degree to which a dialog system is operational. To answer this question, we analyse both systems with respect not only to quantitative metrics such as accuracy but also to user- and corpus-based metrics. User-based metrics are computed based on a questionnaire the users filled in; while corpus-based metrics are manually extracted from the corpus of Player-VC interactions collected during the user-based evaluation. As suggested by evaluation frameworks such as PARADISE (Walker et al., 1997) and SASSI (Hone and Graham, 2000), we show that a multiview evaluation permits a better assessment of how well the dialog system functions "in the real world". The metrics proposed assess dialog success and coherence, as well the costs of dialog components.

The paper is organized as follows. In Section 2,

we present the MP game, the dialogue strategies used in the different dialogs and the dialog data used for training. Section 3 presents the two dialog systems we compare. Section 4 presents the evaluation schemes used to compare these two systems and discusses the results obtained. Section 5 concludes with directions for further research.

2 Dialogues in the MP Game

We begin by describing the MP game, the dialogs in the MP game, the strategies used to guide the hybrid dialog manager and the data used for training.

2.1 The MP Game and Dialogs

The MP game is a multi-player quest where 3 teenagers seek to build a joystick in order to free their uncle trapped in a video game [1]. To build this joystick, the player (who alternatively represents anyone of these three teenagers) must explore the plastic factory and achieve 17 mandatory goals (*find the plans, get the appropriate mould, retrieve some plastic from the storing shed*, etc), as well as 11 optional goals which, when reached, provide them with extra information about the plastic industry (and therefore increases their knowledge of it).

In total, the player can achieve up to 28 game goals by conducting 12 separate dialogs in various parts of the virtual world. Each of the 12 dialogs in the MP game helps players to achieve the game goals. The player interacts with the virtual characters to obtain information that helps her to achieve these goals and, as a consequence, to increase her score in the game. Table 1 summarises the game goals and the contextual parameters (player's role, location in the virtual world, VCs present) associated with each dialog.

2.2 Dialog Data and Annotation

To train both classifiers, the one used by the hybrid and the one used by the QA system, we collected Human-Machine dialog data using a Wizard-of-Oz setting and manually annotated each turn with a dialog move. The resulting corpus (called Emospeech Corpus) and the annotation scheme (as well as the inter-annotator agreement) used are described in detail (Rojas-Barahona et al., 2012). Briefly, the Emospeech Corpus comprises 1249 dialogs, 10454 utterances and 168509 words. It contains 3609 player utterances consisting of 31613 word tokens and 2969 word types, with approximately 100 conversations for each dialog in the game. Turns were annotated with dialog moves (Traum and Larsson, 2003) capturing both domain knowledge (e.g., about the goals set by the game) and the set of core communicative acts.

2.3 Dialog Strategies

We identified four main dialog strategies underlying the 12 MP dialogs and used these to define the plans guiding the rule-based discourse management in the hybrid system. These strategies can be seen as transactions made up of conversational games (Carletta et al., 1997).

Strategy 1. This strategy is used in the first dialog only and consists of a single *Address Request* move by the VC followed by the player's answer: Lucas requests Ben to find the address of the Plastic Enterprise that must be hidden somewhere in the lab. Ben can accept, reject or ask for help. Lucas answers accordingly and ends the conversation.

Strategy 2. Nine dialogues follow this strategy. They include several (up to 5) requests for information and the corresponding system/player's exchange. Appendix A shows an example dialog following this strategy.

Strategy 3: This is a confirmation strategy where the VC first checks that the player has already achieved a given task, before informing her about the next step (e.g. dialogs with Melissa in Table 1).

Strategy 4. This strategy, exemplified in Appendix B, is similar to strategy 2 but additionally includes a negotiation step where the VC asks the player for help.

3 Dialogue Systems

The game and the two dialog systems built were integrated as agents within the Open Agent Architecture as shown in Figure 1. Both systems access a database for starting the appropriate dialogs at the appropriate place in the virtual world while simultaneously storing all interactions in the database.

[1]The MP game was created by Artefacto, http://www.artefacto.fr/index_ok.htm

Id	VC	Player	Goals	Location
1	Lucas	Ben	Find the address of the enterprise.	Uncle's place.
2	M.Jasper	Lucas	The manufacturing first step	Enterprise reception
3	Samir	Julie	Find the plans of the joystick *Optional: job, staff, studies, security policies*	Designing Office
4	Samir	Julie	Find out what to do next *Optional: jobs in the enterprise, staff in the enterprise*	Designing Office
5	Melissa	Lucas	Find the mould, optional where are the moulds	Plant
6	Melissa	Lucas	Find the right machine	Plant
7	Melissa	Lucas	Confirm you have found the right mould and machine and find out what to do next	Plant
8	Operator	Julie	Knowing about the material space and about the job *Optional: find out what to do in the case of failure helping to feed a machine with the right material*	Material Space
9	Serge	Ben	Perform quality tests. *Optional: VC's job*	Laboratory Tests
10	Serge	Ben	Find out what to do next. *Optional: know what happens with broken items*	Laboratory Tests
11	Sophia	Julie	Find the electronic components, knowing about VC's job	Finishing
12	Sophia	Lucas	Finishing process *Optional: know about conditioning the product*	Finishing

Table 1: Description of the 12 dialogs in the MP Game.

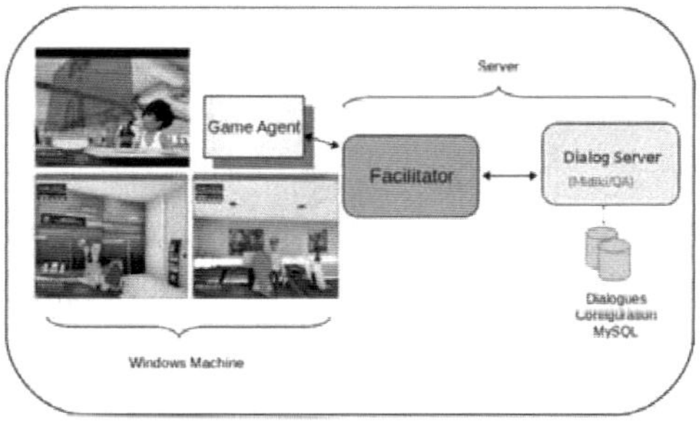

Figure 1: General Architecture for the dialog system: modules are implemented as agents within the Open Agent Architecture.

3.1 The Hybrid Dialogue System

The hybrid system combines an interpreter; a rule based, Information State Approach dialog manager; a generator; and the game/dialog communication components i.e., the OAA interface.

The Interpreter Module In the hybrid system, the interpreter is a classifier trained on the annotated data (cf. section 2.2), which maps the player's utterance to a dialog move. To build the classifier we experimented with both SVM (Support Vector Machine) and LR (Logistic Regression) [2] using different sets of features: utterances were preprocessed by removing stop words and converting content words to unaccented lowercase. Afterwards, we experiment with and without TF*IDF (term frequency*Inverse Document Frequency) filtering and context moves (from 0 to 4 previous dialog moves).

Since the game consist of a number of different dialogs, two options naturally arise: we could either train a single classifier on the whole dataset or train one classifier per dialog. Hence the data sets (and the number of categories to be learned) differ depending on whether we trained one classifier on the whole game data or a classifier for each dialog.

In addition, hand-written rules are used to correct misclassification errors as follows. The best prediction given by the classifier is matched against the expected move determined by the last move stored in the information-state (see below the description of the dialog manager). In case of a mismatch, the interpreter selects a move that is valid in the current context and updates the information state with this move. For instance, if the last move is a yes/no question, *confirm* and *disconfirm* dialog acts are valid moves; for propositional questions, $\texttt{Goal}_i$ is a valid

[2]We used LIBSVM (Chang and Lin, 2001) and MALLET (McCallum, 2002) for the LR classifier with L1 Regularisation.

dialog move [3]; etc. Since the process is non deterministic, this re-interpretation process may improve the system response but it may also be incorrect. For instance, in the following example re-interpretation correctly overrides the dialog move output by the classifier to a move asking the VC (Samir) for the next goal to be achieved.

Samir: Vous avez d'autres questions pour moi?

Do you have other questions ?

Julie: comment cela fonctionne ?

How does it work?

Samir: Eh bien , il va falloir la fabriquer maintenant cette manette . Allez voir Mélissa.

Well, you have to build the joystick now. Go to see Melissa.

In contrast, the dialog below shows a case where re-interpretation fails. Instead of re-interpreting the player's (Julie) input as a request for the next goal, it outputs a request for information about the staff thereby yielding an incoherent exchange.

Samir: D' autres questions ?

Other questions?

Julie: oui qu'est-ce que je peux faire avec ces bouts de papier ?

yes, what can I do with these pieces of paper ?

Samir: Et bien sachez qu'il y a de plus en plus des femmes dans cette industrie ...

you should know there are more and more women in this industry ...

The Dialog Manager We designed a plan for each dialog strategy and extended Midiki (Burke et al., 2003) to support the OAA architecture and access the relational database specifying the configurations of the different dialogs in the game. Each time a new dialog is launched, the information state is loaded with the corresponding dialog-context (e.g., speakers, list of goals to be discussed) and the plan modeling the corresponding dialog strategy. To support dialog management, we implemented a set of update and selection rules for integrating players' moves, handling the information-state and for preparing the agenda according to the plan. More specifically, the following rules are executed at runtime: *Integration*: integrates dialog moves (e.g., questions, answers, acknowledgments) in the information state (questions are listed in the *Question Under Discussion*, answers change the *Commond Ground*, player answers are integrated in response to VCs questions). *Manage Plan*: searches the next action in the plan. *Refill Agenda*: updates the agenda with the next action and *Selection*: selects the next dialog move according to the plan. Once the system move has been selected, the Generator searches an appropriate verbalisation.

[3]The system asks the player for the goal to be discussed: $ask(task(X))$ and the player answers one goal in the situated dialog: $Goal_i$.

The Generator As mentioned above, the generator implements a generation-by-selection strategy. Given the dialog move output by the dialog manager, the generator selects any utterance in this corpus that is labeled with this dialog move and with the identifier of the current dialog.

In addition, two types of dialog moves are given special treatment. The first two moves of each dialog are systematically constrained to be a welcome greeting followed by either a request to pursue a goal (`ask(Goal`$_i$`)` or a proposal to help (`ask(task(X))`). Furthermore, propositional questions (i.e., proposals by the system to discuss additional topics) were annotated separately with their respective dialog goals. For example, Samir's sentence: *Are you interested in hearing about my job, the people that work here or the security policies?*, was annotated with the goals: *job*, *staff* and *security_policies*. For these dialog acts, the generator checks the list of current missing goals so as to retrieve an appropriate propositional question. In this way, the system can coherently direct the player by suggesting possible topics without using vague and repetitive sentences such as *Would you like to know more?*.

3.2 The QA System

The QA system combines a classifier that matches players' turns to system dialog moves with the same generation-by-selection algorithm used in the hybrid system. Like the hybrid system, the QA dialog system maintains a constant interaction with the game to allow for the game coherence and continuity. In particular, at the end of each dialog, the game goals that have been reached through the dialog are returned to the game server so that the game can proceed and be updated with the appropriate score.

For the QA system, we trained a Logistic Regression (LR) classifier for each dialog in the game.

We applied the same preprocessing and extracted the same features used for training the interpreter in the hybrid system.

3.3 Discussion and Interaction Examples

As shown above, while the QA system simply matches the player's input to a system response, the hybrid system has a much more elaborate dialog management policy including re-interpretation and the use of game and dialog history information, to guide the dialog. As a result, the QA dialogs are generally more spontaneous, giving the player more initiative whereas the hybrid system enforces a more System-Driven dialog strategy thereby guiding the player through the game. The following two examples illustrate this point. Sophia is the system and Lucas the player. The game context provides two goals which can be discussed: one mandatory (To find out that finishing the manufacturing process involves conditioning the product), and one optional (To be told what conditioning the product means). The examples show how the hybrid system proposes both goals to the user while the QA engine provides the same information fluently.

Hybrid system

Sophia. Vous avez fait du bon travail les enfants!

You did a great job kids!

Sophia: Bien. Que puis-je faire pour vous ?

What can I do for you?

Lucas: J'ai fini la manette

I've finished the joystick

Sophia: Normalement j'ai encore quelques étapes à réaliser avant l'envoi au client. Vous voulez en savoir plus ?

Normally I still have to condition the product. Do you want to know more about conditioning a product?

Lucas: Oui

Yes, ok

Sophia: Conditionner le produit veut dire l'emballer soigneusement pour pouvoir l'expédier au client. Aldo, le logisticien assure qu'on ne manque pas de stock et de gérer les livraisons et les expéditions.

Conditioning the product means packing it carefully in order to ship it to the customer. Aldo,the logistics coordinator ensures there is no shortage of stock and he is also in charge of the deliveries and shipments.

Sophia: Je vous laisse tester votre manette . Au revoir

I leave you test out your joystick. Goodbye

Question Answer

Sophia: hé bien c'est du bon travail tout ça.

Good! That's a great job kids!

Sophia: Alors , où en sommes nous?

So where are we?

Lucas:voilà nous avons utilisé les composants. Quelle est l'étape suivante?

We used the components, what is the next step?

Sophia: On finis la fabrication par conditionner le produit.

We finish the fabrication by conditioning the product.

Lucas:Ok

Sophia: Conditioner le produit veut dire l'emballer soigneusement pour pouvoir l'expédier au client . Le logisticien assure qu'on ne manque pas de stock et de gérer les livraisons et les expéditions.

Conditioning the product means packing it carefully in order to ship it to the customer. Aldo,the logistics coordinator ensures there is no shortage of stock and he is also in charge of the deliveries and shipments.

Sophia: Et voila, je vous dis au revoir

Ok, I say good bye!

4 Evaluation

In evaluating the two systems, we seek to compare their usability: Which system is best suited for use by real users in the context of the MP serious game? We also seek to better understand which module causes which errors and why. To address these questions we conducted a quantitative evaluation where we compare the accuracy of the interpreter and the dialog manager integrated in each system; a user based evaluation involving 22 subjects using both the QA and the hybrid system; and a corpus based evaluation where we examine such criteria as dialog coherence, dialog success, interpretation and generation errors in the corpus of Human-System interactions collected during the user-based evaluation.

4.1 Quantitative Evaluation

We begin by evaluating the accuracy of the interpreter and the dialog manager used by the hybrid and the QA system respectively. These two classifiers were trained on the Emospeech corpus mentioned above and evaluated with 30-fold cross-validation.

Hybrid System As we mentioned in section 3.1, since the game includes different dialogs, a natural question arise: whether to implement the interpreter with a single classifier for the whole dataset, or using a different classifier for each dialog in the game. To answer this question, we compared the accuracy reached in each case. The details of these experiments are described in (Rojas-Barahona et al., 2012). The highest accuracy is reported when using a single classifier for the *whole game*, reaching an accuracy of 90.26%, as opposed to 88.22% in average *for each dialog*. In both cases, the classifier used is LR, with L1 regularisation and applying the tf*idf filtering. However, although the classifier trained on the whole dialog data has better accuracy (learning a model per dialog often run into the sparse data issue), we observed that, in practice, it often predicted interpretations that were unrelated to the current dialog thereby introducing incoherent responses in dialogs. For instance, in the dialog below, the player wants to know how waste is managed in the factory. The best prediction given by the interpreter is a goal related to another dialog thereby creating a mismatch with the DM expectations. Re-interpretation then fails producing a system response that informs the player of the next goal to be pursued in the game instead of answering the player's request.

Ben: Comment on gère les dechets ici?

How is the waste managed here ?

Serge: Allez voir Sophia pour qu'elle vous fournisse les composants électroniques nécessaires à votre manette.

Go and see Sophia, she'll give you the electronic components you need for your joystick.

For the user based experiment, we therefore use the LR models with one classifier per dialog.

QA System For evaluating the QA classifier, we also compared results with or without tf*idf filtering. The best results were obtained by the LR classifier *for each dialog* with tf*idf filtering yielding an accuracy of 88.27% as shown in Table 2.

Id	w/o Tf*Idf	w Tf*Idf
1	83.33	82.93
2	93.55	91.8
3	72	80.95
4	80	82.47
5	95.24	93.98
6	97.56	97.5
7	97.5	97.44
8	70.59	76
9	92.77	91.14
10	85.53	86.49
11	83.51	87.5
12	94.12	91.04
Avg.	87.14	88.27

Table 2: Results of the LR classifier for mapping players' utterances to system moves, with content-words and a context of four previous system moves, with and without tf*idf filtering.

4.2 Preliminary User-Based Evaluation

The accuracy of the interpreter and the dialog manager used by the hybrid and the QA system only gives partial information on the usability of the dialog engine in a situated setting. We therefore conducted a user-based evaluation which aims to assess the following points: interpretation quality, overall system quality, dialog clarity, game clarity and timing. We invited 22 subjects to play the game twice, once with one system and once with the other. The experiment is biased however in that the players always used the hybrid system first. This is because in practice, the QA system often fail to provide novice players with enough guidance to play the game. This can be fixed by having the player first use the hybrid system. Interestingly, the game guidance made possible by the Information State approach is effective in guiding players through the game e.g., by proposing new goals to be discussed at an appropriate point in the dialog; and by taking dialog history into account.

After playing, each user completed the questionnaire shown in Table 3. For those criteria such as dialog and game clarity, we do not report the scores since these are clearly impacted by how many times the player has played the game. Table 4 shows the mean of the quantitative scores given by the 22 subjects for interpretation, overall system quality and timing. We computed a significance test between the scores given by the subjects, using the Wilcoxon signed-rank test[4]. As shown in the Table, for all criteria, except Q.4, the QA performs significantly ($p < 0.01$) better than the Hybrid system.

[4]The Wilcoxon signed-rank test is the non-parametric alternative to the paired t-test for correlated samples, applicable, e.g. when dealing with measures which cannot be assumed to have equal-interval scales, as is usual with user questionnaires.

	Interpretation
Q.1	Did you have the feeling the virtual characters understood you? (very bad 1 ... 100 very good)
	Overall System Quality
Q.2	Did you find the conversations coherent? (very bad 1 . . . 100 very good)
Q.3	Did you enjoy talking with the virtual characters? (very annoying 1 ... 100 very enjoyable)
Q.4	Would you prefer playing the game without conversations with virtual characters? (yes/no)
Q.5	What is your overall evaluation of the quality of the conversations? (very bad 1 . . . 100 very good)
	Dialogue clarity
Q.6	How easy was it to understand what you were supposed to ask? (very difficult 1 ... 100 very easy)
Q.7	How clear was the information given by the virtual characters? (totally unclear 1 ... 100 very clear)
Q.8	How effective were the instructions at helping you complete the game? (not effective 1 ... 100 very effective)
	Game clarity
Q.9	How easy was it to understand the game? (totally unclear 1 ... 100 very clear)
	Timing
Q.10	Were the system responses too slow (1) / just at the right time (2) / too fast (3)

Table 3: Questionnaire filled by the subjects that played with both dialog systems.

Interpretation. Question Q.1 aims to captures the user's assessment of the dialog system ability to correctly interpret the player's utterances. The QA system scores 0.7 points higher than the Hybrid system suggesting better question/answer coherence for this system. One possible reason is that while the hybrid system detects any incoherence and either tries to fix it using re-interpretation (which as we saw sometimes yields an incoherent dialog) or make it explicit (using a misunderstanding dialog act i.e., a request for rephrasing), the QA system systematically provides a direct answer to the player's input.

The relatively low scores assigned by the user to the interpretation capabilities of the two systems (57.36 and 64.55 respectively) show that the high accuracy of the interpreter and the dialog manager is not a sufficient criteria for assessing the usability of a dialog system.

Timing. One important factor for the usability of a system is of course real time runtimes. The evaluation shows that overall the speed of the QA system was judged more adequate. Interestingly though the difference between the two systems stems no so much from cases where the hybrid approach is too slow than from cases where it is too fast. These cases are due to the fact that while the QA system always issues one-turn answer, the rule based dialog based approach used in the hybrid system often produce two consecutive turns, one answering the player and the other attempting to guide her towards the following game goal.

In sum, although the QA system seems more robust and better at supporting coherent dialogs, the hybrid system seems to be more effective at guiding the player through the game.

	Question	Hybrid	QA
Interpr.	Q.1	57.36	64.55 (*)
	Q.2	57.78	60.68 (*)
	Q.3	60.77	66.45 (*)
Sys Qual.	Q.4/no	86.37	81.82
	Q.5	59.54	65.68 (*)
	Avg.	66.12	68.66 (*)
Timing	Q.10	2.25	2.05 (*)

Table 4: Mean of the quantitative scores given by 22 individuals. (*) denotes statistical significance at $p < 0.01$ (two-tailed significance level).

4.3 Corpus-Based Evaluation

The User-Based evaluation resulted in the collection of 298 dialogs (690 player and 1813 system turns) with the Hybrid system and 261 dialogs (773 player and 1411 system turns) with the QA system. To better understand the causes of the scores derived from the user-filled questionnaire, we performed manual error analysis on this data focusing on dialog incoherences, dialog success, dialog management and generation errors (reported in Table 5).

DM Errors The count of dialog management (DM) errors is the ratio $\frac{WR}{P}$ of wrong system responses on counts of player's input. In essence this metrics permits comparing the accuracy of the QA dialog manager with that of the hybrid system. On average there is no clear distinction between the two systems.

Generation Errors The system response selected by the generation component might be contextually inappropriate for at least two reasons. First, it may contain information which is unrelated to the current context. Second, it might have been imprecisely or incorrectly annotated. For instance, in the dialog below, the annotation of the turn *Yes, thanks. What do you want me to do?* did not indicate that the turn included a *Confirm* dialog move. Selecting this turn in the absence of a yes/no question resulted in a contextually inappropriate system response.

SYSTEM: Bonjour les petits jeunes je suis le préparateur matiére.

Hello kids, I am the raw material responsible

SYSTEM: Oui merci. Vous me voulez quoi en fait ?

Yes, thanks. What do you want me to do?

PLAYER: je veux en savoir plus sur cet endroit.

I would like to know more about this place

As shown in Table 5, for both systems, there were few generation errors.

Id	%DM H.	%DM. QA	%Gen H. & QA
1	0.0	4.55	0.57
2	10.81	12.00	1.02
3	10.38	12.04	1.49
4	16.22	14.86	0.32
5	10.34	2.13	1.46
6	0.0	0.0	0.94
7	9.52	4.0	0.0
8	11.68	7.08	2.06
9	2.13	26.47	0.76
10	15.63	16.13	6.08
11	11.94	8.33	3.19
12	14.29	8.16	3.17
Avg.	9.41	9.65	1.76

Table 5: DM and generation errors detected in the hybrid and the QA systems.

Unsuccessful Dialogs We counted as unsuccessful those dialogs that were closed before discussing the mandatory goals. The results are shown in Table 6. Overall the QA system is more robust leading to the mandatory goals being discussed in almost all dialogs. One exception was dialog 8, where the system went into a loop due to the player repeating the same sequence of dialog moves. We fixed this by integrating a loop detection step in the QA dialog manager. For the hybrid system, dialog 7, a dialog involving the confirmation strategy (cf. section 2) is the most problematic. In this case, the DM rules used to handle this strategy are inappropriate in that whenever the system fails to identify a contextually appropriate response, it simply says so and quits the dialog. The example illustrates the difficulty of developing a complete and coherent DM rule system.

Id	%Uns. H.	%Inco. H.	%Uns. QA.	%Inc. QA.
1	0	0.0	0.0	0.0
2	0	0.0	0.0	0.0
3	6.67	3.33	7.41	0.0
4	7.14	0.0	0.0	4.0
5	3.85	0.0	0.0	0.0
6	0.0	0.0	0.0	0.0
7	21.21	0.0	0.0	0.0
8	3.70	0.0	15.63	3.13
9	0.0	0.0	0.0	4.35
10	0.0	6.67	0.0	16.67
11	3.45	6.90	0.0	3.70
12	4.17	4.17	4.55	4.55
Avg.	4.89	1.76	4.47	3.03

Table 6: Overall dialog errors, the percentage of unsuccessful dialogs

Incoherent Dialogs We counted as incoherent, dialogs where most system answers were unrelated to the player's input. As shown in Table 6, despite interpretation and generation imprecisions, most dialogs were globally coherent. They made sense according to the game context: they were related to the task to be solved by the player in the game, and the generated instructions were correctly understood. The hybrid system produces slightly less incoherent dialogs probably because of its re-interpretation mechanism which permits correcting contextually invalid dialog moves.

5 Conclusion

We have presented a multi-view evaluation of two system architectures for conversational agents situated in a serious game. Although the QA system seems more robust and is easier to deploy, the hybrid dialog engine seems to fare better in terms of game logic in that it guides the player more effectively through the game. The evaluation shows the importance of assessing not only the dialog engine accuracy but also its usability in the setting it was designed for. In future work, we plan to compute a regression model of user satisfaction for applying reinforcement learning and find the optimal strategy. In addition, we plan to extend the comparison to other domains such as language learning and complex negociation dialogs.

6 Acknowledgments

The research presented in this paper was partially supported by the Eurostar EmoSpeech project and by the European Fund for Regional Development within the framework of the INTERREG IV A Allegro Project.

References

C. Burke, C. Doran, A. Gertner, A. Gregorowicz, L. Harper, J. Korb, and D. Loehr. 2003. Dialogue complexity with portability?: research directions for the information state approach. In *Proceedings of the HLT-NAACL 2003 workshop on Research directions in dialogue processing - Volume 7*.

Jean Carletta, Stephen Isard, Gwyneth Doherty-Sneddon, Amy Isard, Jacqueline C. Kowtko, and Anne H. Anderson. 1997. The reliability of a dialogue structure coding scheme. *Comput. Linguist.*, 23(1):13–31, March.

Chih C. Chang and Chih J. Lin, 2001. *LIBSVM: a library for support vector machines*.

David DeVault, Anton Leuski, and Kenji Sagae. 2011. An evaluation of alternative strategies for implementing dialogue policies using statistical classification and hand-authored rules. In *5th International Joint Conference on Natural Language Processing (IJCNLP 2011)*.

Sudeep Gandhe and David Traum. 2007. Creating spoken dialogue characters from corpora without annotations. In *Proceedings of 8th Conference in the Annual Series of Interspeech Events*, pages 2201–2204.

Jonathan Gratch, Jeff Rickel, Elisabeth André, Justine Cassell, Eric Petajan, and Norman Badler. 2002. Creating interactive virtual humans: Some assembly required. *IEEE Intelligent Systems*, 17:54–63, July.

Dennis Hofs, Mariët Theune, and Rieks Akker op den. 2010. Natural interaction with a virtual guide in a virtual environment: A multimodal dialogue system. *Journal on Multimodal User Interfaces*, 3(1-2):141–153, March. Open Access.

Kate S. Hone and Robert Graham. 2000. Towards a tool for the subjective assessment of speech system interfaces (sassi). *Nat. Lang. Eng.*, 6(3-4):287–303, September.

W. L. Johnson, H. H. Vilhjálmsson, and S. Marsella. 2005. Serious games for language learning: How much game, how much AI? In *Artificial Intelligence in Education*.

S. Larsson and D. Traum. 2000. Information state and dialogue management in the TRINDI dialogue move engine toolkit. *Natural Language Engineering*, 6:323–340.

Anton Leuski and David Traum. 2008. A statistical approach for text processing in virtual humans. In *Proceedings of the 26th Army Science Conference*.

Anton Leuski, Ronakkumar Patel, David Traum, and Brandon Kennedy. 2006. Building effective question answering characters. In *Proceedings of the 7th SIGDIAL Workshop on Discourse and Dialogue*, pages 18–27.

Andrew Kachites McCallum. 2002. Mallet: A machine learning for language toolkit. http://mallet.cs.umass.edu.

Lina M. Rojas-Barahona, Alejandra Lorenzo, and Claire Gardent. 2012. Building and exploiting a corpus of dialog interactions between french speaking virtual and human agents. In *Proceedings of the 8th International Conference on Language Resources and Evaluation (to be published)*.

David R. Traum and Staffan Larsson. 2003. The information state approach to dialogue management. In Jan Kuppevelt, Ronnie W. Smith, and Nancy Ide, editors, *Current and New Directions in Discourse and Dialogue*, volume 22 of *Text, Speech and Language Technology*, pages 325–353. Springer Netherlands. 10.1007/978-94-010-0019-2_15.

David R. Traum, Antonio Roque, Anton Leuski, Panayiotis Georgiou, Jillian Gerten, Bilyana Martinovski, Shrikanth Narayanan, Susan Robinson, and Ashish Vaswani. 2007. Hassan: A virtual human for tactical questioning. In *Proceedings of the 8th SIGdial Workshop on Discourse and Dialogue*, page 71–74, September.

David Traum, Stacy C. Marsella, Jonathan Gratch, Jina Lee, and Arno Hartholt. 2008. Multi-party, multi-issue, multi-strategy negotiation for multi-modal virtual agents. In *Proceedings of the 8th international conference on Intelligent Virtual Agents*, IVA '08, pages 117–130, Berlin, Heidelberg. Springer-Verlag.

Marilyn A. Walker, Donald Hindle, Jeanne Fromer, Giuseppe Di Fabbrizio, and Craig Mestel. 1997. Evaluating competing agent strategies for a voice email agent. *CoRR*, cmp-lg/9706019.

A. Example of a dialog with the hybrid system. Translation into English of a dialog between Samir (the system) and Julie (the player) (Strategy 2), it corresponds to the third dialog in Table 1

Samir: Hello my name is Samir, the product designer

Samir: What are you doing here young people?

Julie: we come to build the joystick of Professor Geekman

Samir: You are in the right place. The plans are in the closet

Samir: Before would you like to hear about my job, the studies I did or my colleagues

Julie: Tell me about your job.

Samir: Well, for instance, is me who devise and design the items we construct in this enterprise

Samir: Do you want to know more about my colleagues or about the security measures applied here?

Julie: What do your colleagues do?

Samir: My job is universal! In fact it can please both girls that boys...

Samir: In your opinion, what studies should be done to get there

Julie: Designing studies?

Samir: This is a creative job. Several training can lead to the job arts, industrial design, computer-aided design

Samir: And does the safety standards interest you?

Julie: That is important the safety yes, tell me more

Samir: You know, here you are in a strategic place.

The novelties, the products of tomorrow, is here that they are born. They must be protected. For that reason we control the entrance here.

Samir: Well, Good Luck. Bye!

B. Translation to English of a dialog with the QA system. Dialog between the raw material operator (the system) and Julie (the player), it corresponds to the 8th dialog in Table 1(Strategy 4).

Preparateur1: Hello I am the raw material responsible. I can provide you a lot of information about this place.

Preparateur1: What can I do for you ?

Julie: What do you do here?

Preparateur1: My role is to ensure machines are supplied with the right materials,in good colors. I turn on the drying ovens and the whole supply system.

Julie: How does it work the supply system?

Preparateur1: Well when we get the pellet material, they are wet ...

Julie: What does it happen when there is a problem?

Preparateur1: In that case, I call the technician, he is the best for fixing everything

Julie:Thanks for the information, what should I do now?

Preparateur1: It is not complicated and you will learn things. I have a new machine to supply but I can not find the right material. Would you give me a hand?

Julie: yes

Preparateur1: You must supply this machine with a new generation of plastic. This machine allows the manufacture of plastic bags

Julie: ok

Preparateur1: Let's go!

Julie: Ok, Let's start!

Preparateur1: Great, Thanks!

Preparateur1: You are very kind, thank you.

"Love ya, jerkface": using Sparse Log-Linear Models to Build Positive (and Impolite) Relationships with Teens

William Yang Wang, Samantha Finkelstein, Amy Ogan, Alan W Black, Justine Cassell
School of Computer Science, Carnegie Mellon University
{yww, slfink, aeo, awb, justine}@cs.cmu.edu

Abstract

One challenge of implementing spoken dialogue systems for long-term interaction is how to adapt the dialogue as user and system become more familiar. We believe this challenge includes evoking and signaling aspects of long-term relationships such as rapport. For tutoring systems, this may additionally require knowing how relationships are signaled among non-adult users. We therefore investigate conversational strategies used by teenagers in peer tutoring dialogues, and how these strategies function differently among friends or strangers. In particular, we use annotated and automatically extracted linguistic devices to predict impoliteness and positivity in the next turn. To take into account the sparse nature of these features in real data we use models including Lasso, ridge estimator, and elastic net. We evaluate the predictive power of our models under various settings, and compare our sparse models with standard non-sparse solutions. Our experiments demonstrate that our models are more accurate than non-sparse models quantitatively, and that teens use unexpected kinds of language to do relationship work such as signaling rapport, but friends and strangers, tutors and tutees, carry out this work in quite different ways from one another.

1 Introduction and Related Work

Rapport, the harmonious synchrony between interlocutors, has numerous benefits for a range of dialogue types, including direction giving (Cassell et al., 2007) or contributing to patient recovery (Vowles and Thompson, 2012). In peer tutoring, an educational paradigm in which students of similar ability tutor one another, friendship among tutors and tutees leads to better learning (Gartner et al., 1971). With the burgeoning use of spoken dialogue systems in education, understanding the process by which two humans build and signal rapport during learning becomes a vital step for implementing spoken dialogue systems (SDSs) that can initiate (and, as importantly, maintain) a successful relationship with students over time. However, implementing a tutorial dialogue system that appropriately challenges students in the way that peers do so well (Sharpley et al., 1983), while still demonstrating the rapport that peers can also provide, calls for understanding the differences in communication between peer tutors just meeting and those who are already friends.

The Tickle-Degnen and Rosenthal (1990) model provides a starting point by outlining the components of rapport, including the finding that positivity decreases over the course of a relationship. The popularity of this model, however, has not diminished the disproportionate attention that positivity and politeness receive in analyses of rapport (Brown and Levinson, 1978), including in the vast majority of computational approaches to rapport-building in dialogue (Stronks et al., 2002; Johnson and Rizzo, 2004; Bickmore and Picard, 2005; Gratch et al., 2006; McLaren et al., 2007; Cassell et al., 2007; Baker et al., 2008; Bickmore et al., 2011). The creation and expression of rapport is complex, and can also be signaled through negative, or impolite, exchanges (Straehle, 1993; Watts, 2003; Spencer-Oatey, 2008) that communicate affection and relationship security among intimates who can flout common social norms (Culpeper, 2011; Kienpointner, 1997).

However, it is an open question as to whether such rudeness is likely to impress a new student on the first day of class. We must better understand how and when impoliteness and other negative dialogue moves can contribute to the development and expression of the rapport that is so important in educational relationships. In this analysis, then, we begin with a corpus of tutoring chat data annotated with a set of affectively-charged linguistic devices (e.g. complaining, emoticons), and then differentiate between the linguistic devices that friend and stranger interlocutors employ (with friendship standing as a proxy for pre-existent rapport) and the resulting social effects or functions of those devices on the partners.

Since our ultimate goal is to build an SDS that can adapt to the user's language in real time, we also automatically extract lexical and syntactic features from the conversations. And, in order to determine what the system should say to evoke particular responses, we predict social effects in partner two from the use of the linguistic devices in partner one.

Since we want to understand how the system can deal with newly met peers as well as peers who have become friends, we develop and evaluate our model on dyads of friends and then evaluate the same model with dyads of strangers, to examine whether dyads with less a priori rapport react differently to the same linguistic devices.

Of course, in addition to understanding the phenomenon of rapport in all of its complexity, a major challenge for building rapport-signaling SDS is to construct a compact feature space that capture only reliable rapport signals and generalizes well across different speakers. Of course phenomena such as insults, complaints and pet names, no matter how important, appear relatively rarely in data of this sort. Training discriminative models with maximum likelihood estimators (MLE) on such datasets usually results in assigning too much weight on less frequent signals. This standard MLE training method not only produces dense models, but may also overestimates lower frequency features that might be unreliable signals and overfit to a particular set of speakers. In recent studies on speaker state prediction that use lexical features, it has been shown that MLE estimators demonstrate large performance gaps between non-overlapping speaker datasets (Jeon et al., 2010; Wang et al., 2012a).

On the other hand, recent studies on ℓ_1/ℓ_2 based group penalty for evaluating dialogue systems (González-Brenes and Mostow, 2011), structured sparsity for linguistic structure prediction (Martins et al., 2011), and discovering historical legal opinions with a sparse mixed-effects latent variable model (Wang et al., 2012b) have all shown concrete benefits of modeling sparsity in language-related predictive tasks. We therefore apply sparsity-sensitive models that can prevent less frequent features from overfitting. We start with the ℓ_1-regularized Lasso (Tibshirani, 1994) model, since, compared to other covariance matrix based sparse models, such as sparse Principal Component Analysis (PCA) and sparse Canonical Correlation Analysis (CCA), the Lasso model is straightforward and requires fewer computing resources when the feature dimension is high. Hence, we compare the contributions of both automated features and annotated features using the proposed Lasso model to predict impoliteness and positivity.

In addition to Lasso and a logistic regression baseline, we introduce two alternative penalty models: the non-sparse ridge (le Cessie and van Houwelingen, 1992) estimator, and an elastic net model (Zou and Hastie, 2005). The ridge estimator applies a quadratic penalty for feature selection, resulting in a smooth objective function and a non-sparse feature space, which can be seen as a strong non-sparse penalty model. We investigate the elastic net model, because it balances the pros and cons of Lasso and ridge estimators, and enforces composite penalty. In addition to the model comparisons, by varying the different sizes of feature windows (number of turns in the dialogue history), we empirically show that our proposed sparse log-linear model is flexible, enabling the model to capture long-range dependency.

This approach also allows us to extend previous work on speaker state prediction. Although speaker state prediction has attracted much attention in the dialogue research community, most studies have focused on the analysis of anger, frustration, and other classic emotions (Litman and Forbes-Riley, 2004; Liscombe et al., 2005; Devillers and Vidrascu, 2006; Ai et al., 2006; Grimm et al., 2007; Gupta and Nitendra., 2007; Metallinou et al., 2011). Recently, Wang and Hirschberg (2011) proposed a hierarchical model that detects level of interest of speakers in dialogue, using a multistream prediction feedback technique. However, to the best of our knowledge, we are among the first to study the problem of automatic impoliteness and positivity prediction in dialogue. Because our ultimate goal is to build an SDS that responds to users' language use over time, the features from the user's target turn that the model is aiming to predict are not observable, which renders the task more difficult than previous speaker state detection tasks.

Our main contributions are three-fold: (1) analysis of linguistic devices that function to signal rapport among friends - and their effects on non-friend dyads; (2) detailed analyses of language behavior features that predict these rapport behaviors - both impoliteness and positivity - in the next turn of teenagers' peer tutoring sessions; (3) an evaluation of non-sparse and sparse log-linear models for predicting impoliteness and positivity.

By understanding the signals of rapport that a person is likely to display in response to various linguistic devices, we can begin to build an SDS that can anticipate the social response and adapt to the rapport-signaling efforts of its partner, both as a newly introduced technology, and, over time, as a system with whom the user has a rapport.

2 The Corpus

We use the data from a previous study evaluating the impact of a peer tutoring intervention that monitored students' collaboration and in some cases provided adaptive support (Walker et al., 2011). In the intervention, peer tutors observed the work of their tutee and supported them through a chat interface as they completed algebra problems. The system logged all chat and other information about the problem steps. Participants were 130 high school students (81 female) in grades 7-12 from one American high school with some prior knowledge of the algebra material. Participants were asked to sign up for the study with a friend. Those who were interested but were unable to participate with a friend, were matched with another unmatched participant. In an after-school session, participants first took a 20-minute pre-test on the math concepts, and then spent 20 minutes working alone with the computer to prepare for tutoring. One student in each dyad was then randomly assigned the role of tutor, while the other was given the role of tutee, regardless of relative ability. They spent the next 60 minutes engaging in tutoring. Finally, students were given a domain posttest isomorphic to the pretest.

54 dyads signed up as **friends** and 6 were unmatched **strangers**. To compare behavior between friends and strangers in the face of very different data set sizes we use 48 friend dyads for training, and select 6 friend and 6 stranger dyads as two separate test sets. The total number of utterances in the friend training set, friend test set, and stranger test set are 4538, 468 and 402. To perform turn-based prediction experiments, we concatenate the text in the utterances by the same speaker into a single turn, and perform an "OR" operation[1] on features (See Section 3 for details) in multiple utterances of the same speaker to generate the turn-based binary features.

3 Feature Engineering

In this section, we describe both the annotated and automatically extracted features analyzed.

3.1 Annotated Features and Labels[2]

To understand what linguistic devices participated in positivity and impoliteness during tutoring, we annotated all 60 dyads for surface-level language behaviors such as complaints, challenges (Culpeper, 1996) and praise. We also automatically identified chat features that socially color the communication, such as excessive punctuation[P] or capitalization[Ca]. Utterances could receive more than one code, and inter-rater reliability ranged from K=.71 to K=1.

Because these linguistic behaviors may serve a range of different functions in context, such as rude language serving to cement a relationship (Ardington, 2006), or teasing to increase rapport (Straehle, 1993), we also annotate the **social functionality** of each utterance in context, in terms of positivity (K=.79)[3] and impoliteness (K=.76), which are seen as holding down opposite kinds of social functionality (Terkourafi, 2008). Details of annotation can be found in our recent work (Ogan et al., 2012).

Language Behavior Features

Language behavior features were annotated by two raters, based on previous work on impoliteness (Culpeper, 1996), positivity (Boyer et al., 2008), and computer-mediated communication (Herring and Zelenkauskaite, 2009), as follows:.

- Insults[Di] (κ=1): Personalized negative vocatives or references. *eg. "you are so weird."*
- Challenges[Ch] (κ =.91): Directly questioning partner's decision or ability. *eg. Partner 1: "see I am helping", Partner 2: "barely."*
- Condescensions / brags[C] (κ=1): Asserting authority or partner's inferiority. *eg. Tutee: "nothing you have done has affected me what so ever."*
- Message enforcer[Ef] (κ=.85): Emphasizing text or attracting partner's attention. *eg. "Earth to Erin."*
- Dismissal / Silencer / Curse[Cu] (κ =.76): Asserting unimportance of contribution/partner. *eg. "shuttttt up computer."*
- Pet name[Pe] (κ = .9): Vocatives that may or may not be insulting. *eg. "whats up homie?"*
- Criticisms / exclusive complaints[EC] (κ=.8): Negative evaluation of partner. *eg. "You are so bad at this dude."*
- Inclusive complaints[I] (κ=.78): Complaints directed outside the partner, such as at the task, computers, or study. *eg. "This is really dumb, ya think?"*
- Laughter[L] (κ=1): *eg. "haha", "lol"*
- Off-task[O] (κ=.71): Doesn't pertain to or advance tutorial dialogue. *eg. "Coming over after this?"*

Impoliteness and Positivity Labels

While the surface-level features were coded based on a single utterance, context determined the labels for impoliteness and positivity, including the recent tone of the dialogue and the partner's response to the utterance. Utterances were coded as positivity (κ=.79) when they included goals that directly added positive affect into the exchange through praise, empathy, reassurance, cooperative talk (McLaren et al.,

[1]If any of the utterances within one turn has this feature turned on, then we say that we have observed this feature in this turn.

[2]We thank Erin Walker for data collection and annotation.

[3]We use Cohen's kappa in this study.

2011), task enthusiasm, and making or responding to jokes. Impoliteness (κ=.76) included both cooperatively rude utterances such as teasing (typical eg. "hahah you're the worst tutor ever") and uncooperatively rude utterances that may cause offense (typical eg. "um why don't you try actually explainin urself..") (Kienpointner, 1997).

3.2 Automated Features

To compare the performance between what could be automatically extracted from dialogue and hand annotation, we extracted 2,872 unigram and 12,016 bigram features from the text corpus. Using the Stanford PoS tagger[4] with its attached model, we also extracted 46 common part-of-speech tags from the text. In addition to the above lexical and syntactic features, we automatically extracted the capitalization features[Ca] that have at least one full word (eg. "CALM DOWN") (Chovanec, 2009). Since a recent text prediction task (Wang and McKeown, 2010) observed benefits from modeling punctuation features[P], we extracted the expressive punctuation that included at least one exclamation point or more than one question-mark (eg. "I don't get it?!??!") (Crystal, 2001). We used a smiley dictionary[5] to extract the emoticons[E] that convey emotional states (Sánchez et al., 2006) from text.

4 Sparse Log-Linear Models

We formulate our impoliteness and positivity prediction problems as binary classifications. To do this, we estimate the label $\hat{y}_t \sim Bernoulli(\hat{\theta})$. First, we introduce a standard log-linear parametrization[6] to our predictive tasks:

$$\hat{\theta}_{\vec{y}_t} = \frac{\exp \sum_i \vec{w}_i \vec{f}_i(\vec{y}_t)}{1 + \exp \sum_i \vec{w}_i \vec{f}_i(\vec{y}_t)}, \quad (1)$$

where $\vec{f}(\vec{y}_t)$ is a set of feature functions computed on the observation vector $\vec{y}_t$. The term $\vec{w}_i$ puts a weight on feature i for predicting impoliteness, and our estimation problem is now to set these weights. The log-likelihood and the gradient are:

$$\ell = \sum_t y_t \log \hat{\theta}_{\vec{y}_t} + (1 - y_t) \log(1 - \hat{\theta}_{\vec{y}_t}) \quad (2)$$

$$\frac{\partial \ell}{\partial \vec{w}} = \sum_t \left(\frac{\partial \hat{\theta}_{\vec{y}_t}}{\partial \vec{w}} \right) \left(\frac{y_t}{\hat{\theta}_{\vec{y}_t}} - \frac{1 - y_t}{1 - \hat{\theta}_{\vec{y}_t}} \right) \quad (3)$$

$$\frac{\partial \hat{\theta}_{\vec{y}_t}}{\partial \vec{w}} = \left(\hat{\theta}_{\vec{y}_t} - (\hat{\theta}_{\vec{y}_t})^2 \right) \vec{f}(\vec{y}_t), \quad (4)$$

so the parameters can be set using gradient ascent. To control the overall complexity, we can apply regularized models on the elements of $\vec{w}$. A sparsity-inducing model, such as the Lasso (Tibshirani, 1994) or elastic net (Zou and Hastie, 2005) model, will drive many of these weights to zero, revealing important interactions between the impoliteness/positivity label and other features. Instead of maximizing the log-likelihood, we can minimize the following Lasso model that consists of the negative log-likelihood loss function:

$$\min \Big(-\ell + \sum_i \lambda_1 ||\vec{w}_i|| \Big) \quad (5)$$

Since the Lasso penalty can introduce discontinuities to the original convex function, we can also consider an alternative non-sparse ridge estimator (le Cessie and van Houwelingen, 1992) that has the convex property:

$$\min \Big(-\ell + \sum_i \lambda_2 ||\vec{w}_i||^2 \Big) \quad (6)$$

In addition to the Lasso and ridge estimators, the composite penalty based elastic net model balances the sparsity and smoothness properties of both Lasso and ridge estimators:

$$\min \Big(-\ell + \sum_i \lambda_1 ||w_i|| + \sum_i \lambda_2 ||w_i||^2 \Big) \quad (7)$$

Our log-linear model is quite flexible; by comparing various restrictions, we can test different features when modeling impoliteness and positivity. In addition, the model can incorporate features from previous time windows, which requires much less computational complexity compared to standard high order Markov models. We use the L-BFGS method (Liu and Nocedal, 1989) for the numerical optimization.

5 Empirical Experiments

We predict impoliteness vs. non-impoliteness and positivity vs. non-positivity of an interlocutor in the immediate future turn, given only information from current/previous turns. Because accuracy, precision, recall and F-measure are threshold-based point estimation metrics that might prevent one from observing the big picture of system performance, we consider the Receiver Operating Characteristic (ROC) metric to evaluate the dynamics of the true positive rate vs. the false positive rate (Hanley and McNeil, 1982) in our system. We mainly use Area Under Curve (AUC) as a metric to compare classifiers, since it maps the ROC metric to a single scalar value representing expected performance. A random classifier will have an AUC of 0.5 (Fawcett, 2006).

[4] http://nlp.stanford.edu/software/tagger.shtml

[5] http://www.techdictionary.com/emoticon.html

[6] We thank Jacob Eisenstein for the formulation of logistic regression model.

Models	P	Ca	E	L	O	Ef	Pe	Di	C	EC	Ch	Cu	I
						Impoliteness Prediction							
Tr-Te	.44	-1.10	.62	.72	.09	.64	.09	1.29	.96	.89	.69	.77	-0.19
Te-Tr	-2.48	.54	-0.26	0.15	.59	1.62	.24	.22	.89	.72	.75	.04	-0.18
						Positivity Prediction							
Tr-Te	-0.87	.19	.36	.55	1.06	-0.62	.69	-1.63	-1.57	.16	-0.41	1.22	.86
Te-Tr	-1.39	-0.46	.70	.48	.46	.33	.62	-0.71	.70	-0.65	-0.47	-0.54	.78

Table 1: Comparing the Learned Weights of Different Features when Predicting the Partner's Impoliteness in a Non-Sparse Log-Linear Model. *Tr-Te: predict tutee turn with tutor turn. Te-Tr: predict tutor turn with tutee turn. For full name of features, see Section 3.*

5.1 Comparing the Learned Weights of Different Features

In our previous analysis of these data (Ogan et al., 2012), a PCA method allowed us to group linguistic behaviors in order to address the issue of data sparsity. With the use of log-linear models, we are able to investigate the contributions of individual language behaviors in one student's turn to the prediction of social functions in their partner's next turn. In this experiment, we evaluate the weights of various linguistic devices in a standard logistic regression model. We found that behaviors commonly associated with impoliteness were predictors of partner impoliteness in the next turn, while positive behaviors such as laughter were predictors of upcoming positivity. SDSs can leverage this knowledge to take the partners lead during a tutoring session, using the partners positivity or impoliteness to determine the affect of the systems upcoming move. As we intend to develop a system that acts as a tutee, however, we further divided the analysis by tutoring role, investigating how partners in different roles employ language features differently, such that the system can act in accordance with its given role. Table 1 shows the results.

Similarly to the collapsed factors in our previous work, we found here that tutors and tutees do in fact use language behaviors differently, and to accomplish different social functions. Effectively, this means that certain language behaviors may instigate impoliteness when said by one partner, but lead to positivity when expressed by the other. For example, tutee bragging predicts a response of positivity on behalf of the tutor ($\vec{w}_C^{(TE)}$ = .7), perhaps because the tutor wants to be supportive of a protégé's self-efficacy and success. Conversely, when the tutor brags during a peer tutoring dialogue, the tutee, who may feel threatened by the tutors bravado, is extremely likely to respond with impoliteness ($\vec{w}_C^{(TR)}$ = .96). In a peer tutoring paradigm, when the more powerful partner (the tutor) expresses dominance through self-inflation, the subordinate partner may use impoliteness to regain some social control. On the other hand, some language behaviors actively work to tear down this power imbalance, such as inclusive complaining, where the partners take an us against the task approach, building solidarity through complaining about the experiment. These utterances predict positivity whether used by the tutor ($\vec{w}_I^{(TR)}$ = .86) or tutee ($\vec{w}_I^{(TE)}$ = .78). Other comparisons between weighted features by role demonstrate similarly theoretically-motivated findings that shed light on how language is used to achieve social functions.

5.2 Comparing the Contributions of Different Features on Friend and Stranger Datasets

A previous study (Ogan et al., 2012) on these same data seemed to indicate that negative conversational strategies composed of linguistic devices such as complaining and insults were correlated with learning in the friend dyads and negatively correlated with learning in strangers. However the small number of stranger dyads prevented them from drawing conclusions about particular linguistic devices from the data. Here, we empirically show the predictive performance of different feature sets on both friend and stranger test sets in Table 2 , using a sparse Lasso model with features from only the current turn. In the impoliteness prediction task, when predicting on the test set that consists of only friends, we observe statistically significant improvement over a random baseline, using surface-level language behavior features, lexical, lexical + syntactic, all automatic, and all features. When combining all features, the best AUC is .621. The automatic features, mainly including n-grams and part-of-speech tags, have emerged as a useful automated feature space. On the other hand, we do not observe any significant results on the stranger datasets, suggesting that strangers do not respond with impoliteness in the same way that friends do. When predicting positivity on the friend dataset, we see that the performance of surface-level language behavior features has dropped from the first task, and the statistical t-test is non-significant when comparing to a random baseline. This is not surprising, because we have shown in the previous section that surface-level language behavior features are strong indicators of impoliteness, but might not have advantages in predicting positivity for friends. Interestingly, the automated features outperform the combination of all features, indicating a promising future for the actual deployment of an SDS that can interact using appropriate positivity and impoliteness.

When predicting positivity in the stranger dataset, we find the opposite trend. In contrast to the impoliteness prediction task, the overall performance on the stranger dataset improved, and the lexical, lexical+syntactic, and all feature combination have significantly outperformed the chance baseline. These results suggest that positivity is a predictable behavior among strangers, who may all express uniform positivity across all dyads, while it is the impoliteness that is predictable among friends. Perhaps it is that through the development of a rapport with a partner, the particular ways in which positivity is expressed becomes personalized to the dyad, and can no longer be applied to other groups who have their own expressions of positivity. In other words, unlike in Tolstoy's world, here unhappy families are all alike; every happy family is happy in its own way. We must look to the easily-predictable impoliteness among friends instead, arguing strongly for the inclusion of impoliteness in a model of rapport.

Feature Sets	F-AUC	p	S-AUC	p
Impoliteness Prediction				
Random	.500	-	.500	-
Behavior	.596	.017	.505	.473
Lex	.599	.014	.435	.819
Lex + POS	.605	.009	.425	.857
All Auto	.591	.022	.451	.751
All Features	.621	.003	.427	.850
Positivity Prediction				
Random	.500	-	.500	-
Behavior	.549	.141	.527	.302
Lex	.623	.003	.601	.025
Lex + POS	.646	.001	.587	.047
All Auto	.651	.001	.577	.070
All Features	.641	.001	.608	.019

Table 2: Comparing contributions of different feature streams on both friend and stranger testsets with Lasso model when predicting impoliteness and positivity of the next turn using only features from the current turn. *(F-: the friend test set. S: the stranger test set. p: one-tailed p-value by comparing to a random classifier. Behavior: detailed surface-level language behavior features defined in Section 3. Lex: unigram and bigram. POS: part-of-speech features. All Auto: all automatically extracted features (Lex + POS + punctuation + caps + emoticons).)*

5.3 Comparing Logistic Regression, Lasso, Ridge, and Elastic Net

While our previous work (Ogan et al., 2012) demonstrated that PCA is a useful feature selection method when there are only a dozen features, in this experiment, the dimension of our feature space is substantially higher, which aligns to the size of vocabulary. Thus, covariance-based feature selection methods, such as PCA, might be too slow. Here we compare the performances of standard MLE trained logistic regression, Lasso, non-sparse ridge, and elastic net models. In particular, we demonstrate the predictive power of Lasso and elastic net models, varying distinct levels of sparsity. In the Figure 1, we show the comparison of three different models in the impoliteness prediction task. The horizontal axis represents different values of regularization coefficient λ. For the Lasso model and the elastic net model, increasing the value λ will result in a sparser feature space, and we set the $\lambda = \lambda_1 = \lambda_2$ in the elastic net model to promote same level of sparsity and smoothness. The result at $\lambda = 0$ represents the standard non-sparse logistic regression model, which obtains an AUC of .563. When introducing penalty for large weights in this standard model, .4 to .5 significant improvements ($p = .003$ for Lasso, $p = .007$ for ridge, and $p = .004$ for elastic net) of AUC are observed from Lasso, ridge and elastic net models when $\lambda = 1$. The elastic net model that balances sparsity and smoothness, has obtain the best result in this experiment. The best result of elastic net model is .63 when $\lambda = 7$. This experiment shows that all three penalty models have outperformed the non-sparse logistic regression model. The elastic net model, which balances sparisty and smoothness, obtains the best results when predicting impoliteness. Figure 2 shows the comparison of three models on the friend dataset in the positivity prediction task. When $\lambda = 0$, the standard logistic regression model has an AUC of .638. When increasing the λ to 1, both Lasso and elastic net models have shown significant improvements (both $p < .001$) in AUC, but not the non-sparse ridge estimator. The Lasso model is found to be the best model in this task: we obtain better results when the model gets sparser until the model is too sparse when $\lambda = 6$. In contrast to the experiment in Figure 1, we see that both the ridge and elastic net models do not very strong advantages in this positivity prediction task. We hypothesize that the reason why Lasso works better in the positivity task is that the frequency of positivity labels is substantially higher than the impoliteness labels in our corpus, so that a Lasso model that enforces full ℓ_1 penalty fits better in this task. In contrast, since the impoliteness label is less frequent, a denser elastic net composite penalty model that preserve critical features, works the best in the impoliteness prediction task. In general, we can see that sparse log-linear models outperform standard log-linear models as well as non-sparse ridge estimators in the two tasks.

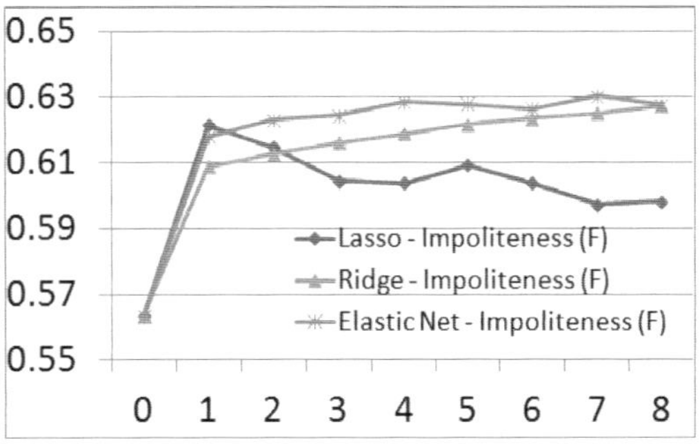

Figure 1: Comparing Impacts of Different Levels of Sparsity on the Friend Dataset When Predicting Impoliteness with Lasso, Ridge, and Elastic Net Models

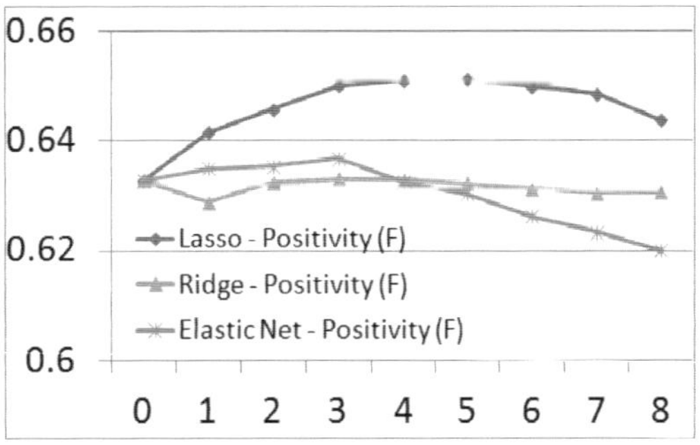

Figure 2: Comparing Impacts of Different Levels of Sparsity on the Friend Dataset When Predicting Positivity with Lasso, Ridge, and Elastic Net Models

5.4 Comparing Impacts of Different Feature Window Sizes

A practical problem for parameter estimation in both generative and discriminative models for dialogue processing is to evaluate how much history the system should take into account, so that it can have enough information to make correct predictions. In this experiment, we investigate the impact of using different feature window sizes using the elastic net model. We compare the two-tailed student t-test between the baseline that only uses features from the current turn and models that use current + previous n turn(s). For the friend dataset, when only using the features from the current turn to predict the impoliteness in the immediate next turn, we observe an AUC of .619. The best result is obtained when we combine the previous two turns together with the current feature turn: an AUC of .635, significantly better ($p = .03$) than only using the current turn window. The patterns on the non-friend dataset are less clear, while the model obtains the best result when window size is +3 previous turns, the improvement is not significant ($p = .962$). In the positivity task, we also observe benefits to incorporating larger feature windows. The AUC on the friend test set starts at .638, when only using the current feature window in the elastic net model. After incorporating larger feature windows, we obtain the best result of .675 at the +4 window ($p = .04$). Similarly, the AUC on non-friend test set initializes at .618, but climbs to .632 at the +4 window.

6 Error Analysis and Discussion

We performed an error analysis to understand the contexts under which our model failed to accurately predict a students' social response, and discuss the implications of these examples based on a theoretical understanding of the roles of tutors and tutees as well as friends and strangers. The following is an example error produced when looking only at the previous turn to predict the current turn:

- Tutee (impolite): *"dude thats def wrong i gotta subract 16m not just 16"* (the current turn)
- Tutor (non-impolite): *"16m is what has to be subtracted from both sides"* (the next turn, predicted incorrectly)

In the segment above the tutee challenges the tutor by pointing out a "def" mistake; the tutor responds with a task-oriented contribution that moves the dialogue forward, but does not escalate the face threat (Ogan et al., 2012). And, in fact, if we look one more turn back in the history, the tutor once again uses calm language: "wait it says youre wrong i dont know why ust wait". The increased window size is implicitly evoking the differential conversational strategies of tutors vs. tutees. And while the current data set is too small to build separate models for tutors and tutees, in this case (and based on the prior work in Ogan et al., 2012), accounting for role distinctions that differentiate strategies taken by tutors and tutees is the likely reason behind the improvement due to window size.

Conversely to the friend data set, the false negatives that occur when predicting impoliteness in the stranger data set are not improved by increasing the window size, as is demonstrated in the following exchange:

- Tutor (non-impolite): "subtract ym from both sides."
- Tutee (non-impolite): "first step? first Step?"
- Tutor (non-impolite): "*subtract hb from both sides*" (the current turn)
- Tutee (impolite): "*first step? FIRST STEP??????????*" (the next turn, predicted incorrectly)

The impolite tutee utterance at turn 4 is predicted to be non-impolite when analysis is limited to the previous turn, as is also shown in the first example in this section. However, unlike the previous example which improved with an expanding window size, looking back to turns 1 and 2 does not improve the model. While we do not have enough stranger dyads to completely explore this phenomenon, it seems clear that strangers' responses do not follow the same patterns as friends. The current unpredictability of strangers can be due to a number of social phenomena, such as less affect (both positive and negative) overall, which results in a different conversational flow. Less overall affect means that there is less likely to be useful information in the previous utterances. This is an important distinction between designing models for dyads with rapport and those without, which is a primary concern in the development of social SDSs. Among strangers, other techniques may need to be used to increase model accuracy, such as looking at the content of the utterances to determine whether or not a speaker had been repeating themselves, as is shown in this example, which could likely be an indicator of rudeness.

As a final example of how the error analysis can reveal important phenomena for future study, when examining the prediction of positivity on the stranger test set, we first observe that emoticons are useful indicators of positivity. However, sometimes emoticons serve quite different social functions, which leads to false positives:

- Tutor (non-positivity): "*Simplify ! :)*" (the current turn)
- Tutee (non-positivity): "*y didnt it chang*" (the next turn, predicted incorrectly)

Here, the smiley face is used by the tutor primarily to mitigate the face threat of an impolite command. However, since the experiment reported in Section 6.1 shows that our model attributes more weight to emoticons when predicting positivity, the model errs on this utterance. Here the error analysis suggests that in fact we might need to investigate more complicated latent variable models to capture the subtle social functionality of some language use in context.

7 Conclusion

Long-term relationships involve the expression of both positive and negative sentiments and, paradoxically, both can serve to increase closeness. In this paper, we have addressed the novel task of predicting impoliteness and positivity in teenagers' peer tutoring conversations, and our results shed light on what kinds of behaviors evoke these social functions for friends and for strangers, and for tutors and tutees. Our investigation has successfully predicted impoliteness and positivity on the basis of both annotated and automatically extracted features, suggesting that a dialogue system will one day be able to employ analyses such as these to signal relationships with users. And while social features such as those we annotated are naturally quite rare in dialogue, our quantitative experiments have demonstrated the capabilities of modeling sparsity in log-linear models: elastic net and Lasso models outperformed standard logistic regression model and the non-sparse ridge penalty model.

We found that positivity is much more predictable for strangers than is impoliteness, while the opposite was true for friends. This could lend support for the importance of positivity as a rapport-signaling function in the early stages of a relationship (as in (Tickle-Degnen and Rosenthal, 1990)), and indicating the need for further research on the increasing importance of impoliteness as a rapport signal over the course of relationship development.

We also found that performance on the prediction tasks increased with larger feature window sizes, particularly for impoliteness among friends and positivity among strangers. From our error analysis, we see that this improvement may arise because different behaviors predict impoliteness and positivity based on the social role of the speaker. Thus tutee bragging predicts positivity in tutors, while tutor bragging negatively predicts positivity among tutees. The power differential between the two may lead tutees to want to take tutors "down a peg" while tutors struggle to maintain the position of power in the dyad.

While results such as these may seem specific to teenage peer tutors, the general conclusion remains, that linguistic devices have different social functions in different contexts, and dialogue systems that intend to spend a lifetime on the job will do well to adapt their language to the stage of relationship with a user, and the social role they play.

References

Hua Ai, Diane J. Litman, Kate Forbes-Riley, Mihai Rotaru, Joel Tetreault, and Amruta Purandare. 2006. Using system and user performance features to improve emotion detection in spoken tutoring dialogs. In *Proceedings of the Ninth International Conference on Spoken Language Processing (Interspeech 2006)*.

Angela M. Ardington. 2006. Playfully negotiated activity in girls talk. *Journal of Pragmatics*, 38(1):73 – 95.

Rachel E. Baker, Alastair J. Gill, and Justine Cassell. 2008. Reactive redundancy and listener comprehension in direction-giving. In *Proceedings of the 9th SIGdial Workshop on Discourse and Dialogue*.

Timothy W. Bickmore and Rosalind W. Picard. 2005. Establishing and maintaining long-term human-computer relationships. *ACM Transactions on Computer-Human Interaction*.

Timothy Bickmore, Laura Pfeifer, and Daniel Schulman. 2011. Relational agents improve engagement and learning in science museum visitors. In *Proceedings of the 10th international conference on Intelligent virtual agents*, IVA'11.

Kristy Elizabeth Boyer, Robert Phillips, Michael Wallis, Mladen Vouk, and James Lester. 2008. Balancing cognitive and motivational scaffolding in tutorial dialogue. In *Proceedings of the 9th international conference on Intelligent Tutoring Systems*, ITS '08.

Penelope Brown and Stephen Levinson. 1978. Universals in language usage: Politeness phenomena. In *Questions and politeness: Strategies in social interaction*.

Justine Cassell, Alastair J. Gill, and Paul A. Tepper. 2007. Coordination in conversation and rapport. In *Proceedings of the Workshop on Embodied Language Processing*, EmbodiedNLP '07, pages 41–50, Stroudsburg, PA, USA. Association for Computational Linguistics.

Jan Chovanec. 2009. Simulation of spoken interaction in written online media texts. *Brno Studies in English*.

David Crystal. 2001. Language and the internet. *Cambridge University Press*.

Jonathan Culpeper. 1996. Towards an anatomy of impoliteness. In *Journal of Pragmatics*.

Jonathan Culpeper. 2011. Impoliteness: Using language to cause offence.

Laurence Devillers and Laurence Vidrascu. 2006. Real-life emotions detection with lexical and paralinguistic cues on human-human call center dialogs. In *Proceedings of the Ninth International Conference on Spoken Language Processing (Interspeech 2006)*.

A Gartner, M Kohler, and F Riessman. 1971. Children teach children: Learning by teaching. In *New York and London: Harper and Row*.

José González-Brenes and Jack Mostow. 2011. Which system differences matter? using l1/l2 regularization to compare dialogue systems. In *Proceedings of the SIGDIAL 2011 Conference*, pages 8–17, Portland, Oregon, June. Association for Computational Linguistics.

Jonathan Gratch, Anna Okhmatovskaia, Francois Lamothe, Stacy Marsella, Mathieu Morales, Rick J. van der Werf, and Louis-Philippe Morency. 2006. Virtual rapport. In *Proceedings of the International Conference on Intelligent Virtual Agents (IVA 2006)*.

M. Grimm, E. Mower K. Kroschel, and S. Narayanan. 2007. Primitives-based evaluation and estimation of emotions in speech. In *Speech Communication*.

P. Gupta and R. Nitendra. 2007. Two-stream emotion recognition for call center monitoring. In *Proceedings of the 8th Annual Conference of the International Speech Communication Association (Interspeech 2007)*.

Susan C. Herring and Asta Zelenkauskaite. 2009. Symbolic capital in a virtual heterosexual market. In *Written Communication*.

Je Hun Jeon, Rui Xia, and Yang Liu. 2010. Level of interest sensing in spoken dialog using multi-level fusion of acoustic and lexical evidence. In *Proceedings of the 11th Annual Conference of the International Speech Communication Association (Interspeech 2010)*, INTERSPEECH 2010.

W. Lewis Johnson and Paola Rizzo. 2004. Politeness in tutoring dialogs: run the factory, thats what id do. In *Intelligent Tutoring Systems*, Lecture Notes in Computer Science.

Manfred Kienpointner. 1997. Varieties of rudeness: types and functions of impolite utterances. In *Functions of Language*.

S. le Cessie and J.C. van Houwelingen. 1992. Ridge estimators in logistic regression. *Applied Statistics*, 41(1):191–201.

Jackson Liscombe, Julia Hirschberg, and Jennifer J. Venditti. 2005. Detecting certainness in spoken tutorial dialogues. In *Proceedings of the 6th Annual Conference of the International Speech Communication Association (Interspeech 2005)*.

D. Litman and K. Forbes-Riley. 2004. Predicting student emotions in computer-human tutoring dialogues. In *Proceedings of the 42nd Annual Meeting of the Association for Computational Linguistics (ACL 2004)*.

Dong C. Liu and Jorge Nocedal. 1989. On the limited memory bfgs method for large scale optimization. *Mathematical Programming*, 45:503–528.

Andre Martins, Noah Smith, Mario Figueiredo, and Pedro Aguiar. 2011. Structured sparsity in structured prediction. In *Proceedings of the 2011 Conference on*

Empirical Methods in Natural Language Processing, pages 1500–1511, Edinburgh, Scotland, UK., July. Association for Computational Linguistics.

Bruce M. McLaren, Sung-Joo Lim, David Yaron, and Ken Koedinger. 2007. Can a polite intelligent tutoring system lead to improved learning outside of the lab? In *Proceedings of the 2007 conference on Artificial Intelligence in Education: Building Technology Rich Learning Contexts That Work*.

Bruce McLaren, DeLeeuwm Krista E., and Richard E. Mayer. 2011. Polite web-based intelligent tutors: Can they im-prove learning in classrooms? In *Computers and Education*.

Angeliki Metallinou, Martin Wollmer, Athanasios Katsamanis, Florian Eyben, Bjorn Schuller, and Shrikanth S. Narayanan. 2011. Context-sensitive learning for enhanced audiovisual emotion classification. *IEEE Transactions on Affective Computing*.

Amy Ogan, Samantha Finkelstein, Erin Walker, Ryan Carlson, and Justine Cassell. 2012. Rudeness and rapport: Insults and learning gains in peer tutoring. In *Proceedings of the 11 International Conference on Intelligence Tutoring Systems (ITS 2012)*.

J. Alfredo Sánchez, Norma P. Hernández, Julio C. Penagos, and Yulia Ostróvskaya. 2006. Conveying mood and emotion in instant messaging by using a two-dimensional model for affective states. In *Proceedings of VII Brazilian symposium on Human factors in computing systems*, IHC '06, pages 66–72, New York, NY, USA. ACM.

A. Sharpley, J. Irvine, and C. Sharpley. 1983. An examination of the effectiveness of a cross-age tutoring program in mathematics for elementary school children. In *American Educational Research Journal*.

Helen Spencer-Oatey. 2008. Face (im)politeness and rapport. In *Culturally Speaking: Culture, Communication and Politeness Theory*.

Carolyn A. Straehle. 1993. "samuel?" "yes dear?" teasing and conversatrion rapport. In *Framing in Discourse*.

Bas Stronks, Anton Nijholt, Paul van Der Vet, Dirk Heylen, and Aaron Machado. 2002. Designing for friendship: Becoming friends with your eca. In *Proceedings of Embodied conversational agents - let's specify and evaluate (AAMAS)*.

Marina Terkourafi. 2008. Toward a unified theory of politeness, impoliteness, and rudeness. *Impoliteness in language: studies on its interplay with power in theory and practice*.

Robert Tibshirani. 1994. Regression shrinkage and selection via the lasso. *Journal of the Royal Statistical Society, Series B*, 58:267–288.

Linda Tickle-Degnen and Robert Rosenthal. 1990. The nature of rapport and its nonverbal correlates. In *Psychological Inquiry*.

Kevin E. Vowles and Miles Thompson. 2012. The patient-provider relationship in chronic pain. In *Psychiatric Management of Pain*.

Erin Walker, Nikol Rummel, and Kenneth R. Koedinger. 2011. Is it feedback relevance or increased accountability that matters? In *Proceedings of the 10th International Conference on Computer-Supported Collaborative Learning (CSCL 2011)*.

William Yang Wang and Julia Hirschberg. 2011. Detecting levels of interest from spoken dialog with multi-stream prediction feedback and similarity based hierarchical fusion learning. In *Proceedings of the 12th annual SIGdial Meeting on Discourse and Dialogue (SIGDIAL 2011)*, Portland, OR., USA, June. ACL.

William Yang Wang and Kathleen McKeown. 2010. "got you!": Automatic vandalism detection in wikipedia with web-based shallow syntactic-semantic modeling. In *Proceedings of the 23rd International Conference on Computational Linguistics (Coling 2010)*, pages 1146–1154, Beijing, China, August. Coling 2010 Organizing Committee.

William Yang Wang, Fadi Biadsy, Andrew Rosenberg, and Julia Hirschberg. 2012a. Automatic detection of speaker state: Lexical, prosodic, and phonetic approaches to level-of-interest and intoxication classification. *Computer Speech & Language*.

William Yang Wang, Elijah Mayfield, Suresh Naidu, and Jeremiah Dittmar. 2012b. Historical analysis of legal opinions with a sparse mixed-effects latent variable model. In *Proceedings of the 50th Annual Meeting of the Association for Computational Linguistics (ACL 2012)*.

Richard J. Watts. 2003. Politeness. *Cambridge University Press*.

Hui Zou and Trevor Hastie. 2005. Regularization and variable selection via the elastic net. *Journal of the Royal Statistical Society, Series B*, 67:301–320.

Enhancing Referential Success by Tracking Hearer Gaze

Alexander Koller
University of Potsdam
koller@ling.uni-potsdam.de

Konstantina Garoufi
University of Potsdam
garoufi@uni-potsdam.de

Maria Staudte
Saarland University
masta@coli.uni-saarland.de

Matthew Crocker
Saarland University
crocker@coli.uni-saarland.de

Abstract

The ability to monitor the communicative success of its utterances and, if necessary, provide feedback and repair is useful for a dialog system. We show that in situated communication, eyetracking can be used to reliably and efficiently monitor the hearer's reference resolution process. An interactive system that draws on hearer gaze to provide positive or negative feedback after referring to objects outperforms baseline systems on metrics of referential success and user confusion.

1 Introduction

Because dialog is interactive, interlocutors are constantly engaged in a process of predicting and monitoring the effects of their utterances. Typically, a speaker produces an utterance with a specific communicative goal in mind—e.g., that the hearer will perform an action or adopt a certain belief—, and chooses one particular utterance because they *predict* that it will achieve this communicative goal. They will then *monitor* the hearer's reactions and infer from their observations whether the prediction actually came true. If they recognize that the hearer misunderstood the utterance, they may *repair* the problem by diagnosing what caused the misunderstanding and giving the hearer *feedback*. In a task-oriented dialog in which the hearer must perform a part of the task, feedback is especially important to inform the hearer when they made a mistake in the task. Ideally, the speaker should even detect when the hearer is *about to* make a mistake, and use feedback to keep them from making the mistake at all.

Many implemented dialog systems include a component for monitoring and repair. For instance, Traum (1994) presents a model for monitoring the grounding status of utterances in the TRAINS system; Young et al. (1994) show how the student's utterances in a dialog system can be used to uncover mistaken assumptions about their mental state; and Paek and Horvitz (1999) discuss an automated helpdesk system that can track grounding under uncertainty. However, most of these systems rely on the user's verbal utterances as their primary source of information; monitoring thus presupposes an (error-prone) language understanding module.

In the context of situated communication, where the speaker and hearer share a physical (or virtual) environment, one type of observation that can potentially give us a very direct handle on the hearer's understanding of an utterance is eye gaze. Eyetracking studies in psycholinguistics have shown that when listeners hear a referring expression, they tend to rapidly attend to the object in a scene to which they resolve this expression (Tanenhaus et al., 1995; Allopenna et al., 1998). For utterances that involve references to objects in the current environment, one can therefore ask whether eyetracking can be used to reliably judge the communicative success of the utterance. This would be of practical interest for implemented dialog systems once eyetracking becomes a mainstream technology; and even today, a system that reliably monitors communicative success using eyetracking could serve as a testbed for exploring monitoring and repair strategies.

In this paper, we present an interactive natural-language generation (NLG) system that uses eyetracking to monitor communicative success. Our system gives real-time instructions that are designed to help the user perform a treasure-hunt task in the virtual 3D environments of the recent Challenges on Generating Instructions in Virtual Environments (GIVE; Koller et al. (2010)). It monitors how the user resolves referring expressions (REs) by mapping the user's gaze to objects in the virtual environment. The system takes gaze to the intended referent as evidence of successful understanding, and gives the user positive feedback; by contrast, gaze to other objects triggers negative feedback. Crucially, this feedback comes before the user interacts with the object in the virtual environment, keeping the user from making mistakes before they happen.

We evaluate our system against one baseline that gives no feedback, and another that bases its feedback on monitoring the user's movements and their field of view. We find that the eyetracking-based system outperforms both on referential success, and that users interacting with it show significantly fewer signs of confusion about how to complete their task. This demonstrates that eyetracking can serve as a reliable source of evidence in monitoring communicative success. The system is, to our knowledge, the first dialog or NLG system that uses the hearer's gaze to monitor understanding of REs.

Plan of the paper. The paper is structured as follows. We first discuss related work in Section 2. We then describe our approach as well as the baselines in Section 3, set up the evaluation in Section 4 and present the results in Section 5. In Sections 6 and 7 we discuss our findings and conclude.

2 Related work

Dialog systems model a process of *grounding*, in which they decide to what extent the user has understood the utterance and the communicative goal has been reached. Observing the user behavior to monitor the state of understanding is a key component in this process. A full solution may require plan recognition or abductive or epistemic reasoning (see e.g. Young et al. (1994), Hirst et al. (1994)); in practice, many systems use more streamlined (Traum, 1994) or statistical methods (Paek and Horvitz, 1999). Most dialog systems focus on the verbal interaction of the system and user, and the user's utterances are therefore the primary source of evidence in the monitoring process. Some *incremental* dialog systems can monitor the user's verbal reactions to the system's utterances in real time, and continuously update the grounding state while the system utterance is still in progress (Skantze and Schlangen, 2009; Buss and Schlangen, 2010).

In this paper, we focus on the generation side of a dialog system—the user is the hearer—and on monitoring the user's *extralinguistic* reactions, in particular their gaze. Tanenhaus et al. (1995) and Allopenna et al. (1998) showed that subjects in psycholinguistic experiments who hear an RE visually attend to the object to which they resolve the RE. The "visual world" experimental paradigm exploits this by presenting objects on a computer screen and using an eyetracker to monitor the subject's gaze. This research uses gaze only as an experimental tool and not as part of an interactive dialog system, and the visual worlds are usually limited to static 2D scenes. Also, such setups cannot account for the reciprocal nature of dialog and the consequences that hearer gaze has for the speaker's monitoring process.

In the context of situated dialog systems, previous studies have employed robots and virtual agents as *speakers* to explore how and when speaker gaze helps human hearers to ground referring expressions (Foster, 2007). For instance, Staudte and Crocker (2011) show that an agent can make it easier for the (human) hearer to resolve a system-generated RE by looking at the intended referent, using head and eye movements. Conversely, the performance of a system for resolving human-produced REs can be improved by taking the (human) speaker's gaze into account (Iida et al., 2011). Gaze has also been used to track the general dynamics of a dialog, such as turn taking (Jokinen et al., in press).

Here we are interested in monitoring the *hearer's* gaze in order to determine whether they have understood an RE. To our knowledge, there has been no research on this; in particular, not in dynamic 3D environments. The closest earlier work of which we are aware comes from the context of the GIVE Challenge, a shared task for interactive, situated natural language generation systems. These systems typically approximate hearer gaze as visibility of objects on the screen and monitor grounding based on this (Denis, 2010; Racca et al., 2011).

Figure 1: A first-person view of a virtual 3D environment.

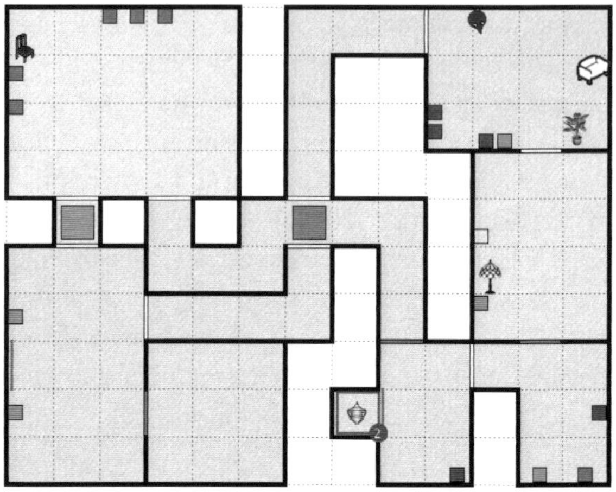

Figure 2: A map of the environment in Fig. 1; note the user in the upper right room.

3 Interactive natural-language generation in virtual environments

In this paper, we consider the communicative situation of the GIVE Challenge (Koller et al., 2010; Striegnitz et al., 2011). In this task, a human user can move about freely in a virtual indoor environment featuring several interconnected rooms and corridors. A 3D view of the environment is displayed on a computer screen as in Fig. 1, and the user can walk forward/backward and turn left/right, using the cursor keys. They can also press buttons attached to the walls, by clicking on them with the mouse once they are close enough. The small and big white circles in Fig. 1, which represent eyetracking information, are not actually visible to the user.

The user interacts with a real-time NLG system in the context of a treasure-hunt game, where their task is to find a trophy hidden in a wall safe. They must press certain buttons in the correct sequence in order to open the safe; however, they do not have prior knowledge of which buttons to press, so they rely on instructions and REs generated by the system. A room may contain several buttons other than the *target*, which is the button that the user must press next. These other buttons are called *distractors*. Next to buttons, rooms also contain a number of landmark objects, such as chairs and plants, which cannot directly be interacted with, but may be used in REs to nearby targets. Fig. 2 shows a top-down map of the virtual environment in which the scene of Fig. 1 arose. We call an entire game up to the successful discovery of the trophy, an *interaction* of the system and the user.

3.1 Monitoring communicative success

NLG systems in the GIVE setting are in an interactive communicative situation. This situation represents one complete half of a dialog situation: Only the system gets to use language, but the user moves and acts in response to the system's utterances. As a result, the system should continuously monitor and react to what the user does, in real time. This is most tangible in the system's use of REs. When a user misinterprets (or simply does not understand) a system-generated RE, there is a high chance that they will end up pressing the wrong button. This will hinder the completion of the task. A system that predicts how the user resolves the RE by monitoring their movements and actions, and that can proactively give the user feedback to keep them from making a mistake, will therefore perform better than one which cannot do this. Furthermore, if the system can give positive feedback when it detects that the user is about to do the right thing, this may increase the user's confidence.

Monitoring communicative success in GIVE interactions and providing the right feedback can be challenging. For example, in the original interaction from which we took the screenshot of Fig. 1, the system instructed the user to "push the right button to the right of the green button", referring to the rightmost blue button in the scene. In response, the user first walked hesitantly towards the far pair of buttons (green and blue), and then turned to face the other pair, as seen in Fig. 3. A typical NLG system used

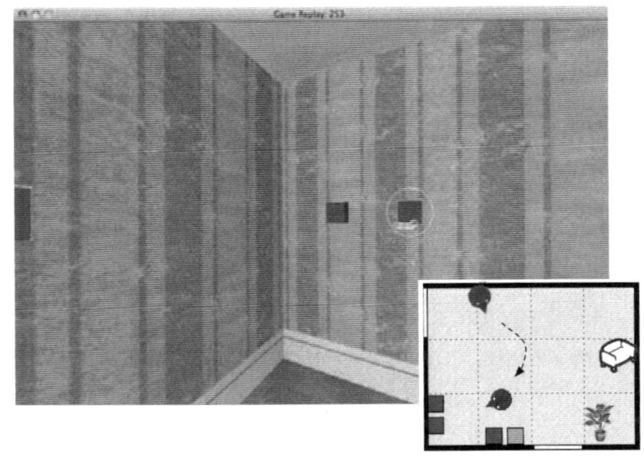

Figure 3: The scene of Fig. 1, after the user moved and turned in response to a referring expression.

in the GIVE Challenge (e.g., Dionne et al. (2009), Denis (2010), Racca et al. (2011)) may try to predict how the user might resolve the RE based on the visibility of objects, timing data, or distances. Relying only on such data, however, even a human observer could have difficulties in interpreting the user's reaction; the user in Fig. 3 ended up closer to the green and blue buttons, but the other buttons (the two blue ones) are, to similar degrees, visually in focus.

The contribution of this paper is to present a method for monitoring the communicative success of an RE based on eyetracking. We start from the hypothesis that when the user resolves an RE to a certain object, they will tend to gaze at this object. In the scene of Fig. 3, the user was indeed looking at the system's intended referent, which they later pressed; the small white circles indicate a trace of recent fixations on the screen, and the big white circle marks the object in the virtual environment to which the system resolved these screen positions. Our system takes this gaze information, which is available in real time, as evidence for how the user has resolved its RE, and generates positive or negative feedback based on this.

3.2 NLG systems

To demonstrate the usefulness of the eyetracking-based approach, we implemented and compared three different NLG systems. All of these use an identical module for generating navigation instructions, which guides the user to a specific location, as well as object manipulation instructions such as "push the blue button"; "the blue button" is an RE that describes an object to the user. The systems generate REs that are optimized for being easy for the hearer to understand, according to a corpus-based model of understandability (Garoufi and Koller, 2011). The model was trained on human instructions produced in a subset of the virtual environments we use in this work. The resulting system computes referring expressions that are correct and uniquely describe the referent as seen by the hearer at the moment in which generation starts.

Unlike in the original GIVE Challenge, the generated instructions are converted to speech by the Mary text-to-speech system (Schröder and Trouvain, 2003) and presented via loudspeaker. At any point, the user may press the 'H' key on their keyboard to indicate that they are confused and request a clarification. This will cause the system to generate an instruction newly; if it contains an RE, this RE may or may not be the same as the one used in the original utterance.

The difference between the three systems is in the way they monitor communicative success and determine when to give feedback to the user.

The no-feedback system. As a baseline system, we used a system which does not monitor success at all, and therefore never gives feedback on its own initiative. Notice that the system still re-generates an RE when the user presses the 'H' key.

Movement-based monitoring. As a second baseline, we implemented a system that attempts to monitor whether a user understood an RE based on their movements. This system is intended to represent the user monitoring that can be implemented, with a reasonable amount of effort, on the basis of immediately available information in the GIVE setting.

The movement-based system gives no feedback until only a single button in the current room is visible to the user, since it can be hard to make a reliable prediction if the user sees several buttons on their screen. Then it tracks the user's distance from this button, where "distance" is a weighted sum of walking distance to the button and the angle the user must turn to face the button. If, after hearing the RE, the user has decreased the distance by more than a given threshold, the system concludes that the hearer has resolved the RE as this button. If that is the button the system intended to refer to, the system utters the positive feedback "yes, that one". For incorrect buttons, it utters the negative feedback "no, not that one". Although the negative feedback is relatively vague, it has the advantage of limiting the variability of the system's outputs, which facilitates evaluation.

Eyetracking-based monitoring. Finally, the eyetracking-based system attempts to predict whether the user will press the correct button or not by monitoring their gaze. At intervals of approximately 15 ms, the system determines the (x,y) position on the screen that the user is looking at. It then identifies the object in the environment that corresponds to this position by casting a ray from the (virtual) camera through the screen plane, and picking the closest object lying within a small range of this ray (Fig. 1; see Staudte et al. (2012) for details). If the user continously looks at the same object for more than a certain amount of time, the system counts this as an inspection of the object; for our experiments, we chose a threshold of 300 ms. Once the system detects an inspection to a button in the room, it generates positive or negative feedback utterances in exactly the same way as the movement system does.

Both the movement-based and the eyetracking-based model withhold their feedback until a first full description of the referent (a *first-mention RE*) has been spoken. Additionally, they only provide feedback once for every newly approached or inspected button and will not repeat this feedback unless the user has approached or inspected another button in the meantime. Example interactions of a user with each of the three systems are presented in Appendix A.

4 Evaluation

We set up a human evaluation study in order to assess the performance of the eyetracking system as compared against the two baselines on the situated instruction giving task. For this, we record participant interactions with the three systems employed in three different virtual environments. These environments were taken from Gargett et al. (2010); they vary as to the visual and spatial properties of the objects they contain. One of these environments is shown in Fig. 2. Overall, 31 participants (12 females) were tested. All reported their English skills as fluent, and all were capable of completing the tasks. Their mean age was 27.6 years.

4.1 Task and procedure

A faceLAB eyetracking system (`http://www.seeingmachines.com/product/facelab`) remotely monitored participants' eye movements on a 24-inch monitor, as in Fig. 4 and 5 of Appendix B. Before the experiment, participants received written instructions that described the task and explained that they would be given instructions by an NLG system. They were encouraged to request additional help any time they felt that the instructions were not sufficient (by pressing the 'H' key).

The eyetracker was calibrated using a nine-point fixation stimulus. We disguised the importance of gaze from the participants by telling them that we videotaped them and that the camera needed calibration. Each participant started with a short practice session to familiarize themselves with the interface and to clarify remaining questions. We then collected three complete interactions, each with a different virtual environment and NLG system (alternated according to a Latin square design). Finally, each participant received a questionnaire which was aimed to reveal whether they noticed that they were eyetracked and that one of the generation systems made use of that, and how satisfied they were with this interaction. The entire experiment lasted approximately 30 minutes.

4.2 Analysis

For the assessment of communicative success in these interactions, we considered as referential scenes the parts of the interaction between the onset of a first-mention RE to a given referent and the participant's reaction (pressing a button or navigating away to another room). To control for external factors that could have an impact on this, we discarded individual scenes in which the systems rephrased their first-mention REs (e.g. by adding further attributes), as well as a few scenes which the participants had to go through a second time due to technical glitches. To remove errors in eyetracker calibration, we included interactions with the eyetracking NLG system in the analysis only when we were able to record inspections (to the referent or any distractor) in at least 80% of all referential scenes. This

system	success all	easy	hard	success w/out confusion all	easy	hard	#scenes all	easy	hard
eyetracking	93.4	100.0	90.4	91.9	100.0	88.2	198	62	136
with feedback	94.3	100.0	91.7	92.8	100.0	89.4	194	62	132
without feedback	50.0	-	50.0	50.0	-	50.0	4	0	4
no-feedback	86.6*	100.0°	80.6*	83.5**	98.9°	76.5**	284	88	196
movement	89.8°	100.0°	85.2°	87.5°	97.8°	82.8°	295	92	203
with feedback	93.9	100.0	90.6	91.9	97.7	88.7	247	88	159
without feedback	68.8	100.0	65.9	64.6	100.0	61.4	48	4	44

Table 1: Mean referential success rate (%) and number of scenes for the systems, broken down by scene complexity and presence of feedback. Differences of overall system performances to the eyetracking system are: significant at ** $p < 0.01$, * $p < 0.05$; ° not significant.

filtered out 9 interactions out of the 93 we collected.

Inferential statistics on this data were carried out using mixed-effect models from the lme4 package in R (Baayen et al., 2008). Specifically, we used logistic regression for modeling binary data, Poisson regression for count variables and linear regression for continuous data.

5 Results

On evaluating the post-task questionnaires, we did not find any significant preferences for a particular NLG system. Roughly the same number of them chose each of the systems on questions such as "which system did you prefer?". When asked for differences between the systems in free-form questions, no participant mentioned the system's reaction to their eye gaze—though some noticed the (lack of) feedback. We take this to mean that the participants did not realize they were being eyetracked.

Below, we report results on objective metrics that do not depend on participants' judgments.

5.1 Confusion

A key goal of any RE generation system is that the user understands the REs easily. One measure of the ease of understanding is the frequency with which participants pressed the 'H' key to indicate their confusion and ask for help. The overall average of 'H' keystrokes per interaction was 1.14 for the eyetracking-based system, 1.77 for the movement-based system, and 2.26 for the no-feedback system. A model fitted to the keystroke distribution per system shows significant differences both between the eyetracking and the no-feedback system (Coeff. = 0.703, SE = 0.233, Wald's Z = 3.012, $p < .01$) and between the eyetracking and the movement-based system (Coeff. = 0.475, SE = 0.241, Wald's Z = 1.967, $p < .05$). In other words, the feedback given by the eyetracking-based system significantly reduces user confusion.

5.2 Referential success

An even more direct way to measure the interaction quality is the ratio of generated REs that the participants were able to resolve correctly. In our evaluation, we looked at two different definitions of success. First, an RE can count as successful if the first button that the user pressed after hearing the RE was the system's intended referent. The results of this evaluation are shown in the leftmost part of Table 1, under "success". A logistic mixed-effects model fitted to the referential success data revealed a marginal main effect of system ($\chi^2(2) = 5.55, p = .062$). Pairwise comparisons further show that the eyetracking system performs significantly better than the no-feedback system (Coeff. = -0.765, SE = 0.342, Wald's Z = $-2.24, p < .05$); no significant difference was found between the eyetracking-based and the movement-based system.

Second, we can additionally require that an RE only counts as successful if the user did not press the 'H' key between hearing the first-mention RE and pressing the correct button. This is a stricter version of referential success, which requires that the system recognized cases of potential confusion and did not force the user to take the initiative in case of difficulties. It is in line with Dethlefs et al.'s (2010) findings that metrics that penalize difficulties the user encountered before successfully completing the task are better predictors of user satisfaction than ones that only consider the eventual task completion. Our results on this metric are shown in the middle part of Table 1, under "success without confusion". We observe again a main effect of system ($\chi^2(2) = 7.78, p < .05$); furthermore, the eyetracking system elicited again more correct buttons than the no-feedback system (Coeff. = -0.813, SE = 0.306, Wald's Z = $-2.66, p < 0.01$).

To obtain a more detailed view of when and to what extent the systems' behavior differed, we distinguished scenes according to their complexity. A scene was classified as *easy* if a) there were no distractors in it, or b) all distractors had different colors from the target, while the system included the color attribute in its RE. All other scenes were considered *hard*. Note that "easy" and "hard" are properties of the scene and not of the system, because every system generated the same REs in each scene.

In the experiments, we found essentially no difference between the success rates of different systems on easy scenes (see the "easy" columns of Table 1): All systems were almost always successful. The differences came almost exclusively from the hard scenes, where the eyetracking system performed significantly better than the no-feedback system (success: Coeff. = -0.793, SE = 0.348, Wald's Z = $-2.28, p < 0.05$; success without confusion: Coeff. = -0.833, SE = 0.315, Wald's Z = $-2.64, p < 0.01$) and, at least numerically, also much better than the movement system.

There was a particularly interesting difference in the feedback behavior of the eyetracking and movement systems on hard scenes (see the rightmost part of Table 1, labeled "#scenes"). In easy scenes, both systems almost always gave feedback (62/62 = 100.0%; 88/92 = 95.6%); but for hard scenes, the ratio of scenes in which the movement system gave feedback at all dropped to 159/203 = 78.3%, whereas the ratio for the eyetracking system remained high. This may have contributed to the overall performance difference between the two systems.

system	#actions (norm.)	distance (norm.)	duration (norm.)	idle (sec)
eyetracking	1.06	1.22	1.49	256.6
no-feedback	1.22*	1.27	1.59	272.5
movement	1.16	1.26	1.56	274.4

Table 2: Mean values of additional metrics. Differences to the eyetracking system are significant at * $p < 0.05$.

5.3 Further performance metrics

Finally, we measured a number of other objective metrics, including the number of actions (i.e., button presses), the distance the user traveled, the total duration of the interaction, and the mean time a participant spent idle. Even though these measures only partly provide statistically significant results, they help to draw a clearer picture of how the eyetracking-based feedback affects performance.

Because the three virtual environments were of different complexity, we normalized the number of actions, distance, and duration by dividing the value for a given interaction by the minimum value for all interactions of the same virtual environment. The resulting measures are shown in Table 2. Participants performed significantly fewer actions in the eyetracking system than in the no-feedback system (Coeff. = 0.174, SE = 0.067, t = 2.57, $p(mcmc) < .05$); there were also trends that users of the eyetracking-based system traveled the shortest distance, needed the least overall time, and spent the least time idle.

The only measure deviating from this trend is movement speed, i.e., the speed at which users reacted to the systems' instructions to press certain buttons. For all successful scenes (without confusion), we computed the speed by dividing the GIVE distance (including turning distance) between the target referent and the user's location at the time of the instruction containing the first-mention RE by the time (in seconds) between hearing the instruction and pressing the target. The mean movement speed is 0.518 for the no-feedback system, 0.493 for the movement system, and 0.472 for the eyetracking system. A marginal main effect of movement speed confirms this trend ($\chi^2(2) = 5.58, p = .061$) and shows that participants moved more slowly when getting eyetracking-based feedback than when getting no feedback at all (Coeff. = 0.0352, SE =

0.0166, t = $-4.97, p(mcmc) < .05$).

6 Discussion

The results in Section 5 demonstrate the usefulness of eyetracking as a foundation for monitoring and feedback. Compared to the no-feedback system, the eyetracking-based system achieved a significantly lower confusion rate and a significantly higher RE success rate, especially on hard instances. The difference increases further if we discount scenes in which the user had to ask for help, thus forcing the system to give feedback anyway. In other words, eyetracking provides reliable and direct access to the hearer's reference resolution process. Real-time dialog systems can use gaze information to monitor the success of REs and generate feedback before the user actually makes a mistake.

Monitoring and feedback could also be achieved without using eyetracking. To explore this alternative, we compared eyetracking against a movement-based system. We found that the former outperformed the latter on hearer confusion and (at least numerically) on referential success, while not performing worse on other measures. This means that the improvement comes not merely from the fact that feedback was given; it is also important when and where feedback is given. The crucial weakness of the movement-based system is that it gave feedback for hard instances much more rarely than the eyetracking system. Increasing recall by lowering the system's confidence threshold would introduce fresh errors. Further improvements must therefore come at the cost of a more complex monitoring system, both conceptually and in terms of implementation effort. From this perspective, eyetracking offers good performance at low implementation cost.

One result that seems to go against the trend is that users of the eyetracking system moved significantly more slowly on their way to a target. We see two possible explanations for this. First, it may be that users needed some time to listen to the feedback, or were encouraged by it to look at more objects. A second explanation is that this is not really a difference in the quality of the systems' behavior, but a difference in the populations over which the mean speed was computed: The speed was only averaged over scenes in which the users resolved the RE correctly, and the eyetracking system achieved communicative success in many cases in which the others did not—presumably complex scenes in which the user had to work harder to find the correct button. This issue bears more careful analysis.

Finally, the eyetracking-based system could be improved further in many ways. On the one hand, it suffers from the fact that all objects in the 3D environment shift on the screen when the user turns or moves. The user's eyes will typically follow the object they are currently inspecting, but lag behind until the screen comes to a stop again. One topic for future work would be to remove noise of this kind from the eyetracker signal. On the other hand, the negative feedback our system gave ("no, not that one") was quite unspecific. More specific feedback ("no, the BLUE button") might further improve the system's performance.

7 Conclusion

We described an interactive NLG system that uses eyetracking to monitor the communicative success of the REs it generates. The communication is situated in a virtual 3D environment in which the user can move freely, and our system automatically maps eyetracking screen coordinates to objects in the environment. A task-based evaluation found that the eyetracking-based system outperforms both a no-feedback system and a system whose feedback is based on the user's movements in the virtual environment, along with their field of view.

Eyetracking is currently widely available in research institutions, which should make our system easy to reimplement in other situated domains. We anticipate that eyetracking may become mainstream technology in the not-too-distant future. But even in a purely research context, we believe that the directness with which eyetracking allows us to observe the hearer's interpretation process may be useful as a testbed for efficient theories of grounding.

Acknowledgments. This research was partly supported by the Cluster of Excellence "Multimodal Computing and Interaction" at Saarland University. We are grateful to Irena Dotcheva for help with data collection as well as to Alexandre Denis and Christoph Clodo for software support, and to Kristiina Jokinen for helpful comments.

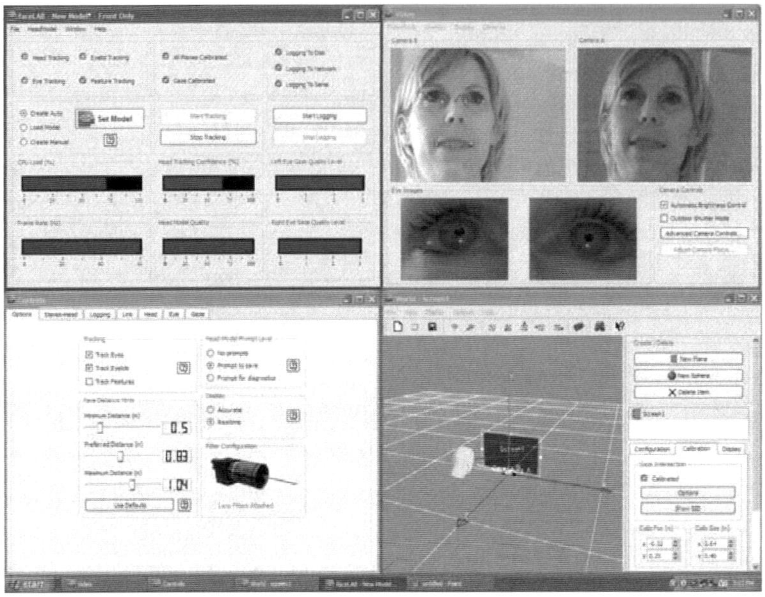

Figure 4: A screenshot from the faceLAB software, including visualization of eye-gaze position in 3D space.

References

Paul Allopenna, James Magnuson, and Michael Tanenhaus. 1998. Tracking the Time Course of Spoken Word Recognition Using Eye Movements: Evidence for Continuous Mapping Models. *Journal of Memory and Language*, 38:419–439.

R.H. Baayen, D.J. Davidson, and D.M. Bates. 2008. Mixed-effects modeling with crossed random effects for subjects and items. *Journal of Memory and Language*, 59:390–412.

Okko Buss and David Schlangen. 2010. Modelling sub-utterance phenomena in spoken dialogue systems. In *Aspects of Semantics and Pragmatics of Dialogue. SemDial 2010, 14th Workshop on the Semantics and Pragmatics of Dialogue*, pages 33–41.

Alexandre Denis. 2010. Generating referring expressions with reference domain theory. In *Proceedings of the 6th International Natural Language Generation Conference*.

Nina Dethlefs, Heriberto Cuayahuitl, Kai-Florian Richter, Elena Andonova, and John Bateman. 2010. Evaluating task success in a dialogue system for indoor navigation. In *Aspects of Semantics and Pragmatics of Dialogue. SemDial 2010, 14th Workshop on the Semantics and Pragmatics of Dialogue*, pages 143–146.

Daniel Dionne, Salvador de la Puente, Carlos León, Pablo Gervás, and Raquel Hervás. 2009. A model for human readable instruction generation using level-based discourse planning and dynamic inference of attributes. In *Proceedings of the 12th European Workshop on Natural Language Generation*.

Mary Ellen Foster. 2007. Enhancing human-computer interaction with embodied conversational agents. In *Proceedings of HCI International 2007*.

Andrew Gargett, Konstantina Garoufi, Alexander Koller, and Kristina Striegnitz. 2010. The GIVE-2 Corpus of Giving Instructions in Virtual Environments. In *Proceedings of the 7th Conference on International Language Resources and Evaluation*.

Konstantina Garoufi and Alexander Koller. 2011. The Potsdam NLG systems at the GIVE-2.5 Challenge. In *Proceedings of the Generation Challenges Session at the 13th European Workshop on Natural Language Generation*.

Graeme Hirst, Susan McRoy, Peter Heeman, Philip Edmonds, and Diane Horton. 1994. Repairing conversational misunderstandings and non-understandings. *Speech Communications*, 15:213–229.

Ryu Iida, Masaaki Yasuhara, and Takenobu Tokunaga. 2011. Multi-modal reference resolution in situated dialogue by integrating linguistic and extra-linguistic clues. In *Proceedings of 5th International Joint Conference on Natural Language Processing*.

K. Jokinen, H. Furukawa, M. Nishida, and S. Yamamoto. in press. Gaze and turn-taking behaviour in casual conversational interactions. *ACM Trans. Interactive Intelligent Systems*. Special Issue on Eye Gaze in Intelligent Human-Machine Interaction.

Alexander Koller, Kristina Striegnitz, Donna Byron, Justine Cassell, Robert Dale, Johanna Moore, and Jon

Oberlander. 2010. The First Challenge on Generating Instructions in Virtual Environments. In Emiel Krahmer and Mariet Theune, editors, *Empirical Methods in Natural Language Generation*, number 5790 in LNCS, pages 337–361. Springer.

Tim Paek and Eric Horvitz. 1999. Uncertainty, utility, and misunderstanding: A decision-theoretic perspective on grounding in conversational systems. In *AAAI Fall Symposium on Psychological Models of Communication in Collaborative Systems*.

David Nicolás Racca, Luciana Benotti, and Pablo Duboue. 2011. The GIVE-2.5 C Generation System. In *Proceedings of the Generation Challenges Session at the 13th European Workshop on Natural Language Generation*.

Marc Schröder and J. Trouvain. 2003. The German Text-to-Speech Synthesis System MARY: A Tool for Research, Development and Teaching. *International Journal of Speech Technology*, 6:365–377.

Gabriel Skantze and David Schlangen. 2009. Incremental dialogue processing in a micro-domain. In *Proceedings of the 12th Conference of the European Chapter of the Association for Computational Linguistics*.

Maria Staudte and Matthew W. Crocker. 2011. Investigating joint attention mechanisms through human-robot interaction. *Cognition*, 120(2):268–291.

Maria Staudte, Alexander Koller, Konstantina Garoufi, and Matthew W. Crocker. 2012. Using listener gaze to augment speech generation in a virtual 3D environment. In *Proceedings of the 34th Annual Conference of the Cognitive Science Society*. To appear.

Kristina Striegnitz, Alexandre Denis, Andrew Gargett, Konstantina Garoufi, Alexander Koller, and Mariet Theune. 2011. Report on the Second Second Challenge on Generating Instructions in Virtual Environments (GIVE-2.5). In *Proceedings of the Generation Challenges Session at the 13th European Workshop on Natural Language Generation*.

Michael K. Tanenhaus, Michael J. Spivey-Knowlton, Kathleen M. Eberhard, and Julie C. Sedivy. 1995. Integration of visual and linguistic information in spoken language comprehension. *Science*, 268:1632–1634.

David Traum. 1994. *A computational theory of grounding in natural language conversation*. Ph.D. thesis, University of Rochester.

Michael Young, Johanna Moore, and Martha Pollack. 1994. Towards a principled representation for discourse plans. In *Proceedings of the Sixteenth Annual Meeting of the Cognitive Science Society*.

A Example interactions

The following interactions between a user (U) and each of the three systems (S) were recorded during the systems' attempts to instruct the user to press the rightmost blue button shown in Fig. 1.

A.1 Eyetracking system

(1) S: *Push the right button to the right of the green button.*
U: (approaches the pair of blue and green button and inspects one of them)
S: *No, not that one!*
. . . (U inspects other buttons in the scene, while S provides appropriate feedback)
U: (inspects the correct target)
S: *Yes, that one!*
U: (presses the correct button)

A.2 Movement system

(2) S: *Push the right button to the right of the green button.*
U: (approaches the pair of blue and green buttons; once the user is very close to the blue button, it happens to become the only button visible on screen)
U: (continues moving closer to the blue button)
S: *No, not that one!*
U: (has no time to react to the system's feedback and presses the wrong blue button)

A.3 No-feedback system

(3) S: *Push the right button to the right of the green button.*
U: (presses the wrong blue button)

B The experimental setup

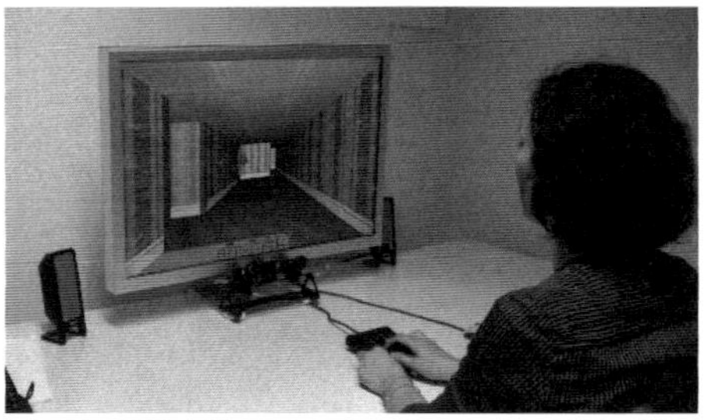

Figure 5: A faceLAB eyetracking system monitored participants' eye movements during the interactions.

Unsupervised Topic Modeling Approaches to Decision Summarization in Spoken Meetings

Lu Wang
Department of Computer Science
Cornell University
Ithaca, NY 14853
luwang@cs.cornell.edu

Claire Cardie
Department of Computer Science
Cornell University
Ithaca, NY 14853
cardie@cs.cornell.edu

Abstract

We present a token-level decision summarization framework that utilizes the latent topic structures of utterances to identify "summary-worthy" words. Concretely, a series of unsupervised topic models is explored and experimental results show that fine-grained topic models, which discover topics at the utterance-level rather than the document-level, can better identify the gist of the decision-making process. Moreover, our proposed token-level summarization approach, which is able to remove redundancies within utterances, outperforms existing utterance ranking based summarization methods. Finally, context information is also investigated to add additional relevant information to the summary.

1 Introduction

Meetings are an important way for information sharing and collaboration, where people can discuss problems and make concrete decisions. Not surprisingly, there is an increasing interest in developing methods for extractive summarization for meetings and conversations (Zechner, 2002; Maskey and Hirschberg, 2005; Galley, 2006; Lin and Chen, 2010; Murray et al., 2010a). Carenini et al. (2011) describe the specific need for *focused summaries* of meetings, i.e., summaries of a particular aspect of a meeting rather than of the meeting as a whole. For example, the decisions made, the action items that emerged and the problems arised are all important outcomes of meetings. In particular, decision summaries would allow participants to review decisions from previous meetings and understand the related topics quickly, which facilitates preparation for the upcoming meetings.

A:We decided our target group is the focus on who can afford it , (1)
B:Uh I'm kinda liking the idea of latex , if if spongy is the in thing . (2)
B:what I've seen , just not related to this , but of latex cases before , is that [vocalsound] there's uh like a hard plastic inside , and it's just covered with the latex . (2)
C:Um [disfmarker] And I think if we wanna keep our costs down , we should just go for pushbuttons , (3)
D:but if it's gonna be in a latex type thing and that's gonna look cool , then that's probably gonna have a bigger impact than the scroll wheel . (2)
A:we're gonna go with um type pushbuttons , (3)
A:So we're gonna have like a menu button , (4)
C:uh volume , favourite channels , uh and menu . (4)
A:Pre-set channels (4)

Decision Abstracts (Summary)
DECISION 1: The target group comprises of individuals who can afford the product.
DECISION 2: The remote will have a latex case.
DECISION 3: The remote will have pushbuttons.
DECISION 4: The remote will have a power button, volume buttons, channel preset buttons, and a menu button.

Figure 1: A clip of a meeting from the AMI meeting corpus (Carletta et al., 2005). A, B, C and D refer to distinct speakers; the numbers in parentheses indicate the associated meeting decision: DECISION 1, 2, 3 or 4. Also shown is the gold-standard (manual) abstract (summary) for each decision.

Meeting conversation is intrinsically different from well-written text, as meetings may not be well organized and most utterances have low density of salient content. Therefore, multiple problems need to be addressed for speech summarization. Consider the sample dialogue snippet in Figure 1 from the AMI meeting corpus (Carletta et al., 2005). Only *decision-related dialogue acts (DRDAs)* — utterances at least one decision made in the meeting[1] — are listed and ordered by time. Each DRDA is labeled numerically according to the decision it supports; so the second and third utterances (in **bold**) support DECISION 2, as do the fifth utterance in the snippet. Manually constructed *decision abstracts* for each decision are shown at the bottom of the figure.

Besides the prevalent dialogue phenomena (such as "Uh I'm kinda liking" in Figure 1), disfluencies and off-topic expressions, we notice that single utterance is usually not informative enough to form a decision. For instance, no single DRDA associated with DECISION 4 corresponds all that well with its decision abstract: "pushbuttons", "menu button" and "Pre-set channels" are mentioned in separate DAs. As a result, extractive summarization methods that select individual utterance to form the summary will perform poorly.

Furthermore, it is difficult to identify the core topic when multiple topics are discussed in one utterance. For example, all of the bold DRDAs supporting DECISION 2 contain the word "latex". However, the last DA in bold also mentions "bigger impact" and "the scroll wheel", which are not specifically relevant for DECISION 2. Though this problem can be approached by training a classifier to identify the relevant phrases and ignore the irrelevant ones or dialogue phenomena, it needs expensive human annotation and is limited to the specific domain.

Note also that for DECISION 4, the "power button" is not specified in any of the listed DRDAs supporting it. By looking at the transcript, we find "power button" mentioned in one of the preceding, but not decision-related DAs. Consequently another challenge would be to add complementary knowledge when the DRDAs cannot provide complete information.

Therefore, we need a summarization approach that is tolerant of dialogue phenomena, can determine the key semantic content and is easily transferable between domains. Recently, topic modeling approaches have been investigated and achieved state-of-the-art results in multi-document summarization (Haghighi and Vanderwende, 2009; Celikyilmaz and Hakkani-Tur, 2010). Thus, topic models appear to be a better ref for document similarity w.r.t. semantic concepts than simple literal word matching. However, very little work has investigated its role in spoken document summarization (Chen and Chen, 2008; Hazen, 2011), and much less conducted comparisons among topic modeling approaches for focused summarization in meetings.

In contrast to previous work, we study the unsupervised token-level decision summarization in meetings by identifying a concise set of key words or phrases, which can either be output as a compact summary or be a starting point to generate abstractive summaries. This paper addresses problems mentioned above and make contributions as follows:

- As a step towards creating the abstractive summaries that people prefer when dealing with spoken language (Murray et al., 2010b), we propose a token-level rather than sentence-level framework for identifying components of the summary. Experimental results show that, compared to the sentence ranking based summarization algorithms, our token-level summarization framework can better identify the summary-worthy words and remove the redundancies.
- Rather than employing supervised learning methods that rely on costly manual annotation, we explore and evaluate topic modeling approaches of different granularities for the unsupervised decision summarization at both the token-level and dialogue act-level. We investigate three topic models — Local LDA (LocalLDA) (Brody and Elhadad, 2010), Multi-grain LDA (MG-LDA) (Titov and McDonald, 2008) and Segmented Topic Model (STM) (Du et al., 2010) — which can utilize the latent topic structure on utterance level instead of document level. Under our proposed token-level summarization framework, three fine-grained models outperform the basic LDA model and two extractive baselines that select the longest and the most representative utterance for each decision, respectively. (ROUGE-SU4 F score of 14.82% for STM vs. 13.58% and 13.46% for the baselines, given the perfect clusterings of DRDAs.)
- In line with prior research that explore the role of context for utterance-based extractive summariza-

[1] These DRDAs are annotated in the AMI corpus and usually contain the decision content. They are similar, but not completely equivalent, to the *decision dialogue acts (DDAs)* of Bui et al. (2009), Fernández et al. (2008), Frampton et al. (2009).

tion (Murray and Renals, 2007), we investigate the role of context in our token-level summarization framework. For the given clusters of DRDAs, We study two types of context information — the DAs preceding and succeeding a DRDA and DAs of high TF-IDF similarity with a DRDA. We also investigate two ways to select relevant words from the context DA. Experimental results show that two types of context have comparable effect, but selecting words from the dominant topic of the center DRDA performs better than from the dominant topic of the context DA. Moreover, by leveraging context, the recall exceeds the provided upperbound's recall (ROUGE-1 recall: 48.10% vs. 45.05% for upperbound by using DRDA only) although the F scores decrease after adding context information. Finally, we show that when the true DRDA clusterings are not available, adding context can improve both the recall and F score.

2 Related Work

Speech and dialogue summarization has become important in recent years as the number of multimedia resources containing speech has grown. A primary goal for most speech summarization systems is to account for the special characteristics of dialogue. Early work in this area investigated supervised learning methods, including maximum entropy, conditional random fields (CRFs), and support vector machines (SVMs) (Buist et al., 2004; Galley, 2006; Xie et al., 2008). For unsupervised methods, maximal marginal relevance (MMR) is investigated in (Zechner, 2002) and (Xie and Liu, 2010). Gillick et al. (2009) introduce a concept-based global optimization framework by using integer linear programming (ILP).

Only in very recent works has decision summarization been addressed in (Fernández et al., 2008), (Bui et al., 2009) and (Wang and Cardie, 2011). (Fernández et al., 2008) and (Bui et al., 2009) utilize semantic parser to identify candidate phrases for decision summaries and employ SVM to rank those phrases. They also train HMM and SVM directly on a set of decision-related dialogue acts on token level and use the classifiers to identify summary-worthy words. Wang and Cardie (2011) provide an exploration on supervised and unsupervised learning for decision summarization on both utterance- and token- level.

Our work also arises out of applying topic models to text summarization (Bhandari et al., 2008; Haghighi and Vanderwende, 2009; Celikyilmaz and Hakkani-Tur, 2010; Celikyilmaz and Hakkani-Tur, 2010). Mostly, the sentences are ranked according to importance based on latent topic structures, and top ones are selected as the summary. There are some works for applying document-level topic models to speech summarization (Kong and shan Leek, 2006; Chen and Chen, 2008; Hazen, 2011). Different from their work, we further investigate the topic models of fine granularity on sentence level and leverage context information for decision summarization task.

Most existing approaches for speech summarization result in a selection of utterances from the dialogue, which cannot remove the redundancy within utterances. To eliminate the superfluous words, our work is also inspired by keyphrase extraction of meetings (Liu et al., 2009; Liu et al., 2011) and keyphrase based summarization (Riedhammer et al., 2010). However, a small set of keyphrases are not enough to concretely display the content. Instead of only picking up keyphrases, our work identifies all of the summary-worthy words and phrases, and removes redundancies within utterances.

3 Summarization Frameworks

In this section, we first present our proposed token-level decision summarization framework — **DomSum** — which utilizes latent topic structure in utterances to extract words from **Dom**inant Topic (see details in Section 3.1) to form **Sum**maries. In Section 3.2, we describe four existing sentence scoring metrics denoted as *OneTopic, MultiTopic, TMM-Sum* and *KLSum* which are also based on latent topic distributions. We adopt them to the utterance-level summarization for comparison in Section 6.

3.1 Token-level Summarization Framework

Domsum takes as input the clusters of DRDAs (with or without additional context DAs), the topic distribution for each DA and the word distribution for each topic. The output is a set of topic-coherent summary-worthy words which can be used directly as the summary or to further generate abstractive summary. We introduce DomSum in two steps according to its input: taking clusters of DRDAs as the input and with additional context information.

DRDAs Only. Given clusters of DRDAs, we use Algorithm 1 to produce the token-level summary for each cluster. Generally, Algorithm 1 chooses the topic with the highest probability as the *dominant topic* given the dialogue act (DA). Then it collects the words with a high joint probability with the dominant topic from that DA.

```
Input  : Cluster C = {DA_i}, P(T_j|DA_i), P(w_k|T_j)
Output: Summary
Summary<- Φ (empty set)
foreach DA_i in C do
    DomTopic<- max_{T_j} P(T_j|DA_i) (*)
    Candidate<- Φ
    foreach word w_k in DA_i do
        SampleTopic<- max_{T_j} P(w_k|T_j)P(T_j|DA_i)
        if DomTopic == SampleTopic then
            Candidate <- Union (Candidate, w_k)
        end
    end
    Summary <- Union (Summary, Candidate)
end
```

Algorithm 1: DomSum — The token-level summarization framework. DomSum takes as input the clusters of DRDAs and related probability distributions.

Leveraging Context. For each DRDA (denoted as "*center DA*"), we study two types of context information (denoted as "*context DAs*"). One is adjacent DAs, i.e., immediately preceding and succeeding DAs, the other is the DAs having top TF-IDF similarities with the center DA. Context DAs are added into the cluster the corresponding center DA in.

We also study two criteria of word selection from the context DAs. For each context DA, we can take the words appearing in the dominant topic of either this context DA or its center DRDA. We will show in Section 6.1 that the latter performs better as it produces more topic-coherent summaries. Algorithm 1 can be easily modified to leverage context DAs by updating the input clusters and assigning the proper dominant topic for each DA accordingly — this changes the step $(*)$ in Algorithm 1.

3.2 Utterance-level Summarization Metrics

We also adopt four sentence scoring metrics based on the latent topic structure for extractive summarization. Though they are developed on different topic models, given the desired topic distributions as input, they can rank the utterances according to their importance and provide utterance-level summaries for comparison.

OneTopic and MultiTopic. In (Bhandari et al., 2008), several sentence scoring functions are introduced based on Probabilistic Latent Semantic Indexing. We adopt two metrics, which are *OneTopic* and *MultiTopic*. For OneTopic, topic T with highest probability $P(T)$ is picked as the central topic per cluster C. The score for DA in C is:

$$P(DA|T) = \frac{\sum_{w \in DA} P(T|DA, w)}{\sum_{DA' \in C, w \in DA'} P(T|DA', w)},$$

MultiTopic modifies OneTopic by taking all of the topics into consideration. Given a cluster C, DA in C is scored as:

$$\sum_T P(DA|T)P(T) = \sum_T \frac{\sum_{w \in DA} P(T|DA, w)}{\sum_{DA' \in C, w \in DA'} P(T|DA', w)} P(T)$$

TMMSum. Chen and Chen (2008) propose a Topical Mixture Model (TMM) for speech summarization, where each dialogue act is modeled as a TMM for generating the document. TMM is shown to provide better utterance-level extractive summaries for spoken documents than other conventional unsupervised approaches, such as Vector Space Model (VSM) (Gong and Liu, 2001), Latent Semantic Analysis (LSA) (Gong and Liu, 2001) and Maximum Marginal Relevance (MMR) (Murray et al., 2005). The importance of a sentence S can be measured by its generative probability $P(D|S)$, where D is the document S belongs to. In our experiments, one decision is made per cluster of DAs. So we adopt their scoring metric to compute the generative probability of the cluster C for each DA:

$$P(C|DA) = \prod_{w_i \in C} \sum_{T_j} P(w_i|T_j)P(T_j|DA),$$

KLSum. Kullback-Lieber (KL) divergence is explored for summarization in (Haghighi and Vanderwende, 2009) and (Lin et al., 2010), where it is used to measure the distance of distributions between the document and the summary. For a cluster C of DAs, given a length limit θ, a set of DAs S is selected as:

$$S^* = \arg\min_{S:|S|<\theta} KL(P_C||P_S) = \arg\min_{S:|S|<\theta} \sum_{T_i} P(T_i|C) log \frac{P(T_i|C)}{P(T_i|S)}$$

4 Topic Models

In this section, we briefly describe the three fine-grained topic models employed to compute the latent topic distributions on utterance level in the meetings. According to the input of Algorithm 1, we are interested in estimating the topic distribution for each DA $P(T|DA)$ and the word distribution for each topic $P(w|T)$. For MG-LDA, $P(T|DA)$ is computed as the expectation of local topic distributions with respect to the window distribution.

4.1 Local LDA

Local LDA (LocalLDA) (Brody and Elhadad, 2010) uses almost the same probabilistic generative model as Latent Dirichlet Allocation (LDA) (Blei et al., 2003), except that it treats each sentence as a separate document[2]. Each DA d is generated as follows:

1. For each topic k:
   (a) Choose word distribution: $\phi_k \sim Dir(\beta)$
2. For each DA d:
   (a) Choose topic distribution: $\theta_d \sim Dir(\alpha)$
   (b) For each word w in DA d:
      i. Choose topic: $z_{d,w} \sim \theta_d$
      ii. choose word: $w \sim \phi_{z_{d,w}}$

4.2 Multi-grain LDA

Multi-grain LDA (MG-LDA) (Titov and McDonald, 2008) can model both the meeting specific topics (e.g. the design of a remote control) and various concrete aspects (e.g. the cost or the functionality). The generative process is:

1. Choose a global topic distribution: $\theta_m^{gl} \sim Dir(\alpha^{gl})$
2. For each sliding window v of size T:
   (a) Choose local topic distribution: $\theta_{m,v}^{loc} \sim Dir(\alpha^{loc})$
   (b) Choose granularity mixture: $\pi_{m,v} \sim Beta(\alpha^{mix})$
3. For each DA d:
   (a) choose window distribution: $\psi_{m,d} \sim Dir(\gamma)$
4. For each word w in DA d of meeting m:
   (a) Choose sliding window: $v_{m,w} \sim \psi_{m,d}$
   (b) Choose granularity: $r_{m,w} \sim \pi_{m,v_{m,w}}$
   (c) If $r_{m,w} = gl$, choose global topic: $z_{m,w} \sim \theta_m^{gl}$
   (d) If $r_{m,w} = loc$, choose local topic: $z_{m,w} \sim \theta_{m,v_{m,w}}^{loc}$
   (e) Choose word w from the word distribution: $\phi_{z_{m,w}}^{r_{m,w}}$

4.3 Segmented Topic Model

The last model we utilize is Segmented Topic Model (STM) (Du et al., 2010), which jointly models document- and sentence-level latent topics using a two-parameter Poisson Dirichlet Process (PDP). Given parameters α, γ, Φ and PDP parameters a, b, the generative process is:

1. Choose distribution of topics: $\theta_m \sim Dir(\alpha)$
2. For each dialogue act d:
   (a) Choose distribution of topics: $\theta_d \sim PDP(\theta_m, a, b)$
3. For each word w in dialogue act d:
   (a) Choose topic: $z_{m,w} \sim \theta_d$
   (b) Choose word: $w \sim \phi_{z_{m,w}}$

[2]For the generative process of LDA, the DAs in the same meeting make up the document, so "each DA" is changed to "each meeting" in LocalLDA's generative process.

5 Experimental Setup

The Corpus. We evaluate our approach on the AMI meeting corpus (Carletta et al., 2005) that consists of 140 multi-party meetings. The 129 scenario-driven meetings involve four participants playing different roles on a design team. A short (usually one-sentence) abstract is manually constructed to summarize each decision discussed in the meeting and used as gold-standard summaries in our experiments.

System Inputs. Our summarization system requires as input a partitioning of the DRDAs according to the decision(s) that each supports (i.e., one cluster of DRDAs per decision). As mentioned earlier, we assume for all experiments that the DRDAs for each meeting have been identified. For evaluation we consider two system input settings. In the **True Clusterings** setting, we use the AMI annotations to create perfect partitionings of the DRDAs as the input; in the **System Clusterings** setting, we employ a hierarchical agglomerative clustering algorithm used for this task in previous work (Wang and Cardie, 2011). The Wang and Cardie (2011) clustering method groups DRDAs according to their LDA topic distribution similarity. As better approaches for DRDA clustering become available, they could be employed instead.

Evaluation Metric. To evaluate the performance of various summarization approaches, we use the widely accepted ROUGE (Lin and Hovy, 2003) metrics. We use the stemming option of the ROUGE software at `http://berouge.com/` and remove stopwords from both the system and gold-standard summaries, same as Riedhammer et al. (2010) do.

Inference and Hyperparameters We use the implementation from (Lu et al., 2011) for the three topic models in Section 4. The collapsed Gibbs Sampling approach (Griffiths and Steyvers, 2004) is exploited for inference. Hyperparameters are chosen according to (Brody and Elhadad, 2010), (Titov and McDonald, 2008) and (Du et al., 2010). In LDA and LocalLDA, α and β are both set to 0.1 . For MG-LDA, α^{gl}, α^{loc} and α^{mix} are set to 0.1; γ is 0.1

and the window size T is 3. And the number of local topic is set as the same number of global topic as discussed in (Titov and McDonald, 2008). In STM, α, a and b are set to 0.5, 0.1 and 1, respectively.

5.1 Baselines and Comparisons

We compare our token-level summarization framework based on the fine-grained topic models to (1) two unsupervised baselines, (2) token-level summarization by LDA, (3) utterance-level summarization by Topical Mixture Model (TMM) (Chen and Chen, 2008), (4) utterance-level summarization based on the fine-grained topic models using existing metrics (Section 3.2), (5) two supervised methods, and (6) an upperbound derived from the AMI gold standard decision abstracts. (1) and (6) are described below, others will be discussed in Section 6.

The LONGEST DA Baseline. As in (Riedhammer et al., 2010) and (Wang and Cardie, 2011), this baseline simply selects the longest DRDA in each cluster as the summary. Thus, it performs utterance-level decision summarization. This baseline and the next allow us to determine summary quality when summaries are restricted to a single utterance.

The PROTOTYPE DA Baseline. Following Wang and Cardie (2011), the second baseline selects the decision cluster prototype (i.e., the DRDA with the largest TF-IDF similarity with the cluster centroid) as the summary.

Upperbound. We also compute an upperbound that reflects the gap between the best possible extractive summaries and the human-written abstracts according to the ROUGE score: for each cluster of DRDAs, we select the words that also appear in the associated decision abstract.

6 Results and Discussion

6.1 True Clusterings

How do fine-grained topic models compare to basic topic models or baselines? Figure 2 demonstrates that by using the DomSum token-level summarization framework, the three fine-grained topic models uniformly outperform the two non-trivial baselines and TMM (Chen and Chen, 2008) (reimplemented by us) that generates utterance-level summaries. Moreover, the fine-grained models also beat basic LDA under the same DomSum token-level summarization framework. This shows the fine-

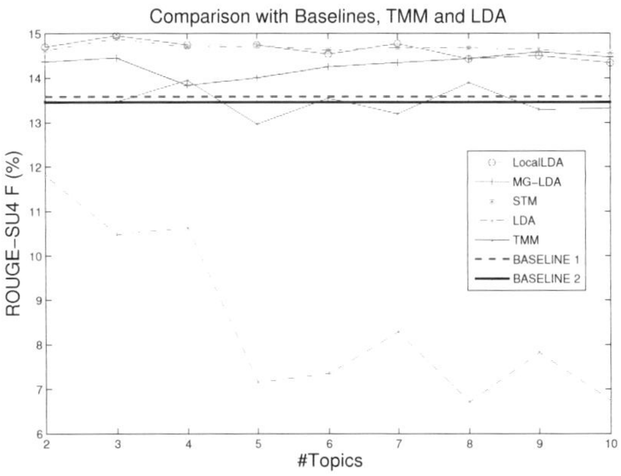

Figure 2: With true clusterings of DRDAs as the input, we use DomSum to compare the performance of LocalLDA, MGLDA and STM against two baselines, LDA and TMM. "# topic" indicates the number of topics for the model. For MGLDA, "# topic" is the number of local topics.

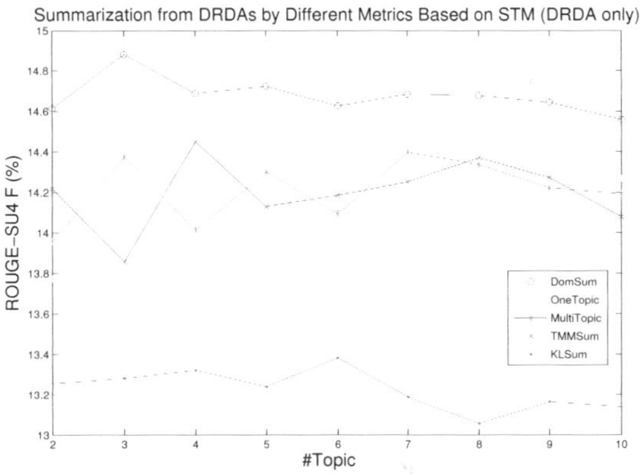

Figure 3: With true clusterings of DRDAs as the input, DomSum is compared with four DA-level summarization metrics using topic distributions from STM. Results from LocalLDA and MGLDA are similar so they are not displayed.

grained topic models that discover topic structures on utterance-level better identify gist information.

Can the proposed token-level summarization framework better identify important words and remove redundancies than utterance selection methods? Figure 3 demonstrates the comparison results for our DomSum token-level summarization framework with four existing utterance scoring metrics discussed in Section 3.2, namely OneTopic, MultiTopic, TMMSum and KLSum. The utterance with highest score is extracted to form the summary. LocalLDA and STM are utilized to compute the input distributions, i.e., $P(T|DA)$ and $P(w|T)$. From Figure 3, DomSum yields the best F scores which

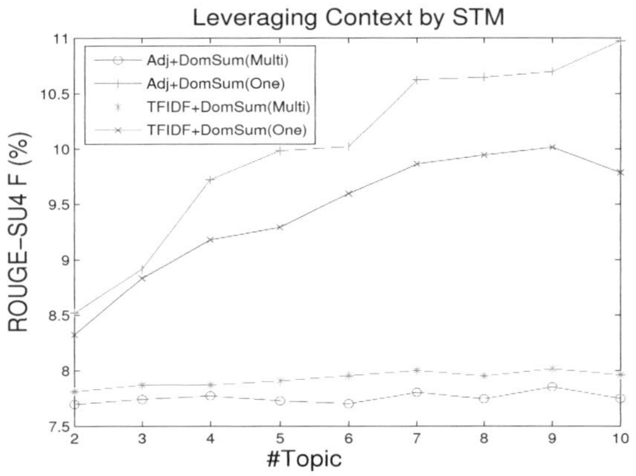

Figure 4: Under DomSum framework, two types of context information are added: Adjacent DA ("Adj") and DAs with high TFIDF similarities ("TFIDF"). For each context DA, selecting words from the dominant topic of center DA ("One") or the current context DA ("Multi") are investigated.

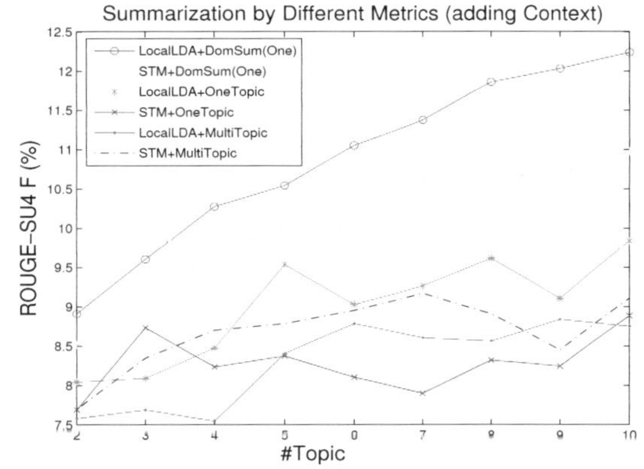

Figure 5: By using adjacent DAs as context, DomSum is compared with two DA-level summarization metrics: OneTopic and MultiTopic. For DomSum, the words of context DA from dominant topic of the center DA ("One") is selected; For OneTopic and MultiTopic, three top ranked DAs are selected.

	True Clusterings				
	R-1			R-2	R-SU4
	PREC	REC	F1	F1	F1
Baselines					
Longest DA	34.06	31.28	32.61	12.03	13.58
Prototype DA	40.72	28.21	33.32	12.18	13.46
Supervised Methods					
CRF	52.89	26.77	35.53	11.48	14.03
SVM	43.24	37.92	40.39	12.78	16.24
Our Approach					
5 topics					
LocalLDA	35.18	38.92	36.95	12.33	14.74
+ *context*	17.26	45.34	25.00	8.40	11.05
STM	34.06	41.30	**37.32**	**12.42**	**14.82**
+ *context*	15.60	***48.10***	23.56	8.16	9.98
10 topics					
LocalLDA	36.20	36.81	36.50	12.04	14.34
+ *context*	21.82	41.57	28.62	9.61	12.24
STM	34.15	40.83	37.19	12.40	14.56
+ *context*	17.87	46.57	25.82	8.89	10.97
Upperbound	100.00	***45.05***	62.12	33.27	34.89

Table 1: ROUGE-1 (R-1), ROUGE-2 (R-2) and ROUGE-SU4 (R-SU4) scores for our proposed token-level summarization approaches along with two baselines, supervised methods and the Upperbound (only using DRDAs). — all use True Clusterings

shows that the token-level summarization approach is more effective than utterance-level methods.

Which way is better for leveraging context information? We explore two types of context information. For adjacent content (*Adj* in Figure 4), 5 DAs immediately preceding and 5 DAs succeeding the center DRDA are selected. For TF-IDF context (*TFIDF* in Figure 4), 10 DAs of highest TF-IDF similarity with the center DRDA are taken. We also explore two ways to extract summary-worthy words from the context DA — selecting words from the dominant topic of either the center DA (denoted as "One" in parentheses in Figure 4) or the current context DA (denoted as "multi" in parentheses in Figure 4). Figure 4 indicates that the two types of context information do not have significant difference, while selecting the words from the dominant topic of the center DA results in better ROUGE-SU4 F scores. Notice that compared with Figure 3, the results in Figure 4 have lower F scores when using the true clusterings of DRDAs. This is because context DAs bring in relevant words as well as noisy information. We will show in Section 6.2 that when true clusterings are not available, the context information can boost both recall and F score.

How do the token-level summarization framework compared to utterance selection methods for leveraging context? We also compare the ability of leveraging context of DomSum to utterance scoring metrics, i.e., OneTopic and MultiTopic. 5 DAs preceding and 5 DAs succeeding the center DA are added as context information. For context DA under DomSum, we select words from the dominant topic of the center DA (denoted as "One" in parentheses in Figure 5). For OneTopic and MultiTopic, the top 3 DAs are extracted as the summary. Figure 5 demonstrates the combination of LocalLDA and STM with each of the metrics. DomSum, as a token-level summarization metrics, dominates other two metrics in leveraging context.

	System Clusterings				
	R-1			R-2	R-SU4
	PREC	REC	F1	F1	F1
Baselines					
Longest DA	17.06	11.64	13.84	2.76	3.34
Prototype DA	18.14	10.11	12.98	2.84	3.09
Supervised Methods					
CRF	46.97	15.25	23.02	6.09	9.11
SVM	39.05	18.45	25.06	6.11	9.82
Our Approach					
5 topics					
LocalLDA	25.57	16.57	20.11	4.03	5.87
+ *context*	20.68	25.96	23.02	3.09	4.48
STM	24.15	17.82	20.51	4.03	5.69
+ *context*	20.64	***30.03***	**24.47**	3.59	4.76
10 topics					
LocalLDA	25.98	15.94	19.76	3.59	4.41
+ *context*	23.98	21.92	22.90	3.45	4.10
STM	26.32	19.14	22.16	**4.07**	**5.88**
+ *context*	22.50	28.40	25.11	3.43	4.15

Table 2: ROUGE-1 (R-1), ROUGE-2 (R-2) and ROUGE-SU4 (R-SU4) scores for our proposed token-level summarization approaches, compared with two baselines and supervised methods. — all use System Clusterings

DRDA (1): I think if we can if we can include them at not too much extra cost, then I'd put them in, **DRDA (2)**: Uh um we we're definitely going in for voice recognition as well as LCDs, mm. **DRDA (3)**: So we've basically worked out that we're going with a simple battery, **context DA (1)**:So it's advanced integrated circuits? **context DA (2)**:the advanced chip **context DA (3)**: and a curved on one side case which is folded in on itself , um made out of rubber
Decision Abstract: It will have voice recognition, use a simple battery, and contain an advanced chip.
Longest DA & Prototype DA: Uh um we we're definitely going in for voice recognition as well as LCDs, mm. **TMM:** I think if we can if we can include them at not too much extra cost, then I'd put them in, **SVM:** cost voice recognition simple battery **CRF:** voice recognition battery **STM:** extra cost, definitely going voice recognition LCDs, simple battery **STM + context:** cost, company, advanced integrated circuits, going voice recognition, simple battery, advanced chip, curved case rubber

Table 3: Sample system outputs by different methods are in the third cell (methods' names are in bold). First cell contains three DRDAs supporting the decision in the second cell and three adjacent DAs of them.

How do our approach perform when compared with supervised learning approaches? For a better comparison, we also provide summarization results by using supervised systems along with an upperbound. We use Support Vector Machines (Joachims, 1998) with RBF kernel and order-1 Conditional Random Fields (Lafferty et al., 2001) — trained with the same features as (Wang and Cardie, 2011) to identify the summary-worthy **tokens** to include in the abstract. A three-fold cross validation is conducted for both methods. ROUGE-1, ROUGE-2 and ROUGE-SU4 scores are listed in Table 1. From Table 1, our token-level summarization approaches based on LocalLDA and STM are shown to outperform the baselines and even the CRF. Meanwhile, by adding context information, both LocalLDA and STM can get better ROUGE-1 recall than the supervised methods, even higher than the provided upperbound which is computed by only using DRDAs. This shows the DomSum framework can leverage context to compensate the summaries.

6.2 System Clusterings

Results using the **System Clusterings** (Table 2) present similar findings, though all of the system and baseline scores are lower. By adding context information, the token-level summarization approaches based on fine-grained topic models compare favorably to the supervised methods in F scores, and also get the best ROUGE-1 recalls.

6.3 Sample System Summaries

To better exemplify the summaries generated by different systems, sample output for each method is shown in Table 3. We see from the table that utterance-level extractive summaries (Longest DA, Prototype DA, TMM) make more coherent but still far from concise and compact abstracts. On the other hand, the supervised methods (SVM, CRF) that produce token-level extracts better identify the overall content of the decision abstract. Unfortunately, they require human annotation in the training phase. In comparison, the output of fine-grained topic models can cover the most useful information.

7 Conclusion

We propose a token-level summarization framework based on topic models and show that modeling topic structure at the utterance-level is better at identifying relevant words and phrases than document-level models. The role of context is also studied and shown to be able to identify additional summary-worthy words.

Acknowledgments This work was supported in part by National Science Foundation Grants IIS-0968450 and IIS-1111176, and by a gift from Google.

References

Harendra Bhandari, Takahiko Ito, Masashi Shimbo, and Yuji Matsumoto. 2008. Generic text summarization using probabilistic latent semantic indexing. In *Proceedings of IJCNLP*, pages 133–140.

David M. Blei, Andrew Y. Ng, and Michael I. Jordan. 2003. Latent dirichlet allocation. *J. Mach. Learn. Res.*, 3:993–1022, March.

Samuel Brody and Noemie Elhadad. 2010. An unsupervised aspect-sentiment model for online reviews. In *Human Language Technologies: The 2010 Annual Conference of the North American Chapter of the Association for Computational Linguistics*, HLT '10, pages 804–812, Stroudsburg, PA, USA. Association for Computational Linguistics.

Trung H. Bui, Matthew Frampton, John Dowding, and Stanley Peters. 2009. Extracting decisions from multi-party dialogue using directed graphical models and semantic similarity. In *Proceedings of the SIGDIAL 2009 Conference*, pages 235–243.

Anne Hendrik Buist, Wessel Kraaij, and Stephan Raaijmakers. 2004. Automatic summarization of meeting data: A feasibility study. In *Proc. Meeting of Computational Linguistics in the Netherlands (CLIN)*.

Giuseppe Carenini, Gabriel Murray, and Raymond Ng. 2011. *Methods for Mining and Summarizing Text Conversations*. Morgan & Claypool Publishers.

Jean Carletta, Simone Ashby, Sebastien Bourban, Mike Flynn, Thomas Hain, Jaroslav Kadlec, Vasilis Karaiskos, Wessel Kraaij, Melissa Kronenthal, Guillaume Lathoud, Mike Lincoln, Agnes Lisowska, and Mccowan Wilfried Post Dennis Reidsma. 2005. The ami meeting corpus: A pre-announcement. In *In Proc. MLMI*, pages 28–39.

Asli Celikyilmaz and Dilek Hakkani-Tur. 2010. A hybrid hierarchical model for multi-document summarization. In *Proceedings of the 48th Annual Meeting of the Association for Computational Linguistics*, ACL '10, pages 815–824, Stroudsburg, PA, USA. Association for Computational Linguistics.

Berlin Chen and Yi-Ting Chen. 2008. Extractive spoken document summarization for information retrieval. *Pattern Recogn. Lett.*, 29:426–437, March.

Lan Du, Wray Buntine, and Huidong Jin. 2010. A segmented topic model based on the two-parameter poisson-dirichlet process. *Mach. Learn.*, 81:5–19, October.

Raquel Fernández, Matthew Frampton, John Dowding, Anish Adukuzhiyil, Patrick Ehlen, and Stanley Peters. 2008. Identifying relevant phrases to summarize decisions in spoken meetings. INTERSPEECH-2008, pages 78–81.

Matthew Frampton, Jia Huang, Trung Huu Bui, and Stanley Peters. 2009. Real-time decision detection in multi-party dialogue. In *Proceedings of the 2009 Conference on Empirical Methods in Natural Language Processing: Volume 3 - Volume 3*, pages 1133–1141.

Michel Galley. 2006. A skip-chain conditional random field for ranking meeting utterances by importance. In *Proceedings of the 2006 Conference on Empirical Methods in Natural Language Processing*, pages 364–372.

Dan Gillick, Korbinian Riedhammer, Benoit Favre, and Dilek Hakkani-Tur. 2009. A global optimization framework for meeting summarization. In *Proceedings of the 2009 IEEE International Conference on Acoustics, Speech and Signal Processing*, ICASSP '09, pages 4769–4772. IEEE Computer Society.

Yihong Gong and Xin Liu. 2001. Generic text summarization using relevance measure and latent semantic analysis. In *Proceedings of the 24th annual international ACM SIGIR conference on Research and development in information retrieval*, SIGIR '01, pages 19–25, New York, NY, USA. ACM.

T. L. Griffiths and M. Steyvers. 2004. Finding scientific topics. *Proceedings of the National Academy of Sciences*, 101(Suppl. 1):5228–5235, April.

Aria Haghighi and Lucy Vanderwende. 2009. Exploring content models for multi-document summarization. In *Proceedings of Human Language Technologies: The 2009 Annual Conference of the North American Chapter of the Association for Computational Linguistics*, NAACL '09, pages 362–370. Association for Computational Linguistics.

Timothy J. Hazen. 2011. Latent topic modeling for audio corpus summarization. In *INTERSPEECH*, pages 913–916.

Thorsten Joachims. 1998. Text categorization with Support Vector Machines: Learning with many relevant features. In Claire Nédellec and Céline Rouveirol, editors, *Machine Learning: ECML-98*, volume 1398, chapter 19, pages 137–142. Berlin/Heidelberg.

Sheng-Yi Kong and Lin shan Leek. 2006. Improved spoken document summarization using probabilistic latent semantic analysis (plsa). In *Proceedings of the 2006 IEEE International Conference on Acoustics, Speech and Signal Processing*, ICASSP '06.

John D. Lafferty, Andrew McCallum, and Fernando C. N. Pereira. 2001. Conditional random fields: Probabilistic models for segmenting and labeling sequence data. In *Proceedings of the Eighteenth International Conference on Machine Learning*, ICML '01, pages 282–289, San Francisco, CA, USA. Morgan Kaufmann Publishers Inc.

Shih-Hsiang Lin and Berlin Chen. 2010. A risk minimization framework for extractive speech summarization. In *Proceedings of the 48th Annual Meeting of the Association for Computational Linguistics*, ACL '10, pages 79–87. Association for Computational Linguistics.

Chin-Yew Lin and Eduard Hovy. 2003. Automatic evaluation of summaries using n-gram co-occurrence statistics. In *Proceedings of the 2003 Conference of the North American Chapter of the Association for Computational Linguistics on Human Language Technology - Volume 1*, pages 71–78.

S.-H. Lin, Y.-M. Yeh, and B. Chen. 2010. Leveraging kullback-leibler divergence measures and information-rich cues for speech summarization.

Feifan Liu, Deana Pennell, Fei Liu, and Yang Liu. 2009. Unsupervised approaches for automatic keyword extraction using meeting transcripts. In *Proceedings of Human Language Technologies: The 2009 Annual Conference of the North American Chapter of the Association for Computational Linguistics*, NAACL '09, pages 620–628, Stroudsburg, PA, USA. Association for Computational Linguistics.

Fei Liu, Feifan Liu, and Yang Liu. 2011. A supervised framework for keyword extraction from meeting transcripts. *IEEE Transactions on Audio, Speech & Language Processing*, 19(3):538–548.

Bin Lu, Myle Ott, Claire Cardie, and Benjamin Tsou. 2011. Multi-aspect sentiment analysis with topic models. In *Workshop on Sentiment Elicitation from Natural Text for Information Retrieval and Extraction.*

Sameer Maskey and Julia Hirschberg. 2005. Comparing Lexical, Acoustic/Prosodic, Structural and Discourse Features for Speech Summarization. In *Proc. European Conference on Speech Communication and Technology (Eurospeech).*

Gabriel Murray and Steve Renals. 2007. Towards online speech summarization. In *INTERSPEECH*, pages 2785–2788.

Gabriel Murray, Steve Renals, and Jean Carletta. 2005. Extractive summarization of meeting recordings. In *in Proceedings of the 9th European Conference on Speech Communication and Technology*, pages 593–596.

Gabriel Murray, Giuseppe Carenini, and Raymond Ng. 2010a. Interpretation and transformation for abstracting conversations. In *Human Language Technologies: The 2010 Annual Conference of the North American Chapter of the Association for Computational Linguistics*, HLT '10, pages 894–902, Stroudsburg, PA, USA. Association for Computational Linguistics.

Gabriel Murray, Giuseppe Carenini, and Raymond T. Ng. 2010b. Generating and validating abstracts of meeting conversations: a user study. In *INLG'10*.

Korbinian Riedhammer, Benoit Favre, and Dilek Hakkani-Tür. 2010. Long story short - global unsupervised models for keyphrase based meeting summarization. *Speech Commun.*, 52(10):801–815, October.

Ivan Titov and Ryan McDonald. 2008. Modeling online reviews with multi-grain topic models. In *Proceeding of the 17th international conference on World Wide Web*, WWW '08, pages 111–120. ACM.

Lu Wang and Claire Cardie. 2011. Summarizing decisions in spoken meetings. In *Proceedings of the Workshop on Automatic Summarization for Different Genres, Media, and Languages*, pages 16–24, Portland, Oregon, June. Association for Computational Linguistics.

Shasha Xie and Yang Liu. 2010. Using confusion networks for speech summarization. In *Human Language Technologies: The 2010 Annual Conference of the North American Chapter of the Association for Computational Linguistics*, HLT '10, pages 46–54. Association for Computational Linguistics.

Shasha Xie, Yang Liu, and Hui Lin. 2008. Evaluating the effectiveness of features and sampling in extractive meeting summarization. In *Proc. of IEEE Spoken Language Technology (SLT).*

Klaus Zechner. 2002. Automatic summarization of open-domain multiparty dialogues in diverse genres. *Comput. Linguist.*, 28:447–485, December.

An Unsupervised Approach to User Simulation: toward Self-Improving Dialog Systems

Sungjin Lee[1,2] and **Maxine Eskenazi**[1]
[1]Language Technologies Institute, Carnegie Mellon University, Pittsburgh, Pennsylvania
[2]Computer Science and Engineering, Pohang University of Science and Technology, South Korea
{sungjin.lee, max}@cs.cmu.edu[1], junion@postech.ac.kr[2]

Abstract

This paper proposes an unsupervised approach to user simulation in order to automatically furnish updates and assessments of a deployed spoken dialog system. The proposed method adopts a dynamic Bayesian network to infer the unobservable true user action from which the parameters of other components are naturally derived. To verify the quality of the simulation, the proposed method was applied to the Let's Go domain (Raux et al., 2005) and a set of measures was used to analyze the simulated data at several levels. The results showed a very close correspondence between the real and simulated data, implying that it is possible to create a realistic user simulator that does not necessitate human intervention.

1 Introduction

For the past decade statistical approaches to dialog modeling have shown positive results for optimizing a dialog strategy with real data by applying well-understood machine learning methods such as reinforcement learning (Henderson et al., 2008; Thomson and Young, 2010; Williams and Young, 2007b). User simulation is becoming an essential component in developing and evaluating such systems. In this paper we describe an unsupervised process to automatically develop user simulators. The motivation for this comes from the fact that many systems are presently moving from being simple lab simulations to actual deployed systems with real users. These systems furnish a constant flow of new data that needs to be processed in some way. Our goal is to minimize human intervention in processing this data. Previously, data had to be hand-annotated, a slow and costly process. Recently crowdsourcing has made annotation faster and less expensive, but all of the data still has to be processed and time must be spent in creating the annotation interface and tasks, and in quality control. Our goal is to process the metadata (e.g. user actions, goals, error typology) in an unsupervised manner. And our method eliminates the need for human transcription and annotation by inferring the user goal from grounding information. We also consider user actions as latent variables which are inferred based on observations from Automatic Speech Recognition (ASR). We used the above inferred user actions paired with the observed actions to build an error model. Since the focus of this work is placed on improving and evaluating the dialog strategy, error simulation can be carried out at the semantic level. This eliminates the need for transcription, which would have necessitated an error simulation at the surface level. The end result here will be a system that has as little human intervention as possible.

This paper is structured as follows. Section 2 describes previous research and the novelty of our approach. Section 3 elaborates on our proposed unsupervised approach to user simulation. Section 4 explains the experimental setup. Section 5 presents and discusses the results. Finally, Section 6 concludes with a brief summary and suggestions for future research.

2 Related Work

Previous user simulation studies can be roughly categorized into rule-based methods (Chung, 2005;

Lopez-Cozar et al., 2006; Schatzmann et al., 2007a) and data-driven methods (Cuayahuitl et al., 2005; Eckert et al., 1997; Jung et al., 2009; Levin et al., 2000; Georgila et al., 2006; Pietquin, 2004). Rule-based methods generally allow for more control over their designs for the target domain while data-driven methods afford more portability from one domain to another and are attractive for modeling user behavior based on real data. Although development costs for data-driven methods are typically lower than those of rule-based methods, previous data-driven approaches have still required a certain amount of human effort. Most intention-level models take a semantically annotated corpus to produce user intention without introducing errors (Cuayahuitl et al., 2005; Jung et al., 2009). Surface-level approaches need transcribed data to train their surface form and error generating models (Jung et al., 2009; Schatzmann et al., 2007b). A few studies have attempted to directly simulate the intention, surface, and error by applying their statistical methods on the recognized data rather than on the transcribed data (Georgila et al., 2006; Schatzmann et al., 2005). Although such approaches can avoid human intervention, the sole incorporation of erroneous user action can propagate those errors to the higher-level discourse features which are computed from them, and thus could result in less realistic user behavior. In this work, the true user action is treated as a hidden variable and, further, its associated dialog history is also viewed as latent so that the uncertainty of the true user action is properly controlled in a principled manner. Syed and Williams (2008) adopted the *Expectation Maximization* algorithm for parameter learning for a latent variable model. But their method still requires a small amount of transcribed data to learn the observation confusability, and it suffers from overfitting as a general property of maximum likelihood. To address this problem, we propose a Bayesian learning method, which requires no transcribed data.

3 Unsupervised Approach to User Simulation

Before describing each component in detail, we present the overall process of user simulation with an example in the Let's Go domain in Figure 1. To begin a dialog, the user simulator first sets the user goal by sampling the goal model. Then the user simulator engages in a conversation with the dialog system until the termination model ends it. At each turn, the termination model randomly determines whether the dialog will continue or not. If the dialog continues, the user model generates user actions at the predicate level with respect to the given user goal and system action. Having the user actions, the error template model transforms some user actions into other actions if necessary and determines which action will receive an incorrect value. After that, the error value model substantiates the values by drawing a confusable value if specified to be incorrect or by using the goal value. Finally, a confidence score will be attached to the user action by sampling the confidence score model which conditions on the correctness of the final user action.

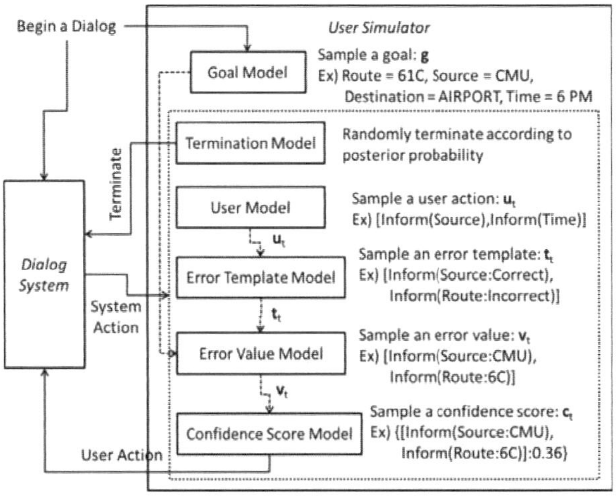

Figure 1: The overall process of user simulation in the Let's Go domain, where users call the spoken dialog system to get bus schedule information for Pittsburgh

3.1 Goal Model

The goal model is the first component to be defined in terms of the working flow of the user simulator. In order to generate a plausible user goal in accordance with the frequency at which it appears in a real situation, the dialog logs are parsed to look for the grounding information[1] that the users have provided. Since the representation of a user goal in this study is a vector of constraints required by a user, for example *[Route:61C, Source:CMU,*

[1]Specifically, we used explicitly confirmed information by the system for this study

Destination:AIRPORT, Time:6 PM], each time we encounter grounding information that includes the constraints used in the backend queries, this is added to the user goal. If two actions contradict each other, the later action overwrites the earlier one. Once all of the user goals in the data have been gathered, a discrete distribution over the user goal is learned using a maximum likelihood estimation. Because many variables later in this paper are discrete, a general notation of a conditional discrete distribution is expressed as follows:

$$p(\mathbf{x}_i|\mathbf{x}_{pa(i)}, \boldsymbol{\theta}) = \prod_{\mathbf{k},k'} \theta_{\mathbf{k},k'}^{\delta(pa(i),\mathbf{k})\delta(\mathbf{x}_i,k')} \quad (1)$$

where $\mathbf{k}$ represents the joint configuration of all the parents of i and $\delta(\cdot,\cdot)$ denotes *Kronecker* delta. Note that $\sum_{k'} \theta_{\mathbf{k},k'} = 1$. Given this notation, the goal model Λ can be written in the following form:

$$g \sim p(\mathbf{g}|\boldsymbol{\Lambda}) = \prod_k \lambda_k^{\delta(\mathbf{g},k)} \quad (2)$$

3.2 User Model

Having generated a user goal, the next task is to infer an appropriate user action for the given goal and system action. This is what the user model does. Since one of key properties of our unsupervised approach is that the true user actions are not observable, the user model should maintain a belief over the dialog state by taking into consideration the observed user actions. Inspired by (Williams et al., 2005), to keep the complexity of the user model tractable, a dynamic Bayesian network is adopted with several conditional independence assumptions, giving rise to the graphical structure which is shown in Figure 2. Unlike belief tracking in a dialog system, the user goal in a user simulation is pre-determined before the beginning of the dialog. As with most previous studies, this property allows the user model to deal with a predicate-level action consisting of a speech act and a concept (e.g. *[Inform(Source), Inform(Time)]*) and is only concerned about whether a given field is specified or not in the user goal (e.g. *Bus:Unspecified, Source:Specified*). This abstract-level handling enables the user model to employ exact inference algorithms such as the *junction tree* algorithm (Lauritzen and Spiegelhalter, 1988) for more efficient reasoning over the graphical structure.

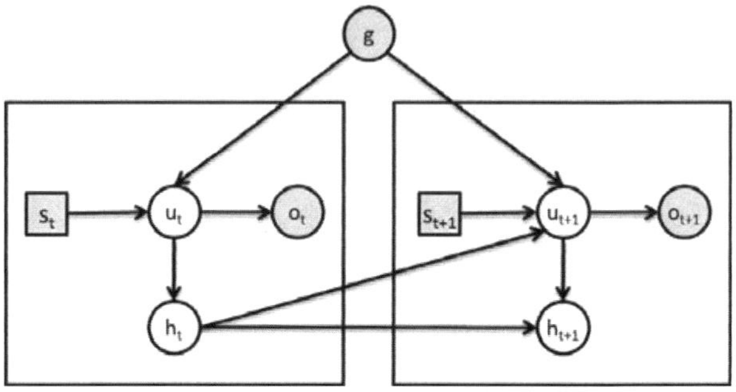

Figure 2: The graphical structure of the dynamic Bayesian network for the user model. $\mathbf{g}$ denotes the user goal and $\mathbf{s}_t, \mathbf{u}_t, \mathbf{h}_t, \mathbf{o}_t$ represents the system action, the user action, the dialog history, and the observed user action for each time slice, respectively. The shaded items are observable and the transparent ones are latent.

The joint distribution for this model is given by

$$\begin{aligned} &p(\mathbf{g}, \mathbf{S}, \mathbf{H}, \mathbf{U}, \mathbf{O}|\boldsymbol{\Theta}) \\ &\quad = p(\mathbf{h}_0|\boldsymbol{\pi}) \prod_t p(\mathbf{u}_t|\mathbf{g}, \mathbf{s}_t, \mathbf{h}_{t-1}, \boldsymbol{\phi}) \\ &\quad \cdot p(\mathbf{h}_t|\mathbf{h}_{t-1}, \mathbf{u}_t, \boldsymbol{\eta}) p(\mathbf{o}_t|\mathbf{u}_t, \boldsymbol{\zeta}) \end{aligned} \quad (3)$$

where a capital letter stands for the set of corresponding random variables, e.g., $\mathbf{U} = \{\mathbf{u}_1, \ldots, \mathbf{u}_N\}$, and $\boldsymbol{\Theta} = \{\boldsymbol{\pi}, \boldsymbol{\phi}, \boldsymbol{\eta}, \boldsymbol{\zeta}\}$ denotes the set of parameters governing the model[2].

For a given user goal, the user model basically performs an inference to obtain a marginal distribution over $\mathbf{u}_t$ for each time step from which it can sample the probability of a user action in a given context:

$$u_t \sim p(\mathbf{u}_t|\mathbf{g}, \mathbf{s}_1^t, \mathbf{u}_1^{t-1}, \boldsymbol{\Theta}) \quad (4)$$

where $\mathbf{s}_1^t$ denotes the set of system actions from time 1 to time t and $\mathbf{u}_1^{t-1}$ is the set of previously sampled user actions from time 1 to time $t-1$.

3.2.1 Parameter Estimation

As far as parameters are concerned, $\boldsymbol{\zeta}$ is a deterministic function that yields a fraction of an observed confidence score in accordance with the degree of agreement between $\mathbf{u}_t$ and $\mathbf{o}_t$:

$$p(\mathbf{o}_t|\mathbf{u}_t) = CS(\mathbf{o}_t) \cdot \left(\frac{|\mathbf{o}_t \cap \mathbf{u}_t|}{|\mathbf{o}_t \cup \mathbf{u}_t|}\right)^p + \epsilon \quad (5)$$

[2]Here, uniform prior distributions are assigned on $\mathbf{g}$ and $\mathbf{S}$

where $CS(\cdot)$ returns the confidence score of the associated observation and p is a control variable over the strength of disagreement penalty[3]. In addition, $\boldsymbol{\pi}$ and $\boldsymbol{\eta}$ are deterministically set by simple discourse rules, for example:

$$p(\mathbf{h}_t = \textit{Informed} | \mathbf{h}_{t-1}, \mathbf{u}_t) = \begin{cases} 1 & \text{if } \mathbf{h}_{t-1} = \textit{Informed} \text{ or } \mathbf{u}_t = \textit{Inform}(\cdot), \\ 0 & \text{otherwise.} \end{cases} \quad (6)$$

The only parameter that needs to be learned in the user model, therefore, is $\boldsymbol{\phi}$ and it can be estimated by maximizing the likelihood function (Equation 7). The likelihood function is obtained from the joint distribution (Equation 3) by marginalizing over the latent variables.

$$p(\mathbf{g}, \mathbf{S}, \mathbf{O} | \boldsymbol{\Theta}) = \sum_{\mathbf{H}, \mathbf{U}} p(\mathbf{g}, \mathbf{S}, \mathbf{H}, \mathbf{U}, \mathbf{O} | \boldsymbol{\Theta}) \quad (7)$$

Since direct maximization of the likelihood function will lead to complex expressions with no closed-form solutions due to the latent variables, the *Expectation-Maximization* (EM) algorithm is an efficient framework for finding maximum likelihood estimates.

As it is well acknowledged, however, that overfitting can arise as a general property of maximum likelihood, especially when only a small amount of data is available, a *Bayesian* approach needs to be adopted. In a Bayesian model, any unknown parameter is given a prior distribution and is absorbed into the set of latent variables, thus it is infeasible to directly evaluate the posterior distribution of the latent variables and the expectations with respect to this distribution. Therefore a deterministic approximation, called *mean field* theory (Parisi, 1988), is applied.

In *mean field* theory, the family of posterior distributions of the latent variables is assumed to be partitioned into disjoint groups:

$$q(\mathbf{Z}) = \prod_{i=1}^{M} q_i(\mathbf{Z}_i) \quad (8)$$

where $\mathbf{Z} = \{\mathbf{z}_1, \ldots, \mathbf{z}_N\}$ denotes all latent variables including parameters and $\mathbf{Z}_i$ is a disjoint group.

[3]For this study, p was set to 1.0

Amongst all distributions $q(\mathbf{Z})$ having the form of Equation 8, we then seek the member of this family for which the divergence from the true posterior distribution is minimized. To achieve this, the following optimization with respect to each of the $q_i(\mathbf{Z}_i)$ factors is to be performed in turn (Bishop, 2006):

$$\ln q_j^*(\mathbf{Z}_j) = E_{i \neq j}\big[\ln p(\mathbf{X}, \mathbf{Z})\big] + const \quad (9)$$

where $\mathbf{X} = \{\mathbf{x}_1, \ldots, \mathbf{x}_N\}$ denotes all observed variables and $E_{i \neq j}$ means an expectation with respect to the q distributions over all groups $\mathbf{Z}_i$ for $i \neq j$.

Now, we apply the *mean field* theory to the user model. Before doing so, we need to introduce the prior over the parameter $\boldsymbol{\phi}$ which is a product of *Dirichlet* distributions[4].

$$\begin{aligned} p(\boldsymbol{\phi}) &= \prod_{\mathbf{k}} Dir(\boldsymbol{\phi}_{\mathbf{k}} | \boldsymbol{\alpha}_{\mathbf{k}}^0) \\ &= \prod_{\mathbf{k}} C(\boldsymbol{\alpha}_{\mathbf{k}}^0) \prod_{l} \phi_{\mathbf{k},l}^{\alpha_{\mathbf{k}}^0 - 1} \end{aligned} \quad (10)$$

where $\mathbf{k}$ represents the joint configuration of all of the parents and $C(\boldsymbol{\alpha}_{\mathbf{k}}^0)$ is the normalization constant for the *Dirichlet* distribution. Note that for symmetry we have chosen the same parameter $\alpha_{\mathbf{k}}^0$ for each of the components.

Next we approximate the posterior distribution, $q(\mathbf{H}, \mathbf{U}, \boldsymbol{\phi})$ using a factorized form, $q(\mathbf{H}, \mathbf{U})q(\boldsymbol{\phi})$. Then we first apply Equation 9 to find an expression for the optimal factor $q^*(\boldsymbol{\phi})$:

$$\begin{aligned} \ln q^*(\boldsymbol{\phi}) &= E_{\mathbf{H},\mathbf{U}}\big[\ln p(\mathbf{g}, \mathbf{S}, \mathbf{H}, \mathbf{U}, \mathbf{O}, \boldsymbol{\Theta})\big] + const \\ &= E_{\mathbf{H},\mathbf{U}}\Big[\sum_t \ln p(\mathbf{u}_t | \mathbf{g}, \mathbf{s}_t, \mathbf{h}_{t-1}, \boldsymbol{\phi})\Big] \\ &\quad + \ln p(\boldsymbol{\phi}) + const \\ &= \sum_t \sum_{i,j,k,l} \Big(E_{\mathbf{H},\mathbf{U}}\big[\boldsymbol{\delta}_{i,j,k,l}\big] \ln \phi_{i,j,k,l} \Big) \\ &\quad + \sum_{i,j,k,l} (\alpha_{i,j,k,l}^o - 1) \ln \phi_{i,j,k,l} + const \\ &= \sum_{i,j,k,l} \Big(\Big(E_{\mathbf{H},\mathbf{U}}[n_{i,j,k,l}] + (\alpha_{i,j,k,l}^o - 1) \Big) \\ &\quad \cdot \ln \phi_{i,j,k,l} \Big) + const \end{aligned} \quad (11)$$

[4]Note that priors over parameters for deterministic distributions (e.i., $\boldsymbol{\pi}$, $\boldsymbol{\eta}$,and $\boldsymbol{\zeta}$) are not necessary.

where $\boldsymbol{\delta}_{i,j,k,l}$ denotes $\delta(\mathbf{g},i)\delta(\mathbf{s}_t,j)\delta(\mathbf{h}_{t-1},k)$ $\delta(\mathbf{u}_t,l)$ and $n_{i,j,k,l}$ is the number of times where $\mathbf{g}=i,\mathbf{s}_t=j,\mathbf{h}_{t-1}=k$, and $\mathbf{u}_t=l$. This leads to a product of *Dirichlet* distributions by taking the exponential of both sides of the equation:

$$q^*(\boldsymbol{\phi})=\prod_{i,j,k} Dir(\boldsymbol{\phi}_{i,j,k}|\boldsymbol{\alpha}_{i,j,k}),$$
$$\alpha_{i,j,k,l}=\alpha^0_{i,j,k,l}+E_{\mathbf{H},\mathbf{U}}[n_{i,j,k,l}] \quad (12)$$

To evaluate the quantity $E_{\mathbf{H},\mathbf{U}}[n_{i,j,k,l}]$, Equation 9 needs to be applied once again to obtain an optimal approximation of the posterior distribution $q^*(\mathbf{H},\mathbf{U})$.

$$\begin{aligned}\ln q^*(\mathbf{H},\mathbf{U}) &= E_{\boldsymbol{\phi}}\big[\ln p(\mathbf{g},\mathbf{S},\mathbf{H},\mathbf{U},\mathbf{O},\boldsymbol{\Theta})\big]+const\\ &= E_{\boldsymbol{\phi}}\Big[\sum_t \ln p(\mathbf{u}_t|\mathbf{g},\mathbf{s}_t,\mathbf{h}_{t-1},\boldsymbol{\phi})\\ &\quad+\ln p(\mathbf{h}_t|\mathbf{h}_{t-1},\mathbf{u}_t)\\ &\quad+\ln p(\mathbf{o}_t|\mathbf{u}_t)\Big]+const\\ &= \sum_t\Big(E_{\boldsymbol{\phi}}\big[\ln p(\mathbf{u}_t|\mathbf{g},\mathbf{s}_t,\mathbf{h}_{t-1},\boldsymbol{\phi})\big]\\ &\quad+\ln p(\mathbf{h}_t|\mathbf{h}_{t-1},\mathbf{u}_t)\\ &\quad+\ln p(\mathbf{o}_t|\mathbf{u}_t)\Big)+const\end{aligned} \quad (13)$$

where $E_{\boldsymbol{\phi}}\big[\ln p(\mathbf{u}_t|\mathbf{g},\mathbf{s}_t,\mathbf{h}_{t-1},\boldsymbol{\phi})\big]$ can be obtained using Equation 12 and properties of the *Dirichlet* distribution:

$$\begin{aligned}&E_{\boldsymbol{\phi}}\big[\ln p(\mathbf{u}_t|\mathbf{g},\mathbf{s}_t,\mathbf{h}_{t-1},\boldsymbol{\phi})\big]\\ &\quad=\sum_{i,j,k,l}\boldsymbol{\delta}_{i,j,k,l}E_{\boldsymbol{\phi}}\big[\ln\phi_{i,j,k,l}\big]\\ &\quad=\sum_{i,j,k,l}\boldsymbol{\delta}_{i,j,k,l}(\psi(\alpha_{i,j,k,l})-\psi(\hat{\boldsymbol{\alpha}}_{i,j,k}))\end{aligned} \quad (14)$$

where $\psi(\cdot)$ is the digamma function with $\hat{\boldsymbol{\alpha}}_{i,j,k}=\sum_l \alpha_{i,j,k,l}$. Because computing $E_{\mathbf{H},\mathbf{U}}[n_{i,j,k,l}]$ is equivalent to summing each of the marginal posterior probabilities $q^*(\mathbf{h}_{t-1},\mathbf{u}_t)$ with the same configuration of conditioning variables, this can be done efficiently by using the *junction tree* algorithm. Note that the expression on the right-hand side for both $q^*(\boldsymbol{\phi})$ and $q^*(\mathbf{H},\mathbf{U})$ depends on expectations computed with respect to the other factors. We will therefore seek a consistent solution by cycling through the factors and replacing each in turn with a revised estimate.

3.3 Error Model

The purpose of the error model is to alter the user action to reflect the prevalent speech recognition and understanding errors. The error generation process consists of three steps: the error model first generates an error template then fills it with erroneous values, and finally attaches a confidence score.

Given a user action, the error model maps it into a distorted form according to the probability distribution of the error template model $\boldsymbol{\Omega}$:

$$\mathcal{T}(u)\sim p(\mathcal{T}(u)|u)=\prod_{k,k'}\omega_{k,k'}^{\delta(u,k)\delta(\mathcal{T}(u),k')} \quad (15)$$

where $\mathcal{T}(\cdot)$ is a random function that maps a predicate of the user action to an error template, e.g. $\mathcal{T}$(*Inform(Time)*) $\rightarrow$ *Inform(Route:incorrect)*. To learn the parameters, the hidden variable $\mathbf{u}_t$ is sampled using Equation 4 for each observation $\mathbf{o}_t$ in the training data and the value part of each observation is replaced with a binary value representing its correctness with respect to the user goal. This results in a set of complete data on which the maximum likelihood estimates of $\boldsymbol{\Omega}$ are learned.

With the error template provided, next, the error model fills it with incorrect values if necessary following the distribution of the error value model $\boldsymbol{\Lambda}$ which is separately defined for each concept, otherwise it will keep the correct value:

$$\mathcal{C}(v)\sim p(\mathcal{C}(v)|v)=\prod_{k,k'}\lambda^{\delta(v,k)\delta(\mathcal{C}(v),k')} \quad (16)$$

where $\mathcal{C}(\cdot)$ is a random function which maps a correct value to a confusable value, e.g. $\mathcal{C}$(*Forbes*) $\rightarrow$ *Forward*. As with the error template model, the parameters of the error value model are also easily trained on the dataset of all pairs of a user goal value and the associated observed value. Because no error values can be observed for a given goal value, an unconditional probability distribution is also trained as a backoff.

Finally, the error model assigns a confidence score by sampling the confidence score model $\boldsymbol{\Gamma}$

which is separately defined for each concept:

$$s \sim p(s|c) = \prod_{k,k'} \gamma^{\delta(c,k)\delta(s,k')} \tag{17}$$

where s denotes the confidence score and c represents the correctness of the value of the user action which is previously determined by the error template model. Since two decimal places are used to describe the confidence score, the confidence score model is represented with a discrete distribution. This lends itself to trivial parameter learning similar to other models by computing maximum likelihood estimates on the set of observed confidence scores conditioned on the correctness of the relevant values.

In sum, for example, having a user action *[Inform(Source:Forbes), Inform(Time:6 PM)]* go through the sequence of aforementioned models possibly leads to *[Inform(Source:Forward), Inform(Route:6C)]*.

3.4 Termination Model

Few studies have been conducted to estimate the probability that a dialog will terminate at a certain turn in the user simulation. Most existing work attempts to treat a termination initiated by a user as one of the dialog actions in their user models. These models usually have a limited dialog history that they can use to determine the next user action. This *Markov* assumption is well-suited to ordinary dialog actions, each generally showing a correspondence with previous dialog actions. It is not difficult, however, to see that more global contexts (e.g., cumulative number of incorrect confirmations) will help lead a user to terminate a failed dialog. In addition, the termination action occurs only once at the end of a dialog unlike the other actions. Thus, we do not need to put the termination action into the user model. In order to easily incorporate many global features involving an entire dialog (Table 1) into the termination model, the *logistic regression* model is adapted. At every turn, before getting into the user model, we randomly determine whether a dialog will stop according to the posterior probability of the termination model given the current dialog context.

Feature	Description
NT	Number of turns
RIC	Ratio of incorrect confirmations
RICW	Ratio of incorrect confirmations within a window
RNONU	Ratio of non-understanding
RNONUW	Ratio of non-understanding within a window
ACS	Averaged confidence score
ACSW	Averaged confidence score within a window
RCOP	Ratio of cooperative turns
RCOPW	Ratio of cooperative turns within a window
RRT_C	Ratio of relevant system turns for each concept
RRTW_C	Ratio of relevant system turns for each concept within a window
NV_C	Number of values appeared for each concept

Table 1: A description of features used for a logistic regression model to capture the termination probability. The window size was set to 5 for this study.

4 Experimental Setup

4.1 Data

To verify the proposed method, three months of data from the Let's Go domain were split into two months of training data and one month of test data. Also, to take the error level into consideration, we classified the data into four groups according to the averaged confidence score and used each group of data to build a different error model for each error level. For comparison purposes, simulated data was generated for both training and test data by feeding the same context of each piece of data to the proposed method. Due to the characteristics of the bus schedule information domain, there are a number of cases where no bus schedule is available, such as requests for uncovered routes and places. Such cases were excluded for clearer interpretation of the result, giving us the data sets described in Table 2.

4.2 Measures

To date, a variety of evaluation methods have been proposed in the literature (Cuayahuitl et al., 2005; Jung et al., 2009; Georgila et al., 2006; Pietquin and

	Training data	Test data
Number of dialogs	1,275	669
Number of turns	9,645	5,103

Table 2: A description of experimental data sets.

Hastie, 2011; Schatzmann et al., 2005; Williams, 2007a). Nevertheless, it remains difficult to find a suitable set of evaluation measures to assess the quality of the user simulation. We have chosen to adopt a set of the most commonly used measures. Firstly, expected precision (EP), expected recall (ER) and F-Score offer a reliable method for comparing real and simulated data even though it is not possible to specify the levels that need to be satisfied to conclude that the simulation is realistic. These are computed by comparison of the simulated and real user action for each turn in the corpus:

$$EP = 100 * \frac{\textit{Number of identical actions}}{\textit{Number of simulated actions}} \quad (18)$$

$$ER = 100 * \frac{\textit{Number of identical actions}}{\textit{Number of real actions}} \quad (19)$$

$$\textit{F-Score} = 100 * \frac{2 * EP * ER}{EP + ER} \quad (20)$$

Next, several descriptive statistics are employed to show the closeness of the real and simulated data in a statistical sense. The distribution of different user action types, turn length and confidence score can show constitutional similarity. It is still possible, however, to be greatly different in their interdependence and cause quite different behavior at the dialog level even though there is a constitutional similarity. Therefore, the dialog-level statistics such as dialog completion rate and averaged dialog length were also computed by running the user simulator with the Let's Go dialog system.

5 Results

As mentioned in Section 4.2, expected precision and recall were measured. Whereas previous studies only reported the scores computed in the predicate level, i.e. speech act and concept, we also measured the scores based on the output of the error template model which is the predicate-level action with an indicator of the correctness of the associated value (Figure 1). The result (Table 3) shows a moderate

Error Mark	Training data		Test data	
	w/o	w/	w/o	w/
EP	58.13	45.12	54.44	41.86
ER	58.40	45.33	54.61	41.99
F-Score	58.27	45.22	54.52	41.93

Table 3: Expected precision, expected recall and F-Score

balance between agreement and variation which is a very desirable characteristic of a user simulator since a simulated user is expected not only to resemble real data but also to cover diverse unseen behavior to a reasonable extent. As a natural consequence of the increased degree of freedom, the scores considering error marking are consistently lower. In addition, the results of test data are slightly lower than those of training data, as expected, yet a suitable balance remains.

Next, the comparative distributions of different actions between real and simulated data are presented for both training and test data (Figure 3). The results are also based on the output of the error template model to further show how errors are distributed over different actions. The distributions of simulated data either from training or test data show a close match to the corresponding real distributions. Interestingly, even though the error ratio of the test data is noticeably different from that of the training data, the proposed method is still able to generate similar results. This means the variables and their conditional probabilities of the proposed method were designed and estimated properly enough to capture the tendency of user behavior with respect to various dialog contexts. Moreover, the comparison of the turn length distribution (Figure 4) indicates that the simulated data successfully replicated the real data for both training and test data. The results of confidence score simulation are presented in Figure 5[5]. For both training and test data, the simulated confidence score displays forms that are very similar to the real ones.

Finally, to confirm the resemblance on the dialog level, the comparative results of dialog completion rate and averaged dialog length are summarized in Table 4. As shown in the dialog completion result, the simulated user is a little harder than the real user

[5]Due to the space limitation, the detailed illustrations for each action type are put in Appendix A.

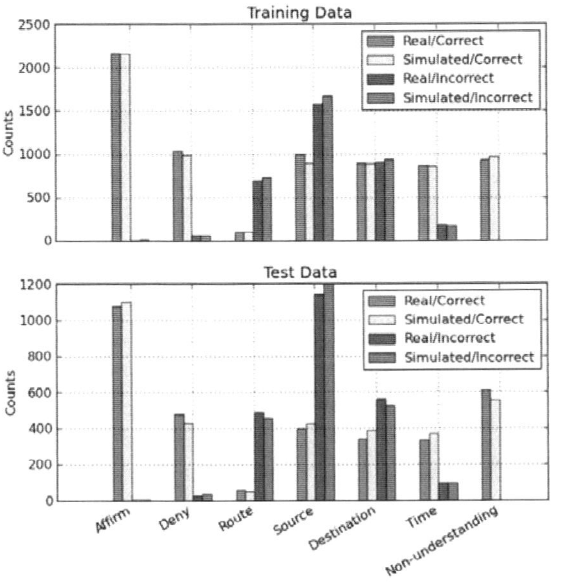

Figure 3: A comparison of the distribution of different actions between real and simulated data for both training and test data

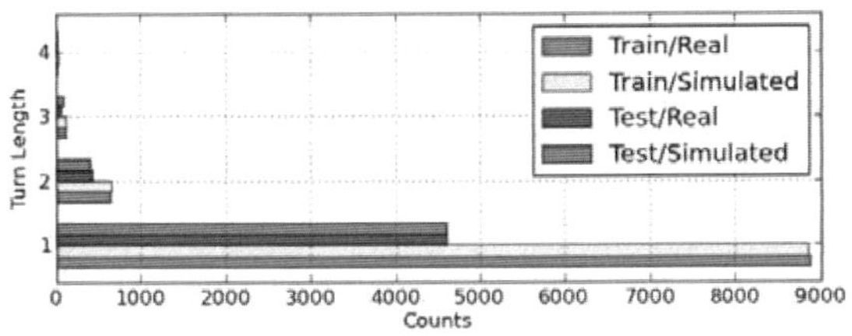

Figure 4: A comparison of the distribution of turn length between real and simulated data for both training and test data

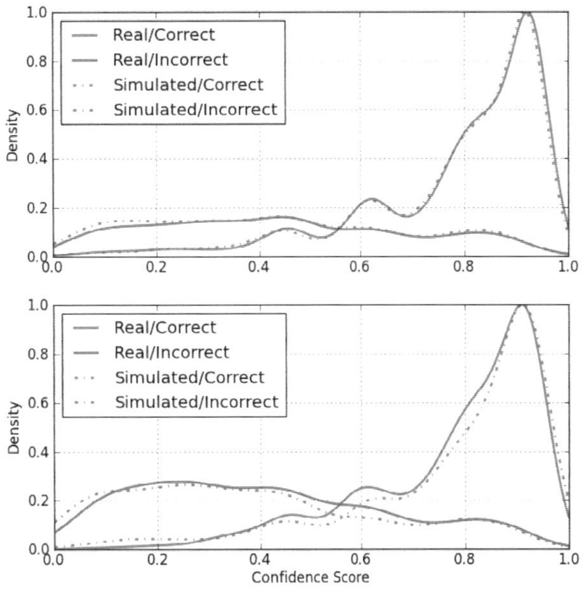

Figure 5: A comparison of the distribution of confidence score between real and simulated data for both training and test data

	Real		**Simulated**	
DCR (%)	59.68		55.04	
ADL	mean	std.	mean	std.
Success	10.62	4.59	11.08	5.10
Fail	7.75	6.20	7.75	8.64
Total	9.46	5.48	9.50	7.12

Table 4: A comparison of dialog completion rate (DCR) and averaged dialog length (ADL) which is presented according to the dialog result.

to accomplish the purpose. Also, the variation of the simulated data as far as turn length is concerned was greater than that of the real data, although the averaged lengths were similar to each other. This might indicate the need to improve the termination model. The proposed method for the termination model is confined to incorporating only semantic-level features but a variety of different features would, of course, cause the end of a dialog, e.g. system delay, acoustic features, spatial and temporal context, weather and user groups.

6 Conclusion

In this paper, we presented a novel unsupervised approach for user simulation which is especially desirable for real deployed systems. The proposed method can cover the whole pipeline of user simulation on the semantic level without human intervention. Also the quality of simulated data has been demonstrated to be similar to the real data over a number of commonly employed metrics. Although the proposed method does not deal with simulating N-best ASR results, the extension to support N-best results will be one of our future efforts, as soon as the Let's Go system uses N-best results. Our future work also includes evaluation on improving and evaluating dialog strategies. Furthermore, it would be scientifically more interesting to compare the proposed method with a supervised approach using a corpus with semantic transcriptions. On the other hand, as an interesting application, the proposed user model could be exploited as a part of belief tracking in a spoken dialog system since it also considers a user action to be hidden.

Acknowledgments

We would like to thank Alan Black for helpful comments and discussion. This work was supported by the second Brain Korea 21 project.

References

C. Bishop, 2006. *Pattern Recognition and Machine Learning*. Springer.

G. Chung, 2004. Developing a Flexible Spoken Dialog System Using Simulation. *In Proceedings of ACL.*

H. Cuayahuitl, S. Renals, O. Lemon, H. Shimodaira, 2005. Humancomputer dialogue simulation using hidden Markov models. *In Proceedings of ASRU.*

W. Eckert, E. Levin, R. Pieraccini, 1997. User modeling for spoken dialogue system evaluation. *In Proceedings of ASRU.*

K. Georgila, J. Henderson, O. Lemon, 2006. User simulation for spoken dialogue systems: Learning and evaluation. *In Proceedings of Interspeech.*

J. Henderson, O. Lemon, K. Georgila, 2008. Hybrid Reinforcement / Supervised Learning of Dialogue Policies from Fixed Datasets. *Computational Linguistics*, 34(4):487-511

S. Jung, C. Lee, K. Kim, M. Jeong, G. Lee, 2009. Data-driven user simulation for automated evaluation of spoken dialog systems. *Computer Speech and Language*, 23(4):479–509.

S. Lauritzen and D. J. Spiegelhalter, 1988. Local Computation and Probabilities on Graphical Structures and their Applications to Expert Systems. *Journal of Royal Statistical Society*, 50(2):157–224.

E. Levin, R. Pieraccini, W. Eckert, 2000. A stochastic model of humanmachine interaction for learning dialogstrategies. *IEEE Transactions on Speech and Audio Processing*, 8(1):11-23.

R. Lopez-Cozar, Z. Callejas, and M. McTear, 2006. Testing the performance of spoken dialogue systems by means of an articially simulated user. *Articial Intelligence Review*, 26(4):291-323.

G. Parisi, 1988. *Statistical Field Theory*. Addison-Wesley.

O. Pietquin, 2004. A Framework for Unsupervised Learning of Dialogue Strategies. *Ph.D. thesis, Faculty of Engineering.*

O. Pietquin and H. Hastie, 2011. A survey on metrics for the evaluation of user simulations. *The Knowledge Engineering Review.*

A. Raux, B. Langner, D. Bohus, A. W Black, and M. Eskenazi, 2005. Let's Go Public! Taking a Spoken Dialog System to the Real World. *In Proceedings of Interspeech.*

J. Schatzmann, K. Georgila, S. Young, 2005. Quantitative evaluation of user simulation techniques for spoken dialogue systems. *In Proceedings of SIGdial.*

J. Schatzmann, B. Thomson, K. Weilhammer, H. Ye, S. Young, 2007. Agenda-based user simulation for bootstrapping a POMDP dialogue system. *In Proceedings of HLT/NAACL.*

J. Schatzmann, B. Thomson, S. Young, 2007. Error simulation for training statistical dialogue systems. *In Proceedings of ASRU.*

U. Syed and J. Williams, 2008. Using automatically transcribed dialogs to learn user models in a spoken dialog system. *In Proceedings of ACL.*

B. Thomson and S. Young, 2010. Bayesian update of dialogue state: A POMDP framework for spoken dialogue systems. *Computer Speech & Language*, 24(4):562-588.

J. Williams, P. Poupart, and S. Young, 2005. Factored Partially Observable Markov Decision Processes for Dialogue Management. *In Proceedings of Knowledge and Reasoning in Practical Dialogue Systems.*

J. Williams, 2007. A Method for Evaluating and Comparing User Simulations: The Cramer-von Mises Divergence. *In Proceedings of ASRU.*

J. Williams and S. Young, 2007. Partially observable Markov decision processes for spoken dialog systems. *Computer Speech & Language*, 21(2):393-422.

Appendices

Appendix A. Distribution of confidence score for each concept

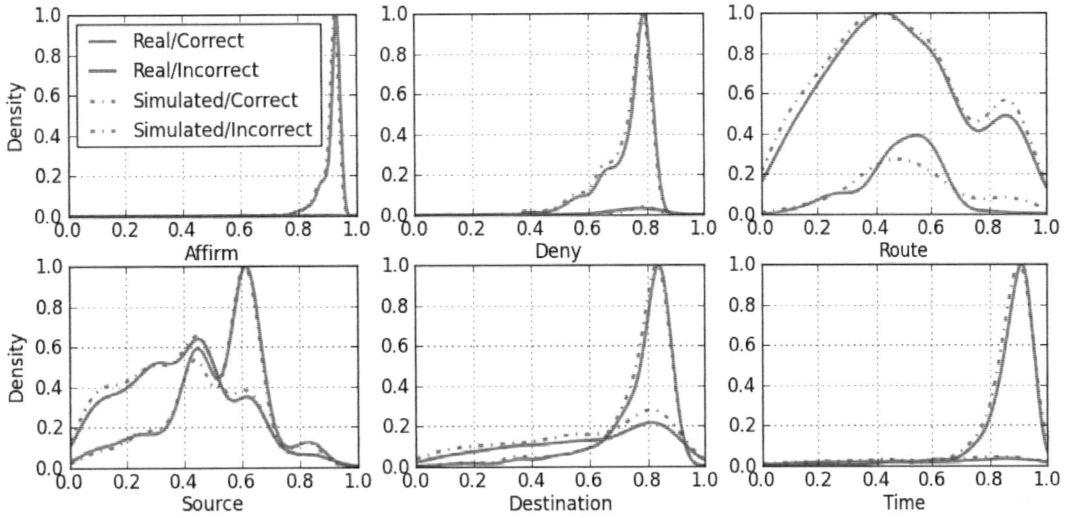

Figure 6: A comparison of the distribution of confidence score between real and simulated data for the training data

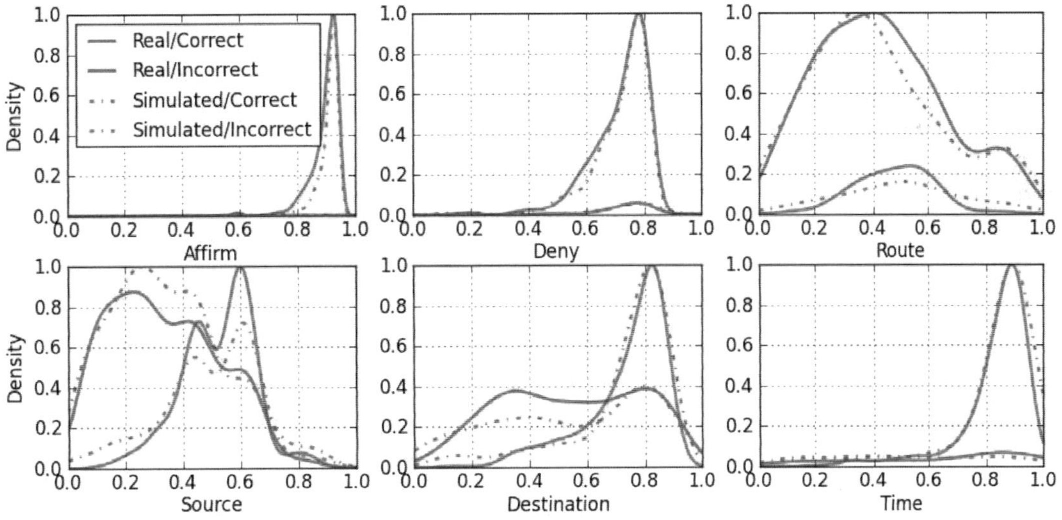

Figure 7: A comparison of the distribution of confidence score between real and simulated data for the test data

Hierarchical Conversation Structure Prediction in Multi-Party Chat

Elijah Mayfield, David Adamson, and Carolyn Penstein Rosé
Language Technologies Institute
Carnegie Mellon University
5000 Forbes Avenue, Pittsburgh, PA 15213
{emayfiel, dadamson, cprose}@cs.cmu.edu

Abstract

Conversational practices do not occur at a single unit of analysis. To understand the interplay between social positioning, information sharing, and rhetorical strategy in language, various granularities are necessary. In this work we present a machine learning model for multi-party chat which predicts conversation structure across differing units of analysis. First, we mark sentence-level behavior using an information sharing annotation scheme. By taking advantage of Integer Linear Programming and a sociolinguistic framework, we enforce structural relationships between sentence-level annotations and sequences of interaction. Then, we show that clustering these sequences can effectively disentangle the threads of conversation. This model is highly accurate, performing near human accuracy, and performs analysis on-line, opening the door to real-time analysis of the discourse of conversation.

1 Introduction

When defining a unit of analysis for studying language, one size does not fit all. Part-of-speech tagging is performed on individual words in sequences, while parse trees represent language at the sentence level. Individual tasks can be performed at the lexical, sentence, or document level, or even to arbitrary length spans of text (Wiebe et al., 2005), while rhetorical patterns are annotated in a tree-like structure across sentences or paragraphs.

In dialogue, the most common unit of analysis is the utterance, usually through dialogue acts. Here, too, the issue of granularity and specificity of tags has been a persistent issue, along with the integration of larger discourse structure. Both theory-driven and empirical work has argued for a collapsing of annotations into fewer categories, based on either marking the dominant function of a given turn (Popescu-Belis, 2008) or identifying a single construct of interest and annotating only as necessary to distinguish that construct. We take the latter approach in this work, predicting conversation structure particularly as it relates to information sharing and authority in dialogue. We use systemic functional linguistics' Negotiation annotation scheme (Mayfield and Rosé, 2011) to identify utterances as either giving or receiving information. This annotation scheme is of particular interest because in addition to sentence-level annotation, well-defined sequences of interaction are incorporated into the annotation process. This sequential structure has been shown to be useful in secondary analysis of annotated data (Mayfield et al., 2012a), as well as providing structure which improves the accuracy of automated annotations.

This research introduces a model to predict information sharing tags and Negotiation sequence structure jointly with thread disentanglement. We show that performance can be improved using integer linear programming to enforce constraints on sequence structure. Structuring and annotation of conversation is available quickly and with comparatively little effort compared to manual annotation. Moreover, all of our results in this paper were obtained using data a real-world, chat-based internet community, with a mix of long-time expert and first-time novice users, showing that the model is robust to the challenges of messy data in natural environments.

The remainder of this paper is structured as follows. First, we review relevant work in annotation at the levels of utterance, sequence, and thread, and applications of each. We then introduce the domain of our data and the framework we use for annotation of conversation structure. In Section 4 we define a supervised, on-line machine learning model which performs this annotation and structuring across granularities. In Section 5, we evaluate this model and show that it approaches or matches human reliability on all tasks. We conclude with discussion of the utility of this conversation structuring algorithm for new analyses of conversation.

2 Related Work

Research on multi-party conversation structure is widely varied, due to the multifunctional nature of language. These structures have been used in diverse fields such as computer-supported collaborative work (O'Neill and Martin, 2003), dialogue systems (Bohus and Horvitz, 2011), and research on meetings (Renals et al., 2012). Much work in annotation has been inspired by speech act theory and dialogue acts (Traum, 1994; Shriberg et al., 2004), which operate primarily on the granularity of individual utterances. A challenge of tagging is the issue of specificity of tags, as previous work has shown that most utterances have multiple functions (Bunt, 2011). General tagsets have attempted to capture multi-functionality through independent dimensions which produce potentially millions of possible annotations, though in practice the number of variations remains in the hundreds (Jurafsky et al., 1998). Situated work has jointly modelled speech act and domain-specific topics (Laws et al., 2012).

Additional structure inspired by linguistics, such as adjacency pairs (Schegloff, 2007) or dialogue games (Carlson, 1983), has been used to build discourse relations between turns. This additional structure has been shown to improve performance of automated analysis (Poesio and Mikheev, 1998). Identification of this fine-grained structure of an interaction has been studied in prior work, with applications in agreement detection (Galley et al., 2004), addressee detection (op den Akker and Traum, 2009), and real-world applications, such as customer service conversations (Kim et al., 2010). Higher-order structure has also been explored in dialogue, from complex graph-like relations (Wolf and Gibson, 2005) to simpler segmentation-based approaches (Malioutov and Barzilay, 2006). Utterance level-tagging can take into account nearby structure, e.g. forward-looking and backward-looking functions in DAMSL (Core and Allen, 1997), while dialogue management systems in intelligent agents often have a plan unfolding over a whole dialogue (Ferguson and Allen, 1998).

In recent years, threading and maintaining of multiple "floors" has grown in popularity (Elsner and Charniak, 2010), especially in text-based media. This level of analysis is designed with the goal of separating out sub-conversations which are independently coherent. There is a common ground emerging in the thread detection literature on best practices for automated prediction. Early work viewed the problem as a time series analysis task (Bingham et al., 2003). Treating thread detection as a clustering problem, with lines representing instances, was given great attention in Shen et al. (2006). Subsequent researchers have treated the thread detection task as based in *discourse coherence*, and have pursued topic modelling (Adams, 2008) or entity reference grids (Elsner and Charniak, 2011) to define that concept of coherence.

Other work integrates local discourse structure with the topic-based threads of discourse. Ai et al. (2007) utilizes information state, a dialogue management component which loosely parallels thread structure, to improve dialogue act tagging. In the context of Twitter conversations, Ritter et al. (2010) suggests using dialogue act tags as a middle layer towards conversation reconstruction. Low-level structure between utterances has also been used as a foundation for modelling larger-level sociological phenomena between speakers in a dialogue, for instance, identifying leadership (Strzalkowski et al., 2011) and rapport between providers and patients in support groups (Ogura et al., 2008). These works have all pointed to the utility of incorporating sentence-level annotations, low-level interaction structure, and overarching themes into a unified system. To our knowledge, however, this work is the first to present a single system for simultaneous an-

Negotiation/Threads				Seq	User	Text
K2				1	C	[M], fast question, did your son have a biopsy?
K2				1	C	or does that happen when he comes home
	K1			2	V	i have 3 dogs.
	K1			2	V	man's best friend
	f			2	S	:-D
	o			2	C	and women
	K2			3	J	what kind of dogs????
		K1		4	C	[D], I keep seeing that you are typing and then it stops
		K2		5	C	how are you doing this week
	K1			3	V	the puppies are a maltese/yorkie mix and the full grown is a pomaranian/yorkie.
K1				1	M	No, he did not have a biopsy.
K1				1	M	The surgeon examined him and said that by feel, he did not think the lump was cancerous, and he should just wait until he got home.
f				1	C	that has to be very hard
			o	7	M	A question, however– [J], you would probably know.
			K2	7	M	He was told that they could not just do a needle biopsy, that he would have to remove the whole lump in order to tell if it was malignant.
		o		8	D	Yes.
		K1		8	D	I was waiting for [M] to answer.
			K1	7	J	That sounds odd to me

Table 1: An example excerpt with Negotiation labels, sequences, and threads structure (columns) annotated.

notation and structuring at all three levels.

3 Data and Annotation

Our data comes from the Cancer Support Community, which provides chatrooms, forums, and other resources for support groups for cancer patients. Each conversation took place in the context of a weekly meeting, with several patient participants as well as a professional therapist facilitating the discussion. In total, our annotated corpus consists of 45 conversations. This data was sampled from three group sizes - 15 conversations from small groups (2 patients, in addition to the trained facilitator), 15 from medium-sized groups (3-4 patients), and 15 from large groups (5 or more patients).

3.1 Annotation

Our data is annotated at the three levels of granularity described previously in this paper: *sentences*, *sequences*, and *threads*. In this section we define those annotations in greater detail. Sentence-level and sequence-level annotations were performed using the Negotiation framework from systemic functional linguistics (Martin and Rose, 2003). Once sequences were identified, those sequences were grouped together into threads based on shared topic.

We annotate our data using an adaptation of the Negotiation framework. This framework has been proven reliable and reproducible in previous work (Mayfield and Rosé, 2011). By assigning aggregate scores over a conversation, the framework also gives us a notion of *Authoritativeness*. This metric, defined later in Section 5, allows us to test whether automated codes faithfully reproduce human judgments of information sharing behavior at a per-user level. This metric has proven to be a statistically significant indicator of outcome variables in direction giving (Mayfield et al., 2011) and collaborative learning domains (Howley et al., 2011).

In particular, Negotiation labels define whether each speaker is a *source* or *recipient* of information. Our annotation scheme has four turn-level codes and a rigidly defined information sharing structure, rooted in sociolinguistic observation. We describe each in detail below.

Sentences containing new information are marked as **K1**, as the speaker is the "primary knower," the source of information. These sentences can be general facts and world knowledge, but can also contain opinions, retelling of narrative, or other contextualized information, so long as the writer acts as the source of that information. Sentences requesting information, on the other hand, are marked **K2**, or "secondary knower," when the writer is signalling that they want information from other participants in the chat. This can be direct question asking, but can also include requests for elaboration or indirect illocutionary acts (e.g. *"I'd like to hear more."*). In addition to these primary moves, we also use a social feedback code, **f**, for sentences consisting of affective feedback or sentiment, but which do not contain new information. These moves can include emoticons, fixed expressions such as "good luck," or purely social banter. All other moves, such as typo correction or floor grabbing, are labelled **o**.

This annotation scheme is highly flexible and adaptive to new domains, and is not specific to medical topics or chatroom-based media. It also gives us a well-defined structure of an interaction: each sequence consists of exactly one primary knower (**K1**) move, which can consist of any number of primary knower sentences from a single speaker. If a **K2** move occurs in the sequence, it occurs before any **K1** moves. Feedback moves (**f**) may come at any time so long as the speaker is responding to another speaker in the same sequence. Sentences labeled **o** are idiosyncratic and may appear anywhere in a sequence. In section 4.3, we represent these constraints formally.

In addition to grouping sentences together into sequences structurally, we also group those sequences into threads. These threads are based on annotator judgement, but generally map to the idea that a single thread should be on a single theme, e.g. "handling visiting relatives at holidays." These threads are both intrinsically interesting for identifying the topics of a conversation, as well as being a useful preprocessing step for any additional, topic-based annotation that may be desired for later analysis.

We iteratively developed a coding manual for these layers of annotation; to test reliability at each iteration of instructions, two annotators each independently annotated one full conversation. Inter-annotator reliability is high for sentence-level annotation ($\kappa = 0.75$). Following Elsner and Charniak (2010), we use micro-averaged f-score to evaluate inter-rater agreement on higher-level structure. We find that inter-annotator agreement is high for both sequence-level structure ($f = 0.82$) and thread-level structure ($f = 0.80$). A detailed description of the annotation process is available in Mayfield et al. (2012b). After establishing reliability, our entire corpus was annotated by one human coder.

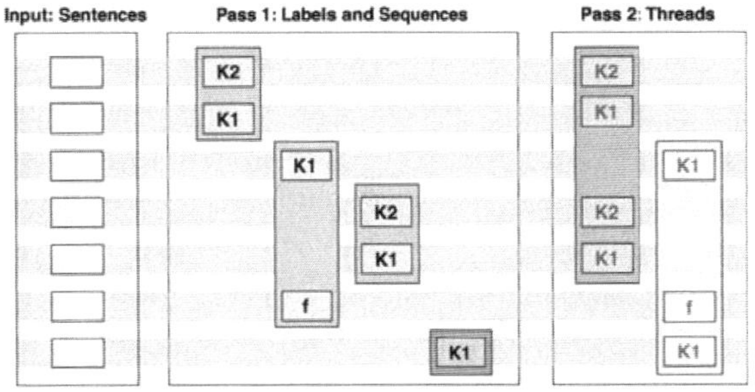

Figure 1: Structured output at each phase of the two-pass machine learning model. In pass one, utterances are grouped into sequences with organizational structure; the second pass groups sequences based on shared themes.

4 Conversation Structure Prediction

In previous work, the Negotiation framework has been automatically coded with high accuracy (Mayfield and Rosé, 2011). However, that work restricted the domain to a task-based, two-person dialogue, and structure was viewed as a segmentation, rather than threading, formulation. At each turn, a sequence could continue or a new sequence could begin.

Here, we extend this automated coding to larger groups speaking in unstructured, social chat, and we extend the structured element of this coding scheme to structure by sequence and thread. To our knowledge, this is also the first attempt to utilize functional sequences of interaction as a preprocessing step for thread disentanglement in chat. We now present a comprehensive machine learning model which annotates a conversation by utterance, groups utterances topics by local structure into sequences, and assigns sequences to threads.

4.1 On-Line Instance Creation

This is a two-pass algorithm. The first pass labels sentences and detects sequences, and the second pass groups these sequences into threads. We follow Shen et al. (2006) in treating the sequence detection problem as a single-pass clustering algorithm. Their model is equivalent to the **Previous Cluster** model described below, albeit with more complex features. In that work a threshold was defined in order for a new message to be added to an existing cluster. If that threshold is not passed, a new cluster is formed. Modelling the probability that a new cluster should be formed is similar to a context-sensitive threshold, and because we do not impose a hard threshold, we can pass the set of probabilities for cluster assignments to a structured prediction system.

4.2 Model Definitions

At its core, our model relies on three probabilistic classifiers. One of these models is a classification model, and the other two treat sequence and thread structure as clusters. All models use the LightSIDE (Mayfield and Rosé, 2010) with the LibLinear algorithm (Fan et al., 2008) for machine learning..

Negotiation Classifier (Neg)

The Negotiation model takes a single sentence as input. The output of this model is a distribution over the four possible sentence-level labels described in section 3.1. The set of features for this model consists of unigrams, bigrams, and part-of-speech bigrams. Part-of-speech tagging was performed using the Stanford tagger (Toutanova et al., 2003) within LightSIDE.

Cluster Classifiers (PC, NC)

We use two models of cluster assignment probability. The Previous Cluster (PC) classifier takes as input a previous set of sentences $C = \{c_1, c_2, \ldots, c_n\}$ and set of new sentences $N = \{N_1, N_2, \ldots, N_m\}$. To evaluate whether c^* should be added to this cluster, we train a binary probabilistic classifier that predicts the probability that the sentences in N belong to the same cluster as the sentences already in C. In the first pass, each input N to the PC classifier is a set containing a single sentence, and each C is the set of sentences in a previously-identified sequence. In the second pass, each N is a sequence as predicted by the first pass.

The PC model uses two features. The first is a time-based feature, measuring the amount of time that has elapsed between the last sentence in C and the first sentence in N. The time feature is represented differently between sequence prediction and thread prediction. Elsner and Charniak (2010) recommends using bucketed nominal values based on the log time, to group together very recent and very distant posts. We follow this for sequence prediction. Due to the more complex structure of the sequence grouping task in the second pass, we use a raw numeric time feature. The second feature is a coherence metric, the cosine similarity between the centroid of C and the centroid of N. We define the centroid based on TF-IDF weighted unigram vectors.

We impose a threshold after which previous clusters are no longer considered as options for the PC classifier. Because sequences are shorter than threads, we set these thresholds separately, at 90 seconds for sequences and 120 seconds for threads. Approximately 1% of correct assignments are impossible due to these thresholds.

The New Cluster (NC) classifier takes as input a set of sentences $n = \{n_1, n_2, \ldots, n_m\}$, and predicts the probability that a given sentence is initiating a new sequence (or, in the second pass, whether a given sequence is initiating a new thread). This model contains only unigram features.

At each sentence s we consider the set of possible previous cluster assignments $C = \{c_1, c_2, \ldots, c_n\}$, and define $p_{sc}(s, c)$ to be the probability that s will be assigned to cluster c. We define $p_{nc}(s) = \lambda_s NC(s)$. The addition of a weight parameter to the output of the NC classifier allows us to tune the likelihood of transitioning to a new cluster. This prediction structure is illustrated in Figure 2. In the first pass, these cluster probabilities are used in conjunction with the output of the Negotiation classifier to form a structured output; in the second pass, the maximum cluster probability is chosen.

4.3 Constraining Sequence Structure with ILP

In past work the Negotiation framework has benefited from enforced constraints of linguistically supported rules on sequence structure (Mayfield and

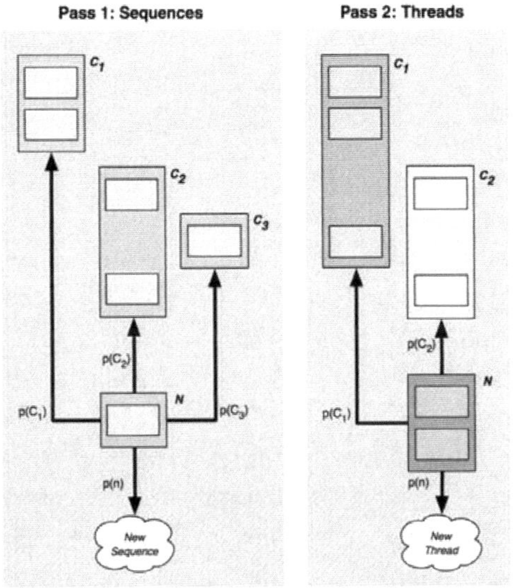

Figure 2: The output of the cluster classifier in either pass is a set of probabilities corresponding to possible cluster assignments, including that of creating a new cluster. In the second pass, the input is a set of sentences (a sequence) rather than a single sentence, and output assignments are to threads rather than sequences.

Rosé, 2011). Constraints on the structure of annotations are easily defined using Integer Linear Programming. Recent work has used boolean logic (Chang et al., 2008) to allow intuitive rules about a domain to be enforced at classification time. ILP inference was performed using Learning-Based Java (Rizzolo and Roth, 2010).

First, we define the classification task. Optimization is performed given the set of probabilities $\mathcal{N}(s)$ as the distribution output of the Neg classifier given sentence s as input, and the set of probabilities $\mathcal{C}(s) = p_{nc}(s) \cup p_{sc}(s, c), \forall c \in C$. Instance classification requires maximizing the objective function:

$$\arg\max_{n \in \mathcal{N}(s), c \in \mathcal{C}(s)} \; n + c$$

We impose constraints on sequence prediction. If the most likely output from this function assigns a label that is incompatible with the assigned sequence, either the label is changed or a new sequence is assigned so that constraints are met. For each constraint, we give the intuition from section 3.1, followed by our formulation of that constraint. u_s is shorthand for the user who wrote sentence s; n_s is shorthand for a proposed Negotiation label of sentence s; while c_s is a proposed sequence assignment for s, c' is shorthand for assignment to a new sequence, and $S_c = \{(n_{c,1}, u_{c,1}), (n_{c,2}, u_{c,2}), \ldots, (n_{c,k}, u_{c,k})\}$ is the set of Negotiation labels n and users u associated with sentences $(s_{c,1} \ldots s_{c,k})$ already in sequence c.

1. **K2** moves, if any, occur before **K1** moves.

   $((c_s = c) \wedge (n_s = \mathbf{K2}))$
   $\rightarrow (\nexists i \in S_c \; s.t. \; n_{c,i} = \mathbf{K1})$

2. **f** moves may occur at any time but must be responding to a different speaker in the same sequence.

   $((c_s = c) \wedge (n_s = \mathbf{f}))$
   $\rightarrow (\exists i \in S_c \; s.t. \; u_{c,i} \neq u_s)$

3. Functionally, therefore, **f** moves may not initiate a sequence).

   $(c_s = c') \rightarrow (n_s \neq \mathbf{f})$

4. Speakers do not respond to their own requests for information (the speakers of **K2** and **K1** moves in the same sequence must be different).

   $((c_s = c) \wedge (n_s = \mathbf{K1}))$
   $\rightarrow (\forall i \in S_c, ((n_{c,i} = \mathbf{K2}) \rightarrow (u_{c,i} \neq u_s)))$

5. Each sequence consists of at most one continuous series of **K1** moves from the same speaker.

   $(c_s = c) \rightarrow ((\exists i \in S_c \; s.t. \; (n_{c,i} = \mathbf{K1}))$
   $\rightarrow ((u_{c,i} = u_s) \wedge (\forall j > i,$
   $(u_{c,j} = u_s) \wedge (n_{c,i} = \mathbf{K1})))$

Human annotators treated these rules as hard constraints, as the classifier does. In circumstances where these rules would be broken (for instance, due to barge-in or trailing off), a new sequence begins.

5 Evaluation

5.1 Methods

To evaluate the performance of this model, we wish to know how it replicates human annotation at each granularity. For Negotiation labels, agreement is measured by terms of absolute accuracy and kappa agreement above chance. We also include a measure of aggregate information sharing behavior per user. This score, which we term *Information Authoritativeness (Auth)*, is defined per user as the percentage of their contentful sentences (K1 or K2) which were giving information (K1). To measure performance on this measure, we measure the r^2 coefficient between user authoritativeness scores calculated from the predicted labels compared to actual labels. This is equivalent to measuring the variance explained by our model, where each data point represents a single user's predicted and actual authoritativeness scores over the course of a whole conversation ($n = 215$).

Sequence and thread agreement is evaluated by micro-averaged f-score (MAF), defined in prior work for a gold sequence i with size n_i, and a proposed sequence j with size n_j, based on precision and recall metrics:

$$P = \frac{n_{ij}}{n_j} \qquad R = \frac{n_{ij}}{n_i} \qquad F(i,j) = \frac{2 \times P \times R}{P+R}$$

MAF across an entire conversation is then a weighted sum of f-scores across all sequences[1]:

$$MAF = \sum_i \frac{n_i}{n} \max_j F(i,j)$$

We implemented multiple baselines to test whether our methods improve upon simpler approaches. For sequence and thread prediction, we implement the following baselines. **Speaker Shift** predicts a new thread every time a new writer adds a line to the chat. **Turn Windows** predicts a new sequence or thread after every n turns. **Pause Length** predicts a new sequence or thread every time that a gap of n seconds has occurred between lines of chat. For both of the previous two baselines, we vary the parameter n to optimize performance and provide a challenging baseline. None of these models use any features or constraints, and are based on heuristics. To compare to our model, we present both an **Unconstrained** model, which uses machine learning and does not impose sequence constraints from Section 4.3, as well as our full **Constrained** model.

Evaluation is performed using 15-fold cross-validation. In each fold, one small, one medium, and one large conversation are held out as a test set, and classifiers are trained on the remaining 42 conversations. Significance is evaluated using a paired student's t-test per conversation ($n = 45$).

Sentence-Level (Human $\kappa = 0.75$)			
Model	Accuracy	κ	Auth r^2
Unconstrained	.7736	.5870	**.7498**
Constrained	**.7777**	**.5961**	.7355
Sequence-Level (Human MAF = 0.82)			
Model	Precision	Recall	MAF
Speaker Shift	.7178	.5140	.5991
Turn Windows	.7207	.6233	.6685
Pause Length	.8479	.6582	.7411
Unconstrained	.7909	.7068	.7465
Constrained	**.8557**	**.7116**	**.7770**
Thread-Level (Human MAF = 0.80)			
Model	Precision	Recall	MAF
Turn Windows	.5994	**.7173**	**.6531**
Pause Length	.6145	.6316	.6229
Unconstrained	**.7132**	.5781	.6386
Constrained	.6805	.6024	.6391

Table 2: Tuned optimal annotation performances of baseline heuristics compared to our machine learning model.

5.2 Results

Results of experimentation show that all models are highly accurate in their respective tasks. With sentence-level annotation approaching 0.6 κ, the output of the model is reliable enough to allow automatically annotated data to be included reliably alongside human annotations. Performance for sequence-based modelling is even stronger, with no statistically significant difference in f-score between the machine learning model and human agreement.

Table 2 reports our best results after tuning to maximize performance of baseline models, our original machine learning model, and the model with ILP constraints enforced between Negotiation labels and sequence. In all three cases, we see machine performance approaching, but not matching, human agreement. Incorporating ILP constraints improves per-sentence Negotiation label classification by a small but significant amount ($p < .001$).

Clustering performance is highly robust, as demonstrated in Figure 3, which shows the effect of changing window sizes and pause lengths and values of λ_s for machine learned models. Our thread disentanglement performance matches our baselines, and

[1]This metric extends identically to a gold thread i and proposed thread j.

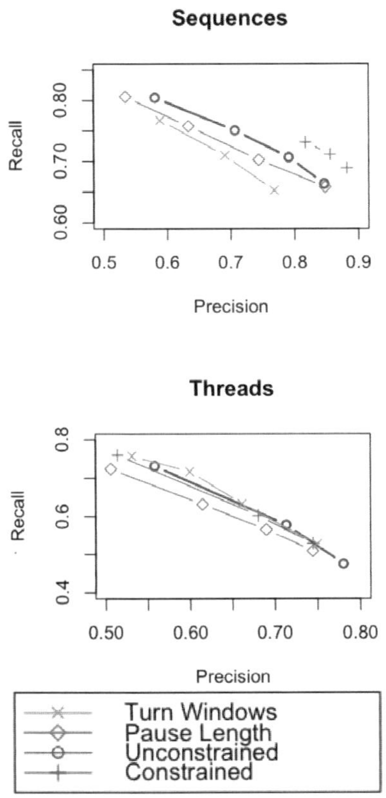

Figure 3: Parameter sensitivity on sequence-level (top) and thread-level (bottom) annotation models.

is in line with heuristic-based assignments from Elsner and Charniak (2010). In sequence clustering, we observe improvement across all metrics. The Constrained model achieves a higher f-score than all other models ($p < 0.0001$). We determine through a two-tailed confidence interval that sequence clustering performance is statistically indistinguishable from human annotation ($p < 0.05$).

Error analysis suggests that the constraints are too punishing on the most constrained labels, **K2** and **f**. The differences in performance between constrained and unconstrained models is largely due to higher recall for both **K1** and **o** move prediction, while recall for **K2** and **f** moves lowered slightly. One possibility for future work may include compensating for this by artificially inflating the likelihood of highly-constrained Negotiation labels. Additionally, we see that the most common mistakes involve distinguishing between **K1** and **f** moves. While many **f** moves are obviously non-content-bearing (*"Wow, what fun!"*), others, especially those based in humor, may look grammatical and contentful (*"We've got to stop meeting this way."*). Better detection of humor and a more well-defined definition of what information is being shared will improve this aspect of the model. Overall, these errors do not limit the efficacy of the model for enabling future analysis.

6 Conclusion and Future Work

This work has presented a unified machine learning model for annotating information sharing acts on a sentence-by-sentence granularity; grouping sequences of sentences based on functional structure; and then grouping those sequences into topic-based threads. The model performs at a high accuracy, approaching human agreement at the sentence and thread level. Thread-level accuracy matched but did not exceed simpler baselines, suggesting that this model could benefit from a more elaborate representation of coherence and topic. At the level of sequences, the model performs statistically the same as human annotation.

The automatic annotation and structuring of dialogue that this model performs is a vital preprocessing task to organize and structure conversational data in numerous domains. Our model allows researchers to abstract away from vocabulary-based approaches, instead working with interaction-level units of analysis. This is especially important in the context of interdisciplinary research, where other representations may be overly specialized towards one task, and vocabulary may differ for spurious reasons across populations and cultures.

Our evaluation was performed on a noisy, real-world chatroom corpus, and still performed very accurately. Coherent interfacing between granularities of analysis is always a challenge. Segmentation, tokenization, and overlapping or inconsistent structured output are nontrivial problems. By incorporating sentence-level annotation, discourse-level sequence structure, and topical thread disentanglement into a single model, we have shown one way to reduce or eliminate this interfacing burden and allow greater structural awareness in real-world systems. Future work will improve this model's accuracy further, test its generality in new domains such as spoken multi-party interactions, and evaluate its usefulness in imposing structure for secondary analysis.

Acknowledgments

The research reported here was supported by National Science Foundation grant IIS-0968485, Office of Naval Research grant N000141110221, and in part by the Pittsburgh Science of Learning Center, which is funded by the National Science Foundation grant SBE-0836012.

References

Paige H. Adams. 2008. *Conversation Thread Extraction and Topic Detection in Text-based Chat*. Ph.D. thesis.

Hua Ai, Antonio Roque, Anton Leuski, and David Traum. 2007. Using information state to improve dialogue move identification in a spoken dialogue system. In *Proceedings of Interspeech*.

Ella Bingham, Ata Kaban, and Mark Girolami. 2003. Topic identification in dynamical text by complexity pursuit. In *Neural Processing Letters*.

Dan Bohus and Eric Horvitz. 2011. Multiparty turn taking in situated dialog. In *Procedings of SIGDIAL*.

Harry Bunt. 2011. Multifunctionality in dialogue. In *Computer Speech and Language*.

Lauri Carlson. 1983. *Dialogue Games: An Approach to Discourse Analysis*. Massachussetts Institute of Technology.

Ming-Wei Chang, Lev Ratinov, Nicholas Rizzolo, and Dan Roth. 2008. Learning and inference with constraints. In *Proceedings of the Association for the Advancement of Artificial Intelligence*.

Mark G Core and James F Allen. 1997. Coding dialogs with the damsl annotation scheme. In *AAAI Fall Symposium on Communicative Action in Humans and Machines*.

Micha Elsner and Eugene Charniak. 2010. Disentangling chat. *Computational Linguistics*.

Micha Elsner and Eugene Charniak. 2011. Disentangling chat with local coherence models. In *Proceedings of the Association for Computational Linguistics*.

Rong-En Fan, Kai-Wei Chang, Cho-Jui Hsieh, Xiang-Rui Wang, and Chih-Jen Lin. 2008. LIBLINEAR: A library for large linear classification.

George Ferguson and James Allen. 1998. Trips: An integrated intelligent problem-solving assistant. In *Proceedings of AAAI*.

Michael Galley, Kathleen McKeown, Julia Hirschberg, and Elizabeth Shriberg. 2004. Identifying agreement and disagreement in conversational speech: Use of bayesian networks to model pragmatic dependencies. In *Proceedings of ACL*.

Iris Howley, Elijah Mayfield, and Carolyn Penstein Rosé. 2011. Missing something? authority in collaborative learning. In *Proceedings of Computer Supported Collaborative Learning*.

Daniel Jurafsky, Rebecca Bates, Noah Coccaro, Rachel Martin, Marie Meteer, Klaus Ries, Elizabeth Shriberg, Andreas Stolcke, Paul Taylor, and Carol Van Ess-Dykema. 1998. Switchboard discourse language modelling final report. Technical report.

Su Nam Kim, Lawrence Cavedon, and Timothy Baldwin. 2010. Classifying dialogue acts in one-on-one live chats. In *Proceedings of the Conference on Empirical Methods in Natural Language Processing*.

M Barton Laws, Mary Catherine Beach, Yoojin Lee, William H. Rogers, Somnath Saha, P Todd Korthuis, Victoria Sharp, and Ira B Wilson. 2012. Provider-patient adherence dialogue in hiv care: Results of a multisite study. *AIDS Behavior*.

Igor Malioutov and Regina Barzilay. 2006. Minimum cut model for spoken lecture segmentation. In *Proceedings of ACL/COLING*.

J.R. Martin and David Rose. 2003. *Working with Discourse: Meaning Beyond the Clause*. Continuum.

Elijah Mayfield and Carolyn Penstein Rosé. 2010. An interactive tool for supporting error analysis for text mining. In *NAACL Demonstration Session*.

Elijah Mayfield and Carolyn Penstein Rosé. 2011. Recognizing authority in dialogue with an integer linear programming constrained model. In *Proceedings of Association for Computational Linguistics*.

Elijah Mayfield, Michael Garbus, David Adamson, and Carolyn Penstein Rosé. 2011. Data-driven interaction patterns: Authority and information sharing in dialogue. In *Proceedings of AAAI Fall Symposium on Building Common Ground with Intelligent Agents*.

Elijah Mayfield, David Adamson, Alexander I Rudnicky, and Carolyn Penstein Rosé. 2012a. Computational representations of discourse practices across populations in task-based dialogue. In *Proceedings of the International Conference on Intercultural Collaboration*.

Elijah Mayfield, Miaomiao Wen, Mitch Golant, and Carolyn Penstein Rosé. 2012b. Discovering habits of effective online support group chatrooms. In *ACM Conference on Supporting Group Work*.

Kanayo Ogura, Takashi Kusumi, and Asako Miura. 2008. Analysis of community development using chat logs: A virtual support group of cancer patients. In *Proceedings of the IEEE Symposium on Universal Communication*.

Jacki O'Neill and David Martin. 2003. Text chat in action. In *Proceedings of the International Conference on Supporting Group Work*.

Rieks op den Akker and David Traum. 2009. A comparison of addressee detection methods for multiparty conversations. In *Workshop on the Semantics and Pragmatics of Dialogue*.

Massimo Poesio and Andrei Mikheev. 1998. The predictive power of game structure in dialogue act recognition: Experimental results using maximum entropy estimation. In *Proceedings of the International Conference on Spoken Language Processing*.

Andrei Popescu-Belis. 2008. Dimensionality of dialogue act tagsets: An empirical analysis of large corpora. In *Language Resources and Evaluation*.

Steve Renals, Hervé Bourlard, Jean Carletta, and Andrei Popescu-Belis. 2012. *Multimodal Signal Processing: Human Interactions in Meetings*.

Alan Ritter, Colin Cherry, and Bill Dolan. 2010. Unsupervised modeling of twitter conversations. In *Proceedings of NAACL*.

Nicholas Rizzolo and Dan Roth. 2010. Learning based java for rapid development of nlp systems. In *Proceedings of the International Conference on Language Resources and Evaluation*.

E. Schegloff. 2007. *Sequence organization in interaction: A primer in conversation analysis*. Cambridge University Press.

Dou Shen, Qiang Yang, Jian-Tao Sun, and Zheng Chen. 2006. Thread detection in dynamic text message streams. In *Proceedings of SIGIR*.

Elizabeth Shriberg, Raj Dhillon, Sonali Bhagat, Jeremy Ang, and Hannah Carvey. 2004. The icsi meeting recorder dialog act (mrda) corpus. In *Proceedings of SIGDIAL*.

Tomek Strzalkowski, George Aaron Broadwell, Jennifer Stromer-Galley, Samira Shaikh, Ting Liu, and Sarah Taylor. 2011. Modeling socio-cultural phenomena in online multi-party discourse. In *AAAI Workshop on Analyzing Microtext*.

Kristina Toutanova, Dan Klein, Christopher Manning, and Yoram Singer. 2003. Feature-rich part-of-speech tagging with a cyclic dependency network. In *Proceedings of NAACL*.

David Traum. 1994. *A computational theory of grounding in natural language conversation*. Ph.D. thesis.

Janyce Wiebe, Theresa Wilson, and Claire Cardie. 2005. Annotating expressions of opinions and emotions in language. *Language Resources and Evaluation*.

Florian Wolf and Edward Gibson. 2005. Representing discourse coherence: A corpus-based study. *Computational Linguistics*.

Rapid Development Process of Spoken Dialogue Systems using Collaboratively Constructed Semantic Resources

Masahiro Araki
Department of Information Science
Kyoto Institute of Technology
Matsugasaki, Sakyo-ku, Kyoto 606-8585, Japan
araki@kit.ac.jp

Abstract

We herein propose a method for the rapid development of a spoken dialogue system based on collaboratively constructed semantic resources and compare the proposed method with a conventional method that is based on a relational database. Previous development frameworks of spoken dialogue systems, which presuppose a relational database management system as a background application, require complex data definition, such as making entries in a task-dependent language dictionary, templates of semantic frames, and conversion rules from user utterances to the query language of the database. We demonstrate that a semantic web oriented approach based on collaboratively constructed semantic resources significantly reduces troublesome rule descriptions and complex configurations in the rapid development process of spoken dialogue systems.

1 Introduction

There has been continuing interest in the development methodology of spoken dialogue systems (SDS). In recent years, statistical methods, such as Williams et al. (2007) and Hori et al. (2009), have attracted a great deal of attention as a data-driven (i.e., corpus-driven) approach, which can reduce the troublesome manual coding of dialogue management rules. Statistical methods can also be applied to other components of SDS, such as semi-automatic construction of semantic interpreters and response generators. However the overall SDS development process still requires some hand coding, for example to establish the connection to the underlying application.

Another data-driven approach was designed to provide all of the SDS components with the goal of rapidly constructing the entire system (Kogure et al., 2001; Heinroth et al., 2009). This approach starts from a data model definition (and so can be regarded as a data-modeling driven approach) and adds rules and templates, which are used as task-dependent knowledge in an SDS. As a data model definition, Kogure et al. (2001) used a relational database (RDB) schema and Heinroth et al. (2009) used OWL, which is an ontology definition language in semantic web applications. Although these data-modeling schemata are familiar to developers of web applications, additional definition of rules and templates needed for an SDS is troublesome for ordinary web developers because such SDS-related rules require specialized knowledge of linguistics and speech application development.

We herein propose a new data-modeling driven approach for rapid development of SDS that is based on collaboratively constructed semantic resources (CSRs). We present an automatic generation mechanism of code and data for a simple SDS. In addition, we compare the proposed approach with an ordinary data-modeling driven approach that is based on a RDB. By using CSRs and the Rails framework of web application development, the troublesome definitions of rules and templates for SDS can be reduced significantly.

The remainder of the present paper is organized as follows. Section 2 describes the proposed approach to a data-modeling driven development process for SDS based on CSRs. Section 3 compares the proposed approach with the previous RDB-based approach. In Section 4, the paper concludes with a discussion of future research.

2 Data-modeling driven approach based on CSRs

In this section, we explain our previous data-modeling driven approach and describe additional new functionality based on CSRs.

2.1 Object-oriented SDS development framework

We previously proposed a data-modeling driven framework for rapid prototyping of SDS (Araki et al., 2011). This includes a class library that is based on the class hierarchy and the attribute definitions of an existing semantic web ontology, i.e., Schema.org[1]. This class library is used as a base class of an application-specific class definition. An example class definition is shown in Figure 1.

```
@DBSearch
@SystemInitiative
class MyBook extends Book {
  int ranking
  static constraints = {
    name(onsearch:"like")
    author(onsearch:"like")
    publisher()
    ranking(number:true)
  }
}
```

Figure 1: Example of class definition extending existing class library.

In this example, the *MyBook* class inherits all of the attributes of the *Book* class of Schema.org in the same manner as object-oriented programming languages. The developer can limit the attributes that are used in the target application by listing them in the constraints section. On the other hand, the developer can add additional attributes (in this class, *ranking* attributes as the type of *integer*) in the definition of the class.

[1] http://schema.org/

The task type and dialogue initiative type are indicated as annotations at the beginning of the class definition. In this example, the task type is DB search and the initiative type is user initiative. This information is used in generating the controller code and view code of the target SDS.

Using Grails[2], which is a Rails web application framework, the proposed framework generates the dialogue controller code of the indicated task type and the view code, which have speech interaction capability on the HTML5 code from this class definition. The overall concept of the object-oriented framework is shown in Figure 2.

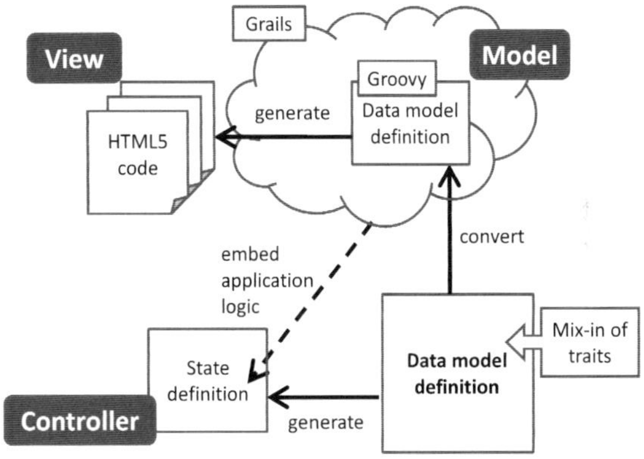

Figure 2: Overview of the object-oriented SDS development framework.

2.2 Usage of CSRs

The disadvantage of our previous framework, described in the previous subsection, is the high dependence on the dictation performance of the speech recognition component. The automatically generated HTML5 code invokes dictation API, irrespective of the state of the dialogue and initiative type. In order to improve speech recognition accuracy, grammar rules (in system initiative dialogue) and/or the use of a task/domain-dependent language model (LM) (in mixed/user initiative dialogue) are necessary. In our previous framework, the developer had to prepare these ASR-related components using language resources, which are beyond the proposed data-driven framework.

In order to overcome this defect, we add the Freebase[3] class library, which is based on large-scale CSRs, because Freebase already includes the

[2] http://grails.org/

[3] http://www.freebase.com/

contents of the data. These contents and a large-scale web corpus facilitate the construction of grammar rules and a LM that is specific to the target task/domain. For example, the Film class of Freebase has more than 191 thousand entries (as of May 2012). These real data can be used as resources to improve SDS accuracy.

In system initiative type dialogue, the contents of each attribute can construct word entries of the grammar rule for each attribute slot. For example, the grammar rule for the user's response to "Which genre of movie are you searching for?" can be constructed from the contents of the genres attribute of the Film class. We implemented a generator of the set of content words specified in the data model definition from the data of Freebase. The generator is embedded as one component of the proposed rapid prototyping system.

In the mixed/user initiative type tasks, since content words and functional words make up the user's utterance, we need a LM for speech recognition and a semantic frame extractor for the construction of semantic data storage queries. We designed and implemented a LM generator and a semantic frame extractor using a functional expression dictionary that corresponds to the attributes of Freebase (Araki, submitted). An example entry of the function expression dictionary is shown in Figure 3 and the flow of the LM generation is shown in Figure 4.

item	value
property	fb:film.performance.actor
phrase pattern	X "ga de te iru" Y
constraints	X rdf:type "/film/actor"
partial graph	Y fb:film.performance.actor X

Figure 3: An entry of function expression dictionary.

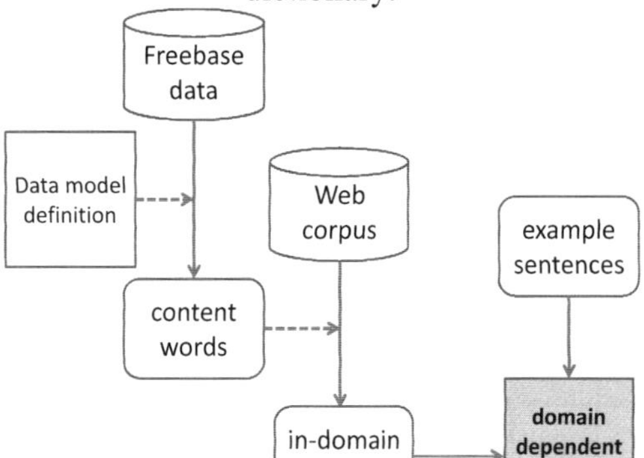

Figure 4: Construction process of LM.

3 Comparison with the RDB-based approach

3.1 Overview of the RDB-based method

As an example of the RDB-based SDS prototyping method, we review the method described in Kogure et al. (2001) (see Figure 5).

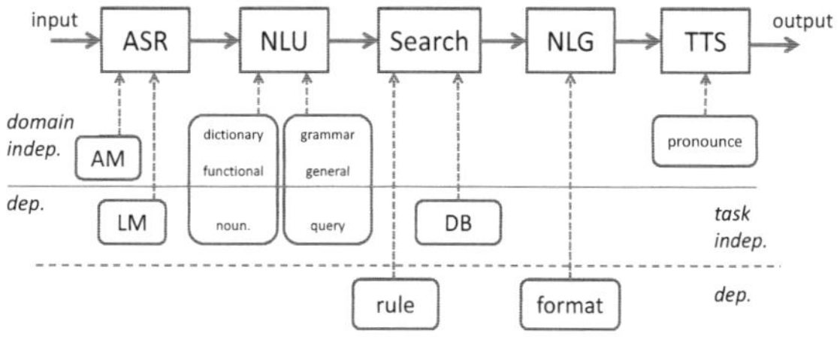

Figure 5: Modules and knowledge of the RDB-based method.

They examined the domain dependency and task dependency of the knowledge that drives SDS. Domain/task-independent knowledge, such as an acoustic model, a general function word dictionary, and a pronunciation dictionary, are prepared in advance for all of the systems. Both domain-dependent/task-independent knowledge, such as the language model, the noun/verb dictionary, and the database schema, and domain/task-dependent knowledge, such as the rule of query generation obtained from the results of semantic analysis and format for output, must be specified by the developer. If the developer wants to change a task within the same domain, the developer can reuse domain-dependent/task-independent knowledge (everything above the dotted line in Figure 4) and must specify task-dependent knowledge (everything below the dotted line in Figure 4).

3.2 Comparison of the data-modeling stage

In the data modeling of the RDB-based method, the developer must specify field names (e.g., title, year), their corresponding data types (e.g., string, integer), and the labels of the fields (i.e., the labels for the language used in the SDS), as in the usual web application with RDB. Since the data model definitions differ from one another, it is difficult to integrate similar systems even if these systems deal with the same domain.

In the CSRs-based approach, the data-modeling process involves selecting necessary attributes of the inherited class and, if needed, adding fields for additional domain/task-specific information. The data type has already been set in the existing data schema, and language-dependent label information can be acquired by the value of *rdfs:label*, where the value of the *lang* attribute is the target language.

3.3 Comparison of code generation stage

In the RDB-based method, the developer must specify the noun and verb dictionary, grammar for parsing, and rules for query generation. In addition, the RDB-based approach must either stick to a fixed dialogue pattern for DB search or make the developer write dialogue management rules.

By combining the CSRs-based approach with the Rails framework, the task dependent dictionary is automatically generated from the data and grammar rules are easily constructed with the functional expression entries of properties. Also in this approach, typical dialogue management patterns are already prepared and can be specified as annotations. For the sake of this setting, all of the basic codes for SDS are automatically generated from the data model definition.

3.4 Comparison of functionality

In the RDB-based method, the developer must make a domain/task dependent LM using language resources outside of the development process. However, in general, it is difficult to acquire a domain/task-dependent corpus. In addition, although the RDB-based method is designed to be robust with respect to the task modification, this method is not robust with respect to porting to different languages. Language specific code tends to be embedded in every component of an SDS.

In the CSRs-based approach, the domain/task-dependent LM is automatically generated, as described in Subsection 2.2. For the sake of this data-modeling driven method and native multilinguality of CSRs, the developer can easily implement multilingual SDS (Araki et al., 2012). Multilingual contents are already prepared in Freebase (although English resources are dominant) and a multilingual web speech API is already implemented, e.g., in the Google Chrome browser, the developer can implement a prototype of other language SDS by dictation. If the developer wants to use domain/task-dependent LMs, he/she must prepare example sentences for the target domain/task in the target language.

4 Conclusions and future research

We have proposed a method for rapid development of a spoken dialogue system based on CSRs and have compared the proposed method with the conventional method, which is based on RDB.

In the current implementation, our system cannot handle the problem of the variation of the named entity which is dealt with by e.g. Hillard et al. (2011). We are planning to examine the extensibility of the proposed framework by combining such refinement methods.

Acknowledgments

The present research was supported in part by the Ministry of Education, Science, Sports, and Culture through a Grant-in-Aid for Scientific Research (C), 22500153, 2010.

References

Masahiro Araki and Yuko Mizukami. 2011. Development of a Data-driven Framework for Multimodal Interactive Systems. In Proc. of IWSDS 2011, 91-101.

Masahiro Araki. submitted. An Automatic Construction Method of Spoken Query Understanding Component from Data Model Definition.

Masahiro Araki and Daisuke Takegoshi. 2012. A Rapid Development Framework for Multilingual Spoken Dialogue Systems. In Proc. of COMPSAC 2012.

Tobias Heinroth, Dan Denich and Gregor Bertrand. 2009. Ontology-based Spoken Dialogue Modeling. In Proc. of the IWSDS 2009.

Dustin Hillard, Asli Çelikyilmaz, Dilek Z. Hakkani-Tür, and Gökhan Tür. 2011. Learning Weighted Entity Lists from Web Click Logs for Spoken Language Understanding. In Proc. of Interspeech 2011, 705-708.

Chiori Hori, Kiyonori Ohtake, Teruhisa Misu,. Hideki Kashioka and Satoshi Nakamura. 2009. Statistical Dialog Management Applied to WFST-based Dialog Systems. In Proc. of ICASSP 2009, 4793-4796.

Satoru Kogure and Seiichi Nakagawa. 2001. A Development Tool for Spoken Dialogue Systems and Its Evaluation. In Proc. of TSD2001, 373-380.

Jason D. Williams and Steve Young. 2007. Partially Observable Markov Decision Processes for Spoken Dialog Systems. Computer Speech and Language, 21(2), 393-422.

The Effect of Cognitive Load on a Statistical Dialogue System

M. Gašić*, **P. Tsiakoulis***, **M. Henderson***, **B. Thomson***, **K. Yu***, **E. Tzirkel**** **and S. Young***
*Cambridge University Engineering Department
Trumpington Street, Cambridge CB2 1PZ, UK
{mg436, pt344, mh521, brmt2, ky219, sjy}@eng.cam.ac.uk
**General Motors Advanced Technical Centre, Israel
eli.tzirkel@gm.com

Abstract

In recent years statistical dialogue systems have gained significant attention due to their potential to be more robust to speech recognition errors. However, these systems must also be robust to changes in user behaviour caused by cognitive loading. In this paper, a statistical dialogue system providing restaurant information is evaluated in a set-up where the subjects used a driving simulator whilst talking to the system. The influences of cognitive loading were investigated and some clear differences in behaviour were discovered. In particular, it was found that users chose to respond to different system questions and use different speaking styles, which indicate the need for an incremental dialogue approach.

1 Introduction

A spoken dialogue system enables a user to obtain information while using their hands to perform some other task, which in many cases is the user's primary task. A typical example is an in-car spoken dialogue system where the spoken interaction is secondary to the main task of driving the car (Weng et al., 2004). This domain is particularly challenging since it involves dealing with the errors caused by the varying noise levels and changes in user behaviour caused by the cognitive load.

A statistical approach to dialogue modelling has been proposed as a means of automatically optimising dialogue policies. In particular, the partially observable Markov decision process (POMDP) model for dialogue provides a representation of varying levels of uncertainty of the user input, yielding more robust dialogue policies (Williams and Young, 2007; Thomson and Young, 2010; Young et al., 2010).

Another thread of research deals with speech interfaces for in-car applications, see (Baron and Green, 2006) for a review. Past research has investigated the extent to which speaking is cognitively less demanding than typing (Gartner et al., 2001; Tsimhoni et al., 2004; Kun et al., 2007). In addition, considerable research has examined how driving safety is influenced by a dialogue system (Lai et al., 2001; Lee et al., 2001; Nielsen et al., 2008). However, to the best of our knowledge, little work has been done to investigate the effect of the cognitive load when interacting with a real conversational spoken dialogue system. The work presented in (Mishra et al., 2004) suggests that the user speech is more disfluent when the user is performing another task. However, this work is based on a Wizard of Oz framework, where a human provides the system's responses. Also, a push-to-talk button was used for every utterance which will have affected the natural flow of the dialogue. It is important to know if the change of cognitive load has an effect on the speaking style and whether the system can alter its behaviour to accommodate for this.

In this paper we try to answer these questions by examining dialogues where users drove a car simulator and talked to an open-microphone fully automated spoken dialogue system at the same time.

The rest of the paper is organised as follows. Section 2 provides an overview of the dialogue system used and section 3 describes the evaluation set-up. The analysis of the results is given in Section 4. Section 5 concludes the paper.

Table 1: Example dialogue task

You are looking for a cheap restaurant and it should be in the east part of town. Make sure you get the address of the venue.

2 System overview

The user speaks to the system, and the acoustic signal is converted by the speech recogniser into a set of sentence hypotheses, which represents a probability distribution over all possible things that the user might have said. The sentence hypotheses are converted into an N-best list of dialogue acts by a semantic decoder. Since the dialogue state cannot be directly observed it maintains a probability distribution over all states, which is called the belief state. The belief state is updated at every user turn using Bayesian inference treating the input dialogue acts as evidence. Based on belief state, the optimal system act is selected using a policy and which is trained automatically using reinforcement learning. The abstract system dialogue act is converted to an appropriate utterance by a natural language generator and then converted to speech by an HMM-based speech synthesiser. To enable in-car speech interaction via mobile phone, a VoIP interface is implemented. The domain is Cambridge restaurant information with a database of about 150 venues and 7 slots that users can query.

3 Evaluation set-up

Our goal is to understand system performance when driving. However, due to the safety restrictions, performance was tested using a driving simulator. The following sections explain the set-up.

3.1 Car simulator

The car simulator used in the evaluation was the same as in (Davies and Robinson, 2011). It consists of a seat, a steering wheel and pedals, which give a realistic cab-like environment for the participants. There is also a projection screen which largely fills the visual field of the driver. The simulation software is a modified version of Rockstar Games' Grand Theft Auto: San Andreas, with over 500 km of roads. For the purpose of the evaluation, the subjects were asked to drive on the main motorway, to keep the lane and not to drive over 70mph.

3.2 Subjects

For the study 28 subjects were recruited, 22 where native speakers. Each subject had to complete three scenarios: (1) to drive the car simulator for 10 minutes, (2) to talk to the system for 7 dialogues and (3) to talk to the system for 7 dialogues while driving. The scenarios were in counter-balanced order.

While they were driving, the speed and the road position were recorded. If the scenario involved talking to the system, the instructor read out the dialogue task (see an example in Table 1) and dialled the phone number. In addition, the subject had the dialogue task displayed on a small screen next to the driving wheel. The subject talked to the system using loud speaker mode on the mobile phone.

4 Results

To examine the influence of cognitive load, the following examinations were performed. First, we investigate if the subjects felt any change in the cognitive load (Section 4.1). Then, in Section 4.2, we examine how the driving was influenced by the subjects talking to the system. Finally, we investigate how successfully the subjects were able to complete the dialogue tasks while driving (Section 4.3). This is followed with an examination of the conversational patterns that occurred when the subjects were driving whilst talking to the system (Section 4.4).

4.1 Cognitive load

After each scenario the subjects were asked to answer five questions based on the NASA-TLX self-reporting scheme for workload measurement. They answered by providing a rating from 1 (very easy) to 5 (very hard). The averaged results are given in Table 2. We performed a Kruskal test, followed by pairwise comparisons for every scenario for each answer and all differences are statistically significant ($p < 0.03$) apart from the differences in the frustration, the stress and the pace between talking and talking and driving. This means that they were clearly able to feel the change in cognitive load.

Table 2: Subjective evaluation of the cognitive load

Driving	Talking	Talking&Driving
How mentally demanding was the scenario?		
1.61	2.21	2.89
How hurried was the pace of the scenario?		
1.21	1.71	1.89
How hard did you have to work?		
1.5	2.32	2.96
How frustrated did you feel during the task?		
1.29	2.61	2.61
How stressed did you feel during the task?		
1.29	2.0	2.32

Table 3: Analysis of driving speed to determine which measures are larger for Talking&Driving than Driving

Measure	Percentage of users	Confidence interval
Higher speed	8%	[1%, 25%]
Larger std.dev	77%	[56%, 91%]
Larger entropy	85%	[65%, 95%]

4.2 Driving performance

For 26 subjects we recorded position on the road and the speed. Since these measurements vary significantly across the subjects, for each subject we calculated the average speed, the standard deviation and the entropy and similarly for the average position in the lane. For the speed, we computed how many subjects had a higher average speed when they were talking and driving versus when they were just talking and similarly for the standard deviation and the entropy. The results are given in Table 3. It can be seen that the user's speed is lower when they are driving and talking, however, the increase in the standard deviation and the entropy suggest that their driving is more erratic. No significant differences were observed for the road position.

4.3 Dialogue task completion

Each participant performed 14 dialogues, 7 for each scenario. In total, there were 196 dialogues per scenario. After each dialogue they told the instructor if they thought the dialogue was successful, and this information was used to compute the subjective completion rate. In addition, all dialogues were transcribed and analysed to see if the system provided information the user asked for and hence calculate an objective completion rate. The results are given in Table 4. These differences are not statistically significant due to the small sample size. However, it can be seen that the trend is that the dialogues where the subject was not performing another task at the same time were more successful. Also, it is interesting that the subjective scores are higher than the objective ones. This can be explained by the fact that the dialogue tasks were predefined and the subjects do not always pay sufficient attention to their task descriptions.

Table 4: Subjective and Objective Task completion (196 Dialogues per scenario)

	Talking	Talking&Driving
Subjective	78.6%	74.0%
Objective	68.4%	64.8%

Table 5: Percentage of turns that are in line with the predefined task

	Talking	Talking&Driving
Percentage of turns that follow the task	98.3%	96.79%
Number of turns	1354	1388

4.4 Conversational patterns

Given that the subjects felt the change of cognitive load when they were talking to the system and operating the car simulator at the same time, we were interested to see if there are any changes in the dialogues which might suggest this.

First, we examine how well they follow the given task on a turn-to-turn basis. For example, if the task is to find a cheap restaurant and if at some point in the dialogue the user says *I'd like an expensive restaurant* that turn is not consistent with the task. The results are given in Table 5 and they are statistically significant ($p < 0.01$).

We then examine the number of contradictions on a turn-to-turn basis. For example, if the user says *I'd like a cheap restaurant* and later on they say *I'd like*

Table 6: User obedience to system questions

1. system requests or confirms and requests		
	Samples	Obedience
Talking	392	67.6%
Talking&Driving	390	63.9%
2. system confirms		
	Samples	Obedience
Talking	91	73.6%
Talking&Driving	92	81.5%

an expensive restaurant the latter turn is clearly a contradiction. The percentage of contradicting turns is less than 1% and the difference between the scenarios is not statistically significant. This suggests that while users tend to forget the task they are given when they are driving, they still act rationally despite the increase in the cognitive load.

The next analysis concerns the user obedience, i.e. the extent to which subjects answer the system questions. We grouped the system questions in two classes. The first class represents the questions where the system requests a value for a particular slot, for instance *What part of town are you looking for?* and the questions where the system confirms and requests at the same time, for instance *You are looking for a cheap restaurant. What part of town are you looking for?* The second class correspond to system confirmations, for example *Did you say you are looking for a cheap restaurant?* The percentage of the obedient user turns per class is given in Table 6. Due to the small sample size these results are not statistically significant. Still, it is interesting to see that when driving the subjects appear to be more obedient to the system confirmations than when they are just talking. When the system makes a confirmation, the user can answer with simple yes or no, whereas when the system requests the value of a particular slot, the user needs to think more to provide an answer.

The number of barge-ins, the number of filler words and the average speech intensity vary considerably among the subjects. Therefore, we average these statistics per user and examine the number of users for which the particular measure is greater for the scenario where they talked to the system and drove the simulator at the same time. The results (Table 7) show that the number of barge-ins and the number of fillers is significantly greater for the scenario when they are talking and driving and the intensity on average tend to be greater.

Table 7: Analysis of measures related to the speaking style which values are larger for Talking&Driving than Talking

Measure	% of users	Conf. interval
More barge-ins	87%	[69%, 96%]
More fillers	73%	[54%, 88%]
Higher intensity	67%	[47%, 83%]

5 Conclusion and Future work

There are several important observations arising from this study. Firstly, dialogues with cognitively loaded users tend to be less successful. This suggests that the system should alter its behaviour to match user behaviour and alleviate the cognitive load in order to maintain the level of performance. This necessitates rapid on-line adaptation of dialogue policies.

The second observation is that cognitively loaded users tend to respond to some types of system questions more than others. This indicates that the user model within a POMDP dialogue system should be conditioned on a measure of cognitive load.

Finally, this study has found that users barge-in and use filler words significantly more often when they are cognitively loaded. This suggests the need for a much richer turn-taking model which allows the system to use back-channels and barge-in when the user hesitates. An obvious candidate is the incremental approach (Schlangen and Skantze, 2009; DeVault et al., 2009) which allows the system to process partial user inputs, back-channels, predict short term user input and interrupt the user during hesitations. While incremental dialogue is a growing area of study, it has not so far been examined in the context of dialogue for secondary tasks. We signpost this as an important area for future work.

Acknowledgments

We would like to thank to Peter Robinson and Ian Davies for their help with the experiments.

References

A Baron and P Green. 2006. Safety and Usability of Speech Interfaces for In-Vehicle Tasks while Driving: A Brief Literature Review. Technical Report UMTRI-2006-5.

I Davies and P Robinson. 2011. Emotional investment in naturalistic data collection. In *International Conference on Affective Computing and Intelligent Interaction*.

D DeVault, K Sagae, and DR Traum. 2009. Can I finish? Learning when to respond to incremental interpretation results in interactive dialogue. In *10th Annual SIGDIAL meeting on Discourse and Dialogue*.

U Gartner, W Konig, and T Wittig. 2001. Evaluation of Manual vs. Speech Input When Using a Driver Information System in Real Traffic. In *International Driving Symposium on Human Factors in Driving Assessment, Training and Vehicle Design*.

A Kun, T Paek, and Ž Medenica. 2007. The effect of speech interface accuracy on driving performance. In *Interspeech*.

J Lai, K Cheng, P Green, and O Tsimhoni. 2001. On the Road and on the Web? Comprehension of synthetic and human speech while driving. In *SIGCHI*.

JD Lee, B Caven, S Haake, and TL Brown. 2001. Speech-based Interaction with In-vehicle Computers: The Effect of Speech-based E-mail on Drivers' Attention to the Roadway. *Human Factors*, 43:631–640.

R Mishra, E Shriberg, S Upson, J Chen, F Weng, S Peters, L Cavedon, J Niekrasz, H Cheng, and H Bratt. 2004. A wizard of Oz framework for collecting spoken human-computer dialogs. In *Interspeech*.

BS Nielsen, B Harsham, B Raj, and C Forlines. 2008. Speech-Based UI Design for the Automobile. *Handbook of Research on User Interface Design and Evaluation for Mobile Technology*, pages 237–252.

David Schlangen and Gabriel Skantze. 2009. A general, abstract model of incremental dialogue processing. In *Proceedings of the 12th Conference of the European Chapter of the Association for Computational Linguistics*, EACL '09, pages 710–718.

B Thomson and S Young. 2010. Bayesian update of dialogue state: A POMDP framework for spoken dialogue systems. *Computer Speech and Language*, 24(4):562–588.

O Tsimhoni, D Smith, and P Green. 2004. Address Entry While Driving: Speech Recognition Versus a Touch-Screen Keyboard. *Human Factors*, 46:600–610.

F Weng, L Cavedon, B Raghunathan, D Mirkovic, H Cheng, H Schmidt, H Bratt, R Mishra, S Peters, L Zhao, S Upson, E Shriberg, and C Bergmann. 2004. Developing a conversational dialogue system for cognitively overloaded users. In *Proceedings of the International Congress on Intelligent Transportation Systems*.

JD Williams and SJ Young. 2007. Partially Observable Markov Decision Processes for Spoken Dialog Systems. *Computer Speech and Language*, 21(2):393–422.

SJ Young, M Gašić, S Keizer, F Mairesse, J Schatzmann, B Thomson, and K Yu. 2010. The Hidden Information State Model: a practical framework for POMDP-based spoken dialogue management. *Computer Speech and Language*, 24(2):150–174.

Predicting Adherence to Treatment for Schizophrenia from Dialogue Transcripts

Christine Howes, Matthew Purver, Rose McCabe, Patrick G. T. Healey, Mary Lavelle
Queen Mary University of London
Mile End Road, London E1 4NS
c.howes@qmul.ac.uk

Abstract

Recent work on consultations between outpatients with schizophrenia and psychiatrists has shown that adherence to treatment can be predicted by patterns of repair – specifically, the pro-activity of the patient in checking their understanding, i.e. patient clarification. Using machine learning techniques, we investigate whether this tendency can be predicted from high-level dialogue features, such as backchannels, overlap and each participant's proportion of talk. The results indicate that these features are not predictive of a patient's adherence to treatment or satisfaction with the communication, although they do have some association with symptoms. However, all these can be predicted if we allow features at the word level. These preliminary experiments indicate that patient adherence is predictable from dialogue transcripts, but further work is necessary to develop a meaningful, general and reliable feature set.

1 Introduction

How conversational partners achieve and maintain shared understanding is of crucial importance in the understanding of dialogue. One such mechanism, other initiated repair (Schegloff, 1992), where one conversational participant queries or corrects the talk of another, has been well documented in both general and task-based dialogues (Colman and Healey, 2011). However, how such shared understanding impacts beyond the level of the conversation has not typically been examined. Exceptions to this have highlighted the role of shared understanding in schizophrenia (McCabe et al., 2002; Themistocleous et al., 2009) and the association between psychiatrist-patient communication and adherence. McCabe et al. (in preparation) found that more patient clarification (i.e. other initiated repair) of the psychiatrist's talk was associated with better treatment adherence six months later. Clarification consists mainly of asking questions to clarify the meaning of the psychiatrist's utterance (checking understanding) and correcting something that the psychiatrist has said (getting the facts straight). Example 1, taken from a consultation, shows the patient requesting clarification of something the psychiatrist has just said about a possible side effect.

(1) **Dr:** Yep, well that is a possible side effect
Pat: Side effect?
Dr: Of the er haloperidol

The patient's request leads to additional explanation by the psychiatrist about the medication which can cause the possible side effect. More patient clarification reflects greater effort to reach a shared understanding. McCabe et al. (in preparation) found that for each unit increase in the patient clarification factor,[1] the odds of good (versus poor) adherence were increased by 5.8 (95% CI 1.3 to 25.8, p=0.02).

Explaining the link between communicative patterns of patients and adherence may create the possibility for new interventions to improve adherence, and has both clinical and theoretical implications.

[1] A regression factor weighted heavily towards patient clarifcations (as in e.g. 1).

However, there is no evidence regarding what factors influence patient clarification and may explain the link with adherence. If patient clarification is a measure of greater communicational effort, or engagement, then we might expect other dialogue measures, such as the amount of acknowledgements or other grounding cues (Traum and Allen, 1992), or the proportion of talk per person, to be correlated with other initiated repair and therefore similarly predictive of subsequent adherence behaviour. This is of particular importance if we wish to build a system to automatically predict possible (lack of) adherence from dialogue transcripts, especially given that the types of patient clarification which carry the highest weight in the patient clarification factor (next-turn repair initiators, Schegloff, 1992) are rare, occurring on average only 1.2 times per dialogue.

Further, although certain types of repair were shown to affect how patients reported they felt the conversation went, self-reports of symptoms and communicational factors are not predictive of adherence. Although micro-communicational behaviour (in the form of other initiated repair) does have a bearing on subsequent adherence behaviour, patients are unaware of this. Additional questions therefore concern whether we can predict patient's symptom levels and subjective analyses of the communication based only on overview dialogue factors.

2 Hypotheses

Factors which we would expect to index patient engagement, and thus be predictive of adherence to treatment are the amount of backchannel responses patients make, and the proportion of questions patients ask, both of which ought to be higher for the more engaged patients. We might also expect that such patients have a greater proportion of the talk overall, and/or longer turns on average, though note that this conversational pattern might also be one in which the patient is not engaged, as they might not be responding to the feedback from their consultant.

For the symptom scores (see below for details), we should expect that patients with high levels of negative symptoms (which includes loss of affect and poverty of speech) would produce less talk overall, and in general produce shorter turns. There should also be more noticeable gaps in the dialogues (defined as greater than approximately 200ms, (Heldner and Edlund, 2010)). Contrarily, for positive symptoms, (including hallucinations and delusions) patients ought to produce longer turns and have a greater proportion of the talk.

We also expect to see effects on how patients felt the conversation went from the amount of overlap, though as overlap can be both intended and interpreted as either interruptive or collaborative (as with e.g. overlapping backchannels) it is unclear which direction such a prediction should take.

3 Method

131 dialogues from outpatient consultations between patients and psychiatrists were analysed according to a number of factors. Each of these factors, detailed in table 1, below, is calculated for each dialogue participant (with the exception of pauses). Each patient featured in only one of the dialogues however, there were only 29 doctors in the study, so the same clinician may have featured in several of the dialogues with different patients. The consultations varied in length, with the shortest consisting of 61 turns (438 words) and the longest 881 turns (13178 words), with an average of 320.5 turns (2706.4 words). In addition, a third party was present in 47 of the consultations.

Following the consultation, each patient was asked questions from standard questionnaires to ascertain their level of symptoms, and their evaluation of aspects of the consultation. The positive and negative syndrome scale (PANSS) (Kay et al., 1987) assesses positive, negative and general symptoms on a 7-point scale of severity (1=absent – 7=extreme). Positive symptoms represent a change in the patients' behaviour or thoughts and include sensory hallucinations and delusional beliefs. Negative symptoms represent a withdrawal or reduction in functioning, including blunted affect, and emotional withdrawal and alogia (poverty of speech). Positive and negative subscale scores ranged from 7 (absent) – 49 (extreme), general symptoms (such as anxiety) scores ranged from 16 (absent) – 112 (extreme).

Patient satisfaction with the communication was assessed using the Patient Experience Questionnaire (PEQ) (Steine et al., 2001). Three of the five subscales (12 questions) were used as the others were not relevant, having been developed for primary care. The three subscales were 'communication experiences', 'communication barriers' and 'emotions immediately after the visit'. For the communication subscales, items were measured on a 5-point Likert scale, with 1=disagree completely and 5=agree completely. The four items for the emotion scale were measured on a 7-point visual analogue scale, with opposing emotions were at either end. A higher score indicates a better experience.

Adherence to treatment was rated by the clinicians as good ($> 75\%$), average ($25 - 75\%$) or poor ($< 25\%$) six months after the consultation. Due to the low incidence of poor ratings (only 8 dialogues), this was converted to a binary score of 1 for good adherence (91 patients), and 0 otherwise (37). Ratings were not available for the remaining dialogues.

Measure	Description
Turns	Total number of turns
Words	Total number of words spoken
Proportion	Proportion of total talk in words (by each participant)
WordsPerTurn	Average length of turn in words
WhPerWord	Proportion of wh-words (e.g. what? who?) per word
OCRPerWord	Proportion of open class repair initiators (e.g. pardon? huh?) per word
BackchannelPerWord	Proportion of backchannels (e.g. uh-huh, yeah) per word
RepeatPerWord	Proportion of words repeated from preceding turn by other person
OverlapAny	Proportion of turns containing any overlapping talk
OverlapAll	Proportion of turns entirely overlapping another turn
QMark	Proportion of turns containing a question mark
TimedPause	Pause of more than approx 200ms, as marked on the transcripts

Table 1: Measures from outpatient consultations

3.1 Classification Experiments

We performed a series of classification experiments using the Weka machine learning toolkit (Hall et al., 2009) to predict each of the outcome measures outlined above (symptom measures, satisfaction measures, and adherence to treatment). In each case, outcome measures were converted to binary high/low scores on an equal frequency basis (i.e. providing approximately equal numbers of high and low instances). Features used were the high-level measures given in Table 1, and/or all unigrams extracted from the transcript; in both cases, features from doctor and patient were treated separately. Unigrams were produced by tokenising the lower-cased transcripts on white space; no stemming or stopword removal was performed, and feature values were binary i.e. indicating only presence or absence of the word spoken by the given speaker in the given dialogue.[2] Given the small size of our dataset (131 instances) and the large feature space resulting (> 6500 features), we selected features based on their predictive ability across the entire dataset (using Weka's CfsSubsetEval selector), reducing the number of features to 50-100. In order to avoid biasing towards doctor-specific features, we used only words spoken by patients in these experiments – each patient only features in one dialogue, so patient-specific vocabulary cannot help performance across dialogues. All unigram features thus selected were used in at least 3 dialogues.[3]

4 Results

Experiments including unigram features used LibSVM's support vector machine implementation (Chang and Lin, 2001) with a radial basis function kernel; experiments with only high-level features used J48 decision trees. In each case, experiments used 5-fold cross-validation.[4] In experiments predicting adherence, the distribution between positive and negative (i.e. good and bad adherence) made it impossible to balance the dataset - as this can be problematic for decision tree classifiers, we also present results for a downsampled dataset with only 71 instances but which provides balance. Performance is shown in Table 2 as overall percentage accuracy, and is compared to a majority-class baseline throughout; results which are significantly different at the 5% level according to a χ^2 test from a

[2]Experiments with frequency counts did not affect the results as reported.

[3]Bi- and tri-gram features were not extracted from this data because of the small amount of data available which we felt would result in models that suffered from overfitting (note that the same concern holds for the unigram features).

[4]Classifiers were trained on 80% and tested on 20% of the sample, with this was repeated 5 times over each possible 80/20 combination so as to test the whole dataset.

random distribution and the majority class distribution are shown marked with *.

	Baseline	Words	High-level
PANSS *positive*	51.1	87.0*	56.5*
PANSS *negative*	49.6	87.8*	56.5*
PANSS *general*	48.4	91.1*	54.0
PEQ *emotions*	51.9	89.1*	53.5
PEQ *communication*	50.8	79.8*	52.4
PEQ *comm. barriers*	51.6	90.6*	51.6
PEQ *overall*	50.8	90.6*	53.9
Adherence	73.2	91.1*	63.4
Adherence (balanced)	53.5	93.0*	52.1

Table 2: Percentage accuracies vs feature set

Results show good performance for all experiments when including lexical features, with all factors being predictable with around 90% accuracy with the exception of PEQ communication at just below 80%. However, using high-level features alone gives negligible performance, except for a small benefit on the PANSS negative and positive symptom measures, though contrary to our hypotheses the most important high-level features were OCRPerWord by the doctor (negative) and WhWords by an other participant (positive).

Examination of the most predictive unigrams shows that sets selected for different outcome measures are different: for example, the 54 features selected for adherence and the 73 selected for PEQ overall have only 1 word in common (*"mates"*). Adherence-related words include words related to conditions, treatment and medication (*"schizophrenic"*, *"sickness"*, *"symptoms"*, *"worse"*, *"pains"*, *"flashbacks"*, *"sodium"*, *"chemical"*, *"monthly"*); PEQ-related words include those related to personal life (*"sundays"*, *"thursdays"*, *"television"*, *"sofa"*, *"wine"*, *"personally"*, *"played"*), and filled pauses (*"eerrmm"*, *"uhhm"*) – although more investigation is required to draw any firm conclusions from these. Table 3 shows the full lists for adherence and PEQ overall.

5 Discussion and Conclusions

The results show that although we can weakly predict symptoms at levels above chance using only high-level dialogue factors, we cannot do so for adherence, or satisfaction measures. Despite the link between patient other initiated repair and adherence, this is also not an effective predictor for our machine learning approach because of the scarcity of the phenomenon, and the fact that many of the consultations for which the patients subsequently exhibited good adherence behaviour do not feature a single patient clarification, which may be linked to psychiatrist clarity rather than lack of effort or engagement on the patient's part.

The high accuracies with lexical features show that some aspects of the consultations do enable accurate prediction of adherence, PEQ measures and symptoms. However, as the features which allow us to achieve such good results rely on specific words used, it is unclear how generalisable or interpretable such results are. The lexical features chosen do generalise over our dataset (in which individual patients appear only once), and exclude doctor talk, so cannot be simply picking out unique unigram signatures relating to individual patients or doctors; however, given the small size of the dataset used for this initial investigation with its constrained domain, genre and topics, and the use of the whole dataset to select predictive words, it is unclear whether these results will scale up to a larger dataset.

We therefore suspect that more general, higher-level dialogue features such as specific interaction phenomena (repair, question-answering) and/or more general models of topic may be required. While unigrams are too low-level to be explanatory and may not generalise, the dialogue features discussed are too high-level to be useful; we are therefore examining mid-level phenomena and models to capture the predictability while remaining general and providing more interpretable features and results. Although the word lists offer clues as to the relevance of specific words for the overall predictability, we would not like to leave it at that. Further experiments are therefore underway to investigate whether we can find a level of appropriate explanatory power and maximal predictivity using an interim level of analysis, for example with n-gram and part-of-speech-based models, topic models based on word distributions, and turn-taking phenomena. Additional experiments also look at the turn-level data to see if the patient led clarification factor can be directly extracted from the transcripts.

Adherence			PEQ overall			
air	grass	schizophrenic	20th	electric	onto	sometime
anyone	grave	sensation	ages	energy	overweight	son
balanced	guitar	sickness	angry	environment	oxygen	standing
bleach	h	simply	anxiety	experiencing	packed	stomach
build	hahaha	sodium	background	facilities	percent	suddenly
building	lager	stable	bladder	friendly	personally	sundays
busy	laying	stock	booked	helps	picture	suppose
challenge	lifting	symptoms	boy	ignore	played	table
chemical	lucky	talks	broken	immediately	programs	team
complaining	mates	teach	bus	increased	progress	television
cup	monthly	terminology	certificate	irritated	provide	thursdays
dates	mouse	throat	dead	kick	public	troubles
en	nowhere	virtually	deep	later	quid	uhhm
fill	pains	was	drunk	lee	radio	upsetting
finished	possibly	wave	earn	loose	realised	walks
fish	pr	weve	eeerrrr	low	reply	watchers
flashbacks	recent	worse	eerrmm	march	sat	wine
	removed	writing	eerrrmm	mates	shaky	
	ri			moments	sofa	

Table 3: Most predictive unigram features

References

Chih-Chung Chang and Chih-Jen Lin, 2001. *LIBSVM: a library for Support Vector Machines*. Software available at `http://www.csie.ntu.edu.tw/~cjlin/libsvm`.

M. Colman and P. G. T. Healey. 2011. The distribution of repair in dialogue. In *Proceedings of the 33rd Annual Meeting of the Cognitive Science Society*, pages 1563–1568, Boston, MA.

Mark Hall, Eibe Frank, Geoffrey Holmes, Bernhard Pfahringer, Peter Reutemann, and Ian H. Witten. 2009. The WEKA data mining software: An update. *SIGDKDD Explorations*, 11(1):10–18.

M. Heldner and J. Edlund. 2010. Pauses, gaps and overlaps in conversations. *Journal of Phonetics*, 38(4):555–568.

S.R. Kay, A. Fiszbein, and L.A. Opfer. 1987. The positive and negative syndrome scale (PANSS) for schizophrenia. *Schizophrenia bulletin*, 13(2):261.

R. McCabe, C. Heath, T. Burns, S. Priebe, and J. Skelton. 2002. Engagement of patients with psychosis in the consultation: conversation analytic study. *British Medical Journal*, 325(7373):1148–1151.

R. McCabe, M. Lavelle, S. Bremner, D. Dodwell, P. G. T. Healey, R. Laugharne, S. Priebe, and A. Snell. in preparation. Shared understanding in psychiatrist-patient communication: Association with treatment adherence in schizophrenia.

E.A. Schegloff. 1992. Repair after next turn: The last structurally provided defense of intersubjectivity in conversation. *American Journal of Sociology*, pages 1295–1345.

S. Steine, A. Finset, and E. Laerum. 2001. A new, brief questionnaire (PEQ) developed in primary health care for measuring patients' experience of interaction, emotion and consultation outcome. *Family practice*, 18(4):410–418.

M. Themistocleous, R. McCabe, N. Rees, I. Hassan, P. G. T. Healey, and S. Priebe. 2009. Establishing mutual understanding in interaction: An analysis of conversational repair in psychiatric consultations. *Communication & Medicine*, 6(2):165–176.

D.R. Traum and J.F. Allen. 1992. A speech acts approach to grounding in conversation. In *Second International Conference on Spoken Language Processing*.

Reinforcement Learning of Question-Answering Dialogue Policies for Virtual Museum Guides

Teruhisa Misu[1]*, Kallirroi Georgila[2], Anton Leuski[2], David Traum[2]
[1]National Institute of Information and Communications Technology (NICT), Kyoto, Japan
[2]USC Institute for Creative Technologies, Playa Vista, CA, USA
teruhisa.misu@nict.go.jp, {kgeorgila,leuski,traum}@ict.usc.edu

Abstract

We use Reinforcement Learning (RL) to learn question-answering dialogue policies for a real-world application. We analyze a corpus of interactions of museum visitors with two virtual characters that serve as guides at the Museum of Science in Boston, in order to build a realistic model of user behavior when interacting with these characters. A simulated user is built based on this model and used for learning the dialogue policy of the virtual characters using RL. Our learned policy outperforms two baselines (including the original dialogue policy that was used for collecting the corpus) in a simulation setting.

1 Introduction

In the last 10 years Reinforcement Learning (RL) has attracted much attention in the dialogue community, to the extent that we can now consider RL as the state-of-the-art in statistical dialogue management. RL is used in the framework of Markov Decision Processes (MDPs) or Partially Observable Markov Decision Processes (POMDPs). In this paradigm dialogue moves transition between dialogue states and rewards are given at the end of a successful dialogue. The goal of RL is to learn a dialogue policy, i.e. the optimal action that the system should take at each possible dialogue state. Typically rewards depend on the domain and can include factors such as task completion, dialogue length, and user satisfaction. Traditional RL algorithms require on the order of thousands of dialogues to achieve good performance. Because it is very difficult to collect such a large number of dialogues with real users, instead, simulated users (SUs), i.e. models that simulate the behavior of real users, are employed (Georgila et al., 2006). Through the interaction between the system and the SUs thousands of dialogues can be generated and used for learning. A good SU should be able to replicate the behavior of a real user in the same dialogue context (Ai and Litman, 2008).

Most research in RL for dialogue management has been done in the framework of slot-filling applications (Georgila et al., 2010; Thomson and Young, 2010), largely ignoring other types of dialogue. In this paper we focus on the problem of learning dialogue policies for question-answering characters. With question-answering systems (or characters), the natural language understanding task is to retrieve the best response to a user initiative, and the main dialogue policy decision is whether to provide this best response or some other kind of move (e.g. a request for repair, clarification, or topic change), when the best answer does not seem to be good enough. Note that often in the literature the term question-answering is used for slot-filling dialogue systems as well, in the sense that the user asks some questions, for example, about restaurants in a particular area, and the system answers by providing a list of options, for example, restaurants. We use the term "question-answering" for systems where user questions can be independent of one another (follow-up questions are possible though) and do not have the objective of reducing the search space and retrieving results from a database of e.g. restaurants, flights, etc. Thus examples of question-answering

* This work was done when the first author was a visiting researcher at USC/ICT.

characters can be virtual interviewees (that can answer questions, e.g. about an incident), virtual scientists (that can answer general science-related questions), and so forth.

For our experiments we use a corpus (Aggarwal et al., 2012) of interactions of real users with two virtual characters, the Twins, that serve as guides at the Museum of Science in Boston (Swartout et al., 2010). The role of these virtual characters is to entertain and educate the museum visitors. They can answer queries about themselves and their technology, generally about science, as well as questions related to the exhibits of the museum. An example interaction between a museum visitor and the Twins is shown in Figure 1. The dialogue policy of the Twins was arbitrarily hand-crafted (see section 7 for details) and many other policies are possible (including Baseline 2, presented in section 7, and taking more advantage of question topics and context). We propose to use RL for optimizing the system's response generation. This is a real-world application for which RL appears to be an appropriate method.

Although there are similarities between question-answering and slot-filling dialogues there are also a number of differences, such as the reward function and the behavior of the users. As discussed later in detail, in question-answering the users have a number of questions that they are planning to ask (stock of queries), which can be increased or decreased depending not only on whether they received the information that they wanted but also on how satisfied they are with the interaction. The system has to plan ahead in order to maximize the number of successful responses that it provides to user queries. At the same time it needs to avoid providing incorrect or incoherent responses so that the user does not give up the interaction.

One of the challenges of our task is to define an appropriate reward function. Unlike slot-filling dialogues, it is not clear what makes an interaction with a question-answering system successful. A second challenge is that in a museum setting it is not clear what constitutes a dialogue session. Often two or more users alternate in asking questions, which further complicates the problem of defining a good reward function. A third challenge is that the domain is not well defined, i.e. users do not know in advance what the system is capable of (what kind of questions the characters can answer). Moreover, there are many cases of "junk" user questions (e.g. "are you stupid?") or even user prompts in languages other than English (e.g. "hola").

User: What are your names? (ASR: `what are your names`)

Ada: My name's Ada.

Grace: And I'm Grace. We're your Virtual Museum Guides. With your help, we can suggest exhibits that will get you thinking! Or answer questions about things you may have seen here.

Ada: What do you want to learn about?

User: Artificial intelligence. (ASR: `is artificial intelligence`)

Grace: One example of AI, or Artificial Intelligence, is 20Q, an online computer activity here at Computer Place that asks you questions to guess what you're thinking.

Ada: I wish we'd been programmed to do that. Nah... on second thought, I prefer just answering your questions.

Grace: That takes AI too.

Figure 1: Example dialogue between the Twins virtual characters and a museum visitor.

We first analyze our corpus in order to build a realistic model of user behavior when interacting with the virtual characters. A SU is built based on this model and used for learning the dialogue policy of the virtual characters using RL. Then we compare our learned policy with two baselines, one of which is the dialogue policy of the original system that was used for collecting our corpus and that is currently installed at the Museum of Science in Boston. Our learned policy outperforms both baselines in a simulation setting.

To our knowledge this is the first study that uses RL for learning this type of question-answering dialogue policy. Furthermore, unlike most studies that use data collected by having paid subjects interact with the system, we use data collected from real users, in our case museum visitors.[1] We also compare our learned dialogue policy with the dialogue policy of the original system that is currently installed at the Museum of Science in Boston.

The structure of the paper is as follows. In sec-

[1]Note that the CMU "Let's Go!" corpus is another case of using real user data for learning dialogue policies for the Spoken Dialogue Challenge.

tion 2 we present related work. Section 3 provides a brief introduction to RL and section 4 describes our corpus. Then in section 5 we explain how we built our SU from the corpus, and in section 6 we describe our learning methodology. Section 7 presents our evaluation results. Finally section 8 presents some discussion and ideas for future work together with our conclusion.

2 Related Work

To date, RL has mainly been used for learning dialogue policies for slot-filling applications such as restaurant recommendations (Jurčíček et al., 2012), sightseeing recommendations (Misu et al., 2010), appointment scheduling (Georgila et al., 2010), etc., largely ignoring other types of dialogue. Recently there have been some experiments on applying RL to the more difficult problem of learning negotiation policies (Heeman, 2009; Georgila and Traum, 2011a; Georgila and Traum, 2011b). Also, RL has been applied to tutoring domains (Tetreault and Litman, 2008; Chi et al., 2011).

There has been a lot of work on developing question-answering systems with dialogue capabilities, e.g. (Jönsson et al., 2004; op den Akker et al., 2005; Varges et al., 2009). Most of these systems are designed for information extraction from structured or unstructured databases in closed or open domains. One could think of them as adding dialogue capabilities to standard question-answering systems such as the ones used in the TREC question-answering track (Voorhees, 2001). Other work has focused on a different type of question-answering dialogue, i.e. question-answering dialogues that follow the form of an interview and that can be used, for example, for training purposes (Leuski et al., 2006; Gandhe et al., 2009). But none of these systems uses RL.

To our knowledge no one has used RL for learning policies for question-answering systems as defined in section 1. Note that Rieser and Lemon (2009) used RL for question-answering, but in their case, question-answering refers to asking for information about songs and artists in an mp3 database, which is very much like a slot-filling task, i.e. the system has to fill a number of slots (e.g. name of band, etc.) in order to query a database of songs and present the right information to the user. As discussed in section 1 our task is rather different.

3 Reinforcement Learning

A dialogue policy is a function from contexts to (possibly probabilistic) decisions that the dialogue system will make in those contexts. Reinforcement Learning (RL) is a machine learning technique used to learn the policy of the system. For an RL-based dialogue system the objective is to maximize the reward it gets during an interaction. RL is used in the framework of Markov Decision Processes (MDPs) or Partially Observable Markov Decision Processes (POMDPs).

In this paper we follow a POMDP-based approach. A POMDP is defined as a tuple (S, A, P, R, O, Z, γ, b_0) where S is the set of states (representing different contexts) which the system may be in (the system's world), A is the set of actions of the system, $P : S \times A \rightarrow P(S, A)$ is the set of transition probabilities between states after taking an action, $R : S \times A \rightarrow \Re$ is the reward function, O is a set of observations that the system can receive about the world, Z is a set of observation probabilities $Z : S \times A \rightarrow Z(S, A)$, and γ a discount factor weighting long-term rewards. At any given time step i the world is in some unobserved state $s_i \in S$. Because s_i is not known exactly, we keep a distribution over states called a *belief state* b, thus $b(s_i)$ is the probability of being in state s_i, with initial belief state b_0. When the system performs an action $\alpha_i \in A$ based on b, following a policy $\pi : S \rightarrow A$, it receives a reward $r_i(s_i, \alpha_i) \in \Re$ and transitions to state s_{i+1} according to $P(s_{i+1}|s_i, \alpha_i) \in P$. The system then receives an observation o_{i+1} according to $P(o_{i+1}|s_{i+1}, \alpha_i)$. The quality of the policy π followed by the agent is measured by the expected future reward also called Q-function, $Q^{\pi} : S \times A \rightarrow \Re$.

There are several algorithms for learning the optimal dialogue policy and we use Natural Actor Critic (NAC) (Peters and Schaal, 2008), which adopts a natural policy gradient method for policy optimization, also used by (Thomson and Young, 2010; Jurčíček et al., 2012). Policy gradient methods do not directly update the value of state S or Q-function (expected future reward). Instead, the policy π (or parameter $\mathbf{\Theta}$, see below) is directly updated so as to increase the reward of dialogue episodes generated by the previous policy.

A system action a_{sys} is sampled based on the following soft-max (Boltzmann) policy:

$$\pi(a_{sys}=k|\Phi) = Pr(a_{sys}=k|\mathbf{\Phi},\mathbf{\Theta}) = \frac{\exp(\sum_{i=1}^{I}\phi_i\cdot\theta_{ki})}{\sum_{j=1}^{J}\exp(\sum_{i=1}^{I}\phi_i\cdot\theta_{ji})}$$

Here, $\mathbf{\Phi} = (\phi_1, \phi_2, \ldots, \phi_I)$ is a basis function, which is a vector function of the belief state. $\mathbf{\Theta} = (\theta_{11}, \theta_{12}, \ldots \theta_{1I}, \ldots, \theta_{JI})$ consists of J (# actions) $\times$ I (# features) parameters. The parameter θ_{ji} works as a weight for the i-th feature of the action j and determines the likelihood that the action j is selected. $\mathbf{\Theta}$ is the target of optimization by RL.

During training, RL algorithms require thousands of interactions between the system and the user to achieve good performance. For this reason we need to build a simulated user (SU) (Georgila et al., 2006), that will behave similarly to a real user, and will interact with the policy for thousands of iterations to generate data in order to explore the search space and thus facilitate learning.

Topic	Example user question/prompt
introduction	Hello.
personal	Who are you named after?
school	Where do you go to school?
technology	What is artificial intelligence?
interfaces	What is a virtual human?
exhibition	What can I do at Robot Park?

Table 1: Topics of user questions/prompts.

4 The Twins Corpus

As mentioned in section 1 the Twins corpus (Aggarwal et al., 2012) was collected at the Museum of Science in Boston (Swartout et al., 2010). The Twins can answer a number of user questions/prompts in several topics, i.e. about themselves and their technology, about science in general, and about exhibits in the museum. We have divided these topics in six categories shown in Table 1 together with an example for each category.

An example interaction between a museum visitor and the Twins is shown in Figure 1. We can also see the output of the speech recognizer. In the part of the corpus that we use for our experiment automatic speech recognition (ASR) was performed by Otosense, an ASR engine developed by the USC SAIL lab. Natural language understanding and dialogue management are both performed as a single task by the NPCEditor (Leuski and Traum, 2010), a text classification system that classifies the user's query to a system's answer using cross-language information retrieval techniques. When the system fails to understand the user's query it can prompt her to do one of the following:

- rephrase her query (from now on referred to as off-topic response 1, OT1), e.g. "please rephrase your question";
- prompt the user to ask a particular question that the system knows that it can handle (from now on referred to as off-topic response 2, OT2), e.g. "you may ask us about our hobbies";
- cease the dialogue and check out the "behind the scenes" exhibit which explains how the virtual characters work (from now on referred to as off-topic response 3, OT3).

The Twins corpus contains about 200,000 spoken utterances from museum visitors (primarily children) and members of staff or volunteers. For the purposes of this paper we used 1,178 dialogue sessions (11,074 pairs of user and system utterances) collected during March to May 2011. This subset of the corpus contains manual transcriptions of user queries, system responses, and correct responses to user queries (the responses that the system should give when ASR is perfect).

5 User Simulation Model

In order to build a model of user behavior we perform an analysis of the corpus. One of our challenges is that the boundaries between dialogue sessions are hard to define, i.e. it is very hard to automatically calculate whether the same or a new user speaks to the system, unless complex voice identification techniques are employed. We make the reasonable assumption that a new dialogue session starts when there are no questions to the system for a time interval greater than 120 sec.

From each session we extract 30 features. A full list is shown in Table 7 in the Appendix. Our goal is to measure the contribution of each feature to the user's decision with respect to two issues: (1) whether the user will cease the dialogue or not, and (2) what kind of query the user will make next, based on what has happened in the dialogue so far. To do that we use the Chi-squared test, which is commonly used for feature selection.

So to measure the contribution of each feature to whether the user will cease the dialogue or not, we give a binary label to each user query in our corpus, i.e. 1 when the query is the last user query in the dialogue session and 0 otherwise. Then we calculate the contribution of each feature for estimating this label. In Table 8, column 1, in the Appendix, we can see the 10 features that contribute the most to predicting whether the user will cease the dialogue. As we can see the dominant features are not whether the system correctly responded to the user's query, but mostly features based on the dialogue history (e.g. the number of the system's off-topic responses so far) and user type information. Indeed, a further analysis of the corpus showed that children tend to have longer dialogue sessions than adults.

Our next step is the estimation of the contribution of each feature for predicting the user's next query. The label we predict here is the topic of the user's utterance (personal, exhibition, etc., see Table 1). We can see the 10 most predictive features in Table 8, column 2, in the Appendix. The contribution of the most recent user's utterance (previous topic category) is larger than that of dialogue history features. This tendency is the same when we ignore repeated user queries, e.g. when the system makes an error and the user rephrases her query (see Table 8, column 3, in the Appendix). The user type is important for predicting the next user query. In Figure 2 we can see the percentages of user queries per user type and topic.

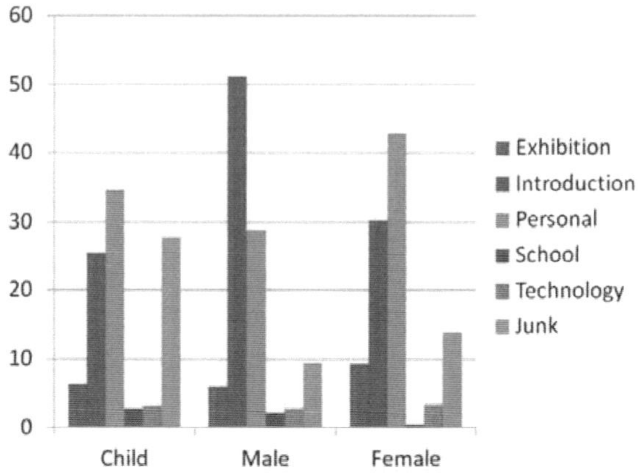

Figure 2: Percentages of user queries per user type and topic.

Based on the above analysis we build a simulated user (SU). The SU simulates the following:

- User type (child, male, female): a child user is sampled with a probability of 51.1%, a male with 31.1%, and a female with 17.8%. These probabilities are estimated from the corpus.

- Number of questions the user is planning to ask (stock of queries): We assume here that the user is planning to ask a number of questions. This number may increase or decrease. For example, it can increase when the system prompts the user to ask about a particular topic (OT2 prompt), and it may decrease when the user decides to cease the dialogue immediately. The number of questions is sampled from a user type dependent Zipf distribution (strictly speaking the continuous version of the distribution; Parato distribution) the parameter of which is estimated from the corpus using the maximum likelihood criterion. We chose Zipf because it is a long-tail distribution that fits our data (users are not expected to ask a large number of questions). According to this distribution a child user is more likely to have a larger stock of queries than a male or female adult.

- User's reaction: The user has to decide on one of the following. Go to the next topic (Go-on); cease the dialogue if there are no more questions in the stock of queries (Out-of-stock); rephrase the previous query (Rephrase); abandon the dialogue (Give-up) regardless of the remaining questions in the stock; generate a query based on a system recommendation, OT2 prompt (Refill). We calculate the user type dependent probability for these actions from the corpus. But the problem here is that it is not possible to distinguish between the case in which the user asked all the questions in the stock of queries (i.e. all the questions she intended to ask) and left, from the case in which she gave up and abandoned the dialogue. We estimate the percentage of "Give-up" as the difference between the ratio of "Cease" after an incorrect response and the ratio of “Cease” after a correct response, assuming a similar percentage of “Out-of-stock” for both correct and incorrect responses. Likewise, the difference in ”Go-on” for OT2 and other responses is attributed to ”Refill”. The probability of “Rephrase” is estimated from the corpus. For example the probability that a child will rephrase after an OT1 system prompt is 54%, after an erroneous system prompt 38%, etc.

- Topic for next user query (e.g. introduction, personal, etc.): The SU selects a new topic based on user type dependent topic transition bigram probabilities estimated from the corpus.

- User utterance: The SU selects a user utterance from the corpus that matches the current user type and topic. We have split the corpus in groups of user utterances based on user type and topic and we sample accordingly.

- Utterance timing: We simulate utterance timing (duration of pause between system utterance and next user query) per user type and user change. The utterance timing is sampled based on a Gaussian distribution the parameters of which are set based on the corpus statistics. For example, the average duration of a session until the user changes is 62.7 sec with a standard deviation of 71.2 sec.

6 Learning Question-Answering Policies

Our goal is to use RL in order to optimize the system’s response generation. As we saw in the previous section the SU generates a user utterance from our corpus. We do not currently use ASR error simulation but instead a real ASR engine. So the audio file that corresponds to the selected user utterance is forwarded to 3 ASR systems, with child, male, and female acoustic models (AMs) respectively. Then these recognition results are forwarded to the NPCEditor that produces an N-best list of possible system responses (retrieval results). That is, as mentioned in section 4, the NPCEditor classifies each ASR result to a system answer using cross-language information retrieval techniques. The policy can choose one of the NPCEditor retrieval results or reject them and instead present one of the three off-topic prompts (OT1, OT2, or OT3). So the system has 10 possible actions to choose between:

- use the response with the best or the second best score retrieved from the NPCEditor based on a child AM (2 actions);

- use the response with the best or the second best score retrieved from the NPCEditor based on a male AM (2 actions);

- use the response with the best or the second best score retrieved from the NPCEditor based on a female AM (2 actions);

- use the response with the best of the 6 aforementioned scores of the NPCEditor;

- use off-topic prompt OT1;

- use off-topic prompt OT2;

- use off-topic prompt OT3.

We use the following features to optimize our dialogue policy (see section 3). We use the 6 retrieval scores of the NPCEditor (the 2 best scores for each user type ASR result), the previous system action, the ASR confidence scores, the voting scores (calculated by adding the scores of the results that agree), the system’s belief on the user type and user change, and the system’s belief on the user’s previous topic. So we need to learn a POMDP-based policy using these 42 features.

Unlike slot-filling dialogues, defining the reward function is not a simple task (e.g. reward the system for filled and confirmed slots). So in order to define the reward function and thus measure the quality of the dialogue we set up a questionnaire. We asked 5 people to rate 10 dialogues in a 5-Likert scale. Each dialogue session included 5 question-answer pairs. Then we used regression analysis to set the reward for each of the question-answer pair categories shown in Table 2. So for example, responding correctly to an in-domain user question is rewarded (+23.2) whereas providing an erroneous response to a junk question, i.e. treating junk questions as if they were in-domain questions, is penalized (-14.7).

One limitation of this reward function (Reward function 1) is that it does not take into account whether the user has previously experienced an off-topic system prompt. To account for that we define Reward function 2. Here we consider the number of off-topic responses in the two most recent system prompts. Reward function 2 is shown in Table 3.

QA Pair	Reward
in-domain → correct	23.2
in-domain → error	-12.2
in-domain → OT1	-5.4
in-domain → OT2	-8.4
in-domain → OT3	-9.6
junk question → error	-14.7
junk question → OT1	4.8
junk question → OT2	10.2
junk question → OT3	6.1
give up	-16.9

Table 2: Reward function 1.

QA Pair	Reward
in-domain → correct	16.9
in-domain → error	-2.0
in-domain → OT1	13.9
in-domain → OT1(2)	7.3
in-domain → OT2	-7.9
in-domain → OT2(2)	4.2
in-domain → OT3	-15.8
in-domain → OT3(2)	-8.3
junk question → error	-4.6
junk question → OT1	4.1
junk question → OT1(2)	4.1
junk question → OT2	43.4
junk question → OT2(2)	-33.1
junk question → OT3	3.1
junk question → OT3(2)	6.1
give up	-19.5

Table 3: Reward function 2.

As we can see, providing an OT2 as the first off-topic response is a poor action (-7.9); it is preferable to ask the user to rephrase her question (OT1) as a first attempt to recover from the error (+13.9). On the other hand, providing an OT2 prompt, after an off-topic prompt has occured in the previous system prompt, is a reasonable action (+4.2).

7 Evaluation

We compare our learned policy with two baselines. The first baseline, Baseline 1, is the dialogue policy that is used by our system that is currently installed at the Museum of Science in Boston. Baseline 1 selects the best ASR result (i.e. the result with the highest confidence score) out of the results with the 3 different AMs (child, male, and female), and forwards this result to the NPCEditor to retrieve the system's response. If the NPCEditor score is higher than an emprically set pre-defined threshold (see (Leuski and Traum, 2010) for details), then the system presents the retrieved response, otherwise it presents an off-topic prompt. The system presents these off-topic prompts in a fixed order. First, OT1, then OT2, and then OT3.

We also have Baseline 2, which forwards all 3 ASR results to the NPCEditor (using child, male, and female AMs). Then the NPCEditor retrieves 3 results, one for each one of the 3 ASR results, and selects the retrieved result with the highest score. Again if this score is higher than a threshold, the system will present this result, otherwise it will present an off-topic prompt.

Each policy interacts with the SU for 10,000 dialogue sessions and we calculate the average accumulated reward for each dialogue. In Tables 4 and 5 we can see our results for Reward functions 1 and 2 respectively. In both cases the learned policy outperforms both baselines. For both reward functions the most predictive feature is the ASR confidence score when combined with the NPCEditor's retrieval score and the previous system action. Also, for both reward functions the second best feature is "voting" when combined with the retrieval score and the previous system action.

In Table 6 we can see how often the learned policy, which is based on Reward function 1 using all features, selects each one of the 10 system actions (200,000 system turns in total).

Policy	Avg Reward
Baseline 1	24.76 (19.29)
Baseline 2	51.63 (49.84)
Learned Policy - Features	
Retrieval score	
+ system action (*)	46.74
(*) + ASR confidence score	61.59
(*) + User type probability	47.28
(*) + Estimated previous topic	47.87
(*) + Voting	59.94
All features	**60.93**

Table 4: Results with reward function 1. The values in parentheses for Baselines 1 and 2 are the rewards when the NPCEditor does not use the pre-defined threshold.

Policy	Avg Reward
Baseline 1	39.40 (38.51)
Baseline 2	55.45 (54.49)
Learned Policy - Features	
Retrieval score	
+ system action (*)	49.15
(*) + ASR confidence score	69.51
(*) + User type probability	50.15
(*) + Estimated previous topic	49.84
(*) + Voting	69.06
All features	**73.59**

Table 5: Results with reward function 2. The values in parentheses for Baselines 1 and 2 are the rewards when the NPCEditor does not use the pre-defined threshold.

System Action	Frequency
Child + 1st best score	10.33%
Child + 2nd best score	2.70%
Male + 1st best score	13.72%
Male + 2nd best score	1.03%
Female + 1st best score	39.73%
Female + 2nd best score	0.79%
Best of scores 1-6	2.38%
OT1	11.01%
OT2	6.86%
OT3	11.45%

Table 6: Frequency of the system actions of the learned policy that is based on Reward function 1 using all features.

8 Discussion and Conclusion

We showed that RL is a promising technique for learning question-answering policies. Currently we use the same SU for both training and testing the policies. One could argue that this favors the learned policy over the baselines. Because our SU is based on general corpus statistics (probability that the user is child or male or female, number of questions the user is planning to ask, probability of moving to the next topic or ceasing the dialogue, utterance timing statistics) rather than sequential information we believe that this is acceptable. We only use sequential information when we calculate the next topic that the user will choose. That is, due to the way the SU is built and its randomness, we believe that it is very unlikely that the same patterns that were generated during training will be generated during testing. Thus we do not anticipate that our results would be different if for testing we used a SU trained on a different part of the corpus, or that the learned policy is favored over the baselines. However, this is something to verify experimentally in future work.

For future work we would also like to do the following. First of all, currently we are in the process of analyzing user satisfaction questionnaires from museum visitors in order to define a better reward function. Second, we would like to use voice identification techniques to automatically estimate from the corpus the statistics of having more than one user or alternating users in the same session. Third, and most important, we would like to incorporate the learned policy into the system that is currently installed in the museum and evaluate it with real users. Fourth, currently our SU is based on only some of our findings from the analysis of the corpus. We intend to build a more complex and hopefully more realistic SU based on our full corpus analysis. Finally, we will also experiment with learning policies directly from the data (Li et al., 2009).

To conclude, we analyzed a corpus of interactions of museum visitors with two virtual characters that serve as guides at the Museum of Science in Boston, in order to build a realistic model of user behavior when interacting with these characters. Based on this analysis, we built a SU and used it for learning the dialogue policy of the virtual characters using RL. We compared our learned policy with two baselines, one of which was the dialogue policy of the original system that was used for collecting the corpus and that is currently installed at the Museum of Science in Boston. Our learned policy outperformed both baselines which shows that RL is a promising technique for learning question-answering dialogue policies.

Acknowledgments

This work was funded by the NSF grant #1117313. The Twins corpus collection was supported by the NSF grant #0813541.

References

Priti Aggarwal, Ron Artstein, Jillian Gerten, Athanasios Katsamanis, Shrikanth Narayanan, Angela Nazarian, and David Traum. 2012. The Twins corpus of museum visitor questions. In *Proc. of the Language Resources and Evaluation Conference (LREC)*, pages 2355–2361, Istanbul, Turkey.

Hua Ai and Diane Litman. 2008. Assessing dialog system user simulation evaluation measures using human judges. In *Proc. of the Annual Meeting of the Association for Computational Linguistics: Human Language Technologies (ACL-HLT)*, pages 622–629, Columbus, OH, USA.

Min Chi, Kurt VanLehn, Diane Litman, and Pamela Jordan. 2011. Empirically evaluating the application of reinforcement learning to the induction of effective and adaptive pedagogical strategies. *User Modeling and User-Adapted Interaction*, 21(1-2):137–180.

Sudeep Gandhe, Nicolle Whitman, David Traum, and Ron Artstein. 2009. An integrated authoring tool for tactical questioning dialogue systems. In *Proc. of the IJCAI Workshop on Knowledge and Reasoning in Practical Dialogue Systems*, Pasadena, CA, USA.

Kallirroi Georgila and David Traum. 2011a. Learning culture-specific dialogue models from non culture-specific data. In *Proc. of HCI International, Lecture Notes in Computer Science Vol. 6766*, pages 440–449, Orlando, FL, USA.

Kallirroi Georgila and David Traum. 2011b. Reinforcement learning of argumentation dialogue policies in negotiation. In *Proc. of Interspeech*, pages 2073–2076, Florence, Italy.

Kallirroi Georgila, James Henderson, and Oliver Lemon. 2006. User simulation for spoken dialogue systems: Learning and evaluation. In *Proc. of Interspeech*, pages 1065–1068, Pittsburgh, PA, USA.

Kallirroi Georgila, Maria K. Wolters, and Johanna D. Moore. 2010. Learning dialogue strategies from older and younger simulated users. In *Proc. of the Annual SIGdial Meeting on Discourse and Dialogue (SIGdial)*, pages 103–106, Tokyo, Japan.

Peter A. Heeman. 2009. Representing the reinforcement learning state in a negotiation dialogue. In *Proc. of the IEEE Automatic Speech Recognition and Understanding Workshop (ASRU)*, Merano, Italy.

Arne Jönsson, Frida Andén, Lars Degerstedt, Annika Flycht-Eriksson, Magnus Merkel, and Sara Norberg. 2004. Experiences from combining dialogue system development with information access techniques. In *New Directions in Question Answering, Mark T. Maybury (Ed)*, pages 153–164. AAAI/MIT Press.

Filip Jurčíček, Blaise Thomson, and Steve Young. 2012. Reinforcement learning for parameter estimation in statistical spoken dialogue systems. *Computer Speech and Language*, 26(3):168–192.

Anton Leuski and David Traum. 2010. Practical language processing for virtual humans. In *Proc. of the 22nd Annual Conference on Innovative Applications of Artificial Intelligence (IAAI)*, Atlanta, GA, USA.

Anton Leuski, Ronakkumar Patel, David Traum, and Brandon Kennedy. 2006. Building effective question answering characters. In *Proc. of the Annual SIGdial Meeting on Discourse and Dialogue (SIGdial)*, pages 18–27, Sydney, Australia.

Lihong Li, Jason D. Williams, and Suhrid Balakrishnan. 2009. Reinforcement learning for dialog management using least-squares policy iteration and fast feature selection. In *Proc. of Interspeech*, pages 2475–2478, Brighton, United Kingdom.

Teruhisa Misu, Komei Sugiura, Kiyonori Ohtake, Chiori Hori, Hideki Kashioka, Hisashi Kawai, and Satoshi Nakamura. 2010. Modeling spoken decision making dialogue and optimization of its dialogue strategy. In *Proc. of the Annual SIGdial Meeting on Discourse and Dialogue (SIGdial)*, pages 221–224, Tokyo, Japan.

Rieks op den Akker, Harry Bunt, Simon Keizer, and Boris van Schooten. 2005. From question answering to spoken dialogue: Towards an information search assistant for interactive multimodal information extraction. In *Proc. of Interspeech*, pages 2793–2796, Lisbon, Portugal.

Jan Peters and Stefan Schaal. 2008. Natural actor-critic. *Neurocomputing*, 71(7-9):1180–1190.

Verena Rieser and Oliver Lemon. 2009. Does this list contain what you were searching for? Learning adaptive dialogue strategies for interactive question answering. *Natural Language Engineering*, 15(1):55–72.

William Swartout, David Traum, Ron Artstein, Dan Noren, Paul Debevec, Kerry Bronnenkant, Josh Williams, Anton Leuski, Shrikanth Narayanan, Diane Piepol, Chad Lane, Jacquelyn Morie, Priti Aggarwal, Matt Liewer, Jen-Yuan Chiang, Jillian Gerten, Selina Chu, and Kyle White. 2010. Ada and Grace: Toward realistic and engaging virtual museum guides. In *Proc. of the International Conference on Intelligent Virtual Agents (IVA)*, pages 286–300, Philadelphia, PA, USA.

Joel R. Tetreault and Diane J. Litman. 2008. A reinforcement learning approach to evaluating state representations in spoken dialogue systems. *Speech Communication*, 50(8-9):683–696.

Blaise Thomson and Steve Young. 2010. Bayesian update of dialogue state: A POMDP framework for spoken dialogue systems. *Computer Speech and Language*, 24(4):562–588.

Sebastian Varges, Fuliang Weng, and Heather Pon-Barry. 2009. Interactive question answering and constraint relexation in spoken dialogue systems. *Natural Language Engineering*, 15(1):9–30.

Ellen M. Voorhees. 2001. The TREC question answering track. *Natural Language Engineering*, 7(4):361–378.

Appendix

Features	Features
average ASR accuracy of user queries	if system correctly answered current user query
# user queries	if system responded with off-topic prompt to current user query
# correct system responses	# times user repeated current query
# incorrect system responses	# successive incorrect system responses
# off-topic system prompts	# successive off-topic system prompts
% correct system responses	# user queries for topic "introduction"
% incorrect system responses	# user queries for topic "personal"
user type (child, male, female)	# user queries for topic "school"
if user asks example query 1	# user queries for topic "technology"
if user asks example query 2	# user queries for topic "interfaces"
if user asks example query 3	# user queries for topic "exhibition"
if user asks example query 4	# user queries for other topics
if system correctly responds to example query 1	if system correctly responds to example query 3
if system correctly responds to example query 2	if system correctly responds to example query 4
# junk user queries	previous topic category

Table 7: List of features used in predicting when the user will cease a session (Cease Dialogue), what the user will say next (Say Next 1), and what the user will say next after removing repeated user queries (Say Next 2). Example query 1 is "who are you named after?"; example query 2 is "are you a computer?"; example query 3 is "what do you like to do for fun?"; example query 4 is "what is artificial intelligence?".

Cease Dialogue	Say Next 1	Say Next 2
average ASR accuracy of user queries	previous topic category	previous topic category
user type (child, male, female)	# user queries for topic "personal"	# junk user queries
# off-topic system prompts	# user queries	# successive incorrect system responses
# successive off-topic system prompts	# junk user queries	if system correctly answered current user query
# incorrect system responses	% correct system responses	user type (child, male, female)
# user queries	% incorrect system responses	% incorrect system responses
# junk user queries	# incorrect system responses	% correct system responses
# user queries for other topics	# user queries for other topics	# incorrect system responses
if system responded with off-topic prompt to current user query	# correct system responses	# off-topic system prompts
% correct system responses	user type (child, male, female)	# user queries

Table 8: List of the 10 most dominant features (in order of importance) in predicting when the user will cease a session (Cease Dialogue), what the user will say next (Say Next 1), and what the user will say next after removing repeated user queries (Say Next 2).

From Strangers to Partners: Examining Convergence within a Longitudinal Study of Task-Oriented Dialogue

Christopher M. Mitchell **Kristy Elizabeth Boyer** **James C. Lester**

Department of Computer Science
North Carolina State University
Raleigh, NC, USA
{cmmitch2, keboyer, lester}@ncsu.edu

Abstract

Convergence is thought to be an important phenomenon in dialogue through which interlocutors adapt to each other. Yet, its mechanisms and relationship to dialogue outcomes are not fully understood. This paper explores convergence in textual task-oriented dialogue during a longitudinal study. The results suggest that over time, convergence between interlocutors increases with successive dialogues. Additionally, for the tutorial dialogue domain at hand, convergence metrics were found to be significant predictors of dialogue outcomes such as learning, mental effort, and emotional states including frustration, boredom, and confusion. The results suggest ways in which dialogue systems may leverage convergence to enhance their interactions with users.

1 Introduction

Convergence is a widely observed phenomenon in dialogue, in which interlocutors adapt to the patterns in each other's utterances (Brennan 1996; Pickering and Garrod 2004). These patterns can include lexical choice (Hirschberg 2008; Ward and Litman 2007), syntactic choice (Reitter et al. 2006; Stoyanchev and Stent 2009) and loudness (Coulston et al. 2002). It is believed that convergence is indicative of shared understanding (Pickering and Garrod 2004), which makes it an important consideration for task-oriented dialogue systems.

In addition to facilitating shared understanding, convergence has also been associated with the success of dialogues in several domains (Steinhauser et al. 2011; Ward and Litman 2007), and can also be leveraged for lexical and syntactic priming that may improve performance of spoken dialogue systems via more accurate speech recognition (Stoyanchev and Stent 2009). While such results have established that convergence is an important dialogue phenomenon, the field does not yet fully understand how convergence is associated with dialogue success.

This paper examines surface-level and lexical convergence within textual task-oriented dialogues. The analysis considers three levels of convergence: utterance-level *short-term* priming effects, *conversation level* convergence effects, and *longitudinal* convergence effects, as interlocutors participate in six conversations together over the course of several weeks. Using these measures, we build multiple regression models that indicate ways in which convergence can predict both desirable and undesirable outcomes of task-oriented dialogues.

This paper makes several contributions. First, by examining convergence at several granularity levels and across multiple dialogues with the same partners, we gain insight into how convergence phenomena unfold over time. Second, the findings provide confirmatory evidence that in some domains, such as the tutorial dialogue considered here, lexical priming be associated with unintended consequences. Finally, we demonstrate that dialogue convergence is also associated with affective components such as frustration, engagement, and confusion. These results contribute to an understanding of convergence that may enable us to harness this phenomenon more effectively within dialogue systems.

2 Related Work

Convergence and the related concepts of alignment and priming have been extensively studied. Alignment, or the development of shared understanding, has been studied by Pickering and Garrod (2004) who propose that alignment on lower-level observable features is indicative of alignment at the level of conceptual models. The influence of shared representation in dialogue has also been explored in the context of learning; for example, Ward and Litman (2007) studied lexical convergence in human-human tutoring and found that the rate of priming, which measures student re-use of tutor words at various distances, was positively associated with learning for students with low initial test scores. Conversely, Steinhauser et al. (2011) analyzed lexical convergence in an automated dialogue-based physics tutor, and found that the level of the student mimicking the tutor was negatively correlated with learning. Thus, the relationship between dialogue convergence and learning is not fully understood, and may be highly dependent on context.

In addition to a theoretical link to shared representations, convergence has practical implications, in particular for speech recognition (Stoyanchev and Stent 2009). Brennan (1996) found that users adapt their lexical choices to match those of an automated system in both text-based and speech-based interactions, even when it is apparent that the system understood the user's original lexical choice. Convergence has even been found to occur in non-lexical aspects of a dialogue, such as users adapting their loudness levels to match that of a software agent (Coulston et al. 2002). Together, these results suggest that convergence has implications beyond lexical and syntactic choice.

3 Corpus

The corpus consists of text-based tutorial dialogues between two interlocutors, a tutor and a student, working together to complete tasks in the domain of introductory computer science (excerpt in Appendix A). The corpus was collected over two semesters, in which 67 first-year university students were selected from an introductory engineering course and assigned to one of seven tutors of varying levels of tutoring experience. Each student engaged in six task-based dialogues with a single tutor over four weeks with the goal of producing a working software artifact during each session. Each session included several subtasks, and time was strictly limited to forty minutes duration. The remote collaboration interface, shown in Figure 1, facilitated a real-time synchronized view of the workspace and dialogue. This paper considers dialogue utterances only, leaving to future work the analysis of task-related artifacts.

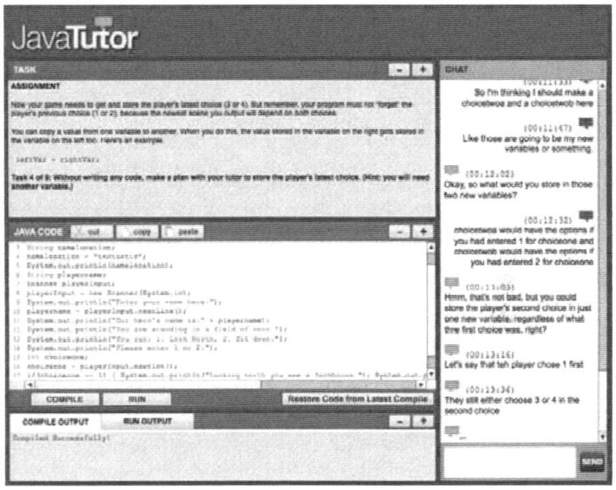

Figure 1. Task-oriented dialogue interface

The effectiveness of the dialogue was measured in several ways. First, student learning was measured as difference in score on pre-test and post-tests. Student engagement, or level of involvement during the dialogue, was measured with a brief survey after each dialogue (O'Brien and Toms 2010), as were student's satisfaction with the exchange, and a rating of how mentally challenging the task was perceived to be (Hart and Staveland 1988). Finally, the tutors were asked to rate their satisfaction with the effectiveness of each session and to report on their perceptions of the affective states of both interlocutors during the session. The students were not asked about their own affective states, as this may have introduced bias in subsequent dialogues.

4 Analysis

The goal of the analysis is to identify the characteristics of the dialogues that are predictive of the outcomes of interest, including learning, engagement, affect, and overall success of the dialogue as rated by the interlocutors. Summary statistics for the dialogues were computed, including time duration of the session, number of utterances, number of words, number of characters, mean word length, and lexicon size (Table 1). Stop words were not excluded from the analysis, in part due to specialized usage of common vocabulary in the computer science domain (e.g., *for*, *if*).

Although not traditionally considered a form of convergence, we were interested in the relationship between the levels of activity of the two interlocutors. To this end, we analyzed the number of utterances, words, and characters used by tutor and student, and found a significant positive correlation on these metrics ($p<0.0001$ for each).

The first convergence phenomenon considered centers on lexical priming, the tendency for one interlocutor to re-use words previously introduced by the other. We have utilized a priming metric computed as follows: Interlocutor A's *Priming Ratio* (PR) is the percent of Interlocutor A's words reused by Interlocutor B at a given distance *d*, where distance is measured in terms of number of Interlocutor B's utterances. Negative slope of PR over distance indicates a priming effect because an interlocutor was more likely to reuse a word shortly after its use by the other interlocutor. This metric has been used to investigate tutor priming (Steinhauser et al. 2011; Ward and Litman 2007), and we generalize it to measure priming for both interlocutors. Note that student PR, which reflects the extent to which the tutor adopted the student's lexical choice, is of particular interest from the perspective of dialogue system design, in which tutor utterances are system-generated.

	Tutor mean (SD)	Student mean (SD)
Surface Features		
Number of utterances	83.7 (28.8)	35.6 (13.1)
Number of words	580.9 (202.3)	170.1 (92.6)
Number of characters	2383.4 (886.6)	667.3 (386.0)
Mean word length	4.1 (0.2)	3.9 (0.3)
Lexicon size	329.7 (87.3)	106.3 (47.3)
Convergence Metrics		
Priming Ratio (1-10)	.030 (.02)	.047 (.02)
ΔPriming Ratio (1-10)	-.011 (.02)	-.017 (.04)
Max Priming Ratio	.052 (.02)	.091 (.04)
Matched Word Ratio	.233 (.09)	.386 (.08)

Table 1. Statistics for each metric

In addition to the Priming Ratio, we also computed a metric to reflect convergence: Interlocutor A's *Matched Word Ratio* (MWR) is the percent of Interlocutor A's words that had been previously used by Interlocutor B at any point in the dialogue history. Because it is backward-looking, this metric is applicable not only in a corpus study, but could also be used within a runtime system to track convergence as the dialogue unfolds.

5 Models and Results

Mean Matched Word Ratio for both interlocutors increased as sessions progressed, reflecting that the two dialogue partners used more of each other's words as they spent more time together. The Priming Ratio also revealed several phenomena in the corpus. Similarly to prior observations from tutorial dialogue (Ward and Litman 2007), we found that student reuse of tutor primes decreased with distance, indicating that a lexical priming effect occurred (Figure 2). This trend also occurred for tutor reuse of student primes (Figure 3). The effect was more pronounced in the tutor's PR than the student's PR; that is, there was more evidence that tutors converged to students in the short term. This finding may be associated in part with the higher number of tutor utterances: a distance in terms of number of tutor utterances represents fewer combined student and tutor utterances than the same distance in terms of student utterances. Additionally, tutor convergence may reflect a dimension of intentional pedagogical choice.

The Priming Ratio is designed to reflect short-term priming. However, there is evidence of a longer-term effect as the two interlocutors engaged in dialogue across multiple sessions. Figures 2 and 3 display Tutor's PR and Student's PR, respectively, by task set, of which there were six in the corpus study. The last task set displays an overall higher level of lexical convergence than the earlier sessions, and there is a general trend of increasing convergence as the number of sessions together increases.

In order to identify the features that were most predictive of dialogue outcomes, all of the convergence metrics and surface summary features were provided as input to a stepwise linear regression model. Standard greedy variable addition and removal was performed, with additional post-processing and re-training to eliminate instances of multicollinearity. The learned models (Appendix B) include a mixture of convergence metrics and surface features, as well as structural features such as the task set number and the time duration of the dialogue. At least one convergence metric was found to be associated with each outcome in the generated models, with the exception of Engagement.

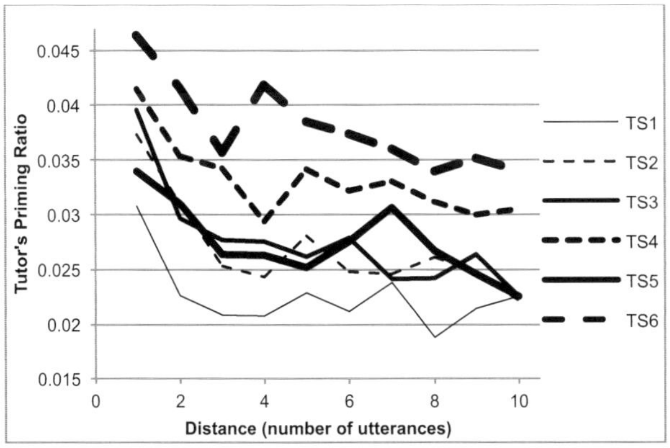

Figure 2. Tutor's Priming Ratio aggregated by task set (TS = Task Set)

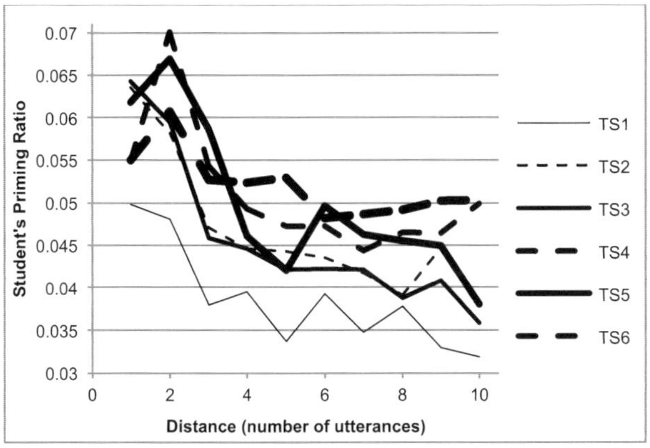

Figure 3. Student's Priming Ratio aggregated by task set (TS = Task Set)

Several significant relationships emerged within the models. We discuss a subset of these here. First, tutor Priming Ratio was a significant predictor for outcomes as rated by both tutor and student. Higher tutor Priming Ratio was associated with higher tutor perception of dialogue success, perhaps because students reflected tutor lexical choice more frequently. The same metric was associated with lower student score for how mentally demanding the tasks were perceived to be, which suggests that a shared lexicon may be associated with decreased cognitive load.

Another significant finding is the relationship between student Priming Ratio and student boredom, confusion, and frustration. In all the models, increased reports of these student emotions by the tutor corresponded to lower student Priming Ratio. This result suggests that tutor reuse of student lexical choice may be associated with positive affective outcomes.

Finally, the tutor's Matched Word Ratio is a significant negative predictor of learning gains, and also a significant negative predictor for student confusion. This finding may be related to the fact that by reusing more student language, the tutor may be effectively introducing fewer novel contributions that might lead to confusion.

6 Conclusion and Future Work

Understanding how convergence unfolds holds significant promise for designing more effective dialogue systems. Toward that end, this paper has explored convergence in task-oriented dialogue at three levels: at the level of pairs of utterances, across a single conversation, and over multiple conversations with the same interlocutors. The results demonstrate that within the corpus, the two interlocutors display increasing levels of convergence longitudinally. Additionally, the results suggest ways in which short-term and long-term convergence are associated with particular positive and negative aspects of dialogue success and user affect.

The findings have significant implications for dialogue systems. First, they suggest that not only may successful lexical priming aid in understanding (Stoyanchev and Stent 2009), it may also be associated with lower cognitive load for users. Additionally, it may be possible to leverage convergence to positively impact users' affective states with respect to emotions such as boredom, confusion, and frustration. These potential relationships suggest that work to further elucidate convergence phenomena is particularly promising because dialogue systems stand to benefit from strategically leveraging convergence and adaptation.

Acknowledgments

This work is supported in part by the National Science Foundation through Grants DRL-1007962 and CNS-1042468. Any opinions, findings, conclusions, or recommendations expressed in this report are those of the participants, and do not necessarily represent the official views, opinions, or policy of the National Science Foundation.

References

Brennan, S. (1996). Lexical Entrainment in Spontaneous Dialog. In *Proceedings of the 1996 International Symposium on Spoken Dialogue*, 41-44.

Coulston, R., Oviatt, S., and Darves, C. (2002). Amplitude Convergence in Children's Conversational Speech with Animated Personas. In *Proceedings of the 7th International Conference on Spoken Language Processing*, 2689–2692.

Hart, S. and Staveland, L. (1988). Development of NASA-TLX (Task Load Index): Results of Empirical and Theoretical Research. In P.A. Hancock and N. Meshkati, eds., *Human Mental Workload*. 1988, 139-183.

Hirschberg, J. (2008). High Frequency Word Entrainment in Spoken Dialogue. In *Proceedings of ACL HLT*, 169-172.

O'Brien, H. and Toms, E. (2010). The Development and Evaluation of a Survey to Measure User Engagement. *Journal of the American Society for Information Science and Technology*, 6(1), 50-69.

Pickering, M. and Garrod, S. (2004). Toward a Mechanistic Psychology of Dialogue. *Behavioral and Brain Sciences*, 27(2), 169-226.

Reitter, D., Moore, J., and Keller, F. (2006). Priming of Syntactic Rules in Task-Oriented Dialogue and Spontaneous Conversation. In *Proceedings of the 28th Annual Conference of the Cognitive Science Society*, 685-690.

Steinhauser, N., Campbell, G., Taylor, L., Scott, C., Dzikovska, M., and Moore, J. (2011). Talk Like an Electrician: Student Dialogue Mimicking Behavior in an Intelligent Tutoring System. In *Proceedings of the 15th International Conference on Artificial Intelligence in Education*, 361-368.

Stoyanchev, S. and Stent, A. (2009). Lexical and Syntactic Priming and Their Impact in Deployed Spoken Dialog Systems. In *Proceedings of NAACL HLT*, 189-192.

Ward, A. and Litman, D. (2007). Dialog Convergence and Learning. In *Proceedings of the 13th International Conference on Artificial Intelligence in Education*, 262-269.

Appendix A. Corpus Excerpt

T: yes so what happens with the other paths?

S: is it because the last statement is fullfilled so it has no need to print the error?
S: i understand what is happening but i do not know how to explain it
T: ok so you noticed that when the if statement directly before it is true then it does not go to the else
T: but if the if statement directly before the else statement is false then it goes to the else statement
S: yes.

S: so i need to make all of them else if statements?

T: yes

Appendix B. Regression Models

	β	p
Norm. Learning Gain, R^2 = .0687		
Tutor's MWR	-.169	.0160
Task set number	-.144	.0392
Engagement (Student-reported) R^2 = .0892		
Tutor's number of characters	-.527	.0007
Student's mean word length	.159	.0033
Tutor's mean word length	-.169	.0053
Tutor's lexicon size	.369	.0189
Mentally demanding (Student-reported) R^2 = .217		
Tutor's PR (distances 1-5)	-.128	.0118
Session length (ms)	.174	.0065
Combined number of utterances	.579	.0005
Tutor's number of utterances	-.475	.0040
Tutor's number of characters	-.439	.0031
Tutor's mean word length	-.118	.0496
Tutor's lexicon size	.627	<.0001
Student confusion*, R^2 = .319		
Student's PR (distances 1-10)	-.233	<.0001
Tutor's number of matched words	1.04	<.0001
Tutor's MWR	-.523	<.0001
Task set number	-.122	.0105
Session length (ms)	.292	<.0001
Student's number of characters	.247	.0048
Combined lexicon size	-.594	<.0001
Student frustration*, R^2 = .300		
Max value of Student's PR	.156	.0035
Session length (ms)	.239	<.0001
Tutor's number of utterances	.460	<.0001
Tutor's number of words	.342	.0135
Tutor's lexicon size	-.748	<.0001
Student boredom*, R^2 = .202		
Student's PR (distances 1-5)	-.234	<.0001
Tutor's number of utterances	.261	.0001
Tutor's lexicon size	-.412	<.0001
Session successful overall*, R^2 = .246		
Tutor's PR (distances 1-3)	.186	.0002
Δ Student's PR (distances 1-10)	.122	.0079
Session length (ms)	-.420	<.0001
Tutor's number of utterances	.518	<.0001
Tutor's number of words	-.473	.0006
Tutor's lexicon size	.275	.0340

* = from tutor perception survey;
β = standardized regression coefficient

The Structure and Generality of Spoken Route Instructions

Aasish Pappu and Alexander Rudnicky
Language Technologies Institute, Carnegie Mellon University
{aasish, air}@cs.cmu.edu

Abstract

A robust system that understands route instructions should be able to process instructions generated naturally by humans. Also desirable would be the ability to handle repairs and other modifications to existing instructions. To this end, we collected a corpus of spoken instructions (and modified instructions) produced by subjects provided with an origin and a destination. We found that instructions could be classified into four categories, depending on their intent such as imperative, feedback, or meta comment. We asked a different set of subjects to follow these instructions to determine the usefulness and comprehensibility of individual instructions. Finally, we constructed a semantic grammar and evaluated its coverage. To determine whether instruction-giving forms a predictable sub-language, we tested the grammar on three corpora collected by others and determined that this was largely the case. Our work suggests that predictable sub-languages may exist for well-defined tasks.

Index Terms: Robot Navigation, Spoken Instructions

1 Introduction

Generating and interpreting instructions is a topic of enduring interest. Cognitive psychologists have examined how people perceive spatial entities and structure route instructions (Daniel and Denis, 1998; Allen, 1997). Linguists and others have investigated how people articulate route instructions in conversation with people or agents (Eberhard et al., 2010; Gargett et al., 2010; Stoia et al., 2008; Marge and Rudnicky, 2010). Artificial intelligence researchers have shown that under supervised conditions autonomous agents can learn to interpret route instructions (Kollar et al., 2010; MacMahon et al., 2006; Matuszek et al., 2010; Bugmann et al., 2004; Chen and Mooney, 2010).

While the subject has been approached from different perspectives, it has been generally held that the language of directions is mostly limited and only parts of the vocabulary (such as location names) will vary from case to case. We are interested in being able to interpret natural directions, as might be given to a robot, and generating corresponding trajectory. But natural directions contain different types of information, some (more-or-less) easily interpreted (e.g., "go to the end of the hall") while others seem daunting (e.g., "walk past the abstract mural with birds"). So the question might actually be "is there enough interpretable data in human directions to support planning a usable trajectory?".

The language of instructions contains a variety of relevant propositions: a preface to a route, an imperative statement, or a description of a landmark. Previous work has proposed both coarse and fine-grained instruction taxonomies. (Bugmann et al., 2004) proposed a taxonomy of 15 primitive categories in a concrete "action" framework. In contrast, (Daniel and Denis, 1998) suggested a five-way categorization based on cognitive properties of instructions.

Instructions vary greatly and can include superfluous detail. (Denis et al., 1999) found that when people were asked to read and assess a set of instructions some of the instructions were deemed unnecessary and could be discarded. There is some evidence (Lovelace et al., 1999; Caduff and Timpf, 2008) that only the mention of significant landmarks along the route leads to better-quality instructions. Computational (rather than descriptive) approaches to this problem include: using sequence labeling approach to capture spatial relations, landmarks, and action verbs (Kollar et al., 2010), generating a frame structure for an instruction (MacMahon et al., 2006), or using statistical machine translation techniques to translate instructions into actions (Matuszek et al., 2010).

We describe a new instructions corpus, its analysis in terms of a taxonomy suitable for automated understanding and a verification that the instructions are in fact usable by humans. With a view to automating understanding, we also constructed a grammar capable of processing this language, and show that it provides good coverage for both our corpus and three other corpora (Kollar et al., 2010; Marge and Rudnicky, 2010; Bugmann et al., 2004)

This paper is organized as following: Section 2 describes the corpus collection study. Then in Section 3, we discuss the taxonomy of route instructions. Section 4 focuses on which categories are important for navigation. In Section 5, we report our results and error analysis on parsing instructions from our corpus and three other corpora containing route instructions, followed by lessons learned and future work.

2 The Navagati[1] Corpus

We collected a corpus of spoken instructions describing how to get from one part of a large building complex to another. To ensure consistency we recruited individuals who were familiar with the environment and consequently could formulate such instructions without reference to maps or other materials. Since we are ultimately interested in how such instructions are edited, we also included conditions in which subjects were asked to modify their instructions in several ways. The corpus is publicly available[2].

2.1 Participants and Procedure

We recruited subjects who were both fluent English speakers and were also familiar with the environment (a university building complex). Subjects were told to imagine that they had encountered a visitor, not familiar with the campus, at a specific location (in front of elevators on a particular floor) who needed instructions to a specific location, a café two buildings away.

For each set of instructions, subjects were asked to think about the route and their instructions, then record them as a single monologue. Subjects sat in front of a computer and wore a close-talking microphone. Initially no map was provided and they were expected to rely on their memory. In subsequent tasks they were shown a floor-plan indicating a specific location of the visitor and asked to modify their instructions. Speech was transcribed using Amazon Mechanical Turk, shown to be a reliable resource for spoken language transcription (Marge et al., 2010). Transcriptions were normalized to standardize spellings (e.g., building names).

2.2 Design

Previous works have focused on eliciting route instructions between multiple pairs of locations. There is a general agreement that the structure of instructions did not vary with the increase in number of start-end location pairs. However previous works have not looked at how instructions would be modified under different situations.

We were interested in two general cases: normal instructions (**Simple** scenario) and repairing existing instructions (**Repair** scenario). Each scenario included three tasks, as described below.

We selected two locations that could be walked between without necessarily going outside. However the subjects were free to to give instructions for a route of their choice between a location pair. The first location (A) was in front of an elevator on the seventh floor of Gates Hillman Center, the second location (B) was a cafe on the fifth floor of Wean Hall. The expected pathway included changes in floor, direction and passing through a different building. It required reasonably detailed instructions.

In the **Simple** scenario, subjects were asked to generate three variants, as follows: (1) instructions for $A \rightarrow B$; (2) for $B \rightarrow A$; and (3) a simplified version of (2).

The motivation behind (2) is to learn whether people would make references about the parts of the route that were previously traversed in the opposite direction. In the case of (3), we were interested in the degree of instruction reuse and the condensation strategy. We explicitly told the subject "Imagine that the visitor found your instructions confusing. They asked you to simplify the instructions. How would you do that?"

The **Repair** scenario was designed to probe how a subject would alter their instructions in response to complications. Subjects were asked to modify their intial Simple instructions ($A \rightarrow B$) to cope with: (1) visitor missing a landmark and takes a wrong turn; (2) an obstruction (construction) blocking the original path; and (3) the visitor getting lost and ends up in an unknown part of the (middle) building. For each case, the subject was given a map (as in figure 1) that marked the visitor's location and had to get the visitor back on track.

Figure 1: Map of the construction area (marked as star)

The tasks in this scenario were designed to see whether people modify directions differently when three different situations are presented. Precisely, we want to know if

[1] Sanskrit root for Navigation meaning "to travel by boat"

[2] http://tts.speech.cs.cmu.edu/apappu/navagati/

there is any difference in the discourse structure and verbosity of the directions.

2.3 Analysis

Nine subjects performed 6 tasks each, producing 54 sets of instructions, for a total of 65 minutes of speech. Please note that other corpora in the route instructions domain have similiar scale (see Figure 5(a)). The transcriptions were segmented semi-automatically into atomic units corresponding to instruction steps. For example, the instruction "Go left, then turn right" was segmented into: "go left", and "then turn right" based on bigram heuristics. We compiled a list of most frequent bigrams and trigrams in the corpus e.g., "and then", "after that" etc. The transcriptions were segmented at the bigram/trigram boundaries and were manually verified for the correctness of a segment. The Simple scenario generated 552 instructions, the Repair part contained 382 instructions, a total of 934. The vocabulary has 508 types and 7937 tokens. Table 1 summarizes the factors measured in both the scenarios. Only two (marked by *) differed between scenarios (t-test at $p < 0.05$). We examined acoustic properties (for example mean pitch) but did not find any significant differences across scenario type.

Table 1: Simple vs Repair Scenario

Factors	Simple	Repair
# Tokens	4461	3476
# Types	351	375
# Instructions	552	382
# Words-per-Instruction*	7.5	8.0
# Landmarks	450	314
# Motion Verbs*	775	506
# Spatial Prepositions	61	60
# Filler Phrases	414	380

We can compare language similarity across scenarios by comparing the perplexity of text in the two scenarios. If the instructions and repairs are similar, we would expect that a model built from one scenario should be able to capture data from the other scenario. We randomly divided data from each scenario into training (70%) and testing data (30%). We built a trigram language model (LM) smoothed with absolute discounting using the CMU-SLM toolkit (Rosenfield, 1995). Then, we computed the perplexity on testing data from each scenario against each model. From Table 2, Simple-LM has lower perplexity compared to Repair-LM on the test sets. The perplexity of Simple-LM on Repair-Test is slightly higher when compared to Simple-Test. This could be due to the lexical diversity of the Repair scenario or simply to the smaller sample size. Table 1 (row 1) indicates that the data in Repair scenario is smaller than data in Simple scenario. To explore the lexical diversity of these two scenarios we conducted a qualitative analysis of the instructions from both the scenarios.

In Task 1 of the Simple scenario, we only observed a sequence of instructions. However in Task 2 of Simple Scenario, we noticed references to instructions from Task 1 via words like "remember", "same route", etc. This suggests that instructions may be considered in context of previous exchanges and that this history should normally be available for interpretation purposes. In Task 3 of the Simple scenario, 7 out of 9 subjects simply repeated the instructions from Task 2 while the rest provided a different version of the same instructions. We did not observe any other qualitative differences across three tasks in the Simple scenario.

In Task 1 of the Repair scenario, all but one subject gave instructions that returned the visitor to the missed landmark, instead of bypassing the landmark. In Task 2, the obstruction on the path could be negotiated through a shorter or longer detour. But only 4 out of 9 participants suggested the shorter detour. In Task 3, we did not observe anything different from Task 2. Despite the difference in the situations, the language of repair was found to be quite similar. The structure of the delivery was organized as follows: (1) Subjects introduced the situation of the visitor; (2) then modified the instructions according to the situation. Introduction of the situation was different in each task, (e.g., "you are facing the workers" vs "looks like you are near office spaces" vs "if you have missed the atrium you took a wrong turn"). But the modification or repair of the instructions was similar across the situations. The repaired instructions are sequences of instructions with a few cautionary statements inserted between instructions. We believe that subjects added cautionary statements in order to warn the visitor from going off-the-route. We observed that 6.3% of the repaired instructions were *cautionary* statements; we did not observe cautionary statements in the original Simple scenario. In order to see the effect of these cautionary statements we removed them from both training and testing sets of the Repair scenario, then built a trigram LM using this condensed training data (Repair–w/o-cautionLM). Table 2 shows that perplexity drops when cautionary statements are excluded from the repair scenario, indicating that Simple and Repair scenarios are similar except for these cautionary statements.

3 Taxonomy of Route Instructions

Taxonomies have been proposed in the past. Daniel and Denis (1998) proposed a taxonomy that reflected attributes of spatial cognition and included 5 classes: (1) Imperatives; (2) Imperatives referring a landmark; (3) Introduction of a landmark without an action; (4) Non-spatial description of landmarks and (5) Meta comments.

Table 2: Perplexity of Simple/Repair Language Models

LM/Test	Simple-Test	Repair-Test	Repair -w/o-caution
Simple-LM	29.6	36.5	30.3
Repair-LM	37.4	37.3	35.6
Repair -w/o-cautionLM	31.9	37.6	26.8

Bugmann et al. (2004) suggested 15 primitive (robot-executable) actions. We present a hierarchical instruction taxonomy that takes into account both cognitive properties and the needs of robot navigation. This taxonomy is based on 934 route instruction monologues. It should be noted that this taxonomy is not based on dialog acts but rather takes the intent of the instruction into the account.

3.1 Categories

We segmented the spoken instructions using a criterion that split individual actions and observations. Our taxonomy is roughly comparable to that of (Daniel and Denis, 1998) but differs in the treatment of landmarks because the mention of the landmarks in an instruction can be of two types: contextual mention and positional mention. Contextual Mention means when a landmark in the surroundings but it is not on the path. On the other hand, positional mention requires the landmark to be on the path. In our taxonomy, contextual mention becomes Advisory instruction and positional mention is called Grounding instruction. The taxonomy has four major categories that subsume 18 sub-categories; these are given in Table 3.

For instance, "You want to take a right" belongs to the Imperative category. "You will see a black door" is an Advisory instruction about the surroundings. "You are on the first floor" denotes Grounding. "Your destination is located in another building and you will walk across three buildings in this route" gives an overview of the route, a Meta Comment. From Figure 2, we see that majority of the route instructions are Imperative.

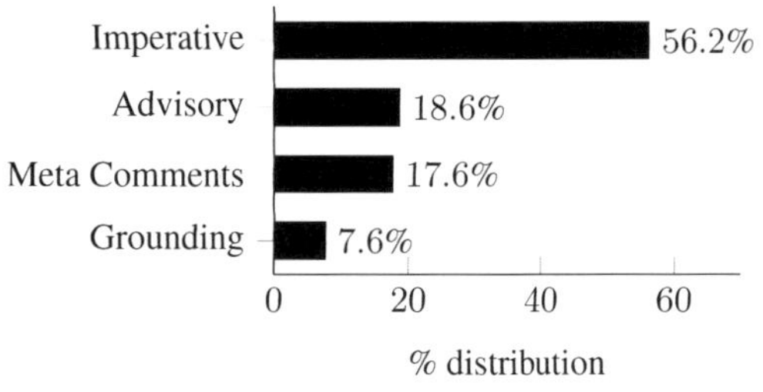

Figure 2: First Tier Instruction Categories

3.1.1 Imperative Instructions

Imperative instructions are executable and can result in physical displacement. We identified seven subcategories of Imperatives that distinguish different contexts (e.g., going along a corridor, changing floors via elevator or stairs, or going to a specific location).

Imperative instructions can also include *preconditions* or *postconditions*. The order of their execution varies based on the directionality of the condition between two instructions. `Continue` is interesting because it can have *travel-distance* and *travel-direction* arguments, or even no arguments. In the latter case the follower continues an action (e.g., "keep walking"), until some unspecified condition ends it.

3.1.2 Advisory Instructions

While giving route instructions people mention landmarks along the route as feedback to the direction-follower. Some of these landmarks are not part of the path but do serve as waypoints for the follower (e.g., "you will see a hallway right there"). We observe that landmarks are distinct either functionally and/or physically. For example, a hallway is both functionally and physically different from an elevator but only physically different from a door because both function as an instrument (or path) to get from one place to another. Based on this distinction, we divided advisory instructions into five sub-categories depending on the type of landmark mentioned in the instruction (see Table 3).

Compound locations (see Table 3) are closely located but physically distinct. They may constitute part-whole relationships e.g., "TV screen with a motion sensor". We observed that compound locations are used to disambiguate when multiple instances of a landmark type are present e.g., "chair near the elevator vs "chair near the hallway".

3.1.3 Grounding Instructions

Grounding instructions report absolute position. These instructions indicate current view or location as opposed to future view or location (indicated through advisory instructions). These instructions constitute a landmark name similar to advisory instructions and also follow the distinction between the type of landmark mentioned in the instruction (see Table 3).

3.1.4 Meta Comments

Meta comments are non-executable instructions added to route instructions. People often make these comments at the beginning of instructions and sometimes in between two imperative statements e.g., a precautionary statement. In our corpus we found meta-comments in two situations: (1) Preface or introduction of the route; (2) Caution against a (metaphorical) pitfall in the route.

Category	SubCategory	Distribution	Example
Imperative	Leave-Location	2.3%	Exit the building; Come out of the room
	Follow-Path	7.0%	Walk along the corridor; go across the bridge
	Floor-Transition	11.2%	Take the elevator to fourth floor; Take the stairs to the fifth
	Turn	24.2%	Turn left
	Go-To	27.2%	Walk to the elevators
	Continue	28.0%	Keep going straight for few steps
Advisory	Floor-Level	5.4%	You will see fourth floor of other building
	Floor-Transition	12.2%	You will see elevators
	Compound-Location	13.4%	You will see a hallway to the right of elevators
	End-of-Pathway	21.5%	You will see end of the hallway
	Landmark	47.5%	You will see a TV screen
Grounding	Compound-Location	5.9%	You are on a hallway right next to the elevators
	End-of-Pathway	8.2%	You are on the bridge leading to other building
	Floor-Level	42.4%	You are on fourth floor of the building
	Landmark	43.5%	You are on standing near TV screen
Meta Comments	Caution	14.7%	You can find it immediately; Don't go that side
	Miscellaneous	36.0%	Let me guide you through it; I guess a simpler way would be
	Preface	49.3%	I will guide you to the cafe in that building

Table 3: Taxonomy of Categories with Examples

Both the example instructions and the distribution of the subcategories are given in Table 3.

The language of meta comments is more diverse than that of the other three categories. If we build trigram language models for each category and measure the perplexity on a held-out set from same category the perplexity is relatively high for Meta (49.6) compared to other categories (Advisory: 19.5; Imperative: 18.5; Grounding: 11.4). This suggests that automatic understanding of meta comments might be problematic, consequently it would be useful to determine the ralative utility of different instruction categories. The next section describes at attempt to do this.

4 Which Instructions are Relevant?

Given a variety of information present in a set of route instructions, we wanted to investigate whether all that information is relevant for navigation. In order to find that out we devised a user study asking people to follow instructions collected in our previous study. (Daniel and Denis, 1998) conducted a similar study where they asked subjects to read a set of instructions and strike-off instructions with too much or too little information. However, people may or may not feel the same when they follow (physically navigate) these instructions. Therefore, in our study the experimenter read instructions (of varying amount of detail) to the subjects while they physically navigated through the environment.

4.1 Participants and Procedure

We chose 5 out of the 9 instruction sets, spoken by different subjects (of average length 26.8 instructions per set) from Task 1 of the Simple scenario discussed above. We did not use the others because they contained few instructions (average of 13.5) and provided fewer instances of instructions in different categories. Also, we did not use instructions from Repair Scenario because those instructions dependent on a scenario and a set of instructions that were already provided to the direction follower.

Our set of instructions included the full set, a set with only imperatives and additional sets adding only one of the remaining categories to the imperative set (see Table 4), producing 25 distinct sets of instructions. Additionally, building names and the destination name (transcribed in the instructions) were anonymized to avoid revealing the destination or the "heading" at the early stage of the route.

We recruited 25 subjects, each doing one variant of the instructions. In the session, the experimenter read one instruction at a time to the subject and walked behind the subject as they proceeded. Subjects were asked to say "done" when ready for the next instruction; they were allowed to ask the experimenter to repeat instructions but otherwise were on their own. The experimenter kept track of how and where a subject got lost on their way to destination. (No systematic effects were observed, but see below.) At the end subjects were handed the entire set of instructions and were asked to mark which instructions were difficult to follow and which were redundant. Remaining instructions were deemed to be useful and interpretable.

Table 4: Variants of an Instruction Set

Variant	Imperative	Advisory	Grounding	Meta
Imp	✓			
Imp+Adv	✓	✓		
Imp+Grnd	✓		✓	
Imp+Meta	✓			✓
Entire Set	✓	✓	✓	✓

Category/Variant	Imp	Imp+Grnd	Imp+Meta	Imp+Adv	Entire Set
Diff-Imp	11	10	12	9	12
Diff-Adv	0	10	5	10	10
Diff-Grnd	0	0	13	0	0
Diff-Meta	4	15	12	4	4
Diff-All	6	9	11	7	9

Category/Variant	Imp	Imp+Grnd	Imp+Meta	Imp+Adv	Entire Set
Redun-Imp	5	8	12	11	8
Redun-Adv	5	10	19	10	29
Redun-Grnd	20	13	47	53	27
Redun-Meta	19	31	65	23	50
Redun-All	9	13	26	17	21

Figure 3: What percent of instructions are Difficult (Diff) or Redundant (Redun)? On the `left:` Darker is Difficult `right:` Darker is More Redundant Instructions

4.2 Analysis

Except for one subject, everybody reached the destination. Subjects found Imperative and Advisory instructions more useful compared to Grounding instructions and Meta comments, irrespective of the instruction-set they followed (see Figure 3). Figure 3(a) shows percentage of category-wise difficult instructions in each variant of an instruction set and 3(b) shows percentage of category-wise redundant instructions in each variant of an instruction set. For e.g., Diff-Imp/Imp+Meta means that 12% of imperative-instructions are difficult in the Imperative+Meta variant.

16 out 25 Subjects got lost at least once i.e., they misinterpreted an instruction, followed along wrong path, then they realized inconsistencies with spatial information and the following instruction, and finally recovered from the misinterpreted instruction. A subject lost thrice in the entire experiment who misunderstood one instruction twice and another instruction once. The subject was lost at an intersection of three hallways and only one of them leads towards the destination. This instruction did not have sufficient information about the next heading. All subjects who recovered from misinterpretation informed that landmark's attributes such as number of floors in a building (if building is the landmark) and the spatial orientation of the landmark helped them in recovery.

Instructions that lacked spatial orientation were found to be particularly difficult to follow. Subjects found a few of the imperative and advisory instructions difficult to follow. While following these difficult instructions, people realized that they got lost and asked the experimenter to repeat the instructions. Examples of difficult instructions and the people's complaint on that instruction are as follows:

- *So you kind of cross the atrium* **Complaint:** participants reported that they were not sure how far they had to walk across the atrium.
- *Go beside the handrails till the other end of this building* **Complaint:** no absolute destination, multiple hallways at the end of handrails
- *Just walk down the hallway exit the building* **Complaint:** multiple exits to the building
- *After you get off the elevator, take a left and then left again* **Complaint:** more than one left confused the subjects
- *You can see the building just in front of you* **Complaint:** there were three buildings standing in front and the target building was slightly to the left.
- *You will see the corridor that you want to take* **Complaint:** there were two corridors and the orientation was unspecified in the instruction

5 Understanding Experiments

The Navagati (NAV) corpus instructions were divided into training set (henceforth abbreviated as NAV-train) and testing set (abbreviated as NAV-test) of size 654 (of 6 subjects) and 280 (of 3 subjects). The training set was used to create a grammar based on the taxonomy described in Section 3.

5.1 Grammar

A domain-specific grammar was written to cover most frequent phrases from the training set using the Phoenix (Ward, 1991) format. Phoenix grammars specify a hierarchy of target concepts and is suited to parsing spontaneous speech. The resulting grammar produced correct and complete parses on 78% of the training data (NAV-train). The remaining training instances were not included due to unusual phrasing and disfluencies. The concepts in the grammar are listed in the Table 5.

5.1.1 Managing Variable Vocabulary

Concepts such as Locations, Pathways and Adjectives-of-Location use vocabulary that is specific to an environment, and the vocabulary of these concepts will change

Corpus	#Instr	Words/Instr	Environmnt	Modality	H/R-H/R
NAV	934	9	UnivCampus	Speech	Human-Human
MIT	684	15	UnivCampus	Written	Human-Human
IBL	769	8	ModelCity	Speech	Human-Robot
TTALK	1619	7	OpenSpace	Speech	Human-Robot

LiftingDevic	PathWays	Landmarks	Adjectives
0.029	0.046	0.169	0.13
0.045	0.016	0.163	0.062
n.a.	0.039	0.076	0.13
n.a.	0.027	0.01	0.039

Figure 4: (a) Nature of the Corpora (b) Type-Token Ratio of Concepts across Corpora

Table 5: Higher level and Leaf node Concepts in Grammar

Category Concepts	Examples
Imperative	GoToPlace, Turn, etc
Conditional Imperative	Move_Until_X where X is a condition
Advisory Instructions	You_Will_See_Location
Grounding Instructions	You_are_at_Location
Auxillary Concepts	**Examples**
Locations	buildings, other landmarks on the route
Adjectives-of-Locations	large, open, black, small etc.
Pathways	hallway, corridor, bridge, doors, etc.
LiftingDevice	elevator, staircase, stairwell, etc.
Spatial Relations	behind, above, on right, on left, etc.
Numbers	turn-angles, distance, etc.
Ordinals	first, second as in floor numbers
Filler phrases	you may want to; you are gonna; etc.

with surroundings. We used an off-the-shelf part-of-speech tagger (Toutanova et al., 2003) on NAV-train to identify "location-based" nouns and adjectives. These were added to the grammar as instances of their respective concepts.

5.2 Parsing NAV Instructions

A parse can fall into one of the following categories: 1) *Complete*: clean and correct parse with all concepts and actions mentioned in the instruction. 2) *Incomplete*: If some arguments for an action are missing. 3) *Misparse*: no usable parse produced for an instruction.

Table 6 shows that 87% of the instructions from the NAV corpus (excluding meta comments) are parsed correctly. Correct parses were produced for 89% of Imperatives, 87% of Advisory and 73% of Grounding instructions. Meta comments were excluded because they do not constitute any valid actions and can be ignored. Nevertheless 20% of the meta comments produced a valid parse (i.e. unintended action).

5.3 Grammar Generality

The results for the NAV corpus seem encouraging but it would be useful to know whether the NAV grammar generalizes to other directions scenarios. We selected three corpora to examine this question: MIT (Kollar et al., 2010), IBL[3] (Bugmann et al., 2004) and TTALK[4] (Marge and Rudnicky, 2010). All were navigation scenarios but were collected in a variety of settings (see Figure 4(a)). Corpus vocabularies were normalized using the process described in 5.1.1 and location specific nouns and adjectives added to the grammar. Punctuation was removed. Figure 4(b) shows the type-token ratios for "variable" concepts. There are more landmarks and adjectives (that tag along landmarks) in NAV and MIT compared to IBL and fewest in TTALK corpus (a closed space with two robots). Since, IBL and TTALK do not involve extensive navigation inside the buildings there are no instances of the elevator concept. However, IBL corpus has "exits, roads, streets" in the city environment which were included in the PathWay concept.

5.4 Performance across Corpora

We randomly sampled 300 instructions from each of the three corpora (MIT, IBL and TTALK) and evaluated their parses against manually-created parses. Table 6) shows results for each type of parse (Complete, Incomplete, or Misparse). Meta comments were excluded, as discussed earlier. The NAV grammar appears portable to three other corpora. As shown in Category-Accuracy of Table 6 Imperatives and Advisory instructions are well-parsed by the grammar. In TTALK corpus, there are very few landmark names but there are certain unusual sentences e.g., "she to the rear left hand wall of the room" causing lower accuracy in Advisory instructions. We noticed that MIT corpus had longer description of the landmarks, leading to lower accuracy for Grounding. From Table 6 11% to 16% of Imperative instructions fail to get parsed across the corpora. We consider these failures/errors below.

5.5 Error Analysis

We found six situations that produced incomplete and misparsed instructions: (1) Underspecified arguments; (2) Unusual or unobserved phrases; (2) False-starts and ungrammatical language; (3) Uncovered words; (4) Prolonged description of landmarks within an instruction;

[3] http://www.tech.plym.ac.uk/soc/staff/guidbugm/ibl/readme1.html
[4] http://www.cs.cmu.edu/~robotnavcps/

Table 6: Parse Results

Parse Results	NAV	MIT	IBL	TTALK
# Instructions	280	300	300	300
% Complete	87%	78.8%	83.8%	83.4%
% Incomplete	3.1%	17%	6.6%	3.7%
% Misparse	9.8%	4.1%	9.5%	13%
Category Accuracy				
Imperative	89%	89.4%	86.5%	84.7%
Advisory	87%	93.4%	87.4%	60%
Grounding	73%	62%	100%	100%

(5) Coreferences; 6) Non-specific instructions (eg. either take the right hallway or the left hallway).

5.5.1 Incomplete and Misparsed Instructions

Out-of-Vocabulary (OOV) words were responsible for the majority of incomplete parses across all the corpora; many were singletons. Unusual phrases such as "as if you are doubling back on yourself" caused incomplete parses. We also observed lengthy descriptions in instructions in the MIT corpus, leading to incomplete parses. This corpus was unusual in that it is composed of written, as opposed to spoken, instructions.

Misparsed instructions were caused due to both ungrammatical phrases and OOV words. Ungrammatical instructions contained either missed key content words like verbs or false starts. These instructions did contain meaningful fragments but they did not form a coherent utterance e.g., "onto a roundabout".

We note that incomplete or otherwise non-understandable utterancess can in principle be recovered through clarification dialog (see e.g., (Bohus and Rudnicky, 2005). Direction giving should perhaps not be limited to monologue delivery.

Table 7: Error Analysis for Incomplete and Misparsed instructions

Incomplete	NAV	MIT	IBL	TTALK
# Incomplete Instructions	8	49	19	10
MissingArgs	50%	8%	0%	0%
UnusualPhrases	0%	28%	35%	60%
Lengthy Descriptions	0%	20.4%	0%	0%
Coreferences	0%	0%	20.2%	0%
Non-concrete phrases	3%	2%	5%	0%
OOVs	47%	41.6%	39.8%	40%
Misparse				
# Misparse Instructions	25	12	27	39
Ungrammatical phrases	24%	44%	16%	10%
OOVs	76%	66%	84%	90%

6 Conclusion

To better understand the structure of instructions and to investigate how these might be automatically processed, we collected a corpus of spoken instructions. We found that instructions can be organized in terms of a straighforward two-level taxonomy. We examined the information contents of different components and found that that the Imperative and Advisory categories appear to be the most relevant, though our subjects had little difficulty dealing with instructions composed of only Imperatives; physical context would seem to matter.

We found that it was possible to design a grammar that reasonably covered the information-carrying instructions in a set of instructions. And that a grammar built from our corpus generalized quite well to corpora collected under different circumstances.

Our study suggests that robust instruction-understanding systems can be implemented and, other than the challenge of dealing with location-specific data, can be deployed in different environments. We believe that this study also highlights the importance of dialog-based clarification and the need for strategies that can recognize and capture out-of-vocabulary words. These capabilities are being incorporated into a robot navigation system that can take instructions from humans.

References

G. Allen. 1997. From knowledge to words to wayfinding: Issues in the production and comprehension of route directions. *Spatial Information Theory A Theoretical Basis for GIS*, pages 363–372.

D. Bohus and A.I. Rudnicky. 2005. Sorry, i didn't catch that!- an investigation of non-understanding errors and recovery strategies. In *6th SIGdial Workshop on Discourse and Dialogue*.

G. Bugmann, E. Klein, S. Lauria, and T. Kyriacou. 2004. Corpus-based robotics: A route instruction example. *Intelligent Autonomous Systems 8*.

D. Caduff and S. Timpf. 2008. On the assessment of landmark salience for human navigation. *Cognitive processing*, 9(4):249–267.

D.L. Chen and R.J. Mooney. 2010. Learning to interpret natural language navigation instructions from observations. *Journal of Artificial Intelligence Research*, 37:397–435.

M.P. Daniel and M. Denis. 1998. Spatial descriptions as navigational aids: A cognitive analysis of route directions. *Kognitionswissenschaft*, 7(1):45–52.

M. Denis, F. Pazzaglia, C. Cornoldi, and L. Bertolo. 1999. Spatial discourse and navigation: An analysis of route directions in the city of venice. *Applied Cognitive Psychology*, 13(2):145–174.

K. Eberhard, H. Nicholson, S. Kubler, S. Gundersen, and M. Scheutz. 2010. The indiana .cooperative remote search task.(crest) corpus. In *Proc. of LREC*, volume 10.

A. Gargett, K. Garoufi, A. Koller, and K. Striegnitz. 2010. The give-2 corpus of giving instructions in virtual environments. In *Proc. of LREC*.

T. Kollar, S. Tellex, D. Roy, and N. Roy. 2010. Toward understanding natural language directions. In *Proceeding of the 5th ACM/IEEE HRI*. ACM.

K. Lovelace, M. Hegarty, and D. Montello. 1999. Elements of good route directions in familiar and unfamiliar environments. *Spatial information theory. Cognitive and computational foundations of geographic information science*, pages 751–751.

M. MacMahon, B. Stankiewicz, and B. Kuipers. 2006. Walk the talk: Connecting language, knowledge, and action in route instructions. *Def*, 2(6):4.

M. Marge and A.I. Rudnicky. 2010. Comparing spoken language route instructions for robots across environment representations. In *SIGDIAL*.

M. Marge, S. Banerjee, and A.I. Rudnicky. 2010. Using the amazon mechanical turk for transcription of spoken language. In *Acoustics Speech and Signal Processing (ICASSP), 2010 IEEE International Conference on*, pages 5270–5273. IEEE.

C. Matuszek, D. Fox, and K. Koscher. 2010. Following directions using statistical machine translation. In *Proceeding of the 5th ACM/IEEE international conference on Human-robot interaction*, pages 251–258. ACM.

R. Rosenfield. 1995. The cmu statistical language modeling toolkit and its use in the 1994 arpa csr evaluation.

L. Stoia, D.M. Shockley, D.K. Byron, and E. Fosler-Lussier. 2008. Scare: A situated corpus with annotated referring expressions. In *LREC 2008*.

K. Toutanova, D. Klein, C.D. Manning, and Y. Singer. 2003. Feature-rich part-of-speech tagging with a cyclic dependency network. In *Proceedings of the 2003 Conference of the North American Chapter of the Association for Computational Linguistics on Human Language Technology-Volume 1*, pages 173–180. Association for Computational Linguistics.

W. Ward. 1991. Understanding spontaneous speech: the phoenix system. In *ICASSP*. IEEE.

Improving Implicit Discourse Relation Recognition Through Feature Set Optimization

Joonsuk Park
Department of Computer Science
Cornell University
Ithaca, NY, USA
jpark@cs.cornell.edu

Claire Cardie
Department of Computer Science
Cornell University
Ithaca, NY, USA
cardie@cs.cornell.edu

Abstract

We provide a systematic study of previously proposed features for *implicit discourse relation identification*, identifying new feature *combinations* that optimize F_1-score. The resulting classifiers achieve the best F_1-scores to date for the four top-level discourse relation classes of the Penn Discourse Tree Bank: COMPARISON, CONTINGENCY, EXPANSION, and TEMPORAL. We further identify factors for feature extraction that can have a major impact on performance and determine that some features originally proposed for the task no longer provide performance gains in light of more powerful, recently discovered features. Our results constitute a new set of baselines for future studies of implicit discourse relation identification.

1 Introduction

The ability to recognize the discourse relations that exist between arbitrary text spans is crucial for understanding a given text. Indeed, a number of natural language processing (NLP) applications rely on it — e.g., question answering, text summarization, and textual entailment. Fortunately, *explicit discourse relations* — discourse relations marked by explicit connectives — have been shown to be easily identified by automatic means (Pitler et al., 2008): each such connective is generally strongly coupled with a particular relation. The connective "because", for example, serves as a prominent cue for the CONTINGENCY relation.

The identification of *implicit discourse relations* — where such connectives are absent — is much harder. It has been the subject of much recent research since the release of the Penn Discourse Treebank 2.0 (PDTB) (Prasad et al., 2008), which annotates relations between adjacent text spans in Wall Street Journal (WSJ) articles, while clearly distinguishing *implicit* from *explicit* discourse relations.[1] Recent studies, for example, explored the utility of various classes of features for the task, including linguistically informed features, context, constituent and dependency parse features, and features that encode entity information or rely on language models (Pitler et al., 2009; Lin et al., 2009; Louis et al., 2010; Zhou et al., 2010).

To date, however, there has not been a systematic study of combinations of these features for implicit discourse relation identification. In addition, the results of existing studies are often difficult to compare because of differences in data set creation, feature set choice, or experimental methodology.

This paper provides a systematic study of previously proposed features for implicit discourse relation identification and identifies feature combinations that optimize F_1-score using forward selection (John et al., 1994). We report the performance of our binary (one vs. rest) classifiers on the PDTB data set for its four top-level discourse relation classes: COMPARISON, CONTINGENCY, EXPANSION, and TEMPORAL. In each case, the resulting classifiers achieve the best F_1-scores for the PDTB to date. We

[1]Research on implicit discourse relation recognition prior to the release of the PDTB instead relied on synthetic data created by removing explicit connectives from explicit discourse relation instances (Marcu and Echihabi, 2002), but the trained classifiers do not perform as well on real-world data (Blair-Goldensohn et al., 2007).

further identify factors for feature extraction that can have a major impact performance, including stemming and lexicon look-up. Finally, by documenting an easily replicable experimental methodology and making public the code for feature extraction[2], we hope to provide a new set of baselines for future studies of implicit discourse relation identification.

2 Data

The experiments are conducted on the PDTB (Prasad et al., 2008), which provides discourse relation annotations between adjacent text spans in WSJ articles. Each training and test instance represents one such pair of text spans and is classified in the PDTB w.r.t. its **relation type** and **relation sense**.

In the work reported here, we use the **relation type** to distinguish examples of *explicit* vs. *implicit* discourse relations. In particular, we consider all instances with a relation type other than *explicit* as implicit relations since they lack an explicit connective between the text spans. The **relation sense** determines the relation that exists between its text span *arguments* as one of: COMPARISON, CONTINGENCY, EXPANSION, and TEMPORAL. For example, the following shows an explicit CONTINGENCY relation between *argument1* (arg1) and **argument2** (arg2), denoted via the <u>connective</u> "because":

> *The federal government suspended sales of U.S. savings bonds* <u>because</u> **Congress hasn't listed the ceiling on government debt.**

The four relation senses comprise the target classes for our classifiers.

A notable feature of the PDTB is that the annotation is done on the same corpus as Penn Treebank (Marcus et al., 1993), which provides parse trees and part-of-speech (POS) tags. This enables the use of gold standard parse information for some features, e.g., the *production rules* feature, one of the most effective features proposed to date.

3 Features

Below are brief descriptions of features whose efficacy have been empirically determined in prior works[3], along with the rationales behind them:

Word Pairs (cross product of unigrams: arg1 × arg2) — A few of these word pairs may capture information revealing the discourse relation of the target spans. For instance, *rain-wet* can hint at CONTINGENCY.

First-Last-First3 (the first, last, and first three words of each argument) — The words in this range may be expressions that function as connectives for certain relations.

Polarity (the count of words in arg1 and arg2, respectively, that hold negated vs. non-negated positive, negative, and neutral sentiment) according to the MPQA corpus (Wilson et al., 2005)) — The change in sentiment from arg1 to arg2 could be a good indication of COMPARISON.

Inquirer Tags (negated and non-negated fine-grained semantic classification tags for the verbs in each argument and their cross product) — The tags are drawn from the General Inquirer Lexicon (Stone et al., 1966)[4], which provides word level relations that might be propagated to the target spans' discourse relation, e.g., rise:fall.

Verbs (count of pairs of verbs from arg1 and arg2 belonging to the same Levin English Verb Class (Levin and Somers, 1993)[5], the average lengths of verb phrases as well as their cross product, and the POS of the main verb from each argument) — Levin Verb classes provide a means of clustering verbs according to their meanings and behaviors. Also, longer verb phrases might correlate with CONTINGENCY, indicating a justification.

Modality (three features denoting the presence of modal verbs in arg1, arg2, or both) — Modal verbs often appear in CONTINGENCY relations.

Context (the connective and the sense of the immediately preceding and following relations (if explicit), and a feature denoting if arg1 starts a paragraph) — Certain relations co-occur.

Production Rules (three features denoting the presence of syntactic productions in arg1, arg2 or both, based on all pairs of parent-children nodes in the argument parse trees) — The syntactic structure of an argument can influence that of the other argument as

[2]These are available from http://www.joonsuk.org.

[3]Word Pairs (Marcu and Echihabi, 2002). First-Last-First3 (Wellner et al., 2006). Polarity, Verbs, Inquirer Tags, Modality, Context (Pitler et al., 2009). Production Rules (Lin et al., 2009).

[4]http://www.wjh.harvard.edu/ inquirer/inqdict.txt

[5]http://www-personal.umich.edu/ jlawler/levin.html

well as its relation type.

4 Experiments

We aim to identify the optimal subsets of the aforementioned features for each of the four top-level PDTB discourse relation senses: COMPARISON, CONTINGENCY, EXPANSION, and TEMPORAL. In order to provide a meaningful comparison with existing work, we carefully follow the experiment setup of Pitler et al. (2009), the origin of the majority of the features under consideration:

First, sections 0-2 and 21-22 of the PDTB are used as the validation and test set, respectively. Then, we randomly down-sample sections 2-20 to construct training sets for each of the classifiers, where each set has the same number of positive and negative instances with respect to the target relation. Since the composition of the corresponding training set has a noticeable impact on the classifier performance we select a down-sampled training set for each classifier through cross validation. All instances of non-explicit relation senses are used; the ENTREL type is considered as having the EXPANSION sense.[6]

Second, Naive Bayes is used not only to duplicate the Pitler et al. (2009) setting, but also because it equaled or outperformed other learning algorithms, such as SVM and MaxEnt, in preliminary experiments, while requiring a significantly shorter training time.[7]

Prior to the feature selection experiments, the best preprocessing methods for feature extraction are determined through cross validation. We consider simple lowercasing, Porter Stemming, PTB-style tokenization[8], and hand-crafted rules for matching tokens to entries in the polarity and General Inquirer lexicons.

Then, feature selection is performed via forward selection, in which we start with the single best-performing feature and, in each iteration, add the feature that improves the F_1-score the most, until no significant improvement can be made. Once the optimal feature set for each relation sense is determined by testing on the validation set, we retrain each classifier using the entire training set and report final performance on the test set.

5 Results and Analysis

Table 5 indicates the performance achieved by employing the feature set found to be optimal for each relation sense via forward selection, along with the performance of the individual features that constitute the ideal subset. The two bottom rows show the results reported in two previous papers with the most similar experiment methodology as ours. The notable efficacy of the *production rules* feature, yielding the best or the second best result across all relation senses w.r.t. both F_1-score and accuracy, confirms the finding of Zhou et al. (2010). In contrast to their work, however, combining existing features enhances the performance. Below, we discuss the primary observations gleaned from the experiments.

Word pairs as features. Starting with earlier works that proposed them as features (Marcu and Echihabi, 2002), some form of *word pairs* has generally been part of feature sets for implicit discourse relation recognition. According to our research, however, these features provide little or no additional gain, once other features are employed. This seems sensible, since we now have a clearer idea of the types of information important for the task and have developed a variety of feature types, each of which aims to represent these specific aspects of the discourse relation arguments. Thus, general features like *word pairs* may no longer have a role to play for implicit discourse relation identification.

Preprocessing. Preprocessing turned out to impact the classifier performance immensely, especially for features like *polarity* and *inquirer tags* that rely on information retrieved from a lexicon. For these features, if a match for a given word is not found in the lexicon, no information is passed on to the classifier.

As an example, consider the General Inquirer lexicon. Most of its verb entries are present tense singular in form; thus, without stemming, dictionary look up fails for a large portion of the verbs. In our case, the F_1-score increases by roughly 10% after stemming.

Further tuning is possible by a few hand-written

[6]Some prior work uses a different experimental setting. For instance, Zhou et al. (2010) only considers two of the non-explicit relations, namely *Implicit* and *NoRel*.

[7]We use classifiers from the nltk package (Bird, 2006).

[8]Stanford Parser (Klein and Manning, 2003).

Feature Type	COMP. vs Rest		CONT. vs Rest		EXP. vs Rest		TEMP. vs Rest	
	F_1	Acc.	F_1	Acc.	F_1	Acc.	F_1	Acc.
1. Polarity	16.49	46.82	28.47	61.39	64.20	56.80	13.58	50.69
2. First-Last-First3	22.54	53.05	37.64	66.71	62.27	56.40	15.24	51.81
3. Inquirer Tags	18.07	82.14	34.88	69.60	77.76	66.38	21.65	80.04
4. Verbs	18.05	55.29	23.61	78.33	68.33	58.37	18.11	58.44
5. Production Rules	30.04	75.84	47.80	71.90	77.64	69.60	20.96	63.36
Best Combination	2 & 4 & 5		2 & 4 & 5		1 & 3 & 4 & 5		1 & 3 & 5	
	31.32	74.66	49.82	72.09	79.22	69.14	26.57	79.32
Pitler '09 (Best)	21.96	56.59	47.13	67.30	76.42	63.62	16.76	63.49
Zhou '10 (Best)[*]	*31.79*	*58.22*	*47.16*	*48.96*	*70.11*	*54.54*	*20.30*	*55.48*

[*] *The experiments are conducted under a slightly different setting, as described in Section 4.*

Table 1: Summary of Classifier Performance. 4-way classifiers have been tested as well, but their performance is not as good as that of the binary classifiers shown here. One major difference is that it is harder to balance the number of instances across all the classes when training 4-way classifiers.

rules to guide lexicon lookup. The word *supplied*, for instance, becomes *suppli* after stemming, which still fails to match the lexicon entry *supply*, unless adjusted accordingly.

Binning. An additional finding regards features that capture numeric, rather than binary, information, such as *polarity*. Since this feature encodes the counts of each type of sentiment word (with respect to each argument and their cross product), and Naive Bayes can only interpret binary features, we first employed a binning mechanism with each bin covering a single value. For instance, if arg1 consists of three positive words, we included *arg1pos1*, *arg1pos2* and *arg1pos3* as features instead of just *arg1pos3*.

The rationale behind binning is that it captures the proximity of related instances. Imagine having three instances each with one, two, and three positive words in arg1, respectively. Without binning, the features added are simply *arg1pos1*, *arg1pos2*, *arg1pos3*, respectively. From the perspective of the classifier, the third instance is no more similar to the second instance than it is to the first instance, even though having three positive words is clearly closer to having two positive words than having one positive word. With binning, this proximity is captured by the fact that the first instance has just one feature in common with the third instance, whereas the second instance has two.

Binning, however, significantly degrades performance on most of the classification tasks. One possible explanation is that these features function as an abstraction of certain lexical patterns, rather than directly capturing similarities among instances of the same class.

6 Conclusion

We employ a simple greedy feature selection approach to identify subsets of known features for implicit discourse relation identification that yield the best performance to date w.r.t. F_1-score on the PDTB data set. We also identify aspects of feature set extraction and representation that are crucial for obtaining state-of-the-art performance. Possible future work includes evaluating the performance without using the gold standard parses. This will give a better idea of how the features that rely on parser output will perform on real-world data where no gold standard parsing information is available. In this way, we can ensure that findings in this area of research bring practical gains to the community.

Acknowledgments

We would like to thank Annie Louis and Yu Xu for helping us reimplement the systems from Louis et al. (2010) and Zhou et al. (2010), respectively. We also thank the anonymous reviewers for their helpful feedback. This work was supported in part by National Science Foundation Grants IIS-1111176 and IIS-0968450, and by a gift from Google.

References

Steven Bird. 2006. Nltk: the natural language toolkit. In *Proceedings of the COLING/ACL on Interactive presentation sessions*, COLING-ACL '06, pages 69–72, Stroudsburg, PA, USA. Association for Computational Linguistics.

Sasha Blair-Goldensohn, Kathleen McKeown, and Owen Rambow. 2007. Building and refining rhetorical-semantic relation models. In *HLT-NAACL*, pages 428–435.

G. John, R. Kohavi, and K. Pfleger. 1994. Irrelevant Features and the Subset Selection Problem. In W. Cohen and H. Hirsh, editors, *Proceedings of the Eleventh International Conference on Machine Learning*, pages 121–129. Morgan Kaufmann.

Dan Klein and Christopher D. Manning. 2003. Accurate unlexicalized parsing. In *IN PROCEEDINGS OF THE 41ST ANNUAL MEETING OF THE ASSOCIATION FOR COMPUTATIONAL LINGUISTICS*, pages 423–430.

Beth Levin and Harold Somers. 1993. *English Verb Classes and Alternations: A Preliminary Investigation*. University Of Chicago Press.

Ziheng Lin, Min-Yen Kan, and Hwee Tou Ng. 2009. Recognizing implicit discourse relations in the penn discourse treebank. In *EMNLP*, pages 343–351.

Annie Louis, Aravind K. Joshi, Rashmi Prasad, and Ani Nenkova. 2010. Using entity features to classify implicit discourse relations. In *SIGDIAL Conference*, pages 59–62.

Daniel Marcu and Abdessamad Echihabi. 2002. An unsupervised approach to recognizing discourse relations. In *ACL*, pages 368–375.

M. Marcus, M. Marcinkiewicz, and B. Santorini. 1993. Building a Large Annotated Corpus of English: The Penn Treebank. *Computational Linguistics*, 19(2):313–330.

Emily Pitler, Mridhula Raghupathy, Hena Mehta, Ani Nenkovak, Alan Lee, and Aravind K. Joshi. 2008. Easily identifiable discourse relations. In *COLING (Posters)*, pages 87–90.

Emily Pitler, Annie Louis, and Ani Nenkova. 2009. Automatic sense prediction for implicit discourse relations in text. In *ACL/AFNLP*, pages 683–691.

Rashmi Prasad, Nikhil Dinesh, Alan Lee, Eleni Miltsakaki, Livio Robaldo, Aravind Joshi, and Bonnie Webber. 2008. The penn discourse treebank 2.0. In Bente Maegaard Joseph Mariani Jan Odjik Stelios Piperidis Daniel Tapias Nicoletta Calzolari (Conference Chair), Khalid Choukri, editor, *Proceedings of the Sixth International Conference on Language Resources and Evaluation (LREC'08)*, Marrakech, Morocco, may. European Language Resources Association (ELRA). http://www.lrec-conf.org/proceedings/lrec2008/.

P J Stone, D C Dunphy, M S Smith, and D M Ogilvie. 1966. *The General Inquirer: A Computer Approach to Content Analysis*, volume 08. MIT Press.

Ben Wellner, Lisa Ferro, Warren R. Greiff, and Lynette Hirschman. 2006. Reading comprehension tests for computer-based understanding evaluation. *Natural Language Engineering*, 12(4):305–334.

Theresa Wilson, Janyce Wiebe, and Paul Hoffmann. 2005. Recognizing contextual polarity in phrase-level sentiment analysis. In *HLT/EMNLP*.

Zhi-Min Zhou, Yu Xu, Zheng-Yu Niu, Man Lan, Jian Su, and Chew Lim Tan. 2010. Predicting discourse connectives for implicit discourse relation recognition. In *COLING (Posters)*, pages 1507–1514.

A Temporal Simulator for Developing Turn-Taking Methods for Spoken Dialogue Systems

Ethan O. Selfridge and Peter A. Heeman
Center for Spoken Language Understanding
Oregon Health & Science University
20000 NW Walker Rd., Beaverton, OR, 97006
selfridg@ohsu.edu, heemanp@ohsu.edu

Abstract

Developing sophisticated turn-taking behavior is necessary for next-generation dialogue systems. However, incorporating real users into the development cycle is expensive and current simulation techniques are inadequate. As a foundation for advancing turn-taking behavior, we present a temporal simulator that models the interaction between the user and the system, including speech, voice activity detection, and incremental speech recognition. We describe the details of the simulator and demonstrate it on a sample domain.

1 Introduction and Background

Effective turn-taking is critical for successful human-computer interaction. Recently, approaches have been proposed to improve system turn-taking behavior that use reinforcement learning (Jonsdottir et al., 2008; Selfridge and Heeman, 2010), decision theory (e.g., Raux and Eskenazi, 2009), and hard-coded policies (e.g., Skantze and Schlangen , 2009). Some of these methods model turn-taking as content-free decisions (Jonsdottir et al., 2008; Skantze and Schlangen, 2009), while others primarily rely on dialogue context (Selfridge and Heeman, 2010) and lexical cues (e.g., Raux and Eskenazi, 2009). Turn-taking continues to be an area of active research and its development is vital for next-generation dialogue systems, especially as they allow for more mixed initiative interaction.

Researchers have turned to simulation since developing a dialogue system with real users is expensive, time consuming, and sometimes impossible. Some turn-taking simulations have been highly stylized and only model utterance content, failing to give a realistic model of timing (Selfridge and Heeman, 2010). Others have modeled a content-free form of turn-taking and *only* attend to timing and prosodic information (Jonsdottir et al., 2008; Baumann, 2008; Padilha and Carletta, 2002). The former is insufficient for the training of deployable real-time systems, and the latter neglect an important aspect of turn-taking: semantic information (Gravano and Hirschberg, 2011).

The overall goal is to develop a simulation environment to train behavior policies that can be transferred with minimal modifications to production systems. This paper presents some first steps towards this goal. We describe a temporal simulator that models the timing and content of both user and system speech, as well as that of incremental speech recognition (ISR) and voice activity detection (VAD). We detail the overall temporal simulator architecture, the design of the individual agents that simulate dialogue, and an instantiation of a simple domain. To demonstrate the utility of the simulator, we implement multiple turn-taking polices and use it to compare these policies under conditions of varying reaction time and speech recognition accuracy.

2 Temporal Simulation Framework

We now describe the details of the temporal simulator. Inspired by the Open Agent Architecture (Martin et al., 1999), it is composed of a number of *agents*, each running as a separate computer process. We first describe the time keeping procedure and then the overall agent communication structure.

Time Keeping: To provide a useful training environment, the simulator must realistically model, and run much faster than, 'real-time'. To do this, the simulator keeps an internal clock that advances to the next time slice when all agents have been run for the current time slice. This structure allows the simulator to run far faster than 'real-time' while supporting realistic communication. This framework is similar to the clock cycle described by Padilha et al (2002).

Agent Communication: Agents use messages to communicate. Messages have three components: the addressee, the content and a time stamp. Time stamps dictate when the content is to be processed and must always be for a future, not the current, time slice, as the alternative would imply instantaneous communication and overly complicate the software architecture. A central hub receives all messages and passes them to the intended recipient agent at the appropriate time. At every slice, each agent runs two procedures: one that retrieves messages and one that can send messages. If there are multiple messages intended for the same time slice, the agent completely processes one before moving to the next.

3 Dialogue Simulator

We use the above temporal simulator to simulate dialogue. At present, we focus on dyadic interaction and have three agents that are run in a strict order at every time slice: User, ISR, and System. Time slices are modeled as 10 millisecond (ms) increments, as this is the time scale that speech recognizers run at.

In general, the User agent sends messages to the ISR agent that sends messages to the System agent. The System agent generally sends messages to both the User agent and the ISR agent. The behavior of all three agents rely on parameters (Table 1) that may either be set by hand or estimated from data. The User and System agents have near identical construction, the primary difference being that the System can misunderstand User speech.

User and System Design: Agent speech is governed by a number of timing parameters. The *Take-Turn* parameter specifies when the agent will begin speaking the selected utterance. The agent gets the first word of the utterance, sets the *Word Length* parameter, and "begins" to speak by sending a speech event message. The agent outputs the word after the specified *Word Length*, and sets the *Inter-Word Pause* parameter that governs when the next word will begin. When the agent completes the utterance, it waits until a future time slice to start another (as governed by the *Inter-Utterance Pause* parameter). However, if the listening agent interrupts mid-utterance, the speaking agent stops speaking and will not complete the utterance. Any dialogue agent architecture can be used, providing the input and output fit with the above specifications.

ISR Design: The ISR agent works as both an Incremental Speech Recognizer and a VAD. We currently model uncertainty in recognition but not in the VAD, though this is certainly a plausible and worthwhile addition. When the ISR agent receives the speech event from the User, it sets the VAD *Speech Start* parameter that models lag in speech detection, and the *Speech End (no word)* parameter that models situations where the user starts speaking but stops mid-word and produces an unrecognizable sound. When the word is received from the User, the *Speech End (word)* parameter is set and a partial phrase result is generated based on the probability that the word will be correctly recognized. This probability is then used as the basis for a confidence score that is packaged with the partial phrase result. A *Recognition Lag* parameter governs the time between User speech and the output of partial phrase results to the System. The form of ISR we model recognizes words cumulatively (see Figure 1 for an example) though the confidence score, at present, is only for the newly recognized word. The recognizer will continue to output partials from User words until the User stops speaking or the System sends a message to stop recognizing. One critical aspect of ISR which we are *not* modeling is partial instability, where partials are revised as recognition progresses. Partial instability is an area of active research (e.g. Baumann et al. 2009) and, while revisions may certainly be modeled in the future, we chose not to for simplicity's sake. We feel that, at present, the *Recognition Lag* parameter is sufficient to model the time for a partial to become stable.

Table 1: Parameters and demonstration values (ms)

Conversant Agents	
Inter-Word pause (Usr)	$\mu = 200, \sigma = 100$
Inter-Word pause (Sys)	100
Inter-Utt. pause	$\mu = 1000, \sigma = 500$
Word Length	400
Take-Turn (Usr)	500/200
Take-Turn (Sys)	750/100
ISR Agent	
Recog. Acc.	variable
Recog. Lag	300
VAD	
Speech Start	100
Speech End (word)	200
Speech End (no word)	600

4 Simulation demonstration

We now demonstrate the utility of the temporal simulator by showing that it can be used to evaluate different turn-taking strategies under conditions of varying ASR accuracy. This is the first step before using it to train policies for use in a live dialogue system.

For this demonstration the conversant agents, the System and User, are built according to the Information State Update approach (Larsson and Traum, 2000), and perform an update for every message associated with the current time slice. The conversant agents are identical except for individual rule sets. Four types of rule sets are common across conversant agents: UNDERSTANDING rules, that update the IS using raw message content; DELIBERATION rules, that update the IS by comparing new information to old; UTTERANCE rules, that select the next utterance based on dialogue context; and TURN rules, that select the time to begin the new utterance by modifying the *Take Turn* parameter. Rule sets are executed in this order with one exception. After the UNDERSTANDING rules, the System agent has ACCEPTANCE rules that use confidence scores to decide whether to understand the recognition or not.

Figure 1: Sample dialogue with timing information

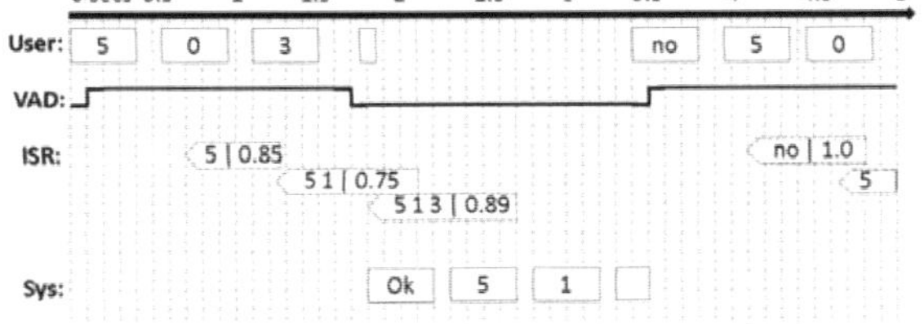

Temporal Simulation Example: We constructed a simple credit card domain, similar to Skantze and Schlangen (2009), where the User says four utterances of four digits each. The System must implicitly confirm every number and if it is correct, the User continues.[1] It can theoretically do this at any time, immediately after the word is recognized, after an utterance, or after multiple utterances. If the system says a wrong number the User interrupts the System with a "no" and begins the utterance again. The System has a Non-Understanding (NU) confidence score threshold set at 0.5. After an NU, the System will not understand any more words and will either confirm any digits recognized before the NU or, if there are no words to confirm, will say an NU utterance ("pardon?"). The User says "yes" to the final, correct confirmation. To maintain simplicity, "yes" and "no" are always accurate. If this were not the case, there would be a number of dialogues that were not successful. The User takes the turn in two ways. It either waits 500 ms after a System utterance to speak or interrupts 200 ms after the System confirms an misrecognized word, which is in line with human reaction time (Fry, 1975).

We implemented three different turn-taking strategies: two *Fixed* and one *Context-based*. Using the Fixed strategy the System either uses a *Slow* policy, waiting 750 ms after no user speech is detected, or a *Fast* policy, waiting only 100 ms. The Fast reaction time results in the System interrupting the User during an utterance when the inter-word pause becomes longer than 200 ms. This is because the VAD *Speech End* parameter is 100 ms and the System is waiting for 100 ms of silence *after Speech End*. The Slow reaction time results in far less interruptions. The Context-based turn-taking strategy uses the recognition score to choose its turn-taking behavior. The motivation is that one would want

[1] Unlike an explicit confirmation ("I heard five. Is that right?"), an implicit confirm ("Ok, five") does not necessitate a strict "yes" or "no" response.

Figure 2: Mean Time and Interruption for different turn-taking polices and ASR accuracy conditions

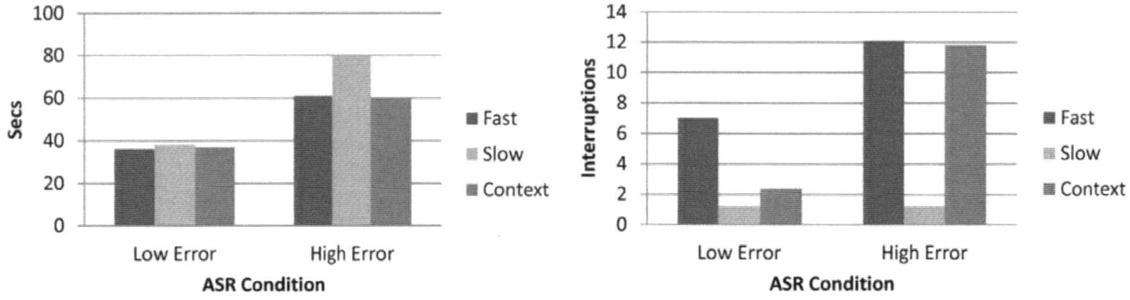

to confirm low-confidence recognitions sooner than those with high confidence. If any unconfirmed result has scores less than 0.8 then the System uses the Fast reaction time to try to confirm or reject as soon as possible. Alternatively, if the results all have high confidences, it can wait until a longer user pause (generally between utterances) by using the Slow reaction time. All parameter values are shown in Table 1.

Figure 1 shows a dialogue fragment of a System using the Context-based turn-taking policy. Numbers are used for the sake of brevity. The start of a box surrounding a word corresponds to when the Speech message was sent (from the User agent to the ISR agent) and the end of the box to when the word has been completed and recognition lag timer begins. The point of the ISR box refers to the time slice when the partial phrase result and score were sent to the System. Note how after the third User word the System interrupts to confirm the utterance, since the confidence score of a previous word dropped below 0.8. Also note how the User interrupts the System after it confirms a wrong number.

Comparing turn-taking policies: We evaluated the three (two Fixed and one Context-based) turn-taking policies in two conditions of ASR accuracy: Low Error, where the probability of correctness was 95%; and High Error, where the probability of correctness was 75%. We compared the mean dialogue time (left Figure 2) and the mean number of interruptions per dialogue (right Figure 2). For dialogue time, we find that all turn-taking policies perform similarly in the Low Error condition. However, in the High Error condition the Slow reaction time performs much worse since it cannot address poor recognitions with the speed of the other two. For interruption, the Fast and Context-driven policies have *far* more than the Slow for the High Error condition. However, in the Low Error condition the Fast policy interrupts far more than the Context-driven. Given that natural behavior is one goal of turn-taking, interruption, while effective at handling High Error rates, should be minimized. The Context-based policy provides support for interruption when it is needed (High Error Condition) and reduces it when it is not (Low Error Condition). The other policies are either unable to interrupt at all (Slow), increasing the dialogue time, or due to a lack the flexibility (Fast), interrupt constantly.

5 Conclusion

We take the first steps towards a simulation approach that characterizes both the content of conversant speech as well as its timing. The temporal simulator models conversant utterances, ISR, and the VAD. The simulator runs quickly (100 times faster than real-time), and is simple and highly flexible. Using an example, we demonstrated that the simulator can help understand the ramifications of different turn-taking policies. We also highlighted both the temporal nature of turn-taking — interruptions, reaction time, recognition lag...etc. — and the content of utterances — speech recognition errors, confidence scores, and wrong confirmations. Plans for future work include adding realistic prosodic modeling and estimating model parameters from data.

Acknowledgments

We thank to the reviewers for their thoughtful suggestions and critique. We acknowledge funding from the NSF under grant IIS-0713698.

References

T. Baumann, M. Atterer, and D. Schlangen. 2009. Assessing and improving the performance of speech recognition for incremental systems. In *Proc. NAACL: HLT*, pages 380–388.

T. Baumann. 2008. Simulating spoken dialogue with a focus on realistic turn-taking. In *Proc. of ESSLLI Student Session*.

D. B. Fry. 1975. Simple reaction-times to speech and non-speech stimuli. *Cortex*, 11(4):355–360.

A. Gravano and J. Hirschberg. 2011. Turn-taking cues in task-oriented dialogue. *Computer Speech & Language*, 25(3):601–634.

G.R. Jonsdottir, K.R. Thorisson, and Eric Nivel. 2008. Learning smooth, human-like turntaking in realtime dialogue. In *Proc. of IVA*, pages 162–175.

S. Larsson and D. Traum. 2000. Information state and dialogue managment in the trindi dialogue move engine toolkit. *Natural Language Engineering*, 6:323–340.

D.L. Martin, Adam J. Cheyer, and Douglas B. Moran. 1999. The open agent architecture: A framework for building distributed software systems. *Applied Artificial Intelligence: An International Journal*, 13(1-2):91–128.

E. Padilha and J. Carletta. 2002. A simulation of small group discussion. In *Proc. of EDILOG*, pages 117–124.

A. Raux and M. Eskenazi. 2009. A finite-state turn-taking model for spoken dialog systems. In *Proc. of HLT/NAACL*, pages 629–637.

G. Skantze and D. Schlangen . 2009. Incremental dialogue processing in a micro-domain. In *Proc. of EACL*, pages 745–753.

E.O. Selfridge and P.A. Heeman. 2010. Importance-Driven Turn-Bidding for spoken dialogue systems. In *Proc. of ACL*, pages 177–185.

Dialogue Act Recognition using Reweighted Speaker Adaptation

Congkai Sun
Institute for Creative Technologies
12015 Waterfront Drive
Playa Vista, CA 90094-2536
csun@ict.usc.edu

Louis-Philippe Morency
Institute for Creative Technologies
12015 Waterfront Drive
Playa Vista, CA 90094-2536
morency@ict.usc.edu

Abstract

In this work we study the effectiveness of speaker adaptation for dialogue act recognition in multiparty meetings. First, we analyze idiosyncracy in dialogue verbal acts by qualitatively studying the differences and conflicts among speakers and by quantitively comparing speaker-specific models. Based on these observations, we propose a new approach for dialogue act recognition based on reweighted domain adaptation which effectively balance the influence of speaker specific and other speakers' data. Our experiments on a real-world meeting dataset show that with even only 200 speaker-specific annotated dialogue acts, the performances on dialogue act recognition are significantly improved when compared to several baseline algorithms. To our knowledge, this work is the first [1] to tackle this promising research direction of speaker adaptation for dialogue act recogntion.

1 Introduction

By representing a higher level intention of utterances during human conversation, dialogue act labels are being used to enrich the information provided by spoken words (Stolcke et al., 2000). Dialogue act recognition is a preliminary step towards deep dialogue understanding. It plays a key role in the design of dialogue systems. Besides, Fernandez et al. (2008) find certain dialogue acts are important cues for detecting decisions in Multi-party dialogue. In Ranganath et al. (2009), dialogue acts are used as important features for flirt detection.

Automatic dialogue act recognition is still an active research topic. The conventional approach is to train one generic classifier using a large corpus of annotated utterances. One aspect that makes it so challenging is that people can express the same idea (or speech act) using a very different set of spoken words. Even more, people can mean different things with the exact same spoken words. These idiosyncratic differences in dialogue acts make the learning of generic classifiers extremely challenging. Luckily, in many applications such as face-to-face meetings or tele-immersion, we have access to archives of previous interactions with the same participants. From these archives, a small subset of spoken utterances can be efficiently annotated. As we will later show in our experiments, even a small number of annotated utterances can make a significant difference.

In this paper, we propose a new approach for dialogue act recognition based on reweighted domain adaptation which effectively balance the influence of speaker specific and other speakers' data. By treating each speaker as one domain, we point out the connection between training speaker specific dialogue act classifier and supervised domain adaptation problem. We analyze idiosyncracy in dialogue verbal acts by qualitatively studying the differences and conflicts among speakers and by quantitively comparing speaker-specific models. We present an extensive set of experiments studying the effect of speaker adaptation on dialogue act recogntion in multi-party meetings using the ICSI-MRDA dataset (Shriberg, 2004).

[1] This paper is an extended version of a poster presented at SemDial 2011, with new experiments and deeper analysis.

The following section presents related work on dialogue act recognition and domain adaptation. Section 3 describes the ICSI-MRDA (Shriberg, 2004) dataset which is used in all our experiments. Section 4 analyze idiosyncracy in dialogue acts, both qualitatively and quantitatively. Section 5 explains our reweighting-based speaker adaptation algorithm. Section 6 contains all experiments to prove the applicability of speaker adaptation to dialogue act recognition. Finally, inspired by the promising results, Section 8 describes some future directions.

2 Previous Work

Automatic dialogue act recognition has been an important problem in the past decades. Different dialogue act labeling standards and datasets have been provided, including Switchboard-DAMSL (Stolcke et al., 2000), ICSI-MRDA (Shriberg, 2004) and AMI (Carletta, 2007). Stolcke et al (2000) is one of the first work using machine learning technique (HMM) to automatically segment and recognize dialogue acts. Rangarajan et al. (2009) demonstrated well-designed prosodic n-gram features are very helpful for Dialogue Act recognition in Maximum Entropy model. And Ang et al (2005) explored joint segmentation and dialogue act classification for speech from ICSI.

Domain adaptation is a popular problem in natural language processing community due to the sparsity of labeled data. Jiang (Jiang, 2007) breaks the analysis of domain adaptation problem into distributional differences in instances and classification functions between source and target data. In Daume's work (2007) several domain adaptation algorithms are described. Our speaker adaptation algorithm is inspired by the reweighting-based adaptation algorithm introduced in this paper.

Recently, dialogue act adaptation has been getting a lot of attention. Tur et al. (2006) successfully use Switchboard-DAMSL to help dialogue act recognition in ICSI-MRDA. Promising results have been obtained by using a regression model to combine the model weights obtained by training on Switchboard-DAMSL and ICSI-MRDA respectively. Following the work by Tur et al. (2006), Guz et al. (2009) further studied the effectiveness of dialogue act domain adaptation in cascaded dialogue act segmentation and recognition system, their results prove adaptation in the intermediate step (segmentation) are also very helpful for the final output (recognition). Jeong et al (2009) use semi-supervised boosting algorithm to leverage labeled data from Switchboard-DAMSL and ICSI-MRDA to help dialogue act recognition in email and forums. Margolis et.al (2010) use a structural correspondence learning technique to adapt dialogue act recognition on automatic translated Spanish genre with the help of Switchboard-DAMSL and ICSI-MRDA. Kolar et al. (2007) explores the difference among speakers for dialogue act segmentation in ICSI-MRDA dataset. Similar to the approach taken in Tur et al. (2006), adaptation is performed through the combination of generic speaker independent Language Model and other speakers' Language Model. Significant improvements have been obtained for most of the selected speakers.

All these previous papers focused on adapting dialogue act models between domains and did not address the person-specific adaptation. The only exception was Kolar et al. (2007) who explored speaker-specific dialogue act segmentation. To our knowledge, this paper is the first work to analyze the effectiveness of speaker adaptation for dialogue act recognition.

3 ICSI-MRDA Corpus

Different Dialogue Act labeling standards and datasets have been provided in recent years, including Switchboard-DAMSL (Stolcke et al., 2000), ICSI-MRDA (Shriberg, 2004) and AMI (Carletta, 2007). ICSI-MRDA is the dataset for our experiments because many of its meetings contain the same speakers, thus making it more suitable for our speaker adaptation study. The tagset in ICSI-MRDA is adapted from DAMSL standard (damsl, 1997) by allowing multiple tags per dialogue act. Each dialogue act in ICSI-MRDA has one general tag and multiple specific tags.

ICSI-MRDA consists of 75 meetings, each roughly an hour long. There are five categories of meetings (three of which we are actively using in our experiments) : *Bed* is about the discussion of natural language processing and neural theories of language, *Bmr* is for the discussion on ICSI meeting corpus, *Bro* is on speech recognition topics and *Bns*

ID	Tag	Type	Nb. Meetings	Nb. DAs
1	mn015	Bed	15	6228
2	me010	Bed	11	5309
3	me013	Bmr	25	9753
4	mn017	Bmr	15	4059
5	fe016	Bmr	18	5500
6	me018	Bro	20	4263
7	me013	Bro	22	11928

Table 1: The 7 speakers from ICSI-MRDA dataset used in our experiments. The table lists: the Speaker ID, original speaker tag, the type of meeting selected for this speaker, the number of meetings this speaker participated and the total number of dialogue acts by this speaker.

is about network and architecture. The last category is *varies* which contains all other topics.

From these 75 meetings, there are 53 unique speakers in total, and an average of about 6 speakers per meeting. 7 speakers[2] having more than 4,000 dialogue acts are selected for our adaptation experiments. Table 1 shows the details of our 7 selected speakers. From the word transcriptions, we created an extended list of linguistic features per utterance. From the 7 selected speakers, we computed 14653 unigram features, 158884 bigram features and 400025 trigram features.

Following the work of Shriberg et al. (2004), we use the 5 general tags in our experiments:

- *Disruption* indicates the current Dialogue Act is interrupted.
- *Back Channel* are utterances which are not made directly by a speaker as a response and do not function in a way that elicits a response either.
- *Floor Mechanism* are dialogue acts for grabbing or maintaining the floor.
- *Question* is for eliciting listener feed back.
- And finally, unless an utterance is completely indecipherable or else can be further described by a general tag, then its default status is *Statement*.

Our dataset consisted of 47040 dialogue acts. The distribution of Dialogue Act is shown in Table 2.

[2]speaker me013 is split into me013-Bmr and me013-Bro to avoid the difference introduced by meeting types.

Tag	proportion
Disruption	14.73%
Back Channel	10.20%
Floor Mechanism	12.40%
Question	7.20%
Statement	55.46%

Table 2: Distribution of dialogue acts in our dataset.

4 Idiosyncrasy in Dialogue Acts

Our goal is to create a dialogue act recognition algorithm that can adapt to specific speakers. Some important questions must be studied before creating such algorithm. The first obvious one is: do speakers really differ in their choice of words and associated dialogue acts? Do we really see a variability on how people express their dialogue intent? If the answers are yes, then we will expect that learning a dialogue act recognizer from speaker-specific utterances should always outperform a recognizer learned from someone else data. Section 4.1 presents a comparative experiment addressing these questions.

To better understand the results from this comparative experiment, we also performed a qualitative analysis presented in Section 4.2 where we look more closely at the differences between speakers. These two qualitative and quantitative analysis are building block for our adaptation algorithm presented in Section 5.

4.1 Speaker-Specific Recognizers

An important assumption when performing speaker adaptation (or more generally domain adaptation) is that data coming from the same speaker should be similar than data coming from another person. In other words, a recognizer trained on a speaker should perform better (when tested on the same person) than a recognizer trained on another speaker. We designed an experiment to test this hypothesis.

We learned 7 speaker-specific recognizers, one for each speaker (see Table 1). We then tested all these recognizers on new utterances from the same 7 speakers. We looked the recognition performance when (1) the recognizer was trained on the same person and (2) when the recognizer was trained on a different person. This experiments quantitatively

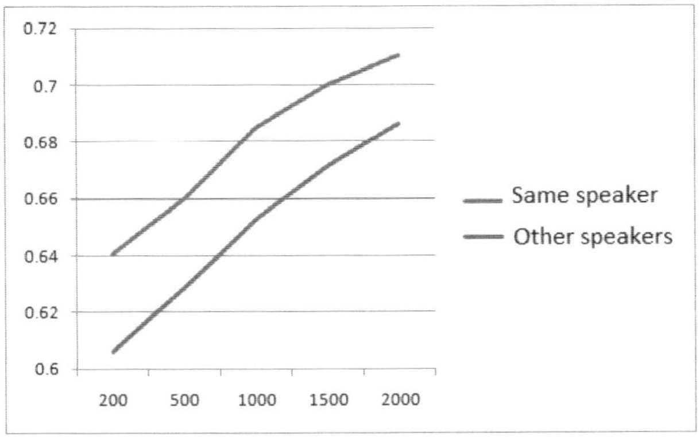

Figure 1: Effect of same-speaker data on dialogue act recognition. We compare two approaches: (1) when a recognizer is trained on the same person and tested on new utterances from the same person, and (2) when the recognizer was trained on another speaker (same test set). We vary the amount of training data to be 200, 500, 1000, 1500 and 2000 dialogue acts. In all cases, using speaker-specific recognizer outperforms recognizer from other speakers.

analyze the the difference among speakers. The experimental methodology used in this experiment is the same as the other experiments described in this paper (see Section 6). We use the Maximum Entropy model(MaxEnt) for all dialogue act recognizers (Ratnaparkhi, 1996). Please refer to Section 6.2 for more details about the experimental methodology.

Figure 1 compares the average performances when testing on the same speaker or on some other speaker. We vary the number of training data for each speaker to be 200, 500, 1000, 1500 and 2000 dialogue acts. For all five cases, the recognizers trained on the same speaker outperforms the average performance when using a recognizer from an other person. Thus speaker specific dialogue acts adaptation fits the assumption of domain adaptation problems.

4.2 Speakers Differences

To better understand the problem, we look more closely at the differences among speakers and their use of dialogue acts. We analyze the problem induced by speaker idiosyncrasy in dialogue acts. During our qualitative analysis of the ICSI-MRDA dataset, we identified three major differences explaining the performances observed in the previous sections: dialogue act conflicts, word distribution and dialogue act label distribution. We describe these three differences with some examples:

Conflicts: These differences happen when two speakers intended to express different meanings while speaking the exact same utterance. To examplify these conflicts, we computed mutual information between a specific utterance and all dialogue act labels. We find interesting examples where for exemple the word *right* is the most important cue for dialogue act *question* when spoken by me013-Bmr, while *right* is also an important cue for dialogue act *back-channel* for speaker me010-Bed. These examples suggest that conflicts exist among speakers and simply trying to learn one generic model may not be able to handle these conflicts. The generic model will learn what most people mean with this utterance, which may be the wrong prediction for our specific speaker.

Word distribution: People have their own vocabulary. Although many words are the same, how often one person use each word will vary. Although we may not have direct conflict here, the problem can also be serious. The learning algorithm may misleadingly focus on optimizing the weights for certain words which are not important(e.g., words that occur more often in other speakers' dialogue acts than his/her own) while under-estimating the important words for this speaker. This observation suggests that our adaptation should take into account word distribution.

Label Distribution: Another interesting observation is to look at the distribution of dialogue act labels for different speakers. Table 2 shows the average distribution over all 7 speakers. When looking more closely at each speaker, we find some interesting differences. For example, speaker 1 made statements 61% of the time while speaker 4 made 49% of the time. While this difference may not look significant, these changes can definitely affect the recognition performance. So the adaptation model should also take into account the dialogue act label distribution.

5 Reweighted Speaker Adaptation

Based on the observations described in the previous sections, we implement a simple reweighting-based domain adaptation algorithm mentioned in (Daume, 2007) based on Maximum Entropy model (MaxEnt) (Ratnaparkhi, 1996). MaxEnt model is a popular and efficient discriminative model which can effectively accommodate large numbers of features. All the unigram, bigram and trigram features are used as input to the maxEnt model, the output is the dialogue act label. MaxEnt model maximizes the log conditional likelihood of all samples:

$$Loss = \sum_{1}^{N} log(p(y_n|x_n)) \quad (1)$$

where N is the number of samples for the training data. x_n represents the feature of the n_{th} sample and y_n is the label. The conditional likelihood is defined as

$$p(y|x) = exp(\sum_i \lambda_i f_i(x,y))/Z(x) \quad (2)$$

where $Z(x)$ is the normalization factor and $f_i(x,y)$ are the n-gram features described in Section 3.

When applied to our problem of speaker adaptation, the *reweighting adaptation model* can be formally defined as

$$Loss = w \sum_{n=1}^{S} log(p(y_n|x_n)) + \sum_{m=1}^{O} log(p(y_m|x_m)) \quad (3)$$

where S is the number of labeled speaker-specific dialogue acts, O is the number for other speakers' labeled dialogue acts. For each speaker, we train one speaker-specific classifier by varying the distribution of training data. We reweight the importance of speaker specific dialogue acts versus other speakers' labeled dialogue acts in the training data. The optimal weight parameter w is automatically estimated through validation.

It is worth mentioning a specific instance of the reweighting adaptation algorithm. When w is set to 1, the reweighting adaptation algorithm is equivalent to simply training a MaxEnt model by putting the speaker-specific and generic data samples together as training data. In our experiments, we will compare the reweighting adaptation approach with this simpler approach, referred as *constant adaptation*.

6 Experiments

Our goal is to get one model specifically adapted for each speaker. We first describes 4 different approaches to be compared in the experiments, and section 6.2 explains our experimental methodology.

6.1 4 Approaches

In these experiments, we compare our approach, called reweighted adaptation, with three more conventional approaches: speaker-specific only, Generic and Constant adaptation.

- ***Speaker Specific Only*** For this approach, we train the dialogue act recognizer using training sentences from the same speaker used during testing.
- ***Generic*** In this case, we train the dialogue act recognizer using utterances from all speakers other than the speaker used during testing.
- ***Constant Adaptation*** For this approach, we train the dialogue act recognizer using all speakers, including the speaker who will later be used for testing. All utterances have the same weight in this case.
- ***Reweighted Adaptation*** This is our proposed approach. As described in Section 5, we train our dialogue act recognizer using all speakers but reweight the utterances from the speaker who will later be used for testing.

6.2 Methodology

In all the following experiments we use MaxEnt models as defined in Section 5. $L2$ regularization is used for MaxEnt to avoid overfitting. The optimal regularization parameter was automatically selected during validation. The following regularization parameters were used: 0.01, 0.1, 1, 10 , 100, 1000 and 0 (no regularization). All the unigram, bigram and trigram features are used in the maxEnt model. The labels are the five dialogue act tags described in Section 3.

All experiments were performed using hold-out testing and hold-out validation. Both validation and test sets consisted of 1000 dialogue acts. The training sets contained only utterances from meetings that were not in the validation set of test set.

Train Data	200	500	1000	1500	2000
Speaker-specific Only	64.07	65.99	68.51	69.99	71.06
Constant adaptation model	76.81	76.96	77.00	77.23	77.53
Our reweighted adaptation model	78.17	78.29	78.67	78.74	78.47

Table 3: Average results among all 7 speakers when train with different combinations of speaker specific data and other speakers' data. The number of speaker specific data is varied from 200, 500, 1000, 1500 to 2000.

In many of our experiments, we analyzed the effect of training set size on the recognition performance. The speaker-specific data size varied from 200, 500, 1000, 1500 and 2000 dialogue acts respectively. When training our reweighting adaptation algorithm described in Section 5, we used the following weights: 10, 30, 50, 75, and 100. The optimal weight factor was selected automatically during validation.

7 Results

In this section we present our approaches to study the importance of speaker adaptation for dialogue act recognition. All following results are calculated based on the overall tag accuracies. We designed three series of experiments for this study:

- Generic Recognizer (Section 7.1)
- Sparsity in speaker-specific data (Section 7.2)
- Effectiveness of Constant Adaptation (Section 7.3)
- Performance of the reweighting algorithm (Section 7.4)

7.1 Generic Recognizer

The first result we get is on average, for each speaker when we use *all other speaker's* data for training, then test on speaker- specific test data. The performance of this generic recognizer is 76.76% is the baseline we try to improve when adding speaker-specific data into consideration. [3]

[3]The performance of our generic model is comparable to the results from Ang et al (2005) when you take into consideration that we used only 47,040 dialogue acts in our experiments (i.e., dialogue acts from our 7 speakers) which is a small fraction compared with Ang et al (2005) .

7.2 Sparsity of speaker-specific data

A second result is the performance when only using speaker-specific data. The row *Speaker Specific Only* in Table 3 shows the average results among all speakers when for each speaker, we train using only data from the same speaker. The number of speaker-specific training data we tried are 200, 500, 1000, 1500, and 2000 respectively. Even with 2000 speaker-specific dialogue acts for training, the best accuracy is 71.06% which is lower than 76.76% when using generic recognizer. Given the challenge in getting 2000 speaker-specific annotated dialogue acts, we are looking at a different approach where we need less speaker-specific data.

7.3 Results of Constant Adaptation

The most straightforward way to combine other speakers' data is to directly add them with speaker-specific data as train. We refer to this approach as constant adaptation. The row *Constant Adaptation* in Table 3 shows the average results among all speakers when for each speaker, we combine the speaker-specific data directly with the *all other speaker's* data. In our experiments, we varied the amount of speaker-specific data included to be 200, 500, 1000, 1500, and 2000 respectively. For all 7 speakers, the performance can always been improved by including speaker-specific data with all other speakers' data for training. Furthermore, the more speaker specific data added, the better performance we get.

7.4 Results of Reweighting Algorithm

Finally, in this section we describe the results for a simple adaptation algorithm based on reweighting, as described in Section 5. Following the same methodology as previous experiments, we vary the amount of speaker-specific data to be 200, 500, 1000, 1500 and 2000. The best reweighting factor is selected through validation on speaker-specific validation data described in section 6.2. The results of all 7 speakers from Reweighting algorithm when we vary the amount of speaker-specific data are shown in Figure 3.

We analyze the influence of the weighting factor on our speaker adaptation by plotting the recognition performance for different weights. Figure 4 il-

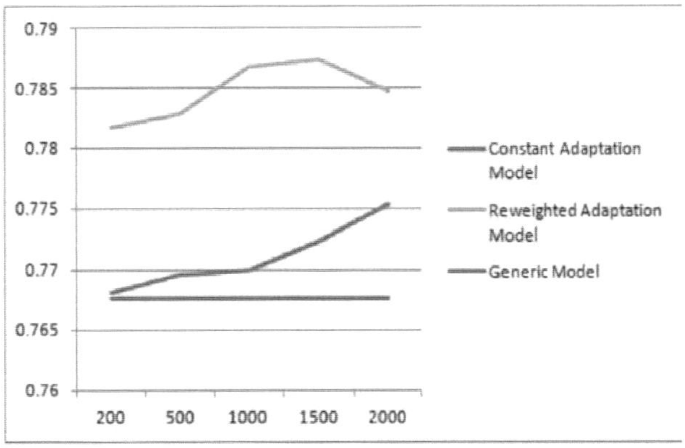

Figure 2: The average results among all 7 speakers when train with different combinations of speaker specific data and other speakers' data are displayed. In both Constant adaptation and Reweighted adaptation models the number of speaker specific data are varied from 200, 500, 1000, 1500 to 2000. In Generic model, only all other speakers' data are used for training data.

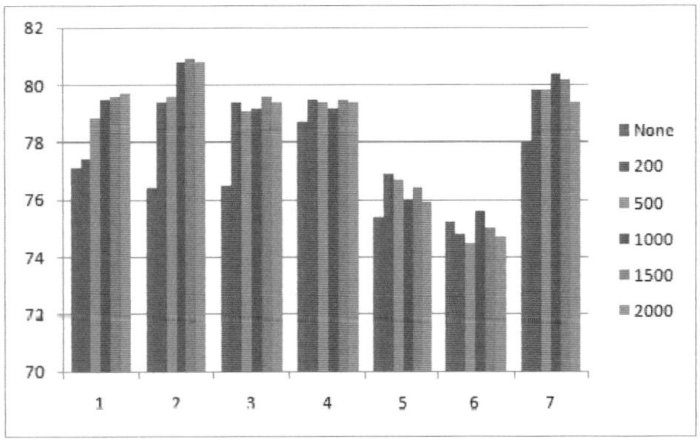

Figure 3: Reweighting algorithm for all 7 Individual Speakers when varying the amount of training data to be 0, 200, 500, 1000, 1500 and 2000.

lustrates the influence of the weight factor on three speaker adaptation cases: None, 500 and 2000. In this case, None represent the Constant Adaptation. We observe the following trend: with more speaker-specific data, the optimal reweighting factor is also lower. This confirms that our reweighting algorithm finds the right balance between speaker-specific data and generic data.

Figure 2 and the row *Reweighted Adaptation* from Table 3 shows the effectiveness of reweighting algorithm. Results shows that even this simple algorithm can efficiently balance the influence of speaker specific data and other speakers' data and

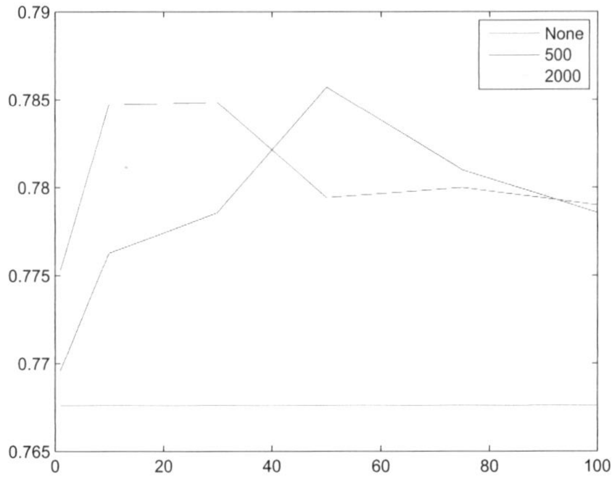

Figure 4: Average results of Reweighting among all 7 speakers when the amount of speaker specific data is 0, 500, 2000

give significantly improved results. And most surprisingly, even with only 200 speaker specific data the reweighting algorithm can give very promising results.

8 Conclusion

In this work we analyze the effectiveness of speaker adaptation for dialogue act recognition. A simple reweighting algorithm is shown to give promising improvement on several baseline algorithms even with only 200 speaker-specific dialogue acts. This paper is a first step toward automatic adaptation for dialogue act recognition. Inspired by the promising results from the simple reweighting algorithm, we plan to evaluate other domain adaptation techniques such as Daume's feature-based approach (2007). It will also be interesting to consider the unlabeled data from each speaker when performing dialogue act recognition.

Acknowledgments

This material is based upon work supported by the National Science Foundation under Grant No. 1118018 and the U.S. Army Research, Development, and Engineering Command (RDECOM). The content does not necessarily reflect the position or the policy of the Government, and no official endorsement should be inferred.

References

Jeremy Ang, Yang Liu, Elizabeth Shriberg 2005. Automatic Dialog Act Segmentation and Classification in Multiparty Meetings. *ICASSP*.

Jean Carletta. 2007. Unleashing the killer corpus: experiences in creating the multi-everything AMI Meeting Corpus. *Language Resources and Evaluation*, 41(2): 181-190

Mark Core and James Allen. 1997. Working Notes: AAAI Fall Symposium. *HLT-NAACL SIGDIAL Workshop*.

Hal Daumé III. 2007. Frustratingly Easy Domain Adaptation. *Proceedings of the 45th Annual Meeting of the Association for Computational Linguistics*.

Raquel Fernandez, Matthew Frampton, Patrick Ehlen, Matthew Purver and Stanley Peters. 2008. Modelling and Detecting Decisions in Multi-Party Dialogue. *Proceedings of the 9th SIGdial Workshop on Discourse and Dialogue*.

Umit Guz, Gokhan Tur, Dilek Hakkani-Tur, and Sebastien Cuendet. 2009. Cascaded model adaptation for dialog act segmentation and tagging. *Computer Speech & Language*, 24(2):289–306.

Minwoo Jeong, Chin-Yew Lin and Gary Lee. 2009. Semi-supervised speech act recognition in emails and forums. *The 2009 Conference on Empirical Methods on Natural Language Processing*.

Jing Jiang and ChengXiang Zhai. 2007. Instance weighting for domain adaptation in NLP. *Proceedings of the 45th Annual Meeting of the Association for Computational Linguistics*.

Jachym Kolar, Yang Liu, and Elizabeth Shriberg. 2007. Speaker Adaptation of Language Models for Automatic Dialog Act Segmentation of Meetings. *Interspeech*, 339–373.

Anna Margolis, Karen Livescu, Mari Ostendorf. 2010. Semi-supervised domain adaptation for automatic dialog act tagging. *ACL 2010 Workshop on Domain Adaptation for Natural Language Processing*.

Rajesh Ranganath, Dan Jurafsky, and Dan McFarland. 2009. It's Not You, it's Me: Detecting Flirting and its Misperception in Speed-Dates. *The 2009 Conference on Empirical Methods on Natural Language Processing*.

Vivek Rangarajan, Srinivas Bangaloreb and Shrikanth Narayanana. 2009. Combining lexical, syntactic and prosodic cues for improved online dialog act tagging. *Computer Speech and Language*, 23(4): 407-422

Adwait Ratnaparkhi. 1996. A maximum entropy model for part-of-speech tagging. *In Proceedings of the Conference on Empirical Methods in Natural Language Processing*.

Elizabeth Shriberg, Raj Dhillon, Sonali Bhagat, Jeremy Ang and Hannah Carvey. 2004. The ICSI Meeting Recorder Dialog Act (MRDA) Corpus. *HLT-NAACL SIGDIAL Workshop*.

Andreas Stolcke, Klaus Ries, Noah Coccaro, Elizabeth Shriberg, Rebecca Bates, Daniel Jurafsky, Paul Taylor, Rachel Martin, Carol V. Ess-dykema and Marie Meteer. 2000. Dialogue Act Modeling for Automatic Tagging and Recognition of Conversational Speech. *Computational Linguistics*, 26:339-373.

Gokhan Tur, Umit Guz and Dilek Hakkani-Tur. 2006. Model Adaptation For Dialogue Act Tagging. *Spoken Language Technology Workshop*.

Estimating Adaptation of Dialogue Partners with Different Verbal Intelligence

K.Zablotskaya
Inst. of Communications Engineering,
University of Ulm, Germany
kseniya.zablotskaya@uni-ulm.de

F.Fernández-Martínez
E.T.S.I. de Telecomunicacíon,
Universidad Politécnica de Madrid, Spain
ffm@die.upm.es

W.Minker
Inst. of Communications Engineering,
University of Ulm, Germany
wolfgang.minker@uni-ulm.de

Abstract

This work investigates to what degree speakers with different verbal intelligence may adapt to each other. The work is based on a corpus consisting of 100 descriptions of a short film (monologues), 56 discussions about the same topic (dialogues), and verbal intelligence scores of the test participants. Adaptation between two dialogue partners was measured using cross-referencing, proportion of "I", "You" and "We" words, between-subject correlation and similarity of texts. It was shown that lower verbal intelligence speakers repeated more nouns and adjectives from the other and used the same linguistic categories more often than higher verbal intelligence speakers. In dialogues between strangers, participants with higher verbal intelligence showed a greater level of adaptation.

1 Introduction

When two speakers are talking to each other, they try to adapt to their dialogue partner and synchronize their verbal behaviours. The adaptation may occur at different levels: lexical (Garrod and Anderson, 1987; Brennan and Clark, 1996), syntactic (Reitter et al., 2006), acoustic (Ward and Litman, 2007), articulation (Bard et al., 2000), comprehension (Levelt and Kelter, 1982), etc. Moreover, synchronization of dialogue partners at one level may cause the adaptation process at any other level (Pickering and Garrod, 2004; Cleland and Pickering, 2003). In this paper we analyse to what degree dialogue partners with different verbal intelligence and levels of acquaintance may adapt to each other during a conversation.

Verbal intelligence (VI) is "the ability to analyse information and to solve problems using language-based reasoning" (Logsdon, 2012). The ability to find suitable words and expressions may be a great help in accomplishing such goals as persuasions, encouragements, explanations, influence, etc. Moreover, there exists a dependency between an individual's verbal intelligence level and his or her success in life (Buzan, 2002).

The first hypothesis we check in this paper is that *both lower and higher verbal intelligence speakers are able to adapt to their dialogue partners; however, this adaptation is reflected by different linguistic features.*

The second hypothesis we check in this work is that *when higher and lower verbal intelligence speakers are talking to a stranger, the former ones adapt better to their dialogue partner than the latter ones.*

This investigation may be helpful for improving the user-friendliness of spoken language dialogue systems. Systems which automatically adapt to users' language styles and change their dialogue strategies may help users to feel free and comfortable when interacting with them.

2 Method

2.1 Corpus Description

For the analysis, a corpus containing 100 monologues, 56 dialogues and 100 verbal intelligence scores of the participants was used. The corpus was collected at the University of Ulm, Germany. All the participants were German native speakers of different genders, ages, educational levels and social status. For the monologue collection, the participants were shown a short film and were asked to describe it with their own words. The candidates were not asked to follow the language style of the film; they were asked to talk as naturally as possible in order to capture their every day conversation styles. Each monologue is about 3 minutes long and contains 370 words on an average. For the dialogue collection, the participants were asked to have a 10-minute conversation with another test person. The topic of the discussions was always the same: the education system in Germany. The average number of turns in the dialogues is 55. Afterwards, verbal intelligence of the candidates was measured using the Hamburg Wechsler Intelligence Test for Adults (Wechsler, 1982). Using this test, we obtained verbal intelligence scores of the test persons with a mean value of 113 and a standard deviation of 7.2. A more detailed description of the corpus can be found in (Zablotskaya et al., 2010; Zablotskaya et al., 2012).

2.2 Clustering

Using the k-means algorithm, the verbal intelligence scores of the test persons were partitioned into:

a) 2 clusters (Cluster L consisted of test persons with lower verbal intelligence, H contained candidates with higher verbal intelligence);

b) 3 clusters (L - lower verbal intelligence, M - average verbal intelligence, H - higher verbal intelligence).

Using the two clusters L and H, all the dialogues were partitioned into the following groups:

c) L-L is a group of dialogues where both partners had lower verbal intelligence scores;

d) H-H is a group of dialogues where both partners had higher verbal intelligence scores;

e) L-H is a group of all the other dialogues.

Using the information about the level of acquaintance of the dialogue partners, the following groups were created:

f) F-F is a group of dialogues with dialogue partners who were friends or relatives;

g) S-S is a group of dialogues with dialogue partners who had not met each other before the experiment (were strangers).

In the following sections the degree of adaptation will be compared between these groups.

3 Measuring Adaptation

There exist different approaches for measuring adaptation of dialogue partners. Reitter et al. (2006) used regression models to show that a speaker in human-human interactions aligns his syntactic structures with those of his dialogue partner. Ward and Litman (2007) modified the measures of convergence offered by Reitter. According to this modification, prime words of the first dialogue partner were determined. For measuring lexical convergence, the use of prime words by the second dialogue partner for each turn was calculated. In (Nenkova et al., 2008) the measurements of adaptation between dialogue partners were based on the usage of high-frequency words. Stoyanchev and Stent (2009) analysed adaptation calculating the number of reused verbs and prepositions by a speaker that occurred in his dialogue partner's turns.

In this work we measure adaptation as cross referencing, proportion of "I", "You" and "We" words, between-subject correlation and similarity between two texts. These approaches are described in the following sections.

3.1 Cross Referencing

Cross referencing is calculated as a number of repeated nouns and adjectives by a speaker P_1 from his dialogue partner P_2 divided by the total number of P_1's words (Sillars et al., 1997).

A one-way analysis of variance (ANOVA) showed significant difference between *Cross referencing* of speakers from the groups L, M and H ($AV_L = 0.08, AV_M = 0.047, AV_H = 0.042, F(2,97) = 8.43, p = 0.00062$). As we may see, speakers with lower verbal intelligence reused more nouns and adjectives of their dialogue partners than speakers with average and higher verbal intelligence.

3.2 "I", "You" and "We" words

The number of "I", "You" and "We" words in a discussion may reflect the degree of closeness of speakers. In Sillars et al. (1997) these measures were used for the analysis of language use in marital conversations and closeness of relationships between partners. It was found out that partners who had lived with each other for a long time and were happy together used "we" pronouns more often than separate pairs. In addition, the proportion of "I" and "You" words were higher for separates. In our investigation we also calculated the proportion of "I", "You" and "We" words for each groups and compared them using ANOVA. Interestingly, the proportion of "I"-words of friends was greater than that of strangers (averaged value of "I"-words for friends $AV_F = 0.0033$, for strangers $AV_S = 0.0017$, $F(1, 109) = 5.33$, $p = 0.024$). This phenomena may be explained in the following way. Even discussing the German education, friends might talk about themselves. People who had not met each other before avoided talking too much about their own experience. On the other hand, the difference of "We"-words was not significant. This means that even friends were not able to linguistically show their closeness discussing such kind of topic.

3.3 Between-Subject Correlation

All the dialogue transcripts were compared with the LIWC dictionary for the German language (Wolf et al., 2008). The dictionary consists of different words sorted by 64 categories. The categories may be divided into the following groups:

- *Language composition*, for example number of words, number of unique words, pronouns, articles, etc.
- *Psychological processes*, for example positive and negative emotions, causal words, words expressing certainty, etc.
- *Relativity*, for example words related to space, motion and time.
- *Topic-related categories*, for example job, school, sleep, etc.

Each word from the dictionary may refer to several categories. For example, the word *traurig* (sad) refers to the categories *Affective Processes*, *Negative emotions* and *Sadness*.

For analysing the degree of adaptation of dialogue participants, Pearson's correlation coefficients between $F(A_i)$ and $F(B_i)$ for each feature F were calculated ($F(A_i)$ is the value of a feature F extracted from the utterances of the first dialogue partner A from a dialogue i, $F(B_i)$ is the value of a feature F extracted from the utterances of the second dialogue partner B from a dialogue i). For participants from the group L-L, 30% of the features showed a significant correlation, for participants from the group H-L this value was 23%, for H-H this value was 12%. Table 1 shows the percentage of features with significant correlation for each LIWC group.

LIWC group	H-H	L-L	H-L
Language composition	28%	37%	9%
Psychological precesses	10%	19%	23%
Relativity	10%	35%	30%
Topic-related categories	11%	37%	27%

Table 1: Percentage of LIWC categories with significant correlation coefficients.

As we can see from the results, for almost all LIWC groups lower verbal intelligence speakers engaged in a conversation showed a higher degree of adaptation.

3.4 Similarity between two Texts

If two dialogue partners adapt to each other during a conversation, the similarity between their utterances should be high. For measuring the similarity between two texts, we calculated the degree of alignment between frequency distributions of certain features (tokens) extracted from the dialogues. For comparing the frequency distributions, the chi-square test was chosen because it does not require the normality of distributions and is easy to implement. A detailed explanation of this method may be found in (Vogel and Lynch, 2007) and (Straker, 2012).

Let F_i and F_j be two text files containing n_i and n_j tokens correspondingly. If F_i and F_j have the same language style, we consider the texts to be taken from the same population and the distributions of tokens from the two files should not be significantly different (null hypothesis). The chi-square statistic is calculated based on the observed and expected values of tokens in both text-files. If the chi-value χ_i^2 is less than a certain significance threshold c_i^2 (based on the degrees of freedom and significance level), the null hypothesis is accepted and the two files may be considered as having a similar language style (making an assumption that the language style is reflected by tokens of this type). For estimating the degree to which the two texts are similar, we calculate the distance between these two values:

$$Similarity_i = S_i = \chi_i^2 - c_i^2.$$

If $-c_i^2 <= S_i <= 0$, the similarity between the texts is significant. If $S_i > 0$, the null hypothesis is rejected: the analysed texts have different language styles.

In this investigation four different types of tokens were extracted: *Letter n-gram distributions*, *Word n-gram distributions*, *Lemma n-gram distributions* and *Part-of-speech n-gram distributions*.

The mean values of S_i for each group were compared to each other using ANOVA. Features with significant ANOVA results for the groups F-F and S-S are shown in Table 2:

Feature	**S_i for F-F**	**S_i for S-S**	**F(1,54)**
Word 3-g	-48.7	-29.8	10.6
Lemma 3-g	-41.8	-23.5	10.1
P.-of-speech 4-g	-38.9	10.0	8.1
P.-of-speech 5-g	-59.4	-34.3	8.6

Table 2: Significant features for F-F and S-S ($p < 0.05$).

The results show that the similarities of language between friends or relatives were greater than between participants who had not met each other before.

Our next purpose was to check whether verbal intelligence plays a certain role if we analyse dialogues between friends and strangers separately. ANOVA was applied to the mean values of the similarity measure S_i calculated for the following groups:

a) L-L, H-H and L-H only for dialogues between friends;

b) L-L, H-H and L-H only for dialogues between strangers.

ANOVA significant feature are shown in Tables 3 and 4.

Feature	**S_i(L-L)**	**S_i(H-H)**	**S_i(L-H)**	**F**
Word 4-g	-77.8	-62.4	-53.81	3.9
P.-of-sp. 6-g	-83.5	-63.7	-53.9	4.7

Table 3: Significant features for L-L, H-H and L-H only for dialogues between friends ($p < 0.05$, $F(1,53)$).

Feature	**S_i(L-L)**	**S_i(H-H)**	**S_i(L-H)**	**F**
Word 4-g.	-59.9	-90.1	-45.2	2.2

Table 4: Significant features for L-L, H-H and L-H only for dialogues between strangers ($p < 0.05$, $F(1,53)$).

As we may see from the results, a lower verbal intelligence speaker may adapt to his dialogue partner if they both are relatives or friends. On the other hand, if dialogue partners have not met each other before, higher verbal intelligence speakers are better able to adapt to their dialogue partner than lower verbal intelligence speakers.

4 Discussions

As we may see from the results, it was difficult for the candidates to linguistically show their closeness discussing the education system in Germany. However, similarity of utterances in dialogues between friends was greater than similarity in dialogues between strangers. Lower verbal intelligence speakers repeated nouns and adjectives from their dialogue partners and used words from the same linguistic dimensions more often than higher verbal intelligence speakers. The first hypothesis is just partly proven because we did not find features that reflect adaptation of higher verbal intelligence speakers. In our future work we are going to further investigate how higher verbal intelligence speakers linguistically show their closeness to the other. The results also showed that speakers with lower verbal intelligence are better able to adapt to the other if they both are relatives or friends. As we suggested in our second hypothesis, if dialogue partners are strangers, higher verbal intelligence speakers show a higher degree of adaptation. In our future work we are going to use this information for improving the classification of speakers into two and three groups according to their verbal intelligence coefficients.

Acknowledgments

This work is partly supported by the DAAD (German Academic Exchange Service).

Parts of the research described in this article are supported by the Transregional Collaborative Research Centre SFB/TRR 62 "Companion-Technology for Cognitive Technical Systems" funded by the German Research Foundation (DFG).

References

Bard, E. G., Anderson, A. H., Sotillo, C., Aylett, M., Doherty-Sneddon, G. and Newlands, A. 2000. Controlling the intelligibility of referring expressions in dialogue. *Journal of Memory and Language*, 42, p.1-22.

Brennan, S. E. and Clark, H. H. 1996. Conceptual pacts and lexical choice in conversation. *Journal of Experimental Psychology: Learning, Memory, and Cognition*, 22, p. 1482-1493.

Buzan, T. 2002. The power of verbal intelligence. HarperCollins Publishers, Inc.

Cleland, A. A. and Pickering, M. J. 2003. The use of lexical and syntactic information in language production: Evidence from the priming of noun-phrase structure. *Journal of Memory and Language*, 49, p.214-230.

Garrod, S. and Anderson, A. 1987. Saying what you mean in dialogue: A study in conceptual and semantic co-ordination. *Cognition*, 27, p. 181-218.

Levelt, W. J. M. and Kelter, S. 1982. Surface form and memory in question answering. *Cognitive Psychology*, 14, p.78-106.

Logsdon, A. 2012. Learning Disabilities. http://www.learningdisabilities.about.com/

Nenkova, A., Gravano, A. and Hirschberg, J. 2008. High frequency word entrainment in spoken dialogue. *Proceedings of ACL/HLT 2008*, p.169-172.

Pickering, M. and Garrod, S. 2004. Toward a mechanistic psychology of dialog. *Behavioral and Brain Sciences*, 27, p.169-190.

Reitter, D., Keller, F. and Moore, J. 2006. Computational modelling of structural priming in dialogue. In Proceedings of the Human Language Technology Conference of the NAACL, companion volume, 2006, p. 121-124.

Sillars A.L., Shellen W., McIntosh A. and Pomegranate M.A. Relational characteristics of language: Elaboration and differentiation in marital conversations. *Western Journal of Communication*, 61, p.403-422.

Stoyanchev, S. and Stent, A. 2009. Lexical and Syntactic Priming and Their Impact in Deployed Spoken Dialog Systems. *Proceedings of NAACL HLT 2009*, Boulder, Colorado, p.189-192.

Straker D. Changing Minds. http://changingminds.org/explanations/research/analysis/chi-square.htm.

Vogel C. and Lynch G. Computational Stylometry: Who's in a Play? In *Proceedings of COST 2102 Workshop (Patras)'2007*, p.169-186.

Ward, A. and Litman, D. 2007. Automatically measuring lexical and acoustic/prosodic convergence in tutorial dialog corpora. In Proceedings of the SLaTE Workshop on Speech and Language Technology in Education.

Wechsler D. 1982. *Handanweisung zum Hamburg-Wechsler-Intelligenztest für Erwachsene (HAWIE)*. Separatdr., Bern; Stuttgart; Wien; Huber.

Wolf M., Horn A.B., Mehl M.R. and Haug S. Äquivalenz und Robustheit der deutschen Version des Linguistic Inquiry and Word Count *Diagnostica*, 54, Heft 2, p.85-98.

Zablotskaya K., Fernández-Martínez F. and Minker W. 2012. Investigating Verbal Intelligence using the TF-IDF Approach. *Proceedings of International Conference on Language Resources and Evaluation (LREC) 2012*, European Language Resources Association (ELRA).

Zablotskaya K., Walter S. and Minker W. 2010. Speech data corpus for verbal intelligence estimation. In *Proceedings of International Conference on Language Resources and Evaluation (LREC) 2010*, European Language Resources Association (ELRA), Valetta, Malta.

A Demonstration of Incremental Speech Understanding and Confidence Estimation in a Virtual Human Dialogue System

David DeVault and **David Traum**
Institute for Creative Technologies
University of Southern California
12015 Waterfront Drive, Playa Vista, CA 90094
{devault,traum}@ict.usc.edu

1 Overview

This demonstration highlights some emerging capabilities for incremental speech understanding and processing in virtual human dialogue systems. This work is part of an ongoing effort that aims to enable realistic spoken dialogue with virtual humans in multi-party negotiation scenarios (Plüss et al., 2011; Traum et al., 2008). In these negotiation scenarios, ideally the virtual humans should demonstrate fluid turn-taking, complex reasoning, and appropriate responses based on factors like trust and emotions. An important component in achieving this naturalistic behavior is for the virtual humans to begin to understand and in some cases respond in real time to users' speech, as the users are speaking (DeVault et al., 2011b). These responses could include relatively straightforward turn management behaviors, like having a virtual human recognize when it is being addressed and turn to look at the user. They could also include more complex responses such as emotional reactions to what users are saying.

Our demonstration is set in an implemented negotiation domain (Plüss et al., 2011) in which two virtual humans, Utah and Harmony (pictured in Figure 1), talk with two human negotiation trainees, who play the roles of Ranger and Deputy. The dialogue takes place inside a saloon in an American town in the Old West. In this scenario, the goal of the two human role players is to convince Utah and Harmony that Utah, who is currently the local bartender, should take on the job of town sheriff. We presented a substantially similar demonstration of this scenario in (DeVault and Traum, 2012).

Figure 1: SASO negotiation in the saloon: Utah (left) looking at Harmony (right).

To support more natural behavior in such negotiation scenarios, we have developed an approach to incremental speech understanding. The understanding models are trained using a corpus of in-domain spoken utterances, including both paraphrases selected and spoken by system developers, as well as spoken utterances from user testing sessions (DeVault et al., 2011b). Every utterance in the corpus is annotated with an utterance meaning, which is represented using a frame. Each frame is an attribute-value matrix (AVM), where the attributes and values represent semantic information that is linked to a domain-specific ontology and task model (Traum, 2003; Hartholt et al., 2008; Plüss et al., 2011). The AVMs are linearized, using a path-value notation, as seen at the lower left in Figure 2. Our framework uses this corpus to train two data-driven models, one for incremental natural language understanding, and a second for incremental confidence modeling. We briefly summarize these two models here; for additional details and motivation for this framework, and discussion of alternative approaches, see (DeVault et al., 2011b; DeVault et al., 2011a).

The first step is to train a predictive incremental understanding model. This model is based on maximum entropy classification, and treats entire individual frames as output classes, with input features extracted from partial ASR results, calculated in increments of 200 milliseconds (DeVault et al., 2011b). Each partial ASR result serves as an incremental input to NLU, which is specially trained for partial input as discussed in (Sagae et al., 2009). NLU is predictive in the sense that, for each partial ASR result, the NLU module tries to output the *complete* frame that a human annotator would associate with the user's *complete* utterance, even if that utterance has not yet been fully processed by the ASR.

The second step in our framework is to train a set of incremental confidence models (DeVault et al., 2011a), which allow the agents to assess in real time, while a user is speaking, how well the understanding process is proceeding. The incremental confidence models build on the notion of NLU F-score, which we use to quantify the quality of a predicted NLU frame in relation to the hand-annotated correct frame. The NLU F-score is the harmonic mean of the precision and recall of the attribute-value pairs (or *frame elements*) that compose the predicted and correct frames for each partial ASR result.

Each of our incremental confidence models makes a binary prediction for each partial NLU result as an utterance proceeds. At each time t during an utterance, we consider the current NLU F-Score F_t as well as the final NLU F-Score F_{final} that will be achieved at the conclusion of the utterance. In (DeVault et al., 2009) and (DeVault et al., 2011a), we explored the use of data-driven decision tree classifiers to make predictions about these values, for example whether $F_t \geq \frac{1}{2}$ (current level of understanding is "high"), $F_t \geq F_{\text{final}}$ (current level of understanding will not improve), or $F_{\text{final}} \geq \frac{1}{2}$ (final level of understanding will be "high"). In this demonstration, we focus on the first and third of these incremental confidence metrics, which we summarize as "Now Understanding" and "Will Understand", respectively.

The incremental ASR, NLU, and confidence outputs are passed to the dialogue managers for each of the agents, Harmony and Utah. These agents then relate these inputs to their own models of dialogue context, plans, and emotions, to calculate pragmatic interpretations, including speech acts, reference resolution, participant status, and how they feel about what is being discussed. A subset of this information is passed to the non-verbal behavior generation module to produce incremental non-verbal listening behaviors (Wang et al., 2011).

2 Demo script

The demonstration begins with the demo operator providing a brief overview of the system design, negotiation scenario, and incremental processing capabilities. The virtual humans Utah and Harmony (see Figure 1) are running and ready to begin a dialogue with the user, who will play the role of the Ranger. The demonstration includes a real-time visualization of incremental speech processing results, which will allow attendees to track the virtual humans' understanding as an utterance progresses. An example of this visualization is shown in Figure 2.

As the user speaks to Utah or Harmony, attendees can observe the real time visualization of incremental speech processing. Further, the visualization interface enables the demo operator to "rewind" an utterance and step through the incremental processing results that arrived each 200 milliseconds.

For example, Figure 2 shows the incremental speech processing state at a moment 4.8 seconds into a user's 7.4 second long utterance, *i've come here today to talk to you about whether you'd like to become the sheriff of this town.* At this point in time, the visualization shows (at top left) that the virtual humans are confident that they are Now Understanding and also Will Understand this utterance. Next, the graph (in white) shows the history of the agents' expected NLU F-Score for this utterance (ranging from 0 to 1). Beneath the graph, the partial ASR result (`HAVE COME HERE TODAY TO TALK TO YOU ABOUT...`) is displayed (in white), along with the currently predicted NLU frame (in blue). For ease of comprehension, an English gloss (*utah do you want to be the sheriff?*) for the NLU frame is also shown (in blue) above the frame.

To the right, in pink, we show some of Utah and Harmony's agent state that is based on the current incremental NLU results. The display shows that both of the virtual humans believe that Utah is being addressed by this utterance, that utah has a positive attitude toward the content of the utterance while harmony does not, and that both have comprehension

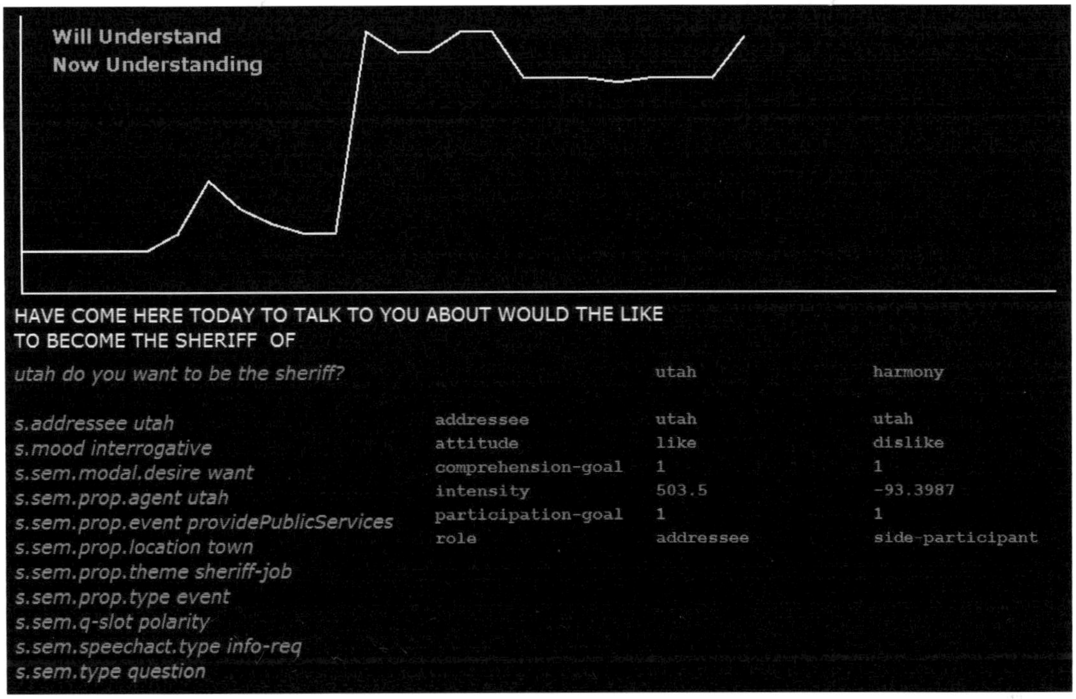

Figure 2: Visualization of Incremental Speech Processing.

and participation goals. Further, Harmony believes she is a side participant at this moment.

Acknowledgments

We thank the entire ICT Virtual Humans team. The project or effort described here has been sponsored by the U.S. Army Research, Development, and Engineering Command (RDECOM). Statements and opinions expressed do not necessarily reflect the position or the policy of the United States Government, and no official endorsement should be inferred.

References

David DeVault and David R. Traum. 2012. Incremental speech understanding in a multi-party virtual human dialogue system. In *Demonstration Proceedings of NAACL-HLT*.

David DeVault, Kenji Sagae, and David Traum. 2009. Can I finish? Learning when to respond to incremental interpretation results in interactive dialogue. In *Proceedings of SIGDIAL*.

David DeVault, Kenji Sagae, and David Traum. 2011a. Detecting the status of a predictive incremental speech understanding model for real-time decision-making in a spoken dialogue system. In *Proceedings of InterSpeech*.

David DeVault, Kenji Sagae, and David Traum. 2011b. Incremental interpretation and prediction of utterance meaning for interactive dialogue. *Dialogue & Discourse*, 2(1).

Arno Hartholt, Thomas Russ, David Traum, Eduard Hovy, and Susan Robinson. 2008. A common ground for virtual humans: Using an ontology in a natural language oriented virtual human architecture. In *Proceedings of LREC*, Marrakech, Morocco, may.

Brian Plüss, David DeVault, and David Traum. 2011. Toward rapid development of multi-party virtual human negotiation scenarios. In *Proceedings of SemDial*.

Kenji Sagae, Gwen Christian, David DeVault, and David R. Traum. 2009. Towards natural language understanding of partial speech recognition results in dialogue systems. In *Short Paper Proceedings of NAACL HLT*.

David Traum, Stacy Marsella, Jonathan Gratch, Jina Lee, and Arno Hartholt. 2008. Multi-party, multi-issue, multi-strategy negotiation for multi-modal virtual agents. In *Proceedings of IVA*.

David Traum. 2003. Semantics and pragmatics of questions and answers for dialogue agents. In *Proc. of the International Workshop on Computational Semantics*.

Zhiyang Wang, Jina Lee, and Stacy Marsella. 2011. Towards more comprehensive listening behavior: Beyond the bobble head. In *Proceedings of IVA*.

Integrating Location, Visibility, and Question-Answering in a Spoken Dialogue System for Pedestrian City Exploration

Srinivasan Janarthanam[1], Oliver Lemon[1], Xingkun Liu[1], Phil Bartie[2], William Mackaness[2], Tiphaine Dalmas[3] and Jana Goetze[4]
[1]Interaction Lab, Heriot-Watt University, Edinburgh
[2] School of GeoSciences, University of Edinburgh
[3]School of Informatics, University of Edinburgh
[4]KTH Royal Institute of Technology, Stockholm, Sweden
sc445,o.lemon,x.liu@hw.ac.uk, philbartie@gmail.com,
william.mackaness@ed.ac.uk,
tiphaine.dalmas@aethys.com, jagoetze@kth.se

Abstract

We demonstrate a spoken dialogue-based information system for pedestrians. The system is novel in combining geographic information system (GIS) modules such as a visibility engine with a question-answering (QA) system, integrated within a dialogue system architecture. Users of the demonstration system can use a web-based version (simulating pedestrian movement using StreetView) to engage in a variety of interleaved conversations such as navigating from A to B, using the QA functionality to learn more about points of interest (PoI) nearby, and searching for amenities and tourist attractions. This system explores a variety of research questions involving the integration of multiple information sources within conversational interaction.

1 Motivation

Although navigation and local information are available to users through smartphone apps, there are still important problems such as how such information is delivered safely and proactively, and without cognitively overloading the user. (Kray et al., 2003) suggested that cognitive load of information presented in textual and speech-based interfaces is medium and low respectively when compared to more complicated visual interfaces. Our objective, therefore, is to build a hands-free and eyes-free system that engages the pedestrian user by presenting all information and receiving user requests through speech only.

In addition, and in contrast to other mobile applications, this system is conversational – meaning that it accumulates information over time, and plans its utterances to achieve long-term goals. It integrates with a city model and a visibility engine (Bartie and Mackaness, 2012) to identify points of interests and visibile landmarks for presentation, a pedestrian tracker to improve the GPS positioning of the user and a question-answering (QA) system to enable users to explore information about the city more freely than with a graphical interface.

Table 1 presents an example dialogue interaction with the system showing the use of visibility information and Question-Answering.

User: Take me to Princes Street.
System: Turn left on to South Bridge and walk towards the tower in front of you.
...
System: Near you is the famous statue of David Hume.
User: Tell me more about David Hume.
System: David Hume is a Scottish philosopher....

Table 1: An example interaction with the system

2 Related work

There are several mobile apps such as *Triposo, Tripwolf*, and *Guidepal* that provide point of interest information, and apps such as *Google Navigation* that provide navigation instructions to users. However, they demand the user's visual attention because they predominantly present information on a mobile screen. In contrast, ours is a speech only interface in order to keep the user's cognitive load low and avoid users from being distracted (perhaps dangerously so) from their primary task.

Generating navigation instructions in the real world for pedestrians is an interesting research problem in both computational linguistics and geo-informatics (Dale et al., 2003; Richter and Duckham, 2008). *CORAL* is an NLG system that generates navigation instructions incrementally upon user requests based on the user's location (Dale et al., 2003). *DeepMap* is a system that interacts with the user to improve positioning using GUI controls (Malaka and Zipf, 2000). *SmartKom* is a dialogue system that presents navigation information multi-modally (Reithinger et al., 2003). There are also several mobile apps developed to help low-vision users with navigation instructions (see (Stent et al., 2010) for example). In contrast to these earlier systems we present navigational, point-of-interest and amenity information in an integrated way with users interacting eyes-free and hands-free through a headset connected to a smartphone.

3 Architecture

The architecture of the current system is shown in figure 1. The server side consists of a dialogue interface (parser, interaction manager, and generator), a City Model, a Visibility Engine, a QA server and a Pedestrian tracker. On the user's side is a web-based client that consists of the simulated real-world and the interaction panel.

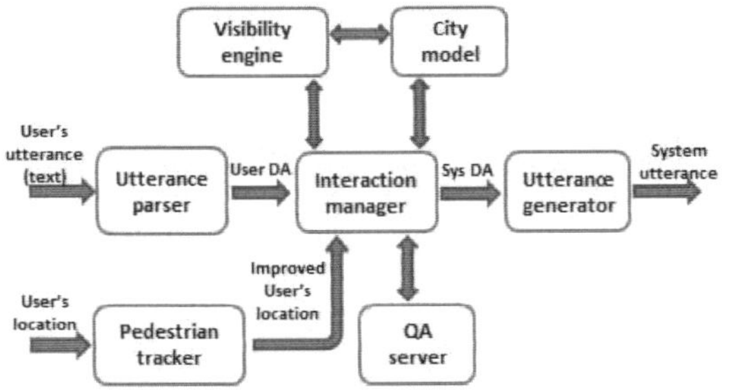

Figure 1: System Architecture

3.1 Dialogue interface

The dialogue interface consists of an utterance parser, an interaction manager and an utterance generator. The interaction manager is the central component of this architecture, which provides the user navigational instructions and interesting PoI information. It receives the user's input in the form of a dialogue act and the user's location in the form of latitude and longitude information. Based on these inputs and the dialogue context, it responds with system output dialogue act (DA), based on a dialogue policy. The utterance generator is a natural language generation module that translates the system DA into surface text, using the Open CCG toolkit (White et al., 2007).

3.2 Pedestrian tracker

Global Navigation Satellite Systems (GNSS) (e.g. GPS, GLONASS) provide a useful positioning solution with minimal user side setup costs, for location aware applications. However urban environments can be challenging with limited sky views, and hence limited line of sight to the satellites, in deep urban corridors. There is therefore significant uncertainty about the user's true location reported by GNSS sensors on smartphones (Zandbergen and Barbeau, 2011). This module improves on the reported user position by combining smartphone sensor data (e.g. accelerometer) with map matching techniques, to determine the most likely location of the pedestrian (Bartie and Mackaness, 2012).

3.3 City Model

The city model is a spatial database containing information about thousands of entities in the city of Edinburgh. These data have been collected from a variety of existing resources such as Ordnance Survey, OpenStreetMap and the Gazetteer for Scotland. It includes the location, use class, name, street address, and where relevant other properties such as build date. The model also includes a pedestrian network (streets, pavements, tracks, steps, open spaces) which can be used to calculate minimal cost routes, such as the shortest path.

3.4 Visibility Engine

This module identifies the entities that are in the user's *vista space* (Montello, 1993). To do this it accesses a *digital surface model*, sourced from LiDAR, which is a 2.5D representation of the city including buildings, vegetation, and land surface elevation. The visibility engine uses this dataset to offer a number of services, such as determining the line of sight from the observer to nominated points (e.g. which junctions are visible), and determining which entities within the city model are visible. These metrics can be then used by the interaction manager to generate effective navigation instructions. E.g. "Walk towards the castle", "Can you see the tower in front of you?", "Turn left after the large building on your left after the junction" and so on.

3.5 Question-Answering server

The QA server currently answers a range of *definition* questions. E.g., "Tell me more about the Scottish Parliament", "Who was David Hume?", etc. QA identifies the entity focused on in the question using machine-learning techniques (Mikhailian et al., 2009), and then proceeds to a textual search on texts from the Gazetteer of Scotland and Wikipedia, and definitions from WordNet glosses. Candidates are reranked using a trained confidence score with the top candidate used as the final answer. This answer is provided as a flow of sentence chunks that the user can interrupt. This information can also be pushed by the system when a salient entity appears in the user's viewshed.

4 Web-based User interface

For the purposes of this (necessarily non-mobile) demonstration, we present a web-based interface that simulates users walking in a 3D city environment. Users will be able to provide speech or text input (if the demonstration environment is too noisy for usable speech recognition as is often the case at conference demonstration sessions).

The web-based client is a JavaScript/HTML program running on the user's web browser. For a detailed description of this component, please refer to (Janarthanam et al., 2012). It consists of two parts: the Streetview panel and the Interaction panel. The Streetview panel presents a simulated real world visually to the user. A Google Streetview client (Google Maps API) is created with an initial user coordinate which then allows the web user to get a panoramic view of the streets around the user's virtual location. The user can walk around using the arrow keys on his keyboard or the mouse. The system's utterances are synthesized using Cereproc text-to-speech engine and presented to the user.

Acknowledgments

The research has received funding from the European Community's 7th Framework Programme (FP7/2007-2013) under grant agreement no. 270019 (SPACEBOOK project http://www.spacebook-project.eu/).

References

P. Bartie and W. Mackaness. 2012. D3.4 Pedestrian Position Tracker. Technical report, The SPACEBOOK Project (FP7/2011-2014 grant agreement no. 270019).

R. Dale, S. Geldof, and J. Prost. 2003. CORAL : Using Natural Language Generation for Navigational Assistance. In *Proceedings of ACSC2003, South Australia.*

S. Janarthanam, O. Lemon, and X. Liu. 2012. A web-based evaluation framework for spatial instruction-giving systems. In *Proc. of ACL 2012, South Korea.*

C. Kray, K. Laakso, C. Elting, and V. Coors. 2003. Presenting route instructions on mobile devices. In *Proceedings of IUI 03, Florida.*

R. Malaka and A. Zipf. 2000. Deep Map - challenging IT research in the framework of a tourist information system. In *Information and Communication Technologies in Tourism 2000*, pages 15–27. Springer.

A. Mikhailian, T. Dalmas, and R. Pinchuk. 2009. Learning foci for question answering over topic maps. In *Proceedings of ACL 2009.*

D. Montello. 1993. Scale and multiple psychologies of space. In A. U. Frank and I. Campari, editors, *Spatial information theory: A theoretical basis for GIS.*

N. Reithinger, J. Alexandersson, T. Becker, A. Blocher, R. Engel, M. Lckelt, J. Mller, N. Pfleger, P. Poller, M. Streit, and V. Tschernomas. 2003. SmartKom - Adaptive and Flexible Multimodal Access to Multiple Applications. In *Proceedings of ICMI 2003, Vancouver, B.C.*

K. Richter and M. Duckham. 2008. Simplest instructions: Finding easy-to-describe routes for navigation. In *Proceedings of the 5th Intl. Conference on Geographic Information Science.*

A. J. Stent, S. Azenkot, and B. Stern. 2010. Iwalk: a lightweight navigation system for low-vision users. In *Proc. of the ASSETS 2010.*

M. White, R. Rajkumar, and S. Martin. 2007. Towards Broad Coverage Surface Realization with CCG. In *Proc. of the UCNLG+MT workshop.*

P. A. Zandbergen and S. J. Barbeau. 2011. Positional Accuracy of Assisted GPS Data from High-Sensitivity GPS-enabled Mobile Phones. *Journal of Navigation*, 64(3):381–399.

A Mixed-Initiative Conversational Dialogue System for Healthcare

Fabrizio Morbini and **Eric Forbell** and **David DeVault** and **Kenji Sagae** and **David R. Traum** and **Albert A. Rizzo**
Institute for Creative Technologies
University of Southern California
Los Angeles, CA 90094, USA
{morbini,forbell,devault,sagae,traum,rizzo}@ict.usc.edu

Abstract

We present a mixed initiative conversational dialogue system designed to address primarily mental health care concerns related to military deployment. It is supported by a new information-state based dialogue manager, FLoReS (**F**orward-**Lo**oking, **Re**ward **S**eeking dialogue manager), that allows both advanced, flexible, mixed initiative interaction, and efficient policy creation by domain experts. To easily reach its target population this dialogue system is accessible as a web application.

Figure 1: Bill Ford, a SimCoach character. SimCoach virtual humans are accessible through a web browser. The user enters natural language input in the text field on the bottom of the screen. The simcoach responds with text, speech and character animation. The text area to the right shows a transcript of the dialogue.

1 Introduction

The SimCoach project is motivated by the challenge of empowering troops and their significant others in regard to their healthcare, especially with respect to issues related to the psychological toll of military deployment. SimCoach virtual humans are not designed to act as therapists, but rather to encourage users to explore available options and seek treatment when needed by fostering comfort and confidence in a safe and anonymous environment where users can express their concerns to an artificial conversational partner without fear of judgment or possible repercussions.

SimCoach presents a rich test case for all components of a dialogue system. The interaction with the virtual human is delivered via the web for easy access. As a trade-off between performance and quality, the virtual human has access to a limited set of pre-rendered animations.

The Natural Language Understanding (NLU) module needs to cope with both chat and military slang and a broad conversational domain. The dialogue policy authoring module needs to support non-dialogue experts given that important parts of the dialogue policy are contributed by experts in psychometrics and mental health issues in the military, and others with familiarity with the military domain.

The dialogue manager (DM) must be able to take initiative when building rapport or collecting the information it needs, but also respond appropriately when the user takes initiative.

2 Supporting Mixed Initiative Dialogues

There is often a tension between system initiative and performance of the system's decision-making for understanding and actions. A strong system-initiative policy reduces the action state space since user actions are only allowed at certain points in the dialogue. System initiative also usually makes it easier for a domain expert to design a dialogue policy that will behave as desired.[1] Such systems can work well if the limited options available to the user are what the user wants to do, but can be problematic otherwise, especially if the user has a choice of whether or not to use the system. In particular, this approach may not be well suited to an application like SimCoach. At the other extreme, some systems allow the user to say anything at any time, but have fairly flat dialogue policies, e.g., (Leuski et al., 2006). These systems can work well when the user is naturally in charge, such as in interviewing a character, but may not be suitable for situations in which a character is asking the user questions, or mixed initiative is desired.

True mixed initiative is notoriously difficult for a manually constructed call-flow graph, in which the system might want to take different actions in response to similar stimuli, depending on local utilities. Reinforcement learning approaches (Williams and Young, 2007; English and Heeman, 2005) can be very useful at learning local policy optimizations, but they require large amounts of training data and a well-defined global reward structure, are difficult to apply to a large state-space and remove some of the control, which can be undesirable (Paek and Pieraccini, 2008).

Our approach to this problem is a forward-looking reward seeking agent, similar to that described in (Liu and Schubert, 2010), though with support for complex dialogue interaction and its authoring. Authoring involves design of local subdialogue networks with pre-conditions and effects, and also qualitative reward categories (goals), which can be instantiated with specific reward values. The dialogue manager, called FLoReS, can locally optimize policy decisions, by calculating the highest overall expected reward for the best sequence of subdialogues from a given point. Within a subdialogue, authors can craft the specific structure of interaction.

Briefly, the main modules that form FLoReS are:

- The **information state**, a propositional knowledge base that keeps track of the current state of the conversation. The information state supports missing or unknown information by allowing atomic formulas to have 3 possible values: true, false and null.
- A set of **inference rules** that allows the system to add new knowledge to its information state, based on logical reasoning. Forward inference facilitates policy authoring by providing a mechanism to specify information state updates that are independent of the specific dialogue context.[2]
- An **event handling** system, that allows the information state to be updated based on user input, system action, or other classes of author-defined events (such as system timeouts).
- A set of **operators**. Operators represent local dialogue structure (trees), and can also be thought of as reusable subdialogues. Each state within the subdialogue can include a *reward* for reaching that state. Rewards are functions of the goals of the system, and are the main method used to decide what to do when there is more than one applicable operator. Operators have preconditions and effects. Effects specify changes to the information state. The preconditions define when an operator can be activated.

3 Sample Dialogue

In this demo, the user will interact with the SimCoach character Bill Ford, using a standard web browser and typing text. The virtual human, driven by FLoReS, will respond using pre-rendered animations encoded as H.264 video, delivered via a standard web server. Table 1 shows an excerpt from a sample conversation with Bill Ford that illustrates some of the features of this dialogue manager.

The excerpt starts from a rapport building smalltalk sub-dialogue on the topic of barbecuing which is interrupted by a user question about confidentiality. The system responds to the user interruption and then re-starts the interrupted smalltalk because it is still the most valuable conversation continuation available at that moment.

[1] Simple structures, such as a call flow graph (Pieraccini and Huerta, 2005) and branching narrative for interactive games (Tavinor, 2009) will suffice for authoring.

[2] For example: every time the user says that s/he has nightmares we want to update the information state to include that s/he also has sleeping problems.

Dialogue transcript	Notes
BBQ Smalltalk Ask anybody about me, and they'll tell you that I love to BBQ	The character is equipped with a few operators for smalltalk about a few topics. BBQ is one of them.
Is this conversation secret?	
Confidentiality QA We don't share your info with anyone who can personally identify you. The techs can see what we say, but just to tell that the site is working. But they have no idea who said it, just what was said Did that help you? *Yes it did.* Great.	Here the system is interrupted by a user question and it decides that answering it is the best course of action.
BBQ Smalltalk Like I was saying, I love to BBQ	After answering the question, the best course of action is to awaken the paused operator about the BBQ smalltalk.
What is PTSD?	
What is PTSD QA PTSD, or post-traumatic stress disorder is an anxiety condition associated with serious traumatic events. It can come with survivor guilt, reliving the trauma in dreams, numbness, and lack of involvement with reality.	Again the BBQ smalltalk is interrupted by another question from the user.
PTSD Topic Interest QA So, is PTSD something you're worried about. I only ask, because you've been asking about it. •••	After answering the second question the system decides to ignore the paused operator and load a follow-up operator related to the important topic raised by the user's question. The selection is based on the expected reward that talking about PTSD can bring to the system.

Table 1: An excerpt of a conversation with Bill Ford that shows opportunistic mixed initiative behavior.

Next, the user asks a question about the important topic of post-traumatic stress disorder (PTSD). That allows operators related to the PTSD topic to become available and at the next chance the most rewarding operator is no longer the smalltalk subdialogue but one that stays on the PTSD topic.

4 Conclusion

We described the SimCoach dialogue system which is designed to facilitate access to difficult health concerns faced by military personnel and their families. To easily reach its target population, the system is available on the web. The dialogue is driven by FLoReS, a new information-state and plan-based DM with opportunistic action selection based on expected rewards that supports non-expert authoring.

Acknowledgments

The effort described here has been sponsored by the U.S. Army. Any opinions, content or information presented does not necessarily reflect the position or the policy of the United States Government, and no official endorsement should be inferred.

References

M.S. English and P.A. Heeman. 2005. Learning mixed initiative dialogue strategies by using reinforcement learning on both conversants. In *HLT-EMNLP*.

Anton Leuski, Ronakkumar Patel, David Traum, and Brandon Kennedy. 2006. Building effective question answering characters. In *Proceedings of the 7th SIGdial Workshop on Discourse and Dialogue*, pages 18–27.

Daphne Liu and Lenhart K. Schubert. 2010. Combining self-motivation with logical planning and inference in a reward-seeking agent. In Joaquim Filipe, Ana L. N. Fred, and Bernadette Sharp, editors, *ICAART (2)*, pages 257–263. INSTICC Press.

Tim Paek and Roberto Pieraccini. 2008. Automating spoken dialogue management design using machine learning: An industry perspective. *Speech Communication*, 50(89):716 – 729. Evaluating new methods and models for advanced speech-based interactive systems.

Roberto Pieraccini and Juan Huerta. 2005. Where do we go from here? Research and commercial spoken dialog systems. In *Proceedings of the 6th SIGdial Workshop on Discourse and Dialogue*, Lisbon, Portugal, September.

Grant Tavinor. 2009. *The art of videogames*. New Directions in Aesthetics. Wiley-Blackwell, Oxford.

J.D. Williams and S. Young. 2007. Scaling POMDPs for spoken dialog management. *IEEE Trans. on Audio, Speech, and Language Processing*, 15(7):2116–2129.

Towards Mediating Shared Perceptual Basis in Situated Dialogue

Changsong Liu, Rui Fang, Joyce Y. Chai
Department of Computer Science and Engineering
Michigan State University
East Lansing, MI, 48864
{cliu,fangrui,jchai}@cse.msu.edu

Abstract

To enable effective referential grounding in situated human robot dialogue, we have conducted an empirical study to investigate how conversation partners collaborate and mediate shared basis when they have mismatched visual perceptual capabilities. In particular, we have developed a graph-based representation to capture linguistic discourse and visual discourse, and applied inexact graph matching to ground references. Our empirical results have shown that, even when computer vision algorithms produce many errors (e.g. 84.7% of the objects in the environment are mis-recognized), our approach can still achieve 66% accuracy in referential grounding. These results demonstrate that, due to its error-tolerance nature, inexact graph matching provides a potential solution to mediate shared perceptual basis for referential grounding in situated interaction.

1 Introduction

To support natural interaction between a human and a robot, technology enabling human robot dialogue has become increasingly important. Human robot dialogue often involves objects and their identities in the environment. One critical problem is *interpretation and grounding of references* - a process to establish mutual understanding between conversation partners about intended references (Clark and Wilkes-Gibbs, 1986). The robot needs to identify referents in the environment that are specified by its human partner and the partner needs to recognize that the intended referents are correctly understood. It is critical for the robot and its partner to quickly and reliably reach the mutual acceptance of references before conversation can move forward.

Despite recent progress (Scheutz et al., 2007b; Foster et al., 2008; Skubic et al., 2004; Kruijff et al., 2007; Fransen et al., 2007), interpreting and grounding references remains a very challenging problem. In situated interaction, although a robot and its human partner are co-present in a shared environment, they have significantly mismatched perceptual capabilities (e.g., recognizing objects in the surroundings). Their knowledge and representation of the shared world are significantly different. When a shared perceptual basis is missing, grounding references to the environment will be difficult (Clark, 1996). Therefore, a foremost question is to understand how partners with mismatched perceptual capabilities mediate shared basis to achieve referential grounding.

To address this problem, we have conducted an empirical study to investigate how conversation partners collaborate and mediate shared basis when they have mismatched visual perceptual capabilities. In particular, we have developed a graph-based representation to capture linguistic discourse and visual discourse, and applied inexact graph matching to ground references. Our empirical results have shown that, even when the perception of the environment by computer vision algorithms has a high error rate (84.7% of the objects are mis-recognized), our approach can still correctly ground those mis-recognized objects with 66% accuracy. The results demonstrate that, due to its error-tolerance nature, inexact graph matching provides a potential solution to mediate shared perceptual basis for referential grounding in situated interaction.

In the following sections, we first describe an empirical study based on a virtual environment to examine how partners mediate their mismatched visual perceptual basis. We then provide details about our graph matching based approach and its evaluation.

2 Related Work

There has been an increasing number of published works on situated language understanding(Scheutz et al., 2007a; Foster et al., 2008; Skubic et al., 2004; Huwel and Wrede, 2006), focusing on interpretation of referents in a shared environment. Different approaches have been developed to resolve visual referents. Gorniak and Roy present an approach that grounds referring expressions to visual objects through semantic decomposition, using context free grammar that connect linguistic structures with underlying visual properties (Gorniak and Roy, 2004a). Recently, they have extended this work by including action-affordances (Gorniak and Roy, 2007). This line of work has mainly focused on grounding words to low-level visual properties. To incorporate situational awareness, incremental approaches have been developed to prune interpretations which do not have corresponding visual referents in the environment (Scheutz et al., 2007a; Scheutz et al., 2007b; Brick and Scheutz, 2007). A recent work applies a bidirectional approach to connect bottom-up incremental language processing to top-down constrains on possible interpretation of referents given situation awareness (Kruijff et al., 2007). Most of these previous works address utterance level processing. Here, we are interested in exploring how the mismatched perceptual capabilities influences the collaborative discourse, and developing a graph-based framework for referential grounding with mismatched perceptions.

3 Empirical Study

It is very difficult to study the collaborative process between partners with mismatched perceptual capabilities. Subjects with truly mismatched perceptual capabilities are difficult to recruit, and the discrepancy between capabilities is difficult to measure and control. The wizard-of-oz studies with

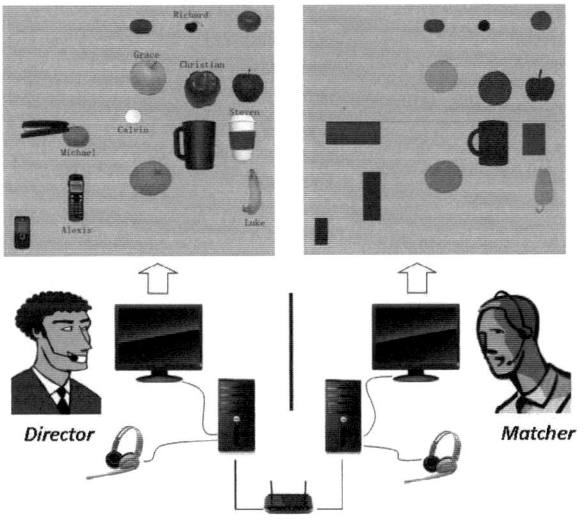

Figure 1: Our experimental system. Two partners collaborate on an object naming task using this system. The *director* on the left side is shown an (synthesized) original image, while the *matcher* on the right side is shown an impoverished version of the original image.

physical robots (e.g., as in (Green and Severinson Eklundh, 2001; Shiomi et al., 2007; Kahn et al., 2008)) are also insufficient since it is not clear what should be the underlying principles to guide the wizard's decisions and thus the perceived robot's behaviors (Steinfeld et al., 2009). To address these problems, motivated by the Map Task (Anderson et al., 1991) and the recent encouraging results from virtual simulation in Human Robot Interaction (HRI) studies (Carpin et al., 2007; Chernova et al., 2010), we conducted an empirical study based on virtual simulations of mismatched perceptual capabilities.

3.1 Experimental System and Task

The setup of our experimental system is shown in Figure 1. In the experiment, two human partners (a *director* and a *matcher*) collaborate on an object naming task. The mismatched perceptual capabilities between partners are simulated by different versions of an image shown to them: the director looks at an original image, while the matcher looks at an impoverished version of the original image.

The original image (the one on the left in Figure 1) was created by randomly selecting images of daily-life items (office supplies, fruits, etc.) from an image database and randomly positioning them onto a background. To create the impoverished image (the one on the right in Figure 1), we applied standard Computer Vision (CV) algorithms to process the original image and then create an abstract representation based on the outputs from the CV algorithms.

More specifically, the original image was fed into a $segmentation \rightarrow feature\ extraction \rightarrow recognition$ pipeline of CV algorithms. First, the OTSU algorithm (Otsu, 1975) was used for image segmentation. Then visual features such as color and shape were extracted from the segmented regions (Zhang and Lu, 2002). Finally, object recognition was done by searching the nearest neighbor (in the shape-feature vector space) from a knowledge base of "known" objects. The impoverished image was then created based on the CV algorithms' outputs. For example, if an object in the original image was recognized as a pear, an abstract illustration of pear would be displayed in the impoverished image at the same position. Other features such like color and size of the object were also extracted from the original image and assigned to the illustration in the impoverished image.

In the naming task, the director's goal is to communicate the "secret names" of some randomly selected objects (i.e., target objects) in his/her image to the matcher, so that the matcher would know which object has what name. As shown in Figure 1, those secret names are displayed only on the director's screen but not the matcher's. Once the matcher believes that he/she correctly acquires the name of an target object, he/she will record the name by mouse-clicking on the target and repeating the name. A task is considered complete when the matcher has recorded the names of all the target objects.

3.2 Examples

Consistent with previous findings (Liu et al., 2011), our empirical study shows that human partners tend to combine object properties and spatial relations to construct their referring expressions. In addition, our empirical study has further demonstrated how partners manage to mediate their perceptual basis through collaborative discourse. Here are two examples from our data:

Example 1.

D[1]: the very top right hand corner, there is a red apple
M: ok
D: and then to the left of that red apple on the top of the screen is a red or black cherry
M: ok
D: and then to the left of that is a brown kiwi fruit
M: ok
D: and the, the red cherry is called Richard
... ...

Example 2.

D: ok, um, so can we start in the top right
M: alright, um, the top right there are two rows of items, they are all circular or apple shaped
D: ok, um, the item in the very top right corner does not have a name
M: um, no name
M: um, to the left of that
D: yes, to the left of that is Richard
M: ok, are there only three items in that row
D: yes, there are only three
M: ok, this is Richard
... ...

As shown in Example 1, the most commonly used object properties include *object class*, *color*, *spatial location*, and others such as *size*, *length* and *shape*. For the relations, the most common one is the projective spatial relations (Liu et al., 2010), such as *right*, *left*, *above*, *below*. Besides, as illustrated by Example 2, descriptions based on grouping of multiple objects are also commonly used. To mediate their shared basis, both the director and the matcher make extra effort to collaborate with each other. For instance, in Example 1, the director applies installment (Clark and Wilkes-Gibbs, 1986) where he utters noun phrases in episodes and the matcher explicitly accepts each installment before the director moves forward. In Example 2, the matcher intends to assist the grounding process by proactively providing what he perceives about the environment.

The data collected from our empirical study have indicated that, to mediate a shared perceptual basis and ground references, a successful method should consider the following issues: (1) It needs to capture the dynamics of the linguistic discourse and identify various relations among different referring expressions throughout discourse. (2) it needs to represent the perceived visual features and topological relations between visual objects in the visual discourse. (3) Because the perceived visual world by

[1] *D* stands for *Director* and *M* for *Matcher*.

the matcher (who represents the lower-calibre artificial agent) very often differs from the perceived visual world by the director (who represents the higher-calibre human partner), reference resolution will need some approximation without enforcing a complete satisfaction of constraints. Based on these considerations, we have developed a graph-based approach for referential grounding. Next we give a detailed account on this approach.

4 A Graph-based Approach to Referential Grounding

In the field of image analysis and pattern recognition, Attributed Relational Graph (ARG) is a very useful data structure to represent an image (Tsai and Fu, 1979; Sanfeliu and Fu, 1983). In an ARG, the underlying unlabeled graph represents the topological structure of the scene. Then each node and edge are labeled with a vector of attributes that represents local features of a single node or the topological features between two nodes. Based on the ARG representations, an inexact graph matching is to find a graph or a subgraph whose *error-transformation cost* with the already given graph is minimum (Eshera and Fu, 1984).

Motivated by the representation power of ARG and the error-correcting capability of inexact graph matching, we developed a graph-based approach to address the referential grounding problem. ARG and probabilistic graph matching have been previously applied in multimodal reference resolution (Chai et al., 2004a; Chai et al., 2004b) by integrating speech and gestures. Here, although we use similar ARG representations, our algorithm is based on inexact graph matching and our focus is on mediating shared perceptual basis.

4.1 Graph Representations

Figure 2 illustrates the key elements and the process of our graph-based method. The key elements of our method are two ARG representations, one of which is called the *discourse graph* and the other called the *vision graph*.

The discourse graph captures the information extracted from the linguistic discourse.[2] To create the discourse graph, the linguistic discourse first needs

[2]Currently we only focus on the utterances from the director.

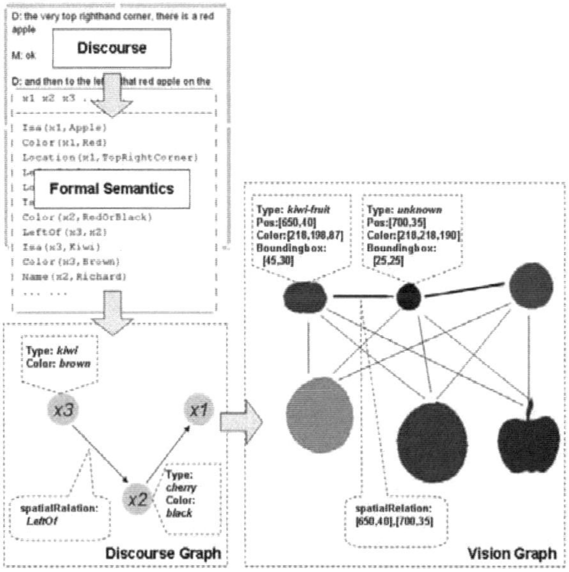

Figure 2: An illustration of graph representations in our method. The discourse graph is created from formal semantic representations of the linguistic discourse; The vision graph is created by applying CV algorithms on the corresponding scene. Given the two graphs, referential grounding is to construct a node-to-node mapping from the discourse graph to the vision graph.

to be processed by NLP components, such as the semantic composition and discourse coreference resolution components. The output of the NLP components are usually in the form of some formal semantic representations, e.g. in the form of first-order logic representations. The discourse graph is then created based on the formal semantics, i.e. each new discourse entity corresponds to a node in the graph, one-arity predicates correspond to node attributes and two-arity predicates correspond to edge attributes. The vision graph, on the other hand, is a representation of the visual features extracted from the scene. Each object detected by CV algorithms is represented as a node in the vision graph, and the attributes of the node correspond to visual features, such as the color, size and position of the object. The edges between nodes represent their relations in the physical space.

Given the discourse graph and the vision graph, now we can formulate referential grounding as constructing a node-to-node mapping from the discourse graph to the vision graph, or in other words, a matching between the two graphs. Note that, the matching we encounter here is different from the original graph matching problem that is often used in the image analysis field. The original version only considers matching between two graphs that have the same type of values for each attribute. But in the case of referential grounding, all the attributes in the discourse graph possess symbolic values since they come from formal semantic representations, whereas the attributes in the vision graph are often numeric values produced by CV algorithms. Our solution is to introduce a set of *symbol grounding functions*, which bridges the heterogeneous attributes of the two graphs and makes general graph matching algorithms applicable to referential grounding.

4.2 Inexact Graph Matching

We formulate referential grounding as a graph matching problem, which has extended the original graph matching approach used in image processing and pattern recognition filed (Tsai and Fu, 1979; Tsai and Fu, 1983; Eshera and Fu, 1984).

First, we give the formal definition of an ARG, which is a doublet of the form

$$G = (N, E)$$

where

- N — The set of attributed-nodes of graph G, defined as $$N = \{(i, a)\,|1 \le i \le |N|\}.$$
- E — The set of directed attributed-edges of graph G, defined as $$E = \{(i, j, e)\,|1 \le i, j \le |N|\}.$$
- $(i, a) \in N$ — Node i with a as its attribute vector, where $a = [v_1, v_2, \cdots, v_K]$ is a vector of K attributes. To simplify the notation, We will denote a node as a_i.
- $(i, j, e) \in E$ — The directed edge from node i to node j with e as its attribute vector, where $e = [u_1, u_2, \cdots, u_L]$ is a vector of L attributes. We will denote an edge as e_{ij}.

In an ARG, the value of a node/edge attribute v_k/u_l can be symbolic, numeric, or as a vector of numeric values. For example, if v_1 is used to represent the color feature of an object, then a possible assignment could be $v_1 = [255, 0, 0]$, which is the rgb color vector.

Suppose we represent referring expressions from the linguistic discourse as a discourse graph G and objects perceived from the environment as a vision graph G', referential grounding then becomes a graph matching problem: given $G = (N, E)$ and $G' = (N', E')$, in which

$$N = \{a_i\,|1 \le i \le I\}, E = \{e_{i_1 i_2}\,|1 \le i_1, i_2 \le I\}$$

$$N' = \{a_j'\,|1 \le j \le J\}, E' = \{e'_{j_1 j_2}\,|1 \le j_1, j_2 \le J\}$$

A matching between G and G' is to find a one-to-one mapping between the nodes in N and the nodes in N'.

Note that it is not necessary for every node in N or N' to be mapped to a corresponding node in the other graph. If a node is not to be mapped to any node in the other graph, we describe it as being mapped to Λ, which denotes an abstract "null" node. To represent the matching result, we re-order N and N' such that the first I'/J' nodes in N/N' are those which have been mapped to their corresponding nodes in the other graph, and the nodes after them are the unmatched nodes, i.e. those matched with Λ. Then the matching result is

$$\begin{aligned} M &= M_1 \cup M_2 \cup M_3 \\ &= \{(i, j)\,|1 \le i \le I', 1 \le j \le J'\} \\ &\quad \cup \{i\,|I' < i \le I\} \\ &\quad \cup \{j\,|J' < j \le J\} \end{aligned}$$

Here M_1 is a set of I' pairs of indices of matched nodes. M_2 and M_3 are the sets of indices of all the unmatched nodes in N and N', respectively. Then M is what we call a matching between G and G'. It is an inexact matching in the sense that we allow both G and G' to have a subset of nodes, i.e. M_2 and M_3, that are not matched with any node in the other graph (Conte et al., 2004). The cost of a matching M is then defined as

$$C(M) = C(M_1) + C(M_2) + C(M_3)$$

To complete the definition of $C(M)$, we use M_{11} to denote the set of all the first indices of the matched pairs in M_1, i.e. $M_{11} = \{i\,|1 \le i \le I'\}$, and $H = \left(N^H, E^H\right)$ is the subgraph of G that is induced by the subset of nodes $N^H = \{a_i\,|i \in M_{11}\}$, then we have

$$\begin{aligned} C(M_1) &= \sum_{a_i \in N^H} C_N(a_i, a'_j) + \\ &\quad \sum_{e_{i_1 i_2} \in E^H} C_E(e_{i_1 i_2}, e'_{j_1 j_2}) \\ C(M_2) &= \sum_{a_i \in (N - N^H)} C_N(a_i, \Lambda) + \\ &\quad \sum_{e_{i_1 i_2} \in (E - E^H)} C_E(e_{i_1 i_2}, \Lambda) \end{aligned}$$

in which $C_N(a_i, a'_j)$ is the cost of mapping a_i to a'_j, $C_E(e_{i_1i_2}, e'_{j_1j_2})$ is the cost of mapping $e_{i_1i_2}$ to $e'_{j_1j_2}$, and $C_N(a_i, \Lambda)/C_E(e_{i_1i_2}, \Lambda)$ is the cost of mapping $a_i/e_{i_1i_2}$ to the null node/edge. They are also called node/edge substitution cost and node/edge insertion cost, respectively (Eshera and Fu, 1984). Note that, in our case we let $C(M_3) = 0$ since we have assumed that the size of G' is bigger than the size of G.

Finally, the optimal matching between G and G' is the one with the minimum matching cost

$$M^* = \arg\min_M \; C(M)$$

which gives us the most feasible result of grounding the entities in the discourse graph with the objects in the vision graph.

Given our formulation of referential grounding as a graph matching problem, the next question is how to find the optimal matching between two graphs. Unfortunately, such a problem belongs to the class of *NP-complete* (Conte et al., 2004). In practice, techniques such as A^* search are commonly used to improve the efficiency, e.g. in (Tsai and Fu, 1979; Tsai and Fu, 1983). But the memory requirement can still be considerably large if the heuristic does not provide a close estimate of the future matching cost (Conte et al., 2004). In our current approach, we use a simple beam search algorithm (Zhang, 1999) to retain the tractability. Following the assumption in (Eshera and Fu, 1984), we set the beam size as hJ^2, where h is the current level of the search tree and J is the size of the bigger graph (in our case G').

4.3 Symbol Grounding Functions

As mentioned in Section 4.1, in referential grounding the discourse graph and the vision graph possess different types of attribute values, therefore we introduce a set of "symbol grounding functions", based on which node/edge substitution and insertion costs can be formally defined.

We start with node substitution cost to give a formal definition of symbol grounding functions. As defined in the previous section, the node substitution cost of mapping (substituting) node a with node a' is[3]

$$C_N(a, a')$$

Recall that in our definition of ARG, each node is represented by a vector of attributes, i.e. $a = [v_1, v_2, \cdots, v_K]$ and $a' = [v'_1, v'_2, \cdots, v'_K]$. Thus, we define the node substitution cost as

$$C_N(a, a') = \sum_{k=1}^{K} - \ln \; f_k(v_k, v'_k)$$

in which $f_k(v_k, v'_k) = p \; (p \in [0, 1])$ is what we call the symbol grounding function for the k-th attribute.

More specifically, a symbol grounding function for the k-th attribute takes two input arguments, namely v_k and v'_k, which are the values of the k-th attribute from node a and a' respectively. The output of the function is a real number p in the range of $[0, 1]$, which can be interpreted as a measurement of the compatibility between a symbol (or word) v_k and a visual feature value v'_k.

Let $\mathcal{L} = \{w_1, w_2, \cdots, w_Z, UNK\}$ be the set of all possible symbolic values of v_k, then $f_k(v_k, v'_k)$ can be further decomposed as

$$f_k(v_k, v'_k) = \begin{cases} f_{k1}(v'_k) & \text{if } v_k = w_1; \\ f_{k2}(v'_k) & \text{if } v_k = w_2; \\ \vdots & \vdots \\ f_{kZ}(v'_k) & \text{if } v_k = w_Z; \\ \lambda_k & \text{if } v_k = UNK. \end{cases}$$

Here the idea is that each value of v_k may specify an unique function that determines the compatibility of a visual feature value v'_k. For example, suppose that we are defining a symbol grounding function for the attribute of "spatial location", i.e. where is an object located in the environment. The symbolic value v can be in the set of $\{Top, Bottom, \cdots, UNK\}$, and the visual feature value v' is the x and y coordinates (in pixels) of the object's center of mass in the image. A grounding function for the symbol *Top* can be defined as[4]

$$f_{Top}(v') = f_{Top}(x, y) = \begin{cases} 1 - \frac{y}{800} & \text{if } y < 400; \\ 0 & \text{otherwise.} \end{cases}$$

Note that we have added a special symbol *UNK* to represent the "unknown" (or "unspecified") value of v_k. When the value of an attribute in the discourse graph is unknown, i.e. the speaker did not mention anything about a particular property, the grounding function will simply return a predefined

[3]For the ease of notation we have dropped the subscript of a node.

[4]Assume that the size of the image is 800×800 pixels and the left-top corner is the origin $(0, 0)$

Type of Error	Number of Objects
No Error	9 (5.1%)
Recognition Error	150 (84.7%)
Segmentation Error	18 (10.2%)
Total	177

Table 1: Types of errors among all the target (named) objects. *Recognition error*: an object is incorrectly recognized as another type of object, or an unknown type. *Segmentation error*: an object is missing, or merged with another object.

Type of Error	Accuracy/Detection Rate	
	Object-properties Only	Object-properties and Relations
No Error	66.7% (6/9)	77.8% (7/9)
Recognition Error	38.7% (58/150)	66% (99/150)
Segmentation Error	33.3% (6/18)	44.4% (8/18)
Overall	39.5% (70/177)	64.4% (114/177)

Table 2: Referential grounding performance of our method. The accuracy/detection rates in the table were obtained by comparing the results with annotated ground truths.

constant, which we denote as λ. The node insertion cost $C_N(a, \Lambda)$ is now defined as[5]

$$C_N(a, \Lambda) = \sum_{k=1}^{K} -\ln \lambda_k$$

Currently we set all the symbol grounding functions' outputs for the unknown value (i.e. the λs) to ε, which is an arbitrarily small real number ($\varepsilon > 0$).

5 Empirical Results

Three pairs of subjects participated in our experiment. Each pair (one acted as the director and the other as the matcher) completed the naming task on 8 randomly created images. In total we collected 24 dialogues with 177 target objects to be named. Table 1 summarizes the errors made by the CV algorithms when the 177 named objects from the original images were processed and represented in the impoverished images, as described in Section 3.1. As shown in the table, only 5% of the objects were correctly represented in the impoverished images. The other 95% of objects were either mis-recognized (about 85%) or mis-segmented (10%).

The evaluation of our approach is based on whether the target objects are correctly grounded by the graph matching method. To focus our current effort on the referential grounding aspect, we ignored all the matchers' contributions to the dialogues. Thus the discourse graphs were built based on only the director's utterances. The formal semantics of each of the director's valid utterances was manually annotated using the DRS (Discourse Representation Structure) representation (Bird et al., 2009). The discourse graphs were then generated from the annotated formal semantics. The vision graphs were generated from the outputs of the CV algorithms. The graph matching method was then applied to return a (sub-) optimal matching between the two graphs.

Table 2 shows the referential grounding performance of our method. To better understand the advantages of the graph-based approach, we have compared two settings. In the first setting, only the object-specific properties are considered for computing the comparability between a linguistic expression and a visual object, and the relations between objects are ignored. This setting is similar to the baseline approach used in (Prasov and Chai, 2008; Prasov and Chai, 2010). In the second setting, the complete graph-based approach is applied, i.e. both the object's properties and the relations be tween objects are considered. As shown in Table 2, although the improvements of performance for the no-error objects and mis-segmented objects are not significant due to the small sample sizes, the performance for the mis-recognized objects is significantly improved by 27.3% ($p < .001$). The improvement for the overall performance is also significant (by 24.9%, $p < .001$). The comparison between two settings have demonstrated the importance of representing and reasoning on relations between objects in referential grounding, and the graph-based approach provides an ideal solution to capture relations.

In particular, even CV error rate is high (due to the simple CV algorithms we used), our method is still able to achieve 66% accuracy of grounding the mis-recognized objects. Furthermore, when a referred object is completely "missing" in the vision graph

[5] The edge substitution/insertion cost is defined in the same way as the node substitution/insertion cost.

due to segmentation error[6], our method is capable to detect such discrepancy between linguistic input and visual perception. The results have shown that 44.4% of those cases have been correctly detected. This is also a very important aspect since information about failures of grounding will allow the dialogue manager and/or the vision system to adapt better strategies.

6 Discussions

The work presented here only represents an initial step in our on-going investigation towards mediating shared perceptual basis in situated dialogue. It consists of several simplifications which will be addressed in our future work.

First, the discourse graph is created only based on contributions from the director, using manual annotations of formal semantics of the discourse. As shown in the examples (Section 3.2), the collaborative discourse has rich dynamics reflecting participants' collaborative behaviors. So our future work is to model these different discourse dynamics and take them into account in the creation of the discourse graph. The discourse graph will be created after each contribution as the conversation unfolds. When utterances are automatically processed, semantics of these utterances often will not be extracted correctly or completely as in their manual annotations. Therefore, our future work will also explore how to efficiently match hypothesized discourse graphs (from automated semantic processing) with vision graphs.

Second, our current symbol grounding functions are very simple and intuitive. Our future work will explore more sophisticated models that have theoretical motivations (e.g., grounding spatial terms based on the Attentional Vector Sum (AVS) model (Regier and Carlson, 2001)) and enable automated acquisition of these functions (Roy, 2002; Gorniak and Roy, 2004b). In addition, we will explore context-based symbol grounding functions where context will be explicitly modeled. Grounding a linguistic term to a visual feature will be influenced by contextual factors such as surroundings of the environment, the discourse history, the speaker's individual preference, and so on.

Lastly, as shown in our examples, the matcher also contributes significantly to ground references. This appears to suggest that, in situated dialogue, lower-calibre partners (i.e., robot, and here the matcher) also make extra effort to ground references. The underlying motivation could be their urge to match what they perceive from the environment to what they are told by their higher-calibre partners (i.e., human). This motivation can be potentially modeled as graph-matching and can be used to guide the design of system responses. We will explore this idea in the future.

[6]For example, if the director refers to "a white ball" but CV algorithm fails to detect that object from the environment, then the node in the discourse graph representing "a white ball" should not be mapped to anything in the vision graph.

7 Conclusion

In situated human robot dialogue, a robot and its human partners have significantly mismatched capabilities in perceiving the environment, which makes grounding of references in the environment especially difficult. To address this challenge, this paper describes an empirical study investigating how human partners mediate the mismatched perceptual basis. Based on this data, we developed a graph-based approach and formulate referential grounding as inexact graph matching. Although our current investigation has several simplifications, our initial empirical results have shown the potential of this approach in mediating shared perceptual basis in situated dialogue.

Acknowledgments

This work was supported by Award #1050004 and Award #0957039 from National Science Foundation and Award #N00014-11-1-0410 from Office of Naval Research.

References

A.H. Anderson, M. Bader, E.G. Bard, E. Boyle, G. Doherty, S. Garrod, S. Isard, J. Kowtko, J. McAllister, J. Miller, et al. 1991. The hcrc map task corpus. *Language and speech*, 34(4):351–366.

S. Bird, E. Klein, and E. Loper. 2009. *Natural language processing with Python*. O'Reilly Media.

T. Brick and M. Scheutz. 2007. Incremental natural language processing for hri. In *Proceeding of the*

ACM/IEEE international conference on Human-Robot Interaction (HRI-07), pages 263–270.

S. Carpin, M. Lewis, J. Wang, S. Balakirsky, and C. Scrapper. 2007. USARSim: a robot simulator for research and education. In *Proceedings of the 2007 IEEE Conference on Robotics and Automation.*

J.Y. Chai, P. Hong, and M.X. Zhou. 2004a. A probabilistic approach to reference resolution in multimodal user interfaces. In *Proceedings of the 9th international conference on Intelligent user interfaces*, pages 70–77. ACM.

J.Y. Chai, P. Hong, M.X. Zhou, and Z. Prasov. 2004b. Optimization in multimodal interpretation. In *Proceedings of the 42nd Annual Meeting on Association for Computational Linguistics*, page 1. Association for Computational Linguistics.

S. Chernova, J. Orkin, and C. Breazeal. 2010. Crowdsourcing hri through online multiplayer games. *AAAI Symposium on Dialogue with Robots.*

H. H. Clark and D. Wilkes-Gibbs. 1986. Referring as a collaborative process. In *Cognition*, number 22, pages 1–39.

H. H. Clark. 1996. *Using language.* Cambridge University Press, Cambridge, UK.

D. Conte, P. Foggia, C. Sansone, and M. Vento. 2004. Thirty years of graph matching in pattern recognition. *International journal of pattern recognition and artificial intelligence*, 18(3):265–298.

M. A. Eshera and K. S. Fu. 1984. A graph distance measure for image analysis. *IEEE transactions on systems, man, and cybernetics*, 14(3):398–410.

M.E. Foster, E.G. Bard, R.L. Hill, M. Guhe, J. Oberlander, and A. Knoll. 2008. Generating haptic- ostensive referring expressions in cooperative, task-based human-robot dialogue. *Proceedings of ACM/IEEE Human-Robot Interaction.*

B. Fransen, V. Morariu, E. Martinson, S. Blisard, M. Marge, S. Thomas, A. Schultz, and D. Perzanowski. 2007. Using vision, acoustics, and natural language for disambiguation. In *Proceedings of HRI07*, pages 73–80.

P. Gorniak and D. Roy. 2004a. Grounded semantic composition for visual scenes. In *Journal of Artificial Intelligence Research*, volume 21, pages 429–470.

P. Gorniak and D. Roy. 2004b. Grounded semantic composition for visual scenes. *J. Artif. Intell. Res. (JAIR)*, 21:429–470.

P. Gorniak and D. Roy. 2007. Situated language understanding as filtering perceived affordances. In *Cognitive Science*, volume 31(2), pages 197–231.

A. Green and K. Severinson Eklundh. 2001. Task-oriented dialogue for CERO: a user centered approach. In *Proceedings of 10th IEEE international workshop on robot and human interactive communication*, September.

Sonja Huwel and Britta Wrede. 2006. Situated speech understanding for robust multi-modal human-robot communication. In *Proceedings of the International Conference on Computational Linguistics (COLING/ACL).*

P. Kahn, N. Greier, T. Kanda, H. Ishiguro, J. Ruckert, R. Severson, and S. Kane. 2008. Design patterns for sociality in human-robot interaction. In *Proceedings of HRI*, pages 97–104.

Geert-Jan M. Kruijff, Pierre Lison, Trevor Benjamin, Henrik Jacobsson, and Nick Hawes. 2007. Incremental, multi-level processing for comprehending situated dialogue in human-robot interaction. In *Symposium on Language and Robots.*

C. Liu, J. Walker, and J.Y. Chai. 2010. Disambiguating frames of reference for spatial language understanding in situated dialogue. In *AAAI Fall Symposium on Dialogue with Robots.*

C. Liu, D. Kay, and J.Y. Chai. 2011. Awareness of partners eye gaze in situated referential grounding: An empirical study. In *2nd Workshop on Eye Gaze in Intelligent Human Machine Interaction.*

N. Otsu. 1975. A threshold selection method from gray-level histograms. *Automatica*, 11:285–296.

Z. Prasov and J.Y. Chai. 2008. What's in a gaze?: the role of eye-gaze in reference resolution in multimodal conversational interfaces. In *Proceedings of the 13th international conference on Intelligent user interfaces*, pages 20–29. ACM.

Z. Prasov and J.Y. Chai. 2010. Fusing eye gaze with speech recognition hypotheses to resolve exophoric references in situated dialogue. In *Proceedings of the 2010 Conference on Empirical Methods in Natural Language Processing*, pages 471–481. Association for Computational Linguistics.

T. Regier and L.A. Carlson. 2001. Grounding spatial language in perception: an empirical and computational investigation. *Journal of Experimental Psychology: General*, 130(2):273.

D.K. Roy. 2002. Learning visually grounded words and syntax for a scene description task. *Computer Speech & Language*, 16(3):353–385.

A. Sanfeliu and K. S. Fu. 1983. A distance measure between attributed relational graphs for pattern recognition. *IEEE transactions on systems, man, and cybernetics*, 13(3):353–362.

M. Scheutz, P. Schermerhorn, J. Kramer, and D. Anderson. 2007a. First steps toward natural human-like HRI. In *Autonomous Robots*, volume 22.

M. Scheutz, P. Schermerhorn, J. Kramer, and D. Anderson. 2007b. Incremental natural language processing for hri. In *Proceedings of HRI.*

M. Shiomi, T. Kanda, S. Koizumi, H. Ishiguro, and N. hagita. 2007. Group attention control for communication robots with wizard of OZ approach. In *Proceedings of HRI*, pages 121–128.

M. Skubic, D. Perzanowski, S. Blisard, A. Schultz, W. Adams, M. Bugajska, and D. Brock. 2004. Spatial language for human-robot dialogs. *IEEE Transactions on Systems, Man and Cybernetics, Part C*, 34(2):154–167.

A. Steinfeld, O. C. Jenkins, and B. Scassellati. 2009. The oz of wizard: Simulating the human for interaction research. In *Proceedings of HRI*, pages 101–107.

W.H. Tsai and K.S. Fu. 1979. Error-correcting isomorphisms of attributed relational graphs for pattern analysis. *Systems, Man and Cybernetics, IEEE Transactions on*, 9(12):757–768.

W.H. Tsai and K.S. Fu. 1983. Subgraph error-correcting isomorphisms for syntactic pattern. *year: 1983*, 13:48–62.

D. Zhang and G. Lu. 2002. An integrated approach to shape based image retrieval. In *Proc. of 5th Asian conference on computer vision (ACCV)*, pages 652–657.

W. Zhang. 1999. *State-space search: Algorithms, complexity, extensions, and applications*. Springer-Verlag New York Inc.

Global Features for Shallow Discourse Parsing

Sucheta Ghosh Giuseppe Riccardi
University of Trento, Italy
{ghosh,riccardi}@disi.unitn.it

Richard Johansson
University of Gothenburg, Sweden
richard.johansson@gu.se

Abstract

A coherently related group of sentences may be referred to as a discourse. In this paper we address the problem of parsing coherence relations as defined in the Penn Discourse Tree Bank (PDTB). A good model for discourse structure analysis needs to account both for local dependencies at the token-level and for global dependencies and statistics. We present techniques on using inter-sentential or sentence-level (global), data-driven, non-grammatical features in the task of parsing discourse. The parser model follows up previous approach based on using token-level (local) features with conditional random fields for shallow discourse parsing, which is lacking in structural knowledge of discourse. The parser adopts a two-stage approach where first the local constraints are applied and then global constraints are used on a reduced weighted search space (n-best). In the latter stage we experiment with different rerankers trained on the first stage n-best parses, which are generated using lexico-syntactic local features. The two-stage parser yields significant improvements over the best performing model of discourse parser on the PDTB corpus.

1 Introduction

There are relevant studies on the impact of global and local features on the models for natural language understanding. In this work we address a similar problem in the context of discourse parsing. Although a good number of the papers in this area heavily rely on local classifiers (Grosz et al., 1995; Soricut et al., 2003; Lapata, 2003; Barzilay et al., 2005), there are still some important works using global and local informations together to form a model of discourse (Grosz et al., 1992; Barzilay et al., 2004; Soricut et al., 2006).

One of the main issues is the basis of the choice between a global or local or a joint model for discourse parsing: it all depends on the criteria to be able to capture maximum amount of information inside the discourse model. The policy for discourse segmentation plays a big role to formulate the maximizing criteria (Grosz et al., 1992). We study in the literature that defining a discourse segment is mostly a data-driven process: some argue for prosodic units, some for intentional structure and some for clause-like structures. We work with PDTB 2.0 annotation framework, therefore use a clause-like structure. Soricut et al. (2003) empirically showed that at the sentence level, there is a strong correlation between syntax and discourse, Ghosh et al. (2011b) found the same. Since the discourse structure may span over multiple sentences, intersentential features are needed to improve the performance of a discourse parser.

Linguistic theory suggests that a core argument frame (i.e. a pair of the `Arg1` and the `Arg2` connected with one and only one connective) is a joint structure, with strong dependencies between arguments (Toutanova et al., 2008). Following this, Ghosh et al. (2011a) also injected some structure-level information through the token-level features, for eg. the previous sentence feature. Still there is a room for improvement with more structure-level information to that discourse model; though it is cost-intensive to modify this discourse model. Therefore in this paper we re-use the model (Ghosh et al., 2011a) and optimize the current loss function adding the global features through reranking of the single-best model.

Reranking has been a popular technique applied in a variety of comparable NLP problems including parsing (Collins, 2000;

Charniak and Johnson, 2005), semantic role labeling (Toutanova et al., 2008), NP Bracketing (Daume III et al., 2004), NER (Collins, 2002), opinion expression detection (Johansson and Moschitti, 2010), now we employ this technique in the area of discourse parsing.

In the next sections, we detail on the backgrounds and motivations of this work, before this we also add a short discussion on PDTB (Penn Discourse TreeBank), i.e. the data we used to train the system. Then we proceed to the reranking approaches and results sections after describing our global feature set. Finally we state and analyze the results.

2 The Penn Discourse Treebank 2.0

The Penn Discourse Treebank (PDTB) is a resource containing one million words from the Wall Street Journal corpus (Marcus et al., 1993) annotated with discourse relations.

Connectives in the PTDB are treated as discourse predicates taking two text spans as *arguments* (`Arg`), i.e. parts of the text that describe events, propositions, facts, situations. Such two arguments in the PDTB are called `Arg1` and `Arg2`, with the numbering not necessarily corresponding to their order in text. Indeed, `Arg2` is the argument syntactically bound to the connective, while `Arg1` is the other one.

In the PDTB, discourse relations can be either overtly or implicitly expressed. However, we focus here exclusively on *explicit* connectives and the identification of their arguments, including the exact spans. This kind of classification is very complex, since `Arg1` and `Arg2` can occur in many different configurations (see Table 1).

Explicit connectives (tokens)	18,459
Explicit connectives (types)	100
`Arg1` in same sentence as connective	60.9%
`Arg1` in previous, adjacent sentence	30.1%
`Arg1` in previous, non adjacent sentence	9.0%

Table 1: Statistics about PDTB annotation from Prasad et al(2008).

In PDTB the senses are assigned according to a three-layered hierarchy: the top-level classes are the most generic ones and include TEMPORAL, CONTINGENCY, COMPARISON and EXPANSION labels. We used these four surface senses only in our task.

2.1 Backgrounds & Motivation

Currently we are using the single-best discourse parser by Ghosh et al. (2011a). This discourse parser can automatically extract of discourse arguments using a pipeline, illustrated in Fig 1. First, we input the explicit discourse connectives (with senses) to the system. These can be the gold labeled or automatically identified (Pitler and Nenkova, 2009); for simplicity here we use Penn Discourse TreeBank (PDTB 2.0) gold-standard connectives (*cf.* see 2). Then a cascaded module is applied extracting the `Arg2` arguments, then the `Arg1`s are extracted.

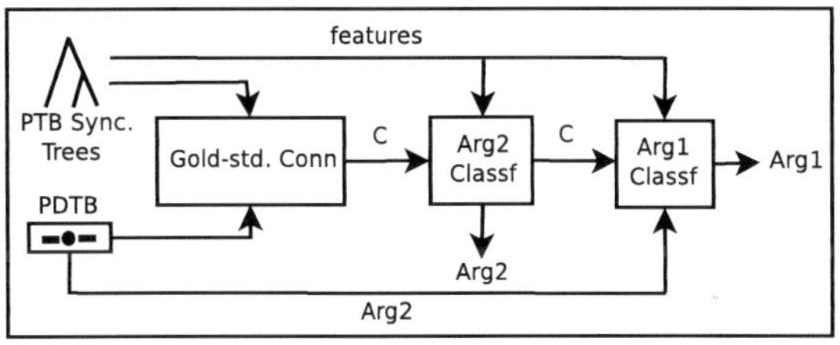

Figure 1: Pipeline for argument detection given a connective.

The `Arg2` and `Arg1` extractors are implemented as conditional random field sequence labelers, which use a set of syntactic and structural features (*cf.* Ghosh et al. (2011a)). In order to reduce the complexities, the sentence containing the connective, and a context window of up to two sentences before and after are supplied to the sequence labelers.

We present a passage of 6 sentences from a nutrition journal article parsed with that parser [1].:

```
<Conn id=1,sense=Comparison>
Although</Conn id=1> <ARG2 id=1>
the mechanism of obesity development
is not fully understood, it is confirmed
<ARG1 id=2>that obesity occurs</ARG1 id=2>
<Conn id=2,sense=Temporal>when</Conn id=2>
<ARG2 id=2>energy intake exceeds energy
expenditure</ARG2 id=2> </ARG2 id=1>.
There are multiple etiologies
for this imbalance, hence,
<Conn id=3, sense=Expansion>
and </Conn id=3> <ARG2 id=3>the rising
prevalence of obesity cannot be addressed
by a single etiology</ARG2 id=3>.
<ARG1 id=4>Genetic factors influence
the susceptibility of a given child to an
obesity-conducive environment</ARG1 id=4>.
<Conn id=4, sense=Comparison>However
```

[1]we used best model of (Ghosh et al., 2011b; Ghosh et al., 2011a) and Stanford lexicalized parser (Klein and Manning, 2003) to parse the text also used AddDiscourse tool to parse the connective and the senses (Pitler and Nenkova, 2009);parser took 17 second to parse

`</Conn id=4>, <ARG2 id=4>`**`environmental factors, lifestyle preferences, and cultural environment seem to play major roles in the rising prevalence of obesity worldwide`**`</ARG2 id=4>. In a small number of cases, childhood obesity is due to genes such as leptin deficiency or medical causes such as hypothyroidism and growth hormone deficiency or side effects due to drugs (e.g. - steroids). Most of the time, <Conn id=5, sense= Comparison>` ***`however`*** `</Conn id=5>, <ARG2 id=5>`**`personal lifestyle choices and cultural environment significantly influence obesity`**`</ARG2 id=5>.`

In the evaluations of Ghosh et al. (2011a), it states that recall was much lower than precision for both the arguments, especially in case of `Arg1`. The system often failed to predict `Arg1`. It is harder to identify since it is not always syntactically bound to the connective, like `Arg2`, moreover it is typically more distant than the `Arg2`s.

We notice the same in the parser output. The parser found all five `Arg2`s for all five connectives, though there may be disagreement on the selected boundaries; the number of parsed `Arg1`s is only two, whereas the second one with id of 4 is a previous sentence argument.

To improve the recall, (Ghosh et al., 2012) implemented a weighted constraint-based *handcrafted* postprocessor to force the Ghosh et al. (2011a) system to output arguments of each type abiding the requirements defined by the PDTB annotation guidelines.

In order to find the best solution with a minimum of constraint violations, the top k analyses output are generated by the CRF (Conditional Random Field) (Lafferty et al., 2001) for every sentence; these analyses can then be combined to form the k top analyses for the whole 5-sentence window around the connective. This combination is most efficiently carried out using a priority queue similar to a chart cell in the k-best parsing algorithm by Huang and Chiang (2005). (see Ghosh et al. (2012) for details)

2.2 Feature Set of Baseline System

We summarize the feature set of the base system (Ghosh et al., 2011a) to emphasize the distinction between the local and global feature set for this work.

The token-level (local) feature set in the Table 2 can be divided into four categories:

Features used for `Arg1` and `Arg2` segmentation and labeling.	
F1.	Token (T)
F2.	Sense of Connective (CONN)
F3.	IOB chain (IOB)
F4.	PoS tag
F5.	Lemma (L)
F6.	Inflection (INFL)
F7.	Main verb of main clause (MV)
F8.	Boolean feature for MV (BMV)
F9.	Previous sentence feature (PREV)
Additional feature used only for `Arg1`	
F10.	`Arg2` Labels

Table 2: Feature sets for `Arg1` and `Arg2` segmentation and labeling in base system (Ghosh et al 2011a).

1. Syntactic. $\{F3, F4, F6\}$ [2]
2. Semantic. $\{F2\}$
3. Lexical $\{F5, F7, F8\}$
4. Structure related token-level features. $\{F9, F10\}$

The remaining one (F1) is the token itself. The sense of the connective feature (F2) extracted from PDTB for the base system, though for the fully automatic one (Ghosh et al., 2011b) it needs the PTB (Penn TreeBank)-style syntactic parse trees as input (Pitler and Nenkova, 2009). The IOB(Inside-Outside-Begin) chain (F3) [3] (F3) is extracted from a full parse tree and corresponds to the syntactic categories of all the constituents on the path between the root note and the current leaf node of the tree. Experiments with other syntactic features proved that IOB chain conveys all deep syntactic information needed in the task, and makes all other syntactic information redundant, for example clause boundaries, token distance from the connective, constituent label, etc.

In order to extract the morphological features needed, we use the *morpha* tool (Minnen et al., 2001), which outputs lemma (F5) and inflection information (F6) of the candidate token. The latter is the ending usually added to the word root to convey inflectional information. It includes for example the *-ing* and *-ed* suffixes in verb endings as well as the *-s* to form the plural of nouns.

As for features (F7) and (F8), they rely on information about the main verb of the current sentence. More specifically, feature (F7) is the main verb token , extracted following the head-finding

[2] Infection can be defined as morpho-syntactic feature.

[3] We extracted this feature using the Chunklink.pl script made available by Sabine Buchholz at ilk.uvt.nl/team/sabine/chunklink/README.html

strategy by Yamada and Matsumoto (2003), while feature (F8) is a boolean feature that indicates for each token if it is the main verb in the sentence or not.[4]

The structure related token-level features do not use any parse tree. The `Arg2` label (F10) features are generated from the word sequence index in PDTB for the base system (for automatic system it is generated by the pipeline (Ghosh et al., 2011b)); this feature is used to classify `Arg1` . The previous sentence feature "Prev" (F9) is a connective-surface feature and is used to capture if the following sentence begins with a connective. This is meant for the classification of the `Arg1` that resides in the previous sentence of the connective. The feature value for each candidate token of a sentence corresponds to the connective token that appears at the beginning of the following sentence, if any. Otherwise, it is equal to 0.

Although both of the structure-related features are strong features according to the feature analysis in Ghosh et al. (2011a), the base system is not able to capture all available global features inside the 5-sentence discourse context, merely uses 2-sentence context. This is due to the fact that CRF classifier uses a narrow window, that can only capture the information nearby the token under consideration. Therefore it becomes impossible to inject more information about the 5-sentence discourse window structure.

3 Global Feature Set

We use a global feature-set. The global features are defined as the data-driven, hand-crafted rule generated and non-grammatical (i.e. no syntactic parse tree is used to generate this features) features.

The model of Ghosh et al. (2011a) is based on Conditional Random Fields (CRF), and incorporating a set of structural and lexical features. At the core part of the model lies a local classifier, which labels each token sequentially with one of the possible argument labels or OTHER in a pipeline. Now global information can be integrated into the model using global features at a longer-distance context, by defining a small set of global constraints (if too many dependencies are encoded, the model will over-fit the training data and will not generalize well).

The global features are computed using each list of k-best lists, in contrast to the lexico-syntactically generated local features for each token item for each sentence of n-best lists. The usage of global feature is meant for exploring the yet undiscovered dimension of the each 5-sentence discourse window. Global feature set consists of the eight features that works on a full 5-sentence discourse window (*cf.* sec. 2.1). The first six (i.e. GF0-GF5) of these are same with the constrained system 2.1.

None of the features are extracted from any parse tree. All the seven features (GF1-GF7) are derived from the generated `Arg` tags of the n-best lists, the first one is the logarithm of posterior probability computed from the CRF posterior probability output for each list of the n-best lists. The finer description of each feature is given below.

GF0. *logarithm of Posterior Probability.* this feature is generated by the base CRF classifier. The CRF generates probability per sentence, for each list of the n-best lists. We calculate sum of the log of each probability during generation of k-best lists forming 5-sentence discourse window.

GF1. *Overgeneration.* It is possible for an argument to be split into more than one part in same sentence, we found these cases several times in PDTB. This constraint is violated if an `Arg1` or `Arg2` is split over multiple sentences. This is a predominant problem for those lists of the n-best lists those are generated with low posteriors. This feature exhibits the problem of overgeneration to the reranker with the counts.

GF2. *Undergeneration.* According to PDTB annotation scheme every connective must have arguments of each type, this constraint is violated if an argument is missing. This is the prevalent problem in the single-best system, especially for the `Arg1` classification. This feature works to specify where a discourse structure missing the argument(s) - one of the main problems that motivated this work.

GF3. *Intersentential Arg2* (used only for `Arg2` reranker). Count of `Arg2`, if any, occurs classified outside connective sentence - this way the system is constrained to have any inter-sentential `Arg2`. This is a hypothetically motivated feature to reduce the complexity of the classification problem; although in fact in PDTB 2.0, there are a few cases

[4]We used the head rules by Yamada & Matsumoto (`http://www.jaist.ac.jp/~h-yamada/`)

of Arg2 of explicit connective (i.e. the 114 out of 18459), where it extends beyond the connectives sentence to include additional sentences in the subsequent discourse (Prasad et al., 2008).

GF4. *Arg1 after the connective sentence.* Count of Arg1, if any, occurs classified after connective sentence. Through this feature we attempt to constrain the system to have Arg1s always occurring in the previous sentence or before the previous sentence of the connective sentence.

GF5. *Argument overlapping with the connective.* Count of the cases if there is any token overlap between Args and connective tokens. This is also not possible for the PDTB-style annotation, so we intend to constrain the overlapping, if any.

GF6. *Argument begins with -I tag.* Count of the cases if the generated Arg chunks begins with the -I (inside) tag, violating the principle of IOB tags for chunking. This is only possible if the CRF chunker fails to tag the boundaries properly.

GF7. *Argument begins with -E tag.* Count of the cases if the generated Arg chunks begins with the -E (end) tag instead of a -B(begin) tag. This is also possible if only the CRF chunker fails to tag the chunk boundaries properly.

We attempt to categorize this feature set according to the properties they bear: $\{GF0\}$ is the *intrinsic* global feature - it is the evidence of confidence on decisions made by the single-best model; $\{GF1, GF2\}$ check the *prevalent problems* seen through the evaluation of decisions by the single best model; $\{GF3, GF4, GF5\}$ are the *hypothetical* global features those reduce classification complexities, they are inspired by the general trends or rules for annotation in PDTB. $\{G6, G7\}$ check the *mistakes* in IOB tagging by the CRF chunker.

4 Reranking Approaches

We formalize the reranking algorithm as follows: for a given sentence s, a reranker selects the best parse $\hat{y}$ among the set of candidates candidate(s) according to some scoring function:

$$\hat{y} = argmax_{y \in \text{candidate}(s)} \text{score}(y) \quad (1)$$

In n-best reranking, candidate(s) is simply a set of n-best parses from the baseline parser, that is, candidate$(s) = \{y_1, y_2, ..., y_n\}$.

In this paper we followed two approaches for the reranking task:

1. Structured Learning Approach: in this case the reranker learns directly from a scoring function that is trained to maximize the performance of the reranking task (Collins and Duffy, 2002). We also investigate two popular and efficient online structured learning algorithms: the structured voted perceptron by Collins and Duffy (2002) and Passive-Aggressive(PA) algorithm by Crammer et al. (2006). The weight-vectors observed from the training phase are averaged following Schapire and Freund (1999). In case of structured perceptron for each of the candidate in a ranked list the scoring function of equation 1 is computed as follows:

$$\text{score}(y_i) = \mathbf{w} \cdot \mathbf{\Phi}(x_{i,j}) \quad (2)$$

where $\mathbf{w}$ is the parameter weight-vector and Φ is the feature representing function of $x_{i,j}$; $x_{i,j}$ denotes the j-th token of the i-th sentence. Since the PA algorithm is based on the theory of large-margin, it attempts find a score that violates the margin maximally by adding an extra cost i.e. $\sqrt{\rho(x_{i,j})}$ to the basic score function for structured perceptron i.e. equation 2. Here ρ is computed as $1 - F(x_{i,j})$, F: F-measure. The online PA also takes care of the learning rate of perceptron, which is considered as 1 in structured perceptron. The learning rate in online PA is min-value between a regularization constant and normalized score function value.

2. Best vs. rest Approach: in the preference kernel approach (Shen and Joshi, 2003) the reranking problem is reduced to a binary classification task on pairs. This reduction enables even a standard support vector machine to optimize the problem. We use a component of this task. We define the best scored discourse window (section 4.1) as a positive example and the rest are the negatives to the system. We use a standard support vector machine (Vapnik, 1995) with linear kernel.

3. Preference Kernel Approach: we also investigated the classical approach of preference kernel, as it is introduced by (Shen and Joshi, 2003). In this method, the reranking problem learning to select the correct candidate h^1 from a candidate set $\{h^1, \cdots, h^k\}$ is reduced to a binary classification problem by creating pairs: positive training instances $\langle h^1, h^2 \rangle, \cdots, \langle h^1, h^k \rangle$ and negative instances $\langle h^2, h^1 \rangle, \cdots, \langle h^k, h^1 \rangle$. The advantage of using this approach is that there are abundant tools for binary machine learning.

If we have a kernel K over the candidate space T, we can construct a *preference* kernel

(Shen and Joshi, 2003) P_K over the space of pairs $T \times T$ as follows:

$$\begin{aligned} P_K &= K(h_1^1, h_2^1) + K(h_1^2, h_2^2) \\ &- K(h_1^1, h_2^2) - K(h_1^2, h_2^1) \end{aligned} \quad (3)$$

In our case, we make pair from the n-best hypotheses h_i as $\langle h_i^1, h_i^2 \rangle$ generated by the base model. We used linear kernel to train the reranker.

Thus we create the feature vectors extracted from the candidate sequences using the features described in Section 3. We then trained linear SVMs (Support Vector Machine) using the LIBLINEAR software (Fan et al., 2008), using L1 loss and L2 regularization.

4.1 Experiments

We use PennDiscourse TreeBank (Prasad et al., 2008) and Penn TreeBank (Marcus et al., 1993) data through this entire work. We keep the split of data as follows: $02 - 22$ folders of PDTB (& PTB) are used for training, $23 - 24$ folders of the same are used for testing; remaining 00-01 folders are meant for development split, it is used only to study the impact of feature (*cf.* 5).

We prepare the n-best outputs of sentences from the base system (*cf.* 2.1). The training data is prepared from the input of n-best lists of the train split, using a oracle module, which generates k-best oracle lists from the n-best single outputs. We procure k-best lists from oracle using the evaluator module (see section 4.2), ordered by the highest to the lowest probability score. Each of the list of the k-best list is a 5-sentence discourse window.

We prepare the test data given the n-best lists of the test split. We obtain k-best list for testing, prepared with the module described in section 2.1. We re-integrate the sentences connected with the same discourse connective id into the 5-sentence discourse window keeping the connective-bearing sentence in the middle. This re-integration done using a priority queue in the style of Huang and Chiang (2005). Each of the list from the k-best list are ordered by the highest to the lowest score with sum of the log of posterior probabilities of each sentence in the n-best list.

Therefore, in short, the n-best list is the list of sentence-level analyses whereas the k-best list is the list of 5-sentence discourse window-level analyses.

Baseline: we consider the performance of the single-best output from the base implementation (*cf.* 2.1) as the baseline.

4.2 Evaluation

We present our results using precision, recall and F1 measures. Following Johansson and Moschitti (2010), we use three scoring schemes: *exact*, *intersection* (or *partial*), and *overlap* scoring. In the exact scoring scheme, a span extracted by the system is counted as correct if its extent exactly coincides with one in the gold standard. We also include two other scoring schemes to have a rough approximation of the argument spans. In the overlap scheme, an expression is counted as correctly detected if it overlaps with a gold standard argument. The intersection scheme assigns a score between 0 and 1 for every predicted span based on how much it overlaps with a gold standard span, so unlike the other two schemes it will reward close matches.

4.3 Classifier Results

	ARG1 Results			ARG2 Results		
Exact	*P*	*R*	*F*	*P*	*R*	*F*
Baseline	69.88	48.51	57.26	83.44	75.14	79.07
Online PA	**66.10**	**53.92**	**59.39**(16)	82.59	76.39	79.37(4)
Struct Per	67.18	52.64	59.03(4)	**82.96**	**76.28**	**79.48**(8)
BestVsRest	66.19	52.83	58.94(8)	81.69	77.14	79.35(4)
Pref-Linear	66.54	53.31	59.20(4)	82.82	76.28	79.42(4)

Table 3: Exact Match Results for four classifiers. Baseline scores in the first row. Used n-best list numbers in parenthesis. The best performances are boldfaced.

We observe that reranking with global features improved the F1 scores for `Arg1` significantly, although for `Arg2` the improvement is insignificant [5]. Since in most of the cases the `Arg2` is syntactically bound with the connective, it is obvious that lexico-syntactically motivated local features help the classification of `Arg2`. On the other hand, the classification of `Arg1` is considerably dependent on non-grammatical, hand-crafted rule generated features. If we compare to our reranking classification results of `Arg1` with that one without previous sentence feature in Ghosh et al. (2011a) then we observe that the global and globally motivated structural feature improved the classification

[5]Throughout this work the permutation test is used to compute the significance of difference, whereas to compute the confidence interval bootstrap resampling is used(Hjorth, 1993). We determined the significant digits for presenting results using the methods illustrated by Weisstein E. W. (Weisstein, 2012)

of `Arg1` by more than 10 points.

We also notice from the table for both the argument classification cases that we achieve balanced scores in terms of the precision and the recall with the structured global features. In fact there is a good improvement of recall without much loss in terms of precision.There is not any significant improvement in case of `Arg2` reranking because the problem of the classification mostly resides on boundary detection of `Arg2`; also we know that estimation of position of an `Arg2` is pretty easy task given the connective is correctly identified.

	ARG1 Results			ARG2 Results		
Exact	P	R	F	P	R	F
Baseline	82.90	61.65	70.72	93.40	84.20	88.56
Online PA	**80.11**	**69.43**	**74.39**(16)	**92.94**	**85.73**	**89.19**(4)
Struct Per	81.18	67.03	73.43(4)	93.20	85.50	89.17(8)
BestVsRest	81.25	66.46	73.11(8)	93.03	85.16	89.1(4)
Pref-linear	80.55	68.49	74.03(4)	93.12	85.56	89.18(4)

Table 4: Partial Match Results for four classifiers. Baseline scores in the first row. Used n-best list numbers in parenthesis. The best performances are boldfaced.

We mark an improvement of the `Arg1` in table 4, with softer partial evaluation metrics; we also observe the same trend in results for `Arg2` classification as in the table 3.

4.3.1 Candidate Set Size

We conduct experiments to study the influence of candidate set size on the quality of reranked output. In addition we also attempt to notice the upper-bound of reranker performance, i.e. the oracle performance. We choose the reranker based on online PA among the four classifier. Since all the four classifiers performed comparably the same way, it is enough to study the performance of one of them on candidate set size, that will reflect the performance of the other classifiers. We also describe and discuss the results on the exact partial measures only, as we notice from the previous section that the effect of reranking is comparable with the exact measure and softer measures.

	Reranked ARG1			Oracle		
k	P	R	F	P	R	F
1	69.88	48.51	57.26	69.88	48.51	57.26
2	67.26	52.34	58.87	81.26	61.70	70.14
4	66.39	53.56	59.29	88.35	71.91	79.29
8	66.11	53.86	59.36	92.47	79.09	85.26
16	66.10	53.92	59.39	93.80	83.77	88.50

Table 5: Oracle and reranker performance as a function of candidate set size of `Arg1`.

In both the tables (5, 6) we notice that the oracle performance is steadily increasing with 16-best lists. We observe that the performance of classification of both `Arg1` and `Arg2` increases at the level of 2-best list then it stagnates after 4-best performance. This nature of increment is may be related to the simple but high-level feature set used in this task of the discourse parsing; and it can also be some issues involved with local feature set, as we observed a huge difference of posterior probabilities between the single-best and the each of the $(n-1)$ lists of a n-best decision by CRF.

	Reranked ARG2			Oracle		
k	P	R	F	P	R	F
1	83.44	75.14	79.07	83.44	75.14	79.07
2	82.90	75.69	79.13	90.13	82.43	86.11
4	82.59	76.39	79.37	92.27	86.53	89.31
8	82.41	76.44	79.32	92.81	88.13	90.41
16	83.41	76.44	79.32	92.82	88.54	90.63

Table 6: Oracle and reranker performance as a function of candidate set size of `Arg2`.

4.3.2 Reranked Intersentential ARG1

We also attempt to observe the effect with respect to inter-sentential classification in case of `Arg1`, with the results obtained with online PA perceptron. As expected, the change we notice the effects in the table 7 is a fraction of potential improvement. We find comparing the inter-sentential vs. overall classification results of `Arg1` that the increment in inter-sentential `Arg1` classification considerably contribute to the overall `Arg1` classification.

		P	R	F1
Baseline	Exact	52.87	27.80	36.44
	Partial	68.93	41.06	51.48
	Overlap	79.62	41.88	54.88
Best Reranked ARG1	Exact	50.41	30.04	37.56
	Partial	66.51	44.95	53.78
	Overlap	76.13	44.54	56.23

Table 7: Inter-sentential Reranked `Arg1` Results.

5 Impact of Feature on ARG1

We study the impact of global features on the performance on `Arg1` reranker with the development set (*cf.* Section 4.1). We are leaving behind the feature performance of the `Arg2`, as the improvement by the reranker for this case is not significant.

The Table 8 shows the results of investigation through an incremental greedy-search based feature selection. All the performance steps are evaluated with a k of 16.

This impact table starts with the *log posterior* only (GF0). This results to the best result achieved by Ghosh et al. (2011a) through the hill-climbing feature analysis. Beside this, we also checked that if we run the reranker with this feature only, then it results to the baseline performance with the test split.

Then the *undergeneration* feature (GF2) is chosen through greedy search among the other features. It gives us, jointly with the log posterior, a significant improvement over the baseline. The impact is predictable as GF2 addresses the basic problem that has driven us to the current task.

The addition of the *overgeneration* (GF1) feature also increased the performance, though non-significantly; this feature is important for the reranker because this is meant for fixing a predominant overgeneration problem in the n-best lists.

We observe that the F1 measure increases significantly after adding the next important feature: *Arg1 after the connective sentence* (GF4); in this case the recall increases more in comparison to the increment in the precision.

In the next step, the feature: *Argument overlapping with connective* (GF5) is added. This decreases the F1 score a bit, though it increases the precision lowering the recall.

We reach to the second-best performance of the `Arg1` reranker after adding the feature: *Argument begins with -I tag* (GF6).

The addition of the feature: *Argument begins with -E tag* (GF7) does not improve the performance much. It is possible that there was no such mistake by CRF inside the test data.

The scores with partial and overlap matches show the same trend so we leave the discussion with them in order to avoid the redundancy.

Additionally, we also perform the individual effect of each of features from the set (GF1,GF2,GF4,GF5,GF6,GF7), jointly with the intrinsic feature GF0, but none other than the undergeneration feature increased the performance over the baseline.

The *intrinsic* GF0 is contributing to achieve the baseline performance; the undergeneration (GF2) feature is also contributing significantly. In summary, the combination of features optimizes the performance of system in terms of F1-measure by decreasing the value of precision and raising the value of recall.

System	*P*	*R*	*F1*
GF0 (Posterior Only)	73.12	50.36	59.64
GF0+GF2	69.62	55.34	61.67
GF0+GF2+GF1	69.92	55.21	61.70
GF0+GF2+GF1+GF4	70.12	56.05	62.30
GF0+GF2+GF1+GF4+GF5	72.36	53.72	61.66
GF0+GF2+GF1+GF4+GF5+GF6	71.10	55.28	62.20
GF0+GF2+GF1+GF4+GF5+GF6+GF7	71.84	54.82	62.19

Table 8: Exact Match Results for `Arg1` through Incremental Feature Selection.

6 Conclusion

We note a significant improvement over the best performing model of discourse parser on the PDTB corpus. This is mostly contributed by the better performance in `Arg1` classification.

We also find that global features have greater impact on `Arg1` classification than that of `Arg2`. We investigate that that the performance of `Arg1` improved by more than 10 points in terms of F1 measure using the global (see Section 3) and structure related features (see Ghosh et al. (2011a)). This happens perhaps due to the fact `Arg2` is syntactically bound to the connective, whereas `Arg1` is not. `Arg2` depends more on local features (*cf.* Section 2.1) than global one. Basically this nature of dependency of `Arg1` on both local and global features are inherited through the PDTB annotation corpus, as well the local feature dependency of `Arg2` are completely data-driven.

The motivation of the paper is to make a balanced classification for both the `Arg1` and `Arg2`, achieved by implementing the constrained-system with global features. This enables to increase a huge recall without losing much in terms of precision.

It is also observed that while the performances of oracle of `Arg1` and `Arg2` are increasing steadily, the performances of both the rerankers stagnate at or before the point of 16-best lists; this is perhaps due to our effective, simple and small feature set.

In this task we emphasized on and studied the data-driven, global and non-grammatical feature set. This syntactic parse tree independent feature set may also be effective with the dialogue data annotated with PDTB annotation style.

7 Acknowledgement

This work was partially funded by IBM Collaborative Faculty Award 2011 grant.

References

[Barzilay et al.2004] Regina Barzilay, Lillian Lee, et al. 2004. Catching the drift: Probabilistic content models, with applications to generation and summarization. In *Proc. of NAACL-HLT, 2004.*

[Barzilay et al.2005] Regina Barzilay, Mirella Lapata, et al. 2005. Modeling local coherence: an entity-based approach. In *Proceedings of the 43rd Annual Meeting of the Association for Computational Linguistics (ACL05).*

[Charniak and Johnson2005] E. Charniak and M. Johnson. 2005. Coarse-to-fine n-best parsing and maxent discriminative reranking. In *Proceedings of the 43rd Annual Meeting of the ACL.*

[Collins and Duffy2002] Michael Collins and Nigel Duffy. 2002. New ranking algorithms for parsing and tagging: Kernels over discrete structures, and the voted perceptron. In *ACL02.*

[Collins2000] Michael Collins. 2000. Discriminative reranking for natural language parsing. In *Computational Linguistics*, pages 175–182. Morgan Kaufmann.

[Collins2002] Michael Collins. 2002. Ranking algorithms for named-entity extraction: Boosting and the voted perceptron. In *Proceedings of ACL 2002.*

[Crammer et al.2006] Koby Crammer, Ofer Dekel, Joseph Keshet, Shai Shalev-Schwartz, and Yoram Singer. 2006. Online passive-aggressive algorithms. *Journal of Machine Learning Research*, 7:551–585.

[Daume III et al.2004] Hal Daume III, Daniel Marcu, et al. 2004. Np bracketing by maximum entropy tagging and svm reranking. In *Proceedings of EMNLP'04.*

[Fan et al.2008] Rong-En Fan, Chih-Jen Lin, Kai-Wei Chang, Xiang-Rui Wang, et al. 2008. Liblinear: A library for large linear classification. *Journal of Machine Learning Research.*

[Ghosh et al.2011a] Sucheta Ghosh, Richard Johansson, Giuseppe Riccardi, and Sara Tonelli. 2011a. Shallow discourse parsing with conditional random fields. In *Proceedings of the 5th International Joint Conference on Natural Language Processing (IJCNLP)*, Chiang Mai, Thailand.

[Ghosh et al.2011b] Sucheta Ghosh, Sara Tonelli, Giuseppe Riccardi, and Richard Johansson. 2011b. End-to-end discourse parser evaluation. In *Proceedings of 5th IEEE International Conference on Semantic Computing*, Palo Alto, CA, USA.

[Ghosh et al.2012] Sucheta Ghosh, Richard Johansson, Giuseppe Riccardi, and Sara Tonelli. 2012. Improving the recall of a discourse parser by constraint-based postprocessing. In *Proceedings of International Conference on Languages Resources and Evaluations (LREC 2012).*

[Grosz et al.1992] B.J. Grosz, J. Hircshberg, et al. 1992. Some intonational characteristics of discourse structure. In Ohala et al., editors, *Proceedings of the International Conference on Spoken Language Processing, Vol. 1*, volume 1, pages 429–432.

[Grosz et al.1995] B.J. Grosz, A. K. Joshi, S. Weinstein, et al. 1995. Centering: A framework for modeling the local coherence of discourse. *Computational Linguistics*, 21(2).

[Hjorth1993] J. S. Urban Hjorth. 1993. *Computer Intensive Statistical Methods.* Chapman and Hall, London.

[Huang and Chiang2005] Liang Huang and David Chiang. 2005. Better k-best parsing. In *Proceedings of the 9th International Workshop on Parsing Technologies (IWPT 2005)*, pages 53–64, Vancouver, Canada.

[Johansson and Moschitti2010] Richard Johansson and Alessandro Moschitti. 2010. Syntactic and semantic structure for opinion expression detection. In *Proceedings of the Fourteenth Conference on Computational Natural Language Learning*, pages 67–76.

[Klein and Manning2003] Dan Klein and Christopher D. Manning. 2003. Fast exact inference with a factored model for natural language parsing. *Advances in Neural Information Processing Systems 15 (NIPS 2002), Cambridge, MA: MIT Press.*

[Lafferty et al.2001] John Lafferty, Andrew McCallum, and Fernando Pereira. 2001. Conditional random fields: Probabilistic models for segmenting and labeling sequence data. In *18th International Conf. on Machine Learning.* Morgan Kaufmann.

[Lapata2003] Mirella Lapata. 2003. Probabilistic text structuring: Experiments with sentence ordering. In *Proceedings of the 41st Meeting of the Association of Computational Linguistics*, pages 545–552.

[Marcus et al.1993] Mitchell P. Marcus, Beatrice Santorini, and Mary Ann Marcinkiewicz. 1993. Building a Large Annotated Corpus of English: the Penn Treebank. *Computational Linguistics*, 19(2):313–330.

[Minnen et al.2001] Guido Minnen, John Carroll, and Darren Pearce. 2001. Applied morphological processing of English. *Natural Language Engineering.*

[Pitler and Nenkova2009] Emily Pitler and Ani Nenkova. 2009. Using syntax to disambiguate explicit discourse connectives in text. In *Proceedings of the 47th Annual Meeting of the Association for Computational Linguistics and the 4th International Joint Conference on Natural Language Processing.*

[Prasad et al.2008] Rashmi Prasad, Nikhil Dinesh, Alan Lee, Eleni Miltsakaki, Livio Robaldo, Aravind Joshi, and Bonnie Webber. 2008. The Penn Discourse Treebank 2.0. In *Proceedings of the 6th*

International Conference on Languages Resources and Evaluations (LREC 2008), Marrakech, Morocco.

[Schapire and Freund1999] Robert E. Schapire and Yoav Freund. 1999. Large margin classification using the perceptron algorithm. *Machine Learning Journal*, 37(3):277–296.

[Shen and Joshi2003] Libin Shen and Aravind Joshi. 2003. An svm based voting algorithm with application to parse reranking. In *CoNLL 2003*.

[Soricut et al.2003] Radu Soricut, Daniel Marcu, et al. 2003. Sentence level discourse parsing using syntactic and lexical information. In *Proceedings of the Human Language Technology and North American Association for Computational Linguistics Conference (HLT/NAACL), May 27-June 1*.

[Soricut et al.2006] Radu Soricut, Daniel Marcu, et al. 2006. Stochastic coherence modeling, parameter estimation and decoding for text planning applications. In *Proceedings of ACL-2006 (Poster)*, pages 803–810.

[Toutanova et al.2008] Kristina Toutanova, Aria Haghighi, Christopher D. Manning, et al. 2008. Kristina toutanova, aria haghighi, and christopher d. manning, a global joint model for semantic role labeling. *Computational Linguistics*.

[Vapnik1995] V. Vapnik. 1995. *The Nature of Statistical Learning Theory*. Springer-Verlag.

[Weisstein2012] Eric W. Weisstein. 2012. "significant digits." from mathworld–a wolfram web resource.

[Yamada and Matsumoto2003] Hiroyasu Yamada and Yuji Matsumoto. 2003. Statistical dependency analysis with support vector machines. In *Proceedings of 8th International Workshop on Parsing Technologies*.

A Reranking Model for Discourse Segmentation using Subtree Features

Ngo Xuan Bach, Nguyen Le Minh, Akira Shimazu
School of Information Science
Japan Advanced Institute of Science and Technology
1-1 Asahidai, Nomi, Ishikawa, 923-1292, Japan
{bachnx,nguyenml,shimazu}@jaist.ac.jp

Abstract

This paper presents a discriminative reranking model for the discourse segmentation task, the first step in a discourse parsing system. Our model exploits subtree features to rerank N-best outputs of a base segmenter, which uses syntactic and lexical features in a CRF framework. Experimental results on the RST Discourse Treebank corpus show that our model outperforms existing discourse segmenters in both settings that use gold standard Penn Treebank parse trees and Stanford parse trees.

1 Introduction

Discourse structure has been shown to have an important role in many natural language applications, such as text summarization (Marcu, 2000; Louis et al., 2010), information presentation (Bateman et al., 2001), question answering (Sun and Chai, 2007), and dialogue generation (Hernault et al., 2008). To produce such kinds of discourse structure, several attempts have been made to build discourse parsers in the framework of Rhetorical Structure Theory (RST) (Mann and Thompson, 1988), one of the most widely used theories of text structure.

In the RST framework, a text is first divided into several elementary discourse units (EDUs). Each EDU may be a simple sentence or a clause in a complex sentence. Consecutive EDUs are then put in relation with each other to build a discourse tree. Figure 1 shows an example of a discourse tree with three EDUs. The goal of the discourse segmentation task is to divide the input text into such EDUs.

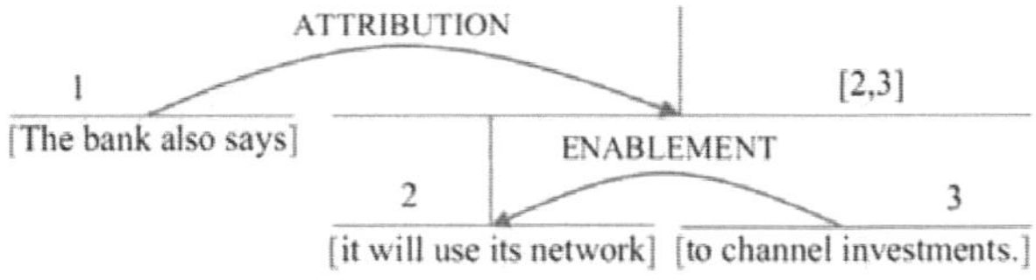

Figure 1: A discourse tree (Soricut and Marcu, 2003).

The quality of the discourse segmenter contributes a significant part to the overall accuracy of every discourse parsing system. If a text is wrongly segmented, no discourse parsing algorithm can build a correct discourse tree.

Existing discourse segmenters usually exploit lexical and syntactic features to label each word in a sentence with one of two labels, *boundary* or *no-boundary*. The limitation of this approach is that it only focuses on the boundaries of EDUs. It cannot capture features that describe whole EDUs.

Recently, discriminative reranking has been used successfully in some NLP tasks such as POS tagging, chunking, and statistical parsing (Collins and Koo, 2005; Kudo et al., 2005; Huang, 2008; Fraser et al., 2009). The advantage of the reranking method is that it can exploit the output of a base model to learn. Based on that output, we can extract long-distance non-local features to rerank.

In this paper, we present a reranking model for the discourse segmentation task. We show how to use subtree features, features extracted from whole EDUs, to rerank outputs of a base model. Experimental results on RST Discourse Treebank (RST-DT) (Carlson et al., 2002) show that our model outperforms existing systems.

The rest of this paper is organized as follows. Section 2 summarizes related work. Section 3 presents our method. Experimental results on RST-DT are described in Section 4. Finally, Section 5 gives conclusions.

2 Related Work

Several methods have been proposed to deal with the discourse segmentation task. Thanh et al. (2004) present a rule-based discourse segmenter with two steps. In the first step, segmentation is done by using syntactic relations between words. The segmentation algorithm is based on some principles, which have been presented in Corston (1998) and Carlson and Marcu (2001), as follows:

1. *The clause that is attached to a noun phrase can be recognised as an embedded unit. If the clause is a subordinate clause, it must contain more than one word.*

2. *Coordinate clauses and coordinate sentences of a complex sentence are EDUs.*

3. *Coordinate clauses and coordinate elliptical clauses of verb phrases (VPs) are EDUs. Coordinate VPs that share a direct object with the main VP are not considered as a separate discourse segment.*

4. *Clausal complements of reported verbs and cognitive verbs are EDUs.*

The segmenter then uses cue phrases to correct the output of the first step.

Tofiloski et al. (2009) describe another rule-based discourse segmenter. The core of this segmenter consists of 12 syntactic segmentation rules and some rules concerning a list of stop phrases, discourse cue phrases, and part-of-speech tags. They also use a list of phrasal discourse cues to insert boundaries not derivable from the parser's output.

Soricut and Marcu (2003) introduce a statistical discourse segmenter, which is trained on RST-DT to label words with *boundary* or *no-boundary* labels. They use lexical and syntactic features to determine the probabilities of discourse boundaries $P(b_i|w_i, t)$, where w_i is the ith word of the input sentence s, t is the syntactic parse tree of s, and $b_i \in \{boundary, no\text{-}boundary\}$. Given a syntactic parse tree t, their algorithm inserts a discourse boundary after each word w for which $P(boundary|w, t) > 0.5$.

Another statistical discourse segmenter using artificial neural networks is presented in Subba and Di Eugenio (2007). Like Soricut and Marcu (2003), they formulate the discourse segmentation task as a binary classification problem of deciding whether a word is the *boundary* or *no-boundary* of EDUs. Their segmenter exploits a multilayer perceptron model with back-propagation algorithm and is also trained on RST-DT.

Hernault et al. (2010) propose a sequential model for the discourse segmentation task, which considers the segmentation task as a sequence labeling problem rather than a classification problem. They exploit Conditional Random Fields (CRFs) (Lafferty et al., 2001) as the learning method and get state-of-the-art results on RST-DT.

In our work, like Hernault et al. (2010), we also consider the discourse segmentation task as a sequence labeling problem. The final segmentation result is selected among N-best outputs of a CRF-based model by using a reranking method with subtree features.

3 Method

3.1 Discriminative Reranking

In the discriminative reranking method (Collins and Koo, 2005), first, a set of candidates is generated using a base model (GEN). GEN can be any model for the task. For example, in the part-of-speech (POS) tagging problem, GEN may be a model that generates all possible POS tags for a word based on a dictionary. Then, candidates are reranked using a linear score function:

$$score(y) = \Phi(y) \cdot W$$

where y is a candidate, $\Phi(y)$ is the feature vector of candidate y, and W is a parameter vector. The final output is the candidate with the highest score:

$$\begin{aligned} F(x) &= argmax_{y \in GEN(x)} score(y) \\ &= argmax_{y \in GEN(x)} \Phi(y) \cdot W. \end{aligned}$$

To learn the parameter W we use the average perceptron algorithm, which is presented as Algorithm 1.

Algorithm 1 Average perceptron algorithm for reranking (Collins and Koo, 2005)

Inputs: Training set $\{(x^i, y^i)|x^i \in R^n, y^i \in C, \forall i = 1, 2, \ldots, m\}$
Initialize: $W \leftarrow 0, W_{avg} \leftarrow 0$
Define: $F(x) = argmax_{y \in GEN(x)} \Phi(y) \cdot W$
for $t = 1, 2, \ldots, T$ **do**
  for $i = 1, 2, \ldots, m$ **do**
    $z^i \leftarrow F(x^i)$
    if $z^i \neq y^i$ **then**
      $W \leftarrow W + \Phi(y^i) - \Phi(z^i)$
    end if
    $W_{avg} \leftarrow W_{avg} + W$
  end for
end for
$W_{avg} \leftarrow W_{avg}/(mT)$
Output: Parameter vector W_{avg}.

In the next sections we will describe our base model and features that we use to rerank candidates.

3.2 Base Model

Similar to the work of Hernault et al. (2010), our base model uses Conditional Random Fields[1] to learn a sequence labeling model. Each label is either *beginning* of EDU (B) or *continuation* of EDU (C). Soricut and Marcu (2003) and Subba and Di Eugenio (2007) use *boundary* labels, which are assigned to words at the end of EDUs. Like Hernault et al. (2010), we use *beginning* labels, which are assigned to words at the beginning of EDUs. However, we can convert an output with *boundary*, *no-boundary* labels to an output with *beginning*, *continuation* labels and vice versa. Figure 2 shows two examples of segmenting a sentence into EDUs and their correct label sequences.

We use the following lexical and syntactic information as features: words, POS tags, nodes in parse trees and their lexical heads and their POS heads[2]. When extracting features for word w, let r be the word on the right-hand side of w and N_p be the deepest node that belongs to both paths from the root to w and r. N_w and N_r are child nodes of N_p that belong to two paths, respectively. Figure 3 shows two partial lexicalized syntactic parse trees. In the first tree, if w = $says$ then r = it, N_p = $VP(says)$, N_w = $VBZ(says)$, and N_r = $SBAR(will)$. We also consider the parent and the right-sibling of N_p if any. The final feature set for w consists of not only features extracted from w but also features extracted from two words on the left-hand side and two words on the right-hand side of w.

Our feature extraction method is different from the method in previous work (Soricut and Marcu, 2003; Hernault et al., 2010). They define N_w as the highest ancestor of w that has lexical head w and has a right-sibling. Then N_p and N_r are defined as the parent and right-sibling of N_w. In the first example, our method gives the same results as the previous one. In the second example, however, there is no node with lexical head "*done*" and having a right-sibling. The previous method cannot extract N_w, N_p, and N_r in such cases. We also use some new features such as the head node and the right-sibling node of N_p.

[The bank also says] [it will use its network] [to channel investments.] (Soricut and Marcu, 2003)

Label sequence: B C C C B C C C C B C C C

[Then,] [when it would have been easier to resist them,] [nothing was done] [and my brother was murdered by the drug mafias three years ago.] (RST Discourse Treebank)

Label sequence: B C B C C C C C C C C B C C B C C C C C C C C C C C

Figure 2: Examples of segmenting sentences into EDUs.

3.3 Subtree Features for Reranking

We need to decide which kinds of subtrees are useful to represent a candidate, a way to segment the input sentence into EDUs. In our work, we consider two kinds of subtrees: *bound trees* and *splitting trees*.

The *bound tree* of an EDU, which spans from word u to word w, is a subtree which satisfies two conditions:

[1]We use the implementation of Kudo (Kudo, CRF++).

[2]Lexical heads are extracted using Collins' rules (Collins, 1999).

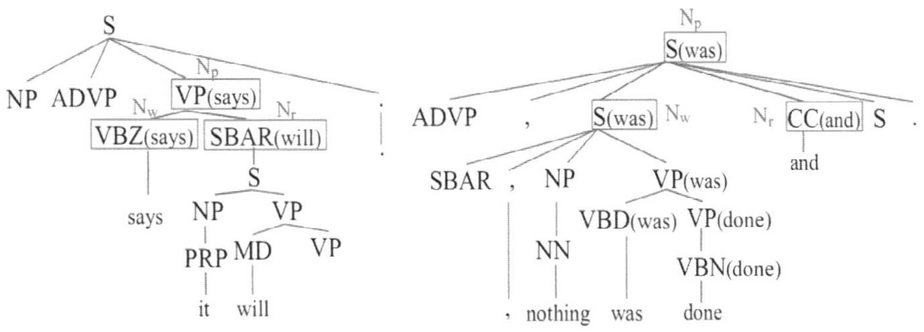

Figure 3: Partial lexicalized syntactic parse trees.

1. its root is the deepest node in the parse tree which belongs to both paths from the root of the parse tree to u and w, and

2. it only contains nodes in two those paths.

The *splitting tree* between two consecutive EDUs, from word u to word w and from word r to word v, is a subtree which is similar to a bound tree, but contains two paths from the root of the parse tree to w and r. Hence, a *splitting tree* between two consecutive EDUs is a *bound tree* that only covers two words: the last word of the first EDU and the first word of the second EDU. Bound trees will cover the whole EDUs, while splitting trees will concentrate on the boundaries of EDUs.

From a bound tree (similar to a splitting tree), we extract three kinds of subtrees: subtrees on the left path (*left tree*), subtrees on the right path (*right tree*), and subtrees consisting of a subtree on the left path and a subtree on the right path (*full tree*). In the third case, if both subtrees on the left and right paths do not contain the root node, we add a pseudo root node. Figure 4 shows the bound tree of EDU "*nothing was done*" of the second example in Figure 3, and some examples of extracted subtrees.

Each subtree feature is then represented by a string as follows:

- A left tree (or a right tree) is represented by concatenating its nodes with hyphens between nodes. For example, subtrees (b) and (e) in Figure 4 can be represented as follows:

  S-NP-NN-nothing, and

  S-VP-VP-VBN-done.

- A full tree is represented by concatenating its left tree and right tree with string ### in the middle. For example, subtrees (g) and (h) in Figure 4 can be represented as follows:

  S-NP-NN###S-VP-VP-VBN, and

  NP-NN-nothing###VP-VP-VBN.

The feature set of a candidate is the set of all subtrees extracted from bound trees of all EDUs and splitting trees between two consecutive EDUs.

Among two kinds of subtrees, splitting trees can be computed between any two adjacent words and therefore can be incorporated into the base model. However, if we do so, the feature space will be very large and contains a lot of noisy features. Because many words are not a boundary of any EDU, many subtrees extracted by this method will never become a *real* splitting tree (tree that splits two EDUs). Splitting trees extracted in the reranking model will focus on a small but compact and useful set of subtrees.

4 Experiments

4.1 Data and Evaluation Methods

We tested our model on the RST Discourse Treebank corpus. This corpus consists of 385 articles from the Penn Treebank, which are divided into a Training set and a Test set. The Training set consists of 347 articles (6132 sentences), and the Test set consists of 38 articles (991 sentences).

There are two evaluation methods that have been used in previous work. The first method measures only *beginning* labels (B labels) (Soricut and Marcu, 2003; Subba and Di Eugenio, 2007). The second

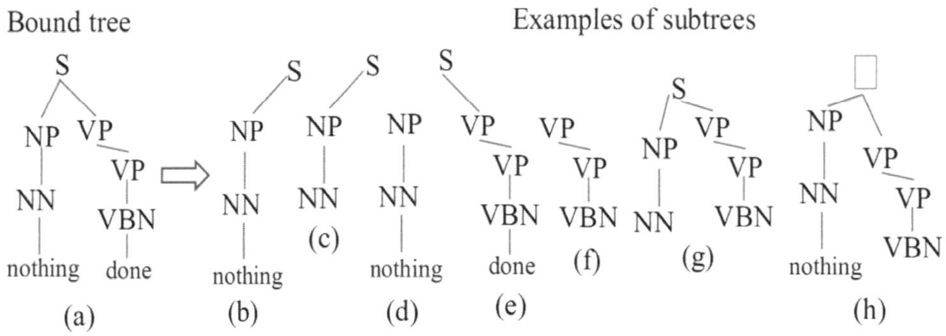

Figure 4: Subtree features.

method (Hernault et al., 2010) measures both *beginning* and *continuation* labels (B and C labels)[3]. This method first calculates scores on B labels and scores on C labels, and then produces the average of them. Due to the number of C labels being much higher than the number of B labels, the second evaluation method yields much higher results. In Hernault et al. (2010), the authors compare their systems with previous work despite using different evaluation methods. Such comparisons are not valid. In our work, we measure the performance of the proposed model using both methods.

Table 1: Performance when evaluating on B labels

Model	Trees	Pre(%)	Re(%)	F_1(%)
SPADE	Penn	84.1	85.4	84.7
NNDS	Penn	85.5	86.6	86.0
CRFSeg	Penn	92.7	89.7	91.2
Base	Penn	92.5	92.5	92.5
Reranking	Penn	**93.1**	**94.2**	**93.7**
CRFSeg	Stanford	91.0	87.2	89.0
Base	Stanford	91.4	90.1	90.7
Reranking	Stanford	**91.5**	**90.4**	**91.0**
Human	-	98.5	98.2	98.3

4.2 Experimental Results

We learned the base model on the Training set and tested on the Test set to get N-best outputs to rerank. To learn parameters of the reranking model, we conducted 5-fold cross-validation tests on the Training set. In all experiments, we set N to 20. To choose the number of iterations, we used a development set, which is about 20 percent of the Training set.

Table 1 shows experimental results when evaluating only *beginning* (B) labels, in which SPADE is the work of Soricut and Marcu (2003), NNDS is a segmenter that uses neural networks (Subba and Di Eugenio, 2007), and CRFSeg is a CRF-based segmenter (Hernault et al., 2010). When using gold parse trees, our base model got 92.5% in the F_1 score, which improves 1.3% compared to the state-of-the-art segmenter (CRFSeg). When using Stanford parse trees (Klein and Manning, 2003), our base model improved 1.7% compared to CRFSeg. It demonstrates the effectiveness of our feature extraction method in the base model. As expected, our reranking model got higher results compared to the base model in both settings. The reranking model got 93.7% and 91.0% in two settings, which improves 2.5% and 2.0% compared to CRFSeg. Also note that, when using Stanford parse trees, our reranking model got competitive results with CRFSeg when using gold parse trees (91.0% compared to 91.2%).

Table 2 shows experimental results when evaluating on both *beginning* and *continuation* labels. Our models also outperformed CRFSeg in both settings, using gold parse trees and using Stanford parse trees (96.6% compared to 95.3% in the first setting, and 95.1% compared to 94.1% in the second setting).

Both evaluation methods have a weak point in that they do not measure the ability to find EDUs exactly. We suggest that the discourse segmentation task should be measured on EDUs rather than boundaries of EDUs. Under this evaluation scheme, our model achieved 90.0% and 86.2% when using

[3]Neither evaluation method counts sentence boundaries.

Table 2: Performance when evaluating on B and C labels

Model	Trees	Pre(%)	Re(%)	F_1(%)
CRFSeg	Penn	96.0	94.6	95.3
Base	Penn	96.0	96.0	96.0
Reranking	Penn	**96.3**	**96.9**	**96.6**
CRFSeg	Stanford	95.0	93.2	94.1
Base	Stanford	95.3	94.7	95.0
Reranking	Stanford	**95.4**	**94.9**	**95.1**

gold parse trees and Stanford parse trees, respectively.

We do not compare our segmenter to systems described in Thanh et al. (2004) and Tofiloski et al. (2009). Thanh et al. (2004) evaluated their system on only 8 texts of RST-DT with gold standard parse trees. They achieved 81.4% and 79.2% in the precision and recall scores, respectively. Tofiloski et al. (2009) tested their system on only 3 texts of RST-DT and used different segmentation guidelines. They reported a precision of 82.0% and recall of 86.0% when using Stanford parse trees.

An important question is which subtree features were useful for the reranking model. This question can be answered by looking at the weights of subtree features (the parameter vector learned by the average perceptron algorithm). Table 3 shows 30 subtree features with the highest weights in absolute value. These features are thus useful for reranking candidates in the reranking model. We can see that most subtree features at the top are *splitting trees*, so *splitting trees* have a more important role than *bound trees* in our model. Among three types of subtrees (*left tree*, *right tree*, and *full tree*), *full tree* is the most important type. It is understandable because subtrees in this type convey much information; and therefore describe *splitting trees* and *bound trees* more precise than subtrees in other types.

4.3 Error Analysis

This section discusses the cases in which our model fails to segment discourses. Note that all errors belong to one of two types, *over-segmentation* type (i.e., words that are not EDU boundaries are mistaken for boundaries) and *miss-segmentation* type (i.e., words that are EDU boundaries are mistaken for not boundaries).

Table 4: Top error words

Word	Percentage among all errors (%)
to	14.5
and	5.8
that	4.6
the	4.6
“	3.5
he	2.3
it	2.3
of	2.3
without	2.3
–	1.7
as	1.7
if	1.7
they	1.7
when	1.7
a	1.2

Tabel 4 shows 15 most frequent words for which our model usually makes a mistake and their percentage among all segmentation errors. Most errors are related to coordinating conjunctions and subordinators (*and*, *that*, *as*, *if*, *when*), personal pronouns (*he*, *it*, *they*), determiners (*the*, *a*), prepositions (*of*, *without*), punctuations (quotes and hyphens), and the word *to*.

Figure 5 shows some errors made by our model. In these examples, gold (correct) EDU boundaries are marked by bracket squares ([]), while predicted boundaries made by our model are indicated by arrows (↓ or ↑). A down arrow (↓) shows a boundary which is predicted correctly, while an up arrow (↑) indicates an *over-segmentation* error. A boundary with no arrow means a *miss-segmentation* error. For example, in Sentence 1, we have a correct boundary and an *over-segmentation* error. Sentences 2 and 3 show two *over-segmentation* errors, and sentences 4 and 6 show two *miss-segmentation* errors.

We also note that many errors occur right after punctuations (commas, quotes, hyphens, brackets, and so on). We analyzed statistics on words that appear before error words. Table 5 shows 10 most frequent words and their percentage among all errors. Overall, more than 35% errors occur right after punctuations.

Table 3: Top 30 subtree features with the highest weights

Type of tree	Type of subtree	Subtree feature	Weight
Splitting tree	Full tree	NP###NP-VP	23.0125
Splitting tree	Full tree	VP###S-VP	19.3044
Splitting tree	Full tree	NP###VBN	18.3862
Splitting tree	Right tree	VP	-18.3723
Splitting tree	Full tree	NP###SBAR	17.7119
Splitting tree	Full tree	NP###NP-SBAR	17.0678
Splitting tree	Full tree	NP###,	-16.6763
Splitting tree	Full tree	NP###VP	15.9934
Splitting tree	Left tree	NP-VP	15.2849
Splitting tree	Full tree	NP###NP	15.1657
Splitting tree	Right tree	SBAR	14.6778
Splitting tree	Full tree	NP###S-NP	14.4962
Splitting tree	Full tree	NP###S	13.1656
Bound tree	Full tree	S-PP###,	12.7428
Splitting tree	Full tree	NP###NP-VP-VBN	12.5210
Bound tree	Full tree	NP###NP	-12.4723
Bound tree	Full tree	VP###VP	-12.1918
Splitting tree	Full tree	NP-VP###S	12.1367
Splitting tree	Right tree	NP-VP	12.0929
Splitting tree	Full tree	NP-SBAR###VP	12.0858
Splitting tree	Full tree	NP-SBAR-S###VP	12.0858
Splitting tree	Full tree	VP###VP-VP	-12.0338
Bound tree	Full tree	VBG###.	11.9067
Bound tree	Right tree	:	11.8833
Bound tree	Full tree	VP###S	-11.7624
Bound trcc	Full tree	S###VP	-11.7596
Bound tree	Full tree	“###”	11.5524
Bound tree	Full tree	S###,	11.5274
Splitting tree	Full tree	NP###VP-VBN	11.3342
Bound tree	Left tree	0	11.2878

Sentence 1: [With the fall social season well under way, name-droppers are out in force,]^{1A} ↓ [trying to impress their betters ↑ and sometimes put down their lessers.]^{1B}

Sentence 2: [But it's not only the stock market ↑ that has some small investors worried.]^{2A}

Sentence 3: ["I am ready at any moment ↑ to compete with a state farm."]^{3A}

Sentence 4: [The Department of Housing and Urban Development has used testers]^{4A} [to investigate discrimination in rental housing.]^{4B}

Sentence 5: [Tell us what measure, ↑short of house arrest, ↑will get this Congress under control.]^{5A}

Sentence 6: [Without machines,]^{6A} [good farms can't get bigger.]^{6B}

Figure 5: Some errors made by our model.

Table 5: Most frequent words that appear before error words

Word	Percentage among all errors (%)
,	24.9
"	5.2
–	2.3
time	1.7
)	1.2
assets	1.2
investors	1.2
month	1.2
plan	1.2
was	1.2

5 Conclusion

This paper presented a reranking model for the discourse segmentation task. Our model exploits subtree features to rerank N-best outputs of a base model, which uses CRFs to learn. Compared with the state-of-the-art system, our model reduces 2.5% among 8.8% errors (28.4% in the term of error rate) when using gold parse trees, and reduces 2% among 11% errors (18.2% in the term of error rate) when using Stanford parse trees. In the future, we will build a discourse parser that uses the described discourse segmenter.

Acknowledgments

This work was partially supported by the 21st Century COE program 'Verifiable and Evolvable e-Society', and Grant-in-Aid for Scientific Research, Education and Research Center for Trustworthy e-Society.

The authors would like to thank the three anonymous reviewers for the time they spent reading and reviewing this paper and Michael Strube for his comments during the revision process of the paper.

References

J. Bateman, J. Kleinz, T. Kamps, and K. Reichenberger. 2001. Towards Constructive Text, Diagram, and Layout Generation for Information Presentation. *Computational Linguistics*, 27(3), pp. 409-449.

L. Carlson and D. Marcu. 2001. Discourse Tagging Manual. *ISI Technical Report*, ISI-TR-545.

L. Carlson, D. Marcu, and M.E. Okurowski. 2002. RST Discourse Treebank. *Linguistic Data Consortium (LDC)*.

M. Collins. 1999. Head-Driven Statistical Models for Natural Language Parsing. *Ph.D. Thesis*, University of Pennsylvania.

S. Corston-Oliver. 1998. Computing Representations of the Structure of Written Discourse. *Ph.D. Thesis*, University of California, Santa Barbara.

M. Collins and T. Koo. 2005. Discriminative Reranking for Natural Language Parsing. *Computational Linguistics*, 31(1), pp. 25-70.

A. Fraser, R. Wang, and H. Schütze. 2009. Rich Bitext Projection Features for Parse Reranking. In *Proceedings of the 12th Conference of the European Chapter of the ACL (EACL)*, pp. 282-290.

H. Hernault, P. Piwek, H. Prendinger, and M. Ishizuka. 2008. Generating Dialogues for Virtual Agents Using Nested Textual Coherence Relations. In *Proceedings of IVA*, pp. 139-145.

H. Hernault, D. Bollegala, and M. Ishizuka. 2010. A Sequential Model for Discourse Segmentation. In *Proceedings of the 11th International Conference on Intelligent Text Processing and Computational Linguistics (CICLing)*, pp. 315-326.

L. Huang. 2008. Forest Reranking: Discriminative Parsing with Non-Local Features. In *Proceedings of the 46th Annual Meeting of the Association for Computational Linguistics (ACL)*, pp. 586-594

D. Klein and C. Manning. 2003. Accurate Unlexicalized Parsing. In *Proceedings of the 41st Annual Meeting of the Association for Computational Linguistics (ACL)*, pp. 423-430.

T. Kudo. CRF++: Yet Another CRF toolkit. Available at http://crfpp.sourceforge.net/

T. Kudo, J. Suzuki, and H. Isozaki. 2005. Boosting-based parse reranking with subtree features. In *Proceedings of the 43rd Annual Meeting of the Association for Computational Linguistics (ACL)*, pp. 189-196.

J. Lafferty, A. McCallum, and F. Pereira. 2001. Conditional random fields: Probabilistic models for segmenting and labeling sequence data. In *Proceedings of the 18th International Conference on Machine Learning (ICML)*, pp.282-289.

A. Louis, A. Joshi, and A. Nenkova 2010. Discourse indicators for content selection in summarization. In *Proceedings of the 11th annual SIGdial Meeting on Discourse and Dialogue (SIGDIAL)* , pp.147-156.

W.C. Mann and S.A. Thompson. 1988. Rhetorical Structure Theory. Toward a Functional Theory of Text Organization. *Text* 8, pp. 243-281.

D. Marcu. 2000. The Theory and Practice of Discourse Parsing and Summarization. MIT Press, Cambridge.

R. Soricut and D. Marcu. 2003. Sentence Level Discourse Parsing using Syntactic and Lexical Information. In *Proceedings of the North American Chapter of the Association for Computational Linguistics (NAACL)*, pp. 149-156.

R. Subba and B. Di Eugenio. 2007. Automatic Discourse Segmentation using Neural Networks. In *Proceedings of the Workshop on the Semantics and Pragmatics of Dialogue (SemDial)*, pp. 189-190.

M. Sun and J.Y. Chai. 2007. Discourse Processing for Context Question Answering Based on Linguistic Knowledge. *Knowledge-Based Systems*. 20(6), pp. 511-526.

H.L. Thanh, G. Abeysinghe, and C. Huyck. 2004. Automated Discourse Segmentation by Syntactic Information and Cue Phrases. In *Proceedings of IASTED*.

M. Tofiloski, J. Brooke, and M. Taboada. 2009. A Syntactic and Lexical-Based Discourse Segmenter. In *Proceedings of the Joint conference of the 47th Annual Meeting of the Association for Computational Linguistics and the 4th International Joint Conference on Natural Language Processing (ACL-IJCNLP)*, pp. 77-80.

Landmark-based Location Belief Tracking in a Spoken Dialog System

Yi Ma
The Ohio State University
Columbus, OH 43210
may@cse.ohio-state.edu

Antoine Raux, Deepak Ramachandran, Rakesh Gupta
Honda Research Institute, USA
425 National Ave, Mountain View, CA 94043
{araux,dramachandran,rgupta}@hra.com

Abstract

Many modern spoken dialog systems use probabilistic graphical models to update their belief over the concepts under discussion, increasing robustness in the face of noisy input. However, such models are ill-suited to probabilistic reasoning about spatial relationships between entities. In particular, a car navigation system that infers users' intended destination using nearby landmarks as descriptions must be able to use distance measures as a factor in inference. In this paper, we describe a belief tracking system for a location identification task that combines a semantic belief tracker for categorical concepts based on the DPOT framework (Raux and Ma, 2011) with a kernel density estimator that incorporates landmark evidence from multiple turns and landmark hypotheses, into a posterior probability over candidate locations. We evaluate our approach on a corpus of destination setting dialogs and show that it significantly outperforms a deterministic baseline.

1 Introduction

Mobile devices such as smart phones and in-car infotainment systems have generated demand for a new generation of location-based services such as local business search, turn-by-turn navigation, and social event recommendation. Accessing such services in a timely manner through speech is a crucial requirement, particularly on the go when the user is unable to resort to other modalities e.g. where safety regulations prohibit drivers from using buttons or a touchscreeen while driving.

In such systems, a Point of Interest (POI) or a destination such as a restaurant, store or a public place is often specified. For example, a car navigation system needs the user to input the destination before giving directions. Similarly, a photo tagging application must allow its users to designate the location where a picture was taken. While postal addresses can be used to unambigously identify locations, they are often either unknown or hard for users to remember. A more natural (though potentially ambiguous) means of specifying locations is to use *landmarks* such as "`the Italian restaurant near Red Rock cafe on Castro Street`" or "`the bakery near that mall with a Subway and a 7 Eleven`". A location-based dialog system that understands referring expressions using landmarks could lead to more succinct dialogs, higher recognition accuracy and a greater appearance of intelligence to the user.

We present a system that performs *belief tracking* over multiple turns of user speech input to infer the most probable target location. The user interacts with the system through speech in order to specify a target location, and may include references to one or more landmarks. Such a system must handle two sources of uncertainty. First, ASR is notoriously error-prone and modern ASR engines provide ranked lists of possible interpretations of speech input rather than single hypotheses. Second, the suitability of a particular landmark or its likelihood of usage by the speaker depends on a number of factors such as distance, size and prominence of the landmark, familiarity of the user and his expectation of common ground for understanding. These factors, or at least the resulting variability, must be taken into account when making inferences about target locations from landmark-based expressions.

The first source of ambiguity (speech understanding) has been the target of research on belief tracking (Mehta et al., 2010; Raux and Ma, 2011; Thomson and Young, 2010). In previous work, the concepts of interest are entities that are ontologically related (i.e. with *is-a* or *has-a* relations), thus discrete probabilistic graphical models such as DBNs have generally sufficed as representations. But these models are ill-suited for dense continuous spatial relations like the distance between any two locations on a map. In this paper, we introduce a *kernel-based belief tracker* as a probabilistic model for inferring target locations from (uncertain) landmarks. The kernel-based representation allows a natural way to weigh the suitability of a landmark and the speech understanding confidence. The output of this tracker is combined with that of a Dynamic Probabilistic Ontology Tree (DPOT) (Raux and Ma, 2011), which performs ontological reasoning over other features of the target location, to give a posterior distribution over the intended location. We evaluate our approach on a new corpus of location setting dialogs specially collected for this work and find it to significantly outperform a deterministic baseline.

2 Related Work

In the context of a location-based dialog system, Seltzer et al. (2007) describes a speech understanding system designed to recognize street intersections and map them to a database of valid intersections using information retrieval techniques. Robustness is achieved by exploiting both words and phonetic information at retrieval time, allowing a soft-matching of the ASR result to the canonical intersection name. Their approach is specifically targeted at intersections, to the exclusion of other types of landmarks. While intersections are frequently used as landmarks in North America (where their study was conducted), this is not always the case in other cultures, such as Japan (Suzuki and Wakabayashi, 2005), where points of interests such as train stations are more commonly used. Also, their approach, which is framed as speech understanding, does not exploit information from previous dialog turns to infer user intention.

Landmarks have been integrated in route directions (Pierre-emmanuel Michon, 2001; Tversky and Lee, 1999) with significant use at origin, destination and decision points. Further, landmarks have been found to work better than street signs in wayfinding (Tom and Denis, 2003). The multimodal system described in (Gruenstein and Seneff, 2007) supports the use of landmarks from a limited set that the user specifies by pointing at the map and typing landmark names. While this allows the landmarks (and their designations) to be of any kind, the burden of defining them is on the user.

Spatial language, including landmarks, has also been the focus of research within the context of human-robot interaction. (Huang et al., 2010; MacMahon et al., 2006) describe systems that translate natural language directions into motion paths or physical actions. These works focus on understanding the structure of (potentially complex) spatial language and mapping it into a representation of the environment. Issues such as imperfect spoken language understanding have not been investigated in this context. Similarly, this vein of spatial language research has traditionally been conducted on small artificial worlds with a few dozen objects and places at most, whereas real-world location-based services deal with thousands or millions of entities.

3 Hybrid Semantic / Location Belief Tracking

Our belief tracking system consists of two trackers running in parallel: a DPOT belief tracker (Raux and Ma, 2011) and a novel kernel-based location tracker. The final inference of user intentions is produced by combining information from the two trackers. The general idea is to rerank the user goals given spatial information provided by the location tracker.

3.1 Semantic Belief Tracker

We perform belief tracking over non-landmark concepts such as business name and street using a Dynamic Probabilistic Ontology Tree (DPOT) (Raux and Ma, 2011). A DPOT is a Bayesian Network composed of a tree-shaped subnetwork representing the (static) user goal (*Goal Network*), connected to

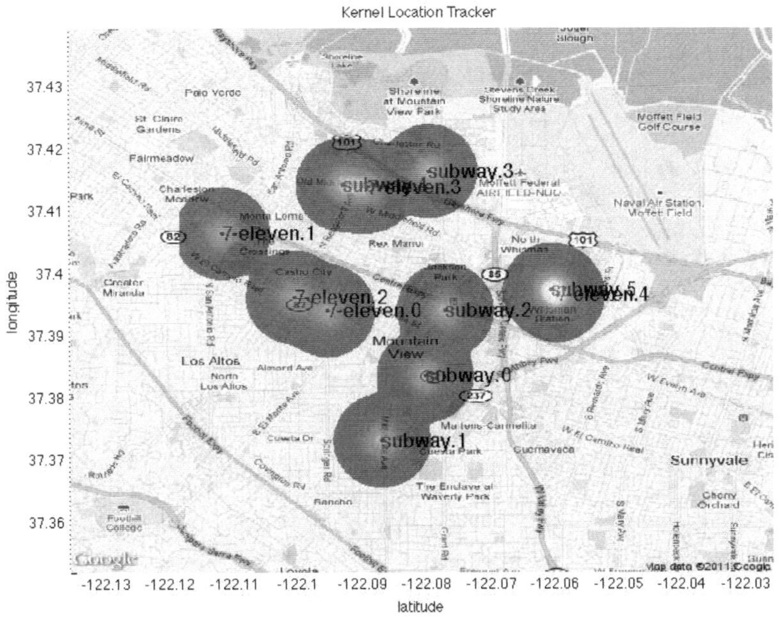

Figure 1: Top view heat map of spatial distribution with landmarks `Subway` and `7 Eleven` over potential target places in Mountain View, CA

a series of subnetworks representing the evidence gathered from each successive dialog turn (*Evidence Networks*). Details of the model and an efficient inference method for posterior probability computations can be found in (Raux and Ma, 2011).

In the context of this paper, the purpose of the semantic tracker is to update a list of the most likely target locations using attributes of that location provided by the user (see Figure 2). In a local business database, such attributes include `Business Name`, `Street`, `Category` (e.g. Japanese restaurant or convenience store), etc. The structure and parameters of the Goal Network encode probabilistic ontological relations between the attributes (e.g. a Mcdonalds would be described as a fast-food restaurant with high probability) that can be exploited during inference. These can be derived from expert knowledge, learned from data, or as is the case in our experimental system, populated from a database of local businesses (see section 4). After each user utterance, the DPOT outputs a ranked list of user goal hypotheses (an example goal hypothesis is [`Category=italian restaurant,Street=castro street`]). Each hypothesis is converted into a query to the backend database, and the posterior probability of the hypothesis is split equally among all matching entries. This results in a ranked list of database entries corresponding to the system's belief over potential target locations, with potentially many entries having the same probability.

3.2 Kernel-based Location Tracker

Landmark concepts extracted by the Natural Language Understanding module (NLU) are passed to the location tracker, which maintains a distribution over coordinates of potential target locations. Each such landmark concept is treated as evidence of spatial proximity of the target to the landmark and the distribution is accordingly updated. Any location in the database can serve as a landmark observation, including major POIs such as train stations or public facilities. If the name of a generic chain store with multiple locations such as `Subway` is used for the landmark, then an observation corresponding to each individual location is added to the tracker.

For each observed landmark ℓ, the location tracker constructs a 2-dimensional Gaussian kernel with mean equal to the longitude and latitude of the landmark ($\mu_\ell = (long_\ell, lat_\ell)$) and a fixed covari-

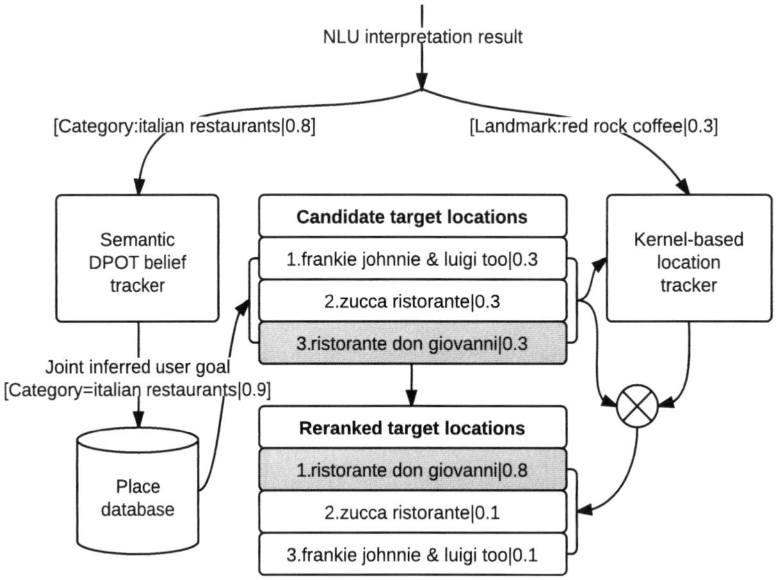

Figure 2: Overview of the hybrid semantic / location belief tracking approach; the database entry in shade is the underlying true target place to which the provided landmark is close

ance matrix Σ_ℓ for each landmark:

$$\boldsymbol{\Phi}_\ell(\boldsymbol{t}) = \frac{1}{2\pi|\Sigma|^{1/2}}\exp(-\frac{1}{2}(\boldsymbol{t}-\mu_\ell)^T\Sigma_\ell^{-1}(\boldsymbol{t}-\mu_\ell))$$

This kernel density determines the conditional probability that the target is at coordinates $\boldsymbol{t} = (long_t, lat_t)$ given the fixed landmark ℓ. The covariance matrix Σ_ℓ and hence the shape of the kernel can be adjusted for different landmarks depending on considerations such as the familiarity, size and prominence of the landmark (a large historic monument is likely to be used as a landmark for locations much further away than a small corner grocery store) etc.

The probability density of the location $\boldsymbol{t}$ being the target is then given by a weighted mixture model:

$$Pr(\boldsymbol{t}|L) = \sum_{\ell \in L} w_\ell \boldsymbol{\Phi}_\ell(\boldsymbol{t}) \quad (1)$$

where L is the set of candidate landmarks returned by the NLU (see Section 4.1) up to the current turn and w_ℓ is set to the confidence score of ℓ from the NLU. Thus candidate landmarks that have higher confidence in the NLU will contribute more strongly to the total likelihood. Since $Pr(\boldsymbol{t}|L)$ is a density function, it is unnormalized. In Figure 1, we show the kernel tracker distribution for a dialog state where `Subway` and `7 Eleven` are provided as landmarks.

The kernel density estimator is a simple approach to probabilistic spatial reasoning. It is easy to implement and requires only a moderate amount of tuning. It naturally models evidence from multiple speech hypotheses and multiple provided landmarks, and it benefits from accumulated evidence across dialog turns. It can also potentially be used to model more general kinds of spatial expressions by using appropriate kernel functions. For example, '`Along Castro street`' can be modeled by a Gaussian with an asymmetric covariance matrix such that the shape of the resulting distribution is elongated and concentrated on the street. While '`Two blocks away from ...`' could be modeled by adding an extra "negative" density kernel that extends from

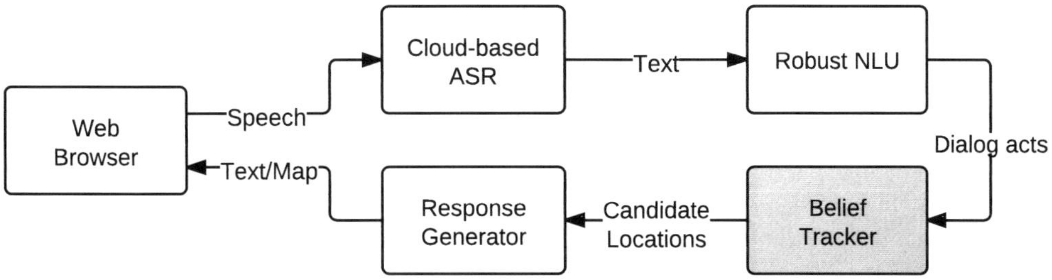

Figure 3: Overview of the Destination Setting System

the center of the landmark to a distance two blocks away.

3.3 Combining the Two Trackers

At each turn, the updated results from the Semantic and Location tracker are combined to give a single ranked list of likely target locations. In Figure 2, this process is illustrated for a dialog turn where two possible concepts are identified – a category attribute [`Category:italian restaurant`] and a landmark [`Landmark:red rock coffee company`]. These are passed to the DPOT tracker and the location tracker respectively. The output of the DPOT is used to retrieve and score matching database entries. The score for each entry is reweighted by the kernel density estimator measured at the coordinates of the location [1]:

$$Pr(e_{ij}) = (\frac{p_i}{N_i})^{\nu} \times Pr(e_{ij}|L) \quad (2)$$

where N_i is the number of matching database entries retrieved from ith goal hypothesis (having joint probability p_i) and e_{ij} is the jth such entry ($j \in [1..N_i]$). The exponent ν for the posterior term is introduced to account for scale difference between the semantic score and the kernel density.

The set of candidate entries can then be reranked according to Eq 2 and returned as the output of the combined belief tracker.

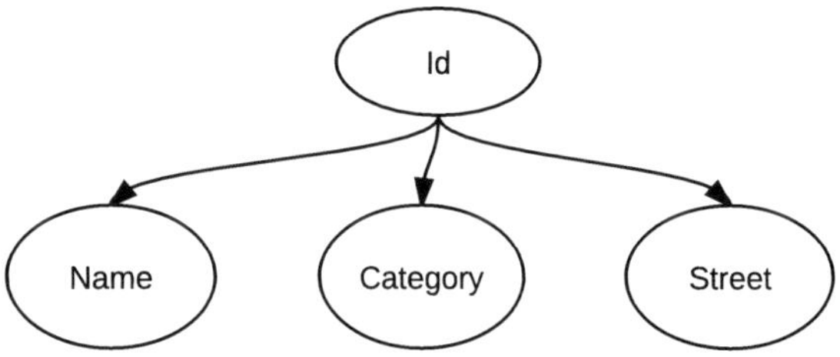

Figure 4: Structure of the Goal Network for the experimental system.

4 Evaluation

4.1 Experimental System

The architecture of our experimental system is shown in Figure 3. The web client, shown in Figure 5, runs in the participant's web browser and displays the target location of the current scenario using the Google Map API. The user's goal is to convey this target location to the system through speech only.

The system backend consists of a database of 2902 businesses located in Mountain View, California with their name, street, street number, business category, latitude and longitude provided. The grammar rules for the NLU and the probability tables in the DPOT are populated from this database.

The web client captures the user speech and sends it to our server with a push-to-talk interface based on the WAMI toolkit (Gruenstein et al., 2008). The server uses a commercial cloud-based ASR service with generic acoustic and language models, which were not adapted to our task. The n-best list of hypotheses from the ASR is sent to our robust natural

[1] The scores are renormalized to between 0 and1.

language understanding module for parsing.

Our NLU uses a hybrid approach combining a weighted finite-state transducer (WFST) with string matching based rescoring of the output. The WFST incorporates out-of-grammar word loops that allow skipping input words at certain points in the parse[2]. This parser robustly maps free form utterances (e.g. "Okay let's go to that Italian place near, uh..., Red Rock Cafe, on Castro") to semantic frames (e.g. [Category=italian restaurant, Street=castro street, Landmark=red rock coffee company]).

The NLU confidence score is computed based on the number of words skipped while parsing, and how close the important concept words match the canonical phrases found in the database. For instance, "Red Rock Cafe" matches the canonical name "Red Rock Coffee Company" with high confidence because rare words (Red, Rock) are identical, and differing but common words (Cafe, Coffee, Company) have a low weight in the score. The string matching score is based on the term-frequency/inverse document frequency (TF-IDF) metric commonly used in information retrieval. In our case, the weight of different terms (IDF) is estimated based on their frequency of occurrence in different database entries (i.e. how uniquely they describe a matching entry). We use the secondstring open-source library (Cohen et al., 2003) for string matching. For any ASR hypothesis, the NLU is likely to generate several parses which are all merged in a global list of candidate parses.

For each candidate parse, the system generates a set of dialog acts (one per concept in the parse) which are input to the belief tracker with their confidence score. Following the approach described in section 3, dialog acts corresponding to the Landmark concept are sent to the kernel-based location belief tracker, while all other concepts are sent to a Dynamic Probabilistic Ontology Trees (DPOT) semantic belief tracker, whose structure is shown in Figure 4. We use a two-level tree. The value of the root node (Id) is never directly observed and represents the database entry targeted by the user. The leaf nodes correspond to the relevant attributes Name, Category, and Street. For any database entry e, attribute a and value of that attribute v_a, the conditional probability $P(a = v_a|Id = e)$ is set to 1 if the value of a is v_a for entry e in the database, and to 0 otherwise. For attributes such as Category, which allow several possible values for each entry, the probability is split equally among valid values. After each user utterance, the network is augmented with a new Evidence Network capturing the possible interpretations and their likelihood, as computed by the NLU. The posterior probability distribution over user goals is computed and rescored using the kernel-based location tracker.

Finally, the Response Generator takes the highest scoring target location from the belief tracker and sends it back to the web client which displays it on the map and also indicates what are the values of the Name, Category, and Street concepts for the top belief (see Figure 5). If the top belief location does not match the goal of the scenario, the user can speak again to refine or correct the system belief. After the user has spoken 5 utterances, they also get the choice of moving on to the next scenario (in which case the dialog is considered a failure).

4.2 Data collection

To evaluate our approach, we ran a data collection experiment using the Amazon Mechanical Turk online marketplace. We defined 20 scenarios grouped into 4 Human Intelligence Tasks (HITs). Figure 5 shows a screen shot of the web interface to the system. In each scenario, the worker is given a target location to describe by referring to nearby landmark information. The target locations were chosen so as to cover a variety of business categories and nearby landmarks. The compensation for completing each set of 5 scenarios is 1 US dollar. Before their first scenario, workers are shown a video explaining the goal of the task and how to use the interface, in which they are specifically encouraged to use landmarks in their descriptions.

At the beginning of each scenario, the target location is displayed on the map with a callout containing a short description using either a generic category (e.g. Italian restaurant, Convenience store) or the name of a chain store (e.g. Subway, Mcdonalds). The worker

[2]This module is implemented using the OpenFST library (Allauzen et al., 2007)

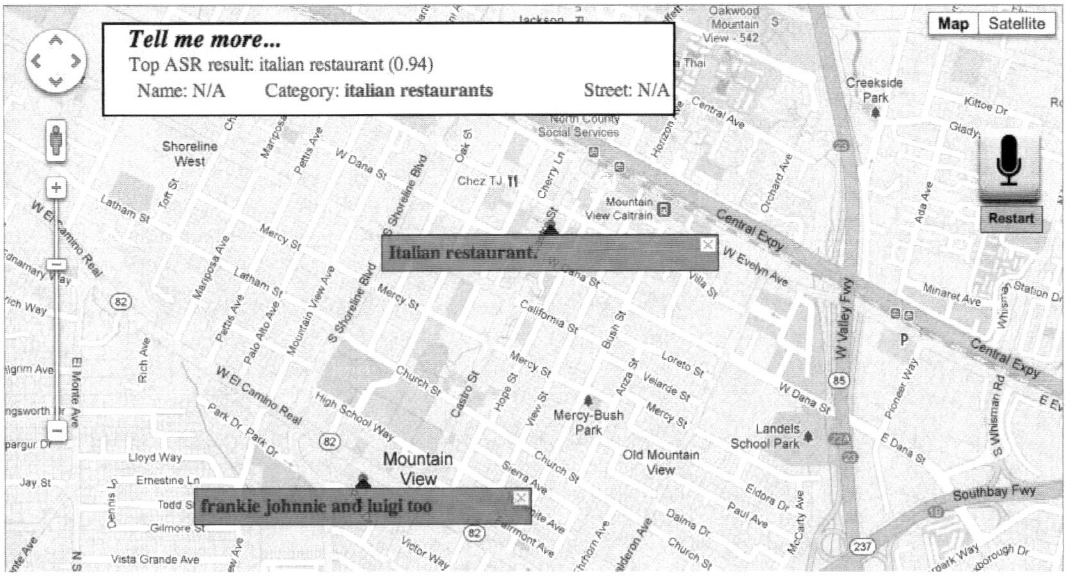

Figure 5: Screen capture of the data collection web interface where the target location is an Italian restaurant (in green, underlying target place is [Ristorante Don Giovanni]) and after the first turn user input 'Italian restaurant' with a system belief [Frankie, Johnnie & Luigi, Too] in blue returned without any landmark information provided so far

then interacts with the system described in section 4.1 until either the system's top belief matches the target location, or they decide to skip the scenario.

4.3 Data Statistics

Overall, 99 workers participated in the data collection, providing 948 dialogs (2,869 utterances, 3 turns per scenario on average), which two of the authors manually transcribed and annotated for dialog acts. 76% of the dialogs (46% of utterances) contained a reference to a landmark. Other strategies commonly used by workers to uniquely identify a location include using a category or chain name and a street, as well as explicitly mentioning the target business name (although workers were explicitly discouraged form doing so). Figure 7 in appendix provides one example dialog from the corpus.

Overall, the workers provided 203 unique landmarks, of which 143 (70%) are in the database.

Workers were able to set the target destination within 5 turns in 60.1% of the dialogs, which we hereafter refer to as task successes. However, based on the manual transcripts, 19.0% of the dialogs could not have succeeded with the current system because the workers used landmark or attributes that do not appear in the database. Since the focus of this study is robustness rather than coverage, we base our evaluation on the remaining 768 dialogs, which we split between a development set of 74 dialogs and a test set of 694 dialogs. On this test set, the live system has a task success rate of 70.6%. By inspecting the log files, we noticed that runtime issues such as timeouts prevented the system from getting any belief from the belief tracker in 6.3% of the dialogs.

The mean Word Error Rate (WER) per worker on the test set is 27.5%. There was significant variability across workers, with a standard deviation 20.7%. Besides the usual factors such as acoustic noise and non-native accents, many of the errors came from the misrecognition of business names, due to the fact that ASR uses an open-ended language model that is tuned neither to Mountain View, nor to businesses, nor to the kind of utterances that our set up tends to yield, which is a realistic situation for large scale practical applications.

Concept precision of the top scoring NLU hypothesis is 73.0% and recall is 57.7%. However, when considering the full list of NLU hypotheses and using an oracle to select the best one for each turn, precision increases to 89.3% and recall to 66.2%, underscoring the potential of using multiple input hypotheses in the belief tracker.

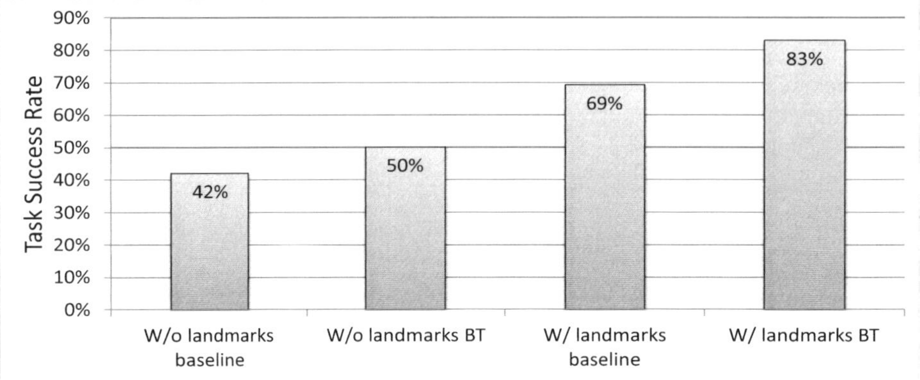

Figure 6: Batch evaluation of the proposed (BT) and baseline approaches with and without landmark information.

4.4 Batch Results

To further analyze the performance of our approach, we conducted a series of batch experiments on the data collected with the runtime system. We first tuned the parameters of the belief tracker ν and Σ_l (see section 3) on the development set ($\nu = 3$ and Σ_l corresponds to a circular Gaussian with standard deviation 500 meters).

We compare the tuned proposed belief tracking system (labeled BT) with three other versions. First, we define a deterministic baseline system which, at each turn, updates its belief by overwriting each concept's value with the value found in the top NLU hypothesis. Based on this (single) user goal hypothesis, we query the database to retrieve matching entries. If the current goal hypothesis contains a `Landmark` concept, the baseline system selects the matching entry that is closest to any location matching the landmark name, by computing the pairwise distance between candidate target locations and landmarks.

We also compute the performance of both the baseline and our proposed approach without using landmark information at all. In these versions, the belief over the attributes (`Name`, `Street`, and `Category`) is updated according to either the top NLU hypothesis (baseline) or the DPOT model (BT) and the first matching database entry is returned, ignoring any landmark information.

Figure 6 shows the task success of each of the four versions on the test set. First, it is clear that landmark information is critical to complete the tasks in this corpus since both systems ignoring landmarks perform significantly worse than their counterparts. Second, the belief tracking approach significantly outperforms the deterministic baseline (83.0% vs 69.3%, $p < 0.001$ using sign test for matched pairs).

To further analyze the performance of the system in different input conditions, we split the dialogs based on their measured concept accuracy (expressed in terms of concept F-measure). All dialogs with an F-measure higher than the median (70.0%) are labeled as high-accuracy, while the other half of the data is labeled as low-accuracy. While both the proposed approach and the baseline perform similarly well for high-accuracy dialogs (task success of resp. 96.0% and 92.8%, difference is not statistically significant), the difference is much larger for low-accuracy dialogs (70.0% vs 45.8%, $p < 0.001$) confirming the robustness of the landmark-based belief tracking approach when confronted with poor input conditions.

5 Conclusion

In this paper, we have explored the possibilities of incorporating spatial information into belief tracking in spoken dialog systems. We proposed a landmark-based location tracker which can be combined with a semantic belief tracker to output inferred joint user goal. Based on the results obtained from our batch experiments, we conclude that integrating spatial information into a location-based dialog system could improve the overall accuracy of belief tracking significantly.

References

Cyril Allauzen, Michael Riley, Johan Schalkwyk, Wojciech Skut, and Mehryar Mohri. 2007. Openfst: A general and efficient weighted finite-state transducer library. In *Proceedings of the Ninth International Conference on Implementation and Application of Automata (CIAA) Lecture Notes in Computer Science*, volume 4783, pages 11–23. Springer.

W.W. Cohen, P. Ravikumar, and S.E. Fienberg. 2003. A comparison of string distance metrics for name-matching tasks. In *Proceedings of the IJCAI-2003 Workshop on Information Integration on the Web (IIWeb-03)*, pages 73–78.

Alexander Gruenstein and Stephanie Seneff. 2007. Releasing a multimodal dialogue system into the wild: User support mechanisms. In *In Proceedings of the 8th SIGdial Workshop on Discourse and Dialogue*, pages 111–119, September.

A. Gruenstein, I. McGraw, and I. Badr. 2008. The wami toolkit for developing, deploying, and evaluating web-accessible multimodal interfaces. In *Proceedings of the 10th international conference on Multimodal interfaces*, pages 141–148. ACM.

Albert Huang, Stefanie Tellex, Abe Bachrach, Thomas Kollar, Deb Roy, and Nick Roy. 2010. Natural language command of an autonomous micro-air vehicle. In *International Conference on Intelligent Robots and Systems (IROS)*.

M. MacMahon, B. Stankiewicz, and B. Kuipers. 2006. Walk the talk: Connecting language, knowledge, and action in route instructions. In *Proceedings of the National Conference on Artificial Intelligence*, volume 21, page 1475. Menlo Park, CA; Cambridge, MA; London; AAAI Press; MIT Press; 1999.

N. Mehta, R. Gupta, A. Raux, D. Ramachandran, and S. Krawczyk. 2010. Probabilistic ontology trees for belief tracking in dialog systems. In *Proceedings of the 11th Annual Meeting of the Special Interest Group on Discourse and Dialogue*, pages 37–46. Association for Computational Linguistics.

Michel Denis Pierre-emmanuel Michon. 2001. When and why are visual landmarks used in giving directions? In D. R. Montello, editor, *Spatial Information Theory, Volume 2205 of Lecture Notes in Computer Science*, pages 292–305. Springer, Berlin.

A. Raux and Y. Ma. 2011. Efficient probabilistic tracking of user goal and dialog history for spoken dialog systems. In *Proceedings of Interspeech 2011*.

Michael L. Seltzer, Yun-Cheng Ju, Ivan Tashev, and Alex Acero. 2007. Robust location understanding in spoken dialog systems using intersections. In *Proceedings of Interspeech 2007*, pages 2813–2816.

K. Suzuki and Y. Wakabayashi. 2005. Cultural differences of spatial descriptions in tourist guidebooks. *Spatial Cognition IV. Reasoning, Action, and Interaction*, 3343:147–164.

B. Thomson and S. Young. 2010. Bayesian update of dialogue state: A pomdp framework for spoken dialogue systems. *Computer Speech & Language*, 24(4):562–588.

Ariane Tom and Michel Denis. 2003. Referring to landmark or street information in route directions: What difference does it make? *Spatial Information Theory. Foundations of Geoghraphic Information Science, Lecture Notes in Computer Science*, 2825/2003:362–374.

Barbara Tversky and Paul U. Lee. 1999. Pictorial and verbal tools for conveying routes. In *Proceedings of the International Conference on Spatial Information Theory: Cognitive and Computational Foundations of Geographic Information Science(COSIT)*. Springer-Verlag London.

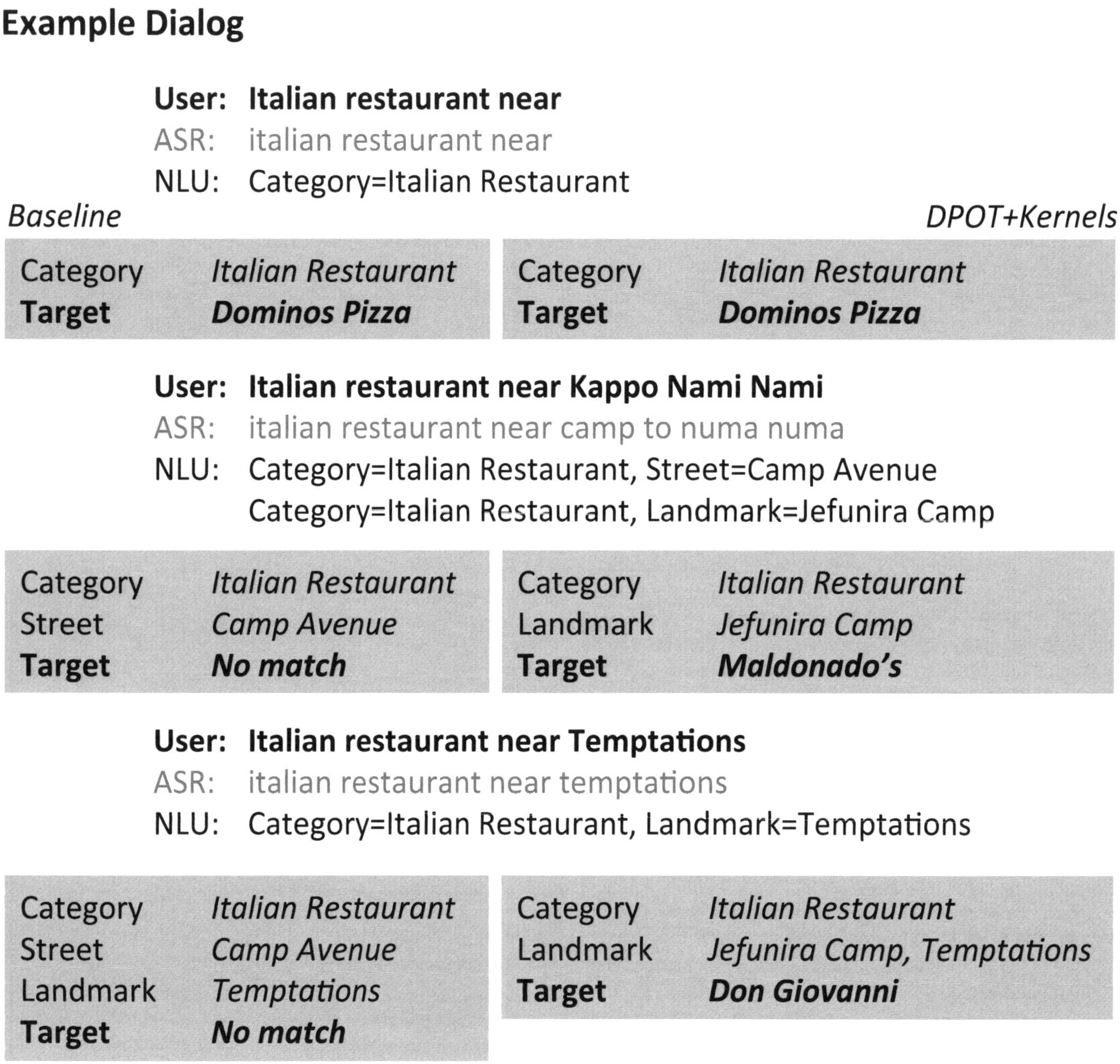

Figure 7: Comparison between baseline and proposed method on an example dialog whose underlying true target is an Italian restaurant called Don Giovanni.

Probabilistic Dialogue Models with Prior Domain Knowledge

Pierre Lison
Department of Informatics
University of Oslo, Norway
plison@ifi.uio.no

Abstract

Probabilistic models such as Bayesian Networks are now in widespread use in spoken dialogue systems, but their scalability to complex interaction domains remains a challenge. One central limitation is that the state space of such models grows exponentially with the problem size, which makes parameter estimation increasingly difficult, especially for domains where only limited training data is available. In this paper, we show how to capture the underlying structure of a dialogue domain in terms of *probabilistic rules* operating on the dialogue state. The probabilistic rules are associated with a small, compact set of parameters that can be directly estimated from data. We argue that the introduction of this abstraction mechanism yields probabilistic models that are easier to learn and generalise better than their unstructured counterparts. We empirically demonstrate the benefits of such an approach learning a dialogue policy for a human-robot interaction domain based on a Wizard-of-Oz data set.

1 Introduction

Spoken dialogue systems increasingly rely on probabilistic models at various stages of their pipeline. Statistical methods have notably been applied to tasks such as disfluency detection (Lease et al., 2006), semantic parsing (Erdogan et al., 2002; He and Young, 2005), dialogue act recognition (Stolcke et al., 2000; Lan et al., 2008), dialogue management (Frampton and Lemon, 2009; Young et al., 2010), natural language generation (Oh and Rudnicky, 2002; Lemon, 2011) and speech synthesis (Zen et al., 2009).

There are two compelling reasons for this growing interest in statistical approaches: first, spoken dialogue is pervaded with noise and uncertainty (due to e.g. speech recognition errors, linguistic and pragmatic ambiguities, and unknown user intentions), which must be dealt with at all processing stages. Second, a decisive advantage of probabilistic models lies in their ability to be automatically optimised from data, enabling statistically-based dialogue systems to exhibit conversational behaviours that are often more robust, flexible and adaptive than hand-crafted systems (Lemon and Pietquin, 2007).

Despite their success, the use of probabilistic models also presents a number of challenges. The most pressing issue is the paucity of appropriate data sets. Stochastic models often require large amounts of training data to estimate their parameters – either directly (Henderson et al., 2008) or indirectly by way of a user simulator (Schatzmann et al., 2007; Cuayáhuitl et al., 2010). Unfortunately, real interaction data is scarce, expensive to acquire, and difficult to transfer from one domain to another. Moreover, many dialogue domains are inherently open-ended, which means they are not limited to the completion of a single task with predefined features but have to represent a varying number of tasks, complex user models and a rich, dynamic environment. Examples of such domains include human-robot interaction (Kruijff et al., 2010), cognitive assistants and companions (Nguyen, 2005; Cavazza et al., 2010), and tutoring systems (Litman and Silliman, 2004; Eskenazi, 2009). In such settings, the dialogue system might need to track a large number of variables in the course of the interaction, which quickly leads to a combinatorial explosion of the state space.

There is an extensive body of work in the machine

learning and planning literature that shows how to address this issue by relying on more expressive representations, able to capture relevant aspects of the problem *structure* in a compact manner. By taking advantage of hierarchical or relational abstractions, system developers can leverage their domain knowledge to yield probabilistic models that are easier to learn (due to a reduced number of parameters) and more efficient to use (since the structure can be exploited by the inference algorithm).

The contributions of this paper are twofold. We first present a new framework for encoding prior knowledge in probabilistic dialogue models, based on the concept of *probabilistic rules*. The framework is very general and can accommodate a wide spectrum of domains and learning tasks, from fully statistical models with virtually no prior knowledge to manually designed models with only a handful of parameters. Second, we demonstrate how this framework can be exploited to learn stochastic dialogue policies with limited data sets using a Bayesian learning approach.

The following pages spell out the approach in more detail. In Section 2, we provide the general background on probabilistic models and their use in spoken dialogue systems. We describe in Section 3 how to encode such models via probabilistic rules and estimate their parameters from data. In Section 4, we detail the empirical evaluation of our approach in a human-robot interaction domain, given small amounts of data collected in Wizard-of-Oz experiments. Finally, we discuss and compare our approach to related work in Section 5.

2 Background

2.1 Bayesian Networks

The probabilistic models used in this paper are expressed as directed graphical models, also known as Bayesian Networks. Let $X_1 ... X_n$ denote a set of random variables. Each variable X_i is associated with a range of mutually exclusive values. In dialogue models, this range is often discrete and can be explicitly enumerated: $Val(X_i) = \{x_i^1, ..., x_i^m\}$.

A Bayesian Network defines the joint probability distribution $P(X_1 ... X_n)$ via conditional dependencies between variables, using a directed graph where each node corresponds to a variable X_i. Each

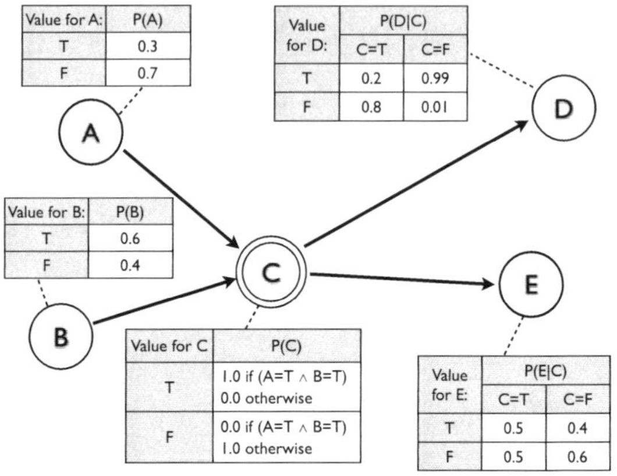

Figure 1: Example of Bayesian network with 5 nodes. The double circles denote a deterministic node. As an example, the query $P(A|D{=}\text{T})$ gives the result $P(A{=}\text{T}|D{=}\text{T}) \approx 0.18$ and $P(A{=}\text{F}|D{=}\text{T}) \approx 0.82$.

edge $X_i \rightarrow X_j$ denotes a conditional dependence between the two nodes, in which case X_i is said to be a *parent* of X_j. A conditional probability distribution $P(X_i|Par(X_i))$ is associated with each node X_i, where $Par(X_i)$ denotes the parents of X_i.

Conditional probability distributions (CPDs) can be defined in various ways, from look-up tables to deterministic distributions (Koller and Friedman, 2009). Together with the directed graph, the CPDs fully determine the joint probability distribution of the Bayesian Network. The network can be used for inference by querying the distribution of a subset of variables, often given some additional evidence, as illustrated by the example in Figure 1.

2.2 Dialogue Models

A dialogue state $\mathbf{s}$ is usually decomposed into a set of state variables $\mathbf{s} = \{s_1, ... s_n\}$ representing relevant features of the interaction. For instance, the state variables for a human-robot interaction scenario might be composed of tasks to accomplish, the interaction history, past events, as well as objects, spatial locations and agents in the environment.

Given the uncertainty present in spoken dialogue, many variables are only partially observable. We thus encode our knowledge of the current state in a distribution $\mathbf{b}(\mathbf{s}) = P(s_1, ..., s_n)$ called the *belief state*, which can be conveniently expressed as a Bayesian Network (Thomson and Young, 2010). This belief state $\mathbf{b}$ is regularly updated as new infor-

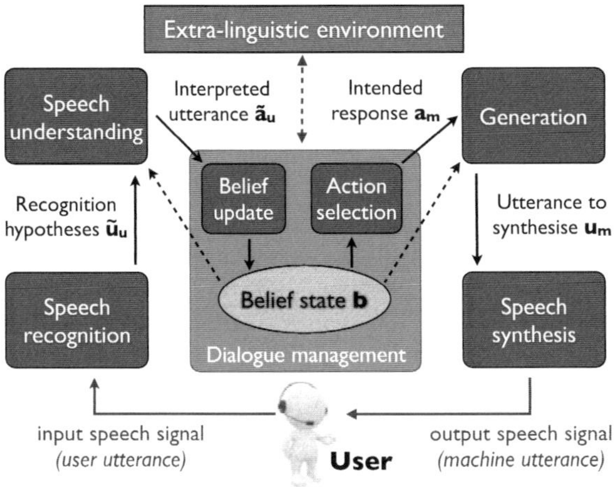

Figure 2: Dialogue system architecture schema.

mation becomes available. As illustrated in Figure 2, the whole system pipeline can be formalised in terms of inference steps over this belief state:

1. Upon detection of a new utterance, the speech recogniser generates the N-best list of recognition hypotheses $\tilde{\mathbf{u}}_\mathbf{u} = P(u_u|o)$;
2. Speech understanding then searches for the most likely dialogue act(s) realised in the utterance: $\tilde{\mathbf{a}}_\mathbf{u} = P(a_u|\tilde{\mathbf{u}}_\mathbf{u}, \mathbf{b})$;
3. The belief state is updated with the new interpreted dialogue act: $\mathbf{b}' = P(\mathbf{s}'|\tilde{\mathbf{a}}_\mathbf{u}, \mathbf{b})$;
4. Based on the updated belief state, the action selection searches for the optimal system action to perform: $a^*_m = \arg\max_{a_m} Q(a_m|\mathbf{b})$;
5. The system action is then realised in an utterance u_m, which is again framed as a search for $u^*_m = \arg\max_{u_m} Q(u_m|\mathbf{b}, a_m)$;
6. Finally, the dialogue state is re-updated given the system action: $\mathbf{b}' = P(\mathbf{s}'|a_m, \mathbf{b})$.

The models defined above use $P(x|\mathbf{b})$ as a notational convenience for $\sum_{\mathbf{s^i} \in Val(\mathbf{s})} P(x|\mathbf{s}{=}\mathbf{s^i})\mathbf{b}(\mathbf{s^i})$. The same holds for the estimated values $\tilde{\mathbf{u}}_\mathbf{u}$ and $\tilde{\mathbf{a}}_\mathbf{u}$: $P(x|\tilde{\mathbf{y}}) = \sum_{y^i \in Val(\tilde{\mathbf{y}})} P(x|y{=}y^i)P(y{=}y^i)$.

3 Approach

The starting point of our approach is the observation that dialogue often exhibits a fair amount of *internal structure*. This structure can take several forms.

We can first note that the probability or utility of a given output variable often depends on only a small subset of input variables, although the number and identity of these variables might naturally differ from action to action. The state variable encoding the physical location of a mobile robot is for instance relevant for answering a user requesting its location, but not for responding to a greeting act.

Moreover, the values of the dependent variables can often be grouped into *partitions* yielding similar outcomes, thereby reducing the problem dimensionality. The partitions can generally be expressed via logical conditions on the variable values. As illustration, consider a dialogue where the user can ask yes/no questions pertaining to the colour of specific objects (e.g. “Is the ball red?”). The utility of the system action $\mathrm{Confirm}$ depends on two variables: the user dialogue act, for instance $a_u = \mathrm{VerifyColour(ball, red)}$, and the object colour, such as $\mathrm{ball.colour} = \mathrm{blue}$. The combination of these two variables can take a wide range of values, but the utility of $\mathrm{Confirm}$ only depends on two partitions: $(\mathrm{VerifyColour(x, y)} \wedge \mathrm{x.colour} = \mathrm{y})$, in which case the utility is positive, and $(\mathrm{VerifyColour(x, y)} \wedge \mathrm{x.colour} \neq \mathrm{y})$, in which case it is negative.

We outline below a generic description framework for expressing this internal structure, based on the concept of *probabilistic rules*. The rules express the distribution of a dialogue model in terms of structured mappings between input and output variables. At runtime, the rules are then combined to perform inference on the dialogue state, i.e. to compute the distribution of the output variables given the input variables. As we shall see, this is done by instantiating the rules and their associated variables to construct an equivalent Bayesian Network used for inference. The probabilistic rules thus function as high-level *templates* for a classical probabilistic model. The major benefit of this approach is that the rule structure is described in exponentially fewer parameters than its plain counterpart, and is thus much easier to learn and to generalise to unseen data.

3.1 Definitions

A probabilistic rule is defined as a condition-effect mapping, where each condition is mapped to a set of alternative effects, each being assigned a distinct probability. The list of conditions is ordered and takes the form of a "**if** ... **then** ... **else**" case expressing the distribution of the output variables depending on the inputs.

Formally, a rule r is defined as an ordered list of cases $\langle c_1, ...c_n \rangle$, where each case c_i is associated with a condition ϕ_i and a distribution over stochastic effects $\{(\psi_i^1, p_i^1), ..., (\psi_i^k, p_i^k)\}$, where ψ_i^j is a stochastic effect and probability $p_i^j = P(\psi_i^j | \phi_i)$, where $p_i^{1...k}$ satisfy the usual probability axioms. The rule reads as such:

$$
\begin{aligned}
&\textbf{if } (\phi_1) \textbf{ then} \\
&\quad \{P(\psi_1^1) = p_1^1, \; ... \; P(\psi_1^k) = p_1^k\} \\
&... \\
&\textbf{else if } (\phi_n) \textbf{ then} \\
&\quad \{P(\psi_n^1) = p_n^1, \; ... \; P(\psi_n^m) = p_n^m\}
\end{aligned}
$$

A final **else** case is implicitly added to the bottom of the list, and holds if no other condition applies. If not overridden, the default effect associated to this last case is void – i.e. it causes no changes to the distribution over the output variables.

Conditions

The rule conditions are expressed as logical formulae grounded in the input variables. They can be arbitrarily complex formulae connected by conjunction, disjunction and negation. The conditions on the input variables can be seen as providing a compact partitioning of the state space to mitigate the dimensionality curse. Without this partitioning in alternative conditions, a rule ranging over m variables each of size n would need to enumerate n^m possible assignments. The partitioning with conditions reduces this number to p mutually exclusive partitions, where p is usually small.

Effects

The rule effects are defined similarly: given a condition holding on a set of input variables, the associated effects define specific *value assignments* for the output variables. The effects can be limited to a single variable or range over several output variables. For action selection, effects can also take the form of assignments of utility values for a particular action, i.e. $Q(a_m = x) = y$, where y is the scalar value for the utility of action x.

Each effect is assigned a probability, and several alternative stochastic effects can be defined for the same case. If a unique effect is specified, it is then implicitly assumed to hold with probability 1.0. The probabilities of stochastic effects and the action utilities are treated as parameters, which can be either hand-coded or estimated from data.

Example

The rules r_1 and r_2 below express the utilities of two actions: the physical action $\text{ExecuteMov}(\text{X})$ (with X representing the movement type), and the clarification request AskRepeat.

$$
\begin{aligned}
r_1: \quad &\textbf{if } (a_u = \text{RequestMov(X)}) \textbf{ then} \\
&\{Q(a_m = \text{ExecuteMov(X)}) = \theta_{r_1}^{(1)}\}
\end{aligned}
$$

$$
\begin{aligned}
r_2: \quad &\textbf{if } (a_u \neq \emptyset \wedge a_m \neq \text{AskRepeat}) \textbf{ then} \\
&\{Q(a_m = \text{AskRepeat}) = \theta_{r_2}^{(1)}\} \\
&\textbf{else if } (a_u \neq \emptyset) \textbf{ then} \\
&\{Q(a_m = \text{AskRepeat}) = \theta_{r_2}^{(2)}\}
\end{aligned}
$$

Rule r_1 specifies that, if the last user action a_u is equal to $\text{RequestMov}(\text{X})$ (i.e. requesting the robot to execute a particular movement X), the utility associated with $\text{ExecuteMov}(\text{X})$ is equal to the parameter $\theta_{r_1}^1$. Similarly, the rule r_2 specifies the utility of the clarification request AskRepeat, provided that the last user action a_u is assigned to a value (i.e. is different than $\emptyset$). Two cases are distinguished in r_2, depending on whether the previous system action was already $AskRepeat$. This partitioning enables us to assign a distinct utility to the clarification request if one follows the other, in order to e.g. penalise for the repeated clarification.

As illustration, assume that $\theta_{r_1}^{(1)} = 2.0$, $\theta_{r_2}^{(1)} = 1.3$, $\theta_{r_2}^{(2)} = 1.1$, and that the belief state contains a state variable a_u with the following distribution:

$$
\begin{aligned}
P(a_u = \text{RequestMov(LiftBothArms)}) &= 0.7 \\
P(a_u = \text{RequestMov(LiftLeftArm)}) &= 0.2 \\
P(a_u = \emptyset) &= 0.1
\end{aligned}
$$

The optimal system action in this case is therefore $\text{ExecuteMov(LiftBothArms)}$ with utility 1.4, followed by AskRepeat with utility 1.17, and $\text{ExecuteMov(LiftLeftArm)}$ with utility 0.4.

3.2 Inference

Given a belief state $\mathbf{b}$, we perform inference by constructing a Bayesian Network corresponding to the application of the rules. Algorithm 1 describes the construction procedure, which operates as follows:

1. We initialise the Bayesian Network with the variables in the belief state;
2. For every rule r in the rule set, we create a condition node ϕ_r and include the conditional dependencies with its input variables;
3. We create an effect node ψ_r conditioned on ϕ_r, expressing the possible effects of the rule;
4. Finally, we create the (chance or value) nodes corresponding to the output variables of the rule, as specified in the effects.

Rule r_2 described in the previous section would for instance be translated into a condition node ϕ_{r_2} with 3 values (corresponding to the specified conditions and a default **else** condition if none applies) and an effect node ψ_{r_2} also containing 3 values (the two specified effects and a void effect associated with the default condition). Figure 3 illustrates the application of rules r_1 and r_2.

Once the Bayesian network is constructed, queries can be evaluated using any standard algorithm for exact or approximate inference. The procedure is an instance of *ground inference* (Getoor and Taskar, 2007), since the rule structure is grounded in a standard Bayesian Network.

3.3 Parameter Learning

The estimation of the rule parameters can be performed using a Bayesian approach by adding parameter nodes $\boldsymbol{\theta} = \theta_1 ... \theta_k$ to the Bayesian Network, and updating their distribution given a collection of training data. Each data sample d is a pair $(\mathbf{b}_d, t_d)$, where $\mathbf{b}_d$ is the belief state for the specific sample, and t_d the target value. The target value depends on the model to learn – for learning dialogue policies, it corresponds to the selected action a_m.

Algorithm 1 : NETWORKCONSTRUCTION $(\mathbf{b}, \mathcal{R})$

Require: $\mathbf{b}$: Current belief state
Require: $\mathcal{R}$: Set of probabilistic rules
$\mathcal{B} \leftarrow \mathbf{b}$
for all rule $r \in \mathcal{R}$ **do**
  $\mathcal{I}_r \leftarrow \text{INPUTNODES}(r)$
  $\phi_r \leftarrow \text{CONDITIONNODE}(r)$
  Add ϕ_r and dependencies $\mathcal{I}_r \rightarrow \phi_r$ to $\mathcal{B}$
  $\psi_r \leftarrow \text{EFFECTNODE}(r)$
  Add ψ_r and dependency $\phi_r \rightarrow \psi_r$ to $\mathcal{B}$
  $\mathcal{O}_r \leftarrow \text{OUTPUTNODES}(r)$
  for all output variable $o \in \mathcal{O}_r$ **do**
    Add/modify node o and dep. $\psi_r \rightarrow o$ to $\mathcal{B}$
  end for
end for
return $\mathcal{B}$

Algorithm 2 : PARAMETERLEARNING $(\mathcal{R}, \boldsymbol{\theta}, \mathcal{D})$

Require: $\mathcal{R}$: Set of probabilistic rules
Require: $\boldsymbol{\theta}$: Parameters with prior distribution
Require: $\mathcal{D}$: Training sample
for all data $d \in \mathcal{D}$ **do**
  $\mathcal{B} \leftarrow \text{NETWORKCONSTRUCTION}(\mathbf{b}_d, \mathcal{R})$
  Add parameters nodes $\boldsymbol{\theta}$ to $\mathcal{B}$
  for all $\theta_i \in \boldsymbol{\theta}$ **do**
    $P(\theta_i'|d) = \alpha \, P(t_d|\mathbf{b}_d, \theta_i) \, P(\theta_i)$
  end for
end for
return $\boldsymbol{\theta}$

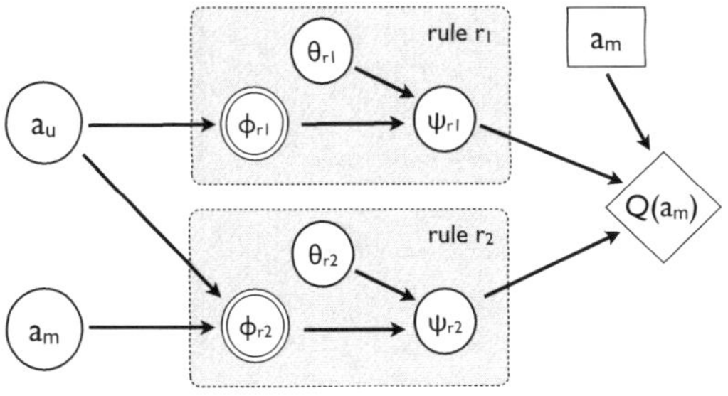

Figure 3: Bayesian Network with the rules r_1 and r_2.

To estimate the parameters $\boldsymbol{\theta}$, we start from an initial prior distribution. Then, for each sample d in the training data, we construct the corresponding Bayesian Network from its belief state $\mathbf{b}_d$ and the rules, including nodes corresponding to the unknown rule parameters. Then, for each parameter θ_i, we compute its posterior distribution given the data (Koller and Friedman, 2009):

$$P(\theta_i'|d) = \alpha \, P(t_d|\mathbf{b}_d, \theta_i) \, P(\theta_i) \quad (1)$$

Given the number of parameters in our example domain and their continuous range, we used approximate inference to calculate the posterior efficiently, via direct sampling from a set of parameter values. The constant α serves as a normalisation factor over the sampled parameter values for θ_i. The procedure is repeated for every sample, as shown in Algorithm 2. The parameter distribution will thus progressively narrow down its spread to the values providing the best fit for the training data.

4 Evaluation

We evaluated our approach in the context of a dialogue policy learning task for a human-robot interaction scenario. The main question we decided to address is the following: how much does the rule structure contribute to the parameter estimation of a given probabilistic model, especially for domains with limited amounts of available data? The objective of the experiment was to learn the rule parameters corresponding to the policy model $Q(a_m|\mathbf{s})$ from a Wizard of Oz data collection. In this particular case, the parameters correspond to the utilities of the various actions. The policy model used in the experiment included a total of 14 rules.

We compared our approach with two baselines which are essentially "flattened" or rolled-out versions of the rule-based model. The input and output variables remain identical, but they are directly connected, without the ϕ and ψ nodes serving as intermediate structures. The two baselines are (1) a plain multinomial model and (2) a linear model of the input variables. We are thus comparing three versions of the $Q(a_m|\mathbf{s})$ model: two baselines where a_m is directly dependent on the state variables, and our approach where the dependency is realised indirectly through condition and effect nodes.

4.1 Experimental Setup

The scenario for the Wizard-of-Oz experiment involved a human user and a Nao robot[1] (see Figure 4). The user was instructed to teach the robot a sequence of basic movements (lift the left arm, step forward, kneel down, etc.) using spoken commands. The interaction included various dialogue acts such as clarification requests, feedbacks, acknowledgements, corrections, etc. Short examples of recorded dialogues are provided in the appendix.

Figure 4: Human user interacting with the Nao robot.

In addition to the policy model, the dialogue system include a speech recognizer (Vocon 3200 from Nuance) connected to the robot microphones, shallow components for dialogue act recognition and generation, a text-to-speech module, and components for planning the robot movements and controlling its motors in real-time. All components are connected to the shared belief state, and read/write to it as they process their data flow.

We collected a total of 20 interactions with 7 users and one wizard playing the role of the policy model, for a total of 1020 system turns, summing to around 1h of interaction. All the interactions were performed in English. The wizard only had access to the N-best list output from the speech recogniser, and could then select which action to perform from a list of 14 alternatives (such as $\mathrm{AskRepeat}$, $\mathrm{DemonstrateMove}$, $\mathrm{UndoMove}$, $\mathrm{AskForConfirmation}$, etc). Each selected action was recorded along with the belief state (including the full probability distribution for every state variable) in effect at the time of the selection.

4.2 Analysis

The data set was split into training (75% of the system turns) and test data (remaining 25%) used to measure the accuracy of our policies. The accuracy is defined as the percentage of actions corresponding to the gold standard action selected by the wizard. The parameter distributions are initialised with uniform priors, and are progressively refined as more data points are processed. We calculated the accuracy by sampling over the parameters, performing inference over the resulting models, and finally averaging over the inference results.

[1] A programmable humanoid robot developed by Aldebaran Robotics, `http://www.aldebaran-robotics.com`.

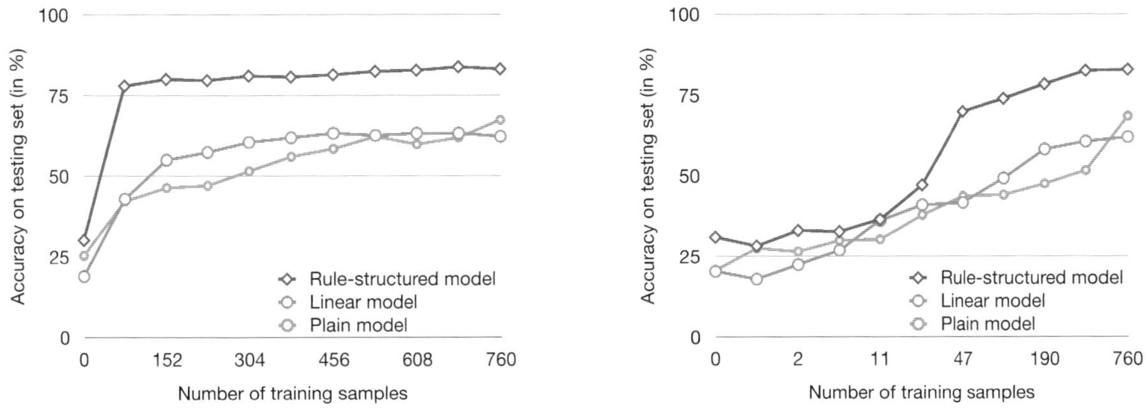

(a) Linear scale

(b) Log-2 scale

Figure 5: Learning curves for the overall accuracy of the learned dialogue policy, on a held-out test set of 255 actions, depending on the size of the training sample. The accuracy results are given for the plain, linear and rule-structured policy models, using linear (left) and logarithmic scales (right).

Table 1 provides the accuracy results. The differences between our model and the baselines are statistically significant using Bonferroni-corrected paired t-tests, with p-value < 0.0001. The 17% of actions labelled as incorrect are mainly due to the high degree of noise in the data set, and the sometimes inconsistent or unpredictable behaviour of the wizard (regarding e.g. clarification requests).

Type of model	*Accuracy (in %)*
Plain model	67.35
Linear model	61.85
Rule-structured model	**82.82**

Table 1: Accuracy results for the three action selection models on a test set, using the full training set.

It is instructive to analyse the learning curve of the three models, shown in Figure 5. Given its smaller number of parameters, the rule-structured model is able to converge to near-optimal values after observing only a small fraction of the training set. As the figure shows, the baseline models do also improve their accuracies over time, but at a much slower rate. The linear model is comparatively faster than the plain model, but levels off towards the end, possibly due to the non-linearity of some dialogue strategies. The plain model continues its convergence and would probably reach an accuracy similar to the rule-structured model if given much larger amounts of training data. Note that since the parameters are initially uniformly distributed, the accuracy is already non-zero before learning, since a random assignment of parameters has a low but non-zero chance of leading to the right action.

5 Discussion and Related Work

The idea of using structural knowledge in probabilistic models has been explored in many directions, both in the fields of decision-theoretic planning and of reinforcement learning (Hauskrecht et al., 1998; Pineau, 2004; Lang and Toussaint, 2010; Otterlo, 2012) and in statistical relational learning (Jaeger, 2001; Richardson and Domingos, 2006; Getoor and Taskar, 2007). The introduced structure may be hierarchical, relational, or both. As in our approach, most of these frameworks rely on the use of expressive representations as *templates* for grounded probabilistic models.

In the dialogue management literature, most structural approaches rely on a clear-cut task decomposition into goals and sub-goals (Allen et al., 2000; Steedman and Petrick, 2007; Bohus and Rudnicky, 2009), where the completion of each goal is assumed to be fully observable, discarding any remaining uncertainty. Information-state approaches to dialogue management (Larsson and Traum, 2000; Bos et al., 2003) also rely on a shared state updated according to a rich repository of rules, but contrary to the approach presented here, these rules are generally deterministic and do not include learnable parameters.

The literature on dialogue policy optimisation with reinforcement learning also contains several approaches dedicated to dimensionality reduction for large state-action spaces, such as function approximation (Henderson et al., 2008), hierarchical reinforcement learning (Cuayáhuitl et al., 2010) and summary POMDPs (Young et al., 2010). Most of these approaches rely on large but weakly structured state spaces (generally encoded as large lists of features), which are suited for slot-filling dialogue applications but are difficult to transfer to more open-ended or relational domains. The idea of state space partitioning, implemented here via high-level conditions, has also been explored in recent papers (Williams, 2010; Crook and Lemon, 2010). Finally, Cuayáhuitl (2011) describes a closely-related approach using logic-based representations of the state-action space for relational MDPs. His approach is however based on reinforcement learning with a user simulator, while the learning procedure presented here relies on supervised learning from a limited data set. He also reduced his belief state to fully observable variables, whereas we retain the partial observability associated with each variable.

An important side benefit of structured representations in probabilistic models is their improved readability for human designers, who are able to use these powerful abstractions to encode their prior knowledge of the dialogue domain in the form of pragmatic rules, generic background knowledge, or task-specific constraints. There has been previous work on integrating expert knowledge into dialogue policy learning, using finite-state policies or ad-hoc constraints to filter a plain statistical model (Williams, 2008; Henderson et al., 2008). The approach presented in this paper is however more general since it does not rely on an external filtering mechanism but directly incorporates prior domain knowledge into the statistical model.

6 Conclusions

We showed in this paper how to represent the underlying structure of probabilistic models for dialogue using *probabilistic rules*. These rules are defined as structured mappings over variables of the dialogue state, specified using high-level conditions and effects. These rules can include parameters such as effect probabilities or action utilities. Probabilistic rules allow the system designer to exploit powerful generalisations in the dialogue domain specification without sacrificing the probabilistic nature of the model. The framework is very general and can express a wide spectrum of models, from classical models fully estimated from data to ones incorporating rich prior knowledge. The choice of model within this spectrum is therefore essentially a design decision dependent on the relative availabilities of training data and domain knowledge.

We have also presented algorithms for constructing Bayesian Networks corresponding to the application of the rules and for estimating their parameters from data using Bayesian inference. The presented approach has been implemented in a spoken dialogue system for human-robot interaction, and validated on a policy learning task based on a Wizard-of-Oz data set. The empirical results have shown that the rule structure enables the learning algorithm to converge faster and with better generalisation performance.

We are currently working on extending this approach in two directions. First, we would like to extend our parameter estimation method to Bayesian model-based reinforcement learning. The current implementation operates in a supervised learning mode, which requires expert data. Alternatively, one could estimate the model parameters in a fully online fashion, without any supervisory input, by incorporating model uncertainty into the inference and continuously adapting the parameter distribution from (real or simulated) interaction experience, using the same Bayesian approach we have outlined in this paper (Ross et al., 2011).

The second direction is the extension of our work to tasks other than action selection. The framework we have presented is not confined to dialogue policy learning but can be used to structure any probabilistic model[2]. It is therefore possible to use probabilistic rules as a unifying framework for all models defined in a given architecture, and exploit it to perform *joint optimisation* of dialogue understanding, action selection and generation.

[2]In fact, the dialogue understanding and generation models used for the evaluation were already structured with probabilistic rules, but with fixed, hand-crafted parameters.

Acknowledgements

The author would like to thank Stephan Oepen, Erik Velldal and Amanda Stent for useful comments on an earlier version of this paper.

References

J. Allen, D. Byron, M. Dzikovska, G. Ferguson, L. Galescu, and A. Stent. 2000. An architecture for a generic dialogue shell. *Natural Language Engineering*, 6:213–228.

D. Bohus and A. I. Rudnicky. 2009. The RavenClaw dialog management framework: Architecture and systems. *Computer Speech & Language*, 23:332–361.

J. Bos, E. Klein, O. Lemon, and T. Oka. 2003. DIPPER: Description and formalisation of an information-state update dialogue system architecture. In *4th SIGdial Workshop on Discourse and Dialogue*, pages 115–124.

M. Cavazza, R. Santos de la Camara, M. Turunen, J. Relaño-Gil, J. Hakulinen, N. Crook, and D. Field. 2010. How was your day? an affective companion ECA prototype. In *Proceedings of the 11th SIGDIAL Meeting on Discourse and Dialogue*, pages 277–280.

P. A. Crook and O. Lemon. 2010. Representing uncertainty about complex user goals in statistical dialogue systems. In *Proceedings of the 11th SIGDIAL meeting on Discourse and Dialogue*, pages 209–212.

H. Cuayáhuitl, S. Renals, O. Lemon, and H. Shimodaira. 2010. Evaluation of a hierarchical reinforcement learning spoken dialogue system. *Computer Speech & Language*, 24:395–429.

H. Cuayáhuitl. 2011. Learning Dialogue Agents with Bayesian Relational State Representations. In *Proceedings of the IJCAI Workshop on Knowledge and Reasoning in Practical Dialogue Systems (IJCAI-KRPDS)*, Barcelona, Spain.

H. Erdogan, R. Sarikaya, Y. Gao, and M. Picheny. 2002. Semantic structured language models. In *Proceedings of the 7th International Conference on Spoken Language Processing (ICSLP)*, Denver, USA.

M. Eskenazi. 2009. An overview of spoken language technology for education. *Speech Commununications*, 51:832–844.

M. Frampton and O. Lemon. 2009. Recent research advances in reinforcement learning in spoken dialogue systems. *Knowledge Engineering Review*, 24(4):375–408.

L. Getoor and B. Taskar. 2007. *Introduction to Statistical Relational Learning*. The MIT Press.

M. Hauskrecht, N. Meuleau, L. P. Kaelbling, T. Dean, and C. Boutilier. 1998. Hierarchical solution of markov decision processes using macro-actions. In *Proceedings of the 14th Conference on Uncertainty in Artificial Intelligence (UAI)*, pages 220–229.

Y. He and S. Young. 2005. Semantic processing using the hidden vector state model. *Computer Speech & Language*, 19(1):85–106.

J. Henderson, O. Lemon, and K. Georgila. 2008. Hybrid reinforcement/supervised learning of dialogue policies from fixed data sets. *Computational Linguistics*, 34:487–511.

M. Jaeger. 2001. Complex probabilistic modeling with recursive relational bayesian networks. *Annals of Mathematics and Artificial Intelligence*, 32(1-4):179–220.

D. Koller and N. Friedman. 2009. *Probabilistic Graphical Models: Principles and Techniques*. MIT Press.

G.-J. M. Kruijff, P. Lison, T. Benjamin, H. Jacobsson, Hendrik Zender, and Ivana Kruijff-Korbayová, 2010. *Situated Dialogue Processing for Human-Robot Interaction*, chapter 8. Springer Verlag, Heidelberg, Germany.

K. C. Lan, K. S. Ho, R. W. Pong Luk, and H. Va Leong. 2008. Dialogue act recognition using maximum entropy. *Journal of the American Society for Information Science and Technology (JASIST)*, pages 859–874.

T. Lang and M. Toussaint. 2010. Planning with noisy probabilistic relational rules. *Journal of Artificial Intelligence Research*, 39:1–49.

S. Larsson and D. R. Traum. 2000. Information state and dialogue management in the TRINDI dialogue move engine toolkit. *Natuarl Language Engineering*, 6(3-4):323–340, September.

M. Lease, M. Johnson, and E. Charniak. 2006. Recognizing disfluencies in conversational speech. *IEEE Transactions on Audio, Speech & Language Processing*, 14(5):1566–1573.

O. Lemon and O. Pietquin. 2007. Machine Learning for Spoken Dialogue Systems. In *Proceedings of the 10th European Conference on Speech Communication and Technologies (Interspeech'07)*, pages 2685–2688.

O. Lemon. 2011. Learning what to say and how to say it: Joint optimisation of spoken dialogue management and natural language generation. *Computer Speech & Language*, 25:210–221.

D. J. Litman and S. Silliman. 2004. ITSPOKE: an intelligent tutoring spoken dialogue system. In *Proceedings of the Conference of the North American Chapter of the Association of Computational Linguistics (HLT-NAACL 2004)*, pages 5–8.

A. Nguyen. 2005. An agent-based approach to dialogue management in personal assistants. In *Proceedings of the 2005 International conference on Intelligent User Interfaces (IUI)*, pages 137–144. ACM Press.

A. Oh and A. I. Rudnicky. 2002. Stochastic natural language generation for spoken dialog systems. *Computer Speech & Language*, 16(3-4):387–407.

M. Otterlo. 2012. Solving relational and first-order logical markov decision processes: A survey. In *Reinforcement Learning*, volume 12 of *Adaptation, Learning, and Optimization*, pages 253–292. Springer Berlin Heidelberg.

J. Pineau. 2004. *Tractable Planning Under Uncertainty: Exploiting Structure*. Ph.D. thesis, Robotics Institute, Carnegie Mellon University, Pittsburgh, USA.

M. Richardson and P. Domingos. 2006. Markov logic networks. *Machine Learning*, 62:107–136.

S. Ross, J. Pineau, B. Chaib-draa, and P. Kreitmann. 2011. A Bayesian Approach for Learning and Planning in Partially Observable Markov Decision Processes. *Journal of Machine Learning Research*, 12:1729–1770.

J. Schatzmann, B. Thomson, K. Weilhammer, H. Ye, and S. Young. 2007. Agenda-based user simulation for bootstrapping a POMDP dialogue system. In *Human Language Technologies 2007: The Conference of the North American Chapter of the Association for Computational Linguistics*, NAACL 2007, pages 149–152.

M. Steedman and R. P. A. Petrick. 2007. Planning dialog actions. In *Proceedings of the 8th SIGDIAL Meeting on Discourse and Dialogue*, pages 265–272, Antwerp, Belgium.

A. Stolcke, N. Coccaro, R. Bates, P. Taylor, C. Van Ess-Dykema, K. Ries, E. Shriberg, D. Jurafsky, R. Martin, and M. Meteer. 2000. Dialogue act modeling for automatic tagging and recognition of conversational speech. *Computional Linguistics*, 26:339–373.

V. Thomson and S. Young. 2010. Bayesian update of dialogue state: A POMDP framework for spoken dialogue systems. *Computer Speech & Language*, 24:562–588, October.

J. D. Williams. 2008. The best of both worlds: Unifying conventional dialog systems and POMDPs. In *International Conference on Speech and Language Processing (ICSLP 2008)*, Brisbane, Australia.

J. D. Williams. 2010. Incremental partition recombination for efficient tracking of multiple dialog states. In *Proceedings of the IEEE International Conference on Acoustics, Speech and Signal Processing (ICASSP)*, pages 5382–5385.

S. Young, M. Gašić, S. Keizer, F. Mairesse, J. Schatzmann, B. Thomson, and K. Yu. 2010. The hidden information state model: A practical framework for pomdp-based spoken dialogue management. *Computer Speech & Language*, 24:150–174.

H. Zen, K. Tokuda, and A. W. Black. 2009. Review: Statistical parametric speech synthesis. *Speech Communications*, 51:1039–1064.

A Example of interaction

We present below two recorded excerpts of Wizard-of-Oz interactions. The user utterances are simplified to show only the hypothesis with highest score (indicated in parenthesis) in the N-best list.

Transcript A.1 Wizard-of-Oz interaction 1

HUMAN: Hi Lenny (*0.74*)
ROBOT: Hello there!
HUMAN: Move your left arm up (*0.41*)
ROBOT: Sure!
[*executing movement, waits a few seconds*]
ROBOT: Was that correct?
HUMAN: Yes (*0.88*)
[*registers movement as confirmed*]
HUMAN: Move your right arm up at the same time (*0.38*)
ROBOT: Let's see
[*executing movement*]
ROBOT: Was that correct?
HUMAN: No (*0.50*)
[*goes back to previous position*]
ROBOT: What should I do then?
[...]

Transcript A.2 Wizard-of-Oz interaction 2

HUMAN: Stand up (*0.41*)
ROBOT: Let's see
[*executing movement*]
HUMAN: Move your right arm forward (*0.35*)
[*last move is implicitly grounded*]
ROBOT: Let's see
[*executing movement*]
HUMAN: Lower the left arm (*0.34*)
ROBOT: Sorry, could you repeat?
HUMAN: Lift your left arm (*0.37*)
ROBOT: Sure
[*executing movement, waits a few seconds*]
ROBOT: Should I do it like this?
[...]

Exploiting Machine-Transcribed Dialog Corpus to Improve Multiple Dialog States Tracking Methods

Sungjin Lee[1,2] and **Maxine Eskenazi**[1]
[1]Language Technologies Institute, Carnegie Mellon University, Pittsburgh, Pennsylvania
[2]Computer Science and Engineering, Pohang University of Science and Technology, South Korea
{sungjin.lee, max}@cs.cmu.edu[1], junion@postech.ac.kr[2]

Abstract

This paper proposes the use of unsupervised approaches to improve components of partition-based belief tracking systems. The proposed method adopts a dynamic Bayesian network to learn the user action model directly from a machine-transcribed dialog corpus. It also addresses confidence score calibration to improve the observation model in a unsupervised manner using dialog-level grounding information. To verify the effectiveness of the proposed method, we applied it to the Let's Go domain (Raux et al., 2005). Overall system performance for several comparative models were measured. The results show that the proposed method can learn an effective user action model without human intervention. In addition, the calibrated confidence score was verified by demonstrating the positive influence on the user action model learning process and on overall system performance.

1 Introduction

With present Automatic Speech Recognition (ASR) and Spoken Language Understanding (SLU) errors, it is impossible to directly observe the true user goal and action. It is crucial, therefore, to efficiently infer this true state from erroneous observations over multiple dialog turns. The Partially Observable Markov Decision Process (POMDP) framework has offered a well-founded theory for this purpose (Henderson et al., 2008; Thomson and Young, 2010a; Williams and Young, 2007; Young et al., 2010). Several approximate methods have also emerged to tackle the vast complexity of representing and maintaining belief states, e.g., partition-based approaches (Gasic and Young, 2011; Williams, 2010; Young et al., 2010) and Bayesian network (BN)-based methods (Raux and Ma, 2011; Thomson and Young, 2010a). The partition-based approaches attempt to group user goals into a small number of partitions and split a partition only when a distinction is required by observations. This property endows it with the high scalability that is suitable for fairly complex domains. However, the parameter learning procedures for the partition-based methods is still limited to hand-crafting or the use of a simple maximum likelihood estimation (Keizer et al., 2008; Roy et al., 2000; Thomson and Young, 2010a; Williams, 2008). In contrast, several unsupervised methods which do not require human transcription and annotation have been recently proposed to learn BN-based models (Jurcicek et al., 2010; Syed and Williams, 2008; Thomson et al., 2010b). In this paper we describe an unsupervised process that can be applied to the partition-based methods. We adopt a dynamic Bayesian network to learn the user action model which defines the likelihood of user actions for a given context. In addition, we propose a simple confidence score calibration method to improve the observation model which represents the probability of an observation given the true user action.

This paper is structured as follows. Section 2 describes previous research and the novelty of our approach. Section 3 and Section 4 elaborate on our proposed unsupervised approach. Section 5 explains the experimental setup. Section 6 presents and discusses the results. Finally, Section 7 concludes with a brief summary and suggestions for future research.

2 Background and Related Work

In order to reduce the complexity of the belief states over the POMDP states, the following factorization of the belief state has been commonly applied to the belief update procedure (Williams et al., 2005):

$$b(\mathbf{g}_t, \mathbf{u}_t, \mathbf{h}_t) \propto \underbrace{p(\mathbf{o}_t|\mathbf{u}_t)}_{\text{observation model}} \sum_{\mathbf{h}_{t-1}} \underbrace{p(\mathbf{h}_t|\mathbf{h}_{t-1}, \mathbf{u}_t, \mathbf{s}_t)}_{\text{dialog history model}} \underbrace{p(\mathbf{u}_t|\mathbf{g}_t, \mathbf{s}_t, \mathbf{h}_{t-1})}_{\text{user action model}} \sum_{\mathbf{g}_{t-1}} \underbrace{p(\mathbf{g}_t|\mathbf{g}_{t-1}, \mathbf{s}_{t-1})}_{\text{user goal model}} \sum_{\mathbf{u}_{t-1}} b(\mathbf{g}_{t-1}, \mathbf{u}_{t-1}, \mathbf{h}_{t-1}) \quad (1)$$

where $\mathbf{g}_t, \mathbf{s}_t, \mathbf{u}_t, \mathbf{h}_t, \mathbf{o}_t$ represents the user goal, the system action, the user action, the dialog history, and the observed user action for each time slice, respectively. The user goal model describes how the user goal evolves. In the partition-based approaches, this model is further approximated by assuming that the user does not change their mind during the dialog (Young et al., 2010):

$$\sum_{\mathbf{g}_{t-1}} p(\mathbf{g}_t|\mathbf{g}_{t-1}, \mathbf{s}_{t-1}) = p(\mathbf{p}_t|\mathbf{p}_{t-1}) \quad (2)$$

where $\mathbf{p}_t$ is a partition from the current turn. The dialog history model indicates how the dialog history changes and can be set deterministically by simple discourse rules, for example:

$$p(\mathbf{h}_t = \textit{Informed}|\mathbf{h}_{t-1}, \mathbf{u}_t, \mathbf{s}_t) = \begin{cases} 1 & \text{if } \mathbf{h}_{t-1} = \textit{Informed} \text{ or } \mathbf{u}_t = \textit{Inform}(\cdot), \\ 0 & \text{otherwise.} \end{cases} \quad (3)$$

The user action model defines how likely user actions are. By employing partitions, this can be approximated by the bigram model of system and user action at the predicate level, and the matching function (Keizer et al., 2008):

$$p(\mathbf{u}_t|\mathbf{g}_t, \mathbf{s}_t, \mathbf{h}_{t-1}) \propto p(\mathcal{T}(\mathbf{u}_t)|\mathcal{T}(\mathbf{s}_t)) \cdot \mathcal{M}(\mathbf{u}_t, \mathbf{p}_t, \mathbf{s}_t) \quad (4)$$

where $\mathcal{T}(\cdot)$ denotes the predicate of the action and $\mathcal{M}(\cdot)$ indicates whether or not the user action matches the partition and system action. However, it turned out that the bigram user action model did not provide an additional gain over the improvement achieved by the matching function according to (Keizer et al., 2008). This might indicate that it is necessary to incorporate more historical information. To make use of historical information in an unsupervised manner, the *Expectation Maximization* algorithm was adopted to obtain maximum likelihood estimates (Syed and Williams, 2008). But these methods still require a small amount of transcribed data to learn the observation confusability, and they suffer from overfitting as a general property of maximum likelihood. To address this problem, we propose a Bayesian learning method, which requires no transcribed data.

The observation model represents the probability of an observation given the true user action. The observation model is usually approximated with the confidence score computed from the ASR and SLU results:

$$p(\mathbf{o}_t|\mathbf{u}_t) \approx p(\mathbf{u}_t|\mathbf{o}_t) \quad (5)$$

It is therefore of vital importance that we obtain the most accurate confidence score as possible. We propose an efficient method that can improve the confidence score by calibrating it using grounding information.

3 User Action Model

To learn the user action model, a dynamic Bayesian network is adopted with several conditional independence assumptions similar to Equation 1. This gives rise to the graphical structure shown in Figure 1. As mentioned in Section 2, the user action model deals with actions at the predicate level[1]. This abstract-level handling enables the user action model to employ exact inference algorithms such as the *junction tree* algorithm (Lauritzen and Spiegelhalter, 1988) for more efficient reasoning over the graphical structure.

[1]To keep the notation uncluttered, we will omit $\mathcal{T}(\cdot)$.

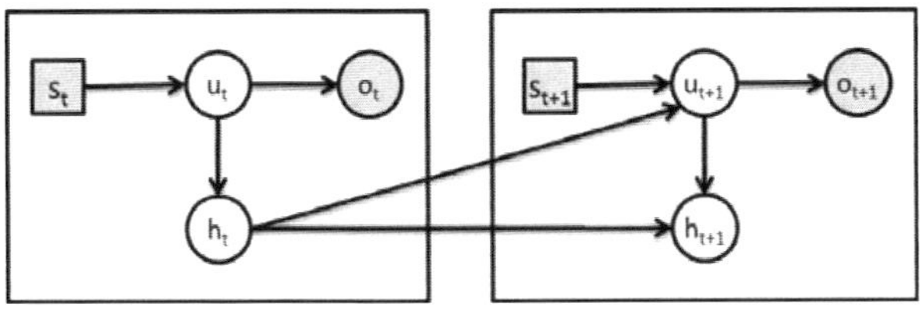

Figure 1: The graphical structure of the dynamic Bayesian network for the user action model. The shaded items are observable and the transparent ones are latent.

The joint distribution for this model is given by

$$p(\mathbf{S}, \mathbf{H}, \mathbf{U}, \mathbf{O}|\boldsymbol{\Theta}) = p(\mathbf{h}_0|\boldsymbol{\pi}) \prod_t p(\mathbf{u}_t|\mathbf{s}_t, \mathbf{h}_{t-1}, \boldsymbol{\phi}) \cdot p(\mathbf{h}_t|\mathbf{h}_{t-1}, \mathbf{u}_t, \boldsymbol{\eta}) p(\mathbf{o}_t|\mathbf{u}_t, \boldsymbol{\zeta}) \quad (6)$$

where a capital letter stands for the set of corresponding random variables, e.g., $\mathbf{U} = \{\mathbf{u}_1, \ldots, \mathbf{u}_N\}$, and $\boldsymbol{\Theta} = \{\boldsymbol{\pi}, \boldsymbol{\phi}, \boldsymbol{\eta}, \boldsymbol{\zeta}\}$ denotes the set of parameters governing the model[2].

Unlike previous research which learns $\boldsymbol{\zeta}$ using maximum likelihood estimation, we use a deterministic function that yields a fraction of an observed confidence score in accordance with the degree of agreement between $\mathbf{u}_t$ and $\mathbf{o}_t$:

$$p(\mathbf{o}_t|\mathbf{u}_t) = CS(\mathbf{o}_t) \cdot \left(\frac{|\mathbf{o}_t \cap \mathbf{u}_t|}{|\mathbf{o}_t \cup \mathbf{u}_t|} \right) + \epsilon \quad (7)$$

where $CS(\cdot)$ returns the confidence score of the associated observation. As mentioned above, $\boldsymbol{\pi}$ and $\boldsymbol{\eta}$ are deterministically set by simple discourse rules (Equation 3). This only leaves the user action model $\boldsymbol{\phi}$ to be learned. In a Bayesian model, any unknown parameter is given a prior distribution and is absorbed into the set of latent variables, thus it is not feasible to directly evaluate the posterior distribution of the latent variables and the expectations with respect to this distribution. Therefore a deterministic approximation, called *mean field* theory (Parisi, 1988), is applied.

In *mean field* theory, the family of posterior distributions of the latent variables is assumed to be partitioned into disjoint groups:

$$q(\mathbf{Z}) = \prod_{i=1}^{M} q_i(\mathbf{Z}_i) \quad (8)$$

where $\mathbf{Z} = \{\mathbf{z}_1, \ldots, \mathbf{z}_N\}$ denotes all latent variables including parameters and $\mathbf{Z}_i$ is a disjoint group. Amongst all distributions $q(\mathbf{Z})$ having the form of Equation 8, we then seek the member of this family for which the divergence from the true posterior distribution is minimized. To achieve this, the following optimization with respect to each of the $q_i(\mathbf{Z}_i)$ factors is to be performed in turn (Bishop, 2006):

$$\ln q_j^*(\mathbf{Z}_j) = E_{i \neq j}\big[\ln(\mathbf{X}, \mathbf{Z})\big] + const \quad (9)$$

where $\mathbf{X} = \{\mathbf{x}_1, \ldots, \mathbf{x}_N\}$ denotes all observed variables and $E_{i \neq j}$ means an expectation with respect to the q distributions over all groups $\mathbf{Z}_i$ for $i \neq j$.

Now we apply the *mean field* theory to the user model. Before doing so, we need to introduce the prior over the parameter $\boldsymbol{\phi}$ which is a product of *Dirichlet* distributions[3].

$$p(\boldsymbol{\phi}) = \prod_{\mathbf{k}} Dir(\boldsymbol{\phi}_{\mathbf{k}}|\boldsymbol{\alpha}_{\mathbf{k}}^0) = \prod_{\mathbf{k}} C(\boldsymbol{\alpha}_{\mathbf{k}}^0) \prod_l \phi_{\mathbf{k},l}^{\alpha_{\mathbf{k}}^0 - 1} \quad (10)$$

where $\mathbf{k}$ represents the joint configuration of all of the parents and $C(\boldsymbol{\alpha}_{\mathbf{k}}^0)$ is the normalization constant for the *Dirichlet* distribution. Note that for symmetry we have chosen the same parameter $\alpha_{\mathbf{k}}^0$ for each of the components.

Next we approximate the posterior distribution, $q(\mathbf{H}, \mathbf{U}, \boldsymbol{\phi})$ using a factorized form, $q(\mathbf{H}, \mathbf{U})q(\boldsymbol{\phi})$. Then we first apply Equation 9 to find an expression for the optimal factor $q^*(\boldsymbol{\phi})$:

[2]Here, a uniform prior distribution is assigned on $\mathbf{S}$

[3]Note that priors over parameters for deterministic distributions (e.i., $\boldsymbol{\pi}$, $\boldsymbol{\eta}$,and $\boldsymbol{\zeta}$) are not necessary.

$$\begin{aligned}\ln q^*(\boldsymbol{\phi}) &= E_{\mathbf{H},\mathbf{U}}\big[\ln p(\mathbf{S},\mathbf{H},\mathbf{U},\mathbf{O},\boldsymbol{\Theta})\big] + const \\ &= E_{\mathbf{H},\mathbf{U}}\Big[\sum_t \ln p(\mathbf{u}_t|\mathbf{s}_t,\mathbf{h}_{t-1},\boldsymbol{\phi})\Big] \\ &\quad + \ln p(\boldsymbol{\phi}) + const \\ &= \sum_t \sum_{i,j,k}\Big(E_{\mathbf{H},\mathbf{U}}\big[\boldsymbol{\delta}_{i,j,k}\big]\ln \phi_{i,j,k}\Big) \\ &\quad + \sum_{i,j,k}(\alpha^o_{i,j,k}-1)\ln\phi_{i,j,k} + const \\ &= \sum_{i,j,k}\Big(\Big(E_{\mathbf{H},\mathbf{U}}[n_{i,j,k}] + (\alpha^o_{i,j,k}-1)\Big) \\ &\quad \cdot \ln\phi_{i,j,k}\Big) + const\end{aligned} \tag{11}$$

where $\delta(\cdot,\cdot)$ denotes *Kronecker* delta and $\boldsymbol{\delta}_{i,j,k}$ denotes $\delta(\mathbf{s}_t,i)\delta(\mathbf{h}_{t-1},j)\ \delta(\mathbf{u}_t,k)$. $n_{i,j,k}$ is the number of times where , $\mathbf{s}_t = i, \mathbf{h}_{t-1} = j$, and $\mathbf{u}_t = k$. This leads to a product of *Dirichlet* distributions by taking the exponential of both sides of the equation:

$$\begin{aligned} q^*(\boldsymbol{\phi}) &= \prod_{i,j} Dir(\boldsymbol{\phi}_{i,j}|\boldsymbol{\alpha}_{i,j}), \\ \alpha_{i,j,k} &= \alpha^0_{i,j,k} + E_{\mathbf{H},\mathbf{U}}[n_{i,j,k}]\end{aligned} \tag{12}$$

To evaluate the quantity $E_{\mathbf{H},\mathbf{U}}[n_{i,j,k}]$, Equation 9 needs to be applied once again to obtain an optimal approximation of the posterior distribution $q^*(\mathbf{H},\mathbf{U})$.

$$\begin{aligned}\ln q^*(\mathbf{H},\mathbf{U}) &= E_{\boldsymbol{\phi}}\big[\ln p(\mathbf{S},\mathbf{H},\mathbf{U},\mathbf{O},\boldsymbol{\Theta})\big] + const \\ &= E_{\boldsymbol{\phi}}\Big[\sum_t \ln p(\mathbf{u}_t|\mathbf{s}_t,\mathbf{h}_{t-1},\boldsymbol{\phi}) \\ &\quad + \ln p(\mathbf{h}_t|\mathbf{h}_{t-1},\mathbf{u}_t) \\ &\quad + \ln p(\mathbf{o}_t|\mathbf{u}_t)\Big] + const \\ &= \sum_t \Big(E_{\boldsymbol{\phi}}\big[\ln p(\mathbf{u}_t|\mathbf{s}_t,\mathbf{h}_{t-1},\boldsymbol{\phi})\big] \\ &\quad + \ln p(\mathbf{h}_t|\mathbf{h}_{t-1},\mathbf{u}_t) \\ &\quad + \ln p(\mathbf{o}_t|\mathbf{u}_t)\Big) + const\end{aligned} \tag{13}$$

where $E_{\boldsymbol{\phi}}\big[\ln p(\mathbf{u}_t|\mathbf{s}_t,\mathbf{h}_{t-1},\boldsymbol{\phi})\big]$ can be obtained using Equation 12 and properties of the *Dirichlet* distribution:

$$\begin{aligned} &E_{\boldsymbol{\phi}}\big[\ln p(\mathbf{u}_t|\mathbf{s}_t,\mathbf{h}_{t-1},\boldsymbol{\phi})\big] \\ &\quad = \sum_{i,j,k}\boldsymbol{\delta}_{i,j,k}E_{\boldsymbol{\phi}}\big[\ln\phi_{i,j,k}\big] \\ &\quad = \sum_{i,j,k}\boldsymbol{\delta}_{i,j,k}(\psi(\alpha_{i,j,k}) - \psi(\hat{\boldsymbol{\alpha}}_{i,j}))\end{aligned} \tag{14}$$

where $\psi(\cdot)$ is the digamma function with $\hat{\boldsymbol{\alpha}}_{i,j} = \sum_k \alpha_{i,j,k}$. Because computing $E_{\mathbf{H},\mathbf{U}}[n_{i,j,k}]$ is equivalent to summing each of the marginal posterior probabilities $q^*(\mathbf{h}_{t-1},\mathbf{u}_t)$ with the same configuration of conditioning variables, this can be done efficiently by using the *junction tree* algorithm. Note that the expression on the right-hand side for both $q^*(\boldsymbol{\phi})$ and $q^*(\mathbf{H},\mathbf{U})$ depends on expectations computed with respect to the other factors. We will therefore seek a consistent solution by cycling through the factors and replacing each in turn with a revised estimate.

4 Confidence Score Calibration

As shown in Section 2, we can obtain a better observation model by improving confidence score accuracy. Since the confidence score is usually computed using the ASR and SLU results, it can be enhanced by adding dialog-level information. Basically, the confidence score represents how likely it is that the recognized input is correct. This means that a well-calibrated confidence score should satisfy that property such that:

$$p(\mathbf{u}_t = a|\mathbf{o}_t = a) \simeq \frac{\sum_k \delta(\mathbf{u}_k,a)\delta(\mathbf{o}_k,a)}{\sum_k \delta(\mathbf{o}_k,a)} \tag{15}$$

However, the empirical distribution on the right side of this equation often does not well match the confidence score measure on the left side. If a large corpus with highly accurate annotation was used, a straightforward remedy for this problem would be to construct a mapping function from the given confidence score measure to the empirical distribution. This leads us to propose an unsupervised method that estimates the empirical distribution and constructs the mapping function which is fast enough to run in real time. Note that we will not construct

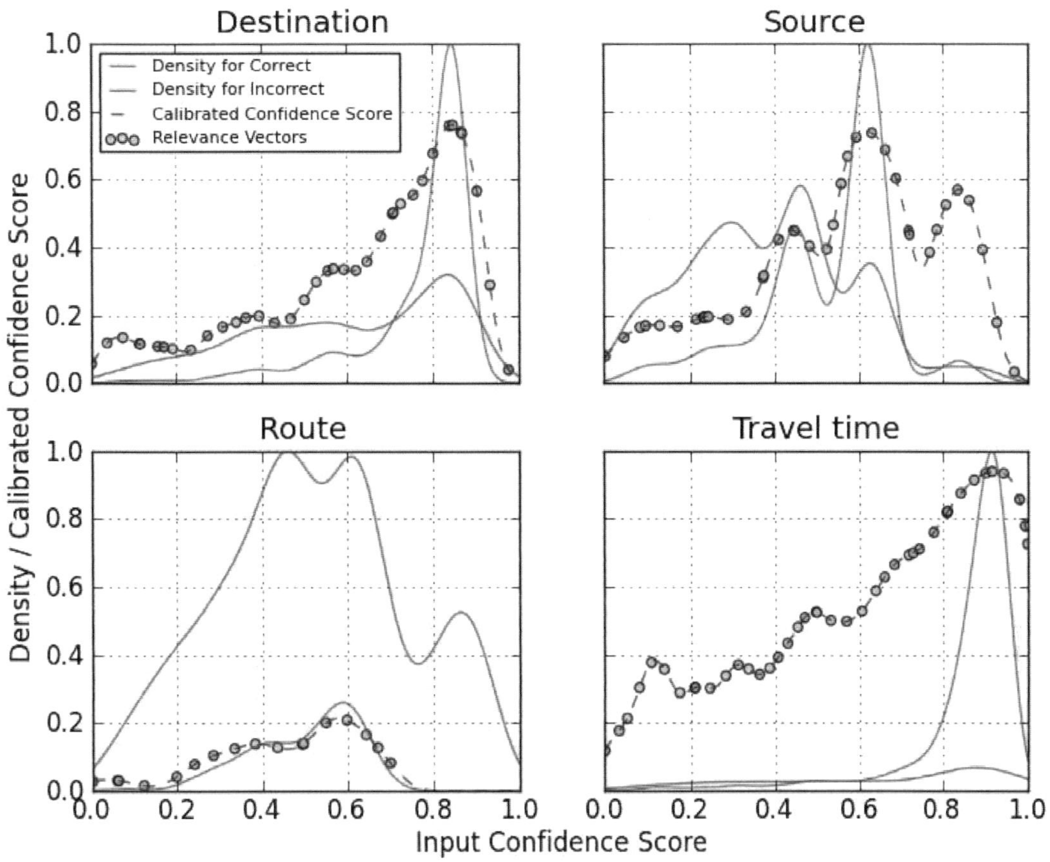

Figure 2: Illustrations of confidence score calibration for the representative concepts in the Let's Go domain

a mapping function for each instance, but rather for each concept, since the former could cause severe data sparseness. In order to estimate the empirical distribution in an unsupervised manner, we exploit grounding information[4] as true labels. We first parse dialog logs to look for the grounding information that the users have provided. Each time we encounter grounding information that includes the constraints used in the backend queries, this is added to the list. If two actions contradict each other, the later action overwrites the earlier one. Then, for each observation in the data, we determine its correctness by comparing it with the grounding information. Next, we gather two sets of confidence scores with respect to correctness, on which we apply a Gaussian kernel-based density estimation. After that, we scale the two estimated densities by their total number of elements to see how the ratio of correct ones over the sum of correct and incorrect ones varies according to the confidence score. The ratio computed above will be the calibrated score:

$$c' = \frac{d_c(c)}{d_c(c) + d_{inc}(c)} \tag{16}$$

where c' indicates the calibrated confidence score and c is the input confidence score. $d_c(\cdot)$ denotes the scaled density for the correct set and $d_{inc}(\cdot)$ is the scaled density for the incorrect set.

Note that this approach tends to yield a more conservative confidence score since correct user actions can exist, even though they may not match the grounding information. Finally, in order to efficiently obtain the calibrated score for a given confidence score, we employ the *sparse Bayesian regression* (Tipping, 2001) with the Gaussian kernel. By

[4]Specifically, we used explicitly confirmed information by the system for this study

virtue of the sparse representation, we only need to consider a few so-called *relevance vectors* to compute the score:

$$y(\mathbf{x}) = \sum_{\mathbf{x}_n \in RV} w_n k(\mathbf{x}, \mathbf{x}_n) + b \qquad (17)$$

where RV denotes the set of relevance vectors, $|RV| \ll |\{\mathbf{x}_n\}|$. $k(\cdot, \cdot)$ represents a kernel function and b is a bias parameter. Figure 2 shows the aforementioned process for several representative concepts in the Let's Go domain.

5 Experimental Setup

To verify the proposed method, three months of data from the Let's Go domain were used to train the user action model and the observation model. The training data consists of 2,718 dialogs and 23,044 turns in total. To evaluate the user action model, we compared overall system performance with three different configurations: 1) the uniform distribution, 2) the user action model without historical information[5] which is comparable to the bigram model of (Keizer et al., 2008), 3) the user action model with historical information included. For system performance evaluation, we used a user simulator (Lee and Eskenazi, 2012) which provides a large number of dialogs with statistically similar conditions. Also, the simulated user enables us to examine how performance changes over a variety of error levels. This simulated user supports four error levels and each model was evaluated by generating 2,000 dialogs at each error level. System performance was measured in terms of average dialog success rate. A dialog is considered to be successful if the system provides the bus schedule information that satisfies the user goal.

To measure the effectiveness of the calibration method, we conducted two experiments. First, we applied the calibration method to parameter learning for the user action model by using the calibrated confidence score in Equation 7. We compared the log-likelihood of two models, one with calibration and the other without calibration. Second, we compared overall system performance with four different settings: 1) the user action model with historical information and the observation model with calibration, 2) the user action model with historical information and the observation model without calibration, 3) the user action model without historical information and the observation model with calibration, 4) the user action model without historical information and the observation model without calibration.

6 Results

The effect of parameter learning of the user action model on average dialog success rate is shown in Figure 3. While, in the previous study, the bigram model unexpectedly did not show a significant effect, our result here indicates that our comparable model, i.e. the model with historical information excluded, significantly outperformed the baseline uniform model. The difference could be attributed to the fact that the previous study did not take transcription errors into consideration, whereas our approach handles the problem by treating the true user action as hidden. However, we cannot directly compare this result with the previous study since the target domains are different. The model with historical information included also consistently surpassed the uniform model. Interestingly, there is a noticeable trend: the model without historical information performs better as the error level increases. This result may indicate that the simpler model is more robust

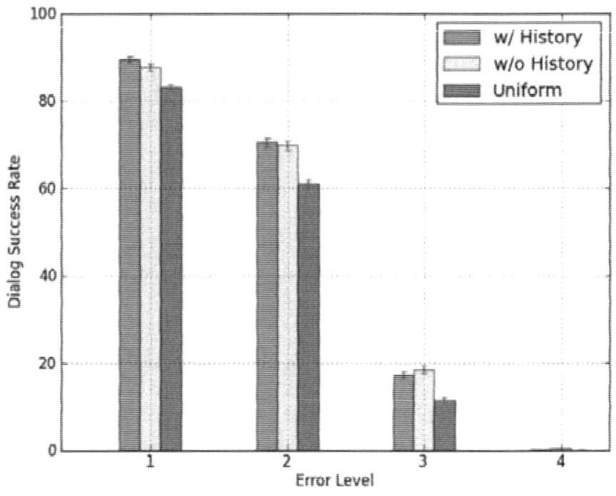

Figure 3: The effect of parameter learning of each user action model on overall system performance. The error bar represents standard error.

[5]This model was constructed by marginalizing out the historical variables.

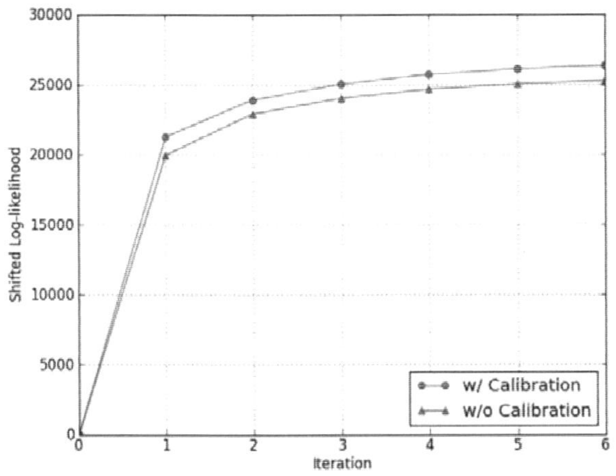

Figure 4: The effect of confidence score calibration on the log-likelihood of the user action model during the training process.

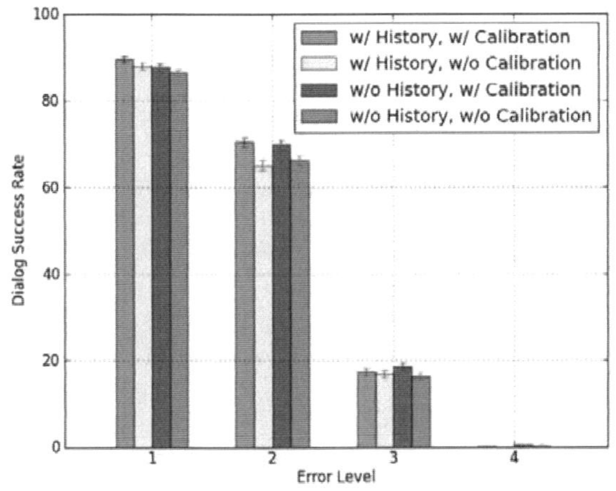

Figure 5: The effect of confidence score calibration for the observation model on overall system performance. The error bar shows standard error.

to error. Although average dialog success rates became almost zero at error level four, this result is a natural consequence of the fact that the majority of the dialogs in this corpus are failed dialogs.

Figure 4 shows the effect of confidence score calibration on the log-likelihood of the user action model during the training process. To take into account the fact that different confidence scores result in different log-likelihoods regardless of the quality of the confidence score, we shifted both log-likelihoods to zero at the beginning. This modification more clearly shows how the quality of the confidence score influences the log-likelihood maximization process. The result shows that the calibrated confidence score gives greater log-likelihood gains, which implies that the user action model can better describe the distribution of the data.

The effect of confidence score calibration for the observation model on average dialog success rate is presented in Figure 5. For both the user action model with historical information included and excluded, the application of the confidence score calibration consistently improved overall system performance. This result implies the possibility of automatically improving confidence scores in a modularized manner without introducing a dependence on the underlying methods of ASR and SLU.

7 Conclusion

In this paper, we have presented novel unsupervised approaches for learning the user action model and improving the observation model that constitute the partition-based belief tracking method. Our proposed method can learn a user action model directly from a machine-transcribed spoken dialog corpus. The enhanced system performance shows the effectiveness of the learned model in spite of the lack of human intervention. Also, we have addressed confidence score calibration in a unsupervised fashion using dialog-level grounding information. The proposed method was verified by showing the positive influence on the user action model learning process and the overall system performance evaluation. This method may take us a step closer to being able to automatically update our models while the system is live. Although the proposed method does not deal with N-best ASR results, the extension to support N-best results will be one of our future directions, as soon as the Let's Go system uses N-best ASR results.

Acknowledgments

This work was supported by the second Brain Korea 21 project.

References

C. Bishop, 2006. *Pattern Recognition and Machine Learning*. Springer.

M. Gasic and S. Young, 2011. Effective handling of dialogue state in the hidden information state POMDP-based dialogue manager. *ACM Transactions on Speech and Language Processing*, 7(3).

J. Henderson, O. Lemon, K. Georgila, 2008. Hybrid Reinforcement / Supervised Learning of Dialogue Policies from Fixed Datasets. *Computational Linguistics*, 34(4):487-511.

F. Jurcicek, B. Thomson and S. Young, 2011. Natural Actor and Belief Critic: Reinforcement algorithm for learning parameters of dialogue systems modelled as POMDPs. *ACM Transactions on Speech and Language Processing*, 7(3).

S. Keizer, M. Gasic, F. Mairesse, B. Thomson, K. Yu, S. Young, 2008. Modelling User Behaviour in the HIS-POMDP Dialogue Manager. *In Proceedings of SLT*.

S. Lauritzen and D. J. Spiegelhalter, 1988. Local Computation and Probabilities on Graphical Structures and their Applications to Expert Systems. *Journal of Royal Statistical Society*, 50(2):157–224.

S. Lee and M. Eskenazi, 2012. An Unsupervised Approach to User Simulation: toward Self-Improving Dialog Systems. *In Proceedings of SIGDIAL*. http://infinitive.lti.cs.cmu.edu:9090.

G. Parisi, 1988. *Statistical Field Theory*. Addison-Wesley.

A. Raux, B. Langner, D. Bohus, A. W Black, and M. Eskenazi, 2005. Let's Go Public! Taking a Spoken Dialog System to the Real World. *In Proceedings of Interspeech*.

A. Raux and Y. Ma, 2011. Efficient Probabilistic Tracking of User Goal and Dialog History for Spoken Dialog Systems. *In Proceedings of Interspeech*.

N. Roy, J. Pineau, and S. Thrun, 2000. Spoken dialogue management using probabilistic reasoning. *In Proceedings of ACL*.

U. Syed and J. Williams, 2008. Using automatically transcribed dialogs to learn user models in a spoken dialog system. *In Proceedings of ACL*.

B. Thomson and S. Young, 2010. Bayesian update of dialogue state: A POMDP framework for spoken dialogue systems. *Computer Speech & Language*, 24(4):562-588.

B. Thomson, F. Jurccek, M. Gasic, S. Keizer, F. Mairesse, K. Yu, S. Young, 2010. Parameter learning for POMDP spoken dialogue models. *In Proceedings of SLT*.

M. Tipping, 2001. Sparse Bayesian Learning and the Relevance Vector Machine. *Journal of Machine Learning Research*, 1:211–244.

J. Williams, P. Poupart, and S. Young, 2005. Factored Partially Observable Markov Decision Processes for Dialogue Management. *In Proceedings of Knowledge and Reasoning in Practical Dialogue Systems*.

J. Williams and S. Young, 2007. Partially observable Markov decision processes for spoken dialog systems. *Computer Speech & Language*, 21(2):393-422.

J. Williams, 2008. Exploiting the ASR N-best by tracking multiple dialog state hypotheses. *In Proceedings of Interspeech*.

J. Williams, 2010. Incremental partition recombination for efficient tracking of multiple dialog states. *In Proceedings of ICASSP*.

S. Young, M. Gasic, S. Keizer, F. Mairesse, J. Schatzmann, B. Thomson and K. Yu, 2010. The Hidden Information State Model: a practical framework for POMDP-based spoken dialogue management. *Computer Speech and Language*, 24(2):150–174.

Cohesion, Entrainment and Task Success in Educational Dialog

Diane Litman
Department of Computer Science and LRDC
University of Pittsburgh
Pittsburgh, PA 15260
litman@cs.pitt.edu

Researchers often study dialog corpora to better understand what makes some dialogs more successful than others. In this talk I will examine the relationship between coherence/entrainment and task success, in several types of educational dialog corpora: 1) one-on-one tutoring, where students use dialog to interact with a human tutor in the physics domain, 2) one-on-one tutoring, where students instead interact with a spoken dialog system, and 3) engineering design, where student teams engage in multi-party dialog to complete a group project. I will first introduce several corpus-based measures of both lexical and acoustic-prosodic dialog cohesion and entrainment, and extend them to handle multi-party conversations. I will then show that the amount of cohesion and/or entrainment positively correlates with measures of educational task success in all of our corpora. Finally, I will discuss how we are using our findings to build better tutorial dialog systems.

A Bottom-Up Exploration of the Dimensions of Dialog State in Spoken Interaction

Nigel G. Ward
Department of Computer Science
University of Texas at El Paso
El Paso, Texas, 79968, USA
nigelward@acm.org

Alejandro Vega
Department of Computer Science
University of Texas at El Paso
El Paso, Texas, 79968, USA
avega5@miners.utep.edu

Abstract

Models of dialog state are important, both scientifically and practically, but today's best build strongly on tradition. This paper presents a new way to identify the important dimensions of dialog state, more bottom-up and empirical than previous approaches. Specifically, we applied Principal Component Analysis to a large number of low-level prosodic features to find the most important dimensions of variation. The top 20 out of 76 dimensions accounted for 81% of the variance, and each of these dimensions clearly related to dialog states and activities, including turn taking, topic structure, grounding, empathy, cognitive processes, attitude and rhetorical structure.

1 Introduction

What set of things should a dialog manager be responsible for? In other words, which aspects of the current dialog state should the dialog manager track?

These questions are fundamental: they define the field of computational dialog modeling and determine the basic architectures of our dialog systems. However the answers common in the field today arise largely from tradition, rooted in the concerns of precursor fields such as linguistics and artificial intelligence (Traum and Larsson, 2003; McGlashan et al., 2010; Bunt, 2011).

We wish to provide a new perspective on these fundamental questions, baed on a bottom-up, empirical investigations of dialog state. We hope thereby to discover new facets of dialog state and to obtain estimates of which aspects of dialog state are most important.

2 Aims

There are many ways to describe dialog state, but in this paper we seek a model with 7 properties:

Orthogonal to Content. While the automatic discovery of content-related dialog states has seen significant advances, we are interested here in the more general aspects of dialog state, those that occur across many if not all domains.

Scalar. While it is descriptively convenient to refer to discrete states (is-talking, is-waiting-for-a-yes-no-answer, and so on), especially for human analysts, in general it seems that scales are more natural for many or all aspects of dialog state, for example, one's degree of confidence, the strength of desire to take the turn, or the solidity of grounding.

Non-Redundant. While various levels and angles are used in describing aspects of dialog state — and many of these are interrelated, correlated, and generally tangled — we would like a set of dimensions which is as concise as possible and mutually orthogonal.

Continuously Varying. While it is common to label dialog states only at locally stable times, for example when neither party is speaking, or only over long spans, for example, utterances, we want a model that can support incremental dialog systems, able to describe the instantaneous state at any point in time, even in the middle of an utterance.

Short-Term. While aspects of dialog state can involve quite distant context, we here focus on the aspects important in keeping the dialog flowing over short time-scales.

Non-Exhaustive. While dialog states can be arbitrarily complex, highly specific, and intricately related to content, a general model can only be expected to describe the frequently important aspects of state.

Prioritized. While no aspects of dialog are uninteresting, we want to know which aspects of dialog state are more important and commonly relevant.

3 Approach

To be as empirical as possible, we want to consider as much data as possible. We accordingly needed to use automatic techniques. In particular, we chose to base our analysis on objective manifestations of dialog state. Among the many possible such manifestations — discourses markers, gesture, gaze, and so on — we chose to use only prosody. This is because the importance of prosody in meta-communication and dialog control has often been noted, because the continuous nature of (most) prosodic features is convenient for our aims, and because prosodic features are relatively easy to compute.

Given our aims and such features, it is natural to do Principal Components Analysis (PCA). This well-known method automatically identifies the factors underlying the observed variations across multiple features. We also hoped that PCA would separate out, as orthogonal factors, aspects of prosody that truly relate to dialog from aspects with lexical, phrasal, or other significance.

4 Related Research

While dialog states have apparently not previously been tackled using PCA, other dimensionality-reduction methods have been used. Clustering has previously been applied as a way to categorize user intention-types and goals, using lexical-semantic features and neighboring-turn features as inputs (Lefevre and de Mori, 2007; Lee et al., 2009), among other methods (Gasic and Young, 2011). Hidden Markov Models have been used to identify dialog "modes" that involve common sequences of dialog-acts (Boyer et al., 2009). There is also work that uses PCA to reduce multi-factor subjective evaluations of emotion, style, or expressiveness into a few underlying dimensions, for example (Barbosa, 2009). In addition, clustering over low-level patterns of turn-taking has been used to identify a continuum of styles (Grothendieck et al., 2011). However analysis of dialog states based on prosodic features has not previously been attempted, nor has analysis of dialog behaviors over time frames shorter than the discourse or the turn sequence.

Reducing the multiplicity of prosodic features to a smaller underlying set has long been a goal for linguists. The traditional method is to start with percepts (for example, that some syllables sound louder) and then look for the acoustic-prosodic features that correlate with these perceptions. More recently the opposite tack has also been tried, starting with acoustic-prosodic features, and trying to infer a higher or deeper level of description. For example, if we discover that for many syllables pitch height, higher volume, and increased duration all correlate, then we can infer some deeper factor underlying all of these, namely stress or prominence. PCA provides a systematic way of doing this for many features at once, and it has been used for various prosodic investigations, including an exploration of the prosodic and other vocal parameters relevant to emotional dimensions (Goudbeek and Scherer, 2010) or levels of vocal effort (Charfuelan and Schröeder, 2011), categorizing glottal-flow waveforms (Pfitzinger, 2008), finding the factors involved in boundaries and accents (Batliner et al., 2001), identifying the key dimensions of variation in pitch contours using Functional Data Analysis (Gubian et al., 2010), and for purely practical purposes (Lee and Narayanan, 2005; Jurafsky et al., 2012). In our own laboratory, Justin McManus applied PCA to 4 left-context, single-speaker prosodic features, and identified the first PC with a continuum from silence to cheerful speech, and the second PC with the continuum from back-channeling to storytelling. However PCA has never before been applied to large set of features, thus we hoped it might reveal important underlying factors in prosody that have not previously been noticed: factors interactionally important, even if not salient.

5 Method

Using Switchboard, a large corpus of smalltalk between strangers over the telephone recorded in two

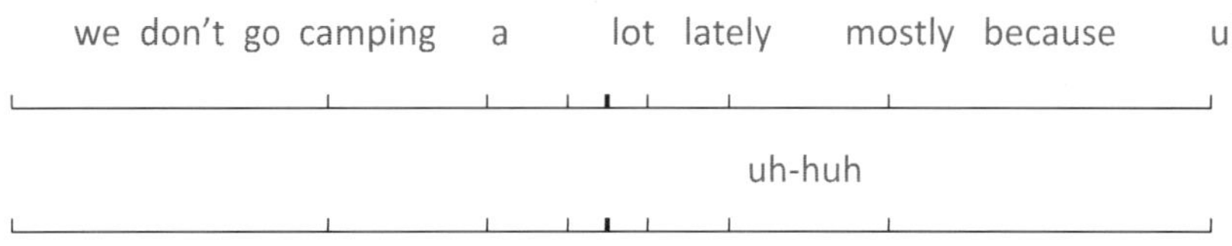

Figure 1: The 16 pitch-height feature windows, centered about a hypothetical occurrence of the word *lot*.

channels (Godfrey et al., 1992), we collected datapoints from both sides of 20 dialogs, totaling almost two hours, taking a sample every 10 milliseconds. This gave us 600,000 datapoints.

For each datapoint we computed 76 prosodic features. These features were taken from both the immediate past and the immediate future, since dialog state, by any definition, relates to both: being dependent on past context and predictive of future actions. The features were taken from both the speaker of interest and his or her interlocutor, since dialog states intrinsically involve the behavior of both parties.

Because our interest is in short-term dialog states, features were computed over only the 3-4 seconds before and after each point of interest. The sequencing of the prosodic features being obviously important, this context was split up into a sequence of windows. Wishing to give more precision and more weight to close context than more distant context, the windows closest to the point of interest were smallest, with the more distant being wider, as illustrated in Figure 1. The window sizes were fixed, not aligned with utterances, words, nor syllables.

The specific features we computed were chosen for convenience, based on a basic set previously found useful for language modeling (Ward et al., 2011). These were 1. a speaking-rate measure, over 325 millisecond windows, 2. volume, over 50 ms windows, 3. pitch height, over 150 ms windows, and 4. pitch range, over 225 ms windows. All were speaker-normalized. The values for the longer regions were obtained by simply averaging the values over two more more adjacent basic features.

In total there were 76 features: 24 volume, 20 pitch range, 16 pitch height, and 16 speaking rate. At times where there was no pitch, the average pitch value was used as substitute. All features were normalized to have mean 0 and standard deviation 1.

PCA was then done. As hoped, a few dimensions explained most of the variance, with the top 4 explaining 55%, the top 10 explaining 70%, and the top 20 explaining 81%.

We then set out to determine, for each of the dimensions, what dialog states or situations, if any, were associated with it.

Our first approach was to examine extreme datapoints. Because we thought that it would be informative to see which words tended to occur at the extremes, we filtered our datapoints to select only those which were at word onsets. For each dimension we then computed, for all of these, the values on that dimension. We then sorted these to find the highest 20 and the lowest 20. Looking at these word lists however was generally not informative, as no word or even word type predominated in any group, in fact, the words were invariably highly diverse. This perhaps indicates that the dimensions of dialog state expressed by prosody do not aligne with those expressed by words, and perhaps confirm that words can correlate with social and dialog functions in unsuspected ways (Tausczik and Pennebaker, 2010).

We next listened to some of some of these datapoints in context. First we listened to a few low-valued ones and came up with informal hypotheses about what they had in common. We then listened to more examples, winnowing and revising hypotheses as we went, until we were satisfied that we had a generalization that held for at least the majority of the cases. Then we did the same thing for the high-valued times. Finally we put the two together and found an opposition, and used this to describe the significance of the dimension as a whole. Sometimes this came easily, but sometimes it required more listening to verify or refine. This was in general easy for the top few dimensions, but more challenging for the lower ones, where the shared properties were generally weaker and more variable.

This process was unavoidably subjective, and must be considered only exploratory. We did not start out with any strong expectations, other than that many of the dimensions would relate to aspects of dialog. Our backgrounds may have predisposed us to be extra alert to turn-taking processes, but often initial hypotheses relating to turn-taking were superseded by others that explained the data better. We did not limit ourselves to terminology from any specific theoretical framework, rather we chose whichever seemed most appropriate for the phenomena.

Our second approach was to look at the loading factors, to see for each dimension which of the input prosodic features were highly correlated with it, both positively and negatively. In every case these confirmed or were compatible with our interpretations, generally revealing heavy loadings on features which previous research or simple logic suggested would relate to the dialog activities and states we had associated with the dimension.

6 Interpretations of the Top Dimensions

The results of our analyses were as follows. These must be taken as tentative, and the summary descriptions in the headings and in the tables must be read as mere mnemonics for the more complex reality that our fuller descriptions capture better, although still far from perfectly.

Dimension 1: Who's speaking?

At points with low values on this dimension the speaker of interest is speaking loudly and continuously without pause while the other is completely silent. At points with high values on this dimension the speaker of interest is producing only back-channels, while the other speaker is speaking continuously. (Points with complete silence on the part of the speaker of interest probably would have been even more extreme, but were not examined since our sample set only included timepoints where the speaker of interest was starting a word.) Unsurprisingly the features with the highest loadings were the volumes for the two speakers. Thus we identify this dimension with "who's speaking." Interestingly, of all the dimensions, this was the only with a bimodal distribution.

Dimension 2: How much involvement is there?

At points with low values on this dimension the dialog appeared to be faltering or awkward, with the lone speaker producing words slowly interspersed with non-filled pauses. High-value points were places where both speakers appeared highly involved, talking at once for several seconds, or one laughing while the other talked. Again the volume features had the highest loadings. Thus we identify this dimension with the amount of involvement.

Dimension 3: Is there a topic end?

At points with low values on this dimension there is generally a quick topic closing, in situations where the speaker had a new topic cued up and wanted to move on to it. An extreme example was when, after hearing clicks indicating call waiting, the speaker said she needed to take the other call. At points with high values on this dimension the topic was constant, sometimes with the less active participant indicating resigned boredom with a half-hearted back-channel. The features with the highest positive loadings were speaking-rate features: fast speech by the interlocutor in the near future correlated with a topic close, whereas fast speech by the current speaker about 1–2 seconds ago correlated with topic continuity. Thus we identify this dimension with topic ending.

Dimension 4: Is the referent grounded yet?

At points with low values on this dimension the speaker is often producing a content word after a filler or disfluent region, and this is soon followed by a back-channel by the other speaker. At points with high values on this dimension the speaker of interest is adding more information to make the point he wanted (starting the comment part of a topic-comment pair) sometimes after the interlocutor had responded with *oh*. Thus this dimension relates to the continuum between trying to ground something and continuing on with something already grounded. Trying to ground correlated with an upcoming fast speaking rate, while proceeding after grounding correlated with a high volume. Thus we identify this dimension with the degree of grounding.

Dimension 5: Does the speaker want to start or stop?

At points with low values on this dimension the speaker of interest is starting a turn strongly, sometimes as a turn-grab or even cutting-off the other speaker. At points with high values on this dimension the speaker is strongly yielding the turn, coupled with the interlocutor very swiftly taking up the turn. Often the turn yield occurs when the speaker is soliciting a response, either explicitly or by expressing an opinion that seems intended to invoke a response. As might be expected, cut-offs correlate with high volume on the part of the interrupting speaker, while clear turn yields correlate with past high volume on the part of the speaker who is ending. Thus we identify this dimension with starting versus stopping.

Dimension 6: Has empathy been expressed yet?

At points with low values on this dimension the speaker is continuing shortly after a high-content, emotionally-colored word that has just been acknowledged by the interlocutor. At points with high values on this dimension, the speaker is acknowledging a feeling or attitude just expressed by the other, by expressing agreement with a short turn such as *that's right* or *yeah, Arizona's beautiful!*. Continuing after empathic grounding correlated with high volume after a couple of seconds; expressing empathy with a short comment correlated with the interlocutor recently having produced a word with high pitch. Thus we identify this dimension with the degree of empathy established.

Dimension 7: Are the speakers synchronized?

At points with low values on this dimension both speakers inadvertently start speaking at the same time. At points with high values on this dimension the speakers swiftly and successfully interleave their speaking, for example by completing each other's turns or with back-channels. The features with the highest positive loadings were those of pitch range and speaking rate with the volume factors having mostly negative loadings. Thus we identify this dimension with the degree of turn synchronization.

Dimension 8: Is the turn end unambiguous?

At points with low values on this dimension the speaker is dragging out a turn which appears, content-wise, to be already finished, producing post-completions, such as *uh* or *or anything like that*. At points with high values on this dimension, often the speaker is definitively ending a turn. The feature with the highest positive loading was pitch range, unsurprisingly since clear turn ends often involve a sharp pitch fall. Thus we identify this dimension with the degree of ambiguity of the turn end.

Dimension 9: Is the topic exhausted?

At points with low values on this dimension a speaker is closing out a topic due to running out of things to say. Often at points with high values on this dimension the speaker is staying with one topic, with continuing interest also from the interlocutor. The most positively correlated feature was the interlocutor's volume 400–800 ms ago, for example during a back-channel or comment showing interest. Thus we identify this dimension with the degree of interest in the current topic.

Dimension 10: Is the speaker thinking?

At points with low values on this dimension the speaker is looking for a word, choosing her words carefully, or recalling something, typically inside a turn but preceded by a short pause or an *um*. At points with high values on this dimension the speaker seems to be giving up on the topic, declaiming any relevant knowledge and/or yielding the turn. The features correlating most with the memory-search/lexical-access state were those of high volume by the speaker 50–1500 milliseconds later; the features correlating most with the giving-up state were speaking rate. Thus we identify this dimension with the degree to which the speaker is putting mental effort into continuing.

Dimension 11: How quick-thinking is the speaker?

Points with low values on this dimension included two types: first where a speaker is ending a false start and about to start over, and second where the speaker is about to be cut off by the interlocutor while saying something noncommittal to end a turn, such as *I guess*. Points with high values included swift echos and confirmations, which seemed to reflect quickness and dominance. Thus we identify this dimension with quickness, confidence and dominance versus the lack thereof.

Dimension 12: Is the speaker claiming or yielding the floor?

Points with low values on this dimension generally seemed to be staking a claim to the floor, revealing the intention to talk on for several seconds, sometimes as topic resumptions. Points with high were generally floor yields, and sometimes sounded negative or distancing. Slow future speaking rate, by both speakers, aligned with the low values, and fast rate with the high values. We identify this dimension with the floor claim/yield continuum.

Dimension 13: How compatible is the proposition with the context?

Points with low values on this dimension occurred in the course of a self-narrative at the beginning of something contradicting what the listener may have inferred, or actually did think and say, for example with *no, we actually don't*. Points with high values of this dimension generally involved a restatement of something said before either by the speaker or the interloctor, for example restating a question after the other failed to answer, or opining that a football team can now expect a few bad years, just a dozen seconds after the interlocutor had already expressed essentially the same thought. The low, contradicting side had high volume and slow speaking rate for a fraction of a second; the restatements were the opposite. Thus we identify this dimension with the continuum between a contrast-type rhetorical structure and a repetition-type one.

Dimension 14: Are the words being said important?

Points with low values on this dimension occur when the speaker is rambling: speaking with frequent minor disfluencies while droning on about something that he seems to have little interested in, in part because the other person seems to have nothing better to do than listen. Points with high values on this dimension occur with emphasis and seemed bright in tone. Slow speaking rate correlated highest with the rambling, boring side of the dimension, and future interlocutor pitch height with the emphasizing side. Thus we identify this dimension with the importance of the current word or words, and the degree of mutual engagement.

Dimension 15: Are the words premature or delayed?

Points with low values on this dimension included examples where the speaker is strongly holding the floor despite a momentary disfluency, for example *uh and* or *well it's it's difficult*, using creaky voice and projecting authority. Points with high value on this dimension overlapped substantially with those high on dimension 14, but in addition seemed to come when the speaker starts sharing some information he had been wanting to talk about but saving up, for in a drawn-out political discussion, a new piece of evidence supporting an opinion expressed much earlier. Thus we identify this dimension with the continuum between talking as soon as you have something to say (or even slightly before) versus talking about something when the time is ripe.

Dimension 16: How positive is the speaker's stance?

Points with low values on this dimension were on words spoken while laughing or near such words, in the course of self-narrative while recounting a humorous episode. Points with high values on this dimension also sometimes occurred in a self narratives, but with negative affect, as in *brakes were starting to fail*, or in deploring statements such as *subject them to discriminatory practices*. Low values correlated with a slow speaking rate; high values with the pitch height. This we identify this a humorous/regrettable continuum.

Other Dimensions

Space does not permit the discussion of further dimensions here, but the end of Table 1 and Table 2 summarize what we have seen in some other dimensions that we have examined for various reasons, some discussed elsewhere (dimensions 25, 62, and 72 in (Ward and Vega, 2012 submitted) and 17, 18, 21, 24, 26, and 72 in (Ward et al., 2012 submitted)). Of course, not all dimensions are mostly about dialog, for example dimension 29 appears to be described best as relating simply to the presence or absence of a stressed word (Ward et al., 2012 submitted), although that of course is not without implications for what dialog activities may cooccur.

7 Discussion

Although prosody is messy and multifunctional, this exploration shows that PCA can derive from raw features a set of dimensions which explain much of the data, and which are surprisingly interpretable.

1	this speaker talking vs. other speaker talking	32%
2	neither speaking vs. both speaking	9%
3	topic closing vs. topic continuation	8%
4	grounding vs. grounded	6%
5	turn grab vs. turn yield	3%
6	seeking empathy vs. expressing empathy	3%
7	floor conflict vs. floor sharing	3%
8	dragging out a turn vs. ending confidently and crisply	3%
9	topic exhaustion vs. topic interest	2%
10	lexical access or memory retrieval vs. disengaging	2%
11	low content and low confidence vs. quickness	1%
12	claiming the floor vs. releasing the floor	1%
13	starting a contrasting statement vs. starting a restatement	1%
14	rambling vs. placing emphasis	1%
15	speaking before ready vs. presenting held-back information	1%
16	humorous vs. regrettable	1%
17	new perspective vs. elaborating current feeling	1%
18	seeking sympathy vs. expressing sympathy	1%
19	solicitous vs. controlling	1%
20	calm emphasis vs. provocativeness	1%

Table 1: Interpretations of top 20 dimensions, with the variance explained by each

21	mitigating a potential face threat vs. agreeing, with humor
24	agreeing and preparing to move on vs. jointly focusing
25	personal experience vs. second-hand opinion
26	signalling interestingness vs. downplaying things
62	explaining/excusing oneself vs. blaming someone/something
72	speaking awkwardly vs. speaking with a nicely cadenced delivery

Table 2: Interpretations of some other dimensions

Overall, the top dimensions covered a broad sampling of the topics generally considered important in dialog research. This can be taken to indicate that the field of dialog studies is mostly already working on the important things after all. However previously unremarked aspects of dialog behavior do appear to surface in some of the lower dimensions; here further examination is needed.

We had hoped that PCA would separate out the dialog-relevant aspects of prosody from the aspects of prosody serving other functions. Generally this was true, although in part because the non-dialog functions of prosody didn't show up strongly at all. While this was probably due in part to the specific feature set used, it still suggests that dialog factors are overwhelmingly important for prosody. Partial exceptions were emotion, attitude, rhetorical structure, speaking styles and interaction styles, all of which appeared as aspects of some dimensions. Some dimensions also seemed to relate to dialects, personality traits, or individuals; for example, many of the most unambiguous turn endings (dimension 8) were by the same few speakers, who seemed to us to be businesslike and dominant.

8 Potential Applications

These dimensions, and similar empirically-derived sets, are potentially useful for various applications.

First, the inferred dimensions could serve as a first-pass specification of the skills needed for a competent dialog agent: suggesting a dialog manager whose core function is to monitor, predict, and guide the development of the dialog in terms of the top 10 or so dimensions. This technique could be very generally useful: since it supports the discovery of dialog dimensions in a purely data-driven way (apart from the subjective interpretations, which are not always needed), this may lead to methods for the automatically generation of dialog models and dialog managers for arbitrary new domains.

Second, for generation and synthesis, given the increased interest in going beyond intelligibility to also give utterances dialog-appropriate wordings and realizations, the inferred dimensions suggest what is needed for dialog applications: we may have identified the most important parameters for adapting and controlling a speech synthesizer's prosodic behavior for dialog applications.

Third, dimensional representations of dialog state could be useful for predicting the speaker's upcoming word choices, that is, useful for language modeling and thus speech recognition, as an improvement on dialog-act descriptions of state or descriptions in terms of raw, non-independent prosodic features (Shriberg and Stolcke, 2004; Ward et al., 2011; Stoyanchev and Stent, 2012). Initial results of conditioning on 25 dimensions gave a 26.8% perplexity reduction (Ward and Vega, 2012 submitted).

These dimensions could also be used for other purposes, including a more-like-this function for audio search based on similarity in terms of dialog context; better characterizing the functions of discourse markers; tracking the time course of action sequences leading to impressions of dominance, friendliness and the like; finding salient or significant events in meeting recordings; and teaching second language learners the prosodic patterns of dialog.

9 Future Work

Our study was exploratory, and there are many obvious ways to improve on it. It would be good to apply this method using richer feature sets, including for example voicing fraction, pitch slope, pitch contour features, spectral tilt, voicing properties, and syllable- and word-aligned features, to get a more complete view of what prosody contributes to dialog. Going further, one might also use temporal features (Ward et al., 2011), features of gaze, gesture, and words, perhaps in a suitable vector-space representation (Bengio et al., 2003). Better feature weighting could also be useful for refining the ranking of the dimensions: while our method treated one standard deviation of variance in one feature as equal in importance to one standard deviation in any other, in human perception this is certainly not the case. It would also be interesting to apply this method to other corpora in other domains: for example in task-oriented dialogs we might expect it to find additional important dimensions relating to task structure, question type, recovery from misunderstandings, uncertainty, and so on. Finally, it would be interesting to explore which of these dimensions of state actually matter most for dialog success (Tetreault and Litman, 2006).

In addition to the identification of specific dimensions of dialog in casual conversations, this paper contributes a new method: that of using PCA over low-level, observable features to identify important dimensions of dialog state, which could be applied more generally.

While we see numerous advantages for quantitative, dimensional dialog state modeling, we do not think that this obsoletes more classical methods. Indeed, it would be interesting to explore how commonly used dialog states and acts relate to these dimensions; for example, to take the set of utterances labeled wh-questions in NXT Switchboard and examine where they are located in the "dialog space" defined by these dimensions (Calhoun et al., 2010; Ward et al., 2012 submitted).

Acknowledgments

This work was supported in part by NSF Award IIS-0914868. We thank Olac Fuentes for suggesting PCA, Justin McManus for the prototype analysis, Shreyas Karkhedkar for help with the basic features, and David Novick for discussion.

References

Plinio Barbosa. 2009. Detecting changes in speech expressiveness in participants of a radio program. In *Interspeech*, pages 2155–2158.

Anton Batliner, Jan Buckow, Richard Huber, Volker Warnke, Elmar Nöth, and Heinrich Niemann. 2001. Boiling down prosody for the classification of boundaries and accents in German and English. In *Eurospeech*, pages 2781–2784.

Yoshua Bengio, Rejean Ducharme, Pascal Vincent, and Christian Jauvin. 2003. A neural probabilistic language model. *Journal of Machine Learning Research*, 3:1137–1155.

Kristy Elizabeth Boyer, Eun Young Ha, Robert Phillips, Michael D. Wallis, Mladen A. Vouk, and James C. Lester. 2009. Inferring tutorial dialogue structure with hidden Markov modeling. In *Proc. NAACL-HLT Workshop on Innovative Uses of NLP for Building Educational Applications*, pages 19–26.

Harry Bunt. 2011. Multifunctionality in dialogue. *Computer Speech and Language*, 25:222–245.

Sasha Calhoun, Jean Carletta, Jason M. Brenier, Neil Mayo, Dan Jurafsky, et al. 2010. The NXT-format Switchboard corpus: a rich resource for investigating the syntax, semantics, pragmatics and prosody of dialogue. *Language Resources and Evaluation*, 44:387–419.

Marcela Charfuelan and Marc Schröeder. 2011. Investigating the prosody and voice quality of social signals in scenario meetings. In *Proc. Affective Computing and Intelligent Interaction*.

Milica Gasic and Steve Young. 2011. Effective handling of dialogue state in the hidden information state POMDP-based dialogue manager. *ACM Transactions on Speech and Language Processing*, 7.

J. J. Godfrey, E. C. Holliman, and J. McDaniel. 1992. Switchboard: Telephone speech corpus for research and development. In *Proceedings of ICASSP*, pages 517–520.

Martijn Goudbeek and Klaus Scherer. 2010. Beyond arousal: Valence and potency/control cues in the vocal expression of emotion. *Journal of the Acoustical Society of America*, 128:1322–1336.

John Grothendieck, Allen L. Gorin, and Nash M. Borges. 2011. Social correlates of turn-taking style. *Computer Speech and Language*, 25:789–801.

Michelle Gubian, Francesco Cangemi, and Lou Boves. 2010. Automatic and data driven pitch contour manipulation with functional data analysis. In *Speech Prosody*.

Dan Jurafsky, Rajesh Ranganath, and Dan McFarland. 2012. Detecting friendly, flirtatious, awkward, and assertive speech in speed-dates. *Computer Speech and Language*, in press.

Chul Min Lee and Shrikanth Narayanan. 2005. Toward detecting emotions in spoken dialogs. *IEEE Transactions on Speech and Audio Processing*, 13:293–303.

Cheongjae Lee, Sangkeun Jung, Kyungduk Kim, and Gary Geunbae Lee. 2009. Automatic agenda graph construction from human-human dialogs using clustering method. In *Proc. NAACL-HLT 2009: Short Papers*, pages 89–92.

Fabrice Lefevre and Renato de Mori. 2007. Unsupervised state clustering for stochastic dialog management. In *ASRU*, pages 550–553.

Scott McGlashan, Daniel C. Burnett, et al. 2010. Voice extensible markup language (VoiceXML) 3.0. Technical report, W3C.

Hartmut R. Pfitzinger. 2008. Segmental effects on the prosody of voice quality. In *Acoustics'08*, pages 3159–3164.

Elizabeth Shriberg and Andreas Stolcke. 2004. Prosody modeling for automatic speech recognition and understanding. In *Mathematical Foundations of Speech and Language Processing, IMA Volumes in Mathematics and Its Applications, Vol. 138*, pages 105–114. Springer-Verlag.

Svetlana Stoyanchev and Amanda Stent. 2012. Concept type prediction and responsive adaptation in a dialogue system. *Dialogue and Discourse*, 3.

Yla R. Tausczik and James W. Pennebaker. 2010. The psychological meaning of words: Liwc and computerized text analysis methods. *Journal of Language and Social Psychology*, 29:24–54.

Joel R. Tetreault and Diane J. Litman. 2006. Comparing the utility of state features in spoken dialogue using reinforcement learning. In *HLT-NAACL*, pages 272–279.

David Traum and S. Larsson. 2003. The information state approach to dialogue management. In Jan van Kuppevelt and Ronnie Smith, editors, *Current and New Directions in Discourse and Dialogue*, pages 325–353. Kluwer.

Nigel G. Ward and Alejandro Vega. 2012, submitted. Towards empirical dialog-state modeling and its use in language modeling. In *Interspeech*.

Nigel G. Ward, Alejandro Vega, and Timo Baumann. 2011. Prosodic and temporal features for language modeling for dialog. *Speech Communication*, 54:161–174.

Nigel G. Ward, David G. Novick, and Alejandro Vega. 2012, submitted. Where in dialog space does uh-huh occur? In *Interdisciplinary Workshop on Feedback Behaviors in Dialog at Interspeech 2012*.

Using Group History to Identify Character-directed Utterances in Multi-child Interactions

Hannaneh Hajishirzi, Jill F. Lehman, and Jessica K. Hodgins
hannaneh.hajishirzi, jill.lehman, jkh@disneyresearch.com

Abstract

Addressee identification is an element of all language-based interactions, and is critical for turn-taking. We examine the particular problem of identifying when each child playing an interactive game in a small group is speaking to an animated character. After analyzing child and adult behavior, we explore a family of machine learning models to integrate audio and visual features with temporal group interactions and limited, task-independent language. The best model performs identification about 20% better than the model that uses the audio-visual features of the child alone.

1 Introduction

Multi-party interaction between a group of participants and an autonomous agent is an important but difficult task. Key problems include identifying when speech is present, who is producing it, and to whom it is directed, as well as producing an appropriate response to its intended meaning. Solving these problems is made more difficult when some or all of the participants are young children, who have high variability in language, knowledge, and behavior. Prior research has tended to look at single children (Oviatt, 2000; Black et al., 2009) or multi-person groups of adults (Bohus and Horvitz, 2009a). We are interested in interactions between animated or robotic characters and small groups of four to ten year old children. The interaction can be brief but should be fun.

Here we focus specifically on the question of deciding whether or not a child's utterance is directed to the character, a binary form of the addressee identification (AID) problem. Our broad goals in this research are to understand how children's behavior in group interaction with a character differs from adults', how controllable aspects of the character and physical environment determine participants' behavior, and how an autonomous character can take advantage of these regularities.

We collected audio and video data of groups of up to four children and adults playing language-based games with animated characters that were under limited human control. An autonomous character can make two kinds of AID mistakes: failing to detect when it is being spoken to, and acting as if it has been spoken to when it has not. The former can be largely prevented by having the character use examples of the language that it can recognize as part of the game. Such exemplification cannot prevent the second kind of mistake, however. It occurs, for example, when children confer to negotiate the next choice, respond emotionally to changes in the game state, or address each other without making eye contact. As a result, models that use typical audio-visual features to decide AID will not be adequate in multi-child environments. By including temporal conversational interactions between group members, however, we can both detect character-directed utterances and ignore the remainder about 20% better than simple audio-visual models alone, with less than 15% failure when being spoken to, and about 20% failure when not addressed.

2 Related Work

Our models explore the use of multimodal features that represent activities among children and adults interacting with a character over time. Prior research has tended to look at single children or multi-person groups of adults and has typically used a less inclusive set of features (albeit in decisions that go beyond simple AID).

Use of multimodal features rests on early work by Duncan and Fiske who explored how gaze and head and body orientation act as important predictors of AID in human-human interactions (Duncan and Fiske, 1977). Bakx and colleagues showed that accuracy can be improved by augmenting facial orientation with acoustic features in an agent's interactions with an adult dyad (Bakx et al., 2003). Others have studied the cues that people use to show their interest in engaging in a conversation (Gravano and Hirschberg, 2009) and how gesture supports selection of the next speaker in turn-taking (Bergmann et al., 2011). Researchers have also looked at combining visual features with lexical features like the parseability of the utterance (Katzenmaier et al., 2004), the meaning of the utterance, fluency of speech, and use of politeness terms (Terken et al., 2007), and the dialog act (Matsusaka et al., 2007). However, all use hand-annotated data in their analysis without considering the difficulty of automatically deriving the features. Finally, prosodic features have been combined with visual and lexical features in managing the order of speaking and predicting the end-of-turn in multi-party interactions (Lunsford and Oviatt, 2006; Chen and Harper, 2009; Clemens and Diekhaus, 2009).

Work modeling the temporal behavior of the speaker includes the use of adjacent utterances (e.g., question-answer) to study the dynamics of the dialog (Jovanovic et al., 2006), the prediction of addressee based on the addressee and dialog acts in previous time steps (Matsusaka et al., 2007), and the use of the speaker's features over time to predict the quality of an interaction between a robot and single adult (Fasel et al., 2009).

Horvitz and Bohus have the most complete (and deployed) model, combining multimodal features with temporal information using a system for multiparty dynamic interaction between adults and an agent (Bohus and Horvitz, 2009a; Bohus and Horvitz, 2009b). In (Bohus and Horvitz, 2009a) the authors describe the use of automatic sensors for voice detection, face detection, head position tracking, and utterance length. They do not model temporal or group interactions in determining AID, although they do use a temporal model for the interaction as a whole. In (Bohus and Horvitz, 2009b) the authors use the speaker's features for the current and previous time steps, but do not jointly track the attention or behavior of all the participants in the group. Moreover, their model assumes that the system is engaged with at most one participant at a time, which may be a valid conversational expectation for adults but is unlikely to hold for children. In (Bohus and Horvitz, 2011), the authors make a similar assumption regarding turn-taking, which is built on top of the AID module.

3 User Study

We use a Wizard of Oz testbed and a scripted mix of social dialog and interactive game play to explore the relationship between controllable features of the character and the complexity of interacting via language with young children. The games are hosted by two animated characters (Figure 1, left). Oliver, the turtle, is the main focus of the social interactions and also handles repair subdialogs when a game does not run smoothly. Manny, the bear, provides comic relief and controls the game board, making him the focus of participants' verbal choices during game play. The game appears on a large flat-screen display about six feet away from participants who stand side-by-side behind a marked line. Audio and video are captured, the former with both close-talk microphones and a linear microphone array.

Oliver and Manny host two games designed to be fun and easy to understand with little explicit instruction. In Madlibs, participants help create a short movie by repeatedly choosing one everyday object from a set of three. The objects can be seen on the board and Oliver gives examples of appropriate referring phrases when prompting for a choice. In Figure 1, for example, he asks, "Should our movie have a robot, a monster, or a girl in it?" After five sets of objects are seen, the choices appear in silly contexts in a short animation; for instance, a robot babysitter may serve a chocolate pickle cake for lunch. In Mix-and-Match (MnM), participants choose apparel and accessories to change a girl's image in unusual ways (Figure 1, right). MnM has six visually available objects and no verbal examples from Oliver, except in repair subdialogs. It is a faster-paced game

Figure 1: Manny and Oliver host Madlibs and a family play Mix-and-Match

with the immediate reward of a silly change to the babysitter's appearance whenever a referring phrase is accepted by the wizard.

The use of verbal examples in Madlibs is expected to influence the children's language, potentially increasing the accuracy of speech recognition and referent resolution in an autonomous system. The cost of exemplification is slower pacing because children must wait while the choices are named. To compensate, we offer only a small number of choices per turn. Removing exemplification, as in MnM, creates faster pacing and more variety of choice each turn, which is more fun but also likely to increase three types of problematic phenomena: out-of-vocabulary choices ("the king hat" rather than "the crown"), side dialogs to establish a referring lexical item or phrase ("Mommy, what is that thing?"), and the use of weak naming strategies based on physical features ("that green hand").

The two games are part of a longer scripted sequence of interactions that includes greetings, goodbyes, and appropriate segues. Overall, the language that can be meaningfully directed to the characters is constrained to a small social vocabulary, yes/no responses, and choices that refer to the objects on the board. The wizard's interface reflects these expectations with buttons that come and go as a function of the game state. For example, *yes* and *no* buttons are available to the wizard after Oliver asks, "Will you help me?" while *robot*, *monster*, and *girl* buttons are available after he asks, "Should our movie have a robot, a monster, or a girl in it?" The wizard also has access to persistent buttons to indicate a long silence, unclear speech, multiple people speaking, or a clear reference to an object not on the board. These buttons launch Oliver's problem-specific repair behaviors. The decomposition of functionality in the interface anticipates replacing the wizard's various roles as voice activity detector, addressee identifier, speech recognizer, referent resolver, and dialog manager in an autonomous implementation.

Although meaningful language to the characters is highly constrained, language to other participants can be about anything. In particular, both games establish an environment in which language among participants is likely to be about negotiating the turn ("Brad, do you want to change anything?"), negotiating the choice ("Billy, don't do the boot") or commenting on the result ("her feet look strange"). Lacking examples of referring phrases by Oliver, MnM also causes side dialogs to discuss how objects should be named. Naming discussions, choice negotiation, and comments define the essential difficulty in AID for our testbed; they are all likely to include references to objects on the board without the intention of changing the game state.

3.1 Data collection and annotation

Twenty-seven compensated children (14 male, 13 female) and six adult volunteers participated. Children ranged in age from four to ten with a mean of 6.4 years. All children spoke English as a first language. Groups consisted of up to four people and always contained either a volunteer adult or the experimenter the first time through the activities. If the experimenter participated, she did not make game choices. Volunteer adults were instructed to support their children's participation in whatever way felt natural for their family. When time permitted, children were given the option of playing one or both games again. Those who played a second time were allowed to play alone or in combination with others, with or without an adult. Data was collected for 25 distinct groups, the details of which are provided in Table 5 in the Appendix.

Data from all sessions was hand-annotated with respect to language, gesture, and head orientation. Labels were based on an initial review of the videos, prior research on AID and turn-taking in adults, and the ability to detect candidate features in our physical environment. A second person segmented and labeled approximately one third of each session for inter-annotator comparison. The redundant third was assigned randomly from the beginning, middle, or end of the session in order to balance across social interactions, Madlibs choices, and MnM choices. Labels were considered to correspond to the same audio or video sequence if the segments overlapped by at least 50%.

For language annotations, audio from the close-talk microphones was used with the video and segmented into utterances based on pauses of at least 50 msec. Typical mispronunciations for young children (e.g., word initial /W/ for /R/) were transcribed as normal words in plain text; non-standard errors were transcribed phonologically. Every utterance was also labeled as being directed to the character (CHAR) or not to the character (NCHAR). Second annotators segmented the audio and assigned addressee but did not re-transcribe the speech. Inter-annotator agreement for segmentation was 95% (κ = .91), with differences resulting from only one annotator segmenting properly around pauses or only one being able to distinguish a given child's voice among the many who were talking. For segments coded by both annotators, CHAR/NCHAR agreement was 94% (κ = .89).

For gesture annotations, video segments were marked for instances of pointing, emphasis, and head shaking yes and no. Emphatic gestures were defined as hand or arm movements toward the screen that were not pointing or part of grooming motions. Annotators agreed on the existence of gestures 74% of the time (κ = .49), but when both annotators interpreted movement as a gesture, they used the same label 98% of the time (κ = .96).

For orientation, video was segmented when the head turned away from the screen and when it turned back. Rather than impose an *a priori* duration or angle, annotators were told to use the turn-away label when the turn was associated with meaningful interaction with a person or object, but not for brief, incidental head movements. Adults could also have segments that were labeled as head-incline if they bent to speak to children. Annotators agreed on the existence of these orientation changes 83% of the time (κ = .62); disagreements may represent simple differences in accuracy or differences in judgments about whether a movement denoted a shift in attention. Orientation changes coded by both annotators had the same label 92% of the time (κ = .85).

The annotated sessions are a significant portion of the training and test data used for our models. Although these data reflect some idiosyncracy due to human variability in speech perception, gesture recognition, and, possibly, the attribution of intention to head movements, they show extremely good agreement with regard to whether participants were talking to the character. Even very young children in group situations give signals in their speech and movements that allow other people to determine consistently to whom they are speaking.

3.2 Analysis of behavior

As intended, children did most of the talking (1371/1895 utterances, 72%), spoke to the characters the majority of the time (967/1371, 71%), and made most of the object choices (666/683, 98%). Adults generally acted in support roles, with 88% of all adult utterances (volunteers and experimenter) directed to the children.

The majority of children's CHAR utterances (71%) were object choices. Although the wizard in our study was free to accept any unambiguous phrase as a valid choice, an automated system must commit to a fixed lexicon. In general, the larger the lexicon, the smaller the probability that a reference will be out-of-vocabulary, but the greater the probability that a reference could be considered ambiguous and require clarification. The lexical entry for each game object contains the simple description given to the illustrator ("alien hands," "pickle") and related terms from WordNet (Fellbaum, 1998) likely to be known by young children (see Table 3 in the Appendix for examples). In anticipation of weak naming strategies, MnM entries also contain salient visual features based on the artwork (like color), as well as the body part the object would replace, where applicable. Entries for Madlibs objects average 2.75 words; entries for MnM average 5.8. With these definitions, only 37/666 (6%) of character-directed choices would have been out-of-vocabulary for a word-spotting speech recognizer with human accuracy. However, Oliver's use of exemplification has a strong effect. In Madlibs, 98% of children's choices were unambiguous repetitions of example phrases. In MnM, 92% of choices contained words in the lexicon, but only 28% indexed a unique object.

Recognition of referring phrases should be a factor in making AID decisions only if it helps to discriminate CHAR from NCHAR utterances. Object references occurred in 62% of utterances to the characters and only 25% of utterances addressed to other participants, but again, Oliver's exemplification mattered. About 20% of NCHAR utterances from children in both games and from adults in Madlibs contained object references. In MnM, however, a third of adults' NCHAR utterances contained object references as they responded to children's requests for naming advice.

Language is not the only source of information available from our testbed. We know adults use both eye gaze and gesture to modulate turn-taking and signal addressee in advance of speech. Because nonverbal mechanisms for establishing joint attention occur early in language development, even children as young as four might use such signals consistently. Although we use head movement as an approximation of eye gaze, we positioned participants side-by-side to make such movements necessary for eye contact. Unfortunately, the game board constituted too strong a "situational attractor" (Bakx et al., 2003). As in their kiosk environment, our adults oriented toward the screen much of the time (68%) they were talking to other participants. Children violated conversational convention more often, orienting toward the screen for 82% of NCHAR utterances.

Gesture information is also available from the video data and reveals distinct patterns of usage for children and adults. The average number of gestures/utterance was more than twice as high in adults. Children were more likely to use emphasis gestures when they were talking to the characters; adults hardly used them at all. Children's gestures overlapped with their speech almost 80% of the time, but adult's gestures overlapped with their speech only half the time. Moreover, when children pointed while talking they were talking to the characters, but when adults pointed while talking they were talking to the children. Finally, adults shook their heads when they were talking to children but not when they were talking to the characters, while children shook their heads when talking to both.

To maintain an engaging experience, object references addressed to the character should be treated as possible choices, while object references addressed to other participants should not produce action. Interactions that violate this rule too often will be frustrating rather than fun. While exemplification in Madlibs virtually eliminated out-of-vocabulary choices, it could not eliminate detectable object references that were not directed to the characters. In both games, such references were often accompanied by other signs that the character was being addressed, like orientation toward the board and pointing. Using all the cues available, human annotators were almost always able to agree on who was being addressed. The next section looks at how well an autonomous agent can perform AID using only the cues it can sense, if it could sense them with human levels of accuracy.

4 Models for Addressee Classification

We cast the problem of automatically identifying whether an utterance is addressed to the character (and so may result in a character action) as a binary classification problem. We build and test a family of models based on distinct sources of information in order to understand where the power is coming from and make it easier for other researchers to compare to our approach. All models in the family are constructed from Support Vector Machines (SVM) (Cortes and Vapnik, 1995), and use the multimodal features in Table 1 to map each 500 msec time slice of a child's speech to CHAR or NCHAR. This basic feature vector combines a subset of the hand-annotated data (Audio and Visual) with automatically generated data (Prosodic and System events). We use a time slice rather than a lexical or semantic boundary for forcing a judgment because in a real-time interaction decisions must be made even when

Audio	speech: presence/absence
Prosodic	pitch: low/medium/high speech power: low/medium/high
System event	character prompt: presence/absence
Visual	orientation: head turn away/back gesture: pointing/emphasis

Table 1: Basic features

lexical or semantic events do not occur.

We consider three additional sources of information: group behavior, history, and lexical usage. Group behavior – the speech, prosody, head orientation, and gestures of other participants – is important because most of the speech that is not directed to the characters is directed to a specific person in the group. History is important both because the side conversations unfold gradually and because it allows us to capture the changes to and continuity of the speaker's features across time slices. Finally, we use lexical features to represent whether the participant's speech contains words from a small, predefined vocabulary of question words, greetings, and discourse markers (see Appendix). Because the behavioral analysis showed significant use of words referring to choice objects during both CHAR and NCHAR utterances, we do not consider those words in determining AID. Indeed, we expect the AID decision to simplify the task of the speech recognizer by helping that component ignore NCHAR utterances entirely.

The full set of models is described by adding to the basic vector zero or more of group (*g*), word (*w*), or history (*h*) features. We use the notation *g*[+/-]*w*[+/-]*h*[(time parameters)/-] to indicate the presence or absence of a knowledge source. The time parameters vary and will be explained in the context of particular models, below. Although we have explored a larger portion of the total model space, we limit our discussion here to representative models (including the best model) that will demonstrate the effect of each kind of information on the two main goals of AID: responding to CHAR utterances and not responding to NCHAR utterances. There are eight models of interest, the first four of which isolate individual knowledge sources:

The *Basic* model (*g-w-h-*) is an SVM classifier trained to generate binary CHAR/NCHAR values based solely on the features in Table 1. It represents the ability to predict whether a child is talking to the

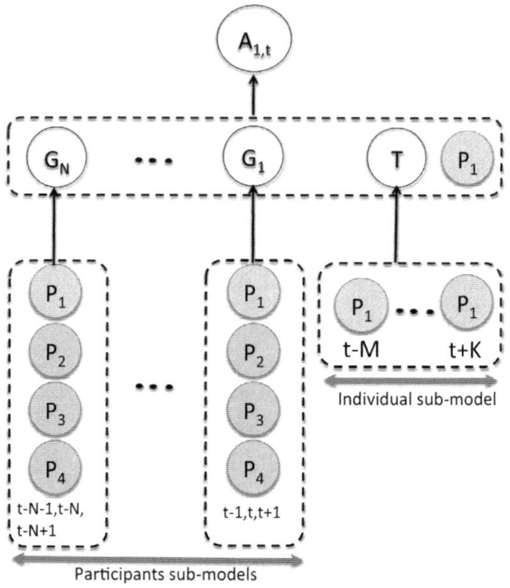

Figure 2: The two-layer *Group-History* model maps group and individual behavior over a fixed window of time slices to a CHAR/NCHAR decision at time t. The decision at time t ($A_{1,t}$) is based on the participant's basic features (P_1), the output of the individual's submodel (T) – which encapsulates the history of the individual for M previous and K subsequent time slices – and the output of N participant submodels, each of which contributes a value based on three times slices.

character independent of speech recognition and focused on only 500 msecs of that child's behavior.

The *Group* model (*g+w-h-*) incorporates group information, but ignores temporal and lexical behavior. This SVM is trained on an extended feature vector that includes the basic features for the other participants in the group together with the speaker's feature vector at each time slice.

The *History* model (*g-w-h*(N,K)) considers only the speaker's basic features, but includes N previous and K subsequent time slices surrounding the slice for which we make the CHAR/NCHAR decision.[1]

The *Word* model (*g-w+h-*) extends the basic vector to include features for the presence or absence of question words, greetings, and discourse markers.

The next three models combine pairs of knowledge sources. The *Group-Word* (*g+w+h-*) and *History-Word* (*g-w+h*(N,K)) models are straight-

[1] A *History* model combining the speaker's basic vector over the previous and current time slices (N = 4 and K = 0) outperformed a Conditional Random Fields (Lafferty et al., 2001) model with $N + 1$ nodes representing consecutive time slices where the last node is conditioned on the previous N nodes.

forward extensions of their respective base models, created by adding lexical features to the basic vectors. The *Group-History* model (*g+w-h*(N,K,M)) is more complex. It is possible to model group interactions over time by defining a new feature vector that includes all the participants' basic features over multiple time slices. As we increase the number of people in a group and/or the number of time slices to explore the model space, however, the sheer size of this simple combination of feature vectors becomes unwieldy. Instead we make the process hierarchical by defining the *Group-History* as a two-layer SVM.

Figure 2 instantiates the *Group-History* model for participant P_1 playing in a group of four. In the configuration shown, the decision for P_1's utterance at time *t* is based on behavior during N previous and K subsequent time slices, meaning each decision is delayed by K time slices with respect to real time. The CHAR/NCHAR decision for time slice *t* depends on P_1's basic feature vector at time *t*, the output from the Individual submodel for time *t*, and the outputs from the Participants submodel for each of the time slices through *t*. A concrete instantiation of the model can be seen in Figure 4 in the Appendix.

The Individual submodel is an SVM that assigns a score to the composite of P_1's basic feature vectors across a window of time (here, $M+K+1$). The Participants submodel is an SVM that assigns a score to the basic features of all members during each three slice sliding subwindow in the full interval. More intuitively: the Individual submodel finds correlations among the child's observable behaviors over a window of time; the Participants submodel captures relationships between members' behaviors that co-occur over small subwindows; and the *Group-History* model combines the two to find regularities that unfold among participants over time, weighted toward P_1's own behavior.

The final model of interest, *Group-History-Word* (*g+w+h*(N,K,M,Q)), incorporates the knowledge from all sources of information. A Lexical submodel is added to the Individual and Participants submodels described above. The Lexical submodel is an SVM classifier trained on the combination of basic and word features for the current and Q previous time slices. The second layer SVM is trained on the scores of the Individual, Participants, and Lexical submodels as well as the combined basic and word feature vector for the child.

Model	Max f1	AUC	TPR	TNR
Basic features				
g-w-h-	0.879	0.504	0.823	0.604
g+w-h-	**0.903**	0.588	**0.872**	0.650
g-w-h(8,1)	0.897	0.626	0.867	0.697
g+w-h(4,1,8)	**0.903**	**0.645**	0.849	**0.730**
Basic + Word features				
g-w+h-	0.904	0.636	**0.901**	0.675
g+w+h-	0.906	0.655	0.863	0.728
g-w+h(8,1)	0.901	0.661	0.886	0.716
g+w+h(4,1,8,4)	**0.913**	**0.701**	0.859	**0.786**

Table 2: Comparison of models

5 Results and Discussions

We used the LibSVM implementation (Chang and Lin, 2011) for evaluation, holding out one child's data at a time during training, and balancing the data set to compensate for the uneven distribution of CHAR and NCHAR utterances in the corpus. As previously noted, we used a time slice of 500 msec in all results reported here. Where history is used, we consider only models with a single time slice of look-ahead ($K = 1$) to create minimal additional delay in the character's response.

Table 2 reports average values, for each model and over all sets of remaining children, in terms of Max F_1, true positive rate (TPR), true negative rate (TNR), and area under the TPR-TNR curve (AUC). TPR represents a model's ability to recognize utterances directed to the character; low TPR means children will not be able to play the game effectively. TNR indicates a model's ability to ignore utterances directed to other participants; low TNR means that the character will consider changing the game state when it hasn't been addressed.

Table 2 (top) shows comparative performance without the need for any speech recognition. F_1 and TPR are generally high for all models. Using only the basic features, however, gives a relatively low TNR and an AUC that is almost random. The *History* model, (*g-w-h(8,1)*), increased performance across all measures compared to the basic features (*g-w-h-*). We found that the *History* model's performance was best when four seconds of the past were considered. Group information within a single time slice also improves performance over the basic features, but the *Group-History* model has the best overall tradeoff in missed CHAR versus ignored NCHAR utterances (AUC). *Group-History's* best performance is achieved using two seconds of group information from the past via the Participants submodel and four seconds of the speaker's past from the Individual submodel.

Comparing the top and bottom halves of Table 2 shows that all models benefit from accurate recognition of a small set of task-independent words. The table shows that word spotting improves both TPR and TNR when added to the *Basic* model, but tends to improve only TNR when added to models with group and history features. Improved TNR probably results from the ability to detect NCHAR utterances when participants are facing the characters and/or pointing during naming discussions and comments.[2]

Table 2 shows results averaged over each held out child. We then recast this information to show, by model, the percentage of children that would experience TPR and TNR higher than given thresholds. Figure 3 shows a small portion of a complete graph of this type; in this case the percentage of children who would experience greater than 0.6 for TPR and greater than 0.5 for TNR under each model. TPR and TNR lines for a model have the same color and share a common pattern.

Better models have higher TPR and TNR for more children. The child who has to keep restating his or her choice (poor TPR) will be frustrated, as will the child who has the character pre-emptively take his or her choice away by "overhearing" side discussions (poor TNR). While we do not know for any child (or any age group) how high a TPR or TNR is required to prevent frustration, Figure 3 shows that without lexical information the *Group-History* and *Group* models have the best balance for the thresholds. *Group-History* gives about 85% of the children a TPR ≥ 0.7 for a TNR ≥ 0.5. The simpler *Group* model, which has no 500 msec delay for lookahead, can give a better TPR for the same TNR but for only 75% of the children. When we add lexical knowledge the case for *Group-History* becomes stronger, as it gives more than 85% of children a TPR ≥ 0.7 for a TNR ≥ 0.6, while *Group* gives 85% of children about the same TPR with a TNR ≥ 0.5.

[2]Results showing the affect of including object choice words in the *w+* models are given in Figure 4 in the Appendix.

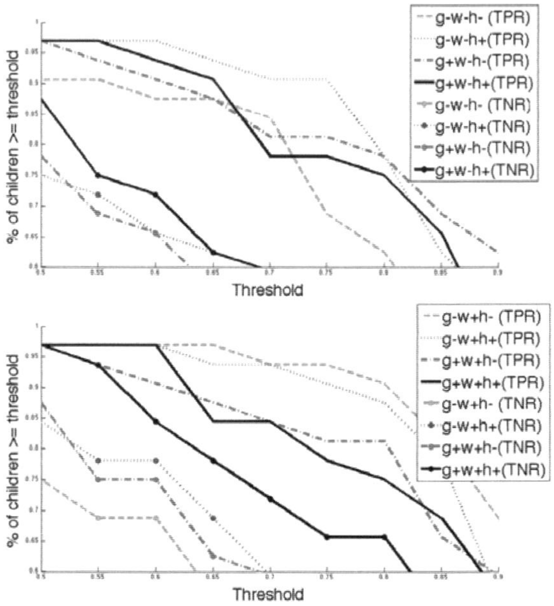

Figure 3: The percentage of children experiencing different TPR/TNR tradeoffs in models with (*bottom*) and without (*top*) lexical knowledge. The g-w-h- model does not fall in the region of interest unless lexical features are used.

6 Conclusions and Future Work

The behavior of the characters, types of games, group make up, and physical environment all contribute to how participants communicate over time and signal addressee. We can manipulate some relationships (e.g., by organizing the spatial layout to promote head movement or having the character use examples of recognizable language) and take advantage of others by detecting relevant features and learning how they combine as behavior unfolds. Our best current model uses group and history information as well as basic audio-visual features to achieve a max F_1 of 0.91 and an AUC of 0.70. Although this model does not yet perform as well as human annotators, it may be possible to improve it by taking advantage of additional features that the behavioral data tells us are predictive (e.g., whether the speaker is an adult or child). Such additional sources of information are likely to be important as we replace the annotated data with automatic sensors for speech activity, orientation, and gesture recognition, and embed addressee identification in the larger context of turn-taking and full autonomous interaction.

References

I. Bakx, K. van Turnhout, and J. Terken. 2003. Facial orientation during multi-party interaction with information kiosks. pages 701–704.

K. Bergmann, H. Rieser, and S. Kopp. 2011. Regulating dialogue with gestures towards an empirically grounded simulation with conversational agents. In *Annual Meeting of the Special Interest Group on Discourse and Dialogue (SIGDIAL)*, pages 88–97.

Matthew Black, Jeannette Chang, Jonathan Chang, and Shrikanth S. Narayanan. 2009. Comparison of child-human and child-computer interactions based on manual annotations. In *Proceedings of the Workshop on Child, Computer and Interaction*, Cambridge, MA.

D. Bohus and E. Horvitz. 2009a. Dialog in the open world: Platform and applications. In *Proceedings of the International Conference on Multimodal Interfaces (ICMI)*, pages 31–38.

D. Bohus and E. Horvitz. 2009b. Learning to predict engagement with a spoken dialog system in open-world settings. In *Annual Meeting of the Special Interest Group on Discourse and Dialogue (SIGDIAL)*, pages 244–252.

D. Bohus and E. Horvitz. 2011. Multiparty turn taking in situated dialog: Study, lessons, and directions. In *Annual Meeting of the Special Interest Group on Discourse and Dialogue (SIGDIAL)*, pages 98–109.

C. Chang and C. Lin. 2011. LIBSVM: A library for support vector machines. *ACM Transaction on Intelligent Systems and Technologies*, 2:27:1–27:27.

L. Chen and M. Harper. 2009. Multimodal floor control shift detection. In *Proceedings of the International Conference on Multimodal Interfaces (ICMI)*.

C. Clemens and C. Diekhaus. 2009. Prosodic turn-yielding cues with and without optical feedback. In *Annual Meeting of the Special Interest Group on Discourse and Dialogue (SIGDIAL)*, pages 107–110.

C. Cortes and V. Vapnik. 1995. Support-vector networks. *Machine Learning Journal*, 20.

S. Duncan and D. W. Fiske. 1977. *Face-to-Face Interaction: Research, Methods and Theory*. Lawrence Erlbaum.

I. Fasel, M. Shiomi, T. Kanda, N. Hagita, P. Chadutaud, and H. Ishiguro. 2009. Multi-modal features for real-time detection of human-robot interaction categories. In *Proceedings of the International Conference on Multimodal Interfaces (ICMI)*, pages 15–22.

Christiane Fellbaum, editor. 1998. *WordNet: An Electronic Lexical Database*. MIT Press, Cambridge, MA.

A. Gravano and J. Hirschberg. 2009. Turn-yielding cues in task-oriented dialogue. In *Annual Meeting of the Special Interest Group on Discourse and Dialogue (SIGDIAL)*, pages 253–261.

N. Jovanovic, H.J.A. op den Akker, and A. Nijholt. 2006. Addressee identification in face-to-face meetings. In *Conference of the European Chapter of the Association for Computational Linguistics (EACL)*, pages 169–176.

M. Katzenmaier, R. Steifelhagen, and T. Schultz. 2004. Identifying the addressee in human-human-robot interactions based on head pose and speech. In *Proceedings of the International Conference on Multimodal Interfaces (ICMI)*, pages 144–151.

John D. Lafferty, Andrew McCallum, and Fernando C. N. Pereira. 2001. Conditional random fields: Probabilistic models for segmenting and labeling sequence data. In *Proceedings of the International Conference on Machine Learning (ICML)*, pages 282–289.

R. Lunsford and S. Oviatt. 2006. Human perception of intended addressee during computer assisted meetings. In *Proceedings of the International Conference on Multimodal Interfaces (ICMI)*, pages 20–27.

Y. Matsusaka, M. Enomoto, and Y. Den. 2007. Simultaneous prediction of dialog acts and address types in three party conversations. In *Proceedings of the International Conference on Multimodal Interfaces (ICMI)*, pages 66–73.

Sharon Oviatt. 2000. Talking to thimble jellies: children's conversational speech with animated characters. pages 877–880.

J. Terken, I. Joris, and L. de Valk. 2007. Multimodal cues for addressee hood in triadic communication with a human information retrieval agent. In *Proceedings of the International Conference on Multimodal Interfaces (ICMI)*.

7 Appendix

Object Choice Words	
	antler, antlers, horn, horns, ear, ears, head, brown
	astronaut, astronauts, space, spaceman, spacemans, spacemen, helmet, head
	bear, bears claw, claws, paw, paws, hand, hands, brown
	bunny, rabbit, bunnies, rabbits, slipper, slippers, foot, feet, white
Task-independent Words	
Discourse marker	hmm, mm, mmm, ok, eww, shh, oopsy
Question words	what, let, where, who, which, when
Greetings	hi, hello, bye, goodbye

Table 3: Excerpts from the dictionary for task-specific and task-independent words

Model	Max f1	AUC	TPR	TNR
Greeting, question & discourse words				
g-w+h-	0.904	0.636	**0.901**	0.675
g+w+h-	0.906	0.655	0.863	0.728
g-w+h(8,1)	0.901	0.661	0.886	0.716
g+w+h(4,1,8,4)	**0.913**	**0.701**	0.859	0.786
With object reference words added				
g-w+h-	0.894	0.576	0.777	0.768
g+w+h-	0.898	0.623	0.782	0.773
g-w+h(7,1)	0.910	0.642	0.838	0.783
g+w+h(4,1,8,4)	0.912	0.685	0.834	**0.799**

Table 4: The effect of adding object reference words

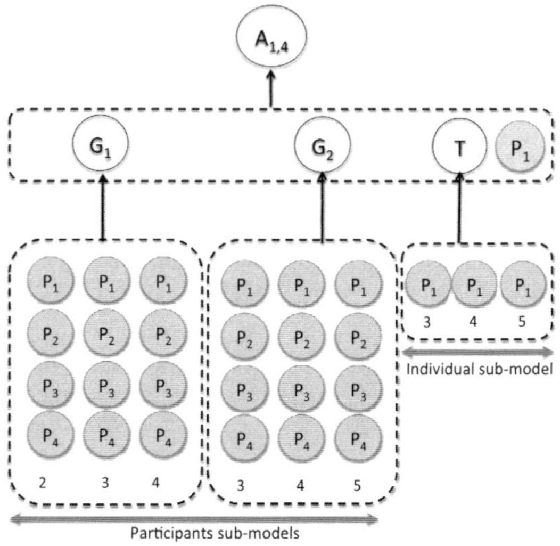

Figure 4: A concrete representation for the *Group-History* model with $N = 2$, $M = 1$, and $K = 1$ at time step $t = 4$. The value at $t = 4$ is delayed one time slice of real time.

Session Type	Group: participant(age)	Duration
full	p1(5), experimenter	9 min
full	p2(7), p3(6), p6(adult)	9 min
full	p4(7), p5 (4), p6(adult)	9 min
replay	p2(7), p3(6), p4(7), p5(4)	8 min
full	p7(10), experimenter	8 min
replay	p7(10)	6 min
full	p8(9), p9(8), experimenter	9 min
full	p10(10), p11(5), experimenter	11 min
full	p12(6), p14(adult)	11 min
full	p13(4), p14(adult)	11 min
full	p15(4), experimenter	8 min
full	p16(9), p17(7), experimenter	12 min
replay	p16(9), experimenter	3 min
full	p18(8), p19(6), p20(8), p21(adult)	12 min
full	p22(5), experimenter	9 min
replay	p22(5), experimenter	3 min
full	p25(6), experimenter	9 min
full	p26(8), p27(4), experimenter	11 min
replay	p26(8), experimenter	6 min
full	p28(7), p29(adult)	12 min
full	p30(5), experimenter	11 min
replay	p30(5), experimenter	4 min
full	p31(6), p32(5), p33(adult)	10 min
full	p34(4), p35(adult)	9 min
replay	p34(4), p35(adult)	4 min

Table 5: Details for sessions used in the analysis (does not include five sessions with corrupted data)

Adapting to Multiple Affective States in Spoken Dialogue

Kate Forbes-Riley
Learning R&D Ctr (LRDC)
University of Pittsburgh
Pittsburgh, PA 15260, USA
forbesk@cs.pitt.edu

Diane Litman
LRDC and Dept. Computer Science
University of Pittsburgh
Pittsburgh, PA 15260, USA
litman@cs.pitt.edu

Abstract

We evaluate a wizard-of-oz spoken dialogue system that adapts to multiple user affective states in real-time: user disengagement and uncertainty. We compare this version with the prior version of our system, which only adapts to user uncertainty. Our analysis investigates how iteratively adding new affect adaptation to an existing affect-adaptive system impacts global and local performance. We find a significant increase in motivation for users who most frequently received the disengagement adaptation. Moreover, responding to disengagement breaks its negative correlations with task success and user satisfaction, reduces uncertainty levels, and reduces the likelihood of continued disengagement.

1 Introduction

State of the art spoken dialogue system research focuses on responding not only to the literal content of users' speech but also to their affective state[1], such that the same literal content may receive one system response when the user is frustrated, and another when the user is confused, etc. The potential benefits are clear: affect-adaptive systems can increase task success (Forbes-Riley and Litman, 2011a; Wang et al., 2008) and other global performance metrics such as user satisfaction (Liu and Picard, 2005; Klein et al., 2002) and motivation (Aist et al., 2002). However, to date most researchers have focused on adapting to a single affective state. The next step is thus to develop and evaluate spoken dialogue systems that respond to multiple user affective states. The problem of how to develop effective affect adaptations is a complex one even as applied to a single affective state, and it multiples with every new state added. For example, it is not clear a priori how responding to one affective state may impact another's frequency and relationship to performance. In this paper we examine this problem in the context of the computer tutoring domain. We previously showed that adapting to user *uncertainty* during spoken dialogue computer tutoring improves task success, both in a wizard-of oz version where a hidden human performed the affect detection and natural language understanding (Forbes-Riley and Litman, 2011b), as well as in a fully automated system version (Forbes-Riley and Litman, 2011a).

We are now taking the next step by incorporating adaptation to a second user affective state: user *disengagement*. We target user disengagement for two reasons: first, our prior manual annotation showed disengagement and uncertainty to be the most frequent user affective states that occur in our system, and second, our prior analyses show that the occurrence of disengagement is negatively correlated with task success and user satisfaction (Forbes-Riley and Litman, 2012).[2] Thus, we hypothesized that providing appropriate system responses to both affective states could have multiple benefits: 1) reduce the frequency of one or both states, 2) "break" the nega-

[1]We use *affect* for emotions and attitudes that affect how users communicate. Other speech researchers also combine concepts of emotion, arousal, and attitudes where emotion is not full-blown (Cowie and Cornelius, 2003).

[2]Redesigning a system in light of correlational analyses can improve performance (Rotaru and Litman, 2009).

tive correlations with performance, and 3) yield further improvements in global and local performance.

In this paper, we test these hypotheses, presenting the results of a controlled experiment evaluating a wizard-of-oz version of our spoken dialogue computer tutor that adapts to both user uncertainty and user disengagement (Section 3). Although we address these states within the tutoring domain, speech researchers from other domains and applications are also focusing on detecting and adapting to user disengagement (e.g., (Schuller et al., 2010; Wang and Hirschberg, 2011)) and uncertainty (e.g. (Pon-Barry and Shieber, 2011; Paek and Ju, 2008)) to improve system performance. Our results should be of interest not only to these researchers but also more generally to any researchers working towards comprehensive affect-adaptive spoken dialogue systems. In particular, our results show that iteratively adding new affect adaptations to an existing affect-adaptive system can yield performance improvements. We find no increase (but also no decrease) in task success or user satisfaction, but we do find an increase in motivation for users who most frequently received the disengagement adaptation (Section 4). Furthermore, we find that responding to disengagement "breaks" negative correlations with task success and user satisfaction (Section 5), and also yields a reduction both in uncertainty levels (Section 4) and in the likelihood of continued disengagement (Section 6).

2 Related Work

User disengagement is highly undesirable because of its potential to increase dissatisfaction and task failure, and there is a growing awareness of its potential to negatively impact commercial applications; thus there has been substantial prior work focused on detecting disengagement (along with the closely related states of boredom and lack of interest) (e.g., (Schuller et al., 2010; Wang and Hirschberg, 2011; Bohus and Horvitz, 2009)). To date, however, only a few disengagement-adaptive systems have been evaluated, and within the tutoring domain these have focused on only one disengagement behavior: *gaming*. For example, responding to gaming with supplementary material reduced gaming and improved task success for users who most frequently gamed (Baker et al., 2006), while adding progress reports and productive learning tips at the end of problems (i.e., without specifically targeting gaming instances) increased task success, engagement, and user satisfaction (Arroyo et al., 2007). Our research builds on this work but is novel in that we focus on speech and dialogue-based disengagement and on adapting to multiple affective states.

More generally, while substantial spoken dialogue and affective systems research has shown that users display a range of affective states when interacting with a system (e.g. (Schuller et al., 2009; Conati and Maclaren, 2009)), to date only a few systems adapt to multiple affective states (e.g., (D'Mello et al., 2010; Aist et al., 2002; Tsukahara and Ward, 2001)). Most have been deployed with wizard-of-oz components, and none have yet shown significant improvements in task success, though other benefits have been shown, including increased user satisfaction (Tsukahara and Ward, 2001), rapport (Acosta and Ward, 2011) and motivation (Aist et al., 2002). Recently, D'Mello et al. (2010) showed that performance can depend on when and to whom the adaptations are provided; higher expertise users never benefited from system responses to their frustration, boredom and confusion, while lower expertise users only benefited after multiple system interactions. While this prior work showed the benefits of adapting to multiple affective states as compared to not adapting to affect at all, it did not test whether these benefits were due to having multiple adaptations, or if any one would have sufficed. Our work is novel in explicitly measuring the value of having multiple adaptations as compared to one.

3 The Experiment

Our prior work showed that our uncertainty-adaptive spoken dialogue system improves performance over not adapting to affect (Forbes-Riley and Litman, 2011b; Forbes-Riley and Litman, 2011a); this system serves as our baseline in the current work.

3.1 Baseline System: UNC_ADAPT ITSPOKE

UNC_ADAPT ITSPOKE (**I**ntelligent **T**utoring **SPOKE**n dialog system)[3] tutors 5 Newtonian

[3]ITSPOKE is a speech-enhanced and modified version of the Why2-Atlas text-based tutor (VanLehn et al., 2002).

physics problems (one per dialogue), using a Tutor Question - User Answer - Tutor Response format.

In the fully automated system, the speech from the user's answer is digitized from head-mounted microphone input and sent to a speech recognizer. The answer's (in)correctness is then automatically classified based on the recognizer's transcription using a semantic analysis component, and the answer's (un)certainty is automatically classified by inputting features of the speech signal (e.g. prosody), the automatic transcript, and the dialogue context into a logistic regression model. The (in)correctness and (un)certainty detection components comprising our system's user model are described in detail elsewhere (Forbes-Riley and Litman, 2011a).

For the present experiment, the affect and (in)correctness labeling are performed by a hidden human wizard. As in our prior work, this allows us to first analyze the impact of an affect adaptation separately from the noise introduced by automating affect and semantic analysis (see Section 7). Figures 1-3 illustrate the binary (dis)engagement (ENG, DISE), (in)correctness (COR, INC), and (un)certainty (CER, UNC) labels.

Finally, the system automatically determines the appropriate response based on the answer's labeled (in)correctness and (un)certainty and this response is sent to the Cepstral text-to-speech system[4], whose audio output is played through the headphones and displayed on a web-based interface (see Figure 4).

The uncertainty label and system adaptation are described in detail elsewhere (Forbes-Riley and Litman, 2011b; Forbes-Riley and Litman, 2011a). Briefly, the *uncertain (UNC)* label is used for turns expressing uncertainty or confusion about the topic being discussed, and the *non-uncertain (CER)* label is used otherwise. The wizard in this experiment displayed interannotator agreement of 0.85 and 0.62 Kappa on correctness and uncertainty, respectively, in prior ITSPOKE corpora. Our uncertainty adaptation is based on the hypothesis that uncertainty and incorrectness are both points of impasse in a dialogue, and that providing additional knowledge can help resolve them. In UNC_ADAPT ITSPOKE, incorrect answers and uncertain answers both receive (in)correctness feedback (e.g., "Right" or "I don't think so"), followed by a (re)statement of the correct answer. Depending on topic difficulty, the system then either provides a brief explanation of reasoning ("Bottom Out") or a more lengthy dialogue exchange that walks the user through the steps of the reasoning ("Remediation Subdialogue"). An example is shown in Figure 1.

3.2 UNC-DISE_ADAPT ITSPOKE

UNC-DISE_ADAPT ITSPOKE adds disengagement detection and adaptation to UNC_ADAPT ITSPOKE. Our disengagement annotation scheme is described in detail elsewhere (Forbes-Riley and Litman, 2011c). It was derived from empirical observation of our data and from prior work, including that mentioned in Section 2 and appraisal theory-based emotion models, which distinguish emotional behaviors from their underlying causes (e.g., (Conati and Maclaren, 2009)). Briefly, the *Disengaged (DISE)* label is used for turns expressing moderate to strong disengagement towards the interaction, i.e., responses given without much effort or caring about appropriateness, and might include signs of boredom or irritation. Clear examples include turns spoken in leaden monotone, with sarcasm, or off-task sounds such as electronics usage. The wizard in this experiment displayed interannotator agreement of 0.55 Kappa on the DISE label in prior ITSPOKE corpora, which is on par with prior affect research, where moderate agreement is common given the difficulty of the task (Forbes-Riley and Litman, 2011c).

Based on the results of the prior research discussed in Section 2 and our own prior research, we have developed one class of system responses for correct+disengaged (COR-DISE) answers and another for incorrect+disengaged (INC-DISE) answers (Forbes-Riley and Litman, 2011c)[5].

Our INC-DISE adaptation builds on the prior finding that supplementary information can help reduce some types of disengagement for highly disengaged users (Baker et al., 2006). We hypothesized that our UNC_ADAPT response to incorrectness (a Bottom Out or Remediation Subdialogue) was insufficient for an INC-DISE turn because the

[4]an outgrowth of Festival (Black and Taylor, 1997).

[5]Originally we distinguished six DISE types, but found this too many to be reliably detected automatically and thus reduced the distinction to two using correctness. Our automatic disengagement detector is discussed further in Section 7.

user had already disengaged. To benefit from this supplementary knowledge, the user first had to reengage. Thus, the UNC-DISE_ADAPT system responds to INC-DISE answers with "productive interaction feedback"[6] followed by an easier "fill in the blank" version of the original question. The purpose of this two-pronged response is to regain the user's attention with the feedback and then provide a path through the impasse with the easier question, thereby keeping the user engaged. An example is shown in Figure 2, where **USER-1** is labeled INC-DISE because the user gives an irrelevant (and obviously incorrect) answer. Note that while most knowledge asymmetry spoken dialogue systems (e.g., problem-solving and troubleshooting (Janarthanam and Lemon, 2008)) use the concept of response *(in)correctness*, a more general version is response *(in)appropriateness*, which can be realized differently across applications, including as the user turn's speech recognition score (Kamm et al., 1998). Since misrecognitions are also a type of dialogue impasse, a similar version of our INC-DISE adaptation could be provided by other spoken dialogue systems for turns where users disengage and their response isn't recognized by the system.

Our COR-DISE adaptation builds on the prior findings that progress reports and productive learning tips can positively impact multiple performance metrics when used without specifically targeting disengagement (Arroyo et al., 2007), but not when used after every user turn (Walonoski and Heffernan, 2006). We hypothesized that these responses might be most beneficial if they targeted COR-DISE turns. Thus, the UNC-DISE_ADAPT system responds to COR-DISE answers with "productive interaction feedback" followed by a progress report graphing the user's correctness both in the current dialogue and over all prior dialogues. Examples are shown in Figures 3-4, where **USER-1** is labeled COR-DISE because the user unnecessarily repeats himself, signaling his lack of interest. As shown, we distinguish two classes of productive interaction feedback. That in "2a" shows the feedback given when the progress report indicates improvement on the current dialogue relative to the prior ones, while "2b" shows the feedback given when there is a decline. Note that a similar combination of productive interaction feedback and progress reports tailored to the domain (e.g., graphs showing subtasks accomplished so far) could be provided by most spoken dialogue systems on turns where users disengage and their response is recognized by the system.[7]

3.3 Experimental Procedure

College students with no college-level physics were recruited and randomly assigned to either the UNC_ADAPT or UNC-DISE_ADAPT condition after balancing for user expertise (pretest score) and gender. Users: (1) read a short physics text, (2) took a pretest and a pre-motivation survey, (3) worked 5 "training" problem dialogues with the system from their condition, (4) took a post-motivation survey and a user satisfaction survey, (5) took a posttest isomorphic to the pretest, and (6) worked a "test" problem dialogue with UNC_ADAPT.

The pre/post tests are the same as those used in multiple prior ITSPOKE experiments (c.f., (Forbes-Riley and Litman, 2011a)). The tests are isomorphic, each containing 26 multiple choice questions querying knowledge of the topics covered in the dialogues. Average pretest and posttest scores were 53% and 81% (out of 100%), respectively.

The pre/post motivation surveys are a reduced version of a widely used motivation survey in the tutoring domain (Pintrich and DeGroot, 1990); our selected questions were relevant to our system and also selected in other recent research (Ward, 2010; Roll, 2009). The two surveys are isomorphic, each containing 19 statements rated on a 7-point Likert scale. Average pre and post scores were 68% and 70% (out of 100%), respectively.

The user satisfaction survey was recently developed and validated for use with spoken dialogue computer tutors (Dzikovska et al., 2011). It contains 40 statements rated on a 5-point Likert scale. Average score was 68% (out of 100%).

The "test" dialogue is isomorphic to the fifth training dialogue, such that all questions are identical except for the identities of the objects discussed. In this way, we can measure how the disengagement

[6] This is our generalization of the concept of "productive learning tip" used in prior work (Arroyo et al., 2007).

[7] Note that our DISE and UNC adaptations are combined if the two states occur simultaneously.

adaptations from the fifth dialogue impact user turns when the questions are repeated in the test dialogue (where no disengagement adaptation is given). We have also used this test dialogue in our prior work (c.f., (Forbes-Riley and Litman, 2011a)).

3.4 Corpus

The resulting corpus contains 228 dialogues (6 per user) and 3518 turns from 38 users, 22 female and 16 male, with 19 subjects per condition.[8] Table 1 shows the distribution of the labeled turns in the corpus.

Table 1: Corpus Description (N=3518)

Turn Label	Total	Percent
Disengaged	622	17.7%
Correct	2825	80.3%
Disengaged+Correct	247	7.0%
Uncertain	537	15.3%

4 Global Performance Evaluation

We use the test and survey instruments described in Section 3.3 to evaluate global performance in UNC-DISE_ADAPT. We measure task success via learning gain; as is typical in the tutoring community, we compute normalized learning gain as (posttest-pretest)/(1-pretest). We compute percent user satisfaction from the survey as (user score)/(maximum possible score). We compute raw motivation gain from the surveys as (post score-pre score).[9] For each metric, we ran a one-way ANOVA with condition as the between-subjects factor. The first two rows of Table 2 show the number of users (N), means (Mn) and standard deviations (sd) for these metrics across condition. Although UNC-DISE_ADAPT shows a small decrease in means for learning gain and user satisfaction, there were no significant differences ($p \leq .05$) or trends ($p \leq .10$) for differences between conditions for any global metric.

As a further comparison, we compared the performance of UNC-DISE_ADAPT to our non-adaptive wizard-of-oz version of ITSPOKE (NO_ADAPT), using the corpus collected from our prior user study comparing UNC_ADAPT and NO_ADAPT; that study showed UNC_ADAPT had significantly higher learning gain than NO_ADAPT (p=.001) (Forbes-Riley and Litman, 2011b).[10] The goal here was to ascertain in a post-hoc way whether adapting to multiple affective states yielded higher task success than not adapting to affect at all. As shown last in Table 2, UNC-DISE_ADAPT and UNC_ADAPT both significantly outperform NO_ADAPT ($p \leq .003$), suggesting that while iteratively adding new affect adaptations to an existing affect-adaptive system does not necessarily yield additive improvements to global performance, it also does not decrease performance.

Table 2: Global Performance Metrics Across Conditions (All UNC vs. UNC-DISE Differences Yield $p >= .274$; All NO-ADAPT Differences Yield $p \leq .003$)

Cond	N	LearnGain		UserSat		MotGain	
		Mn	sd	Mn	sd	Mn	sd
Unc	19	.65	.20	.69	.11	.01	.07
Unc-Dise	19	.58	.19	.66	.09	.01	.07
NoAdapt	21	.38	.20	-	-	-	-

The frequency of disengagement and other affective states can vary widely across system users. In our case, some users showed disengagement on the majority of turns in later dialogues while others showed almost none at all; the average and standard deviation of per user %DISE over conditions are 17.7% and 10.1%, respectively (Table 5 breaks this down by condition). Thus we hypothesized that the global performance improvements of UNC-DISE_ADAPT might have been weakened by including users with low or no disengagement who rarely received the adaptation and thus could not be expected to show improvement. To test this hypothesis, we split users into *high* and *low* DISE based on the median %DISE in the corpus. We ran a two-way ANOVA for each global metric with DISE split and condition as factors. We found a significant interaction effect between condition and DISE

[8]One outlier with negative learning was removed from each condition, because our goal is to investigate the role of affect adaptation when learning is successful.

[9]Total, average or percent satisfaction yielded comparable results, as did raw or normalized motivation and learning gains.

[10]Because this prior corpus was collected in a different experiment, the conclusions here are tenuous. However, both experiments had similar subject populations (local college students) and mean pretest scores (p=.84). The prior experiment used a smaller satisfaction survey and no motivational surveys, so we can only compare learning.

split (F(1,38) = 4.84, p=0.035) for motivation gain. Means for these groups are shown in Table 3. As shown, *low* DISE users had higher motivation gain in UNC_ADAPT, while *high* DISE users had higher motivation gain in UNC-DISE_ADAPT.

Table 3: Motivation Gain Differences Across Condition for High and Low DISE Users (p=.035)

Condition	Split	N	MotGain	
			Mn	sd
UNC	high DISE	9	-.01	.04
UNC-DISE	high DISE	7	.04	.07
UNC	low DISE	10	.03	.08
UNC-DISE	low DISE	12	-.01	.06

In contrast to the tests and surveys, which do not necessarily reflect user performance during the dialogues, the "test" dialogue enables us to measure global performance using dialogue-based metrics. The test dialogue was isomorphic with the final training dialogue, except that the disengagement adaptation was not given; moreover, different system questions could appear in the test dialogue if the user answered a question differently.[11] We hypothesized that responding to the user's disengagement during the training dialogue (UNC-DISE_ADAPT) would yield increased correctness as well as reduced uncertainty and disengagement in the test dialogue.

We tested this hypothesis by computing percent correctness, disengagement, and uncertainty for each user, both alone and in combination, over user answers to tutor questions that were repeated between the training and test dialogues. We ran ANOVAs comparing these metrics across the two conditions. Table 4 presents our results. Interestingly, no differences between conditions were found for transitions from DISE turns. However, the disengagement adaptation did impact other turns in the dialogues apart from the (DISE) ones that triggered it. The first row shows that uncertain answers are more likely to remain uncertain in UNC_ADAPT than in UNC-DISE_ADAPT. The second row shows that incorrect+uncertain+engaged answers are more likely to become correct and certain in UNC-DISE_ADAPT. By more fully engaging users, the disengagement adaptation may thereby enable them to benefit more from the uncertainty adaptation. However, the third row suggests that the adaptation can have a negative impact when users are originally certain about their incorrect answers: incorrect+certain+engaged users turns are more likely to become disengaged in UNC-DISE_ADAPT. This suggests that the disengagement adaptation does not more fully engage certain users (particularly those whose certainty does not reflect correctness).

[11]For example, if a user answered a question incorrectly during training and then answered its isomorph correctly during testing, s/he would not receive the remediation during the test dialogue that s/he received during training.

Table 4: Differences Across Condition for Test Dialogue

Metric	Condition	Mn	sd	p
UNC $\rightarrow$ UNC	UNC	.06	.09	.05
	UNC-DISE	.01	.04	
INC+UNC+ENG $\rightarrow$	UNC	.01	.03	.10
COR+CER+ENG	UNC-DISE	.03	.05	
INC+CER+ENG $\rightarrow$	UNC	.00	.00	.04
INC+CER+DISE	UNC-DISE	.02	.03	

5 Breaking Negative Correlations

As noted in Section 1, in our prior ITSPOKE corpora we found that user disengagement was negatively correlated with task success (measured as learning gain) (p=.01) and user satisfaction (p=.03) (Forbes-Riley and Litman, 2011c; Forbes-Riley and Litman, 2012). Thus, one important standard of evaluation for our disengagement adaptation is to determine whether or not it "breaks" these negative correlations when it is employed with real users (Rotaru and Litman, 2009). A broken correlation would mean that even though disengagement may still occur, it no longer relates to decreased performance.

UNC-DISE_ADAPT responds differently to correct and incorrect DISE turns (Section 3.2). To compare the impacts of these responses both combined and individually, we computed %DISE, %correctDISE (CDISE) and %incorrectDISE (IDISE) for each user (over all five training problems). We then computed bivariate Pearson's correlations within each condition between each DISE metric and both learning and user satisfaction.

Table 5 shows the mean (Mn) and standard deviations (sd) for the DISE metrics within each condition, the coefficient (R) for each correlation, and its significance (p). Consider first task success. The first pair of rows shows that the negative correlation between DISE and learning is still present whether or not the disengagement adaptation is received. However, the second pair of rows shows that the negative correlation between %correctDISE and learning is broken when the disengagement adaptation is received (UNC-DISE), but is still present when not received (UNC). The third pair of rows shows that the disengagement adaptation does not break the negative correlation between %incorrect-DISE and learning. Consider next user satisfaction. The first pair of rows shows that the negative correlation between DISE and user satisfaction is broken when the disengagement adaptation is received (UNC-DISE), but is still present when not received (UNC). The third pair of rows shows that the the negative correlation between %incorrectDISE and user satisfaction is also broken when the disengagement adaptation is received (UNC-DISE), but is still present when not received (UNC). These results suggest that for improving task success, adapting to disengagement is more effective for correct turns than incorrect turns[12], while for improving user satisfaction, adapting to disengagement is effective for incorrect turns and for the dialogue as a whole without considering correctness. Finally, Table 5 shows that while %correctDISE is reduced in UNC-DISE as compared to UNC, %incorrectDISE actually increases in UNC-DISE. This suggests that while a reduction in disengagement due to the adaptation partially explains the broken correlations, the adaptation may also ameliorate the negative performance impact of user disengagement.

6 Local Affect Transition Analyses

In addition to global performance analyses, the impact of affect adaptation can also be evaluated *locally*, i.e., in terms of its immediate impact in the dialogue. We investigate this local effect by computing the likelihoods of transitioning from each user

[12]Users who are more often correct may also be predisposed to learn more. This may explain why %correctDISE has a lesser negative impact on learning than %DISE and %incorrectDISE in UNC and UNC-DISE. However, only the disengagement adaptation can explain why %correctDISE has a lesser negative impact on learning in UNC-DISE than in UNC.

Table 5: Disengagement-Performance Correlations Across Conditions (Bold Indicates "Broken" Correlation)

	Mn	sd	LGain		UserSat	
			R	p	R	p
%DISE in:						
UNC	17.2	12.1	-.77	.01	-.48	**.04**
UNC-DISE	16.9	7.9	-.65	.01	-.16	**.51**
%CDISE in:						
UNC	7.7	7.6	-.45	**.05**	-.14	.56
UNC-DISE	6.1	3.3	.25	**.31**	-.27	.27
%IDISE in:						
UNC	9.5	7.7	-.76	.01	-.61	**.01**
UNC-DISE	10.8	7.7	-.78	.01	-.05	**.83**

disengagement state in turn *n* (DISE or ENG) to each user disengagement state in turn *n+1* (DISE or ENG). We use the *transition likelihood L* metric (D'Mello et al., 2007), which has also previously been used by ourselves and others to compute the likelihood of transitioning from one affective state to another in a dialogue corpus and to compare these likelihoods across different system versions (Forbes-Riley and Litman, 2011a; McQuiggan et al., 2008; D'Mello et al., 2007). As in this prior work, we compute the transition likelihoods for each user (over all 5 training dialogues), then use ANOVAs to determine if there were differences in the likelihoods of all possible transitions from the user state in turn *n*.

Transition likelihood L is computed as shown below, where *n* refers to the disengagement state in turn *n* and *n+1* refers to the state in turn *n+1*. As shown, L computes the likelihood that the n→n+1 transition will occur. L=1 indicates that n+1 always follows n, while L=0 and L<0 indicate that the likelihood of transitioning from n to n+1 is equal to chance, and less than chance, respectively.

$$\mathbf{L(n \rightarrow n+1)} = \frac{P(n+1|n) - P(n+1)}{1 - P(n+1)}$$

We hypothesized that users in the UNC-DISE_ADAPT condition would be less likely to transition into disengagement in turn *n+1*. Mean L values across users for each transition are shown in Table 6 for the two conditions, where the rows represent each turn *n* state and the columns represent each turn *n+1* state. The p-value from the ANOVA for each transition likelihood comparison is also shown. The table shows that in both conditions, an engaged user in turn *n* is significantly more likely to remain engaged in turn *n+1* than s/he is to become disengaged. However, in UNC_ADAPT, a disengaged user is more likely (as a trend, p=.06) to remain disengaged than to become engaged in turn *n+1*. In contrast, in UNC-DISE_ADAPT, a disengaged user is equally likely (p=.14) to become disengaged or remain engaged in turn *n+1*. This analysis thus indicates that the disengagement adaptation also has a benefit at the local performance level, in that it reduces the likelihood of continued disengagement.

Table 6: Mean L Values for Disengagement State Transitions

Condition	Turn n	Turn n+1		
		ENG	DISE	p
UNC-DISE	ENG	.06	-.01	.04
	DISE	-.35	.06	.14
UNC	ENG	.09	-.03	.01
	DISE	-.41	.09	.06

7 Summary and Current Directions

We investigated how iteratively adding new affect adaptation to an affect-adaptive spoken dialogue system impacts global and local performance. We presented a disengagement adaptation that can generalize across domains, and discussed its incorporation into our uncertainty-adaptive computer tutor. We then presented a controlled evaluation comparing these multiply and singly adaptive systems. Our results showed that while the disengagement adaptation did not increase (or decrease) task success or user satisfaction, it demonstrated a slight but significant increase in motivation gain for users with high disengagement. Future analyses will shed further light on how disengagement mediates the effect of condition on motivation. The adaptation also reduced user uncertainty and increased correctness for uncertain answers when repeated in the test dialogue, but increased disengagement for repeated answers that were originally certain and incorrect. It also broke negative correlations between disengaged turns and performance, when measured both as task success and user satisfaction, and showed a trend to reduce disengagement at the local dialogue level.

Our next step is to repeat the experiment with fully automated versions of our affect-adaptive spoken dialogue systems, to determine the impact of adding new affect adaptation when the system performs the affect detection and natural language understanding tasks. We are currently in the last stages of building an automatic disengagement detector that will then be implemented in UNC-DISE_ITSPOKE. Interestingly, our prior work suggests that the fully automated UNC-DISE_ADAPT system may yield greater global performance improvements relative to UNC_ADAPT (Forbes-Riley and Litman, 2012) than the wizard-of-oz version of the system; it may be that users are more responsive to the disengagement adaptation when the affect detection and natural language understanding outputs are "noisier". Future work will also consider other experimental designs to help determine the separate and joint effects of the two affect adaptations.

Acknowledgments

This work is funded by NSF award 0914615. We thank Scott Silliman for experimental support.

References

J. C. Acosta and N. G. Ward. 2011. Achieving rapport with turn-by-turn, user-responsive emotional coloring. *Speech Communication*, 53(9-10):1137–1148.

G. Aist, B. Kort, R. Reilly, J. Mostow, and R. Picard. 2002. Experimentally augmenting an intelligent tutoring system with human-supplied capabilities: Adding human-provided emotional scaffolding to an automated reading tutor that listens. In *Proc. IEEE International Conference on Multimodal Interfaces (ICMI)*, pages 483–492, Washington, DC.

I. Arroyo, K. Ferguson, J. Johns, T. Dragon, H. Merheranian, D. Fisher, A. Barto, S. Mahadevan, and B. Woolf. 2007. Repairing disengagement with non-invasive interventions. In *Proc. Artificial Intelligence in Education (AIED)*, pages 195–202.

R. S. Baker, A. Corbett, K. Koedinger, S. Evenson, I. Roll, A. Wagner, M. Naim, J. Raspat, D. Baker, and J. Beck. 2006. Adapting to when students game an intelligent tutoring system. In *Proceedings Intelligent Tutoring Systems*, pages 392–401.

A. Black and P. Taylor. 1997. Festival speech synthesis system: system documentation (1.1.1). The Centre for Speech Technology Research, University of Edinburgh, http://www.cstr.ed.ac.uk/projects/festival/.

D. Bohus and E. Horvitz. 2009. Models for multiparty engagement in open-world dialog. In *Proceedings of SIGdial*, pages 225–234, London, UK.

C. Conati and H. Maclaren. 2009. Empirically building and evaluating a probabilistic model of user affect. *User Modeling and User-Adapted Interaction*, 19(3):267–303.

R. Cowie and R. R. Cornelius. 2003. Describing the emotional states that are expressed in speech. *Speech Communication*, 40(1-2):5–32.

S. D'Mello, R. S. Taylor, and A. Graesser. 2007. Monitoring affective trajectories during complex learning. In *Proc. Cognitive Science Society*, pages 203–208.

S. D'Mello, B. Lehman, J. Sullins, R. Daigle, R. Combs, K. Vogt, L. Perkins, and A. Graesser. 2010. A time for emoting: When affect-sensitivity is and isn't effective at promoting deep learning. In *Proc. Intelligent Tutoring Systems Conference*, pages 245–254, June.

M. Dzikovska, J. Moore, N. Steinhauser, and G. Campbell. 2011. Exploring user satisfaction in a tutorial dialogue system. In *Proc. SIGDIAL*, pages 162–172, Portland, Oregon, June.

K. Forbes-Riley and D. Litman. 2011a. Benefits and challenges of real-time uncertainty detection and adaptation in a spoken dialogue computer tutor. *Speech Communication*, 53(9–10):1115–1136.

K. Forbes-Riley and D. Litman. 2011b. Designing and evaluating a wizarded uncertainty-adaptive spoken dialogue tutoring system. *Computer Speech and Language (CSL)*, 25(1):105–126.

K. Forbes-Riley and D. Litman. 2011c. When does disengagement correlate with learning in spoken dialog computer tutoring? In *Proceedings of AIED*, Auckland, NZ, June.

K. Forbes-Riley and D. Litman. 2012. Intrinsic and extrinsic evaluation of an automatic user disengagement detector for an uncertainty-adaptive spoken dialogue system. In *Proc. NAACL-HLT*, Montreal, June.

S. Janarthanam and O. Lemon. 2008. User simulations for online adaptation and knowledge-alignment in troubleshooting dialogue systems. In *Proc. SEMdial.*

C. Kamm, D. Litman, and M. Walker. 1998. From novice to expert: The effect of tutorials on user expertise with spoken dialogue systems. In *Proceedings of the 5th International Conference on Spoken Language Processing*, pages 1211–1214.

J. Klein, Y. Moon, and R. Picard. 2002. This computer responds to user frustration: Theory, design, and results. *Interacting with Computers*, 14:119–140.

K. Liu and R. W. Picard. 2005. Embedded empathy in continuous, interactive health assessment. In *CHI Workshop on HCI Challenges in Health Assessment.*

S. W. McQuiggan, J. L Robison, and J. C. Lester. 2008. Affective transitions in narrative-centered learning environments. In *Proc. Intelligent Tutoring Systems Conference*, pages 490–499.

T. Paek and Y.-C. Ju. 2008. Accommodating explicit user expressions of uncertainty in voice search or something like that. In *Proceedings Interspeech)*, pages 1165–1168, Brisbane, Australia, September.

P. Pintrich and E. DeGroot. 1990. Motivational and self-regulated learning components of classroom academic performance. *Journal of Educational Psychology*, 82(1):33–40.

H. Pon-Barry and S. Shieber. 2011. Recognizing uncertainty in speech. *EURASIP Journal on Advances in Signal Processing.*

I. Roll. 2009. *Structured Invention Tasks to Prepare Students for Future Learning: Means, Mechanisms, and Cognitive Processes.* Ph.D. thesis, Carnegie Mellon University.

M. Rotaru and D. Litman. 2009. Discourse structure and performance analysis: Beyond the correlation. In *Proc. SIGDIAL*, pages 178–187, London, UK.

B. Schuller, S. Steidl, and A. Batliner. 2009. The Interspeech 2009 emotion challenge. In *Proc. Interspeech*, pages 312–315, ISCA, Brighton, UK, September.

B. Schuller, S. Steidl, A. Batliner, F. Burkhardt, L. Devillers, C. Muller, and S. Narayanan. 2010. The Interspeech 2010 paralinguistic challenge. In *Proc. Interspeech*, pages 2794–2797, Chiba, Japan, September.

W. Tsukahara and N. Ward. 2001. Responding to subtle, fleeting changes in the user's internal state. In *Proceedings of the SIG-CHI on Human factors in computing systems*, pages 77–84, Seattle, WA. ACM.

K. VanLehn, P. Jordan, C. Rosé, D. Bhembe, M. Böttner, A. Gaydos, M. Makatchev, U. Pappuswamy, M. Ringenberg, A. Roque, S. Siler, R. Srivastava, and R. Wilson. 2002. The architecture of Why2-Atlas: A coach for qualitative physics essay writing. In *Proc. Intelligent Tutoring Systems Conference*, pages 158–167.

J. Walonoski and N. Heffernan. 2006. Prevention of off-task gaming behavior in intelligent tutoring systems. In *Proc. Intelligent Tutoring Systems Conference (ITS)*, pages 722–724.

W. Wang and J. Hirschberg. 2011. Detecting levels of interest from spoken dialog with multistream prediction feedback and similarity based hierarchical fusion learning. In *Proc. SIGDIAL*, pages 152–161, Portland, Oregon, June.

N. Wang, W.L. Johnson, R. E. Mayer, P. Rizzo, E. Shaw, and H. Collins. 2008. The politeness effect: Pedagogical agents and learning outcomes. *International Journal of Human-Computer Studies*, 66(2):98–112.

A. Ward. 2010. *Reflection and Learning Robustness in a Natural Language Conceptual Physics Tutoring System.* Ph.D. thesis, University of Pittsburgh.

APPENDIX

UNC_ADAPT ITSPOKE: What are the forces exerted on the man after he releases his keys?

USER: gravity??? (COR, UNC, ENG)

UNC_ADAPT ITSPOKE: Right. *[Correctness Feedback]* Gravity is the only force acting on the man. This force is also called the weight of the man. It's always present when an object is in earth's gravitational field. *[Bottom Out]*. So what's the direction of the force of gravity on the man (e.g., vertically up)? *[Next Topic Question]*

Figure 1: Annotated Dialogue Example Showing Uncertainty Adaptation

UNC-DISE_ADAPT ITSPOKE-1: Let's begin by looking at the motion of the man and his keys while he's holding them. How does his velocity compare to that of his keys?

USER-1: vertical (INC, UNC, DISE)

UNC-DISE_ADAPT ITSPOKE-2: That doesn't sound right. Let's think about this a little more. *[Productive Interaction Feedback]* Since the man is holding his keys, they aren't moving relative to each other. So their velocities must be WHAT? *[Supplementary Question]*.

Figure 2: Dialogue Example Showing Adaptation for Disengaged+Incorrect Turns

UNC-DISE_ADAPT ITSPOKE-1: Let's begin by looking at the motion of the man and his keys while he's holding them. How does his velocity compare to that of his keys?

USER-1: same same same (COR, CER, DISE)

....

UNC-DISE_ADAPT ITSPOKE-2a: Well done. Here's a quick progress update. Good effort so far!!*[Productive Interaction Feedback When Progress Report Shows Improvement]* Now let's see what happens after the man releases his keys. [...] *[Next Topic Question]*

....

UNC-DISE_ADAPT ITSPOKE-2b: Right. Here's a quick progress update. It might help to remember we will build on the topics we're discussing now.*[Productive Interaction Feedback When Progress Report Shows Decline]* Now let's see what happens after the man releases his keys. [...] *[Next Topic Question]*

Figure 3: Dialogue Example Showing Adaptation for Disengaged+Correct Users

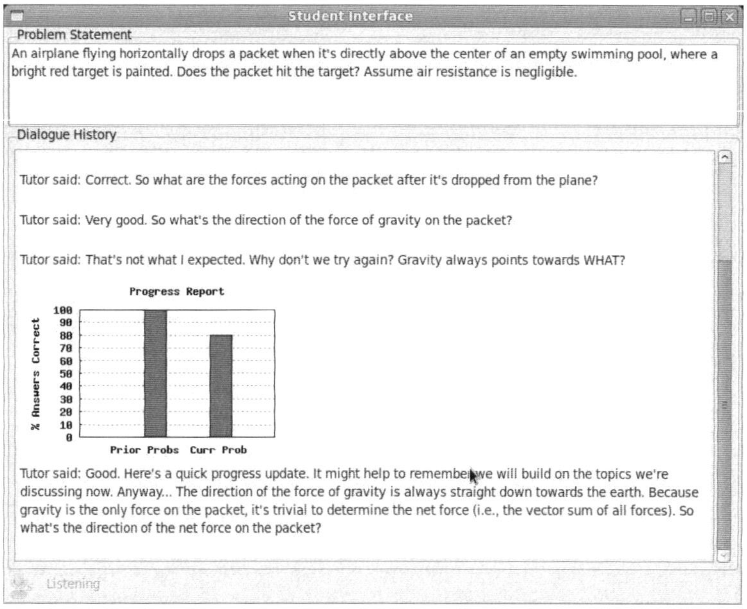

Figure 4: Example Progress Report after Disengaged+Correct Turn

Dialog System Using Real-Time Crowdsourcing and Twitter Large-Scale Corpus

Fumihiro Bessho, Tatsuya Harada, Yasuo Kuniyoshi
The University of Tokyo
Department of Mechano-Informatics
7-3-1 Hongo, Bunkyo-ku, Tokyo 113-8656, Japan
{bessho, harada, kuniyosh}@isi.imi.i.u-tokyo.ac.jp

Abstract

We propose a dialog system that creates responses based on a large-scale dialog corpus retrieved from Twitter and real-time crowdsourcing. Instead of using complex dialog management, our system replies with the utterance from the database that is most similar to the user input. We also propose a real-time crowdsourcing framework for handling the case in which there is no adequate response in the database.

1 Introduction

There is a lot of language data on the Internet. Twitter offers many APIs to retrieve or search post status data, and this data is frequently used in research, such as in stock market prediction (Bollen et al., 2011), the spread of information through social media (Bakshy and Hofman, 2011), and representations of textual content(Ramage et al., 2010). Several models for conversation using Twitter data (Ritter et al., 2010; Higashinaka et al., 2011) have been proposed because of the data's vast size and conversational nature.

Kelly (2009) previously showed that 37% of English tweets are Conversational, of which 69% are two-length (one status post and a reply). In our analysis of over 2.5 million tweets, 37.5% of all Japanese tweets are Conversational, which matches Kelly's data. However, less than 58.3% of these are two-length tweets.

Many chat bots are rule-based, which requires a lot of human effort to create or add new rules. For example, A.L.I.C.E (Wallace, 2009), which won the Loebner Prize three times, creates responses based on a dialog strategy database written in a markup language named AIML. Recently, some other chat bots based on a large-scale dialog corpus have been proposed[1,2].

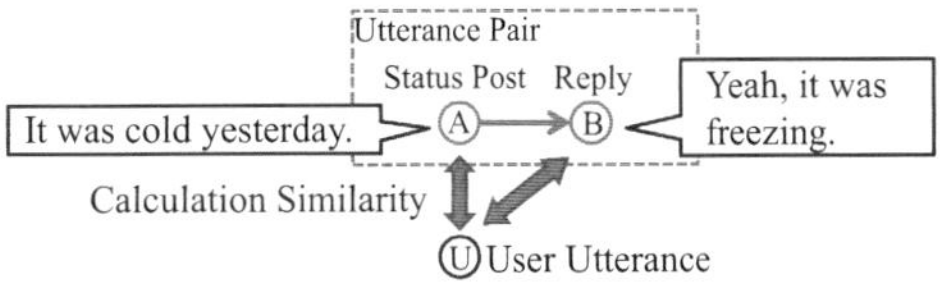

Figure 1: Utterance pair.

In this paper, we propose a novel dialog system (chat bot) that uses real-time crowdsourcing and Twitter large-scale corpus. We evaluate response selection methods based on positive/negative example to judge if each feature could be exploited to judge similarity between uterrances.

2 Method

2.1 Overview

We create an "Utterance Pair" database as shown in Figure 1. Each pair is composed of an utterance (Figure 1, A) and a reply to the utterance (Figure 1, B). Our approach for creating responses is simple and is illustrated in Figure 2. For each user input, the system searches the utterance-pair database for the pair of which the tweet (Figure 1, A) is most similar to that input. The reply contained in this pair (Figure 1, B) forms the system's response to the user's input.

[1] Jabberwacky: http://www.jabberwacky.com
[2] Cleverbot: http://www.cleverbot.com

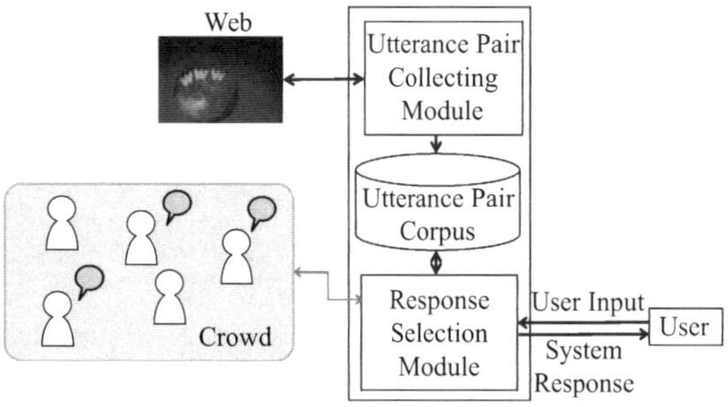

Figure 2: System overview.

If the system cannot find a post that is sufficiently similar to the user's input, then it "outsources" the response to another user.

To build the conversation database, we collected 1.2 million utterance-pairs from the microblogging service, Twitter. We fetched public timeline data using the Streaming API [3] , and then looked for tweets which were written in Japanese [4] and had an in-reply-to field. We followed the replies using the REST API [5].

Raw posts from Twitter included *mentions* (the symbol @ followed by a user name), *quotes* (written with letters "RT"), *hashtags* (a word preceded by the symbol #), and *URLs*. We filtered away this information using regular expressions. Unlike English tweets, in Japanese users placed hashtags at the end of their tweet, separated from the bodytext, making the deletion of hashtags feasible.

2.2 Method for the retrieval of Similar Utterance-pairs

In this section, we define a similarity measure between user input and each utterance data in the database. Each utterance in the database is analyzed by a morphological analyzer after Twitter-specific representations are eliminated as mentioned in Section 2.1. Analyzed data are filtered based on part-of-speech (POS) tags. In this paper we only extract noun, verb and interjection, and because many Japanese tweets include emoticons which cannot be tagged correctly by the morphological analyzer we used. We filtered out emoticons using a key-character-filter.

These documents (tweets) were then converted into document vectors. For a document d_i, the vector element corresponding to word w_j is represented as

$$x_{i,j} = \frac{tf_{i,j}}{n_j}, \quad (1)$$

where $tf_{i,j}$ represents the number of times w_j appears in d_i (term frequency), and n_j represents the length of d_i.

The similarity between two documents is calculated by taking the inner product of the two document vectors, that is

$$Similarity(d_a, d_b) = \boldsymbol{x}_a^{\mathrm{T}} \boldsymbol{x}_b. \quad (2)$$

2.3 Real-Time Crowdsourcing

We propose to integrate the dialog system with "real-time crowdsourcing". When the system fails to find an adequate response to a user input, in other words, when the similarity score of the most similar tweet in the database is below a certain threshold, the system relegates the user's input to other users (crowd). The original user input is a tweet to the chat bot and therefore includes the system's name as the target user. In our experiment, the system exchanges its own name to the address of the crowd and utters the tweet to the crowd. If a crowd member responds to the system before a preset timeout period, the system uses the crowd member's reply as a response to the original user. One of the advantages of this method is that people in the crowd do not know that they are part of a crowd; instead, they think they are being addressed by the system. The original user also thinks (s)he is talking with the system. We implemented this real-time crowdosourcing framework using a Twitter clone, StatusNet[6] as an interface (see Figure 5).

3 Evaluation

We prepared 90 user input examples and extracted 20 utterance-pairs (utterance and responses in the database retrieved from Twitter) per user input, so that a total of 1,800 of triples (a user input and an

[3] https://dev.twitter.com/docs/streaming-api

[4] We assume tweets as Japanese-written which are written by users who set Language as Japanese.

[5] https://dev.twitter.com/docs/api

[6] http://status.net/

utterance pair) were included in our sample. Thirty subjects evaluated the naturalness and versatility of the responses. Each subject evaluated 600 triples. We note that subjects saw only the user input and response in an utterance pair (B in Figure 1), and were not shown A in Figure 1 in the survey sheets. In this paper, versatility of a response corresponds to the number of utterances to which it was rated as sensible response (e.g., "What do you mean?" can serve as a response to almost any input, and is therefore highly versatile). Michael (1994) points out that chat bots have many tricks to fool people, and providing a versatile answer is one of them. We believe our system can avoids versatile answers by using a large-scale database.

In the following, we describe how we evaluate each scoring function (which takes a triplet as an input and the score as the output) using positive/negative learning data. We treat scoring functions as classifiers, that is, when the function receives a triplet as input, we assume that the function judges the triplet as positive data if the output score is above a certain threshold and negative data if it is below it.

Triplets collected in the survey were divided into positive and negative triplets. We consider an utterance pair to be *positive* if it is judged as natural by more than 7 out of 10 subjects and versatile by less than 7 out of 10 subjects. All else were considered *negative* triplets.

The ROC curve is used to illustrate the performance of the classifiers. It is a two-dimensional graph in which true positive rate is plotted on the Y axis and false positive rate is plotted on the X axis. Here, the true positive rate (r_{TP}) and false positive rate (r_{FP}) are given by

$$r_{TP} = \frac{\text{Positives correctly classified}}{\text{Total positives}}, \quad (3)$$

$$r_{FP} = \frac{\text{Negatives incorrectly classified}}{\text{Total negatives}}. \quad (4)$$

The area under the curve (AUC), or the area under the ROC curve, was used to measure classifier performance. A random classifier has an AUC of 0.5, and ideal classifier has an AUC of 1.0. We applied a number of scoring functions to the triples, and then calculated the AUC for each function (classifier) for validation. We chose scoring functions which

Calculate similarity with A or A+B.	A+B
Use tf?	YES
Use idf?	NO
Eliminate Twitter-specific representations?	YES
Filter POS?	YES

Table 1: Scoring function we chose.

- calculate similarity only with A in Figure 1, or A and B in Figure 1,
- use term frequency (tf) when the document vector is calculated, or not,
- use inverse document frequency (idf) when the document vector is calculated, or not,
- eliminate Twitter-specific representations (see Section 2.1) or not,
- normalize by character count or not,
- filter POS or not.

We compared a total of 64 (=2^6) scoring functions. Figure 3 illustrates some or our results. As it shows, when only Twitter-specific expressions are filtered, classifier performance is similar to a random classifier. The addition of word count normalization and POS filter improved to classification performance. This is because longer utterances normally include more specific information, so that the topic is more prone to be missed during the response selection process. Adverbs (e.g. "very") or particles (corresponds preposition in English, e.g. "as") had little effect on the context of an utterance, so POS filtering acts as noise elimination. With respect to tf and idf, the effect of tf varied widely, and idf hindered classification performance (c, d, g, h).

We chose the scoring function with the best performance (see Table 1 for details), of which the AUC is 0.803.

4 Conclusions and Future Work

In this paper, we proposed a new dialog system based on real-time crowdsourcing and a large-scale database which is collected from the web automatically. We also evaluated scoring functions based on positive/negative utterance pairs.

In future work, we will keep on enlarging our utterance pair corpus, and conduct the same experi-

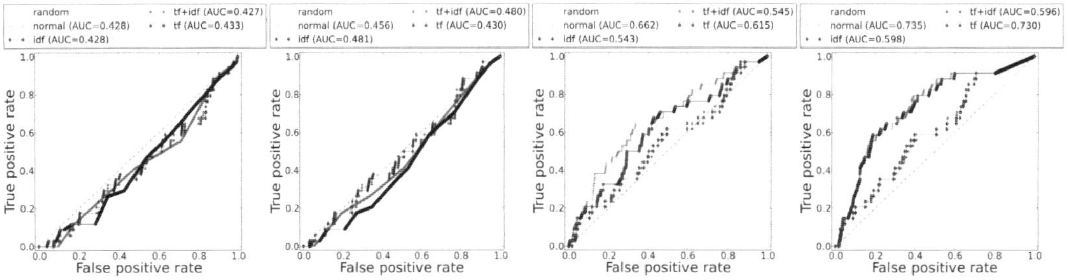

(a) normal (A) (b) eliminated (A) (c) eliminated + normalized (A) (d) eliminated + normalized + POS filter (A)

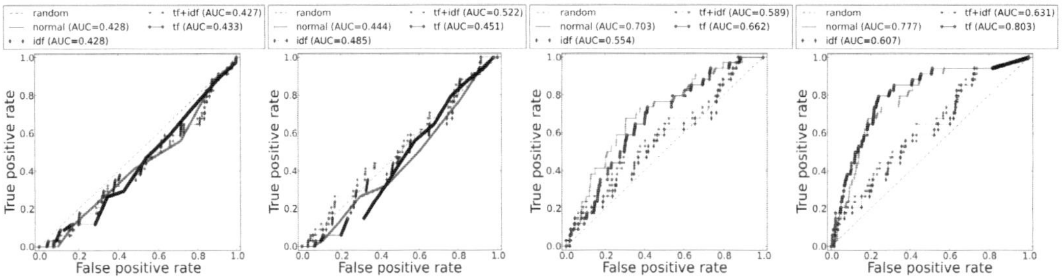

(e) normal (A+B) (f) eliminated (A+B) (g) eliminated + normalized (A+B) (h) eliminated + normalized + POS filter (A+B)

Figure 3: ROC curve for each scoring function. In each graph there are 4 lines, and each line represents whether tf and idf are used to calculate the document vector. Only A in Figure 1 is treated in the first line (a, b, c, d), whereas A and B is considered in the bottom (e, f, g, h). Normal, eliminated, normalized, POS filter mean doing nothing, twitter-specific description is eliminated, normalized by character count, considering only specified POS, respectively.

ments as in this paper on the larger database. We will also use more than two-length tweets for the database. We believe that this approach could lead to a context-aware dialog system (e.g., suppose the user gives "Why?" as the response to the system's utterance "I like dogs.". Our current system cannot handle the topic, "dog", however a system can do so by considering 3 utterances).

References

Eytan Bakshy and Jake M. Hofman. 2011. *Everyone's an Influencer: Quantifying Influence on Twitter.* In Proceedings of International Conference on Web Search and Data Mining.

Johan Bollen, Huina Mao, and Xiaojun Zeng. 2011. *Twitter Mood Predicts the Stock Market.* Journal of Computational Science.

Ryuichiro Higashinaka, Noriaki Kawamae, Kugatsu Sadamitsu, and Yasuhiro Minami. 2011. *Building a Conversational Model from Two-Tweets.* IEEE Workshop on Automatic Speech Recognition and Understanding.

Ryan Kelly. 2009. *Pear Analytics Twitter Study (Whitepaper).*

Michael L. Mauldin. 1994. *Chatterbots, TinyMuds, and the Turing Test Entering the Loebner Prize Competition.* In Proceedings of the National Conference on Artificial Intelligence.

Daniel Ramage, Susan Dumais, and Dan Liebling. 2010. *Characterizing Microblogs with Topic Models.* In Proceedings of the International AAAI Conference on Weblogs and Social Media.

Alan Ritter, Colin Cherry, and Bill Dolan. 2010. *Unsupervised Modeling of Twitter Conversations.* In Proceedings of North American Chapter of the Association for Computational Linguistics - Human Language Technologies.

Richard S. Wallace. 2009. *The Anatomy of A.L.I.C.E..* Parsing the Turing Test.

USER	こんにちは (konnitiha: Hello)
SYSTEM	こんにちは !! こんにちは !! こんにちは !! (konnitiha!! konnnitiha!! konnnitiha!!: Hello!! Hello!! Hello!!)
USER	今日も寒いですよね。(kyou-mo-samui-desu-yone: It's cold today, isn't it?)
SYSTEM	だ、大丈夫ゼロ？上着を羽織って、暖房をつけてみたりした？ (da, daijobu-zero? uwagi-wo-haotte, danbou-wo-tuketemitari-sita?: Are you ok? How about putting on a jacket, and turning on the heater?))
USER	暖房つけてるよ。(danbou-tuketeru-yo.: I've already turned on the heater.)
SYSTEM	暖房ないけどあったかい (＊´～`＊) (danbou-nai-kedo-attakai <emoticon>: There is no heater(in this room), but it's warm <emoticon>)

USER	なんだか熱っぽい。(nandaka-netuppoi: I feel feverish.)
SYSTEM	大丈夫？ (daijoubu?: Are you ok?)
USER	インフルエンザに感染してないといいけど。(Infuruenza-ni-kannsenn-shitenai-to-iikedo.: I hope I'm not ill with flu.)
SYSTEM	インフルエンザ用の効ウィルス剤は感染から 48 時間以内にしかあまり効果がない罠 (infuruenza-you-no-kouuiruzuzai-ha-kannsenn-kara-48jikanninai-ni-shika-amari-kouka-ga-nai-wana: Antiviral drug for flu only works to those who got infected in 48 hours.)
USER	マジか。(majika.: really?)
SYSTEM	寝ろよ！ (neroyo!: You should sleep.)
USER	おとなしく寝ます。(otonashiku-nemasu.: I'll take it easy and sleep.)
SYSTEM	おとなしくするべきだ (otonashiku-suru-beki-da: You should do so.)

Table 2: Dialog examples

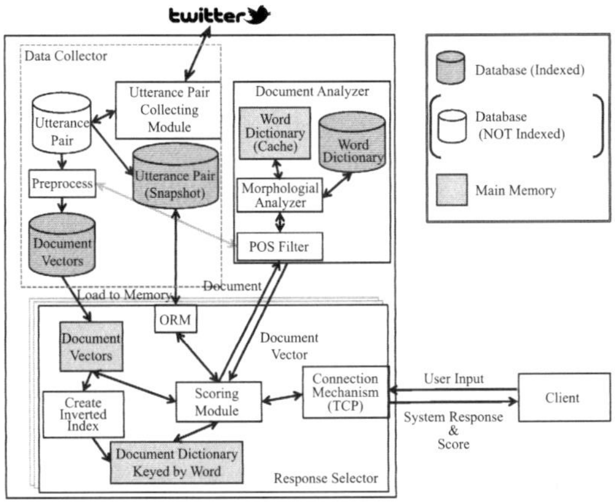

Figure 4: System Implementation.

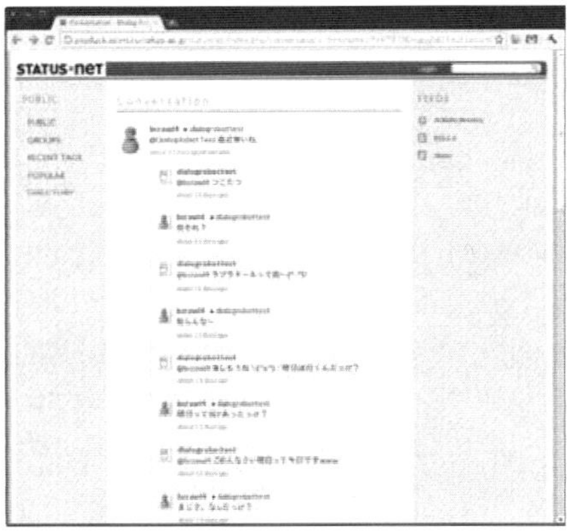

Figure 5: System implementation on StatusNet.

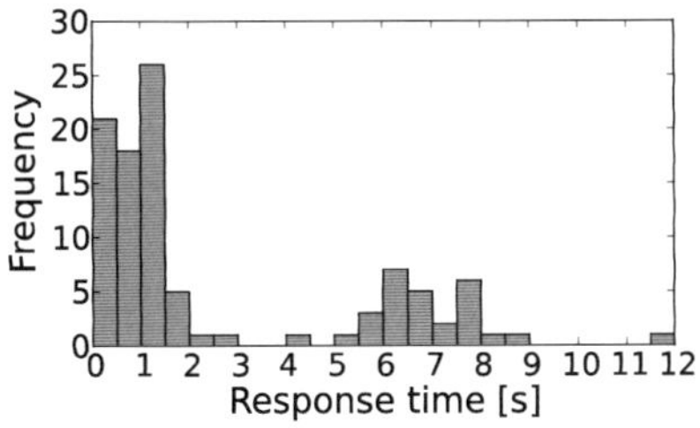

Figure 6: System response time distribution. (datasize = 1,154,621)

Automatically Acquiring Fine-Grained Information Status Distinctions in German

Aoife Cahill
Educational Testing Service,
660 Rosedale Road,
Princeton, NJ 08541, USA
acahill@ets.org

Arndt Riester
Institute for Natural Language Processing (IMS)
Pfaffenwaldring 5b
70569 Stuttgart, Germany
arndt.riester@ims.uni-stuttgart.de

Abstract

We present a model for automatically predicting information status labels for German referring expressions. We train a CRF on manually annotated phrases, and predict a fine-grained set of labels. We achieve an accuracy score of 69.56% on our most detailed label set, 76.62% when gold standard coreference is available.

1 Introduction

The automatic identification of *information status* (Prince, 1981; 1992), i.e. categorizing discourse entities into different classes on the *given-new* scale, has recently been identified as an important issue in natural language processing (Nissim, 2006; Rahman and Ng, 2011; 2012). It is widely acknowledged that information status and, more generally, information structure,[1] is reflected in word order, in the form of referring expressions as well as in prosody. In computational linguistics, the ability to automatically label text with information status, therefore, could be of great benefit to many applications, including surface realization, text-to-speech synthesis, anaphora resolution, summarization, etc.

The task of automatically labeling text with information status, however, is a difficult one. Part of the difficulty arises from the fact that, to a certain degree, such labeling requires world knowledge and semantic comprehension of the text, but another obstacle is simply that theoretical notions of information status are not used consistently in the literature.

In this paper we outline a system, trained on a small amount of data, that achieves encouraging results on the task of automatically labeling transcribed German radio news data with fine-grained information status labels.

2 Learning information status

A simpler variant of the task is *anaphoricity detection* (discourse-new detection) (Bean and Riloff, 1999; Ng and Cardie, 2002; Uryupina, 2003; Denis and Baldridge, 2007; Zhou and Kong, 2011), which divides discourse entities into *anaphoric (given)* and *new*. Identifying discourse-new expressions in texts is helpful as a precursor to coreference resolution, since, by definition, there is no need to identify antecedents for new entities.

In the linguistic literature, referring expressions have been distinguished in much more detail, and there is reason to believe that this could also provide useful information for NLP applications. Nissim (2006) and Rahman and Ng (2011) developed methods to automatically identify three different classes: OLD, MEDIATED and NEW expressions. This classification, which is described in Nissim et al. (2004), has been used for annotating the *Switchboard* dialog corpus (Calhoun et al., 2010), on which both studies are based. Most recently, Rahman and Ng (2012) extend their automatic prediction system to a more fine-grained set of 16 subtypes.

[1] Information structure is usually taken to describe clause-internal divisions into *focus-background, topic-comment, or theme-rheme*, which are in turn defined in terms of contextual factors such as *given-new* information, *salience*, *contrast* and *alternatives*, cf. Steedman and Kruijff-Korbayová (2003), Krifka (2007). *Information status* is the subfield of information structure which exclusively deals with the *given-new* distinction and which is normally confined to referring expressions.

Old. The class of OLD entities in Nissim et al. (2004) is not limited to full-fledged anaphors like in Example (1a) but also includes cases of generic and first/second person pronouns like in (1b), which may or may not possess a previous mention.

(1) a. Shares in *General Electric* rose as investors bet that the US company would take more lucrative engine orders for the A380.
b. I wonder where this comes from.

Mediated. The group of MEDIATED entities mainly has two subtypes: (2a) shows an expression which has not been mentioned before but which is dependent on previous context. Such items have also been called *bridging anaphors* (Poesio and Vieira, 1998). (2b) contains a phrase which is generally known but does not depend on the discourse context.

(2) a. Tomorrow, *the Shenzhou 8 spacecraft* will be in a position to attempt the docking.
b. They hope that he will be given the right to remain in the Netherlands.

New. The label NEW, following Nissim et al. (2004: 1024), applies "to entities that have not yet been introduced in the dialog and that the hearer cannot infer from previously mentioned entities."[2] Two kinds of expressions which fall into this category are unfamiliar definites (3a) and (specific) indefinites (3b).

(3) a. The man who shot a policeman yesterday has not been caught yet.
b. Klose scored a penalty in the 80th minute.

Based on work described in Nissim (2006), Rahman and Ng (2011) develop a machine learning approach to information-status determination. They develop a support vector machine (SVM) model from the annotated Switchboard dialogs in order to predict the three possible classes. In an extension of this work, Rahman and Ng (2012) compare a rule-based system to a classifier with features based on the rules to predict 16 subtypes of the three basic types. On this extended label set on the dialog data, they achieve accuracy of 86.4% with gold standard coreference and 78.7% with automatically detected coreference.

3 Extending Information Status prediction

The work we present here is most similar to that of Rahman and Ng (2012), however, our work differs from theirs in a number of important respects. We (i) experiment with a different information status classification, derived from Riester et al. (2010), (ii) use (morpho-)syntactic and functional features automatically extracted from a deep linguistic parser in our CRF sequence model, (iii) test our approach on a different language (German), (iv) show that high accuracy can be achieved with a limited number of training examples, and (v) that the approach works on a different genre (transcribed radio news bulletins which contain complex embedded phrases like *an offer to the minority Tamil population of Sri Lanka*, not typically found in spoken dialog).

The annotation scheme by Riester et al. (2010) divides referring items differently to Nissim et al. (2004). Arguments are provided in the former paper and in Baumann and Riester (to appear). As it stands, the scheme provides too many labels for our purpose. As a compromise, we group them in seven classes: GIVEN, SITUATIVE, BRIDGING, UNUSED, NEW, GENERIC and EXPLETIVE.

Given. *Givenness* is a central notion in information structure theory. Schwarzschild (1999) defines givenness of individual-type entities in terms of coreference. If desired, GIVEN items can be subclassified, e.g. whether they are pronouns or full noun phrases, and whether the latter are repetitions or short forms of earlier material, or whether they consist of lexically new material (epithets).

Situative. 1st and 2nd person pronouns, locative and temporal adverbials, usually count as deictic expressions since they refer to elements in the utterance situation. We therefore count them as a separate class. SITUATIVE entities may, but need not, corefer.

Bridging. Bridging anaphors, as in (2a) above, have received much attention, see e.g. Asher and Lascarides (1998) or Poesio and Vieira (1998). Although they are discourse-new, they share properties with coreference anaphors since they depend on the discourse context. They represent a class which can be easily identified by human annotators but are difficult to capture by automatic techniques.

Unused. In manual annotation practice, it is very often impossible to decide whether an entity is hearer-known, since this depends on who we assume the hearer to be; and even if we agree on a recipient, we may still be mistaken about their knowledge. For example, *Wolfgang Bosbach, deputy chairman of the*

[2]Note that this definition fails to exclude cases like (2b).

Countable	Boolean	Descriptive
# Words in phrase*	Phrase contains a compound noun	Adverbial type, e.g. locative
# Predicative phrases	Phrase contains coordination	Determiner type, e.g. definite *
# DPs and NPs in phrase	Phrase contains time expression	Left/Right-most POS tag of phrase
# top category children	Phrase contains $<$ *2*, *5* or *10* words	Highest syntactic node label that dominates the phrase
# Labels/titles	Phrase does not have a complete parse	
# Depth of syntactic phrase	Phrase is a pronoun	Grammatical function, e.g. SUBJ *
# Cardinal numbers	Phrase contains more than 1 DP and 1 NP (i.e. phrase contains an embedded argument)	Type of pronoun, e.g. demonstrative
# Depth of syntactic phrase ignoring unary branching		Syntactic shape, e.g. apposition with a determiner and attributive modifier
# Apposition phrases	Head noun appears (partly or completely) in previous 10 sentences *	Head noun type, e.g. common *
# Year phrases		Head noun number, e.g. singular

Table 1: Features of the CRF prediction model (* indicates feature used in baseline model)

CDU parliamentary group may be known to parts of a German audience but not to other people.

We address this by collecting both hearer-known and hearer-unknown definite expressions into one class UNUSED. This does not rule out further subclassification (*known/unknown*) or the possibility of using machine learning techniques to identify this distinction, see Nenkova et al. (2005). The fact that Rahman and Ng (2011) report the highest confusion rate between NEW and MEDIATED entities may have its roots in this issue.

New. Only (specific) indefinites are labeled NEW.

Generic. An issue which is not dealt with in Nissim et al. (2004) are GENERIC expressions as in *Lions have manes*. Reiter and Frank (2010) discuss the task of identifying generic items in a manner similar to the learning tasks presented above, using a Bayesian network. We believe it makes sense to integrate genericity detection into information-status prediction.[3]

4 German data

Our work is based on the DIRNDL radio news corpus of Eckart et al. (2012) which has been hand-annotated with information status labels. We choose a selection of 6668 annotated phrases (1420 sentences). This is an order of magnitude smaller than the annotated Switchboard corpus of Calhoun et al. (2010). We parse each sentence with the German Lexical Functional Grammar of Rohrer and Forst (2006) using the XLE parser in order to automatically extract (morpho-)syntactic and functional features for our model.

5 Prediction Model for Information Status

Cahill and Riester (2009) show that there are asymmetries between pairs of information status labels contained in sentences, i.e. certain classes of expressions tend to precede certain other classes. We therefore treat the prediction of IS labels as a sequence labeling task.[4] We train a CRF using `wapiti` (Lavergne et al., 2010), with the features outlined in Table 1. We also include a basic "coreference" feature, similar to the lexical features of Rahman and Ng (2011), that fires if there is some lexical overlap of nouns (or compound nouns) in the preceding 10 sentences. The original label set described in Riester et al. (2010) contains 21 labels. Here we work with a subset of maximally 12 labels, but also consider smaller subsets of labels and carry out a mapping to the Nissim (2006) label set (Table 2).[5] We run a 10-fold cross-validation experiment and report average prediction accuracy. The results are given in Table 3a. As an informed baseline, we run the same cross-validation experiment with a subset of features that roughly correspond to the features of Nissim (2006). Our models perform statistically significantly better than the baseline ($p < 0.001$, using the approximate randomization test) for all label sets.

[3]Note that in coreference annotation it is an open question whether two identical generic terms should count as coreferent.

[4]Preliminary experimental evidence showed that the CRF performed slightly better than a simple multiclass logistic regression model (e.g. compare 72.19 to 72.43 in Table 3a).

[5]Unfortunately, due to underlying theoretical differences, it is impossible to map between the Riester label set and the extended label set used in Rahman and Ng (2012).

<table>
<tr><th>Total</th><th>Riester 1</th><th>Riester 2</th><th>Riester 3</th><th>Nissim '06</th></tr>
<tr><td>462</td><td>GIVEN-PRONOUN</td><td>GIVEN-PRONOUN</td><td rowspan="5">GIVEN</td><td rowspan="6">OLD</td></tr>
<tr><td>143</td><td>GIVEN-REFLEXIVE</td><td>GIVEN-REFLEXIVE</td></tr>
<tr><td>427</td><td>GIVEN-EPITHET</td><td rowspan="3">GIVEN-NOUN</td></tr>
<tr><td>169</td><td>GIVEN-REPEATED</td></tr>
<tr><td>204</td><td>GIVEN-SHORT</td></tr>
<tr><td>265</td><td>SITUATIVE</td><td>SITUATIVE</td><td>SITUATIVE</td></tr>
<tr><td>449</td><td>BRIDGING</td><td>BRIDGING</td><td>BRIDGING</td><td rowspan="2">MEDIATED</td></tr>
<tr><td>1271</td><td>UNUSED-KNOWN</td><td>UNUSED-KNOWN</td><td rowspan="2">UNUSED</td></tr>
<tr><td>1227</td><td>UNUSED-UNKNOWN</td><td>UNUSED-UNKNOWN</td><td rowspan="3">NEW</td></tr>
<tr><td>1282</td><td>NEW</td><td>NEW</td><td>NEW</td></tr>
<tr><td>632</td><td>GENERIC</td><td>GENERIC</td><td>GENERIC</td></tr>
<tr><td>96</td><td>EXPLETIVE</td><td>EXPLETIVE</td><td>EXPLETIVE</td><td>OTHER</td></tr>
</table>

Table 2: Varying the granularity of the label sets

As expected, the less fine-grained a label set, the easier it is to predict the labels. It remains for future work to show the effect of different label set granularities in practical applications. We approximate gold standard coreference information from the manually annotated labels (e.g. all GIVEN label types are by their nature coreferent), and carry out an experiment with gold-standard approximation of coreference marking. These results are also reported in Table 3a. Here we see a clear performance difference in the effect of gold-standard coreference on the Riester label set (increasing around 6-10%), compared to the Nissim label set (decreasing slightly). This is an artifact of the way the mapping was carried out, deriving the gold standard coreference information from the Riester label set. There is not a one-to-one mapping between OLD and GIVEN, and, in the Riester label set, coreferential entities that are labeled as SITUATIVE (deictic terms) are not recognized as such.

The feature set in Table 1 reflects the morpho-syntactic properties of the phrases to be labeled. Sometimes world knowledge is required in order to be able to accurately predict a label; for example, to know that *the pope* can be categorized as UNUSED-KNOWN, because it can occur discourse-initially, whereas *the priest* must usually be categorized as GIVEN. The BRIDGING relationship is also difficult to capture without some world knowledge. For example, to infer that *the waitress* can be categorized as BRIDGING in the context of *the restaurant* requires information that links the two concepts. Rahman and Ng (2012) also note this and include features based on FrameNet, WordNet and the ReVerb corpus for English.

For German, we address this issue by introducing two further types of features into our model based on the GermaNet resource (Hamp and Feldweg, 1997). The first type is based on the GermaNet synset of the head noun in the phrase and its distance from the root node (the assumption is that entities closer to root are more generic than those further away). The second include the sum and maximum of the Lin semantic relatedness measures (Lin, 1998) of how similar the head noun of the phrase is to the other nouns in current and immediately preceding sentence surrounding the phrase (calculated with GermaNet Pathfinder; Finthammer and Cramer, 2008). The results are given in Table 3b. Here we see a consistent increase in performance of around 4% for each label set over the model that does not include the GermaNet features. Again, we see the same decrease in performance on the Nissim label set when using gold standard coreference information.

Label Set	Accuracy	Gold coref.	Baseline feats.
Riester 1	65.49	72.49	57.25
Riester 2	67.21	76.88	58.82
Riester 3	72.43	82.22	64.20
Nissim '06	76.24	74.06	71.70

(a) Only morpho-syntactic features

Label Set	Accuracy	Gold coreference
Riester 1	69.56	76.62
Riester 2	71.99	79.86
Riester 3	75.82	84.76
Nissim '06	79.61	78.46

(b) Morpho-syntactic + GermaNet features

Table 3: Cross validation accuracy results

6 Conclusion

In this paper we presented a model for automatically labeling German text with fine-grained information status labels. The results reported here show that we can achieve high accuracy prediction on a complex text type (transcribed radio news), even with a limited amount of data.

References

Nicholas Asher and Alex Lascarides. 1998. Bridging. *Journal of Semantics*, 15(1):83–113.

Stefan Baumann and Arndt Riester. to appear. Referential and Lexical Givenness: Semantic, Prosodic and Cognitive Aspects. In G. Elordieta and P. Prieto, editors, *Prosody and Meaning*. Mouton de Gruyter, Berlin.

David L. Bean and Ellen Riloff. 1999. Corpus-Based Identification of Non-Anaphoric Noun Phrases. In *Proceedings of ACL*, pages 373–380, College Park, MD.

Aoife Cahill and Arndt Riester. 2009. Incorporating Information Status into Generation Ranking. In *Proceedings of ACL-IJCNLP*, pages 817–825, Singapore.

Sasha Calhoun, Jean Carletta, Jason Brenier, Neil Mayo, Dan Jurafsky, Mark Steedman, and David Beaver. 2010. The NXT-Format Switchboard Corpus: A Rich Resource for Investigating the Syntax, Semantics, Pragmatics and Prosody of Dialogue. *Language Resources and Evaluation*, 44(4):387–419.

Pascal Denis and Jason Baldridge. 2007. Global Joint Determination of Anaphoricity and Coreference Resolution Usinger Integer Programming. In *Proceedings of ACL-HLT*, Rochester, NY.

Kerstin Eckart, Arndt Riester, and Katrin Schweitzer. 2012. A Discourse Information Radio News Database for Linguistic Analysis. In C. Chiarcos et al., editors, *Linked Data in Linguistics*, pages 65–76, Berlin. Springer.

Marc Finthammer and Irene Cramer. 2008. Exploring and Navigating: Tools for GermaNet. In *Proceedings of LREC*, Marrakech, Morocco.

Birgit Hamp and Helmut Feldweg. 1997. GermaNet – a Lexical-Semantic Net for German. In *Proceedings of the ACL Workshop Automatic Information Extraction and Building of Lexical Semantic Resources for NLP Applications*, pages 9–15.

Manfred Krifka. 2007. Basic Notions of Information Structure. In C. Féry and M. Krifka, editors, *The Notions of Information Structure*, pages 57–68. Universitätsverlag Potsdam.

Thomas Lavergne, Olivier Cappé, and François Yvon. 2010. Practical Very Large Scale CRFs. In *Proceedings of ACL*, pages 504–513.

Dekang Lin. 1998. An Information-Theoretic Definition of Similarity. In *International Conference on Machine Learning*, pages 296–304.

Ani Nenkova, Advaith Siddharthan, and Kathleen McKeown. 2005. Automatically Learning Cognitive Status for Multi-Document Summarization of Newswire. In *Proceedings of HLT/EMNLP*, pages 241–248, Vancouver.

Vincent Ng and Claire Cardie. 2002. Identifying Anaphoric and Non-Anaphoric Noun Phrases to Improve Coreference Resolution. In *Proceedings of COLING*, pages 730–736, Taipei, Taiwan.

Malvina Nissim, Shipra Dingare, Jean Carletta, and Mark Steedman. 2004. An Annotation Scheme for Information Status in Dialogue. In *Proceedings of LREC*, Lisbon.

Malvina Nissim. 2006. Learning Information Status of Discourse Entities. In *Proceedings of EMNLP*, pages 94–102, Sydney.

Massimo Poesio and Renata Vieira. 1998. A Corpus-Based Investigation of Definite Description Use. *Computational Linguistics*, 24(2).

Ellen F. Prince. 1981. Toward a Taxonomy of Given-New Information. In P. Cole, editor, *Radical Pragmatics*, pages 233–255. Academic Press, New York.

Ellen F. Prince. 1992. The ZPG Letter: Subjects, Definiteness and Information Status. In W. Mann and S. Thompson, editors, *Discourse Description*, pages 295–325. Benjamins, Amsterdam.

Altaf Rahman and Vincent Ng. 2011. Learning the Information Status of Noun Phrases in Spoken Dialogues. In *Proceedings of EMNLP*, pages 1069–1080, Edinburgh.

Altaf Rahman and Vincent Ng. 2012. Learning the Fine-Grained Information Status of Discourse Entities. In *Proceedings of EACL 2012*, Avignon, France.

Nils Reiter and Anette Frank. 2010. Identifying Generic Noun Phrases. In *Proceedings of ACL*, pages 40–49, Uppsala, Sweden.

Arndt Riester, David Lorenz, and Nina Seemann. 2010. A Recursive Annotation Scheme for Referential Information Status. In *Proceedings of LREC*, Valletta, Malta.

Christian Rohrer and Martin Forst. 2006. Improving Coverage and Parsing Quality of a Large-Scale LFG for German. In *Proceedings of LREC*, Genoa, Italy.

Roger Schwarzschild. 1999. GIVENness, AvoidF, and other Constraints on the Placement of Accent. *Natural Language Semantics*, 7(2):141–177.

Mark Steedman and Ivana Kruijff-Korbayová. 2003. Discourse Structure and Information Structure. *Journal of Logic, Language and Information*, 12:249–259.

Olga Uryupina. 2003. High-precision Identification of Discourse New and Unique Noun Phrases. In *Proceedings of the ACL Student Workshop*, pages 80–86, Sapporo.

Guodong Zhou and Fang Kong. 2011. Learning Noun Phrase Anaphoricity in Coreference Resolution via Label Propagation. *Journal of Computer Science and Technology*, 26(1).

A Unified Probabilistic Approach to Referring Expressions

Kotaro Funakoshi Mikio Nakano
Honda Research Institute Japan Co., Ltd.
8-1 Honcho, Wako,
Saitama 351-0188, Japan
{funakoshi,nakano}@jp.honda-ri.com

Takenobu Tokunaga Ryu Iida
Tokyo Institute of Technology
2-12-1 Ookayama, Meguro,
Tokyo 152-8550, Japan
{take,ryu-i}@cl.cs.titech.ac.jp

Abstract

This paper proposes a probabilistic approach to the resolution of referring expressions for task-oriented dialogue systems. The approach resolves descriptions, anaphora, and deixis in a unified manner. In this approach, the notion of reference domains serves an important role to handle context-dependent attributes of entities and references to sets. The evaluation with the REX-J corpus shows promising results.

1 Introduction

Referring expressions (REs) are expressions intended by speakers to identify entities to hearers. REs can be classified into three categories: descriptions, anaphora, and deixis; and, in most cases, have been studied within each category and with a narrowly focused interest. Descriptive expressions (such as "the blue glass on the table") exploit attributes of entities and relations between them to distinguish an entity from the rest. They are well studied in natural language generation, e.g., (Dale and Reiter, 1995; Krahmer et al., 2003; Dale and Viethen, 2009). Anaphoric expressions (such as "it") refer to entities or concepts introduced in the preceding discourse and are studied mostly on textual monologues, e.g., (Kamp and Reyle, 1993; Mitkov, 2002; Ng, 2010). Deictic (exophoric) expressions (such as "this one") refer to entities outside the preceding discourse. They are often studied focusing on pronouns accompanied with pointing gestures in physical spaces, e.g., (Gieselmann, 2004).

Dialogue systems (DSs) as natural human-machine (HM) interfaces are expected to handle all the three categories of referring expressions (Salmon-Alt and Romary, 2001). In fact, the three categories are not mutually exclusive. To be concrete, a descriptive expression in conversation is either deictic or anaphoric. It is, however, not easy to tell whether a RE is deictic or anaphoric in advance of a resolution (regardless of whether the RE is descriptive or not). Therefore, we propose a general unified approach to the above three kinds of REs.

We employ a Bayesian network (BN) to model a RE. Dealing with continuous information and vague situations is critical to handle real world problems. Probabilistic approaches enable this for reference resolvers. Each BN is dynamically constructed based on the structural analysis result of a RE and contextual information available at that moment. The BN is used to estimate the probability with which the corresponding RE refers to an entity.

One of the two major contributions of this paper is our probabilistic formulation that handles the above three kinds of REs in a unified manner. Previously Iida et al. (2010) proposed a quantitative approach that handles anaphoric and deictic expressions in a unified manner. However it lacks handling of descriptive expressions. Our formulation subsumes and extends it to handle descriptive REs. So far, no previously proposed method for reference resolution handles all three types of REs.

The other contribution is bringing *reference domains* into that formulation. Reference domains (Salmon-Alt and Romary, 2000) are sets of referents implicitly presupposed at each use of REs. By considering them, our approach can appropriately interpret context-dependent attributes. In addition, by treating a reference domain as a referent, REs referring to sets of entities are handled, too. As far as the authors know, this work is the first that takes a probabilistic approach to reference domains.

1.1 Reference domains

First, we explain reference domains concretely. Reference domains (RDs) (Salmon-Alt and Romary, 2000; Salmon-Alt and Romary, 2001; Denis, 2010) are theoretical constructs, which are basically sets of entities presupposed at each use of REs. RDs in the original literature are not mere sets of entities but mental objects equipped with properties such as *type, focus, or saliency* and internally structured with *partitions*. In this paper, while we do not explicitly handle partitions, reference domains can be nested as an approximation of partitioning, that is, an entity included in a RD is either an individual entity or another RD. Each RD d has its focus and degree of saliency (a non-negative real number). Hereafter, two of them are denoted as $\mathrm{foc}(d)$ and $\mathrm{sal}(d)$ respectively. RDs are sorted in descending order according to saliency.

We illustrate reference domains with figure 1. It shows a snapshot of solving a Tangram puzzle (the puzzle and corpus are explained in section 3.1). RDs are introduced into our mental spaces either linguistically (by hearing a RE) or visually (by observing a physical situation). If one says "the two big triangles" in the situation shown in figure 1, we will recognize a RD consisting of pieces 1 and 2. If we observe one moves piece 1 and attaches it to piece 2, we will perceptually recognize a RD consisting of pieces 1, 2, and 6 due to proximity (Thórisson, 1994). In a similar way, a RD consisting of pieces 5 and 7 also can be recognized. Hereafter, we indicate a RD with the mark @ with an index, and denote its elements by enclosing them with [ ]. E.g., $@_1 = [1, 2]$, $@_2 = [1, 2, 6]$, $@_3 = [5, 7]$. The focused entity is marked by '*'. Thus, $\mathrm{foc}([1*, 2]) = 1$.

The referent of a RE depends on which RD is presupposed. That is, if one presupposes $@_1$ or $@_2$, the referent of "the right piece" should be piece 1. If one presupposes $@_3$, the referent of the same RE should be piece 5. This is the context-dependency mentioned above.

Previous work on RDs (Salmon-Alt and Romary, 2000; Salmon-Alt and Romary, 2001; Denis, 2010) employ not probabilistic but formal approaches.

1.2 Probabilistic approaches to REs

Here, previous probabilistic approaches to REs are explained and differences between ours and theirs are highlighted. Bayesian networks (Pearl, 1988; Jensen and Nielsen, 2007) have been not often but occasionally applied to problems in natural language processing/computational linguistics since (Charniak and Goldman, 1989). With regard to REs, Burger and Connolly (1992) proposed a BN specialized for anaphora resolution. Weissenbacher (2005; 2007) proposed a BN for the resolution of non-anaphoric "it" and also a BN for the resolution of pronominal anaphora. They used pre-defined fixed BNs for their tasks while our approach dynamically tailors a BN for each RE.

Cho and Maida (1992) and Roy (2002) adopted not exactly BNs but similar probabilistic approaches for reference resolution and generation respectively. However, their foci are only on descriptions.

Lison et al. (2010) proposed an approach using Markov logic networks (MLNs) (Richardson and Domingos, 2006) to reference resolution. They dealt with only deictic and descriptive REs. Even though MLNs are also a probabilistic framework, it is difficult for DS developers to provide quantitative domain knowledge needed to resolve REs because MLNs accept domain knowledge in the form of formal logic rules with weights, which must be determined globally. In contrast, BNs are more flexible and easy in providing quantitative knowledge to DSs in the form of conditional probability tables, which can be determined locally.

As just described, there are several probabilistic approaches to REs but none of them incorporates reference domains. In the next section, we introduce our *REBNs (Referring Expression Bayesian Networks)*, a novel Bayesian network-based modeling approach to REs that incorporates reference domains.

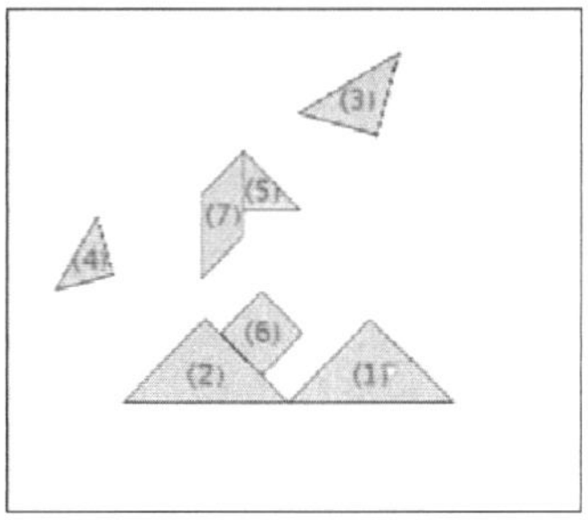

Figure 1: Tangram puzzle. (The labels 1 to 7 are for illustration purposes and not visible to participants.)

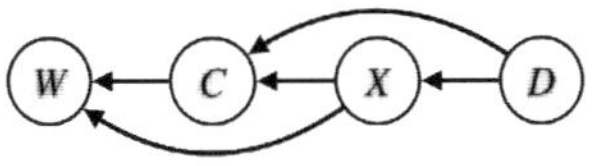

Figure 2: WCXD fundamental structure.

2 Bayesian Network-based Modeling of Referring Expressions

Each REBN is dedicated for a RE in the context at the moment. Its structure is determined by the syntactic and semantic information in the RE and probability tables are determined by the context.

2.1 Structures

Figure 2 shows the fundamental network structure of REBNs. We call this structure WCXD. The four nodes (random variables) W, C, X, and D represent an observed word, the concept denoted by the word, the referent of the RE, and the presupposed RD, respectively. Here, a *word* means a lexical entry in the system dictionary defined by the DS developer (concept dictionary; section 3.2.1).

Each REBN is constructed by modifying or multiply connecting the WCXD structure as shown in figures 3 and 4. Figure 3 shows the network for REs indicating one referent such as "that table." Each W_i node has a corresponding word w_i. Figure 4 shows the network for REs indicating two referents such as "his table." We call the class of the former REs *s-REX* (simple Referring EXpression) and the class of the latter REs *c-REX* (compound Referring EXpression). Although REBNs have the potential to deal with c-REX, hereafter we concentrate on s-REX because the page space is limited and the corpus used for evaluation contains very few c-REX instances.

Although, in section 1, we explained that (Iida et al., 2010) handles anaphoric and deictic expressions in a unified manner, it handles anaphora to instances only and does not handle that to concepts. Therefore, it cannot satisfactorily resolve such an expression "Bring me the red box, and the blue one, too." Here, "one" does not refer to the physical referent of "the red box" but refers to the concept of "box". The C nodes will enable handling of such references to concepts. This is one of the important features of REBNs but will be investigated in future work.

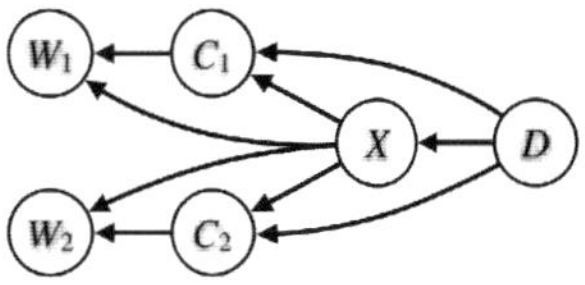

Figure 3: BN for two-word REs indicating one referent.

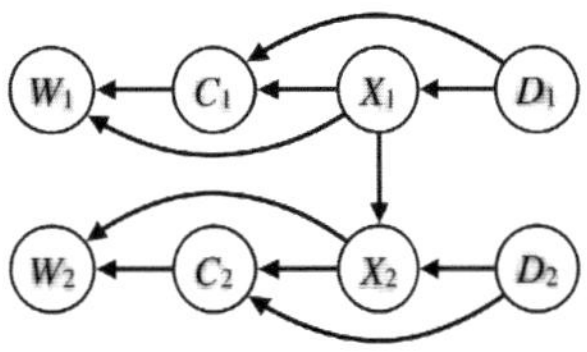

Figure 4: BN for two-word REs indicating two referents.

2.2 Domains of random variables

A REBN for an s-REX instance of N words has $2N + 2$ discrete random variables: $W_1, \ldots, W_N, C_1, \ldots, C_N, X$, and D. The domain of each variable depends on the corresponding RE and the context at the moment. Here, $\mathfrak{D}(V)$ denotes the domain of a random variable V.

$\mathfrak{D}(W_i)$ contains the corresponding observed word w_i and a special symbol ω that represents other possibilities, i.e., $\mathfrak{D}(W_i) = \{w_i, \omega\}$. Each W_i has a corresponding node C_i.

$\mathfrak{D}(C_i)$ contains M concepts that can be expressed by w_i and a special concept Ω that represents other possibilities, i.e., $\mathfrak{D}(C_i) = \{c_i^1, \ldots, c_i^M, \Omega\}$. c_i^j ($j = 1 \ldots M$) are looked up from the concept dictionary (see section 3.2.1, table 2).

$\mathfrak{D}(D)$ contains $L + 1$ RDs recognized up to that point in time, i.e., $\mathfrak{D}(D) = \{@_0, @_1, \ldots, @_L\}$. $@_0$ is the ground domain that contains all the individual entities to be referred to in a dialogue. At the beginning of the dialogue, $\mathfrak{D}(D) = \{@_0\}$. Other L RDs are incrementally added in the course of the dialogue.

$\mathfrak{D}(X)$ contains all the possible referents, i.e., K individual entities and $L + 1$ RDs. Thus, $\mathfrak{D}(X) = \{x_1, \ldots, x_K, @_0, \ldots, @_L\}$. Including RDs enables handling of references to sets.

Then reference resolution is formalized as below:

$$x' = \underset{x \in \mathfrak{D}(X)}{\arg\max}\, P(X = x | W_1 = w_1, \ldots, W_N = w_N). \quad (1)$$

$P(X|W_1, \ldots, W_N)$ is obtained by marginalizing the joint probabilities that are computed with the probability tables described in the next subsection.

2.3 Probability tables

Probability distributions are given as (conditional) probability tables since all the random variables used in a REBN are discrete. Here, four types of probability tables used by REBNs are described.

2.3.1 $P(W_i|C_i, X)$

$P(W_i = w|C_i = c, X = x)$ is the probability that a hearer observes w from c and x which the speaker intends to indicate.

In most cases, W_i does not depend on X, i.e., $P(W_i|C_i, X) \equiv P(W_i|C_i)$. X is, however, necessary to handle individualized terms (names).

There are several conceivable ways of probability assignment. One simple way is: for each c_i^j, $P(W = w_i|C = c_i^j) = 1/T, P(W = \omega|C = c_i^j) = (T-1)/T$, and for Ω, $P(W = w_i|C = \Omega) = \epsilon, P(W = \omega|C = \Omega) = 1 - \epsilon$. Here T is the number of possible words for c_i^j. ϵ is a predefined small number such as 10^{-8}. We use this assignment in the evaluation.

2.3.2 $P(C_i|X, D)$

$P(C_i = c|X = x, D = d)$ is the probability that concept c is chosen from $\mathfrak{D}(C_i)$ to indicate x in d.

The developers of DSs cannot provide $P(C_i|X, D)$ in advance because $\mathfrak{D}(C_i)$ is context-dependent. Therefore, we take an approach of composing $P(C_i|X = x, D = d)$ from $R(c_i^j, x, d)$ ($c_i^j \in \mathfrak{D}(C_i)\backslash\{\Omega\}$). Here $R(c_i^j, x, d)$ is the relevancy of concept c_i^j to referent x with regard to d, and $0 \leq R(c_i^j, x, d) \leq 1$. 1 means full relevancy and 0 means no relevancy. 0.5 means neutral. For example, a concept BOX will have a high relevancy to a suitcase such as 0.8 but a concept BALL will have a low relevancy to the suitcase such as 0.1. If x is not in d, $R(c_i^j, x, d)$ is 0. Algorithm 1 in appendix A shows an algorithm to compose $P(C_i|X = x, D = d)$ from $R(c_i^j, x, d)$. Concept Ω will be assigned a high probability if none of $c_i^j \in \mathfrak{D}(C_i)\backslash\{\Omega\}$ has a high relevancy to x.

If c_i^j is static,[1] $R(c_i^j, x, d)$ is numerically given in advance in the form of a table. If not static, it is implemented as a function by the DS developer, that is, $R(c_i^j, x, d) = f_{c_i^j}(x, d, I)$. Here I is all the information available from the DS.

[1]Whether a concept is static or not depends on each DS.

For example, given a situation such as shown in figure 1, the relevancy function of a positional concept LEFT (suppose a RE such as "the left piece") can be implemented as below:

$$f_{\text{LEFT}}(x, d, I) = (u_x - u_r)/(u_l - u_r). \quad (2)$$

Here, u_x, u_l and u_r are respectively the horizontal coordinates of x, the leftmost piece in d, and the rightmost piece in d, which are obtained from I. If x is a RD, the relevancy is given as the average of entities included in the RD.

2.3.3 $P(X|D)$

$P(X = x|D = d)$ is the probability that entity x in RD d is referred to, which is estimated according to the contextual information at the time the corresponding RE is uttered but irrespective of attributive information in the RE. The contextual information includes the history of referring so far (discourse) and physical statuses such as the gaze of the referrer (situation). We call $P(X = x|D = d)$ the *prediction model*.

The prediction model can be constructed by using a machine learning-based method. We use a ranking-based method (Iida et al., 2010). The score output by the method is input into the standard sigmoid function and normalized to be a probability. If x is not in d, $P(X = x|D = d)$ is 0.

2.3.4 $P(D)$

$P(D = d)$ is the probability that RD d is presupposed at the time the RE is uttered. We cannot collect data to estimate this probabilistic model because RDs are implicit. Therefore, we examine three a priori approximation functions based on the saliency of d. Saliency is proportional to recency.[2]

Uniform model This model ignores saliency. This is introduced to see the importance of saliency.

$$P(D = d) = 1/|\mathfrak{D}(D)| \quad (3)$$

Linear model This model distributes probabilities in proportion to saliency. This is an analogy of the method used in (Denis, 2010).

$$P(D = d) = \frac{\text{sal}(d)}{\sum_{d' \in \mathfrak{D}(D)} \text{sal}(d')} \quad (4)$$

[2]Assignment of saliency is described in section 3.2.3.

Exponential model This model puts emphasis on recent RDs. This function is so called soft-max.

$$P(D = d) = \frac{\exp(\text{sal}(d))}{\sum_{d' \in \mathfrak{D}(D)} \exp(\text{sal}(d'))} \quad (5)$$

3 Experimental Evaluation

We evaluated the potential of the proposed framework by using a situated human-human (HH) dialogue corpus.

3.1 Corpus

We used the REX-J Japanese referring expression corpus (Spanger et al., 2010). The REX-J corpus consists of 24 HH dialogues in each of which two participants solve a Tangram puzzle of seven pieces (see figure 1). The goal of the puzzle is combining seven pieces to form a designated shape (such as a swan). One of two subjects takes the role of operator (OP) and the other takes the role of solver (SV). The OP can manipulate the virtual puzzle pieces displayed on a PC monitor by using a computer mouse but does not know the goal shape. The SV knows the goal shape but cannot manipulate the pieces. The states of the pieces and the mouse cursor operated by the OP are shared by the two subjects in real time. Thus, the two participants weave a collaborative dialogue including many REs to the pieces. In addition to REs, the positions and directions of the pieces, the position of the mouse cursor, and the manipulation by the OP were recorded with timestamps and the IDs of relevant pieces.

3.1.1 Annotation

Each RE is annotated with its referent(s) as shown in table 1. The 1st RE *okkiisankaku*[3] big triangle "a big triangle" in the table is ambiguous and refers to either piece 1 or 2. The 7th and 8th REs refer to the set of pieces 1 and 2. The other REs refer to an individual piece.

To skip the structural analysis of REs to avoid problems due to errors in such analysis, we have additionally annotated the corpus with intermediate structures, from which REBNs are constructed. Because we focus on s-REX only in this paper, the intermediate structures are straightforward:[4] parenthesized lists of separated words as shown in table 1. The procedure to generate a REBN of s-REX from such an intermediate structure is also straightforward and thus it is not explained due to the page limitation.

3.2 Implementations

We use BNJ[5] for probabilistic computation. Here we describe the implementations of resources and procedures that are more or less specific to the task domain of REX-J.

3.2.1 Concept dictionary

Table 2 shows an excerpt of the concept dictionary defined for REX-J. We manually defined 40 concepts by observing the dialogues.

3.2.2 Static relevancy table and relevancy functions

For 13 concepts out of 40, their relevancy values were manually determined by the authors. Table 3 shows an excerpt of the static relevancy table defined for the seven pieces shown in figure 1. TRI is relevant only to pieces 1 to 5, and SQR is relevant only to pieces 6 and 7 but is not totally relevant to piece 7 because it is not a square in a precise sense. FIG is equally but not very relevant to all the pieces,[6]

For the remaining 27 concepts, we implemented relevancy functions (see appendix B).

3.2.3 Updating the list of RDs

In our experiment, REs are sequentially resolved from the beginning of each dialogue in the corpus. In the course of resolution, RDs are added into a list and updated by the following procedure. RDs are sorted in descending order according to saliency.

At each time of resolution, we assume that all the previous REs are correctly resolved. Therefore, after each time of resolution, if the correct referent of the last RE is a set, we add a new RD equivalent to the set into the list of RDs, unless the list contains another equivalent RD already. In either case, the saliency of the RD equivalent to the set is set to $\sigma + 1$ unless the RD is at the head of the list already.

[3]Words are not separated by white spaces in Japanese.

[4]In the case of c-REX, graph-like structures are required.

[5]http://bnj.sourceforge.net/

[6]This is because concept FIG in REX-J is usually used to refer to not a single piece but a shaped form (combined pieces).

D-ID	Role	Start	End	Referring expression	Referents	Intermediate structure
0801	SV	17.345	18.390	*okkiisankaku* big triangle	1 or 2	(*okkii sankaku*)
0801	SV	20.758	21.368	*sore* it	1	(*sore*)
0801	SV	23.394	24.720	*migigawanookkiisankaku* right big triangle	1	(*migigawano okkii sankaku*)
0801	SV	25.084	25.277	*kore* this	1	(*kore*)
0801	SV	26.512	26.671	*sono* that	1	(*sono*)
0801	SV	28.871	29.747	*konookkiisankaku* this big triangle	2	(*kono okkii sankaku*)
0801	OP	46.497	48.204	*okkinasankakkei* big triangle	1, 2	(*okkina sankakkei*)
0801	OP	51.958	52.228	*ryôhô* both	1, 2	(*ryôhô*)

"D-ID" means dialogue ID. "Start" and "End" mean the end points of a RE.

Table 1: Excerpt of the corpus annotation (w/ English literal translations).

Concept	Words
TRI	triangle, right triangle
SQR	quadrate, square, regular tetragon
FIG	figure, shape

Table 2: Dictionary (excerpted and translated in English).

Concept	Relevancy values by piece						
	(1)	(2)	(3)	(4)	(5)	(6)	(7)
TRI	1	1	1	1	1	0	0
SQR	0	0	0	0	0	1	0.8
FIG	0.3	0.3	0.3	0.3	0.3	0.3	0.3

Table 3: Static relevancy table.

Here, σ is the largest saliency value in the list at the moment (the saliency value of the head RD).

Before each time of resolution, we check whether the piece that is most recently manipulated after the previous RE constitutes a perceptual group by using the method explained in section 3.2.4 at the onset time of the target RE. If such a group is recognized, we add a new RD equivalent to the recognized group unless the list contains another equivalent RD. In either case, the saliency of the RD equivalent is set to $\sigma + 1$ unless the RD is at the head of the list already, and the focus of the equivalent RD is set to the most recently manipulated piece.

When a new RD $@_m$ is added to the list, a complementary RD $@_n$ and a subsuming RD $@_l$ are also inserted just after $@_m$ in the list. Here, $@_n = @_0 \backslash @_m$ and $@_l = [@_m*, @_n]$. This operation is required to handle a concept REST, e.g., "the remaining pieces."

3.2.4 Perceptual grouping

There is a generally available method of simulated perceptual grouping (Thórisson, 1994). It works well in a spread situation such as shown in figure 1 but tends to produce results that do not match our intuition when pieces are tightly packed at the end of a dialogue. Therefore, we adopt a simple method that recognizes a group when a piece is attached to another. This method is less general but works satisfactorily in the REX-J domain due to the nature of the Tangram puzzle.

3.2.5 Ranking-based prediction model

As mentioned in section 2.3.3, a ranking-based method (Iida et al., 2010) using SVM^{rank} (Joachims, 2006) was adopted for constructing the prediction model $P(X|D)$. This model ranks entities according to 16 binary features such as *whether the target entity is previously referred to* (a discourse feature), *whether the target is under the mouse cursor* (a mouse cursor feature), etc.[7]

When a target is a set (i.e., a RD), discourse features for it are computed as in the case of a piece; meanwhile, mouse cursor features are handled in a different manner. That is, if one of the group members meets the criterion of a mouse cursor feature, the group is judged as meeting the criterion.

In (Iida et al., 2010), preparing different models for pronouns and non-pronouns achieved better performance. Therefore we trained two linear kernel SVM models for pronouns and non-pronouns with the 24 dialogues.

3.3 Experiment

We used the 24 dialogues for evaluation.[8] As mentioned in section 2.1, we focused on s-REX. These 24 dialogues contain 1,474 s-REX instances and 28 c-REX instances. In addition to c-REX, we excluded REs mentioning complicated concepts, for which it is difficult to implement relevancy functions in a short time.[9] After excluding those REs,

[7]Following the results shown in (Iida et al., 2010), we did not use the 6 manipulation-related features (CO1 ... CO6).

[8]We used the same data to train the SVM-rank models. This is equivalent to assuming that we have data large enough to saturate the performance of the prediction model.

[9]Mostly, those are metaphors such as "neck" and concepts related to operations such as "put." For example, although

$P(D)$ model	Most-recent			Mono-domain			Uniform			Linear			Exponential		
Category	Single	Plural	Total	Single	Plural	Total	Single	Plural	Total	Single	Plural	Total	Single	Plural	Total
w/o S/P info.	42.4	28.8	40.0	77.5	47.3	73.3	77.1	40.6	72.0	78.3	45.1	73.7	76.2	48.4	72.3
w/ S/P info.	44.3	35.4	42.7	84.8	58.8	81.2	84.4	55.0	80.3	85.6	61.0	82.1	83.4	68.1	81.3

Table 4: Results of reference resolution (Accuracy in %).

1,310 REs were available. Out of the 1,310 REs, 182 REs (13.9%) refers to sets, and 612 REs (46.7%) are demonstrative pronouns such as *sore* "it."

3.3.1 Settings

We presupposed the following conditions.

Speaker role independence: We assumed REs are independent of speaker roles, i.e., SV and OP. All REs were mixed and processed serially.

Perfect preprocessing and past information: As mentioned in sections 3.1.1 and 3.2.3, we assumed that no error comes from preprocessing including speech recognition, morphological analysis, and syntactic analysis;[10] and all the correct referents of past REs are known.[11]

No future information: In HH dialogue, sometimes information helpful for resolving a RE is provided after the RE is uttered. We, however, do not consider such future information.

Numeral information: Many languages including English grammatically require indication of numeral distinctions by using such as articles, singular/plural forms of nouns and copulas, etc. Although Japanese does not have such grammatical devices,[12] it would be possible to predict such distinctions by using a machine learning technique with linguistic and gestural information. Therefore we observed the effect of providing such information. In the following experiment we provide the singular/plural distinction information to REBNs by looking at the annotations of the correct referents in advance. This is achieved by adding a special evidence node C_0, where $\mathfrak{D}(C_0) = \{\mathrm{S}, \mathrm{P}\}$. $P(C_0 = \mathrm{S}|X = x) = 1$ and $P(\mathrm{P}|x) = 0$ if x is a piece. On the contrary, $P(\mathrm{S}|x) = 0$ and $P(\mathrm{P}|x) = 1$ if x is a set.

3.3.2 Baselines

To our best knowledge, there is no directly comparable method. We set up two baselines. The first baseline uses the most recent as the resolved referent for each RE (Initial resolution of each dialogue always fails). This baseline is called *Most-recent*.

As the second baseline, we prepared another $P(D)$ model in addition to those explained in section 2.3.4, which is called *Mono-domain*. In Mono-domain, $\mathfrak{D}(D)$ consists of only a single RD $@'_0$, which contains individual pieces and the RDs recognized up to that point in time. That is, $@'_0 = \mathfrak{D}(X)$. Resolution using this model can be considered as a straightforward extension of (Iida et al., 2010), which enables handling of richer concepts in REs[13] and handling of REs to sets[14].

3.3.3 Results

The performance of reference resolution is presented by category and by condition in terms of accuracy (# of correctly resolved REs/# of REs).

We set up the three categories in evaluating resolution, that is, Single, Plural, and Total. Category Single is the collection of REs referring to a single piece. Plural is the collection of REs referring to a set of pieces. Total is the sum of them. Ambiguous REs such as the first one in table 1 are counted as "Single" and the resolution of such a RE is considered correct if the resolved result is one of the possible referents.

"putting a piece" and "getting a piece out" are distinguished due to speakers' intentions, they are (at least superficially) homogeneous in the physical data available from the corpus and difficult for machines to distinguish each other.

[10] In general, the speech and expressions in human-machine (HM) dialogue are less complex and less difficult to process than those in HH dialogue data. This is typcially observed as fewer disfluencies (Shriberg, 2001) and simpler sentences with fewer omissions (Itoh et al., 2002). Therefore, when we apply our framework to real DSs, we can expect clearer and simpler input and thus better performance. We supposed that the condition of perfect preprocessing in HH dialogue approximates the results to those obtained when HM dialogue data is used.

[11] If a reference is misinterpreted (i.e., wrongly resolved) in a dialogue, usually that misinterpretation will be repaired by the interlocutors in the succeeding interaction once the misinterpretation becomes apparent. Therefore, accumulating all past errors in resolution is rather irrational as an experimental setting.

[12] Japanese has a plurality marker *-ra* (e.g., *sore-ra*), but use of it is not mandatory (except for personal pronouns).

[13] (Iida et al., 2010) used only object types and sizes. Other concepts such as LEFT were simply ignored.

[14] (Iida et al., 2010) did not deal with REs to sets.

"w/o S/P info." indicates experimental results without singular/plural distinction information. "w/ S/P info." indicates experimental results with it.

Table 4 shows the results of reference resolution per $P(D)$ modeling method.[15] Obviously S/P information has a significant impact.

While the best performance for category Single was achieved with the Linear model, the best performance for Plural was achieved with the Exponential model. If it is possible to know whether a RE is of Single or Plural, that is, if S/P information is available, we can choose a suitable $P(D)$ model. Therefore, by switching models, the best performance of Total with S/P information reached 83.4%, and a gain of 2.0 points against Mono-domain was achieved (sign test, $p < 0.0001$).

Because the corpus did not include many instances to which the notion of reference domains is effective, the impact of RDs may appear small on the whole. In fact, the impact was not small. By introducing RDs, resolution in category Plural achieved a significant advancement. The highest gain from Mono-domain was 9.3 points (sign test, $p < 0.005$). Moreover, more REs containing positional concepts such as LEFT and RIGHT were correctly resolved in the cases of Uniform, Linear, and Exponential. Table 5 summarizes the resolution results of four positional concepts (with S/P information). While Mono-domain resolved 65% of them, Linear correctly resolved 75% (sign test, $p < 0.05$).

As shown in table 4, the performance of the Uniform model was worse than that of Mono-domain. This indicates that RDs introduced without an appropriate management of them would be harmful noise. Conversely, it also suggests that there might be a room for improvement by looking deeply into the management of RDs (e.g., *forgetting* old RDs).

4 Conclusion

This paper proposed a probabilistic approach to reference resolution, REBNs, which stands for Referring Expression Bayesian Networks. At each time of resolution, a dedicated BN is constructed for the RE in question. The constructed BN deals with either descriptive, deictic or anaphoric REs in a unified manner. REBNs incorporate the notion of reference domains (RDs), which enables the resolution of REs with context-dependent attributes and handling of REs to sets. REBNs are for task-oriented dialogue systems and presuppose a certain amount of domain-dependent manual implementation by developers. Therefore, REBNs would not be suited to general text processing or non-task-oriented systems. However, REBNs have the potential to be a standard approach that can be used for any and all task-oriented applications such as personal agents in smart phones, in-car systems, service robots, etc.

The proposed approach was evaluated with the REX-J human-human dialogue corpus and promising results were obtained. The impact of incorporating RDs in the domain of the REX-J corpus was recognizable but not so large on the whole. However, in other types of task domains where grouping and comparisons of objects occur frequently, the impact would be larger. Note that REBNs are not limited to Japanese, even though the evaluation used a Japanese corpus. Evaluations with human-machine dialogue are important future work.

Although this paper focused on the simple type of REs without relations, REBNs are potentially able to deal with complex REs with relations. The evaluation for complex REs is necessary to validate this potential of REBN. Currently REBN assumes REs whose referents are concrete entities. An extension for handling abstract entities (Byron, 2002; Müller, 2007) is important future work. Another direction would be generating REs with REBNs. A generate-and-test approach is a naive application of REBN for generation. More efficient method is, however, necessary.

Concept	Count	Mono	Uni.	Lin.	Exp.
LEFT	21	11	12	16	13
RIGHT	33	23	23	25	27
UPPER	9	6	6	6	4
LOWER	6	5	4	5	4
Total	69	45	45	52	48

(*Count means the numbers of occurrence of each concept. Mono, Uni., Lin., and Exp. correspond to Mono-domain, Uniform, Linear and Exponential.*)

Table 5: Numbers of correctly resolved REs containing positional concepts.

[15] According to the results of preliminary experiments, even in the case of the Uniform/Linear/Exponential models, we resolved the REs having demonstratives with the Mono-domain model. This is in line with the finding of separating models between pronouns and non-pronouns in (Iida et al., 2010).

References

John D. Burger and Dennis Connoly. 1992. Probabilistic resolution of anaphoric reference. In *Proceedings of the AAAI Fall Symposium on Intelligent Probabilistic Approaches to Natural Language*, pages 17–24.

Donna Byron. 2002. Resolving pronominal reference to abstract entities. In *Proceedings of the 40th Annual Meeting of the Association for Computational Linguistics (ACL)*, pages 80–87.

Eugene Charniak and Robert Goldman. 1989. A semantics for probabilistic quantifier-free first-order languages with particular application to story understanding. In *Proceedings of the Eleventh International Joint Conference on Artificial Intelligence (IJCAI)*, pages 1074–1079, Menlo Park, CA, USA.

Sehyeong Cho and Anthony Maida. 1992. Using a Bayesian framework to identify the referent of definite descriptions. In *Proceedings of the AAAI Fall Symposium on Intelligent Probabilistic Approaches to Natural Language*, pages 39–46.

Robert Dale and Ehud Reiter. 1995. Computational interpretations of the Gricean maxims in the generation of referring expressions. *Cognitive Science*, 18:233–263.

Robert Dale and Jette Viethen. 2009. Referring expression generation through attribute-based heuristics. In *Proceedings of the the 12th European Workshop on Natural Language Generation (ENLG)*, pages 59–65, Athens, Greece, March.

Alexandre Denis. 2010. Generating referring expressions with reference domain theory. In *Proceedings of the 6th International Natural Language Generation Conference (INLG)*, pages 27–35.

Petra Gieselmann. 2004. Reference resolution mechanisms in dialogue management. In *Proceedings of the 8th workshop on the semantics and pragmatics of dialogue (CATALOG)*, pages 28–34, Barcelona, Italy, July.

Ryu Iida, Shumpei Kobayashi, and Takenobu Tokunaga. 2010. Incorporating extra-linguistic information into reference resolution in collaborative task dialogue. In *Proceedings of the 48th Annual Meeting of the Association for Computational Linguistics*, pages 1259–1267, Uppsala, Sweden, July.

Toshihiko Itoh, Atsuhiko Kai, Tatsuhiro Konishi, and Yukihiro Itoh. 2002. Linguistic and acoustic changes of user's utterances caused by different dialogue situations. In *Proceedings of the 7th International Conference on Spoken Language Processing (ICSLP)*, pages 545–548.

Finn V. Jensen and Thomas D. Nielsen. 2007. *Bayesian Networks and Decision Graphs*. Springer, second edition.

Thorsten Joachims. 2006. Training linear SVMs in linear time. In *Proceedings of the ACM Conference on Knowledge Discovery and Data Mining (KDD)*, pages 217–226, Philadelphia, PA, USA, August.

Hans Kamp and Uwe Reyle. 1993. *From Discourse to Logic*. Kluwer Academic Publishers.

Emiel Krahmer, Sebastiaan van Erk, and André Verleg. 2003. Graph-based generation of referring expressions. *Computational Linguistics*, 29:53–72.

Pierre Lison, Carsten Ehrler, and Geert-Jan M. Kruijff. 2010. Belief modelling for situation awareness in human-robot interaction. In *Proceedings of the 19th International Symposium on Robot and Human Interactive Communication (RO-MAN)*, pages 138–143, Viareggio, Italy, September.

Ruslan Mitkov. 2002. *Anaphora Resolution*. Studies in Language and Linguistics. Pearson Education.

Christoph Müller. 2007. Resolving it, this, and that in unrestricted multi-party dialog. In *Proceedings of the 45th Annual Meeting of the Association for Computational Linguistics (ACL)*, pages 816–823.

Vincent Ng. 2010. Supervised noun phrase coreference research: The first fifteen years. In *Proceedings of the 48th Annual Meeting of the Association for Computational Linguistics*, pages 1396–1411, Uppsala, Sweden, July.

Judea Pearl. 1988. *Probabilistic Reasoning in Intelligent Systems: Networks of Plausible Inference*. Morgan Kaufmann, San Mateo, CA, USA.

Matthew Richardson and Pedor Domingos. 2006. Markov logic networks. *Machine Learning*, 62(1–2):107–136.

Deb K. Roy. 2002. Learning visually-grounded words and syntax for a scene description task. *Computer Speech and Language*, 16(3):353–385.

Susanne Salmon-Alt and Laurent Romary. 2000. Generating referring expressions in multimodal contexts. In *Proceedings of the INLG 2000 workshop on Coherence in Generated Multimedia*, Mitzpe Ramon, Israel, June.

Susanne Salmon-Alt and Laurent Romary. 2001. Reference resolution within the framework of cognitive grammar. In *Proceedings of the International Colloqium on Cognitive Science*, San Sebastian, Spain, May.

Elizabeth Shriberg. 2001. To 'errrr' is human: ecology and acoustics of speech disfluencies. *Journal of the International Phonetic Association*, 31(1):153–169.

Philipp Spanger, Masaaki Yasuhara, Ryu Iida, Takenobu Tokunaga, Asuka Terai, and Naoko Kuriyama. 2010. REX-J: Japanese referring expression corpus of situated dialogs. *Language Resources and Evaluation*. Online First, DOI: 10.1007/s10579-010-9134-8.

Kristinn R. Thórisson. 1994. Simulated perceptual grouping: An application to human-computer interaction. In *Proceedings of the 16th Annual Conference of the Cognitive Science Society*, pages 876–881, Atlanta, GA, USA.

Davy Weissenbacher and Adeline Nazarenko. 2007. A Bayesian approach combining surface clues and linguistic knowledge: Application to the anaphora resolution problem. In *Proceedings of the International Conference Recent Advances in Natural Language Processing (RANLP)*, Borovets, Bulgaria.

Davy Weissenbacher. 2005. A Bayesian network for the resolution of non-anaphoric pronoun it. In *Proceedings of the NIPS 2005 Workshop on Bayesian Methods for Natural Language Processing*, Whistler, BC, Canada.

A Algorithm to compose $P(C|X, D)$

Algorithm 1 Composing $P(C|X = x, D = d)$.

Input: $\mathfrak{D}(C)$; $R(c, x, d)$ for all $c \in \mathfrak{D}(C)\backslash\{\Omega\}$
Output: $P(C|X = x, D = d)$

```
n ← 0, s ← 0, S = 𝔇(C)\{Ω}
for all c ∈ S do
    r[c] ← R(c, x, d) #{Relevancy of concept c}
    s ← s + r[c] #{Sum of relevancy r[c]}
    n ← n + (1 − r[c]) #{Sum of residual (1 − r[c])}
end for
r[Ω] ← n/|S|
s ← s + r[Ω]
for all c ∈ 𝔇(C) do
    P(C = c|X = x, D = d) ← r[c]/s
end for
```

(#{...} is a comment.)

B Relevancy functions

As explained in section 2.3.2, the relevancy functions for positional concepts such as LEFT and RIGHT were implemented as geometric calculations. Here several other relevancy functions are shown with corresponding example REs.

"this *figure*":

$$R(\text{FIG}, x, d) = \begin{cases} 0.3 & : \text{ if single(x)} \\ 1 & : \text{ if not single}(x) \text{ and shape}(x) \\ 0 & : \text{ otherwise} \end{cases}$$

(single(x) means x is a single piece. shape(x) means x is a set of pieces that are concatenated and form a shape. 0.3 comes from the static relevancy table.)

"*both* the triangles":

$$R(\text{BOTH}, x, d) = \begin{cases} 1 & : \text{ if } |x| = 2 \\ 0 & : \text{ otherwise} \end{cases}$$

"*another* one":

$$R(\text{ANOTHER}, x, d) = \begin{cases} 1 & : \text{ if foc}(d) \neq x \\ 0 & : \text{ otherwise} \end{cases}$$

"the *remaining* ones":

$$R(\text{REST}, x, d) = \begin{cases} 1 & : \text{ if } d = [x, y*] \\ 0 & : \text{ otherwise} \end{cases}$$

(REST requires $|d| = 2$, and both x and y are sets. ANOTHER does not.)

"*all*":

$$R(\text{ALL}, x, d) = \begin{cases} 1 & : \text{ if } x = d \\ 0 & : \text{ otherwise} \end{cases}$$

(ALL does not always refer to $@_0$.)

Combining Verbal and Nonverbal Features to Overcome the 'Information Gap' in Task-Oriented Dialogue

Eun Young Ha, Joseph F. Grafsgaard, Christopher M. Mitchell, Kristy Elizabeth Boyer, and James C. Lester
Department of Computer Science
North Carolina State University
Raleigh, NC, USA
{eha, jfgrafsg, cmmitch2, keboyer, lester}@ncsu.edu

Abstract

Dialogue act modeling in task-oriented dialogue poses significant challenges. It is particularly challenging for corpora consisting of two interleaved communication streams: a dialogue stream and a task stream. In such corpora, information can be conveyed implicitly by the task stream, yielding a dialogue stream with seemingly missing information. A promising approach leverages rich resources from both the dialog and the task streams, combining verbal and non-verbal features. This paper presents work on dialogue act modeling that leverages body posture, which may be indicative of particular dialogue acts. Combining three information sources (dialogue exchanges, task context, and users' posture), three types of machine learning frameworks were compared. The results indicate that some models better preserve the structure of task-oriented dialogue than others, and that automatically recognized postural features may help to disambiguate user dialogue moves.

1 Introduction

Dialogue act classification is concerned with understanding users' communicative intentions as reflected in their utterances. It is an important first step toward building automated dialogue systems. To date, the majority of work on dialogue act modeling has addressed spoken dialogue (Samuel et al., 1998; Stolcke et al., 2000; Surendran and Levow, 2006; Bangalore et al., 2008; Sridhar et al., 2009; Di Eugenio et al., 2010). However, with the increasing popularity of computer-mediated means of conversation, such as instant messaging and social networking services, automated analysis of textual dialogue holds much appeal. Dialogue act modeling for textual conversations has many practical application areas, which include web-based intelligent tutoring systems (Boyer et al., 2010a), chat-based online customer service (Kim et al., 2010), and social media analysis (Joty et al., 2011).

Human interaction involves not only verbal communication but also nonverbal communication. Research on nonverbal communication (Knapp and Hall, 2006; Mehrabian, 2007; Russell et al., 2003) has identified a range of nonverbal cues, such as posture, gestures, eye gaze, and facial and vocal expressions. However, the utility of these nonverbal cues has not been fully explored within the context of dialogue act classification research. Previous research has leveraged prosodic cues (Sridhar et al., 2009; Stolcke et al., 2000) and facial expressions (Boyer et al., 2011) for automatic dialogue act classification, but other types of nonverbal cues remain unexplored. As a first step toward a dialogue system that learns its behavior from a human corpus, this paper proposes a novel approach to dialogue act classification that leverages information about users' posture. Posture has been found to be a significant indicator of a broad range of emotions (D'Mello and Graesser, 2010; Kapoor et al., 2007; Woolf et al., 2009). Based on the premise that emotion plays an important role in dialogue, this work hypothesizes that adding posture features will improve the performance of automatic dialogue act models.

The domain considered in this paper is task-oriented textual dialogue collected in a human tutoring study. In contrast to conventional task-oriented dialogue corpora (e.g., Carletta et al., 1997; Jurafsky et al., 1998; Ivanovic, 2008) in which conversational exchanges are carried out within a single channel of dialogue between the dialogue participants, the corpus used in this work utilizes two separate and interleaved streams of communication. One stream is the textual conversation between a student and a tutor (*dialogue stream*). The other is the student's problem-solving activity (*task stream*). As will be described in Section 3, the interface used in the corpus collection was designed to allow the tutor to monitor the student's problem-solving activities. Thus, the student's problem-solving activities and the tutor's monitoring of those activities functioned as an implicit communication channel. This characteristic of the corpus poses significant challenges for dialogue act modeling. First, because the dialogue stream and the task stream are interleaved, the dialogue stream alone may not be coherent. Second, since information can be exchanged implicitly via the task stream, the dialogue likely contains substantial *information gaps*[1].

Addressing these challenges, the dialogue act models described in this paper combine three sources of information: the verbal information from the dialogue stream, the task-related context from the task stream, and information about users' posture. This paper makes several contributions to the dialogue research community. First, it is the first effort to explore posture as a nonverbal cue for dialogue act classification. Second, the proposed approach is fully automatic and ready for real-world application. Third, this paper explicitly defines the notion of *information gap* in task-oriented dialogue consisting of multiple communication channels, which has only begun to be explored in the context of dialogue act classification (Boyer et al., 2010a). Finally, this paper examines adaptability of previous dialogue act classification approaches in conventional task-oriented domains by comparing three classifiers previously applied to dialogue act modeling for task-oriented dialogue.

2 Related Work

A rich body of research has addressed data-driven approaches for dialogue act modeling. Russell et al. (2003) applied a transformation-based learning approach for dialogue act tagging for spoken dialogue, using speaker direction, punctuation, marks, and cue phrases. Stolcke et al. (2000) modeled the structure of dialogue as an HMM, treating the dialogue acts as the observations emitted from the hidden states of the learned HMM. More recently, Bangalore et al. (2008) proposed a unified approach to task-oriented dialogue, in which both the user dialogue act classification and the system dialogue act selection were informed by a shared maximum entropy dialogue act classifier. Sridhar et al. (2009) also used a maximum entropy model, exploring the utility of different representations of prosodic features. Di Eugenio et al. (2010) used a memory-based classifier, in combination with a modified latent semantic analysis (LSA) technique by augmenting the original word-document matrix in LSA with rich linguistic features.

While most work on dialogue act modeling has focused on spoken dialogue, a recent line of investigation has explored the analysis of textual conversation, such as asynchronous online chat conversation (Wu et al., 2005; Forsyth, 2007; Reitter et al., 2010; Joty et al., 2011) and synchronous online chat conversation (Ivanovic, 2008; Kim et al., 2010; Boyer et al., 2010a). Wu et al. (2005) proposed a transformation-based learning approach for an asynchronous chat posting domain, utilizing regular expression-based selection rules. For a similar domain, Forsyth (2007) applied neural networks and Naïve Bayes classification technique using lexical cues. Ritter et al. (2010) and Joty et al. (2011) applied unsupervised learning approaches to dialogue act modeling for Twitter conversations, in which dialogue acts were automatically discovered by clustering raw utterances. Work by Ivanovic (2008) and Kim et al. (2010) analyzed one-to-one synchronous online chat dialogue in a task-oriented

[1] In this paper, *information gap* is defined as the information that is missing from the explicit verbal exchanges between the dialogue participants but conveyed by the implicit task stream.

customer service domain. Ivanovic (2008) applied maximum entropy, naïve Bayes, and support vector machines using word *n*-gram features. Kim et al. (2010) compared the CRF, HMM-SVM, and Naïve Bayes classifiers using word *n*-grams and features extracted from the dialogue structure, in which CRF achieved the highest performance. Boyer et al. (2010a) investigated dialogue act modeling for task-oriented tutorial dialogue, applying a logistic regression approach using lexical, syntactic, dialogue structure, and task structure features.

Some previous dialogue act modeling work (Boyer et al., 2011; Sridhar et al., 2009; Stolcke et al., 2000) leveraged nonverbal information such as prosodic cues (Sridhar et al., 2009; Stolcke et al., 2000) and facial expressions (Boyer et al., 2011). Stolcke et al. (2000) combined various prosodic features such as pitch, duration, and energy. Sridhar et al. (2009) represented the sequence of prosodic features as *n*-grams. Boyer et al. (2011) leveraged confusion-related facial expressions for tutorial dialogue.

Like Boyer et al. (2010a), this work addresses dialogue act classification for task-oriented textual conversation in a web-based tutoring domain. In contrast to Boyer et al. (2010a), whose approach directly leveraged manually annotated features, making it challenging to apply the proposed model to a real-world system, the present work is fully automatic and ready for real-world application. A novel feature of this work is its utilization of nonverbal cues carried by users' posture. This is the first dialogue act classification work that leverages posture information.

3 Data

The corpus used in this paper consists of textual exchanges between a student and a tutor in a web-based remote-tutoring interface for introductory programming in Java. The corpus was collected from a series of six tutoring lessons, covering progressive topics in computer science over the course of four weeks. The tutoring interface consisted of four windows: a *task* window displaying the current programming task; a *code* window in which the student writes Java code; an *output* window for displaying the result of compiling and running the code; and a *chat* window for instant exchange of textual dialogue between the student and tutor. With this tutoring interface, the student and the tutor were able to exchange textual dialogue and share a synchronized view of the task. Apart from sending dialogue messages, the only action the tutor could perform to affect the student's interface was advancing to the next programming task.

3.1 Data Collection

The data collection conducted in Fall 2011 paired 42 students with one of four tutors for six forty-minute tutoring sessions on introductory computer science topics. The students were chosen from a first-year engineering course and were pre-screened to filter out those with significant programming experience. The tutors were graduate students with previous tutoring or teaching experience in Java programming. Students were compensated for their participation with partial course credit. The students worked with the same tutor for the entire study. Each lesson consisted of between four and thirteen distinct subtasks.

During each tutoring session, the dialogue text exchanged between the student and the tutor was logged to a database. Additional runtime data including content of the student's Java code, the result (e.g., success or failure) of compiling and running the student's code, and the IDs of the subtask were logged. All logged data were time-stamped at a millisecond precision. Students' body posture was recorded at a rate of 8 frames per second with a Kinect depth camera, which emits infrared rays to measure distance for each pixel in a depth image frame. The camera was positioned above the student's computer monitor, ensuring the student's upper body is centered in the recorded image. Tutors were not recorded.

3.2 Dialogue Act Annotation

For the work described in this paper, a subset of the collected data was manually annotated, which include the first of the six tutoring lessons from 21 students. This corpus contains 2564 utterances (1777 tutor, 787 student). The average number of utterances per tutoring session was 122 (min = 74; max = 201). The average number of tutor utterances per session was 84.6 (min = 51; max = 137) and the average number of student utterances per session was 37.4 (min = 22; max = 64).

Extending a previous annotation scheme used for similar task-oriented tutorial dialogue (Boyer et al., 2010b), the scheme used in this work consists of 13 dialogue act tags (Appendix). The dialogue turns that contained more than one dialogue function were segmented into multiple utterances before being assigned a dialogue act tag. The annotation scheme did not constrain any of the dialogue act tags as applying either to students' or tutors' utterances only; however, the resulting distribution of the tags in the annotated corpus show certain dialogue act tags were more relevant to either students' or tutors' utterances. Figure 1 depicts an excerpt from the corpus with the manually applied dialogue act annotations.

Tutor: hang on :) [S]
Tutor: When we show you example code, it is not the code you need to write. [S]
Tutor: Look at the task again. [H]

Student writes programming code

Tutor: YUP [PF]
Tutor: Perfect [PF]
Tutor: OK. Go ahead and test. [DIR]
Student: And I don't need anything in the parentheses? [Q]
Tutor: Line 9 is correct. You do NOT need anything inside the parentheses. [A]
Student: Ok [ACK]

Student compiles and runs code successfully

Tutor: Good. [PF]
Tutor: Moving on. [S]

Tutor advances to the next task.

Student writes programming code

Tutor: Syntactically correct. But there is a logic error [LF]
Tutor: When will the output statement display your request to the player? [Q]
Student: AFTER they put in their name [A]
Tutor: Exactly [PF]

Figure 1. Corpus Excerpt with Dialogue Act Annotation

Three human annotators were trained to apply the scheme. The training consisted of an iterative process involving collaborative and independent tagging, followed by refinements of the tagging protocol. At the initial phase of training, the annotators tagged the corpus collaboratively. In later phases annotators tagged independently. To compute agreement between different annotators, 24% (5 of the 21 sessions) of the corpus were doubly annotated by two annotators. All possible pairs of the annotators participated in double annotation. The aggregate agreement was .80 in Cohen's Kappa (Cohen, 1960).

3.3 Posture Estimation

Posture has been found to be a significant indicator of a broad range of emotions such as anxiety, boredom, confusion, engaged concentration (or flow), frustration, and joy (D'Mello and Graesser, 2010; Kapoor et al., 2007; Woolf et al., 2009). Early investigations into posture utilized pressure-sensitive chairs which provided indirect measures of upper-body posture (D'Mello and Graesser, 2010; Kapoor et al., 2007; Woolf et al., 2009). Newer, computer vision-based techniques provide more detailed postural data (Sanghvi et al., 2011). The present work uses a posture estimation algorithm developed to automatically detect the head, mid torso, and lower torso through depth image recordings of seated individuals (Grafsgaard et al., 2012). With this estimation algorithm, posture is represented as a triple of *head depth* (distance between camera and head), *mid torso depth*, and *lower torso depth*.

A dataset of depth camera recordings from the first of the six tutoring lessons consists of 512,977 depth image frames collected across 18.5 hours of computer-mediated human-human tutoring among 33 participants.[2] For each depth image frame, the posture algorithm scanned through the three middle regions that corresponded to head, mid-torso, and lower-torso of the recorded person, and selected a single representative depth pixel from each region. The boundaries for each region were heuristically determined relying on the placement of the students' chairs in the middle of the depth recording view at a common distance. Given these constraints, the model was manually verified by two independent human judges to have 95.1% accuracy across 1,109 depth image snapshots corresponding to one-minute intervals across the dataset. The algorithm output for each depth image was labeled as erroneous if either judge found that any of the posture tracking points did not coincide with its target region. Example output of the algorithm is shown in Figure 2.

[2] The other 9 sessions were not successfully recorded because of technical errors.

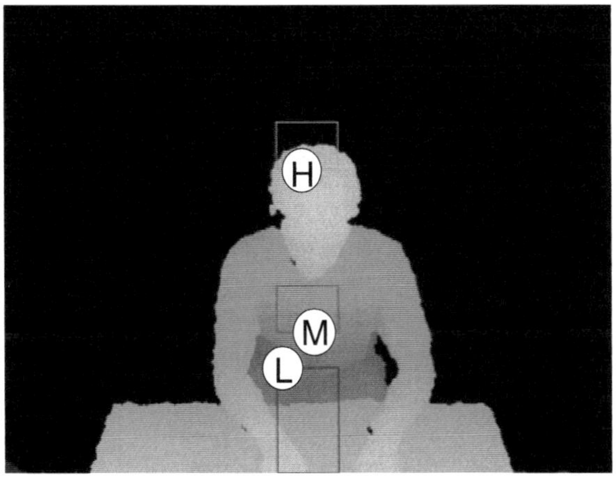

Figure 2. Automatically detected posture points (H = *headDepth*, M = *midTorsoDepth*, L = *lowerTorsoDepth*)

4 Features

For web-based one-to-one dialogue systems, it is important to achieve efficient runtime performance. To maximize real-world feasibility of the learned dialogue act classifiers, this work only considers the features that can be automatically extracted at runtime. In addition, the use of linguistic analysis software, such as a part-of-speech tagger and a syntactic parser, is intentionally restrained. One might argue that rich linguistic analysis may provide additional information to dialogue act classifiers, potentially improving the performance of learned models. However, there is a trade-off between additional information obtained by rich linguistic analysis and processing time. In addition, previous work (Boyer et al., 2010a) found part-of-speech and syntax features did not provide obvious benefit for dialogue act classification in a domain similar to the one considered in this work. The dialogue act classifiers described in this paper integrate four classes of features automatically extracted from three sources of information: the textual dialogue utterances, task-related runtime information logged into the database, and the images of the students recorded by depth cameras. Each feature class is explained in the following subsections.

4.1 Lexical Features

Based on previous dialogue act classification research (Bangalore et al., 2008; Boyer et al., 2010a; Kim et al., 2010), this work utilizes word *n*-grams as features for dialogue act classification. In the experiment reported in Section 5, unigrams and bigrams were used. Adding higher order *n*-grams did not improve model accuracies. In our corpus (Section 3), the nature of the student dialogues is informal and utterances contain many typos. To remove undesirable noise in the data such as typos and rare words, *n*-grams were filtered out according to their frequency in the training data (i.e., *n*-grams that appear less than a predefined cutoff threshold in the training data are not included as features). The value of the cutoff threshold was empirically determined by testing the values between 0 and 10 on a development data set that consisted of 20% of randomly selected dialogue sessions. The value of 3 was selected as it yielded the highest classification accuracy.

4.2 Dialogue Context Features

While lexical features characterize the intrinsic nature of individual utterances, the context of the utterance within a larger dialogue structure provides additional information about a given utterance in relation with other utterances. This work considers the following dialogue context features:

- ***Utterance Position:*** Specifies the relative position of an utterance at a given turn. The value of this feature indicates whether the utterance is the first one in a given turn, the second or later one in a given turn, or the given turn consists of a single utterance.
- ***Length:*** Specifies the number of a given utterance in terms of individual word tokens.
- ***Previous Author:*** Indicates whether the author of the previous utterance was *student* or *tutor*.
- ***Previous Tutor Dialogue Act:*** Specifies dialogue act of the most recent tutor utterance. The value of this feature is directly extracted from the manual annotation in the corpus, because in the broader context of our work, tutor dialogue moves will be determined by an external dialogue management module.

4.3 Task Context Features

In our data, students' problem-solving activities (e.g., reading the problem description, writing computer programming code, and compiling and running the code) functioned as an implicit communication channel between students and tutors (Section 1). Because of the existence of this implicit communication channel, the dialogue exchanges between students and tutors likely contain substantial information gaps. To overcome such information gaps, it is important to identify effective task context features. The present work leverages the following task context features, which can be automatically extracted during runtime:

- ***Previous Task Action:*** Specifies the type of the most recent problem-solving action performed by the student. The value could be *message* (writing a textual message to the tutor) *code* (writing code in the code window), or *compile_run* (compiling or running the code).
- ***Task Begin Flag:*** A binary feature that indicates whether a given utterance is the first one since the current problem task was posted.
- ***Task Activity Flag:*** Another binary feature indicating that a given utterance was preceded by a student's task activity.
- ***Last Compile/Run Status:*** Specifies the status (e.g., *begin*, *stop*, *success*, *error*, *input sent*) of the most recent compile/run action performed by the students.

In addition to the listed task context features, the utility of time information was also explored, such as the amount of time taken for previous coding activity and the elapsed time since the beginning of the current task. However, these features did not positively impact the performance of the learned models and were thus excluded.

4.4 Posture Features

After preprocessing recorded image frames with the estimation algorithm (Section 3.3), students' postures were represented as tuples of three different integer values, each respectively representing *head depth, mid torso depth, and lower torso depth*. To extract posture features, the time window of n seconds directly preceding a given utterance was compared with the previous time window of the same size in terms of *min*, *max*, *median*, *average*, and *variance* of each depth value. The indicators of whether each of these values has *increased*, *decreased* or *remained the same* were considered as potential posture features. To avoid introducing errors to the model by insignificant changes in posture, an error tolerance τ was allowed (i.e., the two compared postures were considered the same unless the amount of the change in the posture was greater than τ).

Optimal values for n and τ were empirically determined, selecting the values that maximized classification accuracy on the development data set. For n, the values between 0 and 60 were compared at an interval of 10. The value of 50 was selected for head depth and 60 for both mid torso depth and lower torso depth. Similarly, the value of τ was determined by comparing the values between 0 and 200 with an increment of 10. The selected value was 100.

All the potential posture features were examined in an informal experiment, in which each of the potential posture features were added to the combination of the lexical, the dialogue context, and the task context features. The posture features that improved the classification accuracy after adding them were included in the present dialogue act models. The selected posture features are *min of head depth* and *max, median, and average of lower torso depth*. None of the *mid torso depth* features were selected.

5 Experiment

The goal of this experiment is twofold: (1) to evaluate the effectiveness of the feature classes and (2) to compare the performance of three classifiers: maximum entropy (ME), naïve Bayes (NB), and conditional random field (CRF). These classifiers are chosen because they have been shown effective for dialogue act modeling in traditional task-oriented textual dialogue, in which conversational exchanges were carried out by a single channel of dialogue (Ivanovic, 2008; Kim et al., 2010). Previous result by Kim et al. (2010) suggests a structured model such as CRF yields more accurate dialogue act model compared to unstructured models (e.g., Naïve Bayes), because of its ability to model the sequential patterns in target classification labels. This experiment examines whether a similar finding is observed for our domain, which exhibits substantial information gaps due to the existence of an implicit communication channel, the task stream.

5.1 Dialogue Act Modeling

All classifiers were built using the MALLET package (McCallum, 2002). This experiment used the manually annotated portion of the data described in Section 3. The original dialogue scheme (Section 3.2) was slightly modified by introducing an additional dialogue act, *GR*, in order to distinguish conventional expressions, such as *greetings* and *thanks*, from other information-delivering utterances. For this modified scheme, annotator agreement was 0.81 in Cohen's Kappa on the doubly annotated portion of the corpus. 6 among the 21 dialogue sessions in the annotated data do not have accompanying images due to technical problems with the depth camera, thus these sessions were excluded from this experiment. Table 1 shows the distribution of the student dialogue act tags in the resulting corpus of 15 dialogues used in this experiment. The most frequent tag was *A* (*answer*), followed by *ACK* (*acknowledgement*) and *Q* (*question*). The features were extracted by aligning three sources of information (the textual dialogue corpus, the task-related runtime log data, and the recorded images) by timestamp. Word boundaries in the dialogue corpus were recognized by the surrounding white spaces and punctuations.

The dialogue context features (D) leveraged in this paper includes *previous tutor dialogue act*. This feature takes the manually annotated value in the corpus, because this work assumes the existence of an external dialogue manager. However, since the external dialogue manager is not likely to achieve 100% accuracy in predicting human tutor dialogue acts, it would be informative to estimate a reasonable range of the accuracies of the student dialogue act model, taking into account the errors introduced by the dialogue manager. For this reason, two versions of the dialogue context features were considered in this experiment: one that leverages the full set of dialogue context features (D) and the other that excludes previous tutor dialogue act (D-). These respectively provide the maximum and the minimum expected accuracy of the student dialogue act model, when used with a dialogue manager.

The models were trained and tested using five-fold cross validation, in which the 15 dialogue sessions were partitioned into 5 non-overlapping sets of the same size (i.e., 3 sessions per partition). Each set was used for testing exactly once.

Student Dialogue Act	Distribution
A (answer)	192 (34.7%)
ACK (acknowledgement)	124 (22.4%)
Q (question)	92 (16.6%)
S (statement)	76 (13.7%)
GR (greeting and thanks)	52 (9.4%)
C (clarification)	6 (1.0%)
RF (request for feedback)	5 (.9%)
RC (request confirmation)	2 (.4%)
O (other)	5 (.9%)
Total	**554**

Table 1. Student dialogue acts in the experiment data

5.2 Results

Table 2 reports the average classification accuracies from the five-fold cross validation. The majority baseline accuracy for our data is .347, when the classifier always chooses the most frequent dialog act (*A*). The first group of rows in Table 3 report the accuracies of individual feature classes. All of the individual features performed better than the baseline. The improvement from the baseline was significant except for D- with CRF. The most powerful feature class was dialogue context class when the full set was used. The second group in Table 3 shows the effects of incrementally combining the feature classes. Adding dialogue act features to the lexical features (L + D) brought significant improvement in the classification accuracy for ME and CRF. Adding posture features (L + D + T + P) also improved the accuracy of ME by a statistically significant margin. The last group shows similar results for ME when the previous tutor dialogue act was excluded from the dialogue context, except that the improvement achieved by adding the posture features (L + D- + T + P) was not significant.

	Features	ME	NB	CRF
Individual	Lexical (L)	$.696^{**}$	$.703^{**}$	$.599^{**}$
	Dialogue (D)	$\mathbf{.711}^{**}$	$\mathbf{.715}^{**}$	$\mathbf{.696}^{**}$
	Dialogue- (D-)	$.477^{**}$	$.473^{**}$	.405
	Task (T)	$.405^{**}$	$.396^{*}$	$.386^{*}$
	Posture (P)	$.382^{*}$	$.385^{*}$	$.399^{*}$
Max	L + D	$.772^{\S\S}$	.724	$.692^{\S\S}$
	L + D + T	.777	.729	.694
	L + D + T + P	$\mathbf{.789}^{\ddagger}$	.714	.682
Min	L + D-	$.724^{\S\S}$	.681	.606
	L + D- + T	.733	.671	.627
	L + D- + T + P	**.750**	.676	.644

Table 2. Classification accuracies ($^{*}p < .05$, $^{**}p < .01$ compared to baseline; $^{\S\S}p < .01$ compared to L; and $^{\ddagger}p < .05$ compared to L + D + T, with paired-samples t-test)

The highest accuracy was achieved by ME when using all four classes of the features, with maximum (L + D + T + P) .789 and minimum (L + D- + T + P) .750. For both the maximum and the minimum conditions, the differences among the classifiers were significant ($p < .01$, one-way repeated measure ANOVA), with post-hoc Tukey HSD tests revealing ME was significantly better than both NB ($p < .05$) and CRF ($p < .01$). There was no significant difference between NB and CRF.

6 Discussion

The experiment described in Section 5 compared the utility of lexical, dialogue context, task context, and posture features for dialogue act classification. The results indicate the effectiveness of these features. Particularly, adding the dialogue context and the posture features improved the accuracy of the maximum entropy model. Although the margin of improvement achieved by adding posture features was relatively small, the improvement was statistically significant ($p < .05$) for the maximum condition (L + D + T + P), which suggests that the users' posture during computer-mediated textual dialogue conveys important communicative messages.

The experiment also compared three classifiers: maximum entropy, naïve Bayes, and CRF. Interestingly, CRF was the worst-performing model for our data, contradicting the previous finding by Kim et al. (2010), in which CRF (a structured classifier) performed significantly better than Naïve Bayes (a non-structured classifier). This contradictive result suggests that, in our domain, the presence of an implicit communication channel resulted in substantial information gaps in the dialogue and it poses new challenges that were not encountered by conventional task-oriented domains consisting of a single communication channel.

The maximum entropy classifier achieved the best overall performance, reaching accuracy of .789. This is an encouraging result compared to previous work in a similar domain. Boyer et al. (2010a) reported an accuracy of .628 for dialogue act classification in a similar domain. However, a direct comparison is not applicable since different data were used in their work.

7 Conclusions and Future Work

Dialogue act modeling for a task-oriented domain in which the dialogue stream is interleaved with the task stream poses significant challenges. With the goal of effective dialogue act modeling, this work leverages information about users' posture as non-verbal features. An experiment found that posture is a significant indicator of dialogue acts, in addition to lexical features, dialogue context, and task context. The experiment also compared three statistical classifiers: maximum entropy, naive Bayes, and CRF. The best performing model was maximum entropy. Using all features, the maximum entropy achieved .789 in accuracy.

Several directions for future work are promising. First, given the encouraging finding that nonverbal information plays a significant role as a communicative means for task-oriented dialogue, various types of non-verbal information can be investigated, such as gesture and facial expressions. Second, incorporating richer task features, such as in our case, deep analysis of student code, may contribute to more accurate dialogue act modeling. Third, it is important to generalize the findings to a larger data set, including across other task-oriented domains. Finally, the community is embracing a move toward annotation-lean approaches such as unsupervised or semi-supervised learning, which hold great promise for dialogue modeling.

Acknowledgments

This research was supported by the National Science Foundation under Grant DRL-1007962. Any opinions, findings, and conclusions expressed in this material are those of the authors and do not necessarily reflect the views of the National Science Foundation.

References

Bangalore, S., Di Fabbrizio, G., & Stent, A. (2008). Learning the structure of task-driven human-human dialogs. *IEEE Transactions on Audio, Speech, and Language Processing*, *16*(7), 1249-1259.

Boyer, K. E., Grafsgaard, J. F., Ha, E. Y., Phillips, R., & Lester, J. C. (2011). An affect-enriched dialogue act classification model for task-oriented dialogue. *Proceedings of the 49th Annual Meeting of the Association for Computational Linguistics: Human*

Language Technologies (pp. 1190-1199). Portland, OR.

Boyer, K. E., Ha, E. Y., Phillips, R., Wallis, M. D., Vouk, M. A., & Lester, J. C. (2010a). Dialogue Act Modeling in a Complex Task-Oriented Domain. *Proceedings of the 11th Annual SIGDIAL Meeting on Discourse and Dialogue* (pp. 297-305). Tokyo, Japan.

Boyer, K. E., Phillips, R., Ingram, A., Ha, E. Y., Wallis, M., Vouk, M., & Lester, J. (2010b). Characterizing the effectiveness of tutorial dialogue with hidden markov models. *Proceedings of the 10th international conference on Intelligent Tutoring Systems* (pp. 55-64). Pittsburgh, PA.

Carletta, J., Isard, A., Isard, S., Kowtko, J., Doherty-Sneddon, G., & Anderson, A. (1997). The reliability of a dialogue structure coding scheme. *Computational Linguistics*, *23*, 13–31.

Cavicchio, F. (2009). The modulation of cooperation and emotion in dialogue: The REC corpus. *Proceedings of the ACL-IJCNLP 2009 Student Research Workshop* (pp. 81 - 87). Suntec, Singapore.

Cohen, J. (1960). A coefficient of agreement for nominal scales. *Educational and Psychological Measurement*, *20*(1), 37 - 46.

Di Eugenio, B., Xie, Z., & Serafin, R. (2010). Dialogue act classification, instance-based learning, and higher order dialogue structure. *Dialogue and Discourse*, *1*(2), 81 - 104.

D'Mello, S., & Graesser, A. (2010). Mining Bodily Patterns of Affective Experience during Learning. *Proceedings of the 3rd International Conference on Educational Data Mining* (pp. 31-40). Pittsburgh, PA.

Forsyth, E. N. (2007). *Improving Automated Lexical and Discourse Analysis of Online Chat Dialog*. Master's thesis. Naval Postgraduate School.

Grafsgaard, J. F., Boyer, K. E., Wiebe, E. N., & Lester, J. C. (2012). Analyzing Posture and Affect in Task-Oriented Tutoring. *Proceedings of the 25th Florida Artificial Intelligence Research Society Conference* (pp. 438-443). Marco Island, FL.

Ivanovic, E. (2008). *Automatic instant messaging dialogue using statistical models and dialogue acts*. Master's thesis. The University of Melbourne.

Joty, S. R., Carenini, G., & Lin, C.-Y. (2011). Unsupervised Modeling of Dialog Acts in Asynchronous Conversations. *Proceedings of the 22nd International Joint Conference on Artificial Intelligence* (pp. 1807-1813). Barcelona, Catalonia, Spain.

Jurafsky, D., Bates, R., Coccaro, N., Martin, R., Meteer, M., Ries, K., Shriberg, E., et al. (1998). *Switchboard discourse language modeling project report*. Baltimore, MD.

Kapoor, A., Burleson, W., & Picard, R. W. (2007). Automatic prediction of frustration. *International Journal of Human-Computer Studies*, *65*(8), 724-736.

Kim, S. N., Cavedon, L., & Baldwin, T. (2010). Classifying dialogue acts in one-on-one live chats. *Proceedings of the 2010 Conference on Empirical Methods in Natural Language Processing* (pp. 862-871). Cambridge, MA.

Knapp, M. L., & Hall, J. A. (2006). *Nonverbal Communication in Human Interaction* (6th ed.). Belmont, CA: Wadsworth/Thomson Learning.

McCallum, A. K. (2002). MALLET: A Machine Learning for Language Toolkit. Available from http://mallet.cs.umass.edu

Mehrabian, A. (2007). *Nonverbal Communication*. New Brunswick, NJ: Aldine Transaction.

Ritter, A., Cherry, C., & Dolan, B. (2010). Unsupervised modeling of twitter conversations. *Proceedings of Human Language Technologies: The 2010 Annual Conference of the North American Chapter* (pp. 172 - 180). Los Angeles, CA.

Russell, J. A., Bachorowski, J. A., & Fernandez-dols, J. M. (2003). Facial and vocal expressions of emotion. *Annual Review of Psychology*, *54*, 329-349.

Sanghvi, J., Castellano, G., Leite, I., Pereira, A., McOwan, P. W., & Paiva, A. (2011). Automatic analysis of affective postures and body motion to detect engagement with a game companion. *Proceedings of the 6th international conference on Human-robot interaction* (pp. 305-312). Lausanne, Switzerland.

Sridhar, R., Bangalore, S., & Narayanan, S. (2009). Combining lexical, syntactic and prosodic cues for improved online dialog act tagging. *Computer Speech and Language*, *23*(4), 407 - 422.

Stolcke, A., Ries, K., Coccaro, N., Shriberg, E., Bates, R., Jurafsky, D., Taylor, P., et al. (2000). Dialogue act modeling for automatic tagging and recognition of conversational speech. *Computational Linguistics*, *26*(3), 339-373.

Surendran, D., & Levow, G.-A. (2006). Dialog act tagging with support vector machines and hidden

Markov models. *Proceedings of Interspeech* (pp. 1950 - 1953). Pittsburgh, PA.

Woolf, B., Burleson, W., Arroyo, I., Dragon, T., Cooper, D., & Picard, R. W. (2009). Affect-aware tutors recognising and responding to student affect. *International Journal of Learning Technology, 4*(3/4), 129-164.

Wu, T., Khan, F. M., Fisher, T. A., Shuler, L. A., & Pottenger, W. M. (2005). Posting Act Tagging Using Transformation-Based Learning. In T. Y. Lin, S. Ohsuga, C.-J. Liau, X. Hu, & S. Tsumoto (Eds.), *Foundations of Data Mining and knowledge Discovery* (pp. 319 - 331). Springer.

Appendix. Dialogue Act Annotation Scheme and Inter-rater Agreement

Tag	Description	Frequency	Agreement (*k*)
H	**Hint:** The tutor gives advice to help the student proceed with the task	Tutor: 133 Student: 0	.50
DIR	**Directive:** The tutor explicitly tells the student the next step to take	Tutor: 121 Student: 0	.63
ACK	**Acknowledgement:** Either the tutor or the student acknowledges previous utterance; conversational grounding	Tutor: 41 Student: 175	.73
RC	**Request for Confirmation:** Either the tutor or the student requests confirmation from the other participant (e.g., *"Make sense?"*)	Tutor: 11 Student: 2	Insufficient data
RF	**Request for Feedback:** The student requests an assessment of performance or work from the tutor	Tutor: 0 Student: 5	1.0
PF	**Positive Feedback:** The tutor provides a positive assessment of the student's performance	Tutor: 327 Student: 0	.90
LF	**Lukewarm Feedback:** The tutor provides an assessment that has both positive and negative elements	Tutor: 13 Student: 0	.80
NF	**Negative Feedback:** The tutor provides a negative assessment of the student's performance	Tutor: 1 Student: 0	.40
Q	**Question:** A question regarding the task that is not a direct request for confirmation or feedback	Tutor: 327 Student: 120	.95
A	**Answer:** An answer to an utterance marked Q	Tutor: 96 Student: 295	.94
C	**Correction:** Correction of a typo in a previous utterance	Tutor: 10 Student: 6	.54
S	**Statement:** A statement regarding the task that does not fit into any of the above categories	Tutor: 681 Student: 174	.71
O	**Other:** Other utterances, usually containing only affective content	Tutor: 6 Student: 10	.69

Semantic Specificity in Spoken Dialogue Requests

Ben Hixon
Hunter College of The
City University of New York
New York, NY, USA
shixon@hunter.cuny.edu

Rebecca J. Passonneau
Columbia University
New York, NY, USA
becky@cs.columbia.edu

Susan L. Epstein
Hunter College, and
The Graduate Center of The
City University of New York
New York, NY, USA
susan.epstein@hunter.cuny.edu

Abstract

Ambiguous or open-ended requests to a dialogue system result in more complex dialogues. We present a semantic-specificity metric to gauge this complexity for dialogue systems that access a relational database. An experiment where a simulated user makes requests to a dialogue system shows that semantic specificity correlates with dialogue length.

1 Introduction

A dialogue system (DS) and its users have asymmetric knowledge. The DS has access to knowledge the user is not privy to, and the user has intentions that the DS attempts to recognize. When the user's intentions are difficult for her to specify fully, the user and DS must collaborate to formulate the intention. The thesis of this work is that a DS can assess the specificity of its knowledge with respect to the user intentions it is designed to address. Our principal result is that, for a DS that queries a relational database, measures of the ambiguity of database attributes can be used both to assess the scope of the DS's task and to guide its dialogue strategy. To demonstrate our thesis, we have developed a *semantic specificity* metric applicable to any DS that queries a relational database. This metric measures the degree to which one or more attributes can uniquely specify an item in the database. Attributes whose values are more often ambiguous have lower semantic specificity.

CheckItOut is a book request DS that references a copy of the catalogue at the Heiskell Braille and Talking Book Library with its 71,166 books (Epstein et al., In Press). We focus on three book attributes: AUTHOR, TITLE and CALL NUMBER. Only the latter is guaranteed to identify a unique book. Of the 64,907 distinct TITLE values, a large majority return a unique book (N=59,236; 91.3%). Of the 28,045 distinct AUTHOR values, about two thirds return a unique book (N=17,980; 64.1%).

Query return size	Distinct TITLE values	Distinct AUTHOR values
1	59236	17980
2	5234	4377
3	345	1771
...		
10	2	168
...		
184	–	1
Total	64907	28045

Table 1: When used as a query, many TITLE values return unique books, but AUTHOR values are less specific.

To compare the specificity of TITLE and AUTHOR, we calculated *query return size*, the number of distinct books in the Heiskell database returned by each possible attribute value. Table 1 tallies how many attribute values have the same query return size. TITLE partitions the books into 10 subsets, where the two most ambiguous TITLE values, *Collected Stories* and *Sanctuary*, each return 10 distinct books. AUTHOR produces 89 subsets; its most ambiguous value, Louis L'Amour, returns 184 distinct books. Clearly, TITLE has higher specificity than AUTHOR.

After a survey of related work, this paper defines a semantic specificity metric that is a weighted sum of the number of query return sizes for one or more attributes. We show through simulation that dialogue length varies with semantic specificity for a DS with a simple system-initiative dialogue strategy.

2 Related Work

Little work has been reported on measures of the relationship between dialogue complexity and the semantic structure of a DS application's database. Zadrozny (1995) proposes Q-Complexity, which roughly corresponds to vocabulary size, and is essentially the number of questions that can be asked about a database. Pollard and Bierman (2000) describe a similar measure that considers the number of bits required to distinguish every object, attribute, and relationship in the semantic space.

Gorin et al. (2000) distinguish between semantic and linguistic complexity of calls to a spoken DS. Semantic complexity is measured by inheritance relations between call types, the number of type labels per call, and how often calls are routed to human agents. Linguistic complexity is measured by utterance length, vocabulary size and perplexity.

Popescu et al. (2003) identify a class of "semantically tractable" natural language questions that can be mapped to an SQL query to return the question's unique correct answer. Ambiguous questions with multiple correct answers are not considered semantically tractable. Polifroni and Walker (2008) address how to present informative options to users who are exploring a database, for example, to choose a restaurant. When a query returns many options, their system summarizes the return using attribute value pairs shared by many of the members.

3 Semantic Specificity

The database queried by a DS can be regarded as the system's knowledge. Consequently, the semantic structure of the database and the way it is populated constrain the requests the system can address and how much information the user must provide. Intuitively, Table 1 shows that TITLE has a higher semantic specificity than AUTHOR. Our goal is to quantify the query ambiguity engendered by the instantiation of any database table.

Often a user does not know in advance which combination of attribute values uniquely communicates her intent to the system. In addition, the DS does not know what the user wants until it has offered an item that the user confirms, whether explicitly or implicitly. The remainder of this section defines the specificity of individual and multiple attributes with respect to a set of database instances.

3.1 Specificity for Single Attributes

When a user requests information about one or more entities, the request can map to many more database instances than intended. Let I be a set of instances (rows) in a database relation, and let α be an attribute of I with values V that occur in I. Denote by $q(v, \alpha)$ the *query return size* for $v \in V$ on α, the number of instances of I returned by the query $\alpha = v$. Whenever $q(v, \alpha) = 1$, the query returns exactly one instance in I; attributes with more such values have higher specificity. If $q(v, \alpha) = 1$ for every v, then α is *maximally specific* with respect to I.

Let Q_α be the set of d_α distinct query return sizes $q(v, \alpha)$ returned on I. We call Q_α the *query return size partition* for α. Q_α induces a partition of V into subsets $V_j, j \in Q_\alpha$ such that a query on every value in a given subset returns the same number of instances. Table 1 shows two such partitions. We now define the specificity $S(\alpha, I)$ of attribute α with respect to I as a weighted sum of the sizes of the subsets in the partition induced by α, normalized by $|I|$, the number of instances in I:

$$S(\alpha, I) = \frac{1}{|I|} \sum_{j \in Q_\alpha} w(j) \cdot |V_j| \quad (1)$$

The weight function w in (1) addresses the number of distinct values in each subset of Q_α. A larger query return size indicates a more ambiguous attribute, one less able to distinguish among instances in I. To produce specificity values in the range $[0, 1]$, $w(j)$ should decrease as j increases, but not penalize any query that returns a single instance, that is, $w(1) = 1$. The faster w decreases, the more it penalizes an ambiguous attribute. Here we take as w the inverse of the query return size, $w(j) = \frac{1}{j}$.

For our CheckItOut example, equation (1) scores TITLE's specificity as 0.871 and AUTHOR's specificity much lower, at 0.300. This matches our intuition. The third attribute with which a user can order a book, CALL NUMBER, was designed as a primary key and so has a perfect specificity of 1.000.

3.2 Specificity for Multiple Attributes

The specificity of a set $\beta = \{\alpha_1, \alpha_2, ..., \alpha_k\}$ of k attributes on a set of instances I measures to what degree a *combination* (one value for each attribute in β) specifies a restricted set of instances in I. Let V be the combinations for β that occur in I, and let $q(v, \beta)$ be the query return size for $v \in V$. Then Q_β, the set of d_β distinct query return sizes, induces a partition on V into subsets $V_j, j \in Q_\beta$ where combinations in the same subset return the same number of instances. We take $w(j,k) = \frac{1}{j^k}$ to penalize ambiguity more heavily when there are more attributes. Then the specificity of β with respect to I is

$$S(\beta, I) = \frac{1}{|I|} \sum_{j \in Q_\beta} w(j,k) \cdot |V_j| \qquad (2)$$

Using this equation, the specificity of $\beta = \{$TITLE, AUTHOR$\}$ is 0.880. Interestingly, this is not much higher than the 0.871 TITLE specificity alone, which indicates that, in this particular database instantiation, AUTHOR has little ability to disambiguate a TITLE query. This is because many "books" in the Heiskell catalog appear in two formats, Braille and audio. This duplication creates an ambiguity that is better resolved by prompting the user for CALL NUMBER or FORMAT. In some cases, a value for FORMAT might still result in ambiguity; for example, different recorded readers produce different audio versions of the same title and author. In contrast, the large difference between AUTHOR's very low specificity (0.300) and that of $\{$TITLE, AUTHOR$\}$ (0.880) suggests that, given an ambiguous author, it would in general be a good strategy for the DS to then prompt the user for the title.

Because specificity is a function of a database instantiation, specificity can be used to guide dialogue strategy. For the books in Heiskell's catalogue that cannot be uniquely identified by AUTHOR and TITLE alone, it can be determined *a priori* that some book requests cannot be disambiguated without additional attribute values.

4 Specificity in Simulated Dialogues

A DS faced with an ambiguous query should enter a disambiguation subdialogue. It can either offer a list of matching instances that must be individually confirmed or rejected by the user, or indicate to the user that an attribute value is ambiguous and request additional information. In general, a less specific user request should increase the dialogue length.

We tested this hypothesis with a simulated user that interacted with the CheckItOut book-order DS through a text interface. As in our work where human subjects called CheckItOut, a new scenario for each call included "patron" identification data and a list of four books with their authors, titles, and call numbers. In each dialogue, the simulator received a scenario, the DS confirmed the simulator's "identity," and then the simulator requested the books.

The simulator uses a rule-based dialogue strategy with some parameters, such as persistence in re-ordering the same book, that can be set or randomized to represent a set of real users more realistically. For this experiment, the simulator was set to request books only by author, and to be willing to engage in a disambiguation subdialogue of arbitrary length. When the system cannot uniquely identify a requested book, it begins a disambiguation subdialogue, an example of which is shown in Figure 1. To avoid addressing information presentation issues such as those explored in (Polifroni and Walker, 2008), CheckItOut followed a simple strategy of offering each next candidate book in a query return, and user studies with CheckItOut restricted query return size to a maximum of three books. For the simulations, we expect an inverse relationship between specificity and dialogue length.

S: NEXT BOOK?
U: Dan Simmons
S: DID YOU SAY DAN SIMMONS?
U: Yes
S: WOULD YOU LIKE ENDYMION BY THIS AUTHOR?
U: No
S: WOULD YOU LIKE THE CROOK FACTORY
BY THIS AUTHOR?
U: Yes

Figure 1: Sample disambiguation subdialogue.

We randomly sampled Heiskell's full set of 71,166 books to create five smaller instantiations of 1000 books each. We deliberately sampled at different frequencies within each subset of the original partition induced by AUTHOR, so that $S(\text{AUTHOR}, T)$ for instantiation T ranged from 0.3528 to 1.000. For each instantiation we simulated 25 dialogues. Conditions of relatively lower speci-

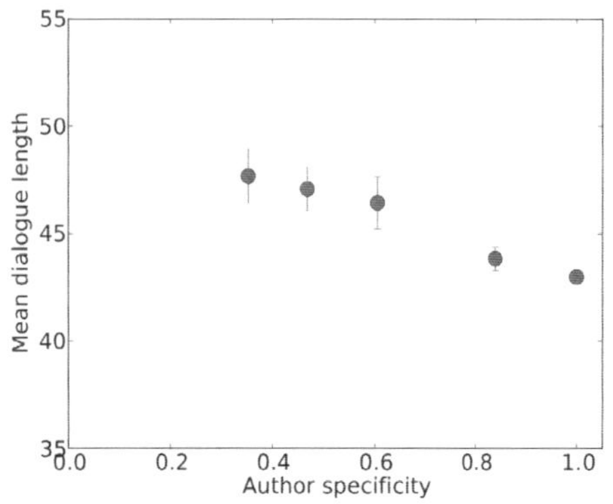

Figure 2: Dialogue length averaged across 25 simulated dialogues for each run of 5 different attribute specificity levels, shown with 95% confidence intervals.

ficity result in more dialogues like the one shown in Figure 1, with multiple turn exchanges where the DS offers the simulator different books by the requested author. As specificity approaches 1.0, the first book offered by the DS is more frequently the requested book, so no disambiguation is required, and the minimum dialogue length of 43 turns is achieved. Figure 2 compares the mean dialogue length for each sub-instantiation to its author specificity, and clearly shows that dialogue length increases as author specificity decreases. The error bars shrink as specificity increases because there is less variation in dialogue length when there are fewer candidate books for CheckItOut to offer.

5 Conclusion and Future Work

Semantic specificity has two important applications. Because it predicts how likely a value for a database attribute (or a combination for a set of attributes) is to return a single database instance, semantic specificity can help formulate subdialogues with a priority order in which the DS should prompt users for attributes. Because it is a predictor for dialogue length, semantic specificity could also be used to evaluate whether a DS dialogue strategy incurs the expected costs. Of course, many factors other than semantic specificity affect DS dialogue complexity, particularly the relation between users' utterances and the semantics of the database. In the examples given here, the way users refer to books corresponds directly to attribute values in the database. Other domains may require a more complex procedure to map between the semantics of the database and the semantics of natural language expressions.

Finally, how well semantic specificity with respect to a database instantiation predicts dialogue length depends in part on how closely the database attributes correspond to information that users can readily provide. Here, AUTHOR and TITLE are convenient both for users and for the database semantics. However, the maximally specific CALL NUMBER is often unknown to the user. For DSs where the database attributes differ from those that can be extracted from user utterances, we intend to explore enhanced or additional metrics to predict dialogue length and guide dialogue strategy.

Acknowledgments

We thank Julia Hirschberg for helpful comments, and Eric Schneider for help with the user simulator. National Science Foundation awards IIS-0745369, IIS-0744904 and IIS-084966 funded this project.

References

Susan L. Epstein, Rebecca J. Passonneau, Tiziana Ligorio, and Joshua Gordon. In Press. Data mining to support human-machine dialogue for autonomous agents. In *Proceedings of Agents and Data Mining Interaction (ADMI 2011)*. Springer-Verlag.

A. L. Gorin, J. H. Wright, G. Riccardi, A. Abella, and T. Alonso. 2000. Semantic information processing of spoken language. In *Proceedings of ATR Workshop on MultiLingual Speech Communication*, pages 13–16.

Joseph Polifroni and Marilyn Walker. 2008. Intensional summaries as cooperative responses in dialogue: Automation and evaluation. In *Proceedings of ACL-08: HLT*, pages 479–487, Columbus, Ohio, June. Association for Computational Linguistics.

Shannon Pollard and Alan W. Bierman. 2000. A measure of semantic complexity for natural language systems. In *NAACL-ANLP 2000 Workshop: Syntactic and Semantic Complexity in Natural Language Processing Systems*, pages 42–46, Stroudsburg, PA, USA. Association for Computational Linguistics.

Ana-Maria Popescu, Oren Etzioni, and Henry Kautz. 2003. Towards a theory of natural language interfaces to databases. In *Proceedings of the 8th international conference on Intelligent user interfaces*, IUI '03, pages 149–157, New York, NY, USA. ACM.

Wlodek Zadrozny. 1995. Measuring semantic complexity. In Moshe Koppel, Eli Shamir, and Martin Golumbic, editors, *Proceedings of the Fourth Bar Ilan Symposium on Foundations of Artificial Intelligence (BISFAI 1995)*, pages 245–254.

Contingency and Comparison Relation Labeling and Structure Prediction in Chinese Sentences

Hen-Hsen Huang
Department of Computer Science and Information Engineering,
National Taiwan University,
Taipei, Taiwan
hhhuang@nlg.csie.ntu.edu.tw

Hsin-Hsi Chen
Department of Computer Science and Information Engineering,
National Taiwan University,
Taipei, Taiwan
hhchen@csie.ntu.edu.tw

Abstract

Unlike in English, the sentence boundaries in Chinese are fuzzy and not well-defined. As a result, Chinese sentences tend to be long and consist of complex discourse relations. In this paper, we focus on two important relations, *Contingency* and *Comparison*, which occur often inside a sentence. We construct a moderate-sized corpus for the investigation of intra-sentential relations and propose models to label the relation structure. A learning based model is evaluated with various features. Experimental results show our model achieves accuracies of 81.63% in the task of relation labeling and 74.8% in the task of relation structure prediction.

1 Introduction

Discourse relation labeling has attracted much attention in recent years due to its potential applications such as opinion mining, question answering, etc. The release of the Penn Discourse Treebank (Joshi and Webber, 2004; Prasad et al., 2008) has advanced the development of English discourse relation recognition (Lin et al., 2009; Pitler et al., 2009; Pitler and Nenkova, 2009; Wang et al., 2010). For Chinese, a discourse corpus is not publicly available yet. Thus, the research on Chinese discourse relation recognition is relatively rare. Most notably, Xue (2005) annotated discourse connectives in the Chinese Treebank. Our previous work labeled four types of relations, including temporal, contingency, comparison and expansion, between two successive sentences, and reported an accuracy of 88.28% and an F-score of 62.88% (Huang and Chen, 2011). The major issue of our work is the determination of discourse boundaries. Each Chinese sentence is always treated as one of the two arguments in their annotation and many instances of the Contingency and the Comparison remain uncaught.

As suggested by the Penn Discourse Treebank annotation guidelines, an argument is possibly some clauses in a sentence, a sentence, or several successive sentences. In Chinese, the Contingency and the Comparison relations are likely to occur within a sentence. Thus, a lot of the Contingency relations and the Comparison relations are missing from annotation in the corpus used in our previous work, and the classification performance for these two relations, especially the Contingency relation, is especially poor (Huang and Chen, 2011).

In contrast to Chinese inter-sentential discourse relation detection (Huang and Chen, 2011) and the study of English coherence evaluation (Lin et al., 2011), this paper focuses on the Contingency relation and the Comparison relations that occur inside a sentence. In Chinese, the relations usually occur in the sentences which contain many clauses. For example, two relations occur in sample (S1).

(S1) 管理處雖嘗試要讓長期來作為大台北後花園的陽明山區更回歸自然 ("Although the

management office tried to make the Yangmingshan area a more natural environment as the long-term garden of Taipei"), 但隨著週休二日、經濟環境改善 ("But due to the two-day weekend and the improved economic conditions"), 遊客帶來停車、垃圾等間接影響卻更為嚴重 ("The issues of tourists parking, garbage, and other indirect effects become more serious")。

In (S1), the long sentence consists of three clauses, and such a Chinese sentence is expressed as multiple short sentences in English. Figure 1 shows that a *Comparison* relation occurs between the first clause and the last two clauses, and a *Contingency* relation occurs between the second clause and the third clause. An explicit paired discourse marker 雖 (although) ... 但 (but) denotes a Comparison relation in (S1), where the first clause is the first argument of this relation, and the second and the third clauses are the second argument of this relation. In addition, an implicit Contingency relation also occurs between the second and the third clauses. The second clause is the cause argument of this Contingency relation, and the third clause is its effect. It shows a nested relation, which makes relation labeling and relation structure determination challenging.

In Chinese, an explicit discourse marker does not always uniquely identify the existence of a particular discourse relation. In sample (S2), a discourse marker 而 "moreover" appears, but neither Contingency nor Comparison relation exists between the two clauses. The discourse marker 而 has many meanings. Here, It has the meaning of "and" or "moreover", which indicates an Expansion relation. In other usages, it may have the meaning of "but" or "however", which indicates a Comparison relation.

(S2) 而大陸經濟開放１０年以來，其進步更令人刮目相看。("Moreover, the progress of mainland is more impressive due to its economic openness for the last 10 years.")

Note that the relation structure of a sentence cannot be exactly derived from the parse tree of the sentence. Shown in Figure 2 is the structure of sample (S3) based on the syntactic tree generated by the Stanford parser. However, it is clear that the correct structure of (S3) is the one shown in Figure 3.

(S3) 目前雖然還只能在圖片上讓女性露露臉 ("Although women only appear in the pictures"), 但未來女性的貢獻 ("The contribution of women"), 將是教科書另一個著墨的重點 ("Will be another major focus in textbooks in the future")。

This shows that the Stanford parser does not capture the information that the last two clauses form a unit, which in turn is one of the two arguments of a Comparison relation.

In this work, we investigate intra-sentential relation detection in Chinese. Given a Chinese sentence, our model will predict if Contingency or Comparison relations exist, and determine their relation structure. In Section 2, the development of a corpus annotated with Contingency and Comparison relations is presented. The methods and the features are proposed in Section 3. In Section 4, the experimental results are shown and discussed. Finally, Section 5 concludes this paper.

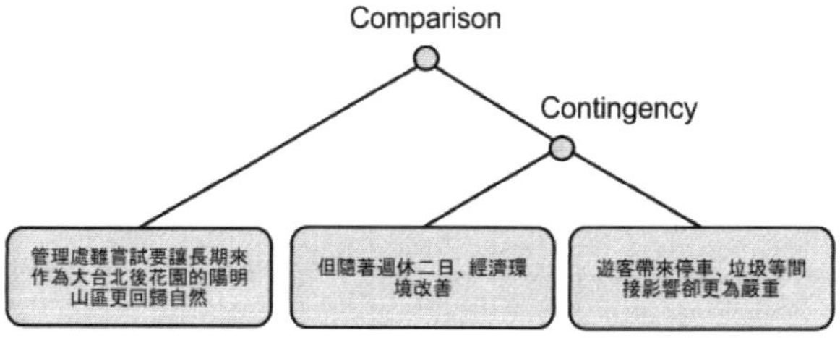

Figure 1: Relation structure of sample (S1).

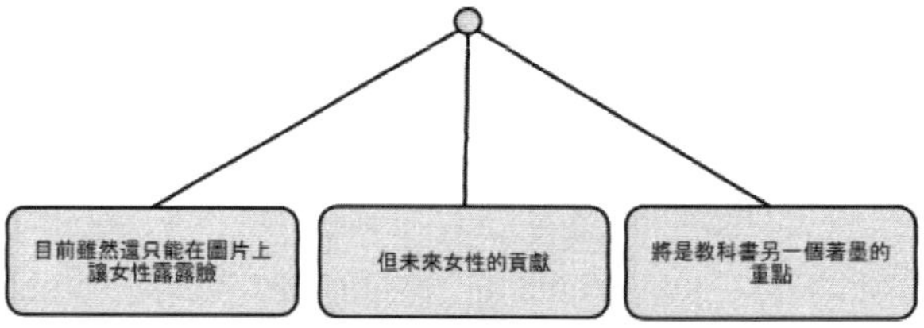

Figure 2: Structure of sample (S3) based on the syntactic tree generated by the Stanford parser.

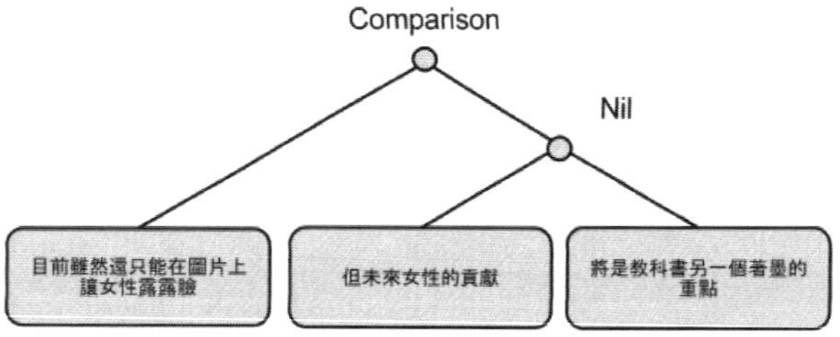

Figure 3: Correct structure of sample (S3)

2 Dataset

The corpus is based on the Sinica Treebank (Huang et al., 2000). A Total of 81 articles are randomly selected from the Sino and Travel sets. All the sentences that consist of two, three, and four clauses are extracted for relation and structure labeling by native Chinese speakers.

A web-based system is developed for annotation. The annotation scheme is designed as follows. An annotator first signs in to the annotation system, and a list of sentences that are assigned to the annotator are given. The annotator labels the sentences one by one in the system. A sentence is split into clauses along commas, and all of its feasible binary tree structures are shown in the interface. The annotator decides if a Contingency/Comparison relation occurs in this sentence. The sentence will be marked as "Nil" if no relation is found. If there is at least one relation in this sentence, the annotator then chooses the best tree structure of the relations, and the second page is shown.

The previously chosen tree structure is presented again, and at this time the annotator has to assign a suitable relation type to each internal node of the tree structure. The relation type includes Contingency "因果", Comparison "轉折", and Nil. For example, in sample (S4), its three internal nodes are annotated with three relation types as shown in Figure 4.

(S4) 即使沒有傳承的使命感 ("Even without the sense of mission of the heritage")，為了尋求更好的治療方式 ("In order to seek better treatments")，也會驅使這些醫學工作者跨越領域區隔 ("These medical workers will be driven crossing domain areas")，去尋找資源 ("To find resources")。

The number of feasible relation structures of a sentence may be very large depending on the number of clauses. For a sentence with n clauses, the number of its feasible structures is given as the recursive function $f(n)$ as follows, and the number of its feasible relation structures is $3^{n-1}f(n)$.

$$f(n) = \begin{cases} 1, & n = 1 \\ \sum_{i=1}^{n-1} f(n-i)f(i), & n > 1 \end{cases}$$

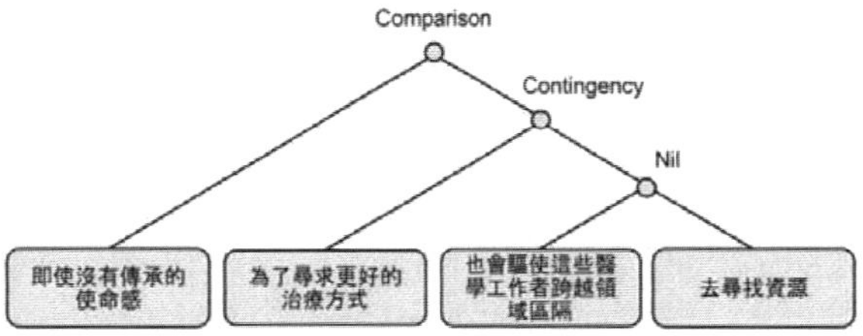

Figure 4: Relation structure of sample (S4).

Explicit/ implicit	Relations	2-Clause	3-Clause	4-Clause	Total	%
Explicit	Both	0	5	6	11	0.89%
	Contingency	59	72	45	176	14.31%
	Comparison	41	57	22	120	9.76%
	Nil	269	249	169	687	55.85%
Implicit	Both	0	0	0	0	0.00%
	Contingency	11	8	0	19	1.54%
	Comparison	6	0	0	6	0.49%
	Nil	125	56	4	211	17.15%
All		511	447	272	1,230	100.00%

Table 1: Statistics of the dataset.

For a two-clause sentence, there are only one tree structure and three possible relation tags (Contingency, Comparison, and Nil) for the only one internal node, the root. For a three-clause sentence, there are two candidate tree structures and nine combinations of the relation tags. For a four-clause sentence, there are five candidate tree structures and 27 combinations of the relation tags. There are theoretically 3, 18, and 135 feasible relation structures for the two-, three-, and four-clause sentences, respectively, though only 49 types of relations structures are observed in the dataset.

Each sentence is shown to three annotators, and the majority is taken as the ground-truth. The Fleiss-Kappa of the inter-annotator agreement is 0.44 (moderate agreement). A final decider is involved to break ties. The statistics of our corpus are shown in Table 1. The explicit data are those sentences which have at least one discourse marker. The rest of the data are implicit. A total of 11 explicit sentences which contain both Contingency and Comparison relations form complex sentence compositions. The implicit samples are relatively rare.

3 Methods

To predict the intra-sentential relations and structures, two learning algorithms, the modern implementation of the decision tree algorithm,

C5.0[1], and the support vector machine, SVMlight[2], are applied. The linguistic features are the crucial part in the learning-based approaches. Various features from different linguistic levels are evaluated in the experiments as shown below.

Word: The bags of words in each clause. The Stanford Chinese word segmenter[3] is applied to all the sentences to tokenize the Chinese words. In addition, the first word and the last word in each clause are extracted as distinguished features.

POS: The bags of parts of speech (POS) of the words in each clause are also taken as features. All the sentences in the dataset are sent to the Stanford parser[4] that parses a sentence from a surface form into a syntactic tree, labels POS for each word, and generates all the dependencies among the words. In addition, the POS tags of the first word and the last word in each clause are extracted as distinguished features.

Length: Several length features are considered, including the number of clauses in the sentence and the number of words for each clause in the sentence.

Connective: In English, some words/phrases called connectives are used as discourse markers. For example, the phrase "due to" is a typical connective that indicates a Contingency relation, and the word "however" is a connective that indicates a Comparison relation.

Similar to the connectives in English, various words and word pair patterns are usually used as discourse markers in Chinese. A dictionary that contains several types of discourse markers is used. The statistics of the connective dictionary and samples are listed in Table 2. An intra-sentential phrase pair indicates a relation which occurs only inside a sentence. In other words, a relation occurs when the two phrases of an intra-sentential pair exist in the same sentence no matter whether they are in the same clause or not. In contrast, an inter-sentential connective indicates a relation that can occur across neighboring sentences. Some connectives belong to both intra-sentential and inter-sentential types. Each connective in each clause is detected and marked with its corresponding type. For example, the phrase 相對的 "In contrast" will be marked as a connective that belongs to Comparison relation. The number of types and scopes of the connectives in a sentence are used as features.

Dependency: The dependencies among all words in a sentence are used as features. The Stanford parser generates dependency pairs from the sentence. A dependency pair consists of two arguments, i.e., the governor and the dependent, and their types. We are interested in those dependency pairs that are across two clauses. That is, the two arguments of a pair are from different clauses. In our assumption, the clauses have a closer connection if some dependencies occur between them. All such dependency pairs and their types are extracted and counted.

Structure: Recent research work reported improved performance using syntactic information for English discourse relation detection. In the work of Pilter and Nenkova (2009), the categories of a tree node, its parent, its left sibling, and its right sibling are taken as features. In the work of Wang et al. (2010), the entire paragraph is parsed

Relation	**Type**	**#**	**Samples**
Temporal	Single Phrase	41	目前 "now" 之後 "after"
	Intra-Sent Phrase Pair	80	接著...再 "Then...again" 當初...曾 "At first...ever"
	Inter-Sent Phrase Pair	30	當初...後來 "Initially...Later" 最早...緊接著 "At first...Then"
Contingency	Single Phrase	62	如此一來 "As a result" 假設 "If"
	Intra-Sent Phrase Pair	180	如果...則 "If ... then" 無論...都 "Whether ..."
	Inter-Sent Phrase Pair	14	既然...看來 "Since... It seems" 幸而...不然 "Fortunately... otherwise"
Comparison	Single Phrase	34	相對的 "In contrast" 未料 "Unexpectedly"
	Intra-Sent Phrase Pair	38	即使...卻 "Even ... but" 雖然...仍 "Although...still"
	Inter-Sent Phrase Pair	15	雖說...其實 "Although... In fact" 儘管...然而 "Although... However"
Expansion	Single Phrase	182	除此之外 "in addition" 而且 "moreover"
	Intra-Sent Phrase Pair	106	不只...而且 "Not only...but also" 或者...或者 "or...or"
	Inter-Sent Phrase Pair	26	首先...其次 "Firstly...Secondly" 既然...況且 "Since...Furthermore"

Table 2: Statistics of connectives (discourse markers).

[1] http://www.rulequest.com/see5-unix.html
[2] http://svmlight.joachims.org/
[3] http://nlp.stanford.edu/software/segmenter.shtml
[4] http://nlp.stanford.edu/software/lex-parser.shtml

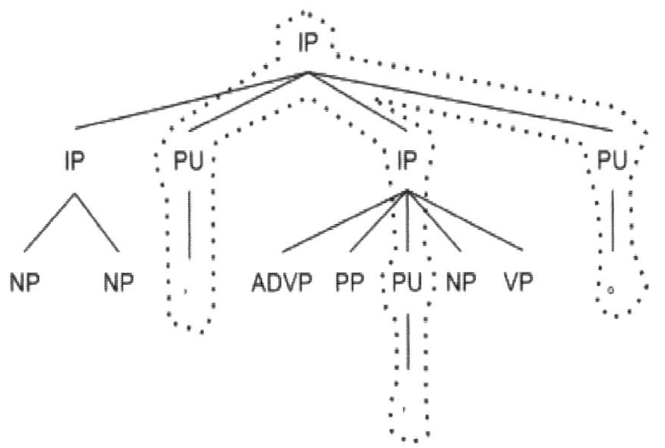

Figure 5: The upper three level sub-tree of (S1) and the punctuation sub-tree of (S1).

as a syntactic tree, and three levels of tree expansions are extracted as structured syntactic features.

To capture syntactic structure, we get the syntactic tree for each sentence using the Stanford parser, and extract the sub-tree of the upper three levels, which represents the fundamental composition of this sentence. In addition, all the paths from the root to each punctuation node in a sentence are extracted. From the paths, the depth of each comma node is counted, and the common parent node of every adjacent clause is also extracted. For example, the upper three level sub-tree of the syntactic tree of (S1) is shown in Figure 5. In addition, the sub-tree in the dotted line forms the structure of the punctuations in the (S1).

Polarity: A Comparison relation implies its two arguments are contrasting, and some contrasts are presented with different polarities in the two arguments. For example, sample (S5) is a case of Comparison.

(S5) 儘管天然環境如此優越，人為的不幸還是叫高棉子民不得好過，遍嚐戰亂的痛楚。("Despite such favorable natural environment, man-made disasters still make the Khmer people unfortunate to suffer from the pain of war.")

The first clause in (S5) is positive ("favorable natural environment"), while the last two clauses are negative ("unfortunate to suffer from the pain of war"). Besides the connectives 儘管 "despite" and 還是 "still", the opposing polarity values between the first and the last two clauses is also a strong clue to the existence of a Comparison relation. In addition, the same polarity of the last two clauses is also a hint that no Comparison relation occurs between them.

To capture polarity information, we estimate the polarity of each clause and detect the negations from the clause. The polarity score is a real number estimated by a sentiment dictionary-based algorithm. For each clause, the polarity score, and the existence of negation are taken as features.

4 Experiments and Discussion

4.1 Experimental Results

All the models in the experiments are evaluated by 5-fold cross-validation. The metrics are accuracies and macro-averaged F-scores. The t-test is used for significance testing.

We firstly examine our model for the task of two-way classification. In this task, binary classifiers are trained to predict the existence of Contingency and Comparison relations in a given sentence. For meaningful comparison, a majority classifier is used as a baseline model, which always predicts the majority class. In the dataset, 72.6% of the sentences involve neither Contingency nor Comparison. Thus, the major class is "Nil", and the accuracy and the F-score of the baseline model is 72.6% and 42.06%, respectively.

The experimental results for the two-way classification task are shown in Table 3. In the table, the symbol † denotes the lowest accuracy which has a significant improvement over the baseline at p=0.05 for the two models. The symbol ‡ denotes the adding of a single feature yields a significant improvement for the model at p=0.005.

The performance of the decision tree and the SVM are similar in terms of accuracy and F-score. Overall, the decision tree model achieves better accuracies. In the two-way classification task, the decision tree model with only the Word feature achieves an accuracy of 76.75%, which is significantly better than the baseline at p=0.05. For both the decision tree and the SVM, Connective is the most useful feature: performance is significantly improved with the addition of Connective.

Besides the binary classification task, we extend our model to tackle the task of finer classification. In the second task, four-way classifiers are trained

	Decision Tree		SVM	
Features	Accuracy	F-Score	Accuracy	F-Score
Word	†76.75%	58.94%	72.36%	56.54%
+POS	77.15%	61.72%	72.28%	60.53%
+Length	77.15%	61.72%	72.60%	61.09%
+Connective	‡81.63%	71.11%	‡78.05%	69.17%
+Dependency	81.14%	70.79%	77.80%	68.79%
+Structure	81.30%	70.78%	†77.48%	69.08%
+Polarity	81.30%	70.78%	77.64%	69.09%

Table 3: Performance of the two-way classification.

	Decision Tree		SVM	
Features	Accuracy	F-Score	Accuracy	F-Score
Word	†76.50%	34.72%	73.58%	31.54%
+POS	76.99%	36.77%	72.52%	34.44%
+Length	76.99%	36.77%	72.36%	34.54%
+Connective	79.84%	44.08%	‡77.89%	45.26%
+Dependency	79.92%	44.47%	†77.07%	44.42%
+Structure	79.92%	44.47%	77.15%	44.69%
+Polarity	79.92%	44.47%	77.40%	44.80%

Table 4: Performance of the four-way classification.

	Decision Tree		SVM	
Features	Accuracy	F-Score	Accuracy	F-Score
Word	73.66%	3.00%	70.00%	3.62%
+POS	73.66%	3.00%	69.84%	4.29%
+Length	73.66%	3.00%	70.00%	5.08%
+Connective	74.80%	4.90%	74.39%	7.66%
+Dependency	74.72%	4.61%	72.60%	5.60%
+Structure	74.72%	4.61%	73.01%	5.49%
+Polarity	74.72%	4.61%	72.76%	5.23%

Table 5: Performance of the 49-way classification.

Task	Explicit		Implicit	
	Accuracy	F-score	Accuracy	F-score
2-way	77.97%	69.26%	88.98%	50.64%
4-way	76.06%	42.54%	88.98%	31.39%
49-way	71.33%	4.88%	89.41%	1.92%

Table 6: Performances for explicit cases and implicit cases.

to predict a given sentence with four classes: existence of Contingency relations only, existence of Comparison relations only, existence of *Both* relations, and Nil. The experimental results of the four-way classification task are shown in Table 4. Consistent with the results of the two-way classification task, the addition of Connective to the SVM yields a significant improvement at p=0.005. The performance between the decision tree and the SVM is still similar, but the SVM achieves a slightly better F-score of 45.26% in comparison with the best F-score of 44.47% achieved by the decision tree.

We further extend our model to predict the full relation structure of a given sentence as shown in Figure 1 and Figure 4. This is a 49-way classification task because there are 49 types of the full relation structures in the dataset. Not only as many as 49-ways, 72.6% of instances belong to the Nil relation, which yields an unbalanced classification problem. The experimental results are shown in Table 5. In the most challenging case, the SVM achieves a better F-score of 7.66% in comparison with the F-score of 4.90% achieved by the decision tree. Connective is still the most helpful feature. Comparing the F-scores of the SVM in the three tasks with the F-scores of the decision tree, it shows that the SVM performs better for predicting finer classes.

4.2 Explicit versus Implicit

We compare the performances between the explicit instances and the implicit instances for the three tasks with the decision tree model trained on all features. The results are shown in Table 6.

The higher accuracies and the lower F-scores of the implicit cases are due to the fact that the classifier tends to predict the sentences as Nil when no connective is found, and most implicit samples are Nil. For example, the relation of Contingency in implicit sample (S6) should be inferred from the meaning of 帶給 "brought".

(S6) 得天獨厚的地理環境，的確帶給這個百年港埠無窮的財富。("The unique geographical environment, it really brought the infinite wealth to this hundred-year port.")

In addition, some informal/spoken phrases are useful clues for predicting the relations, but they are not present in our connective dictionary. For example, the phrase 的話 "if" implies a Contingency relation in (S7). This issue can be addressed by using a larger connective dictionary that contains informal and spoken phrases.

(S7) 想要以自助旅行的方式進行的話，那麼隨團旅遊呢？ ("If you want to backpacking, how about an organized tour?")

We regard an instance as explicit if there is at least one connective in the sentence. However, many explicit instances are still not easy to label even with the connectives. As a result, predicting explicit samples is much more challenging than the task of recognizing explicit discourse relations in English. One reason is the ambiguous usage of connectives as shown in (S2). The following sentence depicts another issue. The word 但是 "however" in (S8) is a connective used as a marker of an inter-sentential relation. That is, the entire sentence is one of the arguments of an inter-sentential Comparison relation, but it does not contain any intra-sentential relation inside the sentence itself.

(S8) 但是，操一口流利中文的傅吾康則公開批評這種看法。("However, Fu Wu Kang, who speaks fluent Chinese, openly criticizes this opinion.")

The fact that connectives possess multiple senses is one of the important reasons for their misclassification. This issue can be addressed by employing contextual information such as the neighboring sentences.

4.3 Number of Clauses

We compare the performance among the 2-clause instances, the 3-clause instances, and the 4-clause instances for the three tasks with the decision tree model trained on all the features. The accuracies (A) and F-scores (F) are reported in Table 7.

Comparing the two-way classification and the four-way classification tasks, the performance of the longer instances decreases a little in relation labeling. Although sentence complexity increases with length, a longer sentence provides more information at the same time. In the 49-way classification, the model should predict the sentence structure and the relation tags from the 49 candidate classes. The performances are greatly decreased because the feasible classes are substantially increased along with the number of clauses.

4.4 Contingency versus Comparison

The confusion matrix of the decision tree model trained on all features for the four-way classification is shown in Table 8. Each row represents the samples in an actual class, while each column of the matrix represents the samples in a predicted class. The precision (P), recall (R), and F-score (F) for each class are provided on the right side of the table. The class *Both* is too small to train the model, thus our model does not correctly predict the samples in the *Both* class. The confusion matrix shows that the confusions between the classes Contingency and Comparison are very rare. The major issue is to distinguish Contingency and Comparison from the largest class, Nil. The lower recall of the Contingency and Comparison relations also show that our model tends to predict the instances as the largest class.

Task	2-Clause		3-Clause		4-Clause	
	A (%)	F (%)	A (%)	F (%)	A (%)	F (%)
2-way	81.80	66.39	78.52	70.32	79.41	69.32
4-way	79.84	49.98	75.62	42.64	80.88	46.73
49-way	80.23	29.62	70.02	9.56	69.85	2.25

Table 7: Performances of clauses of different lengths.

Actual Class	Predicted Class				Performance		
	Cont.	Comp.	Both	Nil	P (%)	R (%)	F (%)
Cont.	61	3	0	131	81.33	31.28	45.19
Comp.	3	40	0	83	74.07	31.75	44.44
Both	2	4	0	5	0	0	0
Nil	9	7	0	882	80.11	98.22	88.24

Table 8: Confusion matrix of the best model in the 4-way classification.

Feature instance	Category	Usages
The first token in the third clause is the word 但 "but; however"	Word	100%
The first token in the second clause is the word 但 "but; however"	Word	99%
The first token in the third clause is a single connective of Contingency	Connective	98%
The first token in the first clause is the word 由於 "because; due to"	Word	96%
There is at least one word 以免 "in order to avoid" in the entire sentence	Word	95%
The first token in the second clause is the word 而 "moreover; while; but"	Word	94%
The first token in the third clause is a single connective of Comparison	Connective	93%
The second clause contains a single connective of Contingency	Connective	92%
The first token in the second clause is a single connective of Contingency	Connective	91%
The first clause contains a single connective of Contingency	Connective	90%

Table 9: Instances of the top ten useful features for the decision tree model

4.5 Features

The top ten useful feature instances reported by the decision tree model in the 49-way classification are shown in Table 9. Word and Connective provide useful information for the classification. Moreover, seven of the ten feature instances are about the word or the connective category of the first token in each clause. This result shows that it is crucial to employ the information of the first token in each clause as distinguished features. Certain words, for example, 但 "but; however", 由於 "because; due to", and 而 "moreover; while; but" are especially useful for deciding the relations. For this reason, labeling these words carefully is necessary. All the synonyms for each of these words should be clustered and assigned the same category. In addition, a dedicated extractor should be involved in accurately fetching these words from the sentence in order to reduce tokenization errors introduced by the Chinese word segmenter.

The advanced features such as Dependency, Structure, and Polarity are not helpful as expected. One possible reason is that the training data is still not enough to model the complex features. In such a case, the surface features are even more useful.

Sample (S1) shows an interesting case of the use of polarity information. The first clause of (S1) is positive (嘗試要讓長期來作為大台北後花園的陽明山區更回歸自然 "tried to make the Yangmingshan area a more natural state as the long-term garden of Taipei"), the second clause of (S1) is also positive (但隨著週休二日、經濟環境改善 "the two-day weekend and the improved economic conditions."), while the last clause of (S1) is negative (遊客帶來停車、垃圾等間接影響卻更為嚴重 "the issues of tourists parking, garbage, and other indirect effects"). The polarity of the last clause is opposite to those of the second clause, but they do not form a Comparison relation. Instead, a Contingency relation occurs between the last two clauses. Likewise, the polarities of the first and second clauses are both positive, but a Comparison relation occurs after the first clause. In fact, we realize that this is a complex case after performing an in-depth analysis. Because the last clause plays the role of effect in the Contingency relation, the negative polarity of the last clause makes the last two clauses form a negative polarity. For this reason, a Comparison relation occurs between the first argument with positive polarity and the second argument (i.e., the last two clauses) with negative polarity without a doubt. The polarity diagram of sample (S1) is shown in Figure 6.

Figure 6: Polarity diagram of (S1).

Overall, the interaction among structure, relation, and polarity is complicated. The surface polarity information we extract by using the sentiment dictionary-based algorithm does not capture such complexity well. A dedicated structure-sensitive polarity tagger will be utilized in future work.

5 Conclusion and Future Work

In this paper, we addressed the problem of intra-sentential Contingency and Comparison relation detection in Chinese. This is a challenging task because Chinese sentences tend to be very long and therefore contain more clauses. To tackle this problem, we constructed a moderate-sized corpus and proposed a learning-based approach that achieves accuracies of 81.63%, 79.92%, and 74.80% and F-scores of 71.11%, 45.26%, and 7.66% in the two-way, the four-way, and the 49-way classification tasks, respectively.

From the experiments, we found that performance could be significantly improved by adding the Connective feature. The next step is to enlarge the connective dictionary automatically by a text mining approach, in particular with those informal connectives, in order to boost performance. The advanced features such as Dependency, Structure, and Polarity are not as helpful as expected due to the small size of the corpus. In future work, we plan to construct a large Chinese discourse Treebank based on the methodology proposed in Section 2 and release the corpus to the public.

Naturally, the intra-sentential relations are important cues for discourse relation detection at the inter-sentential level. How to integrate cues from these two levels will be investigated. Besides, relation labeling and structure prediction are tackled at the same time with the same learning algorithm in this study. We will explore different methods to tackle the two problems separately to reduce the complexity.

References

Chu-Ren Huang, Feng-Yi Chen, Keh-Jiann Chen, Zhao-ming Gao, and Kuang-Yu Chen. 2000. Sinica Treebank: Design Criteria, Annotation Guidelines, and On-line Interface. In *Proceedings of 2nd Chinese Language Processing Workshop (Held in conjunction with the 38th Annual Meeting of the Association for Computational Linguistics, ACL-2000)*, pages 29-37.

Hen-Hsen Huang and Hsin-Hsi Chen. 2011. Chinese Discourse Relation Recognition. In *Proceedings of 5th International Joint Conference on Natural Language Processing (IJCNLP 2011)*, pages 1442-1446.

Aravind Joshi and Bonnie L. Webber. 2004. The Penn Discourse Treebank. In *Proceedings of the Language and Resources and Evaluation Conference*, Lisbon.

Ziheng Lin, Min-Yen Kan, and Hwee Tou Ng. 2009. Recognizing Implicit Discourse Relations in the Penn Discourse Treebank. In *Proceedings of the 2009 Conference on Empirical Methods in Natural Language Processing (EMNLP 2009)*, Singapore.

Ziheng Lin, Hwee Tou Ng, and Min-Yen Kan. 2011. Automatically Evaluating Text Coherence Using Discourse Relations. In *Proceedings of the 49th Annual Meeting of the Association for Computational Linguistics (ACL 2011)*, pages 997-1006.

Emily Pitler and Ani Nenkova. 2009. Using Syntax to Disambiguate Explicit Discourse Connectives in Text. In *Proceedings of the ACL-IJCNLP 2009 Conference Short Papers*, pages 13-1, Singapore.

Emily Pitler, Annie Louis, and Ani Nenkova. 2009. Automatic Sense Prediction for Implicit Discourse Relations in Text. In *Proceedings of the Joint Conference of the 47th Annual Meeting of the ACL and the 4th International Joint Conference on Natural Language Processing of the AFNLP (ACL-IJCNLP 2009)*, Singapore.

Rashmi Prasad, Nikhil Dinesh, Alan Lee, Eleni Miltsakaki, Livio Robaldo, Aravind Joshi, and Bonnie Webber. 2008. The Penn Discourse Treebank 2.0. In *Proceedings of the 6th International Conference on Language Resources and Evaluation (LREC)*.

WenTing Wang, Jian Su, and Chew Lim Tan. 2010. Kernel Based Discourse Relation Recognition with Temporal Ordering Information. In *Proceedings of the 48th Annual Meeting of the Association for Computational Linguistics (ACL 2010)*, Uppsala, Sweden, July.

Nianwen Xue. 2005. Annotating Discourse Connectives in the Chinese Treebank. In *Proceedings of the Workshop on Frontiers in Corpus Annotation II: Pie in the Sky*, pages 84-91.

A Study in How NLU Performance Can Affect the Choice of Dialogue System Architecture

Anton Leuski and David DeVault
USC Institute for Creative Technologies
12015 Waterfront Drive, Playa Vista, CA 90094
{leuski,devault}@ict.usc.edu

Abstract

This paper presents an analysis of how the level of performance achievable by an NLU module can affect the optimal modular design of a dialogue system. We present an evaluation that shows how NLU accuracy levels impact the overall performance of a system that includes an NLU module and a rule-based dialogue policy. We contrast these performance levels with the performance of a direct classification design that omits a separate NLU module. We conclude with a discussion of the potential for a hybrid architecture incorporating the strengths of both approaches.

1 Introduction

Recently computer-driven conversational characters or virtual humans have started finding real-life applications ranging from education to health services and museums (Traum et al., 2005; Swartout et al., 2006; Kenny et al., 2009; Jan et al., 2009; Swartout et al., 2010). As proliferation of these systems increases, there is a growing demand for the design and construction of virtual humans to be made more efficient and accessible to people without extensive linguistics and computer science backgrounds, such as writers, designers, and educators. We are specifically interested in making the language processing and dialogue management components in a virtual human easier for such potential authors to develop. Some system building steps that can be challenging for such authors include annotating the meaning of user and system utterances in a semantic formalism, developing a formal representation of information state, and writing detailed rules that govern dialogue management.

We are generally interested in the extent to which these various authoring steps are necessary in order to achieve specific levels of system performance. In this paper, we present a case study analysis of the performance of two alternative architectures for a specific virtual human. The two architectures, which have been developed and evaluated in prior work (DeVault et al., 2011b; DeVault et al., 2011a), differ substantially in their semantic annotation and policy authoring requirements. We describe these architectures and our evaluation corpus in Section 2. We focus our new analysis specifically on how the overall performance of one of the architectures, which uses a natural language understanding (NLU) module and hand-authored rules for the dialogue policy, depends on the performance of the NLU module. In Section 3, we describe our finding that, depending on the attainable level of NLU accuracy, this modular approach may or may not perform better than a simpler direct classification design that omits a separate NLU module and has a lower annotation and rule authoring burden. In Section 4, we present an initial exploration of whether a hybrid architecture may be able to combine these approaches' strengths.

2 Summary of Data Set and Prior Results

This work is part of an ongoing research effort into techniques for developing high quality dialogue policies using a relatively small number of sample dialogues and low annotation requirements (DeVault et al., 2011b; DeVault et al., 2011a). This section briefly summarizes our prior work and data set.

2.1 Data Set

For our experiments we use the dataset described in (DeVault et al., 2011b). It contains 19 Wizard of Oz dialogues with a virtual human called Amani (Gandhe et al., 2009). The user plays the role of an Army commander whose unit has been attacked by a sniper. The user interviews Amani, who was a witness to the incident and has some information about the sniper. Amani is willing to tell the interviewer what she knows, but she will only reveal certain information in exchange for promises of safety, secrecy, and money (Artstein et al., 2009).

Each dialogue turn in the data set includes a single user utterance followed by the response chosen by a human Amani role player. There are a total of 296 turns, for an average of 15.6 turns/dialogue. User utterances are modeled using 46 distinct speech act (SA) labels. The dataset also defines a different set of 96 unique SAs (responses) for Amani. Six external referees analyzed each user utterance and selected a single character response out of the 96 SAs. Thus the dataset defines a one-to-many mapping between user utterances and alternative system SAs.

2.2 Evaluation Metric

We evaluate the dialogue policies in our experiments through 19-fold cross-validation of our 19 dialogues. In each fold, we hold out one dialogue and use the remaining 18 as training data. To measure policy performance, we count an automatically produced system SA as correct if that SA was chosen by the original wizard or at least one external referee for that dialogue turn. We then count the proportion of the correct SAs among all the SAs produced across all 19 dialogues, and use this measure of *weak accuracy* to score dialogue policies.

We can use the weak accuracy of one referee, measured against all the others, to establish a performance ceiling for this metric. This score is .79; see DeVault et al. (2011b).

2.3 Baseline Systems

We consider two existing baseline systems in our experiments here. The first system (Rules-NLU-SA) consists of a statistical NLU module that maps a user utterance to a single user SA label, and a rule-based dialogue policy hand-crafted by one of the authors. The NLU uses a maximum-entropy model (Berger et al., 1996) to classify utterances as one of the user SAs using shallow text features. Training this model requires a corpus of user utterances that have been semantically annotated with the appropriate SA.

We developed our rule-based policy by manually writing the simple rules needed to implement Amani's dialogue policy. Given a user SA label A_t for turn t, the rules for determining Amani's response R_t take one of three forms:

$$(a)\text{if} A_t = \text{SA}_i \text{ then } R_t = \text{SA}_j$$
$$(b)\text{if} A_t = \text{SA}_i \wedge \ \exists k A_{t-k} = \text{SA}_l \text{ then } R_t = \text{SA}_j$$
$$(c)\text{if} A_t = \text{SA}_i \wedge \neg\exists k A_{t-k} = \text{SA}_l \text{ then } R_t = \text{SA}_j$$

The first rule form specifies that a given user SA should always lead to a given system response. The second and third rule forms enable the system's response to depend on the user having previously performed (or not performed) a specific SA. One the system developers, who is also a computational linguist, created the current set of 42 rules in about 2 hours. There are 30 rules of form (a), 6 rules of form (b), and 6 rules of form (c).

The second baseline system (RM-Text) is a statistical classifier that selects system SAs by analyzing shallow features of the user utterances and system responses. We use the Relevance Model (RM) approach pioneered by Lavrenko et al. (2002) for cross-lingual information retrieval and adapted to question-answering by Leuski et al. (2006). This method does not require semantic annotation or rule authoring; instead, the necessary training data is defined by linking user utterances directly to the appropriate system responses (Leuski and Traum, 2010).

Table 1 summarizes the performance for the baseline systems (DeVault et al., 2011a). The NLU module accuracy is approximately 53%, and the weak accuracy of .58 for the corresponding system (Rules-NLU-SA) is relatively low when compared to the RM system at .71. For comparison we provide a third data point: for Rules-G-SA, we assume that our NLU is 100% accurate and always returns the correct ("gold") SA label. We then run the rule-based dialogue policy on those labels. The third column (Rules-G-SA) shows the resulting weak accuracy value, .79, which is comparable to the weak accuracy score achieved by the human referees (DeVault et al., 2011b).

Rules-NLU-SA	RM-Text	Rules-G-SA
.58	.71	.79

Table 1: Weak accuracy results for baseline systems.

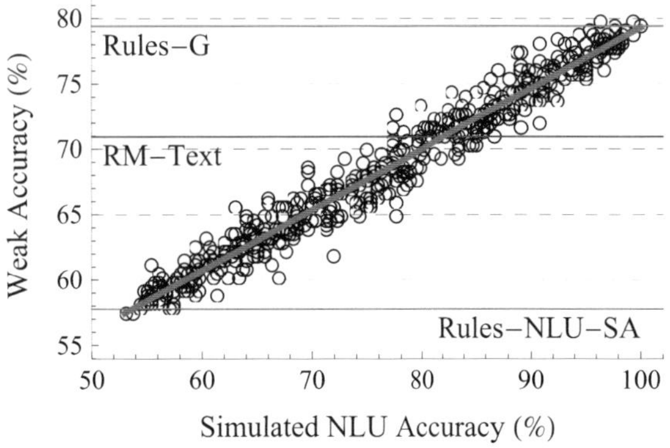

Figure 1: Weak accuracy of the Rules system as a function of simulated NLU accuracy.

3 NLU Accuracy and System Performance

We conducted two experiments. In the first, we studied the effect of NLU accuracy on the performance of the Rules-NLU-SA system. One of our goals was to find how accurate the NLU would have to be for the Rules-NLU-SA system to outperform RM-Text.

To investigate this, we simulated NLU performance at different accuracy levels by repeatedly sampling to create a mixture of the SAs from the trained NLU classifier and from the correct (gold) set of SAs. Specifically, we set a fixed value p ranging from 0 to 1 and then iterate over all dialogue turns in the held out dialogue, selecting the the correct SA label with probability p or the trained NLU module's output with probability $1 - p$. Using the sampled set of SA labels, we compute the resulting simulated NLU accuracy, run the Rules dialogue policy, and record the weak accuracy result. We repeat the process 25 times for each value of p. We let p range from 0 to 1 in increments of .05 to explore a range of simulated accuracy levels.

Figure 1 shows simulated NLU accuracy and the corresponding dialogue policy weak accuracy as a point in two dimensions. The points form a cloud with a clear linear trend that starts at approximately 53% NLU accuracy where it intersects with the Rules-NLU-SA system performance and then goes up to the Rules-G performance at 100% NLU accuracy. The correlation is strong with $R^2 = 0.97$.[1]

The existence of a mostly linear relationship comports with the fact that most of the policy rules (30 of 42), as described in Section 2.3, are of form (a). For such rules, each individual correct NLU speech act translates directly into a single correct system response, with no dependence on the system having understood previous user utterances correctly. In contrast, selecting system responses that comply with rules in forms (b) and (c) generally requires correct understanding of multiple user utterances. Such rules create a nonlinear relationship between policy performance and NLU accuracy, but these rules are relatively few in number for Amani.

The estimated linear trend line (in purple) crosses the RM-Text system performance at approximately 82% NLU accuracy. This result suggests that our NLU component would need to improve from its current accuracy of 53% to approximately 82% accuracy for the Rules-NLU-SA system to outperform the RM-Text classifier. This represents a very substantial increase in NLU accuracy that, in practice, could be expected to require a significant effort involving utterance data collection, semantic annotation, and optimization of machine learning for NLU.

4 Hybrid System

In our second experiment we investigated the potential to integrate the Rules-NLU-SA and RM-Text systems together for better performance. Our approach draws on a confidence score θ from the NLU maximum-entropy classifier; specifically, θ is the probability assigned to the most probable user SA.

Figure 2 shows an analysis of NLU accuracy, Rules-NLU-SA, and RM-Text that is restricted to those subsets of utterances for which NLU confidence θ is greater than or equal to some threshold τ. Two important aspects of this figure are (1) that raising the minimum confidence threshold also raises the NLU accuracy on the selected subset of utterances; and (2) that there is a threshold NLU confidence level beyond which Rules-NLU-SA seems to

[1] This type of analysis of dialogue system performance in terms of internal component metrics is somewhat similar to the regression analysis in the PARADISE framework (Walker et al., 2000). However, here we are not concerned with user satisfaction, but are instead focused solely on the modular system's ability to reproduce a specific well-defined dialogue policy.

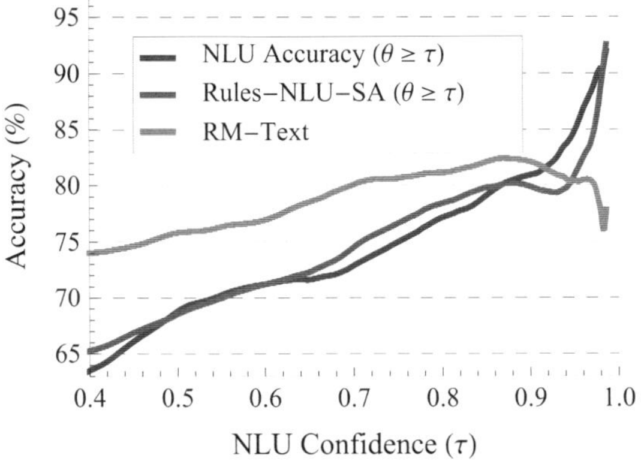

Figure 2: Weak accuracy of Rules-NLU-SA and RM-Text on utterance subsets for which NLU confidence $\theta \geq \tau$. We also indicate the corresponding NLU accuracy at each threshold. In all cases a rolling average of 30 data points is shown to more clearly indicate the trends.

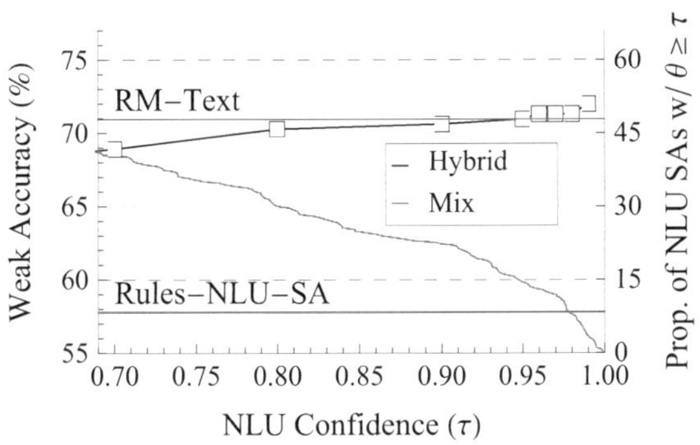

Figure 3: Weak accuracy of the Hybrid system as a function of the NLU confidence score.

outperform RM-Text. This confidence level is approximately 0.95, and it identifies a subset of user utterances for which NLU accuracy is 83.3%. These results therefore suggest that NLU confidence can be useful in identifying utterances for which NLU speech acts are more likely to be accurate and Rules-NLU-SA is more likely to perform well.

To explore this further, we implemented a hybrid system that chooses between Rules-NLU-SA or RM-Text as follows. If the confidence score is high enough ($\theta \geq \tau$, for some fixed threshold τ), the Hybrid system uses the NLU output to run the Rules dialogue policy to select the system SA; otherwise, it discards the NLU SA, and applies the RM classifier to select the system response directly.

Figure 3 shows the plot of the Hybrid system performance as a function of the threshold value τ. We see that with sufficiently high threshold value ($\tau \geq 0.95$) the Hybrid system outperforms both the Rules-NLU-SA and the RM-Text systems. The second line, labeled "Mix" and plotted against the secondary (right) axis, shows the proportion of the NLU SAs with the confidence score that exceed the threshold ($\theta \geq \tau$). It indicates how often the Hybrid system prefers the Rules-NLU-SA output over the RM-Text system output. We observe that approximately 42 of the NLU outputs over all 296 dialogue turns (15%) have confidence values $\theta \geq 0.95$. However, for most of these dialogue turns the outputs for the Rules-NLU-SA and RM-Text dialogue policies are the same. While we observe a small improvement in the Hybrid system weak accuracy values over the RM-Text system at thresholds of 0.95 and higher, the difference is not statistically significant.

Despite the lack of statistical significance in the initial Hybrid results in this small data set, we interpret the complementary evidence from both experiments, which support the potential for Rules-NLU-SA to perform well when NLU accuracy is high, and the potential for a hybrid system to identify a subset of utterances that are likely to be understood accurately at run-time, as indicating that a hybrid design is a promising avenue for future work.

5 Conclusions and Future Work

We presented a case study analysis of how the level of performance that is achievable in an NLU module can provide perspective on the design choices for a modular dialogue system. We found that NLU accuracy must be substantially higher than it currently is in order for the Rules-NLU-SA design, which carries a greater annotation and rule authoring burden, to deliver better performance than the simpler RM-Text design. We also presented evidence that a hybrid architecture could be a promising direction.

Acknowledgments

The project or effort described here has been sponsored by the U.S. Army Research, Development, and Engineering Command (RDECOM). Statements and opinions expressed do not necessarily reflect the position or the policy of the United States Government, and no official endorsement should be inferred.

References

Ron Artstein, Sudeep Gandhe, Michael Rushforth, and David R. Traum. 2009. Viability of a simple dialogue act scheme for a tactical questioning dialogue system. In *DiaHolmia 2009: Proceedings of the 13th Workshop on the Semantics and Pragmatics of Dialogue*, page 43–50, Stockholm, Sweden, June.

Adam L. Berger, Stephen D. Della Pietra, and Vincent J. D. Della Pietra. 1996. A maximum entropy approach to natural language processing. *Computational Linguistics*, 22(1):39–71.

David DeVault, Anton Leuski, and Kenji Sagae. 2011a. An evaluation of alternative strategies for implementing dialogue policies using statistical classification and rules. In *Proceedings of the 5th International Joint Conference on Natural Language Processing (IJCNLP)*, pages 1341–1345, Nov.

David DeVault, Anton Leuski, and Kenji Sagae. 2011b. Toward learning and evaluation of dialogue policies with text examples. In *Proceedings of the 12th annual SIGdial Meeting on Discourse and Dialogue*, pages 39–48.

Sudeep Gandhe, Nicolle Whitman, David R. Traum, and Ron Artstein. 2009. An integrated authoring tool for tactical questioning dialogue systems. In *6th Workshop on Knowledge and Reasoning in Practical Dialogue Systems*, Pasadena, California, July.

Dusan Jan, Antonio Roque, Anton Leuski, Jackie Morie, and David R. Traum. 2009. A virtual tour guide for virtual worlds. In Zsófia Ruttkay, Michael Kipp, Anton Nijholt, and Hannes Högni Vilhjálmsson, editors, *IVA*, volume 5773 of *Lecture Notes in Computer Science*, pages 372–378. Springer.

Patrick G. Kenny, Thomas D. Parsons, and Albert A. Rizzo. 2009. Human computer interaction in virtual standardized patient systems. In *Proceedings of the 13th International Conference on Human-Computer Interaction. Part IV*, pages 514–523, Berlin, Heidelberg. Springer-Verlag.

Victor Lavrenko, Martin Choquette, and W. Bruce Croft. 2002. Cross-lingual relevance models. In *Proceedings of the 25th annual international ACM SIGIR conference on Research and development in information retrieval*, pages 175–182, Tampere, Finland.

Anton Leuski and David Traum. 2010. NPCEditor: A tool for building question-answering characters. In *Proceedings of The Seventh International Conference on Language Resources and Evaluation (LREC)*.

Anton Leuski, Ronakkumar Patel, David Traum, and Brandon Kennedy. 2006. Building effective question answering characters. In *Proceedings of the 7th SIGdial Workshop on Discourse and Dialogue*, Sydney, Australia, July.

W. Swartout, J. Gratch, R. W. Hill, E. Hovy, S. Marsella, J. Rickel, and D. Traum. 2006. Toward virtual humans. *AI Mag.*, 27(2):96–108.

William R. Swartout, David R. Traum, Ron Artstein, Dan Noren, Paul E. Debevec, Kerry Bronnenkant, Josh Williams, Anton Leuski, Shrikanth Narayanan, and Diane Piepol. 2010. Ada and grace: Toward realistic and engaging virtual museum guides. In Jan M. Allbeck, Norman I. Badler, Timothy W. Bickmore, Catherine Pelachaud, and Alla Safonova, editors, *IVA*, volume 6356 of *Lecture Notes in Computer Science*, pages 286–300. Springer.

David Traum, William Swartout, Jonathan Gratch, Stacy Marsella, Patrick Kenney, Eduard Hovy, Shri Narayanan, Ed Fast, Bilyana Martinovski, Rahul Bhagat, Susan Robinson, Andrew Marshall, Dagen Wang, Sudeep Gandhe, and Anton Leuski. 2005. Dealing with doctors: Virtual humans for non-team interaction training. In *Proceedings of ACL/ISCA 6th SIGdial Workshop on Discourse and Dialogue*, Lisbon, Portugal, September.

Marilyn Walker, Candace Kamm, and Diane Litman. 2000. Towards developing general models of usability with PARADISE. *Nat. Lang. Eng.*, 6(3-4):363–377.

Integrating Incremental Speech Recognition and POMDP-based Dialogue Systems

Ethan O. Selfridge[†], **Iker Arizmendi**[‡], **Peter A. Heeman**[†], **and Jason D. Williams**[1]

[†] Center for Spoken Language Understanding, Oregon Health & Science University, Portland, OR, USA
[‡]AT&T Labs – Research, Shannon Laboratory, Florham Park, NJ, USA
[1]Microsoft Research, Redmond, WA, USA
{selfridg,heemanp}@ohsu.edu
iker@research.att.com jason.williams@microsoft.com

Abstract

The goal of this paper is to present a first step toward integrating Incremental Speech Recognition (ISR) and Partially-Observable Markov Decision Process (POMDP) based dialogue systems. The former provides support for advanced turn-taking behavior while the other increases the semantic accuracy of speech recognition results. We present an *Incremental Interaction Manager* that supports the use of ISR with strictly turn-based dialogue managers. We then show that using a POMDP-based dialogue manager with ISR substantially improves the semantic accuracy of the incremental results.

1 Introduction and Background

This paper builds toward integrating two distinct lines of research in spoken dialogue systems: incremental speech recognition (ISR) for input, and Partially Observable Markov Decision Processes (POMDPs) for dialogue management.

On the one hand, ISR improves on whole-utterance speech recognition by streaming results to the dialogue manager (DM) in real time (Baumann et al., 2009; Skantze and Schlangen, 2009). ISR is attractive because it enables sophisticated system behavior such as interruption and back-channeling. However, ISR output is particularly error-prone, and often requires a specialized dialogue manager to be written (Buß and Schlangen, 2011; Schlangen and Skantze, 2009).

On the other hand, POMDP-based dialogue managers improve on traditional approaches by (in part) tracking a distribution over many possible dialogue states, rather than just one, thereby improving robustness to speech recognition errors (Williams and Young, 2007; Thomson and Young, 2010; Young et al., 2010). The overall aim of combining these two lines of research is to improve the robustness of error-prone ISR output.

To our knowledge only one study to date has combined ISR and POMDPs. Lu et al. (2011) show how 1-best ISR hypotheses can be used within a single dialogue turn. This work is different than the present paper, where we use N-Best lists of ISR results across multiple turns of a dialogue.

Specifically, this paper makes two contributions. First, as a foundation, we introduce an *Incremental Interaction Manager* (IIM) that enables ISR to be used within the traditional turn-based dialogue management framework. The IIM confers many, but not all, of the benefits of ISR without requiring modification to a traditional dialogue manager. Thus, in theory, any existing dialogue system architecture could use ISR with the addition of an IIM. Second, we show that pairing our IIM with a POMDP-based dialogue manager yields a substantial improvement in accuracy for incremental recognition results at the dialogue level.

The paper is organized as follows. Section 2 describes the IIM, section 3 describes the POMDP integration, sections 4 and 5 describe experiments and results, and section 6 concludes.

[1]Work done while at AT&T Labs - Research

Table 1: Example IIM operation. P = partial ISR result; A = dialogue action.

ISR	IIM	Original DM state	Copied DM state	DM Action
Prompt: "Where are you leaving from?"				
yew	Rej. P	0	0	-
ridge	Acc. P / Rej. A	0	0	"I'm sorry..."
mckee	Acc. P / Acc. A	0	1	"Ok, Mckee..."
mckeesport	Acc. P / Acc. A	0	2	"Ok, Mckeesport.."
mckeesport center	Acc. P / Rej. A	0	2	"Ok, Mckeesport.."
Prompt: "Ok, Mckeesport. Where are you going to?"				
pitt	Acc. P / Rej. A	2	4	"I'm sorry..."
pittsburgh	Acc. P / Acc. A	2	5	"Ok, Pittsburgh..."

2 Incremental Interaction manager

The Incremental Interaction Manager (IIM) mediates communication between the incremental speech recognizer and the DM. The key idea is that the IIM evaluates potential dialogue moves by applying ISR results to temporary instances of the DM. The IIM *copies* the current state of the DM, provides the copied DM with a recognition result, and inspects the action that the copied DM would take.[2] If the action does not sufficiently advance the dialogue (such as re-asking the same question), the action is rejected and the copied DM is discarded. If the action advances the dialogue (such as asking for or providing new information), then that action is immediately executed.

The system should gracefully handle revisions following a premature action execution, and a copying procedure is a viable solution for any DM. When a revision is received, a *second* copy of the original DM is made and the new ISR result is passed to that second copy; if that second copy takes an action that advances the dialogue *and is different* from the action generated by the first copy, then the first action is terminated, the first copy of the DM is discarded, the second action is initiated, and the second copy assumes the position of the first copy. Additional revisions can be handled by following the same procedure. Terminating a speech action and immediately starting another can be jarring ("Say a city / Ok, Boston..."), which can be mitigated by preceding actions with either a sound or simple silence (at the expense of some response delay). Once recognition is complete, the copied DM is installed as the new original DM.

Many ISR results can be discarded before passing them to the DM. First, only incremental results that could correspond to complete user utterance are considered: incomplete results are discarded and never passed to the DM. In addition, ISR results are often unstable, and it is undesirable to proceed with an ISR result if it will very likely be revised. Thus each candidate ISR result is scored for stability (Selfridge et al., 2011) and results with scores below a manually-set threshold are discarded.

Table 1 shows an example of the recognizer, the IIM, and the DM. For sake of clarity, stability scores are not shown. The system asks "Where are you leaving from?" and the user answers "Mckeesport Center." The IIM receives five ISR results (called *partials*), rejecting the first, *yew*, because its stability score is too low (not shown). With the second, *ridge*, it copies the DM, passes *ridge* to the copy, and discards the action of the copied DM (also discarded) because it does not advance the dialogue. It accepts and begins to execute the action generated by the third partial, *mckee*. The fourth partial revises the action, and the fifth action is rejected since it is the same. The original DM is then discarded and the copied DM state is installed in its place.

Overall, the IIM enables a turn-based DM to enjoy many of the benefits of ISR – in particular, the ability to make turn-taking decisions with a complete account of the dialogue history.

[2]If the DM design does *not* force a state transition following a result then the DM supplies the the action without copying.

3 Integrating ISR with a POMDP-based dialogue manager

A (traditional) dialogue manager based on a partially observable Markov decision process (POMDP DM) tracks a probability distribution over multiple hidden dialogue states called a *belief state* (Williams and Young, 2007).[3] As such, POMDP DMs readily make use of the entire ASR N-Best list, even for low-confidence results — the confidence level of each N-Best list item contributes proportionally to the probability of its corresponding hidden state.

It is straightforward to integrate ISR and a POMDP DM using the IIM. Each item on the N-Best list of an incremental result is assigned a confidence score (Williams and Balakrishnan, 2009) and passed to the POMDP DM as if it were a complete result, triggering a belief state update. Note that this approach is not *predicting* future user speech from partial results (DeVault et al., 2009; Lu et al., 2011), but rather (tentatively) assuming that partial results are complete.

The key benefit is that a belief state generated from an incremental result incorporates all of the contextual information available to the system *from the start of the dialogue until the moment of that incremental result.* By comparison, an isolated incremental result includes only information from the current utterance. If the probability models in the POMDP are estimated properly, belief states should be more accurate than isolated incremental results.

4 Experimental design

For our experiments we used a corpus of 1037 calls from real users to a single dialogue system that provides bus timetable information for Pittsburgh, PA (a subsequent version of Williams (2011)). This dialogue system opened by asking the caller to say a bus route number or "I don't know"; if the system had insufficient confidence following recognition, it repeated the question. We extracted the first 3 responses to the system's bus route question. Often the system did not need to ask 3 times; our experimental set contained 1037 calls with one or more attempts, 586 calls with two or more attempts, and 356 calls with three or more attempts. These utterances were all transcribed, and tagged for the bus route they contained, if any: 25% contained neither a route nor "I don't know".

We ran incremental speech recognition on each utterance using Lattice-Aware Incremental Speech Recognition (Selfridge et al., 2011) on the AT&T WATSON^{SM} speech recognizer (Goffin et al., 2005) with the same rule-based language models used in the production system. On average, there were 5.78, 5.44, and 5.11 incremental results per utterance (plus an utterance-final result) for the first, second, and third attempts. For each incremental result, we noted its time stamp and interpretation: *correct*, if the interpretation was present and correct, otherwise *incorrect*. Each incremental result included an N-Best list, from which we determined oracle accuracy: *correct* if the correct interpretation was present anywhere on the most recent ISR N-Best list, otherwise *incorrect*.

Each incremental result was then passed to the IIM and POMDP DM. The models in the POMDP DM were estimated using data collected from a different (earlier) time period. When an incremental result updated the belief state, the top hypothesis for the route was extracted from the belief state and scored for correctness. For utterances in the first attempt, the belief state was initialized to its prior; for subsequent attempts, it incorporated all of the prior (whole-turn) utterances. In other words, each attempt was begun assuming the belief state had been running up to that point.

5 Results and Discussion

We present results by showing instantaneous semantic accuracy for the raw incremental result (baseline), the top belief state, and oracle. Instantaneous semantic accuracy is shown with respect to the *percent* of the total recognition time the partial is recognized at. An utterance is incorrect if it has no incremental result before a certain percentage.

We show 2 sets of plots. Figure 1 shows only incremental recognition results and excludes the end-of-utterance (*phrase*) results; Figure 2 shows incremental recognition results and includes phrase results. It is useful to view these separately since the phrase result, having access to all the speech, is sub-

[3]It also uses reinforcement learning to choose actions, although in this paper we are not concerned with this aspect.

Figure 1: Instantaneous semantic accuracy of incremental results, excluding phrase-final results

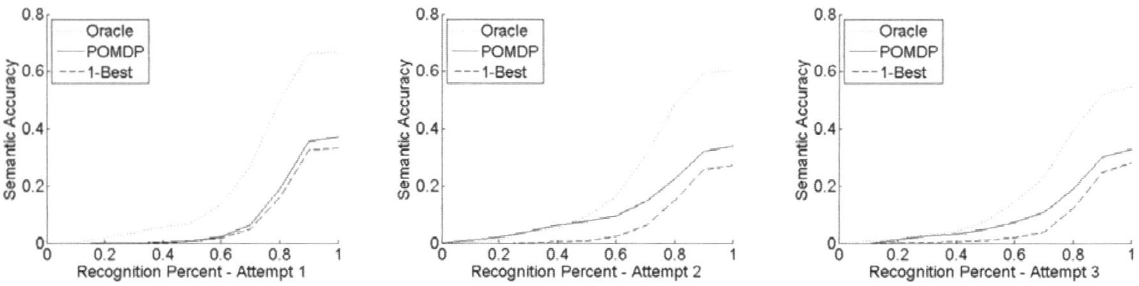

Figure 2: Instantaneous semantic accuracy of incremental and phrase-final results

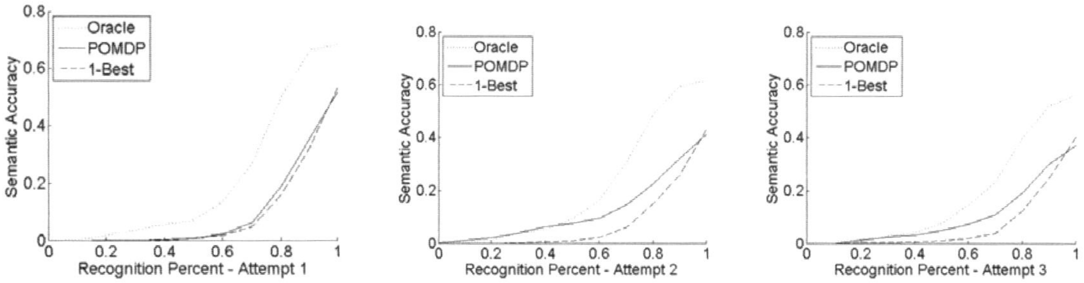

stantially more accurate than the incremental results.

Figure 1 shows that the POMDP is more accurate than the raw incremental result (excluding end-of-phrase results). Its performance gain is minimal in attempt 1 because the belief is informed only by the prior. In attempt 2 and 3, the gain is larger since the belief also benefits from the previous attempts. Since the top POMDP result in subsequent attempts is sometimes already correct (because it incorporates past recognitions), the POMDP sometimes meets and occasionally exceeds the oracle during the early portions of attempts 2 and 3.

Figure 2 shows that when end-of-phrase recognition results are included, the benefit of the belief state is limited to the initial portions of the second and third turns. This is because the POMDP models are not fit well to the data: the models were estimated from an earlier version of the system, with a different user base and different functionality. Identifying and eliminating this type of mismatch is an important issue and has been studied before (Williams, 2011).

Taken as a whole, we find that using belief tracking increases the accuracy of partials by over 8% (absolute) in some cases. Even though the final phrase results of the 1-best list are more accurate than the belief state, the POMDP shows better accuracy on the volatile incremental results. As compared to the whole utterance results, incremental results have lower 1-best accuracy, yet high oracle accuracy. This combination is a natural fit with the POMDPs belief state, which considers the whole N-Best list, effectively re-ranking it by synthesizing information from dialogue history priors.

6 Conclusion

This paper has taken a step toward integrating ISR and POMDP-based dialogue systems. The Incremental Interaction Manager (IIM) enables a traditional turn-based DM to make use of incremental results and enjoy many their benefits. When this IIM is paired with a POMDP DM, the interpretation accuracy of incremental results improves substantially. In the future we hope to build on this work by incorporating Reinforcement Learning into turn-taking and dialogue action decisions.

Acknowledgments

Thanks to Vincent Goffin for help with this work, and to the anonymous reviewers for their comments and critique. We acknowledge funding from the NSF under grant IIS-0713698.

References

T. Baumann, M. Atterer, and D. Schlangen. 2009. Assessing and improving the performance of speech recognition for incremental systems. In *Proc. NAACL: HLT*, pages 380–388. Association for Computational Linguistics.

O. Buß and D. Schlangen. 2011. Dium–an incremental dialogue manager that can produce self-corrections. *Proceedings of semdial*.

David DeVault, Kenji Sagae, and David Traum. 2009. Can i finish? learning when to respond to incremental interpretation results in interactive dialogue. In *Proceedings of the SIGDIAL 2009 Conference*, pages 11–20, London, UK, September. Association for Computational Linguistics.

V. Goffin, C. Allauzen, E. Bocchieri, D. Hakkani-Tur, A. Ljolje, S. Parthasarathy, M. Rahim, G. Riccardi, and M. Saraclar. 2005. The AT&T WATSON speech recognizer. In *Proceedings of ICASSP*, pages 1033–1036.

D. Lu, T. Nishimoto, and N. Minematsu. 2011. Decision of response timing for incremental speech recognition with reinforcement learning. In *Automatic Speech Recognition and Understanding (ASRU), 2011 IEEE Workshop on*, pages 467–472. IEEE.

D. Schlangen and G. Skantze. 2009. A general, abstract model of incremental dialogue processing. In *Proceedings of the 12th Conference of the European Chapter of the Association for Computational Linguistics*, pages 710–718. Association for Computational Linguistics.

E.O. Selfridge, I. Arizmendi, P.A. Heeman, and J.D. Williams. 2011. Stability and accuracy in incremental speech recognition. In *Proceedings of the SIGdial 2011*.

G. Skantze and D. Schlangen. 2009. Incremental dialogue processing in a micro-domain. In *Proceedings of the 12th Conference of the European Chapter of the Association for Computational Linguistics*, pages 745–753. Association for Computational Linguistics.

B. Thomson and S. Young. 2010. Bayesian update of dialogue state: A pomdp framework for spoken dialogue systems. *Computer Speech & Language*, 24(4):562–588.

J.D. Williams and S. Balakrishnan. 2009. Estimating probability of correctness for asr n-best lists. In *Proc SIGDIAL, London, United Kingdom*.

J.D. Williams and S. Young. 2007. Partially observable markov decision processes for spoken dialog systems. *Computer Speech & Language*, 21(2):393–422.

J.D. Williams. 2011. An empirical evaluation of a statistical dialog system in public use. In *Proceedings of the SIGDIAL 2011 Conference*, pages 130–141. Association for Computational Linguistics.

S. Young, M. Gasic, S. Keizer, F. Mairesse, J. Schatzmann, B. Thomson, and K. Yu. 2010. The hidden information state model: A practical framework for pomdp-based spoken dialogue management. *Computer Speech & Language*, 24(2):150–174.

A Regression-based Approach to Modeling Addressee Backchannels

Allison Terrell, Bilge Mutlu
Department of Computer Sciences, University of Wisconsin–Madison
1210 West Dayton Street, Madison, WI 53705, USA
{aterrell,bilge}@cs.wisc.edu

Abstract

During conversations, addressees produce conversational acts—verbal and nonverbal *backchannels*—that facilitate turn-taking, acknowledge speakership, and communicate common ground without disrupting the speaker's speech. These acts play a key role in achieving fluent conversations. Therefore, gaining a deeper understanding of how these acts interact with speaker behaviors in shaping conversations might offer key insights into the design of technologies such as computer-mediated communication systems and embodied conversational agents. In this paper, we explore how a regression-based approach might offer such insights into modeling predictive relationships between speaker behaviors and addressee backchannels in a storytelling scenario. Our results reveal speaker eye contact as a significant predictor of verbal, nonverbal, and bimodal backchannels and utterance boundaries as predictors of nonverbal and bimodal backchannels.

1 Introduction

Conversations involve a dynamic shifting of speakership, one party playing the role of the "speaker" and the other(s) the role of the "addressee" at any given moment (Goodwin, 1981; Levinson, 1988; Clark, 1996). In these roles, while speakers produce the majority of the conversational content, addressees play a major role in facilitating speakership by performing *backchannels*—verbal and nonverbal acts such as "uh huh" and head nods that indicate the addressee's understanding and involvement and acknowledge that the speaker has and may continue to have the floor (Yngve, 1970; Drummond and Hopper, 1993).

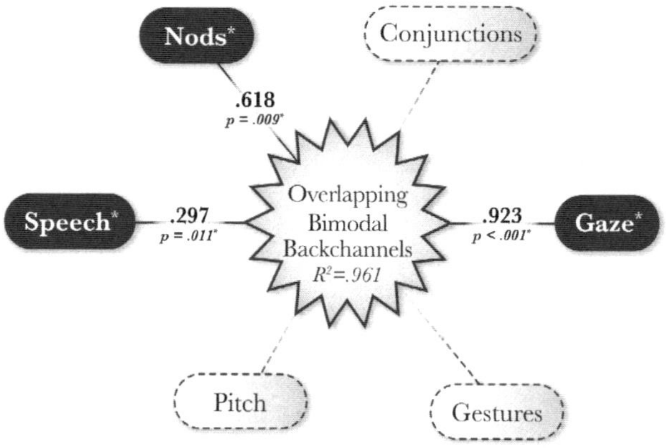

Figure 1: A mapping of the predictive relationships between speaker behaviors and overlapping bimodal addressee backchannels. β coefficients show the relative importance of significant predictors of backchannel behaviors.

Backchannels serve as a mechanism for cooperation between speakers and addressees to achieve efficient communication (Brunner, 1979; Grice, 1989) and to establish rapport (Drolet and Morris, 2000). The design of conversational technologies such as computer-mediated communication systems will have to facilitate the use of backchannel mechanisms to help their users achieve efficient conversations. Similarly, embodied conversational agents will have to use these mechanisms to achieve efficient interactions with their users. However, these developments require a deeper understanding of backchannel behavior and models of the relationship between backchannel acts and speaker behaviors.

Research across many communities including discourse processes, dialog systems, and human-computer interaction has explored the use of backchannels in conversations and sought to model the relationships between backchannel acts and other conversational processes using techniques that range from contingency analyses (Truong et al., 2011) to model training (Morency et al., 2010). In this paper, we propose a complementary, regression-based approach to untangle the *predictive* relationships between speaker behaviors and addressee backchannels. This approach provides us with an understanding of what speaker behaviors are significant predictors of addressee backchannels and of the relative contributions of each behavior in these predictions. The resulting models inform us of what speaker behaviors are important to support in interactive systems and communication technologies to facilitate addressee backchannels and complement finer-granulated analyses of specific backchannel mechanisms.

We contextualize our exploration in a storytelling scenario, which requires addressees to rely on and frequently use backchannels to participate in the discourse while maintaining consistency in conversational roles, using a multimodal data corpus collected from 24 dyads. Our analysis includes verbal and nonverbal backchannels, focusing on continuers and assessments in the verbal channel and head nods in the nonverbal channel. In the remainder of the paper, we review related work, describe our methodology, present our results, and discuss our findings and their implications for future research and the design of communication and interactive technologies.

2 Background

Conversations involve a cooperative process in which interlocutors manage the floor, negotiate turns, and provide feedback with the aid of subtle linguistic and extralinguistic cues—*backchannels*—that might not significantly contribute to the substance of the conversation (Yngve, 1970; Brunner, 1979; Grice, 1989; Drummond and Hopper, 1993). These backchannels allow parties, particularly addressees, to exchange information on their intentions and statuses and to participate in the conversation without disrupting ongoing speech (Morris and Desebrock, 1977; White, 1989). Backchannels differ from "backchannel inviting cues," which might indicate what might be an appropriate time for a backchannel (Gravano and Hirschberg, 2011). While backchannels are produced universally, individual characteristics such as gender (Helweg-Larsen et al., 2004) and cultural background (White, 1989; Ward and Tsukahara, 2000) significantly shape their production and interpretation.

2.1 Backchannel Cues

Researchers have sought to distinguish and categorize the wide range of backchannels based on how they are expressed by addressees (Jenkins and Parra, 2003) and how they contribute to the conversation(Young and Lee, 2004). The majority of research on backchannels considers *verbal* or linguistic cues and offers several categorizations. One of these categorizations distinguishes *continuers* from *assessments* (Young and Lee, 2004). Continuers are short, nondescript verbal segments such as "uh huh" and "yeah" that prompt the speaker to continue talking, while assessments are longer verbal segments such as "oh, wow" and "really?" that offer commentary or request clarification on the speaker's statements.

Another classification of verbal backchannels distinguishes among *non-lexical*, *phrasal*, and *substantive* backchannels (Iwasaki, 1997; Young and Lee, 2004). Non-lexical backchannels include vocalizations such as "hmm" or "uh huh" that offer little or no meaning but indicate the addressee's engagement in the conversation. Phrasal backchannels involve simple, well-established expressions such as "Really?" or "Are you serious?" that indicate acknowledgment. Finally, substantive backchannels involve the addressee taking the floor for brief periods and include repetitions, summary statements, clarifying questions about the speaker's speech, repair, and collaborative completions.

Research on backchannels also describes *nonverbal* or extralinguistic cues such as smiling (Brunner, 1979) and gaze (Rosenfeld and Hancks, 1980) as common backchannel behaviors that indicate agreement, understanding, or engagement in the conversation (Jenkins and Parra, 2003). Nodding is a particularly common nonverbal backchannel behavior that plays a range of roles from indicating agreement to conveying sympathy and understanding with the speaker's perspective (Stivers, 2008). While verbal and nonverbal backchannels play similar communicative roles, the specific context of the conversation, such as whether the conversation involves a negotiation or a discussion, shapes how participants perform and interpret the two forms of backchannels (Jenkins and Parra, 2003). Addressees often display both verbal and nonverbal backchannels (Truong et al., 2011), such as concurrently nodding and saying "yeah" to express agreement.

2.2 Modeling Backchannels

Research on conversational backchannels involves a wide range of modeling approaches including *rule-based models* (Duncan, 1972), *contingency analysis* (Truong et al., 2011), and *trained models* (Morency et al., 2010) across a wide range of conversational contexts from telephone conversations (Ward and Tsukahara, 2000) to face-to-face interactions (Truong et al., 2011). Rule-based models capture relationships between backchannels and other conversational behaviors based on prototypical examples of commonly observed behaviors. Contingency analysis offers a quantitative basis for modeling these relationships through pairwise analyses of co-occurrences. Finally, statistical learning techniques allow researchers to train machine learning algorithms, such as Support Vector Machines (SVM) and Hidden Markov models (HMM), on data that capture these relationships in order to estimate the timing of backchannels.

2.3 Regression-based Modeling

While it remains unexplored in the context of modeling backchannel behaviors, regression-based approaches are commonly used in modeling complex relationships among many variables. In the context of modeling discourse and dialog, frameworks such as PARADISE (PARAdigm for DIalogue System Evaluation) build on regression-based approaches to identify predictive relationships between several elements of dialog and objective or subjective outcomes of the dialog (Walker et al., 1997). Researchers have used these frameworks to evaluate the effectiveness of spoken dialog in interactive systems (Foster et al., 2009; Peltason et al., 2012).

3 Method

Due to the broad range of verbal and nonverbal backchannels, we chose to focus on a limited subset of verbal and nonverbal cues, including continuers and assessments as verbal backchannels and head nods as nonverbal backchannels. Although there are numerous possible speaker behaviors, which may predict backchannels, we focused on six cues based on previous research: (1) speaker's *gaze* (directed toward the addressee), (2) *nods*, (3) *gestures*, (4) *speech* (whether the speaker is speaking or not), (5) *conjunctions* in the speaker's speech, and (6) *pitch variance* in the speaker's speech. These six predictors were then used to build models for five dependent variables: (1) *nonverbal backchannels*, (2) *verbal backchannels*, (3) *concurrent verbal and nonverbal backchannels* (e.g., a nod and an "OK" starting simultaneously), (4) *overlapping verbal and nonverbal backchannels* (e.g., a nod followed by an "OK" towards the end of the nod), and (5) *independent bimodal backchannels* (the presence of either verbal or nonverbal backchannels). We modeled the relationships between these predictors and dependent variables using stepwise regression.

3.1 Participants and Data Corpus

A total of 48 subjects from the University of Wisconsin–Madison participated in this study. They studied a diverse set of fields and were aged between 18 and 28. All participants were native English speakers. We assigned participants into dyads and conversational roles following a fully stratified design to control for the effects of gender composition of the dyads. We discarded data from one dyad, because the participants did not conform to the conversational roles that they were asked to follow. With this omission, our final dataset consisted of 23 dyads.

Our experimental setup followed common conventions of face-to-face conversations. Two participants unfamiliar with one another were seated across from each other at a "social distance" of five feet (Hall, 1963). An illustration of our experimental setup can be seen in Figure 2. The data collection equipment consisted of three high-definition video cameras at 1080p resolution and 30p frame rate, two high-fidelity lapel microphones, and an omni-

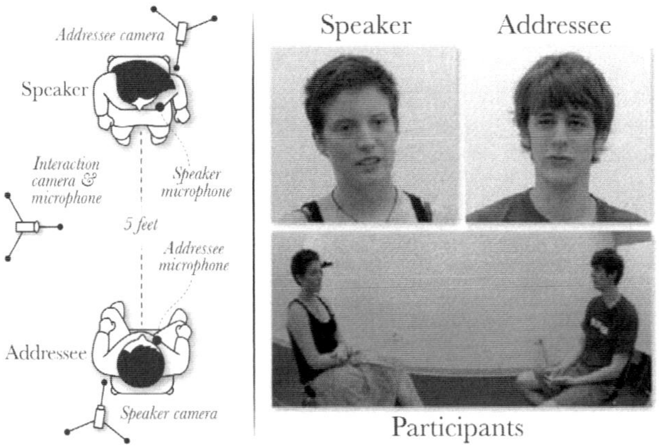

Figure 2: The experimental setup (left) shows the placement of the participants at a "social distance" and of the equipment for capturing data. The snapshots (right) show the vantage point from each of the three cameras.

directional microphone. Two of the video cameras were positioned across from each participant, capturing their upper torso from a direct frontal angle, while the lapel microphones captured their speech. The third camera and the omni-directional microphone recorded the speech and nonverbal behaviors of both participants from a side angle. The final datas corpus consisted of 1 hour and 31 minutes of audio and video. The average video length was 3 minutes and 57 seconds.

3.2 Procedure

The experimental task involved partaking in a *storytelling* scenario that aimed to elicit a wide range of behavioral and interactional mechanisms. In this scenario, one of the participants took on the role of the speaker and narrated the plot of their favorite movie to the second participant who took on the role of the addressee. We expected this scenario to provide us with a rich context to observe backchannels.

Participants were first given a brief description of the experiment and asked to review and sign a consent form. The experimenter then seated the participants, assigned them conversational roles, and set up the data collection equipment. Participants first performed an acclimation task (getting to know one another) that was not considered part of the experimental task. The participants then performed the storytelling scenario. Following the experiment, the experimenter debriefed the participants. Participants were paid $10 for their time.

3.3 Measurements

Based on a preliminary analysis of our data, we identified five forms of addressee backchannels as dependent variables: (1) nonverbal backchannels, (2) verbal backchannels, (3) concurrent verbal and nonverbal backchannels (e.g., a nod and an "OK" starting simultaneously), (4) overlapping verbal and nonverbal backchannels (e.g., a nod followed by an "OK" towards the end of the nod), and (5) independent bimodal backchannels (either verbal or nonverbal backchannels).

Our independent variables consisted of speaker behaviors that previous research suggested as likely predictors of addressee backchannels and that a real-time interactive system might be able to capture and interpret. These variables included visible and audible features from the speaker's movements and speech, such as the presence or absence of speech and pitch variability, and specific linguistic features that might signal discourse structure, such as conjunctions. Drawing on these considerations, our analysis included speaker's *gaze* (directed toward the addressee), *nods*, *gestures*, *speech* (whether the speaker is speaking or not), *conjunctions* in the speaker's speech, and *pitch variance* measurements of the speaker's speech.

In our measurement of pitch, we sought to capture computationally feasible, high-level intonational characteristics of the speech by calculating the variability in pitch in the entire conversation. Low pitch variability indicated more monotonous speakers, whereas high pitch variability represented more expressive speech. This measure was calculated by finding the average pitch of the speaker throughout the conversation and aggregating the difference between the average pitch and the pitch value at each frame, as expressed below:

$$pitch\_variance = \sum_{i=0}^{n} |\overline{pitch} - pitch_i|$$

Here, the number of measurements in the conversation is represented by n; each individual measurement is represented by i; the speaker's average pitch in the entire conversation is represented by $\overline{pitch}$; and the pitch value at each individual measurement is represented by $pitch_i$.

The data was labeled using a combination of manual and computational techniques. All speaker and

Measure (y)	*Function* ($\beta_0 + \beta_1 x_1 + \ldots + \beta_n x_n + e$)	R^2	*Significance*
Nonverbal backchannels	$.138 + .635 \times N(gaze) + .374 \times N(speech) + .089$	.911	*gaze* $p < .001$ *speech* $p = .008$
Verbal backchannels	$.034 + .875 \times N(gaze) + .067$	.977	*gaze* $p < .001$
Concurrent bimodal backchannels	$.019 + .471 \times N(gaze) + .822 \times N(speech) + .059$	.940	*gaze* $p < .001$ *speech* $p < .001$
Overlapping bimodal backchannels	$.013 + .923 \times N(gaze) + .618 \times N(nods) + .297 \times N(speech) + .061$	.966	*gaze* $p < .001$ *nods* $p = .009$ *speech* $p = .011$
Independent bimodal backchannels	$.134 + .483 \times N(gaze) + .212 \times N(pitch) + .074$	.896	*gaze* $p < .001$ *pitch* $p = .014$

Figure 3: The final models for each dependent variable after elimination in the stepwise regression analysis including only the significant predictors. Gaze was a significant predictor in all five models. Speech was significant in three models. Pitch variability and nods each significantly predicted one type of backchannel.

addressee utterances were transcribed using Praat. Speech and conjunctions measurements were drawn from this transcription. Only pauses that were longer than 500 milliseconds were considered as absence of speech; speech segments that were separated by shorter pauses were combined into a single segment. The pitch variability was automatically extracted using Praat. A primary coder labeled 100% of the remaining attributes (addressee nods, speaker nods, speaker gestures, and speaker gaze). To evaluate reliability, a second coder labeled 10% of a randomly sampled subset of the data. The inter-rater reliability showed substantial agreement for all attributes; addressee nods (94% agreement, Cohen's $\kappa = 0.72$), speaker nods (92% agreement, Cohen's $\kappa = 0.71$), speaker gesture (87% agreement, Cohen's $\kappa = 0.67$), and speaker gaze (96% agreement, Cohen's $\kappa = 0.75$).

All variables except pitch variability were binary: 0 for *not occurring* and 1 for *occurring* of events. Pitch variability was a normalized continuous variable that varied between 0 and 1. We considered variables as co-occurring when they overlapped with each other within a window that spanned 200 milliseconds before the onset and after the end of each variable, following criteria from previous research (Truong et al., 2011). The data corpus included measurements of all variables every 33.3 milliseconds.

The data corpus for each dependent variable included aggregate counts of measurements for all variables for each video. The aggregate counts for each video were normalized by dividing them by the length of the video in seconds. Finally, each variable across all videos were normalized to vary between 0 (least frequent) and 1 (most frequent). The resulting data corpus included five data tables of size 23x7 (data from 23 dyads on seven variables—the dependent variable and six predictors) for five types of backchannel behaviors.

3.4 Analysis

Our analysis followed a *stepwise multiple linear regression* to model the relationships between our predictors and dependent variables. Each analysis started with the following linear form:

$$y = (\beta_0 + \beta_1 x_1 + \beta_2 x_2 + \ldots + \beta_n x_n) + e$$

Here, β_0 is a constant, whereas $\beta_1 \ldots \beta_n$ are coefficient weights for each of n predictors. The values of each predictor for each measurement are represented by $x_1 \ldots x_n$. The error term for the model is e, which is assumed to be mean zero and independent and identically distributed (i.i.d.).

Our use of stepwise regression followed a *backward elimination* algorithm in which the final model is constructed by gradually excluding predictors that do not sufficiently contribute to the model. For the purposes of our study, we excluded any predictor with a p-value above .25. The final model is comprised of predictors left which are statistically sig-

	Nonverbal backchannels (R^2 = .912)		*Verbal backchannels* (R^2 = .968)		*Concurrent bimodal backchannels* (R^2 = .938)		*Overlapping bimodal backchannels* (R^2 = .962)		*Independent bimodal backchannels* (R^2 = .889)	
Predictor	*β*	*p*	*β*	*p*	*β*	*p*	*β*	*p*	*β*	*p*
Nods	.297	.542	.209	.242	.332	.227	**.579**	**.015**	.530	.205
Gaze	**.621**	**< .001**	**.952**	**< .001**	**.574**	**.001**	**.848**	**< .001**	**.542**	**.001**
Gestures	−.134	.275	−.033	.834	.052	.735	.235	.113	−.066	.489
Speech	**.388**	**.043**	.067	.644	**.631**	**.005**	.205	.091	.072	.775
Conjunctions	.129	.779	.323	.372	n/a	n/a	−.191	.622	.397	.325
Pitch	.012	.148	.003	.721	−.001	.761	.009	.655	.402	.118

Figure 4: The results of the model for each dependent variable before elimination in the stepwise regression analysis.

nificant ($p < .050$). The β coefficients in the model provide the relative contribution of each independent variable in predicting the dependent variable. Our analysis considered the number of addressee backchannels that occurred in each dyad as the metric of success.

3.5 Results

In all five of our models, the independent variables accounted for a significant proportion of variance in the dependent variables, varying between 89.9% and 96.6%. These results are summarized in Figure 3.

In the first model, speaker behaviors accounted for a significant portion of addressee nonverbal backchannels, $R^2 = .911, F(2,20) = 113.6, p < .001$. Speaker gaze and speech significantly predicted these backchannels, $\beta = .635$, $t(21) = 6.02$, $p < .001$ and $\beta = .374$, $t(21) = 2.90$, $p = .008$, respectively. Gaze also significantly predicted addressee verbal backchannels, $\beta = .875$, $t(22) = 27.24$, $p < .001$, and explained a significant portion of the variance in them, $R^2 = .977, F(1,21) = 702.5, p < .001$.

Results from the third model showed that gaze and speech explained a significant proportion of the variance in concurrent bimodal backchannels, $R^2 = .940, F(2,20) = 172.3, p < .001$, and significantly predicted these backchannels, $\beta = .471$, $t(21) = 3.98$, $p < .001$ and $\beta = .822$, $t(21) = 7.92$, $p < .001$, respectively. In the fourth model, speaker behaviors explained a significant proportion of the variance in overlapping bimodal backchannels, $R^2 = .966, F(3,19) = 180, p < .001$. Speaker gaze, speech, and nods were significant predictors of these backchannels, $\beta = .923$, $t(20) = 12.3$, $p < .001$, $\beta = .297$, $t(20) = 2.80$, $p = .011$, $\beta = .618$, $t(20) = 2.93$, $p = .009$, respectively.

Finally, results from the fifth model showed that speaker behaviors explained a significant proportion of the variance in independent bimodal backchannels, $R^2 = .896, F(2,20) = 94.63, p < .001$. The speaker's gaze and the variability in the pitch of the speaker's speech significantly predicted these addressee behaviors, $\beta = .483$, $t(21) = 6.74$, $p < .001$ and $\beta = .212$, $t(21) = 2.83$, $p = .014$, respectively.

4 Discussion

The results of our statistical analysis show key relationships between speaker behaviors and addressee backchannels, reaffirming findings from previous studies and revealing new relationships. The paragraphs below provide a discussion of these findings and support them with examples of addressee backchannels that we frequently observed in our data. These examples are illustrated in Appendix A in three episodes of interaction. We also discuss the implications of our approach for modeling conversational mechanisms.

Our results are summarized in Figures 3 and 4, which show our final models after elimination and the models before elimination, respectively. The results in Figure 3, consistent with previous work (Bavelas et al., 2002), highlight the importance of gaze in eliciting addressee backchannels. Gaze is included in all five of our models and is consistently the most important predictor of addressee backchannels in four of our five models. In Appendix A, all six instances of the addressee backchannels across three illustrated episodes occur either when the speaker is looking toward the addressee or almost concurrently with the speaker shifting gaze away from the addressee.

The results also show speech to be a significant predictor of addressee backchannels. Three of our models included speech as a predictor, which suggests that more frequent pauses in speech provides the addressee with more opportunities to provide backchannels; that frequent pauses prompt addressees to provide more backchannels to facilitate the continuation of the speaker's speech; and/or that the addressees produce more backchannels, because speakers present more information. Four instances of backchannels shown in Appendix A occur immediately after an utterance has ended, which exemplify pauses as opportune moments for the addressee to produce backchannels.

The significance of pitch variability in predicting independent bimodal backchannels offers a different perspective on the relationship between attributes of speaker pitch and addressee backchannels than previous research does. Although previous work suggested that pitch attributes do not have a significant relationship with addressee backchannels in face-to-face conversations (Truong et al., 2011), pitch variability significantly predicted independent bimodal backchannels in our models. We speculate that pitch variability captures the speaker's overall ability to engage their addressees in their speech and, thus, predicts addressee backchannels. However, our results show that this predictive relationship only exists with independent bimodal backchannels and not with verbal or nonverbal backchannels. This discrepancy might be a result of variability across individuals in their preferences to use verbal and nonverbal backchannels, which is not captured by our models for these individual backchannels but is captured by the model that considers either type of backchannels.

Speech did not significantly predict the addressee's verbal or independent bimodal backchannels, while it predicted nonverbal and concurrent and overlapping backchannels. This finding suggests that frequent pauses in speech elicit primarily nonverbal backchannels and elicit verbal backchannels only in the presence of nonverbal backchannels. A possible explanation of this finding is that addressees might prefer nonverbal backchannels to verbal backchannels when they wish to facilitate the continuation of speech.

A key contribution of our work is an exploration of the relationship between verbal and nonverbal backchannels by modeling the concurrent onsets and overlaps between these backchannels. These models indicate that gaze and speech are significant predictors of concurrent onsets and overlaps in verbal and nonverbal backchannels and that speaker nods also significantly predict overlaps.

Our analysis also identified overlapping bimodal backchannels as a new form of backchannel behavior that has not been considered by previous research (Truong et al., 2011). These backchannels involve the addressee producing a nonverbal backchannel towards the end of the speaker's speech and then producing a verbal backchannel when the speaker had stopped talking. We speculate that this behavior allows the addressee to express agreement during the speaker's speech using nonverbal backchannels without disrupting the speech and reassert agreement using verbal backchannels when the speaker's utterance is completed. Episode B in Appendix A illustrates an instance of overlapping bimodal backchannels.

A final contribution of this work is an illustration of the use of a regression-based approach in modeling predictive relationships between speaker behaviors and addressee backchannels. This approach allowed us to explore the relationships among many aspects of speaker and addressee behavior and to quantify the relative significance of each aspect of the speaker's behaviors in predicting addressee behaviors. Our results confirmed findings from previous research and produced new findings, revealing novel relationships between these behaviors. These relationships will serve as a basis for future research to create more nuanced models of speaker and addressee behavior. They will also inform the design of future communication technologies and interactive systems that incorporate mechanisms to support the communication of key predictors of addressee backchannels.

While the primary goal of our study was to better understand relationships among conversational behaviors, our models might also serve as coarse estimation models. The models shown in Figure 3 might be used to estimate $\hat{y}$—how frequently addressee backchannels should appear—using the predictor coefficients β and values for known speaker behaviors x. These estimations might complement finer-granulated models of backchannel mechanisms in generating opportune backchannel behaviors for artificial agents and predict when these backchannels might occur in human-computer interaction scenarios.

4.1 Limitations

Our work also has a number of limitations. First, because our approach uses aggregate counts of behaviors from the entire interaction, it does not account for the temporal relationships among these variables. Therefore, the insights offered by our approach are limited to high-level conclusions on the relationships between these behaviors and illustrations of these relationships in example episodes of interaction. Future work should include complementary modeling techniques to build finer-granulated models of backchannel mechanisms.

Although participants in each conversation were explicitly assigned to one of the roles of speaker and addressee, we did not specifically tell addressees not to speak, which led to a greater amount of variability in their participation in the conversation, some offering up their opinions or asking questions throughout the speaker's story and others limiting their behaviors to a small number of backchannels. While this variability enabled more natural conversations, this lack of control might have limited the power of our statistical models.

In this paper, we focused on a set of high-level predictors that allow for real-time capture and interpretation, ignoring underlying conversational mechanisms such as repair, which might also serve as significant predictors of backchannels. The relationships between these mechanisms and backchannel behavior would be a fruitful area of exploration for future research.

Finally, the generalizability of our results suffers from the limited extent of the conversational context and participation structure of our experimental setup. Future work should seek to extend this exploration to a broader set of conversational settings, such as interview and discussion scenarios, and participation structures, such as multi-party conversations.

5 Conclusion

Backchannels are essential behaviors for achieving fluent and effective conversations. Gaining a deeper understanding of how these behaviors shape conversations might offer key insights into the design of technologies such as computer-mediated communication systems and embodied conversational agents. In an exploratory study, we used a stepwise regression approach to model the relationships between various types of addressee backchannels and speaker behaviors in a storytelling scenario. We found that gaze significantly predicted all types of backchannel behaviors including verbal, nonverbal, and bimodal backchannels. Our results also showed that speech, speaker nods, and pitch variability predicted some types of backchannel behaviors. While these results have some limitations due to our methodological choices, they suggest directions for future work and offer preliminary insights toward a deeper understanding of backchannel behaviors and how interactive systems and communication technologies might be designed to support these behaviors.

Acknowledgments

We would like to thank Faisal Khan for his help in data collection and processing. This work was supported by National Science Foundation award 1149970.

References

J.B. Bavelas, L. Coates, and T. Johnson. 2002. Listener responses as a collaborative process: The role of gaze. *Journal of Communication*, 52(3):566–580.

L.J. Brunner. 1979. Smiles can be back channels. *Journal of Personality and Social Psychology*, 37(5):728.

H.H. Clark. 1996. *Using language*. Cambridge University Press.

A.L. Drolet and M.W. Morris. 2000. Rapport in conflict resolution: Accounting for how face-to-face contact fosters mutual cooperation in mixed-motive conflicts. *Journal of Experimental Social Psychology*, 36(1):26–50.

K. Drummond and R. Hopper. 1993. Back channels revisited: Acknowledgment tokens and speakership incipiency. *Research on Language and Social Interaction*, 26(2):157–177.

S. Duncan. 1972. Some signals and rules for taking speaking turns in conversations. *Journal of personality and social psychology*, 23(2):283.

M.E. Foster, M. Giuliani, and A. Knoll. 2009. Comparing objective and subjective measures of usability in a human-robot dialogue system. In *Proc ACL/AFNLP*, volume 2, pages 879–887. Association for Computational Linguistics.

C. Goodwin. 1981. *Conversational organization: Interaction between speakers and hearers*. Academic Press New York.

A. Gravano and J. Hirschberg. 2011. Turn-taking cues in task-oriented dialogue. *Computer Speech & Language*, 25(3):601–634.

P. Grice. 1989. *Studies in the Way of Words*. Harvard University Press.

E.T. Hall. 1963. A system for the notation of proxemic behavior. *American anthropologist*, 65(5):1003–1026.

M. Helweg-Larsen, S.J. Cunningham, A. Carrico, and A.M. Pergram. 2004. To nod or not to nod: An observational study of nonverbal communication and status in female and male college students. *Psychology of Women Quarterly*, 28(4):358–361.

S. Iwasaki. 1997. The northridge earthquake conversations: The floor structure and the 'loop' sequence in japanese conversation. *Journal of Pragmatics*, 28(6):661–693.

S. Jenkins and I. Parra. 2003. Multiple layers of meaning in an oral proficiency test: The complementary roles of nonverbal, paralinguistic, and verbal behaviors in assessment decisions. *The Modern Language Journal*, 87(1):90–107.

S.C. Levinson, 1988. *Putting linguistics on a proper footing: Explorations in Goffman's concepts of participation.*, pages 161–227. Oxford, England: Polity Press.

L.P. Morency, I. de Kok, and J. Gratch. 2010. A probabilistic multimodal approach for predicting listener backchannels. *Autonomous Agents and Multi-Agent Systems*, 20(1):70–84.

D. Morris and G. Desebrock. 1977. *Manwatching: A field guide to human behaviour*. HN Abrams New York, NY.

J. Peltason, N. Riether, B. Wrede, and I. Lütkebohle. 2012. Talking with robots about objects: a system-level evaluation in hri. In *Proceedings of the seventh annual ACM/IEEE international conference on Human-Robot Interaction*, HRI '12, pages 479–486, New York, NY, USA. ACM.

H.M. Rosenfeld and M. Hancks, 1980. *The nonverbal context of verbal listener responses*, pages 193–206. The hague: Mouton Publishers.

T. Stivers. 2008. Stance, alignment, and affiliation during storytelling: When nodding is a token of affiliation. *Research on Language and Social Interaction*, 41(1):31–57.

K.P. Truong, R.W. Poppe, I.A. de Kok, and D.K.J. Heylen. 2011. A multimodal analysis of vocal and visual backchannels in spontaneous dialogs. In *Proc Interspeech*, pages 2973–2976. International Speech Communication Association.

M.A. Walker, D.J. Litman, C.A. Kamm, and A. Abella. 1997. Paradise: A framework for evaluating spoken dialogue agents. In *Proc EACL*, pages 271–280. Association for Computational Linguistics.

N. Ward and W. Tsukahara. 2000. Prosodic features which cue back-channel responses in english and japanese. *Journal of Pragmatics*, 32(8):1177–1207.

S. White. 1989. Backchannels across cultures: A study of americans and japanese. *Language in society*, 18(1):59–76.

V.H. Yngve. 1970. On getting a word in edgewise. In *Sixth Regional Meeting of the Chicago Linguistic Society*, volume 6, pages 657–677.

R.F. Young and J. Lee. 2004. Identifying units in interaction: Reactive tokens in korean and english conversations. *Journal of Sociolinguistics*, 8(3):380–407.

Appendix A. Contextual Examples

Below are three example episodes drawn from our data. Each episode displays all occurrences of all the predictors we measured in real time. All six instances of backchannels highlight the importance of the speaker's gaze and speech in eliciting addressee backchannels.

Episode **A**

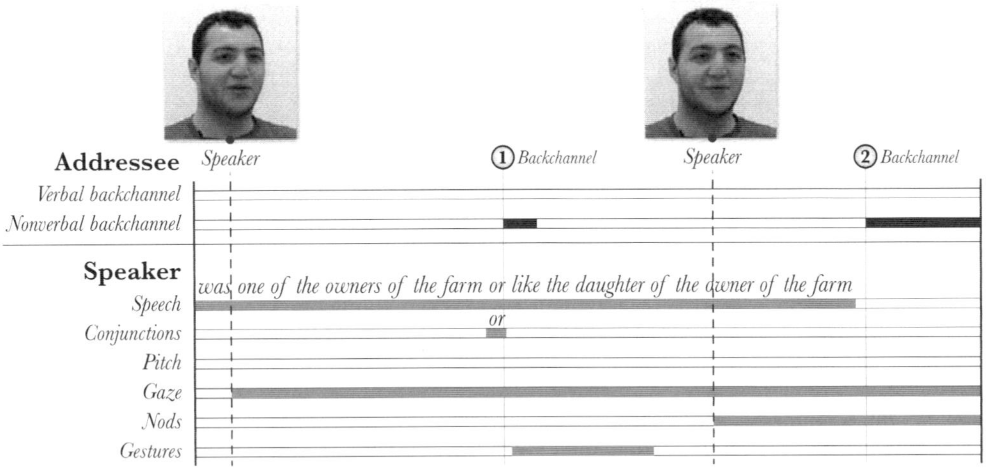

Episode **B**

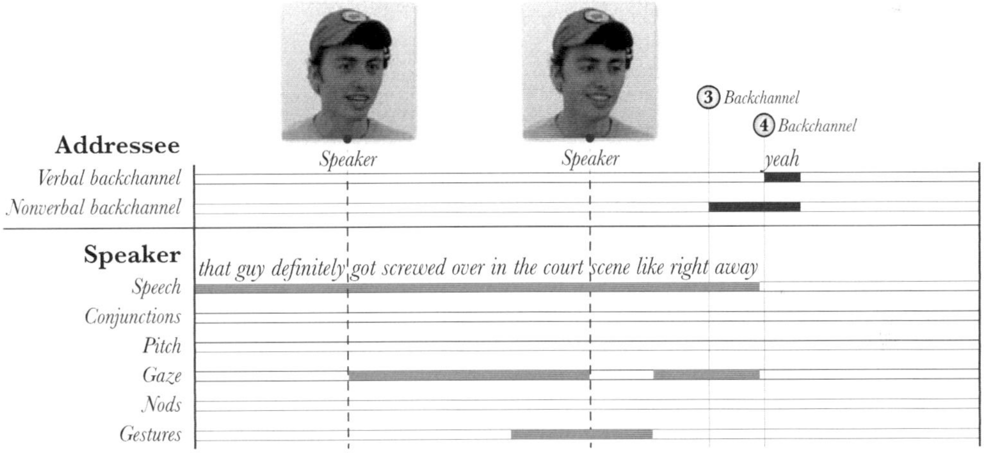

Episode **C**

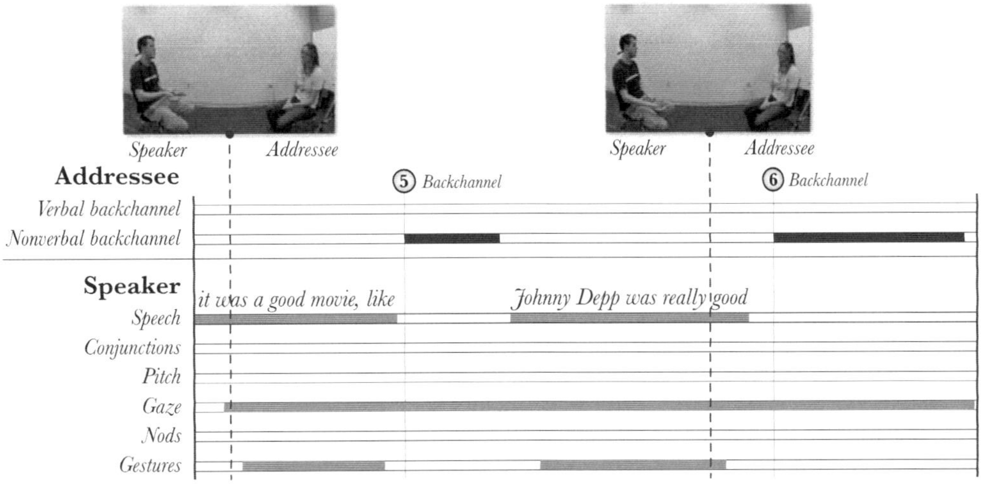

Improving Sentence Completion in Dialogues with Multi-Modal Features

Anruo Wang, Barbara Di Eugenio, Lin Chen
Department of Computer Science
University of Illinois at Chicago
851 S Morgan ST, Chicago, IL 60607, USA
awang28, bdieugen, lchen43@uic.edu

Abstract

With the aim of investigating how humans understand each other through language and gestures, this paper focuses on how people understand incomplete sentences. We trained a system based on interrupted but resumed sentences, in order to find plausible completions for incomplete sentences. Our promising results are based on multi-modal features.

1 Introduction

Our project, called RoboHelper, focuses on developing an interface for elderly people to effectively communicate with robotic assistants that can help them perform Activities of Daily Living (ADLs) (Krapp, 2002), so that they can safely remain living in their home (Di Eugenio et al., 2010; Chen et al., 2011). We are developing a multi-modal interface since people communicate with each other using a variety of verbal and non-verbal signals, including haptics, i.e., force exchange (as when one person hands a bowl to another person, and lets go only when s/he senses that the other is holding it). We collected a medium size multi-modal human-human dialogue corpus, then processed and analyzed it. We observed that a fair number of sentences are incomplete, namely, the speaker does not finish the utterance. Because of that, we developed a core component of our multi-modal interface, a sentence completion system, trained on the set of interrupted but eventually completed sentences from our corpus. In this paper, we will present the component of the system that predicts reasonable completion structures for an incomplete sentence.

Sentence completion has been addressed within information retrieval, to satisfy user's information needs (Grabski and Scheffer, 2004). Completing sentences in human-human dialogue is more difficult than in written text. First, utterances may be informal, ungrammatical or dis-fluent; second, people interrupt each other during conversations (DeVault et al., 2010; Yang et al., 2011). Additionally, the interaction is complex, as people spontaneously use hand gestures, body language and gaze besides spoken language. As noticed by (Bolden, 2003), during face-to-face interaction, the completion problem is not only an exclusively verbal phenomenon but "an action embedded within a complex web of different meaning-making fields". Accordingly, among our features, we will include pointing gestures, and haptic-ostensive (H-O) actions, e.g., referring to an object by manipulating it in the real world (Landragin et al., 2002; Foster et al., 2008).

The paper is organized as follows. In Section 2 we describe our data collection and multi-modal annotation. In Section 3 we discuss how we generate our training data, and in Section 4 the model we train for sentence completion, and the results we obtain.

2 Dataset

In contrast with other sentence completion systems that focus on text input, the dataset we use in this paper is a subset of the ELDERLY-AT-HOME corpus, a multi-modal corpus in the domain of elderly care, which includes collaborative human-human dialogues, pointing gestures and haptic-ostensive (H-O) actions. Our experiments were conducted in a fully functional apartment and included a helper

(HEL) and an elderly person (ELD). HEL helps ELD to complete several realistic tasks, such as putting on shoes, finding a pot, cooking pasta and setting the table for dinner. We used 7 web cameras to videotape the whole experiment, one microphone each to record the audio and one data glove each to collect haptics data. We ran 20 realistic experiments in total, and then imported the videos and audios (in avi format), haptics data (in csv format) and transcribed utterances (in xml format) into Anvil (Kipp, 2001) to build the multi-modal corpus.

Among other annotations (for example Dialogue Acts) we have annotated these dialogues for ***Pointing gestures and H-O actions***. Due to the setting of our experiments, the targets of pointing gestures and H-O actions are real life objects, thus we designed a reference index system to annotate them. We give pre-defined indices to targets which cannot be moved, such as cabinets, draws, and fridge. We also assign runtime indices to targets which can be moved, like pots, glasses, and plates. For example, "Glass1" refers to the first glass that appears in one experiment. In our annotation, a "Pointing" gesture is defined as a hand gesture without any physical contact between human and objects. Hand gestures with physical contact to objects are annotated as H-O actions. H-O actions are further subdivided into 7 subtypes, including "Holding", "Touching","Open" and "Close". In order to verify the reliability of our annotations, we double coded 15% of the pointing gestures and H-O actions. Kappa values of 0.751 for pointing gestures, and of 0.703 for H-O actions, are considered acceptable, especially considering the complexity of these real life tasks (Chen and Di Eugenio, 2012).

In this paper, we focus on specific sub-dialogues in the corpus, which we call interruptions. An interruption can occur at any point in human-human dialogues: it happens when presumably the interrupter (ITR) thinks s/he has already understood what the speaker (SPK) means before listening to the entire sentence. By observing the data from our corpus, we conclude that there are generally three cases of interruptions. First, the speaker (SPK) stops speaking and does not complete the sentence – these are the incomplete sentences whose completion a robot would need to infer. In the second type of interruption, after being interrupted SPK continues with (a) few words, and then stops without finishing the whole sentence: hence, there is a short time overlap between two sentences (7 cases). The third case occurs when the SPK ignores the ITR and finishes the entire sentence. In this case, the SPK and the ITR speak simultaneously (198 cases). The number of interruptions ranges from 1 to 37 in each experiment. An excerpt from an interruption with a subsequent completion (an example of case 3) is shown below. The interruption occurs at the start of the overlap between the two speakers, marked by < and >. This example also includes annotations for pointing gestures and for H-O actions.

Elder:	I need some glasses from < that cabinet >. [Point (Elder, Cabinet1)]
Helper:	< From this > cabinet? [Point (Helper, Cabinet2)]
Helper:	Is this the glass you < 're looking for? > [Touching (Helper, Glass1)]
Elder:	< No, that one.> [Point (Elder, Cabinet1, Glass2)]

As concerns annotation for interruptions, it proceeds from identifying *interrupted sentences* to finding *<interrupted sentences, candidate structure>* pairs which will be used for generating grammatical completion for an incomplete sentence. Each interrupted sentence is marked with two categories: incomplete form, from the start of the sentence to where it is interrupted, such as "I need some glasses"; complete form, from the start of a sentence to where the speaker stops, "I need some glasses from that cabinet."

Table 2 shows distribution statistics for our ELDERLY-AT-HOME corpus. It contains a total of 4839 sentences, which in turn contain 7219 clauses. 320 sentences are incomplete in the sense of case 1 (after interruption SPK never completes his/her sentence); whereas 205 sentences are completed after interruption (cases 2 and 3).

Sentences	4,839
Clauses	7,219
Pointing Gestures	362
H-O Actions	629
Incomplete sentences	320
Interrupted sentences	205

Table 1: Corpus Distributions

3 Candidate Pairs Generation

The question is now, how to generate plausible training instances to predict completions for incomplete sentences. We use the 205 sentences that have been interrupted **but** for which we have completions; however, we cannot only use those pairs for training, since we would run the risk of overfitting, and not being able to infer appropriate completions for other sentences. To generate additional <*Interrupted sentences, candidate structure*> pairs, we need to match an interrupted sentence **IntS** with its potential completions – basically, to check whether IntS can match the prefix of other sentences in the corpus. We do so by comparing the POS sequence and parse tree of IntS with the POS sequence and parse tree of the prefix of another sentence. Both IntS and other sentences in the corpus are parsed via the Stanford Parser (Klein and Manning, 2003).

Before discussing the details though, we need to deal with one potential problem: the POS sequence for the incomplete portion of IntS may not be correctly assigned. For example, when the sentence 'The/DT, top/JJ, cabinet/NN.' is interrupted as 'The/DT, top/NN', the POS tag of NN is assigned to 'top'; this is incorrect, and engenders noise for finding correct completions.

We first pre-process a dialogue by splitting turns into sentences, tokenizing sentences into tokens, and POS tagging tokens. Although for the interrupted sentences, we could obtain a correct POS tag sequence by parsing the incomplete and resumed portions together, this would not work for a truly incomplete sentence (whose completion is our goal). Thus, to treat both interrupted sentences and incomplete sentences in the same way, we train a POS tag Correction Model to correct fallaciously assigned POS tags. The POS tag Correction Model's feature set includes the POS tag of the token, the word, and the previous tokens' POS tags in a window size of 3. The model outputs the corrected POS tags.

The POS tag Correction model described above was implemented using the Weka package (Hall et al., 2009). Specifically, we experimented with J48 (a decision tree implementation), Naive Bayes (NB), and LibSVM (a Support Vector Machine implementation). All the results reported below are calculated using 10 fold cross-validation.

	J48	NB	LibSVM
Accuracy	0.829	0.680	0.532

Table 2: POS tag Correction Model Performance

The results in Table 2 are not surprising, since detecting the POS tag of a known word is a simple task. Additionally, it is not surprising that J48 is more accurate than NB, since NB is known to often behave as a baseline method. What is surprising though is the poor performance of SVMs, which are generally among the top performers for a broad variety of tasks. We are investigating why this may be the case. At any rate, by applying the J48 model, we obtain more accurate POS tag assignments for interrupted sentences (and in our future application, for the incomplete sentence we need to complete).

Once we have corrected the POS assignments for each interrupted sentence IntS, we retrieve potential grammatical structures for IntS, by comparing IntS with the prefixes of all complete sentences in the corpus via POS tags and parse trees. Note that due to the complexity of building a parse tree correction model in our corpus, we only build a model to correct the POS tags, but ignore the possible incorrect parse trees of the incomplete portion of an interrupted sentence. The matching starts from the last word in IntS back to the first word, with weights assigned to each position in decreasing order. Due to the size of our corpus, it is not possible to find exactly matched POS tag sequences for every incomplete sentence; thus, we also consider the parsed tree structures and mismatched POS tags between IntS's and complete sentences by reducing weights according to the size of the matched phrases and distances of mismatched POS tags. After this, a matching score is calculated for each incomplete and candidate structure pair.

Due to the large number of candidate structures, only the top 150 candidate structures for each IntS are selected and manually annotated with three classifications: "R", when the candidate structure provides a grammatically "reasonable" structure, which can be used as a template for completion; "U", which means the candidate structure gives an "ungrammatical" structure, thus this candidate structure cannot be used as template for completion;

"T", the candidate structure is exactly the same as what the speaker was originally saying, as judged based on the video and audio records. An example of an incomplete sentence with candidate structures in each of the three categories is shown below.

It/PRP, feels/VBZ | It/PRP, feels/VBZ, good/JJR
[R] It/PRP, 's/VBZ, fine/JJ, like/IN, this/DT]
[U] We/PRP, did/VBD, n't/RB
[T] It/PRP, is/VBZ, better/JJR

10543 interrupted sentences and candidate pairs are generated. 5268 of those 10543 pairs (49.97%) were annotated as "Reasonable", 4727 pairs (44.85%) were annotated as "Unreasonable", and 545 pairs (5.17%) were annotated as "Same with original sentence".

Incomplete Sentence and Structure pairs	10,543
Reasonable structures (R)	5,268
Unreasonable structures (U)	4,729
Exactly same structures (T)	545

Table 3: Distribution of completion classifications

4 Results and Discussion

On the basis of the annotation, we trained a "Reasonable Structure Selection (RSS)" model via supervised learning methods. For each pair <IntS, Candidate>, the feature set includes word and POS tag of the tokens of IntS and its candidate structure sentence. Co-occurring pointing gestures and H-O actions for both IntS and Candidate are also included in the model. Co-occurrence is defined as temporal overlap between the gesture (pointing or H-O action) and the duration of the utterance. For each training instance, we include the following features:
IntS: <words, POS tags>, <Pointing (Person / Object / Location)>, <H-O action (Person / Object / Location / Type)>;
Candidate: <words/POS tags)>, <Pointing (Person / Object / Location)>, <H-O action (Person / Object / Location / Type)>;
<Matching Score>;
<Classification: R, U, or T>.
We trained the RSS model also using the Weka package. The same methods mentioned earlier (J48, NB and SVM) are used, with 10-fold cross-validations. Results are shown in Table 4. We

		J48	NB	LibSVM
Precision	R, U, T	0.822	0.724	0.567
	R, U	0.843	0.761	0.600
Recall	R, U, T	0.820	0.725	0.512
	R, U	0.842	0.762	0.563
F-Measure	R, U, T	0.818	0.711	0.390
	R, U	0.841	0.761	0.440

Table 4: Reasonable Structure Selection models

ran two different sets of experiments using two versions of training instances: Classification with three classes, R, U and T, and classification with two classes, R and U. When training with only two classes, the T instances are marked as R. We experimented with collapsing R and T candidates since T candidates may lead to overfitting, and some R candidates might even provide better structures for an incomplete sentence than what exactly one speaker had originally said. Not surprisingly, results improve for two-way classification. Based on the J48 model, we observed that the POS tag features play a significant part in classification, whereas the word features are redundant. Further, pointing gestures and H-O actions do appear in some subtrees of the larger decision tree, but not on every branch. We speculate that this is due to the fact that pointing gestures or H-O actions do not accompany every utterance.

5 Conclusions and Future Work

In this paper, we introduced our multi-modal sentence completion schema which includes pointing gestures and H-O actions in the corpus ELDERLY-AT-HOME. Our data shows that it is possible to predict what people will say, even if the utterance is not complete. Our promising results include multi-modal features, which as we have shown elsewhere (Chen and Di Eugenio, 2012) improve traditional co-reference resolution models. In the near future, we will implement the last module of our sentence completion system, the one that fills the chosen candidate structure with actual words.

References

G.B. Bolden. 2003. Multiple modalities in collaborative turn sequences. *Gesture*, 3(2):187–212.

L. Chen and B. Di Eugenio. 2012. Co-reference via pointing and haptics in multi-modal dialogues. In *The 2012 Conference of the North American Chapter of the Association for Computational Linguistics: Human Language Technologies*. Association for Computational Linguistics. short paper, to appear.

L. Chen, A. Wang, and B. Di Eugenio. 2011. Improving pronominal and deictic co-reference resolution with multi-modal features. In *Proceedings of the SIGDIAL 2011 Conference*, pages 307–311. Association for Computational Linguistics.

David DeVault, Kenji Sagae, and David Traum. 2010. Incremental interpretation and prediction of utterance meaning for interactive dialogue. *Dialogue and Discourse*, 2(1):143170.

B. Di Eugenio, M. Zefran, J. Ben-Arie, M. Foreman, L. Chen, S. Franzini, S. Jagadeesan, M. Javaid, and K. Ma. 2010. Towards effective communication with robotic assistants for the elderly: Integrating speech, vision and haptics. In *2010 AAAI Fall Symposium Series*.

M.E. Foster, E.G. Bard, M. Guhe, R.L. Hill, J. Oberlander, and A. Knoll. 2008. The roles of haptic-ostensive referring expressions in cooperative, task-based human-robot dialogue. In *Proceedings of the 3rd ACM/IEEE international conference on Human robot interaction*, pages 295–302. ACM.

K. Grabski and T. Scheffer. 2004. Sentence completion. In *Proceedings of the 27th annual international ACM SIGIR conference on Research and development in information retrieval*, pages 433–439. ACM.

Mark Hall, Eibe Frank, Geoffrey Holmes, Bernhard Pfahringer, Peter Reutemann, and Ian H. Witten. 2009. The WEKA data mining software: An update. *SIGKDD Explorations*, 11(1). http://www.cs.waikato.ac.nz/ml/weka/.

M. Kipp. 2001. Anvil-a generic annotation tool for multimodal dialogue. In *Seventh European Conference on Speech Communication and Technology*.

D. Klein and C.D. Manning. 2003. Accurate unlexicalized parsing. In *Proceedings of the 41st Annual Meeting on Association for Computational Linguistics-Volume 1*, pages 423–430. Association for Computational Linguistics.

K.M. Krapp. 2002. *The Gale Encyclopedia of Nursing & Allied Health: DH*, volume 2. Gale Cengage.

F. Landragin, N. Bellalem, L. Romary, et al. 2002. Referring to objects with spoken and haptic modalities.

F. Yang, P.A. Heeman, and A.L. Kun. 2011. An investigation of interruptions and resumptions in multi-tasking dialogues. *Computational Linguistics*, 37(1):75–104.

Combining Incremental Language Generation and Incremental Speech Synthesis for Adaptive Information Presentation

Hendrik Buschmeier[1], **Timo Baumann**[3], **Benjamin Dosch**, **Stefan Kopp**[1], **David Schlangen**[2]
[1]Sociable Agents Group, CITEC and Faculty of Technology, Bielefeld University
[2]Dialogue Systems Group, Faculty of Linguistics and Literary Studies, Bielefeld University
{hbuschme,bdosch,skopp,david.schlangen}@uni-bielefeld.de
[3]Natural Language Systems Division, Department of Informatics, University of Hamburg
baumann@informatik.uni-hamburg.de

Abstract

Participants in a conversation are normally receptive to their surroundings and their interlocutors, even while they are speaking and can, if necessary, adapt their ongoing utterance. Typical dialogue systems are not receptive and cannot adapt while uttering. We present combinable components for incremental natural language generation and incremental speech synthesis and demonstrate the flexibility they can achieve with an example system that adapts to a listener's acoustic understanding problems by pausing, repeating and possibly rephrasing problematic parts of an utterance. In an evaluation, this system was rated as significantly more natural than two systems representing the current state of the art that either ignore the interrupting event or just pause; it also has a lower response time.

1 Introduction

Current spoken dialogue systems often produce prescripted system utterances or use templates with variable substitution during language generation. If a dialogue system uses grammar-based generation at all, it produces complete utterances that are then synthesised and realised in one big chunk. As systems become increasingly more conversational, however, the need arises to make output generation[1] more flexible. In particular, capabilities for *incrementally* generating output become desirable, for two kinds of reasons.

(a) In situations where fast system responses are important, production of output can begin before the content that is to be presented is fully specified – even if what is being produced is just a turn-taking signal (Skantze and Hjalmarsson, 2010).

(b) A system that produces its output incrementally can react to events happening while it is realising an utterance. This can be beneficial in domains where the state of the world that the system relays information about can change mid-utterance, so that a need may arise to adapt while speaking. It should also improve naturalness by allowing the system to react to dialogue phenomena such as concurrent feedback signals from the user (Buschmeier and Kopp, 2011).

We present work towards enabling such capabilities. We have implemented and connected a component for incremental natural language generation (iNLG) that works with specifications of sub-utterance-sized communicative intentions and a component for incremental speech synthesis (iSS) that can handle sub-utterance-sized input and modifications to not-yet-spoken parts of the utterance with very low latencies. To explore whether such an output generation capability can indeed be advantageous, we have created a test system that can react to random noise events that occur during a system utterance by repeating and modifying the last sub-utterance chunk. In an evaluation, we found that this system is in general more reactive than a non-incremental variant and that humans rate its behaviour to be more natural than two non-incremental and non-responsive systems.

2 Related Work

Psycholinguistic research has identified incrementality as an important property of human language production early on and it has been incorporated into several models (e. g., Kempen and Hoenkamp, 1987;

[1]We will use the term 'output generation' here to cover both natural language generation and speech synthesis.

Levelt, 1989). Guhe (2007) presents a computational model of incremental conceptualisation. However, work on iNLG itself is rare, partly because NLG research focusses on text (instead of spoken language).

Notable exceptions are the in-depth analysis of requirements for and properties of incremental generation by Kilger and Finkler (1995), who describe the LTAG-based incremental syntactic generator VM-GEN. It takes incremental input, processes it and produces output as soon as at least a prefix of the final sentence is syntactically complete. If VM-GEN notices that it committed itself to a prefix too early, it can initiate an overt repair. More recently, Skantze and Hjalmarsson (2010) presented a system that performs incremental generation in the context of a spoken dialogue system. It can already start to produce output when the user has not yet finished speaking and only a preliminary interpretation exists. By flexibly changing what to say and by being able to make self-repairs the system can recover from situations where it selected and committed on an inadequate speech plan. Both systems, however, are not able to flexibly adapt the language that they generate to changing requirements due to changes in the situation or changing needs on the side of the user.

Real-time on-the-fly control of speech synthesis is rare, especially the full integration into a dialogue system. Matsuyama et al. (2010) describe a system that feeds back to the dialogue system the word at which it has been interrupted by a barge-in. Edlund (2008) additionally enables a system to continue at the point where it was interrupted. He also outlines some requirements for incremental speech synthesis: to *give constant feedback* about what has been delivered, to *be interruptible* (and possibly continue from that position), and to *run in real time*. Edlund's system, which uses diphone synthesis, performed non-incrementally before delivery starts. We go beyond this in also enabling changes during delivery and conducting synthesis steps *just-in-time*.

Dutoit et al. (2011) present an incremental HMM optimiser which allows to change pitch and tempo of upcoming phonemes. However, as that system is fed from a (non-incrementally produced) label file, it cannot easily be used in an incremental system.

A predecessor of our iSS component (which was not yet fully incremental on the HMM level) is described in detail in (Baumann and Schlangen, 2012a).

3 Incremental and Adaptive NLG

3.1 The SPUD microplanning framework

The NLG component presented here is based on the SPUD microplanning framework (Stone et al., 2003) and realised in DeVault's (2008) implementation 'Java SPUD'. SPUD frames microplannig as a constraint satisfaction problem, solving the tasks that are involved in generating a sentence (lexical and syntactic choice, referring expression generation and aggregation) in an integrated manner. Generation starts from a communicative goal that specifies constraints for the final utterance. The generation process is further shaped by (a) general constraints that model pragmatic properties of language use such as the Gricean maxims (a principle called 'textual economy'); (b) specific constraints imposed through the communicative status of the propositions to be communicated (i. e., what knowledge can be presupposed and what needs to be communicated explicitly); and (c) linguistic resources (a context-free tree rewriting formalism based on LTAG; Stone, 2002).

To deal efficiently with the infinite search space spanned by the linguistic resources, SPUD uses a heuristic search algorithm to find an utterance that satisfies the imposed constraints (Stone et al., [2003] describe the heuristic function). In each search step, the algorithm expands the 'provisional' utterance by adding the linguistic resource that maximally reduces the estimated distance to the final utterance.

If the generation process runs into a dead-end state, it could in principle deal with the situation by tracking back and expanding a different branch. This, however, is impractical, as it becomes impossible to project when – if at all – generation will finish. Hence, in that case, SPUD stops without providing a result, delegating the problem back to the preceding component in the generation pipeline.

3.2 *Partially* incremental generation

SPUD generates utterances incrementally in the sense that the completeness of the provisional utterance increases monotonically with every step. This, however, does not mean that the surface structure of provisional utterances is constructed incrementally (i. e., from left to right) as well, which would only be possible, if (a) the search strategy would always expand the leftmost non-lexicalised node in the provisional

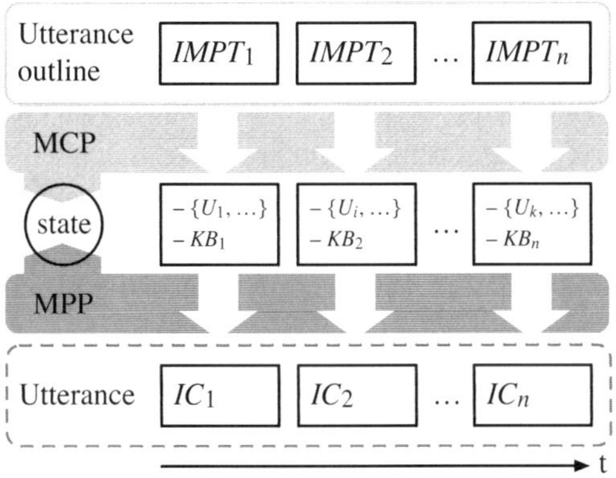

Figure 1: Incremental microplanning consists of two processes, micro content planning (MCP) and microplanning-proper (MPP). The former provides incremental microplanning tasks from an utterance outline to the latter, which incrementally transforms them into communicative intent and intonation unit-sized chunks of natural language.

utterance first and if (b) the linguistic resources are specified (and ordered) in a way that allows left-to-right expansion of the trees in all possible situations. In practice, both requirements are difficult to meet and full word-by-word incrementality in natural language microplanning is not within reach in the SPUD framework. Because of this, we take a slightly more coarse grained approach to incremental microplanning and choose chunks of the size of intonation phrases instead of words as our incremental units. We say that our microplanner does *'partially* incremental generation'.

Our incremental microplanner comprises two interacting processes, *micro content planning* and *microplanning-proper* (MCP and MPP; schematised in Figure 1), each of which fulfils a distinct task and operates on different structures.

MCP takes as input *utterance outlines* that describe the communicative goal (a set of desired updates U_x) intended to be communicated in an utterance and the presuppositions and private knowledge needed to do so. Importantly, utterance outlines specify how the communicative goal can be decomposed into an ordered list of incremental microplanning-tasks $IMPT_x$. Each such task comprises (a) a subset of the communicative goal's desired updates that belong together and fit into one intonation unit sized chunk of speech and (b) knowledge KB_x used in generation.

MPP takes one incremental microplanning-task at a time and uses SPUD to generate the IMPT's communicative intent as well as its linguistic surface form IC_x. The communiciative intent is added to a representation ('state' in Figure 1) that is shared between the two processes. While processing the IMPTs of an utterance outline, MCP can access this representation, which holds information about all the desired updates that were achieved before, and thus knows that a desired update that is shared between subsequent IMPTs has already been communicated. MPP can also take this information into account during generation. This makes it possible that an utterance is coherent and adheres to pragmatic principles even though generation can only take local decisions.

3.3 Adaptive generation

Being able to generate language in sub-utterance chunks makes it possible to dynamically adapt later increments of an utterance to changes in the situation that occur while the utterance is being realised. Decisions about these adaptations need not be taken almost until the preceding increment finishes, making the generation process very responsive. This is important to be able to deal with interactive dialogue phenomena, such as communicative feedback of the interlocutor (Allwood et al., 1992) or compound contributions (Howes et al., 2011), in a timely manner.

Adaptation may happen in both parts of incremental microplanning. In MCP, adaptation takes the form of dynamically changing the choice of which IMPT to generate next or changing the internal structure of an IMPT; adaptation in MPP changes the choices the generation process makes while transforming IMPTs into communicative intent and surface form. Adaptation in MCP is triggered top-down, by higher-level processes such as dialogue management. Adaptation in MPP on the other hand depends on the task given and on the status of the knowledge used during generation. The details are then governed by global parameter settings MPP uses during generation.

If there is, for example, reason for the system to believe that the current increment was not communicated clearly because of noise in the transmission channel, the MCP process might delay future IMPTs and initiate a repair of the current one by re-inserting it at the beginning of the list of upcoming IMPTs of this utterance outline. The MPP process' next task is then to re-generate the same IMPT again. Due to

Table 1: Surface forms generated from the same IMPT (desired updates = {hasSubject(event6, 'Vorlesung Linguistik')}; KB = {event6}) but with different levels of verbosity.

Verbosity	Generated sub-utterance chunk
0	'Vorlesung Linguistik' *(lecture Linguistcs)*
1	'Betreff: Vorlesung Linguistik' *(subject: lecture Linguistics)*
2	'mit dem Betreff Vorlesung Linguistik' *(with the subject: lecture Linguistics)*

changes in the state information and situation that influence microplanning, the resulting communicative intent and surface form might then differ from its previous result.

3.4 Adaptation mechanisms

As a proof of concept, we integrated several adaptation mechanism into our NLG-microplanning system. The goal of these mechanisms is to respond to a dialogue partner's changing abilities to perceive and/or understand the information the system wants to convey. Some of the mechanisms operate on the level of MCP, others on the level of MPP. The mechanisms are implemented either with the knowledge and its conversational status used in generation or by altering the decision structure of SPUD's search algorithm's heuristic function. Similar to the approach of flexible NLG described by Walker et al. (2007), most of the mechanism are conditioned upon individual flags, that in our case depend on a numeric value that represents the level of understanding the system attributes to the user. Here we describe the two most relevant mechanisms used to adapt verbosity and redundancy.

Verbosity The first mechanism aims at influencing the length of a sub-utterance chunk by making it either more or less verbose. The idea is that actual language use of human speakers seldom adheres to the idealised principle of textual economy. This is not only the case for reasons of cognitive constraints during speech production, but also because words and phrases that do not contribute much to an utterance's semantics can serve a function, for example by drawing attention to specific aspects of an utterance or by giving the listener time to process.

To be able to vary utterance verbosity, we annotated the linguistic resources in our system with values of their verbosity (these are hand-crafted similar to the rule's annotation with production costs). During generation in MPP the values of all linguistic resources used in a (provisional) utterance are added up and used as one factor in SPUD's heuristic function. When comparing two provisional utterances that only deviate in their verbosity value, the one that is nearer to a requested verbosity level is chosen. Depending on this level, more or less verbose constructions are chosen and it is decided whether sub-utterance chunks are enriched with additional words. Table 1 shows the sub-utterance chunk 'Betreff: Vorlesung Linguistik' *(subject: lecture Linguistics)* generated with different levels of verbosity.

Redundancy The second adaptation mechanism is redundancy. Again, redundancy is something that an ideal utterance does not contain and by design SPUD penalises the use of redundancy in its heuristic function. Two provisional utterances being equal, the one exhibiting less redundancy is normally preferred. But similar to verbosity, redundancy serves communicative functions in actual language use. It can highlight important information, it can increase the probability of the message being understood (Reiter and Sripada, 2002) and it is often used to repair misunderstanding (Baker et al., 2008).

In incremental microplanning, redundant information can be present both within one sub-utterance chunk (e. g., 'tomorrow, March 26, ... ' vs. 'tomorrow ... ') or across IMPTs. For the former case, we modified SPUD's search heuristic in order to conditionally either prefer an utterance that contains redundant information or an utterance that only contains what is absolutely necessary. In the latter case, redundancy only becomes an option when later IMPTs enable the choice of repeating information previously conveyed and therefore already established as shared knowledge. This is controlled via the internal structure of an IMPT and thus decided on the level of MCP.

4 Incremental Speech Synthesis

In this section we describe our component for incremental speech synthesis. We extend Edlund's (2008) requirements specification cited in Section 2, requiring additionally that an iSS supports changes to as-yet unspoken parts of an ongoing utterance.

We believe that the ISS's requirements of interruptability, changeability, responsiveness, and feedback are best resolved by a processing paradigm in which processing takes place *just-in-time*, i. e., taking processing steps as late as possible such as to avoid re-processing if assumptions change. Before we describe these ideas in detail, we give a short background on speech synthesis in general.

4.1 Background on speech synthesis

Text-to-speech (TTS) synthesis functions in a top-down processing approach, starting on the utterance level and descending onto words and phonemes, in order to make good decisions (Taylor, 2009). For example, top-down modelling is necessary to assign stress patterns and sentence-level intonation which ultimately lead to pitch and duration contours, and to model co-articulation effects.

TTS systems start out assigning intonation patterns to the utterance's words and then generate a *target phoneme sequence* which is annotated with the targets' durations and pitch contour; all of this is called the linguistic pre-processing step. The synthesis step proper can be executed in one of several ways with HMM-based and unit-selection synthesis currently producing the perceptually best results.

In HMM-based synthesis, the target sequence is first turned into a sequence of HMM states. A global optimisation then determines a stream of vocoding features that optimise both HMM emission probabilities and continuity constraints (Tokuda et al., 2000). The stream may also be enhanced to consider global variance of features (Toda and Tokuda, 2007). The parameter frames are then fed to a vocoder which generates the final speech audio signal.

Unit-selection, in contrast, searches for the best sequence of (variably sized) units of speech in a large, annotated corpus, aiming to find a sequence that closely matches the target sequence while having few and if possible smooth joints between units.

We follow the HMM-based approach for our component for the following reasons: (a) even though only global optimisation is optimal for both techniques, the influence of look-ahead on the continuity constraints of HMM-based synthesis is linear leading to a linear loss in optimality with smaller look-aheads (whereas unit-selection with limited look-ahead may jump erratically between completely different unit sequences). (b) HMM-based synthesis nicely separates the production of vocoding parameter frames from the production of the speech audio signal which allows for fine-grained concurrent processing (see next subsection). (c) Parameters in the vocoding frames are partially independent. This allows us to independently manipulate, e. g., pitch without altering other parameters or deteriorating speech quality (in unit-selection, a completely different unit sequence might become optimal even for slight changes of pitch).

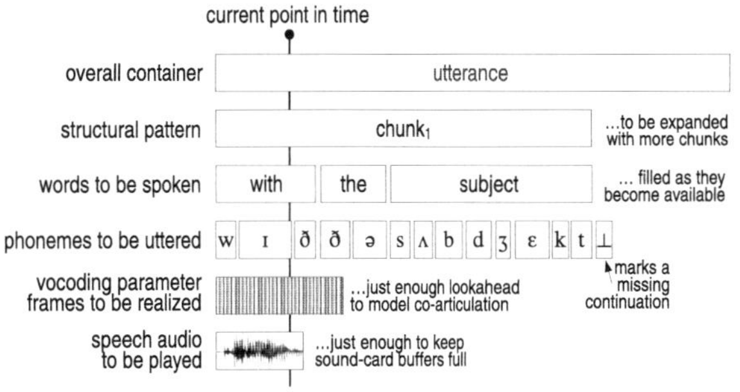

Figure 2: Hierarchical structure of incremental units describing an example utterance as it is being produced during delivery.

4.2 Incrementalising speech synthesis

As explained in the previous subsection, speech synthesis is performed top-down, starting at the utterance and progressing down to the word, target and finally, in the HMM approach, vocoding parameter and signal processing levels. It is, however, not necessary that all details at one level of processing are worked out before starting to process at the next lower level. To be precise, some syntactic structure is sufficient to produce sentence-level intonation, but all words need not be known. Likewise, post-lexical phonological processes can be computed as long as a local context of one word is available and vocoding parameter computation (which must model co-articulation effects) should in turn be satisfied with about one phoneme of context. Vocoding itself does not need any lookahead at all (aside from audio buffering considerations).

Thus, we generate our data structures incrementally in a top-down and left-to-right fashion with different amounts of pre-planning and we do this using several processing modules that work concurrently. This results in a 'triangular' structure as shown in

Figure 2. At the top stands a pragmatic plan for the full utterance from which a syntactic plan can be devised. This plan is filled with words, as they become available. On the vocoding parameter level, only a few frames into the future have been computed so far – even though much more context is already available. That is, we generate structure *just-in-time*, only shortly before it is needed by the next processor. This holds very similarly for the vocoding step that produces the speech signal just-in-time.

The just-in-time processing approach, combined with the increasing temporal granularity of units towards the lower levels has several advantages: (a) little utterance-initial processing (only what is necessary to produce the beginning of the signal) allows for very responsive systems; and (b) changes to the initial plan result only in a modest processing overhead because little structure has to be re-computed.

4.3 Technical overview

As a basis, we use MaryTTS (Schröder and Trouvain, 2003), but replace Mary's internal data structures and processing strategies with structures from our incremental SDS architecture, the INPROTK toolkit (Schlangen et al., 2010; Baumann and Schlangen, 2012b), which implements the IU model for incremental dialogue processing (Schlangen and Skantze, 2009). The model conceptualises – and the toolkit implements – incremental processing as the processing of *incremental units* (IUs), which are the smallest 'chunks' of information at a specific level (the boxes in Figure 2). IUs are interconnected to form a *network* (e. g., words keep links to their associated phonemes and neighbouring words and vice-versa) which represents the system's information state.

The component is fed with chunk IUs which contain some words to be synthesised (on their own or appended to an ongoing utterance). For simplicity, all units below the chunk level are currently generated using Mary's (non-incremental) linguistic preprocessing capabilities to obtain the target phoneme sequence. For continuations, the preceding parts of the utterance are taken into account when generating prosodic characteristics for the new chunk. Also, our component is able to revoke and exchange chunks (or unspoken parts thereof) to change what is to be spoken; this capability however is not used in the example system presented in Section 5.

The lowest level module of our component is what may be called a *crawling vocoder*, which actively moves along the phoneme IU layer and executes two processing steps: (a) for each phoneme it generates the sequence of HMM parameter frames using a local optimisation technique (using up to four neighbouring phonemes as context) similar to the one described by Dutoit et al. (2011); and (b) vocoding the HMM parameters into an audio stream which contains the actual speech signal.

IUs have a 'progress' field which is set by the crawling vocoder to one of 'upcoming', 'ongoing', or 'completed', as applicable. IUs provide a generic update mechanism to support notification about progress changes in delivery. The next section describes how this is used to drive the system.

5 Integrating iNLG and iSS for Adaptive Information Presentation

Integrating incremental microplanning with incremental speech synthesis in one incremental output generation architecture allows us to test and explore how their capabilities act in a coordinated way. As a first example, we implemented a system that presents information about events in an appointment database (e. g., new, conflicting or rescheduled appointments) and is able to cope with external noise burst events, as they might for example occur on a bad telephone line or when using a dialogue system next to a busy street. The focus is on the incremental capabilities of the system which enable its adaptive behaviour.

5.1 Component interplay

iNLG and iSS are implemented as IU modules in the INPROTK architecture. The control flow of the system (Figure 3) is managed without special coupling between the modules, relying only on the left-to-right processing capabilities of INPROTK combined with its generic IU update mechanism for transporting feedback from iSS to iNLG. Both modules can be (and have been) combined with other IU modules.

To communicate an appointment event, the iNLG module starts by generating two initial chunk IUs, the first to be expressed immediately, the second as additional prosodic context (chunk lengths differ with an average of about 4 words). The iNLG registers as a 'progress listener' on each chunkIU, which registers

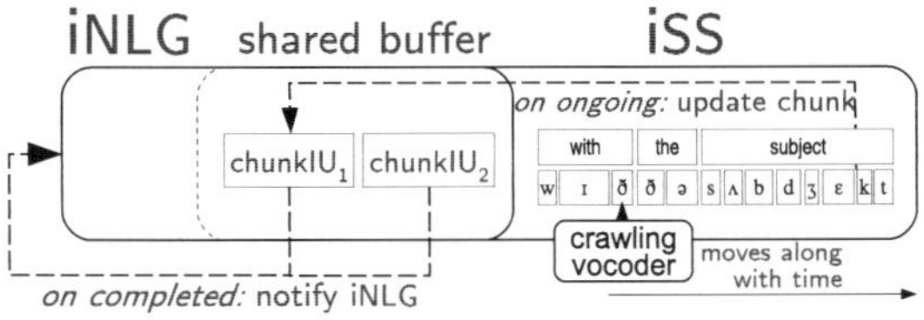

Figure 3: Information flow (dashed lines) between iNLG and iSS components (rounded boxes) and incremental units (rectangular boxes). The vocoder crawls along with time and triggers the updates.

Table 2: Processing time per processing step before delivery can begin (in ms; averaged over nine stimuli taking the median of three runs for each stimulus; calculated from log messages; code paths preheated for optimisation).

	non-incr.	**incr.**
NLG-microplanning	361	52
Synthesis (ling. pre-processing)	217	447[2]
Synthesis (HMM and vocoding)	1004	21
total response time	1582	519

as a progress listener on a phonemeIUnear its end. Shortly before iSS finishes speaking the chunk, iNLG is thus informed and can generate and send the next chunk to iSS *just-in-time*.

If adaptation to noise is needed, iNLG re-generates and re-sends the previous chunk, taking altered parameters into account. Again, a subsequent chunk is immediately pre-generated for additional prosodic context. This way of generating sub-utterance chunks ensures that there is always one chunk lookahead to allow the iSS module to compute an adequate intonation for the current chunk, while maintaining the single chunk as increment size for the system and minimising redundant work on the side of iNLG (this lookahead is not required for iSS; but if it is unavailable, sub-utterance chunks may be inadequately connected prosodically).

5.2 Responding to a noise event

A third module, the noise detector connects to both iSS and iNLG. On noise onset, it informs iSS to interrupt the ongoing utterance after the current word (this works by breaking the links between words so that the crawling vocoder finishes after the currently ongoing word). Once a noise burst ends, iNLG is informed, re-generates the interrupted sub-utterance chunk with the verbosity level decreased by one and the assumed understanding value increased by one (this degree of adaptation results in a noticeable difference, it is, however, not based on empirical study). The values are then reset, the following chunk is generated and both chunks are sent to iSS.

It should be noted, that we have not implemented a real noise source and noise detector. Instead, our random noise simulator generates bursts of noise of 1000 ms after a random time interval (between 2 and 5 seconds) and directly informs the system 300 ms after noise starts and ends. We think it is reasonable to assume that a real noise detector should be able to give accurate information with a similar delay.

6 Evaluation

6.1 Quantitative evaluation

One important argument in favour of incremental processing is the possibility of speeding up system response time, which for non-incremental systems is the sum of the times taken by all processors to do their work. An incremental system, in contrast, can *fold* large amounts of its processing time into the ongoing speech output; what matters is the sum of the *onset times* of each processor, i. e., the time until a first output becomes available to the next processor.

Table 2 summarises the runtime for the three major steps in output production of our system using nine utterances from our domain. Both NLG and speech synthesis' onset times are greatly reduced in the incremental system.[2] Combined, they reduce system response time by more than a second. This is mostly due to the almost complete folding of HMM optimisation and vocoding times into the spoken utterance. NLG profits from the fact that at the beginning of an utterance only two chunks have to be generated (instead of an average of 6.5 chunks in the non-incremental system) and that the first chunk is often very simple.

6.2 Subjective evaluation

To further test whether the system's behaviour in noisy situations resembles that of a human speaker

[2]The iSS component by mistake takes the symbolic pre-processing step twice. Unfortunately, we found this bug only after creating the stimuli used in the subjective evaluation.

in a similar situation, we let humans rate utterances produced by the fully incremental, adaptive system and utterances produced by two non-incremental and less responsive variants (we have not used non-incremental TTS in combination with iNLG as another possible base-line as pretests showed this to sound very unnatural due to the missing prosodic linkage between phrases). The participants were to rate whether they agree to the statement *'I found the behaviour of the system in this situation as I would expect it from a human speaker'* on a 7-point Likert-scale.

In condition A, full utterances were generated non-incrementally, synthesised non-incrementally and played without responding to noise-interruptions in the channel (as if the system did not notice them). Utterances in condition B were generated and synthesised as in condition A, but playback responded to the noisy channel, stopping when the noise was noticed and continuing when noise ended. For condition C, utterances were generated with the fully incremental and adaptive system described in Section 5. Upon noise detection, speech synthesis is interrupted and, when the noise ends, iNLG will re-generate the interrupted sub-utterance chunk – using the adaptation strategy outlined in Section 5.2. This then triggers iSS into action and shortly after, the system continues speaking. Nine system runs, each producing a different utterance from the calendar domain, were recorded in each of the three conditions, resulting in a total of 27 stimuli.

Before the actual stimuli were presented, participants listened to two example stimuli without noise interruptions to get an impression of how an average utterance produced by the system sounds. After the presentation of these two examples, the 27 stimuli were presented in the same random order. Participants listened once to each stimulus and rated it immediately after every presentation.

Twelve PhD-students (3 female, 9 male; mean age 30.5 years; 11 with German as one of their first languages; none with uncorrected hearing impairment) from Bielefeld University participated in our study and listened to and rated the 27 stimuli.

A Friedman rank sum test revealed a highly significant difference between the perceived human-likeness of the three systems ($\chi^2 = 151, p < .0001$). Median values of stimulus ratings in the conditions *A*, *B* and *C* were 2, 2 and 6 respectively, indicating that the fully incremental system was rated considerably more human-like. This was also shown through a *post-hoc* analysis with Wilcoxon signed rank tests which found no significant difference between condition A and B ($V = 1191.5, p = .91$)[3]. Conditions A and C, however, differed highly significantly ($V = 82, p < .0001$), as did conditions B and C ($V = 22.5, p < .0001$) – even after applying a Bonferroni correction to correct for a possible cumulation of α-errors.

7 Conclusion

We have presented what is – to the best of our knowledge – the first integrated component for incremental NLG and speech synthesis and demonstrated the flexibility that an incremental approach to output generation for speech systems offers by implementing a system that can repair understanding problems.

From the evaluation we can conclude that incremental output generation (both iNLG and iSS in isolation or combined) is able to greatly speed up system response time and can be used as a means to speed up system response even in an otherwise non-incremental system. Furthermore, we showed that the behaviour of our fully incremental and adaptive system was perceived as significantly more human-like than the non-incremental and the non-incremental but responsive baseline systems.

The understanding problem that our demonstrator system tackled was of the simplest kind, namely acoustic non-understanding, objectively detectable as the presence of noise. In principle, however, the same mechanisms of stopping and rephrasing can be used to tackle more subjective understanding problems as can be signalled by linguistic feedback. Our incremental output generation component gives us an ideal basis to explore such problems in future work.

Acknowledgements This research is partially supported by the Deutsche Forschungsgemeinschaft (DFG) in the Center of Excellence in 'Cognitive Interaction Technology' (CITEC) and through an Emmy Noether Fellowship to the last author.

[3]This suggests that it does not matter whether a system responds to problems in the communication channel by waiting or totally ignores these problems. Notice, however, that we did not test recall of the calendar events. In that case, condition B should outperform A, as some information was clearly inaudible in A.

References

Jens Allwood, Joakim Nivre, and Elisabeth Ahlsén. 1992. On the semantics and pragmatics of linguistic feedback. *Journal of Semantics*, 9:1–26.

Rachel Baker, Alastair Gill, and Justine Cassell. 2008. Reactive redundancy and listener comprehension in direction-giving. In *Proceedings of the 9th SIGdial Workshop on Discourse and Dialogue*, pages 37–45, Columbus, OH.

Timo Baumann and David Schlangen. 2012a. INPRO_iSS: A component for just-in-time incremental speech synthesis. In *Proceedings of ACL System Demonstrations*, Jeju, South Korea.

Timo Baumann and David Schlangen. 2012b. The INPROTK 2012 release. In *Proceedings of the NAACL-HLT Workshop on Future directions and needs in the Spoken Dialog Community: Tools and Data*, pages 29–32, Montréal, Canada.

Hendrik Buschmeier and Stefan Kopp. 2011. Towards conversational agents that attend to and adapt to communicative user feedback. In *Proceedings of the 11th International Conference on Intelligent Virtual Agents*, pages 169–182, Reykjavik, Iceland.

David DeVault. 2008. *Contribution Tracking: Participating in Task-oriented Dialogue Under Uncertainty*. Ph.D. thesis, Rutgers, The State University of New Jersey, New Brunswick, NJ.

Thierry Dutoit, Maria Astrinaki, Onur Babacan, Nicolas d'Alessandro, and Benjamin Picart. 2011. pHTS for Max/MSP: A streaming architecture for statistical parametric speech synthesis. Technical Report 1, numediart Research Program on Digital Art Technologies, Mons, Belgium.

Jens Edlund. 2008. Incremental speech synthesis. In *Second Swedish Language Technology Conference*, pages 53–54, Stockholm, Sweden, November. System Demonstration.

Markus Guhe. 2007. *Incremental Conceptualization for Language Production*. Lawrence Erlbaum, Mahwah, NJ.

Christine Howes, Matthew Purver, Patrick G. T. Healey, Gregory Mills, and Eleni Gregoromichelaki. 2011. On incrementality in dialogue: Evidence from compound contributions. *Discourse & Dialogue*, 2:279–311.

Gerard Kempen and Edward Hoenkamp. 1987. An incremental procedural grammar for sentence formulation. *Cognitive Science*, 11:201–258.

Anne Kilger and Wolfgang Finkler. 1995. Incremental generation for real-time applications. Technical Report RR-95-11, Deutsches Forschungszentrum für Künstliche Intelligenz, Saarbrücken, Germany.

Willem J. M. Levelt. 1989. *Speaking: From Intention to Articulation*. The MIT Press, Cambridge, UK.

Kyoko Matsuyama, Kazunori Komatani, Ryu Takeda, Toru Takahashi, Tetsuya Ogata, and Hiroshi G. Okuno. 2010. Analyzing user utterances in barge-in-able spoken dialogue system for improving identification accuracy. In *Proceedings of INTERSPEECH 2010*, pages 3050–3053, Makuhari, Japan.

Ehud Reiter and Somayajulu Sripada. 2002. Human variation and lexical choice. *Computational Linguistics*, 28:545–553.

David Schlangen and Gabriel Skantze. 2009. A general, abstract model of incremental dialogue processing. In *Proceedings of the 12th Conference of the European Chapter of the Association for Computational Linguistics*, pages 710–718, Athens, Greece.

David Schlangen, Timo Baumann, Hendrik Buschmeier, Okko Buß, Stefan Kopp, Gabriel Skantze, and Ramin Yaghoubzadeh. 2010. Middleware for incremental processing in conversational agents. In *Proceedings of SIGdial 2010: the 11th Annual Meeting of the Special Interest Group in Discourse and Dialogue*, pages 51–54, Tokyo, Japan.

Marc Schröder and Jürgen Trouvain. 2003. The German text-to-speech synthesis system MARY: A tool for research, development and teaching. *International Journal of Speech Technology*, 6:365–377.

Gabriel Skantze and Anna Hjalmarsson. 2010. Towards incremental speech generation in dialogue systems. In *Proceedings of SIGDIAL 2010: the 11th Annual Meeting of the Special Interest Group on Discourse and Dialogue*, pages 1–8, Tokyo, Japan.

Matthew Stone, Christine Doran, Bonnie Webber, Tonia Bleam, and Martha Palmer. 2003. Microplanning with communicative intentions: The SPUD system. *Computational Intelligence*, 19:311–381.

Matthew Stone. 2002. Lexicalized grammar 101. In *Proceedings of the ACL-02 Workshop on Effective Tools and Methodologies for Teaching Natural Language Processing and Computational Linguistics*, pages 77–84, Philadelphia, PA.

Paul Taylor. 2009. *Text-to-Speech Synthesis*. Cambridge Univ Press, Cambridge, UK.

Tomoki Toda and Keiichi Tokuda. 2007. A speech parameter generation algorithm considering global variance for HMM-based speech synthesis. *IEICE TRANSACTIONS on Information and Systems*, 90:816–824.

Keiichi Tokuda, Takayoshi Yoshimura, Takashi Masuko, Takao Kobayashi, and Tadashi Kitamura. 2000. Speech parameter generation algorithms for HMM-based speech synthesis. In *Proceedings of ICASSP 2000*, pages 1315–1318, Istanbul, Turkey.

Marylin Walker, Amanda Stent, François Mairesse, and Rashmi Prasad. 2007. Individual and domain adaptation in sentence planning for dialogue. *Journal of Artificial Intelligence Research*, 30:413–456.

Focused Meeting Summarization via Unsupervised Relation Extraction

Lu Wang
Department of Computer Science
Cornell University
Ithaca, NY 14853
luwang@cs.cornell.edu

Claire Cardie
Department of Computer Science
Cornell University
Ithaca, NY 14853
cardie@cs.cornell.edu

Abstract

We present a novel unsupervised framework for focused meeting summarization that views the problem as an instance of relation extraction. We adapt an existing in-domain relation learner (Chen et al., 2011) by exploiting a set of task-specific constraints and features. We evaluate the approach on a decision summarization task and show that it outperforms unsupervised utterance-level extractive summarization baselines as well as an existing generic relation-extraction-based summarization method. Moreover, our approach produces summaries competitive with those generated by supervised methods in terms of the standard ROUGE score.

1 Introduction

For better or worse, meetings play an integral role in most of our daily lives — they let us share information and collaborate with others to solve a problem, to generate ideas, and to weigh options. Not surprisingly then, there is growing interest in developing automatic methods for meeting summarization (e.g., Zechner (2002), Maskey and Hirschberg (2005), Galley (2006), Lin and Chen (2010), Murray et al. (2010a)). This paper tackles the task of *focused meeting summarization* , i.e., generating summaries of a particular aspect of a meeting rather than of the meeting as a whole (Carenini et al., 2011). For example, one might want a summary of just the DECISIONS made during the meeting, the ACTION ITEMS that emerged, the IDEAS discussed, or the HYPOTHESES put forth, etc.

Consider, for example, the task of summarizing the decisions in the dialogue snippet in Figure 1. The figure shows only the *decision-related dialogue acts (DRDAs)* — utterances associated with one or more decisions.[1] Each DRDA is labeled numerically according to the decision it supports; so the first two utterances support DECISION 1 as do the final two utterances in the snippet. Manually constructed *decision abstracts* for each decision are shown at the bottom of the figure.[2] These constitute the *decision-focused summary* for the snippet.

Notice that many portions of the DRDAs are not relevant to the decision itself: they often begin with phrases that identify the utterance within the discourse as potentially introducing a decision (e.g., "Maybe that could be", "It seems like you're gonna have"), but do not themselves describe the decision. We will refer to this portion of a DRDA (underlined in Figure 1) as the **Decision Cue**.

Moreover, the decision cue is generally directly followed by the actual **Decision Content** (e.g., "be a little apple", "have rubber cases"). Decision Content phrases are denoted in Figure 1 via italics and square brackets. Importantly, it is just the decision content portion of the utterance that should be considered for incorporation into the focused summary.

[1]These are similar, but not completely equivalent, to the *decision dialogue acts (DDAs)* of (Bui et al., 2009), (Fernández et al., 2008), (Frampton et al., 2009).

[2]Murray et al. (2010b) show that users much prefer *abstractive summaries* over extracts when the text to be summarized is a conversation. In particular, extractive summaries drawn from group conversations can be confusing to the reader without additional context; and the noisy, error-prone, disfluent text of speech transcripts is likely to result in extractive summaries with low readability.

C: Say the standby button is quite kinda separate from all the other functions. (1)
C: Maybe that could *be* [a little apple]. (1)
C: It seems like you're gonna *have* [rubber cases], as well as [buttons]. (2)
A: [Rubber buttons] *require* [rubber case]. (2)
A: You could *have* [your company badge] and [logo]. (3)
A: I mean a lot of um computers for instance like like on the one you've got there, it actually *has* a sort of um [stick on badge]. (3)
C: Shall we *go* [for single curve], just to compromise? (2)
B: We'll *go* [for single curve], yeah. (2)
C: And the rubber push buttons, rubber case. (2)
D: And then are we going for sort of [one button] *shaped* [like a fruit]. <vocalsound> Or veg. (1)
D: Could *be* [a red apple], yeah. (1)

Decision Abstracts (Summary)
DECISION 1: The group decided to make the standby button in the shape of an apple.
DECISION 2: The remote will also feature a rubber case and rubber buttons, and a single-curved design.
DECISION 3: The remote will feature the company logo, possibly in a sticker form.

Figure 1: Clip from the AMI meeting corpus (Carletta et al., 2005). A, B, C and D refer to distinct speakers; the numbers in parentheses indicate the associated meeting decision: DECISION 1, 2 or 3. Also shown is the gold-standard (manual) abstract (summary) for each decision. Colors indicate overlapping vocabulary between utterances and the summary. Underlining, *italics*, and [bracketing] are decscribed in the running text.

This paper presents an unsupervised framework for focused meeting summarization that supports the generation of abstractive summaries. (Note that we do not currently generate actual abstracts, but rather aim to identify those **Content** phrases that should comprise the abstract.) In contrast to existing approaches to focused meeting summarization (e.g., Purver et al. (2007), Fernández et al. (2008), Bui et al. (2009)), *we view the problem as an* **information extraction** *task and hypothesize that existing methods for domain-specific relation extraction can be modified to identify salient phrases for use in generating abstractive summaries.*

Very generally, information extraction methods identify a lexical "trigger" or "indicator" that evokes a relation of interest and then employ syntactic information, often in conjunction with semantic constraints, to find the "target phrase" or "argument constituent" to be extracted. Relation instances, then, are represented by **indicator-argument** pairs (Chen et al., 2011).

Figure 1 shows some possible indicator-argument pairs for identifying the Decision Content phrases in the dialogue sample. Content **indicator** words are shown in *italics*; the Decision Content target phrases are the **arguments**. For example, in the fourth DRDA, "require" is the indicator, and "rubber buttons" and "rubber case" are both arguments. Although not shown in Figure 1, it is also possible to identify relations that correspond to the **Decision Cue** phrases.[3]

Specifically, we focus on the task of *decision summarization* and, as in previous work in meeting summarization (e.g., Fernández et al. (2008), Wang and Cardie (2011)), assume that all decision-related utterances (DRDAs) have been identified. We adapt the unsupervised relation learning approach of Chen et al. (2011) to separately identify relations associated with decision cues vs. the decision content within DRDAs by defining a new set of task-specific constraints and features to take the place of the domain-specific constraints and features of the original model. Output of the system is a set of extracted indicator-argument decision content relations (see the "OUR METHOD" sample summary of Table 6) that can be used as the basis of the decision abstract.

We evaluate the approach (using the AMI corpus (Carletta et al., 2005)) under two input settings — in the **True Clusterings** setting, we assume that the DRDAs for each meeting have been perfectly grouped according to the decision(s) each supports; in the **System Clusterings** setting, an automated system performs the DRDA-decision pairing. The results show that the relation-based summarization approach outperforms two extractive summarization baselines that select the longest and the most representative utterance for each decision, respectively. (ROUGE-1 F score of 37.47% vs. 32.61% and 33.32% for the baselines given the True Clusterings of DRDAs.) Moreover, our approach performs admirably in comparison to two supervised learning alternatives (scores of 35.61% and 40.87%) that aim to identify the important **tokens** to include in the decision abstract given the DRDA clusterings. In contrast to our approach which is transferable to different domains or tasks, these methods would require labeled data for retraining for each new meeting corpus.

[3]Consider, for example, the phrases underlined in the sixth and seventh DRDAs. "I mean" and "shall we" are two typical Decision Cue phrases where "mean" and "shall" are possible indicators with "I" and "we" as their arguments, respectively.

Finally, in order to compare our approach to another *relation-based* summarization technique, we modify the multi-document summarization system of Hachey (2009) to the single-document meeting scenario. Here again, our proposed approach performs better (37.47% vs. 34.69%). Experiments under the System Clusterings setting produce the same overall results, albeit with lower scores for all of the systems and baselines.

In the remainder of the paper, we review related work in Section 2 and give a high-level description of the relation-based approach to focused summarization in Section 3. Sections 4, 5 and 6 present the modifications to the Chen et al. (2011) relation extraction model required for its instantiation for the meeting summarization task. Sections 7 and 8 provide our experimental setup and results.

2 Related Work

Most research on spoken dialogue summarization attempts to generate summaries for full dialogues (Carenini et al., 2011). Only recently, however, has the task of focused summarization, and decision summarization, in particular, been addressed. Fernández et al. (2008) and Bui et al. (2009) employ supervised learning methods to rank phrases or words for inclusion in the decision summary. In comparison, Fernández et al. (2008) find that the phrase-based approach yields better recall than token-based methods, concluding that phrases have the potential to support better summaries. Input to their system, however, is narrowed down (manually) from the full set of DRDAs to the subset that is useful for summarization. In addition, they evaluate their system w.r.t. informative phrases or words that have been manually annotated within this DRDA subset. We are instead interested in comparing our extracted relations to the abstractive summaries.

In contrast to our phrase-based approach, we previously explored a collection of supervised and unsupervised learning methods for utterance-level (i.e., dialogue act) and token-level decision summarization (Wang and Cardie, 2011). We adopt here the two unsupervised baselines (utterance-level summaries) from that work for use in our evaluation. We further employ their supervised summarization methods as comparison points for token-level summarization, adding additional features for consistency with the other approaches in the evaluation. Murray et al. (2010a) develop an integer linear programming approach for focused summarization at the utterance-level, selecting sentences that cover more of the entities mentioned in the meeting as determined through the use of an external ontology.

The most relevant previous work is Hachey (2009), which uses relational representations to facilitate sentence-ranking for multi-document summarization. The method utilizes generic relation extraction to represent the concepts in the documents as relation instances; summaries are generated based on a set cover algorithm that selects a subset of the sentences that best cover the weighted concepts. Thus, the goal of Hachey's approach is sentence extraction rather than phrase extraction. Although his relation extraction method, like ours (see Section 4), is probabilistic and unsupervised (he uses Latent Dirichelt Allocation (Blei et al., 2003)), the relations are limited to pairs of named-entities, which is not appropriate for our decision summarization setting. Nevertheless, we will adapt his approach for comparison with our relation-based summarization technique and include it for evaluation.

3 Focused Summarization as Relation Extraction

Given the DRDAs for each meeting grouped (not necessarily correctly) according to the decisions they support, we put each cluster of DRDAs (ordered according to time within the cluster) into one "decision document". The goal will be to produce one decision abstract for each such decision document. We obtain constituent and dependency parses using the Stanford parser (Klein and Manning, 2003; de Marneffe et al., 2006). With the corpus of constituent-parsed decision documents as the input, we will use and modify Chen et al. (2011)'s system to identify decision cue relations and decision content relations for each cluster.[4] (Section 6 will make clear how the learned decision cue relations will be used to identify decision content relations.) The salient decision content relation instances will be returned as decision summary com-

[4]Other unsupervised relation learning methods might also be appropriate (e.g., Open IE (Banko et al., 2007)), but they generally model relations between pairs of entities and group relations only according to lexical similarity.

ponents.

Designed for in-domain relation discovery from standard written texts (e.g., newswire), however, the Chen et al. (2011) system cannot be applied to our task directly. In our setting, for example, neither the number of relations nor the relation types is known in advance.

In the following sections, we describe the modifications needed for the spoken meeting genre and decision-focused summarization task. In particular, Chen et al. (2011) provide two mechanisms that allow for this type of tailoring: the **feature set** used to cluster potential relation instances into groups/types, and a set of **global constraints** that characterize the general qualities (e.g., syntactic form, prevalence, discourse behavior) of a good relation for the task.

4 Model

In this section, we describe the Chen et al. (2011) probabilistic relation learning model used for both **Decision Cue** and **Decision Content** relation extraction. The parameter estimation and constraint encoding through posterior inference are presented in Section 5.

The relation learning model takes as input clusters of DRDAs, sorted according to utterance time and concatenated into one decision document. We assume one decision will be made per document. The goal for the model is to explain how the decision documents are generated from the latent relation variables. The posterior regularization technique (Section 5) biases inference to adhere to the declarative constraints on relation instances. In general, instead of extracting relation instances strictly satisfying a set of human-written rules, features and constraints are designed to allow the model to reveal diverse relation types and to ensure that the identified relation instances are coherent and meaningful. For each decision document, we select the relation instance with highest probability for each relation type and concatenate them to form the decision summary.

We restrict the eligible indicators to be a noun or verb, and eligible arguments to be a noun phrase (NP), prepositional phrase (PP) or clause introduced by "to" (S). Given a pre-specified number of relation types K, the model employs a set of features $\phi^i(w)$ and $\phi^a(x)$ (see Section 6) to describe the indicator

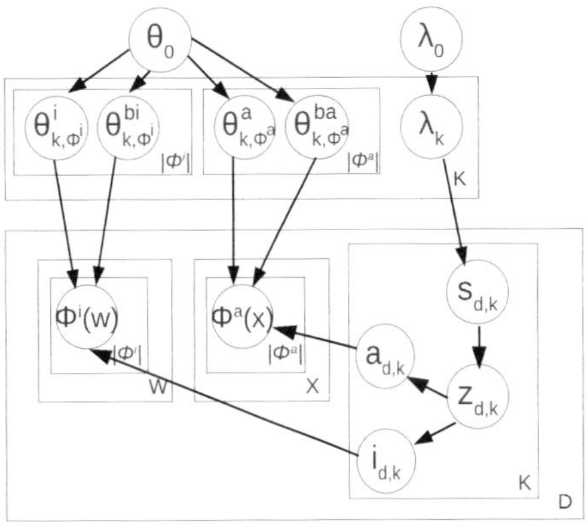

Figure 2: Graphical model representation for the relation learning model. D is the number of decision documents (each decision document consists of a cluster of DRDAs). K is the number of relation types. W and X represent the number of indicators and arguments in the decision document. $|\phi^i|$ and $|\phi^a|$ are the number of features for indicator and argument.

word w and argument constituent x. Each relation type k is associated with a set of *feature distributions* θ_k and a *location distribution* λ_k. θ_k include four parameter vectors: θ_k^i for indicator words, θ_k^{bi} for non-indicator words, θ_k^a for argument constituents, and θ_k^{ba} for non-argument constituents. Each decision document is divided into L equal-length segments and the location parameter vector λ_k describes the probability of relation k arising from each segment. The plate diagram for the model is shown in Figure 2. The generative process and likelihood of the model are shown in Appendix A.

5 Parameter Estimation and Inference via Posterior Regularization

In order to specify global preferences for the relation instances (e.g. the syntactic structure of the expressions), we impose inequality constraints on expectations of the posterior distributions during inference (Graca et al., 2008).

5.1 Variational inference with Constraints

Suppose we are interested in estimating the posterior distribution $p(\theta, z|x)$ of a model in general, where θ, z and x are parameters to estimate, latent variables and observations, respectively. We aim to find a distribution $q(\theta, z) \in Q$ that minimizes the KL-divergence to the true posterior

$$\mathrm{KL}(q(\theta, z)\|p(\theta, z|x)) \quad (1)$$

A mean-field assumption is made for variational inference, where $q(\theta, z) = q(\theta)q(z)$. Then we can minimize Equation 1 by performing coordinate descent on $q(\theta)$ and $q(z)$. Now we intend to have fine-level control on the posteriors to induce meaningful semantic parts. For instance, we would like most of the extracted relation instances to satisfy a set of pre-defined syntactic patterns. As presented in (Graca et al., 2008), a general way to put constraints on posterior q is through bounding expectations of given functions: $E_q[f(z)] \leq b$, where $f(z)$ is a deterministic function of z, and b is a pre-specified threshold. For instance, define $f(z)$ as a function to count the number of generated relation instances that meet the pre-defined syntactic patterns, then most of the extracted relation instances will have the desired syntactic structures.

By using the mean-field assumption, the model in Section 4 is factorized as

$$
\begin{aligned}
&q(\theta, \lambda, z, i, a) = \\
&\prod_{k=1}^{K} q(\lambda_k; \hat{\lambda}_k) q(\theta_k^i; \hat{\theta}_k^i) q(\theta_k^{bi}; \hat{\theta}_k^{bi}) q(\theta_k^a \hat{\theta}_k^a) q(\theta_k^{ba}; \hat{\theta}_k^{ba}) \\
&\times \prod_{d=1}^{D} q(z_{d,k}, i_{d,k}, a_{d,k}; \hat{c}_{d,k}) \qquad (2)
\end{aligned}
$$

The constraints are encoded in the inequalities $E_q[f(z, i, a)] \geq b$ or $E_q[f(z, i, a)] \leq b$, and affect the inference as described above. Updates for the parameters are discussed in Appendix B.

5.2 Task-Specific Constraints.

We define four types of constraints for the decision relation extraction model.

Syntactic Constraints. Syntactic constraints are widely used for information extraction (IE) systems (Snow et al., 2005; Banko and Etzioni, 2008), as it has been shown that most relations are expressed via a small number of common syntactic patterns. For each relation type, we require at least 80%[5] of the induced relation instances in expectation to match one of the following syntactic patterns:

- The indicator is a verb and the argument is a noun phrase. The headword of the argument is the direct object of the indicator or the nominal subject of the indicator.
- The indicator is a verb and the argument is a prepositional phrase or a clause starting with "to". The indicator and the argument have the same parent in the constituent parsing tree.
- The indicator is a noun and is the headword of a noun phrase, and the argument is a prepositional phrase. The noun phrase with the indicator as its headword and the argument have the same parent in the constituent parsing tree.

For relation k, let $f(z_k, i_k, a_k)$ count the number of induced indicator i_k and argument a_k pairs that match one of the patterns above, and b is set to $0.8D$, where D is the number of decision documents. Then the syntactic constraint is encoded in the inequality $E_q[f(z_k, i_k, a_k)] \geq b$.

Prevalence Constraints. The prevalence constraint is enforced on the number of times a relation is instantiated, in order to guarantee that every relation has enough instantiations across the corpus and is task-relevant. Again, we require each relation to have induced instances in at least 80% of decision documents.

Occurrence Constraints. Diversity of relation types is enforced through occurrence constraints. In particular, for each decision document, we restrict each word to trigger at most two relation types as indicator and occur at most twice as part of a relation's argument in expectation. An entire span of argument constituent can appear in at most one relation type.

Discourse Constraints. The discourse constraint captures the insight that the final decision on an issue is generally made, or at least restated, at the end of the decision-related discussion. As each decision document is divided into four equal parts, we restrict 50% of the relation instances to be from the last quarter of the decision documents.

6 Features

Table 1 lists the features we use for discovering both the decision cue relations and decision content relations. We start with a collection of domain-independent BASIC FEATURES shown to be useful in relation extraction (Banko and Etzioni, 2008; Chen et al., 2011). Then we add MEETING FEATURES, STRUCTURAL FEATURES and SEMANTIC FEATURES that have been found to be good predictors for decision detection (Hsueh and Moore, 2007) or meeting and decision summarization (Gal-

[5] Experiments show that this threshold is suitable for decision relation extraction, so we adopt it from (Chen et al., 2011).

Basic Features
unigram (stemmed)
part-of-speech (POS)
constituent label (NP, VP, S/SBAR (start with "to"))
dependency label
Meeting Features
Dialogue Act (DA) type
speaker role
topic
Structural Features (Galley, 2006) (Wang and Cardie, 2011)
in an Adjacency Pair (AP)?
if in an AP, AP type
if in an AP, the other part is decision-related?
if in an AP, the source part or target part?
if in an AP and is source part, is the target positive feedback?
if in an AP and is target part, is the source a question?
Semantic Features (from WordNet) (Miller, 1995)
first Synset of head word with the given POS
first hypernym path for the first synset of head word
Other Features (only for Argument)
number of words (without stopwords)
has capitalized word or not
has proper noun or not

Table 1: Features for **Decision Cue** and **Decision Content** relation extraction. All features, except the last type of features, are used for both the indicator and argument. (An Adjacency Pair (AP) is an important conversational analysis concept (Schegloff and Sacks, 1973). In the AMI corpus, an AP pair consists of a source utterance and a target utterance, produced by different speakers.)

Decision Cue Relations	**Relation Instances**
Group Wrap-up / Recap	we have, we are, we say, we want
Personal Explanation	I mean, I think, I guess, I (would) say
Suggestion	do we, we (could/should) do
Final Decision	it is (gonna), it will, we will

Table 2: Sample **Decision Cue** relation instances. The words in parentheses are filled for illustration purposes, while they are not part of the relation instances.

Discourse Features
clause position (first, second, other)
position to the first decision cue relation if any (before, after)

Table 3: Additional features for **Decision Content** relation extraction, inspired by **Decision Cue** relations. Both indicator and argument use those features.

ley, 2006; Murray and Carenini, 2008; Fernández et al., 2008; Wang and Cardie, 2011). Features employed only for argument's are listed in the last category in Table 1.

After applying the features in Table 1 and the global constraints from Section 5 in preliminary experiments, we found that the extracted relation instances are mostly derived from decision cue relations. Sample decision cue relations and instances are displayed in Table 2 and are not necessarily surprising: previous research (Hsueh and Moore, 2007) has observed the important role of personal pronouns, such as "we" and "I", in decision-making expressions. Notably, the decision cue is always followed by the decision content. As a result, we include two additional features (see Table 3) that rely on the cues to identify the decision content. Finally, we disallow content relation instances with an argument containing just a personal pronoun.

7 Experiment Setup

The Corpus. We evaluate our approach on the AMI meeting corpus (Carletta et al., 2005) that consists of 140 multi-party meetings with a wide range of annotations. The 129 scenario-driven meetings involve four participants playing different roles on a design team. Importantly, the corpus includes a short (usually one-sentence), manually constructed abstract summarizing each decision discussed in the meeting. In addition, all of the dialogue acts that support (i.e., are relevant to) each decision are annotated as such. We use the manually constructed decision abstracts as gold-standard summaries.

System Inputs. We consider two system input settings. In the **True Clusterings** setting, we use the AMI annotations to create perfect partitionings of the DRDAs for input to the summarization system; in the **System Clusterings** setting, we employ a hierarchical agglomerative clustering algorithm used for this task in previous work (Wang and Cardie, 2011). The Wang and Cardie (2011) clustering method groups DRDAs according to their LDA topic distribution similarity. As better approaches for DRDA clustering become available, they could be employed instead.

Evaluation Metrics. We use the widely accepted ROUGE (Lin and Hovy, 2003) evaluation measure. We adopt the ROUGE-1 and ROUGE-SU4 metrics from (Hachey, 2009), and also use ROUGE-2. We choose the stemming option of the ROUGE software at `http://berouge.com/` and remove stopwords from both the system and gold-standard summaries.

Training and Parameters. The Dirichlet hyperparameters are set to 0.1 for the priors. When training the model, ten random restarts are performed and each run stops when reaching a convergence threshold (10^{-5}). Then we select the posterior with the lowest final free energy. For the parameters used in posterior constraints, we either adopt them from (Chen et al., 2011) or choose them arbitrarily without tuning in the spirit of making the approach domain-independent.

We compare our decision summarization approach with (1) two unsupervised baselines, (2) the unsupervised relation-based approach of Hachey (2009), (3) two supervised methods, and (4) an upperbound derived from the gold standard decision abstracts.

The LONGEST DA **Baseline.** As in Riedhammer et al. (2010) and Wang and Cardie (2011), this baseline simply selects the longest DRDA in each cluster as the summary. Thus, this baseline performs utterance-level decision summarization. Although it's possible that decision content is spread over multiple DRDAs in the cluster, this baseline and the next allow us to determine summary quality when summaries are restricted to a single utterance.

The PROTOTYPE DA **Baseline.** Following Wang and Cardie (2011), the second baseline selects the decision cluster prototype (i.e., the DRDA with the largest TF-IDF similarity with the cluster centroid) as the summary.

The Generic Relation Extraction (GRE) Method of Hachey (2009). Hachey (2009) presents a generic relation extraction (GRE) for multi-document summarization. Informative sentences are extracted to form summaries instead of relation instances. Relation types are discovered by Latent Dirichlet Allocation, such that a probability is output for each relation instance given a topic (equivalent to relation). Their relation instances are named entity(NE)-mention pairs conforming to a set of pre-specified rules. For comparison, we use these same rules to select noun-mention pairs rather than NE-mention pairs, which is better suited to meetings, which do not contain many NEs.[6]

	True Clusterings				
	R-1			R-2	R-SU4
	PREC	REC	F1	F1	F1
Baselines					
Longest DA	34.06	31.28	32.61	12.03	13.58
Prototype DA	40.72	28.21	33.32	12.18	13.46
GRE					
5 topics	38.51	30.66	34.13	11.44	13.54
10 topics	39.39	31.01	34.69	11.28	13.42
15 topics	38.00	29.83	33.41	11.40	12.80
20 topics	37.24	30.13	33.30	10.89	12.95
Supervised Methods					
CRF	53.95	26.57	35.61	11.52	14.07
SVM	42.30	41.49	40.87	12.91	16.29
Our Method					
5 Relations	39.33	35.12	37.10	12.05	14.29
10 Relations	37.94	37.03	**37.47**	**12.20**	**14.59**
15 Relations	37.36	37.43	37.39	11.47	14.00
20 Relations	37.27	***37.64***	37.45	11.40	13.90
Upperbound	100.00	***45.05***	62.12	33.27	34.89

Table 4: ROUGE-1 (R-1), ROUGE-2 (R-2) and ROUGE-SU4 (R-SU4) scores for summaries produced by the baselines, GRE (Hachey, 2009)'s best results, the supervised methods, our method and an upperbound — all with perfect/true DRDA clusterings.

Supervised Learning (SVMs and CRFs). We also compare our approach to two supervised learning methods — Support Vector Machines (Joachims, 1998) with RBF kernel and order-1 Conditional Random Fields (Lafferty et al., 2001) — trained using the same features as our system (see Tables 1 and 3) to identify the important **tokens** to include in the decision abstract. Three-fold cross validation is conducted for both methods.

Upperbound. We also compute an upperbound that reflects the gap between the best possible extractive summaries and the human-written abstracts according to the ROUGE score: for each cluster of DRDAs, we select the words that also appear in the associated decision abstract.

8 Results and Discussion

Table 4 illustrates that, using **True (DRDA) Clusterings** our method outperforms the two baselines and the generic relation extraction (GRE) based system in terms of F score in ROUGE-1 and ROUGE-SU4 with varied numbers of relations. Note that for GRE based approach, we only list out their best results for utterance-level summarization. If using the salient relation instances identified by GRE as the summaries, the ROUGE results will be significantly

[6] Because an approximate set cover algorithm is used in GRE, one decision-related dialogue act (DRDA) is extracted each time until the summary reaches the desired length. We run two sets of experiments using this GRE system with different output summaries — one selects one entire DRDA as the final summary (as Hachey (2009) does), and another one outputs the relation instances with highest probability conditional on each relation type. We find that the first set of experiments gets better performance than the second, so we only report the best results for their system in this paper.

	System Clusterings				
	R-1			R-2	R-SU4
	PREC	REC	F1	F1	F1
Baselines					
Longest DA	17.06	11.64	13.84	2.76	3.34
Prototype DA	18.14	10.11	12.98	2.84	3.09
GRE					
5 topics	17.10	9.76	12.40	3.03	3.41
10 topics	16.28	10.03	12.35	3.00	3.36
15 topics	16.54	10.90	13.04	2.84	3.28
20 topics	17.25	8.99	11.80	2.90	3.23
Supervised Methods					
CRF	47.36	15.34	23.18	6.12	9.21
SVM	39.50	18.49	25.19	6.15	9.86
Our Method					
5 Relations	16.12	18.93	17.41	3.31	5.56
10 Relations	16.27	18.93	17.50	3.32	5.69
15 Relations	16.42	19.14	**17.68**	**3.47**	**5.75**
20 Relations	16.75	18.25	17.47	3.33	5.64

Table 5: ROUGE-1 (R-1), ROUGE-2 (R-2) and ROUGE-SU4 (R-SU4) scores for summaries produced by the baselines, GRE (Hachey, 2009)'s best results, the supervised methods and our method — all with system clusterings.

DRDA (1): Uh the batteries, uh we also thought about that already, **DRDA (2)**: uh will be chargeable with uh uh an option for a mount station **DRDA (3)**: Maybe it's better to to include rechargeable batteries **DRDA (4)**: We already decided that on the previous meeting. **DRDA (5)**: which you can recharge through the docking station. **DRDA (6)**: normal plain batteries you can buy at the supermarket or retail shop. Yeah.
Decision Abstract: The remote will use rechargeable batteries which recharge in a docking station.
Longest DA & Prototype DA: normal plain batteries you can buy at the supermarket or retail shop. Yeah. **GRE:** 1st: normal plain batteries you can buy at the supermarket or retail shop. Yeah. 2nd: which you can recharge through the docking station. 3rd: uh will be chargeable with uh uh an option for a mount station **SVM:** batteries include rechargeable batteries decided recharge docking station **CRF:** chargeable station rechargeable batteries **Our Method:** <option, for a mount station>, <include, rechargeable batteries>, <decided, that on the previous meeting>, <recharge, through the docking station>, <buy, normal plain batteries>

Table 6: Sample system outputs by different methods are in the third cell (methods' names are in bold). First cell contains the six DRDAs supporting the decision abstracted in the second cell.

lower. When measured by ROUGE-2, our method still have better or comparable performances than other unsupervised methods. Moreover, our system achieves F scores in between those of the supervised learning methods, performing better than the CRF in both recall and F score. The recall score for the upperbound in ROUGE-1, on the other hand, indicates that there is still a wide gap between the extractive summaries and human-written abstracts: without additional lexical information (e.g., semantic class information, ontologies) or a real language generation component, recall appears to be a bottleneck for extractive summarization methods that select content only from decision-related dialogue acts (DRDAs).

Results using the **System Clusterings** (Table 5) are comparable, although all of the system and baseline scores are much lower. Supervised methods get the best F scores largely due to their high precision; but our method attains the best recall in ROUGE-1.

Discussion. To better exemplify the summaries generated by different systems, sample output for each method is shown in Table 6. The GRE system uses an approximate algorithm for set cover extraction, we list the first three selected DRDA in order. We see from the table that utterance-level extractive summaries (Longest DA, Prototype DA, GRE) make more coherent but still far from concise and compact abstracts. On the other hand, the supervised methods (SVM, CRF) that produce token-level extracts better identify the overall content of the decision abstract. Unfortunately, they require human annotation in the training phase; in addition, the output is ungrammatical and lacks coherence. In comparison, our system presents the decision summary in the form of phrase-based relations that provide a relatively comprehensive expression.

9 Conclusions

We present a novel framework for focused meeting summarization based on unsupervised relation extraction. Our approach is shown to outperform unsupervised utterance-level extractive summarization baselines as well as an existing generic relation-extraction-based summarization method. Our approach also produces summaries competitive with those generated by supervised methods in terms of the standard ROUGE score. Overall, we find that relation-based methods for focused summarization have potential as a technique for supporting the generation of abstractive decision summaries.

Acknowledgments This work was supported in part by National Science Foundation Grants IIS-0968450 and IIS-1111176, and by a gift from Google.

References

Michele Banko and Oren Etzioni. 2008. The Tradeoffs Between Open and Traditional Relation Extraction. In *Proceedings of ACL-08: HLT*, Columbus, Ohio.

Michele Banko, Michael J Cafarella, Stephen Soderl, Matt Broadhead, and Oren Etzioni. 2007. Open information extraction from the web. In *In IJCAI*, pages 2670–2676.

David M. Blei, Andrew Y. Ng, and Michael I. Jordan. 2003. Latent dirichlet allocation. *J. Mach. Learn. Res.*, 3:993–1022, March.

Trung H. Bui, Matthew Frampton, John Dowding, and Stanley Peters. 2009. Extracting decisions from multi-party dialogue using directed graphical models and semantic similarity. In *Proceedings of the SIGDIAL 2009 Conference*, pages 235–243.

Giuseppe Carenini, Gabriel Murray, and Raymond Ng. 2011. *Methods for Mining and Summarizing Text Conversations*. Morgan & Claypool Publishers.

Jean Carletta, Simone Ashby, Sebastien Bourban, Mike Flynn, Thomas Hain, Jaroslav Kadlec, Vasilis Karaiskos, Wessel Kraaij, Melissa Kronenthal, Guillaume Lathoud, Mike Lincoln, Agnes Lisowska, and Mccowan Wilfried Post Dennis Reidsma. 2005. The ami meeting corpus: A pre-announcement. In *In Proc. MLMI*, pages 28–39.

Harr Chen, Edward Benson, Tahira Naseem, and Regina Barzilay. 2011. In-domain relation discovery with meta-constraints via posterior regularization. In *Proceedings of the 49th Annual Meeting of the Association for Computational Linguistics: Human Language Technologies - Volume 1*, HLT '11, pages 530–540, Stroudsburg, PA, USA. Association for Computational Linguistics.

Marie-Catherine de Marneffe, Bill MacCartney, and Christopher D. Manning. 2006. Generating typed dependency parses from phrase structure trees. In *LREC*.

Raquel Fernández, Matthew Frampton, John Dowding, Anish Adukuzhiyil, Patrick Ehlen, and Stanley Peters. 2008. Identifying relevant phrases to summarize decisions in spoken meetings. INTERSPEECH-2008, pages 78–81.

Matthew Frampton, Jia Huang, Trung Huu Bui, and Stanley Peters. 2009. Real-time decision detection in multi-party dialogue. In *Proceedings of the 2009 Conference on Empirical Methods in Natural Language Processing: Volume 3 - Volume 3*, pages 1133–1141.

Michel Galley. 2006. A skip-chain conditional random field for ranking meeting utterances by importance. In *Proceedings of the 2006 Conference on Empirical Methods in Natural Language Processing*, pages 364–372.

Joao Graca, Kuzman Ganchev, and Ben Taskar. 2008. Expectation maximization and posterior constraints. In J.C. Platt, D. Koller, Y. Singer, and S. Roweis, editors, *Advances in Neural Information Processing Systems 20*, pages 569–576. MIT Press, Cambridge, MA.

Ben Hachey. 2009. Multi-document summarisation using generic relation extraction. In *Proceedings of the 2009 Conference on Empirical Methods in Natural Language Processing: Volume 1 - Volume 1*, EMNLP '09, pages 420–429, Stroudsburg, PA, USA. Association for Computational Linguistics.

Pei-yun Hsueh and Johanna Moore. 2007. What decisions have you made: Automatic decision detection in conversational speech. In *In NAACL/HLT 2007*.

Thorsten Joachims. 1998. Text categorization with Support Vector Machines: Learning with many relevant features. In Claire Nédellec and Céline Rouveirol, editors, *Machine Learning: ECML-98*, volume 1398, chapter 19, pages 137–142. Berlin/Heidelberg.

Dan Klein and Christopher D. Manning. 2003. Accurate unlexicalized parsing. In *Proceedings of the 41st Annual Meeting on Association for Computational Linguistics - Volume 1*, ACL '03, pages 423–430, Stroudsburg, PA, USA. Association for Computational Linguistics.

John D. Lafferty, Andrew McCallum, and Fernando C. N. Pereira. 2001. Conditional random fields: Probabilistic models for segmenting and labeling sequence data. In *Proceedings of the Eighteenth International Conference on Machine Learning*, ICML '01, pages 282–289, San Francisco, CA, USA. Morgan Kaufmann Publishers Inc.

Shih-Hsiang Lin and Berlin Chen. 2010. A risk minimization framework for extractive speech summarization. In *Proceedings of the 48th Annual Meeting of the Association for Computational Linguistics*, ACL '10, pages 79–87, Stroudsburg, PA, USA. Association for Computational Linguistics.

Chin-Yew Lin and Eduard Hovy. 2003. Automatic evaluation of summaries using n-gram co-occurrence statistics. In *Proceedings of the 2003 Conference of the North American Chapter of the Association for Computational Linguistics on Human Language Technology - Volume 1*, pages 71–78.

Sameer Maskey and Julia Hirschberg. 2005. Comparing Lexical, Acoustic/Prosodic, Structural and Discourse Features for Speech Summarization. In *Proc. European Conference on Speech Communication and Technology (Eurospeech)*.

George A. Miller. 1995. Wordnet: a lexical database for english. *Commun. ACM*, 38:39–41, November.

Gabriel Murray and Giuseppe Carenini. 2008. Summarizing spoken and written conversations. In *Proceed-*

ings of the Conference on Empirical Methods in Natural Language Processing, pages 773–782.

Gabriel Murray, Giuseppe Carenini, and Raymond Ng. 2010a. Interpretation and transformation for abstracting conversations. In *Human Language Technologies: The 2010 Annual Conference of the North American Chapter of the Association for Computational Linguistics*, HLT '10, pages 894–902, Stroudsburg, PA, USA. Association for Computational Linguistics.

Gabriel Murray, Giuseppe Carenini, and Raymond T. Ng. 2010b. Generating and validating abstracts of meeting conversations: a user study. In *INLG'10*.

Matthew Purver, John Dowding, John Niekrasz, Patrick Ehlen, Sharareh Noorbaloochi, and Stanley Peters. 2007. Detecting and summarizing action items in multi-party dialogue. In *in Proceedings of the 8th SIGdial Workshop on Discourse and Dialogue*.

Korbinian Riedhammer, Benoit Favre, and Dilek Hakkani-Tür. 2010. Long story short - global unsupervised models for keyphrase based meeting summarization. *Speech Commun.*, 52(10):801–815, October.

E. A. Schegloff and H. Sacks. 1973. Opening up closings. *Semiotica*, 8(4):289–327.

Rion Snow, Daniel Jurafsky, and Andrew Y. Ng. 2005. Learning Syntactic Patterns for Automatic Hypernym Discovery. In Lawrence K. Saul, Yair Weiss, and Léon Bottou, editors, *Advances in Neural Information Processing Systems 17*, pages 1297–1304. MIT Press, Cambridge, MA.

Lu Wang and Claire Cardie. 2011. Summarizing decisions in spoken meetings. In *Proceedings of the Workshop on Automatic Summarization for Different Genres, Media, and Languages*, pages 16–24, Portland, Oregon, June. Association for Computational Linguistics.

Klaus Zechner. 2002. Automatic summarization of open-domain multiparty dialogues in diverse genres. *Comput. Linguist.*, 28:447–485, December.

Appendix A Generative Process

The entire generative process is as follows ("Dir" and "Mult" refer to the Dirichlet distribution and multinomial distribution):

1. For each relation type k:
   (a) For each indicator feature ϕ^i, draw feature distributions $\theta^i_{k,\phi^i}, \theta^{bi}_{k,\phi^i} \sim \text{Dir}(\theta_0)$
   (b) For each argument feature ϕ^a, draw feature distributions $\theta^a_{k,\phi^a}, \theta^{ba}_{k,\phi^a} \sim \text{Dir}(\theta_0)$
   (c) Draw location distribution $\lambda_k \sim \text{Dir}(\lambda_0)$
2. For each relation type k and decision document d:
   (a) Select decision document segment $s_{d,k} \sim \text{Mult}(\lambda_k)$
   (b) Select DRDA $z_{d,k}$ uniformly from segment $s_{d,k}$, and indicator $i_{d,k}$ and argument constituent $a_{d,k}$ uniformly from DRDA $z_{d,k}$
3. For each indicator word w in every decision document d:
   (a) For each indicator feature $\phi^i(w) \sim \text{Mult}(\frac{1}{Z}\Pi_{k=1}^{K}\theta_{k,\phi^i})$, where θ_{k,ϕ^i} is θ^i_{k,ϕ^i} if $i_{d,k} = w$ and θ^{bi}_{k,ϕ^i} otherwise. Z is the normalization factor.
4. For each argument constituent x in every decision document d:
   (a) For each indicator feature $\phi^a(x) \sim \text{Mult}(\frac{1}{Z}\Pi_{k=1}^{K}\theta_{k,\phi^a})$, where θ_{k,ϕ^a} is θ^a_{k,ϕ^a} if $a_{d,k} = x$ and θ^{ba}_{k,ϕ^a} otherwise. Z is the normalization factor.

Given θ_0 and λ_0, The joint distribution of a set of feature parameters $\boldsymbol{\theta}$, the location distributions $\boldsymbol{\lambda}$, a set of DRDAs $\boldsymbol{z}$, and the selected indicators $\boldsymbol{i}$ and arguments $\boldsymbol{a}$ is:

$$
\begin{aligned}
&P(\boldsymbol{\theta}, \boldsymbol{\lambda}, \boldsymbol{z}, \boldsymbol{i}, \boldsymbol{a}; \theta_0, \lambda_0) = \\
&\prod_{k=1}^{K} P(\theta^i_k; \theta_0) P(\theta^{bi}_k; \theta_0) P(\theta^a_k | \theta_0) P(\theta^{ba}_k; \theta_0) P(\lambda_k; \lambda_0) \\
&\times (\prod_{d=1}^{D} P(i_{d,k}; z_{d,k}) P(a_{d,k}; z_{d,k}) P(z_{d,k}; s_{d,k}) P(s_{d,k}; \lambda_k) \\
&\times (P(w = i_{d,k}; \theta^i_k) \prod_{w \neq i_{d,k}} P(w; \theta^{bi}_k)) \\
&\times (P(x = a_{d,k}; \theta^a_k) \prod_{x \neq a_{d,k}} P(x; \theta^{ba}_k)))
\end{aligned}
$$

Appendix B Updates for the Parameters

The constraints put on the posterior will only affect the update for $q(z)$. For $q(\theta)$, the update is

$$q(\theta) = \underset{q(\theta)}{\text{argmin}}\, \text{KL}(q(\theta) \| q'(\theta)), \tag{3}$$

where $q'(\theta) \propto \exp \text{E}_{q(z)}[\log p(\theta, z, x)]$, and $q(\theta)$ is updated to $q'(\theta)$. For $q(z)$, the update is

$$
\begin{aligned}
q(z) &= \underset{q(z)}{\text{argmin}}\, \text{KL}(q(z) \| q'(z)) \\
&s.t.\ E_{q(z)}[f_c(z)] \leq b_c,\ \forall c \in C
\end{aligned} \tag{4}
$$

where $q'(z) \propto \exp \text{E}_{q(\theta)}[\log p(\theta, z, x)]$. Equation 4 is easily solved via the dual (Graca et al., 2008) (Chen et al., 2011).

Markov Logic Networks for Situated Incremental Natural Language Understanding

Casey Kennington **David Schlangen**

CITEC Dialogue Systems Group and Faculty of Linguistics and Literary Studies
Universität Bielefeld, Bielefeld, Germany
ckennington@cit-ec.uni-bielefeld.de
david.schlangen@uni-bielefeld.de

Abstract

We present work on understanding natural language in a situated domain, that is, language that possibly refers to visually present entities, in an incremental, word-by-word fashion. Such type of understanding is required in conversational systems that need to act immediately on language input, such as multi-modal systems or dialogue systems for robots. We explore a set of models specified as *Markov Logic Networks*, and show that a model that has access to information about the visual context of an utterance, its discourse context, as well as the linguistic structure of the utterance performs best. We explore its incremental properties, and also its use in a joint parsing and understanding module. We conclude that MLNs offer a promising framework for specifying such models in a general, possibly domain-independent way.

1 Introduction

We speak situated in time and space. Speech by necessity unfolds sequentially in time; and in a conversation, all speech but that of the opening utterance is preceded by other speech belonging to the same conversation. In many, if not most, conversational situations speaker and addressee are co-located in space, and their speech may refer to their shared situation.

Most current spoken dialogue systems attempt to abstract from this fact, however. They work in domains where physical co-location is not necessary, such as information look-up, and they quantize time into discrete turn units by endpointing utterances (see discussion in (Aist et al., 2007; Schlangen and Skantze, 2009)).

In this paper we present our current work on overcoming these abstractions for the task of natural language understanding (NLU). We have created a statistical model that can be trained on conversational data and which can be used as an NLU module for an incremental, situated dialogue system (such as that described in (Buß et al., 2010)). We show that this model beats baseline approaches by a wide margin, and that making available the full set of information comprising visual context, discourse context, and linguistic structure gives significantly better results than any subset of these information sources on their own.

The paper is structured as follows: we first discuss related work and introduce some background, and then describe in detail our set of experiments, and present and analyse our results. We close with a general discussion of this work and possible future extensions.

2 Related Work and Background

The work in this paper builds on, connects and extends several strands of research: grounded semantics (Roy, 2005), which worries about the connection between language and the situation in which it is used, but often does not go beyond the word level to include linguistic structure information and does not work incrementally;[1] statistical NLU (see e.g. (Zettlemoyer and Collins, 2009; Liang et al.,

[1]But see (Spranger et al., 2010); for recent attempts that partially overcome these limitations.

2011)), which tries to infer linguistic structures automatically, but normally stops at generating, not interpreting semantic representations, and works with (the text of) full utterances and not incrementally on speech data; and incremental NLU, which is a less intensely studied field, but where previous contributions (such as (DeVault et al., 2009; Devault et al., 2011; Aist et al., 2007; Schlangen and Skantze, 2009)) have not dealt with learned grounded semantics.

We go beyond this earlier work in that we study a model that is incremental, can use linguistic structure, and learns from conversational data a semantics that connects the utterance to its visual and discourse context. We have looked at individual components of this before (grounded semantics in (Siebert and Schlangen, 2008); incremental reference resolution in (Schlangen et al., 2009); incremental general NLU in (Heintze et al., 2010); interaction between incremental parsing and reference resolution in (Peldszus et al., 2012)), but use a more sophisticated model in this work and show that tackling these tasks jointly improves performance.

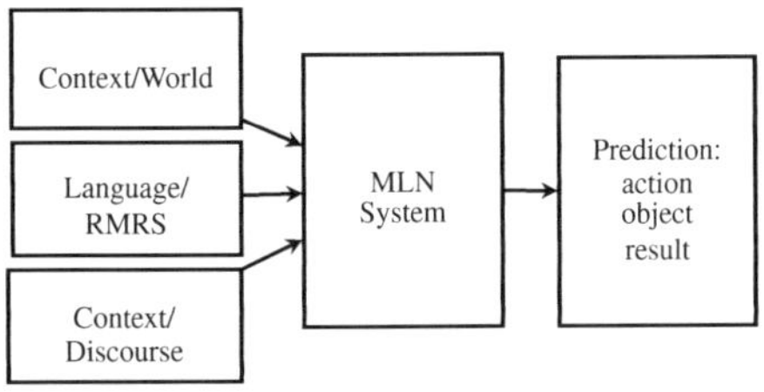

Figure 1: NLU Data Flow

We apply Markov Logic Networks (MLNs, (Richardson and Domingos, 2006)) as the machine learning technique in our experiments. MLNs have recently received attention in language processing fields like co-reference resolution (Chen, 2009), semantic role labeling (Meza-Ruiz and Riedel, 2009), spoken (albeit neither situational nor incremental) NLU (Meurs et al., 2008), and web information extraction (Satpal et al., 2011). The framework offers a convenient way of specifying factor functions on sets of random variables for undirected graphical models (Markov Random Fields, see (Kindermann and Snell, 1980)), in such a way that the factors correspond to weighted first order formulae and the joint distribution of random variables corresponds to probabilities of groundings of formulae. In this way, MLNs offer a helpful bridge between symbolic *representation* and stochastic *inference*. Weights of formulae can be specified by hand or learned from data; we used the latter capability.

Figure 1 shows data flow in our task. We use combinations of situated context, previous context, and linguistic information as evidence to an MLN, and infer what action is to be taken, what object is to be acted upon, and specifications of the manner of execution.

3 Experiments

We will now describe our experiments with using Markov Logic Networks for situated incremental natural language understanding.

3.1 Data and Task

For our experiments, we used task-oriented conversational data from the *Pentomino* domain (Fernández et al., 2007); more specifically, we worked with the corpus also used recently in (Heintze et al., 2010) and (Peldszus et al., 2012). This corpus was collected in a Wizard-of-Oz study, where the user goal was to instruct the computer to pick up, delete, rotate or mirror puzzle tiles on a rectangular board (as in Figure 2), and place them onto another one. For each utterance, the corpus records the state of the game board before the utterance, the immediately preceding system action, and the intended interpretation of the utterance (as understood by the Wizard) in the form of a semantic frame specifying action-type and arguments, where those arguments are objects occurring in the description of the state of the board. The language of the corpus is German.

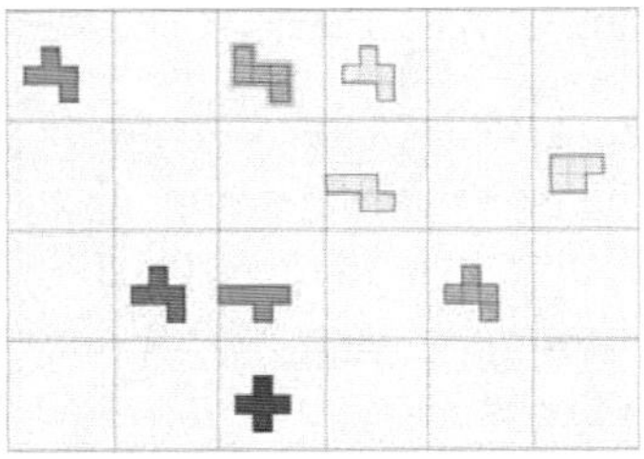

Figure 2: Example Pentomino Board

For this study, we were interested in the potential contribution of linguistic structure to the NLU task.

To this end, we produced for each utterance an incremental sequence of parses and corresponding semantic representations (as RMRS structures (Copestake, 2007), i.e. underspecified semantic representations), using the parser described in (Peldszus et al., 2012). These representations were not further manually checked for appropriateness, and hence do not necessarily represent ground truth.

As in (Peldszus et al., 2012), we discarded utterances without clear semantic alignments. One major difference from them is that we do include the 661 utterances that used pronouns to refer to pieces, leaving us with 1687 utterances, 5.43 words per utterance (sd 2.36), with a vocabulary of 237 distinct words. These were transcribed utterances and not automatic speech recognition output, so our results represent an upper-bound on real world performance.

The task that we wanted our model to tackle can then be stated as follows: given information about the current state of the world (i.e., the game board), the previous system action, and about the (possibly still not-yet completed) utterance, predict an interpretation for the utterance, in the form of such a frame. The elements of the frame may be specified separately; as argued in (Heintze et al., 2010), this is the most appropriate format for incremental processing since it provides a rough alignment between parts of the utterance and parts of its interpretation. Figure 3 illustrates such a desired output from the model. In more general terms, what we want our model to learn then is how, in a given discourse context, language connects to the world. To explore what information contributes to this, we will systematically vary in our experiments what is available to the learner.

n	**word**	**interpretation**
1	*rotate*	`action:rotate`
2	*the*	`...`
3	*yellow*	`argument:`*`yellow objects`*
4	*piece*	`argument:`*`yellow pieces`*
5	*next*	`...`
6	*to*	`...`
7	*the*	`...`
8	*yellow*	`argument:`*`yellow pieces by yellow objects`*
9	*plus*	`argument:`*`yellow piece next to unique yellow plus`*
10	*clockwise*	`option:clockwise`

Figure 3: Incremental interpretation of a 10-word utterance. Only changes to the frame are shown, e.g. when predictions about different frame elements are made. For illustration, sets of objects are represented by descriptions; in the system, these would be sets of object identifiers.

3.2 Representation

As mentioned above, Markov Logic allows the specification of knowledge bases through first order formulae. A straightforward representation of the game board would simply assert salient properties of the individual objects such as their colour, shape, position, etc.; for the topmost object in Figure 2 this could be $colour(yellow) \wedge shape(g) \wedge pos(2, 1)$. However, in pre-experiments on held-out data, we found that a more parsimonious representation actually worked better, in which there is only one abstract property that only implicitly does a typing into different features of the objects; again, for the topmost piece from the figure this would be $piece(p) \wedge property(p, yellow) \wedge property(p, g) \wedge property(p, row0) \wedge property(p, col1)$. This representation follows a Davidsonian form of representing the relations between predicates.

The properties of the objects that we represented in this way were colour, shape, its row and column, horizontal percentage from the center and vertical percentage from the center.

The utterance itself forms another source of information about the situation. In the simplest form, it could be represented just through assertions of the words which are part of it, e.g. $word(rotate) \wedge word(the) \wedge word(yellow) \wedge \ldots$. As mentioned above, we were interested in whether a more detailed linguistic analysis could provide more useful information to a model of situated semantics; we represented this information by extracting some of the relations of the RMRS representation for each utterance (-prefix) and converting them to a slightly simpler form. Figure 4 shows the RMRS representation of an example utterance and the corresponding simplified representation that we derive from it (*labels* as defined by RMRS and quotes required by and the MLN are removed for simplicity). We represent words as RMRS EPs (elementary predicates); i.e., by their lemma and with additional identifiers as arguments, which can be used to relate the EP to other RMRS structure. In the variants of the model that only look at words, the other arguments can simply be ignored in the MLN template. The final argument for EP is the board identifier, which remains unchanged during an utterance.

RMRS	MLN
a33:yellow(e34)	EP(a33,yellow,e34,1)
a19:NN(x14)	EP(a19,NN,x14,1)
ARG1(a49,x14)	RMRS(ARG1,a49,x14,1)
ARG2(a49,x53)	RMRS(ARG2,a49,x53,1)
a49:nextto(e50)	EP(a49,nextto,e50,1)
BV(a52,x53)	RMRS(BV,a52,x53,1)
RSTR(a52,h60)	EP(a52,def,,1)
BODY(a52,h61)	RMRS(ARG1,a72,x53,1)
a52:def()	EP(a72,yellow,e73,1)
ARG1(a72,x53)	EP(a58,plus,x53,1)
a72:yellow(e73)	
a58:plus(x53)	

Figure 4: RMRS and MLN for *yellow piece next to the yellow plus*

Finally, the previous system action and, during learning but not testing, the interpretation that is to be predicted needs to be represented. This is done through predicates $action(), argument()$ and $option()$ for the interpretation of the current utterances and corresponding predicates for that of the previous one.

To summarise, each problem instance is hence represented as a conjunction of predicates encoding a) the (world) situational context (the state of the game board), b) the discourse context (in the form of the previous action), and c) the (possibly as-yet partial) utterance, linguistically analysed.

3.3 Model and Decision Rule

The actual model is now formed by the MLN templates that specify the relations between the predicates; in particular those between those representing the available information (evidence) and the predicates that represent the information that is to be predicted (or, in MLN terminology, whose most likely values are to be inferred). Figure 5 illustrates graphically how our model makes these connections, separately for each frame element that is to be predicted.

These graphs show that for `action` and `option`, we assume an influence both of the words

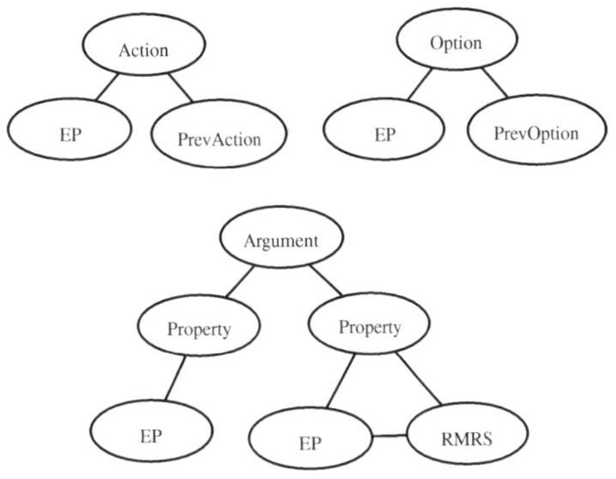

Figure 5: MLN relations between predicates

present in the utterance (denoted by EP; see above) and of the previous value of these slots on the current one. The previous context that is used for training and evaluation is taken from the corpus annotation files. The structure for `argument` is somewhat more complicated; this is where the linguistic information coming from the RMRSs comes into play, and also where the connection between language and properties of the visual scene is made. The actual template that defines our MLN is shown in Figure 6.

1 $EP(a1, a2, +w, a3, b) \Rightarrow Action(+a, b)$
2 $PrevAction(+a, b) \Rightarrow Action(+a, b)$
3 $EP(a1, a2, +w, a3, b)) \Rightarrow Option(+o, b)$
4 $PrevOption(+o, b) \Rightarrow Option(+o, b)$
5 $EP(a1, a2, +w, a3, b)) \wedge Property(p, +pr, b)$
$\Rightarrow Argument(p, b)$
6 $EP(a1, a2, w1, a3, b) \wedge RMRS(+t, a4, a3, b)$
$\wedge RMRS(+t, a4, a5, b) \wedge EP(a5, a6, w2, a5,)$
$\wedge Property(p, +pr, b) \Rightarrow Argument(p, b)$

Figure 6: The MLN template specifying our model

Our MLN system gives us probability distributions over all possible groundings of the frame predicates, but as we are interested in single best candidates (or the special value `unknown`, if no guess can be made yet), we applied an additional decision rule to the output of the MLN component. If the probability of the highest candidate is below a threshold, `unknown` is returned, otherwise that candidate is returned. Ties are broken by random selection. The thresholds for each frame element / predicate were determined empirically on held-out data so that a satisfactory trade-off between letting through wrong predictions and changing correct re-

Type	Class	Acc.
Action majority	put	33.55
Argument majority	tile-3	20.98
Option majority	na	27.08
Frame majority	take, tile-3, na	3.67
Action Contextual		42.24

Table 1: Majority class and Action contextual baselines

sults to unknown was achieved.

3.4 Parameter Training Procedure, Baselines, Metrics

All results reported below were obtained by averaging results of a 10-fold validation on 1489 Pento boards (i.e., utterances + context). We used a separate set of 168 boards for small-scale, held-out experiments. For learning and inference we used the *Alchemy* system (Domingos et al., 2006), using the discriminative training option (Singla and Domingos, 2005).[2] Inference was performed on the $Action$, $Argument$, and $Option$ predicates; a single answer was derived from the distributions delivered by alchemy in the way described in the previous section.

To be able to assess our results, we devised two kinds of baselines for the full utterance. The simplest is just the majority class. Table 1 shows accuracy when choosing the majority class, both for the frame elements individually (where this baseline is quite high) and for the most frequent full frame (which, unsurprisingly, only reaches a very low accuracy). $Action$ can be predicted with somewhat more accuracy if not the overall most frequent value is chosen but that given the previous action (i.e., when $Action$ is conditioned on $PreviousAction$). The accuracy for this method, where the conditional distribution was determined on the 1489 boards and tested on the remaining 168 boards, is shown in the Table under "action contextual".

We give our results below as f-score, slot accuracy and frame accuracy based on comparison to a gold representation. To compute the f-score, we count a prediction of unknown as a false negative (since for our test utterance a value should always have been predicted) and a wrong prediction as a false positive; i.e., a frame with one correct slot and the rest as unknown has perfect precision, but only 1/3 recall. Slot accuracy counts the number of slots that are correct, and frame accuracy only counts fully correct frames. Hence, these metrics are successively more strict. Which one most accurately predicts performance of the model in the context of a dialogue system depends on properties of the further components: if they can act on partial frames, then an f-score that start highs and continually improves as the utterance goes on is desired; if not, then what's relevant is when in the utterance high frame accuracy can be reached.

Using the best model variant, we further compare two parsing/NLU *feedback* strategies, where the feedback is to provide aid to the syntactic/RMRS parser as to which parses to prune (as in (Peldszus et al., 2012)). If a candidate parse does not resolve to anything, then the parse score is degraded. (Peldszus et al., 2012) use a rule-based reference resolution component to provide this feedback signal. We explore what the effects are of exchanging this for a learned feedback strategy using our MLN model. This model, however, does not provide discrete referent sets, but instead gives a probability distribution over all possible pieces. We therefore simply multiplied each parse by the probability of the highest probable piece, so that low probabilities effectively result in pruning a parse.

On the incremental level, we followed Schlangen et al. (2009) by using a subset of their incremental metrics, with a modification on the edit overhead:
first correct: how deep into the utterance do we make the first correct guess?
first final: how deep into the utterance do we make the correct guess, and don't subsequently change our minds?
edit overhead: ratio of unnecessary edits / sentence length, where the only *necessary* edit is that going from unknown to the final, correct result anywhere in the sentence)

We also follow their assumption that as the sentence progresses incrementally, the earlier the frame prediction can be made, the better. This is an important part of our threshold decision rule, because we also assume that no decision is better than a bad decision. A comparison between *first correct* and *first final* would reveal how well this assumption is real-

[2]http://alchemy.cs.washington.edu/

W	E	R	P	FScore	Slot	Frame
×	×	×	×	**92.18**	**88.88**	**74.76** [1]
				{86.76}	{81.61}	{61.21}
×	×	×		81.06	72.59	34.36
				{68.20}	{58.61}	{19.19}
×	×		×	91.63	88.03	72.68 [2]
				{86.47}	{80.69}	{58.18}
×	×			75.44	65.72	22.55
×		×	×	72.29	61.61	24.56
×		×		18.15	12.10	0.0
×			×	72.34	61.67	24.63
×				18.32	12.21	0.0
	×	×	×	90.68	85.68	63.75 [4]
	×	×		68.94	56.26	0.0
	×		×	90.67	85.68	63.89 [3]
	×			69.10	56.39	0.0
		×	×	72.29	61.61	24.56
		×		18.15	12.10	0.0
			×	72.30	61.63	24.69
				18.15	12.10	0.0

Table 2: Comparison of combinations using **W**orld, **E**Ps (words), **R**MRS and **P**revious context. Number in brackets are for tests on automatically transcribed speech.

ized. A good model would have the two numbers fairly close together, and the prediction would be best if both were lower, meaning good predictions earlier in the sentence. The edit overhead further sheds light on this distinction by showing what percentage of the time edits were made unnecessarily throughout a sentence.

The procedure on the incremental level is similar to the full utterance procedure, except that for incremental evaluation the f-score, slot accuracy, and frame accuracies were calculated word for word against the final gold representation.

3.5 Results

Since we were interested in the relative contributions of our different kinds of information sources (visual context, discourse context, words, linguistic structure), we trained and tested variant of the model described above that had access to only parts of the full information (by removing the appropriate predicates from the MLN template). We report results in Table 2 for these different variants; here just as results after the final word of the utterance, i.e., we're not yet

Feedback	Predictor	FScore	Slot	Frame
HC	HC		38.2	
HC	Full	92.26	88.94	74.69
none	Full	92.18	88.88	74.76
Full	Full	**92.29**	**89.01**	**74.96**

Table 3: Feedback strategies comparison for hard-coded (HC), automatic (MLN) and no feedback (none)

looking at the incremental performance. For easier reference, some lines are indexed with their rank according to frame accuracy. The tope three lines also contain a bracketed entry which represents automatically transcribed utterances (also trained on manually transcribed data as in (Peldszus et al., 2012)).

First, it should be pointed out that the full model (which has access to all information types) performs rather well, giving a fully correct interpretation for 74% of all frames. As the somewhat higher f-score indicates, some of the loss of frame accuracy is not due to wrong predictions but rather to staying undecided (choosing `unknown`)—a behaviour that could be advantageous in some applications.

The next line shows that much of the information required to reach this accuracy comes not from the visual context or an analysis of the language but from the discourse context; without access to it, accuracy drops to 22%. However, the advantage of having access to discourse context only really comes out when access to the utterance is given as well (rows indexed with 3 and 4, and 1 and 2). The model that just goes by previous context can only achieve an accuracy of 24%

Connecting discourse context to language alone only brings accuracy to around 65% (rows 3 and 4); only when the visual context is provided as well can the best accuracy be reached. This is a pleasing result, as it shows that the model is indeed capable of making the desired connection between language and world; as none of it was not explicitly given, which words and linguistic structure linked to which properties was completely learned by the discriminative training.

For the automatically transcribed results, all versions take a hit especially with regards to frame accuracy. These also show that previous context and linguistic structure contribute to increased performance.

`action`	1-6	7-8	9-14
first correct (% into utt.)	4.43	9.17	6.80
first final (% into utt.)	29.47	31.57	28.47
edit overhead	4.28		
`argument`	1-6	7-8	9-14
first correct (% into utt.)	12.12	11.14	8.08
first final (% into utt.)	38.26	36.10	30.84
edit overhead	5.72		
`option`	1-6	7-8	9-14
first correct (% into utt.)	7.62	27.75	26.73
first final (% into utt.)	45.13	56.68	59.36
edit overhead	13.96		

Table 4: Incremental Results for Action, Argument, and Option with varying sentence lengths

3.5.1 Feedback Results

Table 3 shows the various feedback strategies. *HC* refers to the hard-coded version of feedback as in (Peldszus et al., 2012). *None* means no feedback was used, which is the setting of the parser as it was used for the RMRS structures used in Table 2. *MLN* refers using our learned model to provide feedback. The column "Predictor" shows what model was used to make the final prediction at the end of the utterance. Overall, MLN performed much better on predicting the frame than the HC system (first row vs the other rows); but one should keep in mind that much of that improvement is presumably due to it having access to discourse context.

The last three lines show that, as (Peldszus et al., 2012) observed, providing feedback during parsing does offer benefits; both HC-MLN and MLN-MLN significantly improve over NONE-MLN (for f-score: one-sided $t(1489) = -3.313$, p-value < 0.001, and $t(1489) = -3.67$, p-value < 0.001, respectively; significance-level Bonferroni corrected for multiple comparisons; similar numbers for other metrics). There was no significance when comparing HC with MLN. This is an interesting result, indicating that even though our model performs better at accurately picking out referents, it provides a less useful feedback signal. This may be due to the way we compute this signal; we leave further exploration to future work.

3.5.2 Incremental Results

Table 4 shows the incremental results. Rows involving *first correct* and *first final* represent average percentage into the utterance, where the utterances were binned for lengths 1-6, 7-8, and 10-17 ("short", "normal", "long" utterances, respectively). The boundaries of the bins were determined by looking at the distribution of utterance lengths, which looked like a normal distribution with 7 and 8-word utterances having the highest representation. Our model makes very early predictions (low *first correct*), but those predictions don't always remain stable, and there is an *edit overhead* which leads to a final correct decision only later in the sentence (*first final*). For `action` and `argument`, the final decision is typically made within the first third of the utterance. For `option`, it comes between the first and second third of the sentence; this reflects typical utterance structure, where the words that describe the option ("spiegle es *horizontal*"; *mirror it horizontally*) usually come later in the sentence.

A final way to show incremental progress is in Figures 7 and 8 for sentences of "normal" length (7-8 words). These show how accurate the prediction was for each incremental step into the sentence, both for the model with and that without access to discourse context. Where *first correct* and *first final* help identify specific points in the processing of an utterance, for this graph each incremental step is compared with the gold result. Figure 8, for the model variant without access to discourse context, shows that there is little impact on prediction of `action` or `option`, but a significant and constant impact on the quality of predicting *argument* (i.e., of doing reference resolution); this is due to some extent to the presence of anaphoric references which simply cannot be resolved without access to context.

Taken together, the incremental statistics help determine an "operating point" for later modules that consume NLU output. Under the assumption that the ongoing utterance will be one of normal length (this of course cannot be known in advance), the strength with which a decision of the predictor can be believed at the current point into the utterance can be read off the graphs.

Some discussion on speed efficiency: Using

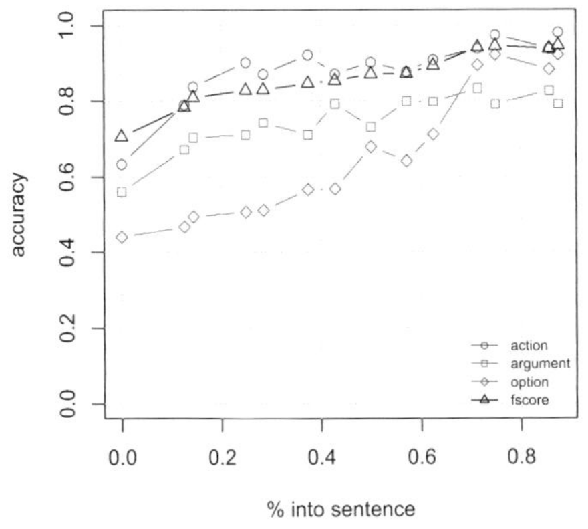

Figure 7: incremental accuracies

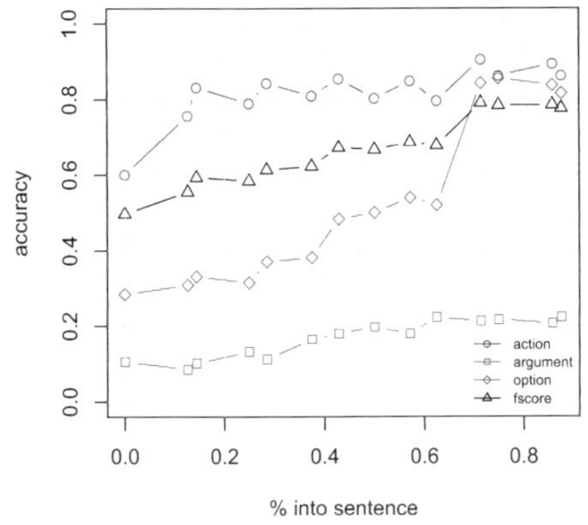

Figure 8: incremental accuracies, no discourse context

MLNs did not introduce any noticeable speed efficiency reduction in non-feedback models. In feedback models which used Auto, many more calls to MLN were used, which greatly slowed down the model.

3.6 Model Analysis

Examining the utterances that were not correctly interpreted, we found that words dealing with the argument occured most frequently, specifically words involving spatial language where the argument was described in relation to another piece. This is somewhat disappointing, as we were hoping that RMRS structure might help learn such constructions.

However, basic spatial expressions were learned successfully, as can be illustrated by Figure 9. It shows shows the probability distributions for the utterances *left* and *bottom right*, on a 5x5 board we generated for analysis, where each field was filled with the same kind of piece of the same colour (thus making these properties non-distinguishing). The darker the gradient in the Figure the higher the probability. The Figure shows that model successfully marks the fields closer to the left (or bottom-right, respectively) as having higher probability. Interestingly, "left" seems to have some confusability with "right" for the model, indicating perhaps that it picked up on the general type of description ("far side"). Further investigation of model properties is left to future work, however.

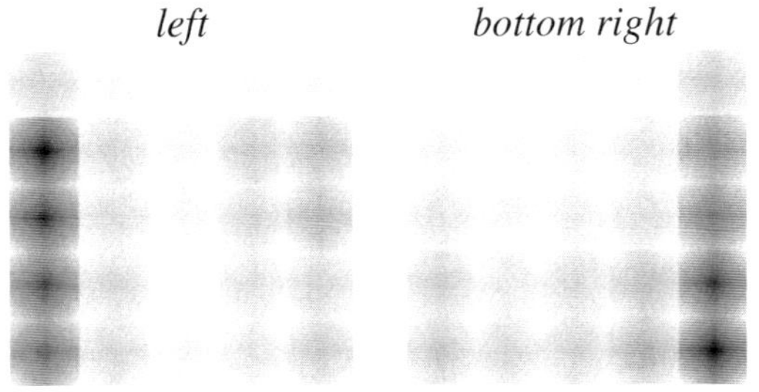

Figure 9: probability gradient for *left* and *bottom right*

4 Conclusions

Markov logic networks are effective in expressing models for situated incremental natural language understanding in a domain like Pentomino. We have shown that various aspects of situated language use, like previous context and the current state of the world, all play a role in NLU. We have also shown that semantic representations like RMRS can improve performance, and we further verified that incremental feedback between parser and NLU can improve performance (Peldszus et al., 2012). MLNs also provide an easy-to-read trained model which can be easily analyzed. However, there is a trade-off in that MLNs take some time to design, which still is an intellectual task. Furthermore, inference in MLNs is still not as efficient as other methods, which can cause a slowdown in applications where very many inference steps are required, such as the feedback model.

In future work, we will further explore how to best integrate linguistic information from the RMRSs, specifically in spatial language; as well as look into improvements in speed performance. Future work will focus on interaction with live ASR. We will also investigate using this setup for automatically trained natural language generation.

Acknowledgements: Thanks to Andreas Peldszus for help with data and to the reviewers.

References

Gregory Aist, James Allen, Ellen Campana, Carlos Gomez Gallo, Scott Stoness, Mary Swift, and Michael K. Tanenhaus. 2007. Incremental understanding in human-computer dialogue and experimental evidence for advantages over nonincremental methods. In *Proceedings of Decalog 2007, the 11th International Workshop on the Semantics and Pragmatics of Dialogue*, Trento, Italy.

Okko Buß, Timo Baumann, and David Schlangen. 2010. Collaborating on utterances with a spoken dialogue system using an isu-based approach to incremental dialogue management. In *Proceedings of the SIGdial 2010 Conference*, pages 233–236, Tokyo, Japan, September.

Fei Chen. 2009. Coreference Resolution with Markov Logic. *Association for the Advancement of Artificial Intelligence*.

Ann Copestake. 2007. Semantic composition with (robust) minimal recursion semantics. In *Proceedings of the Workshop on Deep Linguistic Processing - DeepLP '07*, page 73, Morristown, NJ, USA. Association for Computational Linguistics.

D. DeVault, Kenji Sagae, and David Traum. 2009. Can I finish?: learning when to respond to incremental interpretation results in interactive dialogue. In *Proceedings of the SIGDIAL 2009 Conference: The 10th Annual Meeting of the Special Interest Group on Discourse and Dialogue*, number September, pages 11–20. Association for Computational Linguistics.

David Devault, Kenji Sagae, and David Traum. 2011. Incremental Interpretation and Prediction of Utterance Meaning for Interactive Dialogue. *Dialoge & Discourse*, 2(1):143–170.

Pedro Domingos, Stanley Kok, Hoifung Poon, and Matthew Richardson. 2006. Unifying logical and statistical AI. *American Association of Artificial Intelligence*.

Raquel Fernández, Tatjana Lucht, and David Schlangen. 2007. Referring under restricted interactivity conditions. In *Proceedings of the 8th SIGdial Workshop on Discourse and Dialogue*, pages 136–139.

Silvan Heintze, Timo Baumann, and David Schlangen. 2010. Comparing local and sequential models for statistical incremental natural language understanding. In *Proceedings of the 11th Annual Meeting of the Special Interest Group on Discourse and Dialogue*, pages 9–16. Association for Computational Linguistics.

Ross Kindermann and J. Laurie Snell. 1980. Markov random fields and their applications. In *In Practice*, volume 1 of *Contemporary Mathematics*, page 142. American Mathematical Society.

Percy Liang, Michael Jordan, and Dan Klein. 2011. Learning Dependency-Based Compositional Semantics. In *Proceedings of the 49th Annual Meeting of the Association for Computational Linguistics: Human Language Technologies*, pages 590–599, Portland, Oregon. Association for Computational Linguistics.

Marie-jean Meurs, Frederic Duvert, Fabrice Lefevre, and Renato De Mori. 2008. Markov Logic Networks for Spoken Language Interpretation. *Information Systems Journal*, (1978):535–544.

Ivan Meza-Ruiz and Sebastian Riedel. 2009. Jointly identifying predicates, arguments and senses using Markov logic. In *Proceedings of Human Language Technologies: The 2009 Annual Conference of the North American Chapter of the Association for Computational Linguistics on - NAACL '09*, number June, page 155, Morristown, NJ, USA. Association for Computational Linguistics.

Andreas Peldszus, Okko Buß, Timo Baumann, and David Schlangen. 2012. Joint Satisfaction of Syntactic and Pragmatic Constraints Improves Incremental Spoken Language Understanding. In *Proceedings of the 13th Conference of the European Chapter of the Association for Computational Linguistics*, pages 514–523, Avignon, France, April. Association for Computational Linguistics.

Matthew Richardson and Pedro Domingos. 2006. Markov logic networks. *Machine Learning*, 62(1-2):107–136.

Deb Roy. 2005. Grounding words in perception and action: computational insights. *Trends in Cognitive Sciences*, 9(8):389–396, August.

Sandeepkumar Satpal, Sahely Bhadra, S Sundararajan Rajeev, and Rastogi Prithviraj. 2011. Web Information Extraction Using Markov Logic Networks. *Learning*, pages 1406–1414.

David Schlangen and Gabriel Skantze. 2009. A General, Abstract Model of Incremental Dialogue Processing. In *Proceedings of the 12th Conference of the European Chapter of the ACL (EACL 2009)*, number April, pages 710–718, Athens, Greece. Association for Computational Linguistics.

David Schlangen, Timo Baumann, and Michaela Atterer. 2009. Incremental Reference Resolution: The Task, Metrics for Evaluation, and a {B}ayesian Filtering Model that is Sensitive to Disfluencies. In *Proceedings of the SIGDIAL 2009 Conference*, number September, pages 30–37, London, UK. Association for Computational Linguistics.

Alexander Siebert and David Schlangen. 2008. A Simple Method for Resolution of Definite Reference in a Shared Visual Context. In *Proceedings of the 9th SIGdial Workshop on Discourse and Dialogue*, number June, pages 84–87, Columbus, Ohio. Association for Computational Linguistics.

Parag Singla and Pedro Domingos. 2005. Discriminative Training of Markov Logic Networks. *Computing*, 20(2):868–873.

Michael Spranger, Martin Loetzsch, and Simon Pauw. 2010. Open-ended Grounded Semantics. In *European Conference on Artificial Intelligence 2010*, Lisbon, Portugal. Volume 215 Frontiers in Artificial Intelligence and Applications.

Luke S. Zettlemoyer and Michael Collins. 2009. Learning context-dependent mappings from sentences to logical form. *Proceedings of the Joint Conference of the 47th Annual Meeting of the ACL and the 4th International Joint Conference on Natural Language Processing of the AFNLP: Volume 2 - ACL-IJCNLP '09*, 2:976.

Author Index